EX LIBRIS

KEYS
TO HAPPINESS

KEYS TO HAPPINESS

A Reader's Digest Guide to Successful Living

THE READER'S DIGEST ASSOCIATION

Pleasantville, N. Y.

PRINTED IN THE UNITED STATES OF AMERICA

Contents

The Perfect Blueprint for HAPPINESS

By T. E. Murphy   Condensed from The Rotarian

FOR THREE MONTHS I have been asking friends and acquaintances how familiar they were with the greatest blueprint for a happy life that was ever drawn. Of course they had all heard of this famous code of human relations. But not one of 70 persons questioned—most of them churchgoers—could quote a line of it.

The document they failed to remember was the Sermon on the Mount—the Magna Carta of Christian faith. Three months ago, I should have assumed that most persons knew something of what Jesus said in his most notable utterance. Now I am sure comparatively few people have any clear memory of either the words or their meaning. Yet, as recorded in St. Matthew, Chapters V to VII, the Sermon teaches not only the deepest spiritual truths but also practical techniques by which anyone may find health, success and tranquillity; peace of mind and peace of soul.

Now these are keys most sought after. The best-seller books have largely to do with man and his frustrations. Increasing armies of neurotic, discouraged people attest a spreading emptiness in modern life.

Yet the anxieties of average people are generally out of proportion to their problems. Most of our difficulties are fairly simple: the job, the people we work with, the children; our need to be loved, to feel important, to be a part of things.

Why, then, are so many people leading lives of what Thoreau called "quiet desperation"? May it not be because they have wandered from some great foundation of faith, which should be to us as rivers of water in a dry place, as the shadow of a great rock in a weary land?

The remedy for the desperate life, the prescription for heartache and all the thousand shocks that flesh is heir to, lies ready at hand, simple and sure, in one great, neglected utterance — the Sermon's unsurpassed Golden Rule for human relations:

Therefore all things whatsoever ye would that men should do to you, do ye even so to them.

The Sermon is studded throughout with sound advice on personal conduct in everyday affairs. The human tendency to criticize others, with no blame to ourselves, is thus denounced:

Judge not, that ye be not judged. For with what judgment ye judge, ye shall be judged: and with what measure ye mete, it shall be measured to you again.

That rule worked for Abraham Lincoln, bringing him strength and faith to hold the Union together and keeping him free of bitterness. No other historical figure quoted so often from the Sermon on the Mount.

Not only must we refrain from condemning; we must forgive. For many of us that is the hardest teaching of all. But physicians and psychologists today agree that it is also, by far, the most necessary:

Ye have heard that it hath been said, Thou shalt love thy neighbor, and hate thine enemy. But I say unto you, Love your enemies, bless them that curse you, do good to them that hate you, and pray for them which despitefully use you.

You may think that the teaching is unworkable, asking too much of human nature. Yet every mother, every father, must constantly turn the other cheek; forgiving while correcting children—forgiving and going right on loving, trying to help. In the same spirit of love and helpfulness, the Sermon urges us to try to understand, try to forgive, try to love everybody. In the struggle of self-conquest, the Sermon gives us a solemn compact—that the Father is to forgive us our trespasses only as we forgive those who trespass against us.

Once this apparently unrealistic doctrine of love is tried, its practicality appears. Mrs. Jones moved into a tightly knit New England town. Soon she learned that her neighbor Mrs. Smith, noted for a sharp tongue, had been making unkind remarks about her. She restrained an impulse to rush next door and demand a showdown. A few days later she met a close friend of her detractor. She introduced herself. The other woman shrank back as though well briefed in Mrs. Jones's defects. "I live next door to Mrs. Smith," Mrs. Jones said brightly, "and I just can't resist telling you what a fine neighbor she is. I feel lucky to be near her." A few days later Mrs. Smith appeared at Mrs. Jones's door and said rather shamefacedly, "I really would like to be a good neighbor. Maybe I haven't been as good as you think I've been." No mention of the gossip was ever made and they became fast friends.

If we are at odds with our fellows we are blocked in other relations. Nowhere is that more evident than in the problem of drunkenness. Psychiatrists are able to help only about two percent of alcoholic patients, but Alcoholics Anonymous reports success with 80 percent. What is the difference? Alcoholics Anonymous makes a direct attack on all resentments: "We can't do a thing for you until you get all resentments and hatreds out of your heart."

Forgiveness, release from grudges, as taught in the Sermon, is important also in physical health. In the past 20 years physicians have come to a realization that worry, fear, anger and hatred are poisons that can cripple and destroy the body as well as the mind; grudges can bring arthritis, rage can bring about the need for surgery. A man's thoughts are the theater of his soul.

An eminent doctor, Charles T. Bingham, once said: "Worry, fear and anger are the greatest disease causers. If we had perfect faith we wouldn't worry. Faith is the great healer."

A New York businessman, vice-president of his firm, expected to be chosen president when the founder died. But the directors chose an outsider. The resentment of the vice-president became a secret but all-powerful obsession; he could not sleep or concentrate. One day he was shocked to overhear two office boys talking about him; people were saying he was going to pieces. In despair he asked a wise friend what to do. "Love the man you resent," was the answer. "Help him!"

Next morning he tried it; forced himself to make a suggestion. The new president heartily thanked him. "I'm scared of this new job," he said. "You know more about it than I do. Please help me." Life changed then and there for them both.

To those who spend their lives piling up moneybags for selfish ends, there comes this warning:

> Therefore take no thought, saying, What shall we eat? or, What shall we drink? or, Wherewithal shall we be clothed? ... But seek ye first the kingdom of God, and his righteousness; and all these things shall be added unto you.

From childhood I have watched this promise being fulfilled before my eyes. My mother believed in it completely, her faith never shaken even at grim times when we were down, literally, to a last crust of bread. But, as Mother expected, things would invariably change for the better, and in ample time.

True, the instructions in the Sermon are not easy to follow. If I really worked at them I should become generous and openhanded, forgiving, loving, free from greed and malice. I should possess superb confidence that things would eventually come out all right and so I should not waste my strength, or ruin my digestion, through worry.

Those who follow these teachings and trust in these promises, so the Sermon declares, are "the light of the world." And the Sermon reminds us to set a decent example in the world:

Let your light so shine before men, that they may see your good works.

There is also a security we discover, that comes to one only from living the good life:

Therefore whosoever heareth these sayings of mine, and doeth them, I will liken him unto a wise man, which built his house upon a rock: and the rain descended, and the floods came, and the winds blew, and beat upon that house; and it fell not: for it was founded upon a rock. And every one that heareth these sayings of mine, and doeth them not, shall be likened unto a foolish man, which built his house upon the sand: and the rain descended, and the floods came, and the winds blew, and beat upon that house; and it fell: and great was the fall of it.

Perhaps it is not remarkable that so many have forgotten the profoundest sermon of all time, because its richness is expressed in such simplicity: it is natural, no doubt, for the smart and sophisticated to recoil from such homely faith. But the less faith a man has in his God, the less he has in himself; the more insecure, fearful and purposeless life becomes.

A man may read these forgotten words a thousand times and find within them fresh beauty and wisdom. In the ancient day when Christ first spoke the words, Matthew recorded: "The people were astonished." You will be astonished, too, to discover how pertinent the Sermon on the Mount is when applied to your daily life.

GAYELORD HAUSER's dedication of his book *Look Younger, Live Longer:* "For Lady Mendl, who long ago did what I hope every reader of this book will do: She fell in love with life."

—Published by Farrar, Straus

In a Chinese Garden

By Frederic Loomis, M.D.
Condensed from "The Bond Between Us"

A FEW years ago the aphorism above, which is the inspiration for this little story, was widely used. It was, in part, the theme of a poem written years ago by Robert Service. It was used in 1938 as the title of a book by Max Lerner on the perils of democracy. If Robert Service coined the expression, if others saw and read it in a Chinese garden, or if like other Chinese sayings it made its way into our lives by other means, I do not know.

I have told many times the story of a certain letter, which I received years ago, because the impression it made on me was very deep; and I have never told it, on ships in distant seas or by quiet firesides nearer home, without a reflective, thoughtful response from those around me. The letter:

Peking, China

Dear Doctor:

Please don't be too surprised in getting a letter from me. I am signing only my first name. My surname is the same as yours.

You won't even remember me. Two years ago I

was in your hospital under the care of another doctor. I lost my baby the day it was born.

That same day my doctor came in to see me, and as he left he said, "Oh, by the way, there is a doctor here with the same name as yours who noticed your name on the board, and asked me about you. He said he would like to come in to see you, because you might be a relative. I told him you had lost your baby and I didn't think you would want to see anybody, but it was all right with me."

And then in a little while you came in. You put your hand on my arm and sat down for a moment beside my bed. You didn't say much of anything but your eyes and your voice were kind and pretty soon I felt better. As you sat there I noticed that you looked tired and that the lines in your face were very deep. I never saw you again but the nurses told me you were in the hospital practically night and day.

This afternoon I was a guest in a beautiful Chinese home here in Peking. The garden was enclosed by a high wall, and on one side, surrounded by twining red and white flowers, was a brass plate about two feet long. I asked someone to translate the Chinese characters for me. They said:

Enjoy Yourself
It Is Later Than You Think

I began to think about it for myself. I had not wanted another baby because I was still grieving for the one I lost. But I decided that moment that I should not wait any longer. Perhaps it may be later than I think, too.

And then, because I was thinking of my baby, I thought of you and the tired lines in your face, and the moment of sympathy you gave me when I so needed it. I don't know how old you are but I am quite sure you are old enough to be my father; and I know that those few minutes you spent with me meant little or nothing to you of course—but they meant a great deal to a woman who was desperately unhappy.

So I am so presumptuous as to think that in turn I can do something for you too. Perhaps for you it is later than you think. Please forgive me, but when your work is over, on the day you get my letter, please sit down very quietly, all by yourself, and think about it.

Marguerite

Usually I sleep very well when I am not disturbed by the telephone, but that night I woke a dozen times seeing the brass plate in the Chinese wall. I called myself a silly old fool for being disturbed by a letter from a woman I couldn't even remember, and dismissed the thing from my mind; and before I knew it I found myself saying again to myself: "Well, maybe it *is* later than you think; why don't you do something about it?"

I went to my office next morning and told them I was going away for three months.

It is a wholesome experience for any man who thinks he is important in his own organization to step out for a few months. The first time I went away on a long trip, some years before this letter came, I felt sure that everything would go to pieces. When I returned I found there were just as many patients as when I left, every one had recovered just as fast or faster, and most of my patients did not even know I had been away. It is humiliating to find how quickly and competently one's place is filled, but it is a very good lesson.

I telephoned to Shorty, a retired colonel who was perhaps my closest friend, and asked him to come to my office. On his arrival I told him that I wanted him to go home and pack a grip and come on down to South America with me. He replied that he would like to but that he had so much to attend to in the next few months that it was out of the question to be away even for a week.

I read him the letter. He shook his head. "I can't go," he said. "Of course I'd like to, but for weeks now I've been waiting to close a deal. I'm sorry, old man, but maybe sometime—sometime—" his words came more slowly. "What was that thing again that woman said? 'It is later than you think'? Well—"

He sat quietly for a moment. Neither of us spoke. I could almost see the balance swaying as he weighed the apparent demands of the present against the relatively few years each of us still had to live, exactly as I had the night before.

At last he spoke. "I waited three months for those people to make up their minds. I am not going to wait any longer. They can wait for me now. When would you like to go?"

We went to South America. We spent day after day at sea on a comfortable freighter, feeling our burdens slip off with the miles and our tired bodies being made over by the winds that swept across the Pacific from China. In the course of time we found ourselves in one of the great cities of South America. By good fortune, we were entertained by one of the prominent men of the country, a man who had built enormous steel plants and whose industries were growing rapidly.

During the visit Shorty asked our host if he played golf. He replied: "Señor, I play a little, I would like to play more. My wife is on a vacation in the United States with our children. I would like to join her. I have beautiful horses here which I would love to ride. I can do none of these things because I am too busy. I am 55 years old and in five years more I shall stop. It is true I said the same thing five years ago, but I did not know how much we should be growing. We are building a new plant; we are making steel such as South America has never known. I cannot let go even for an afternoon of golf. My office boy has better leisure."

"Señor," I said, "do you know why I am in South America?"

"Because," he said, "because perhaps you had not too much to do and had the necessary time and money to permit it."

"No," I replied, "I had a great deal to do and I did not have too much of either time or money. We are sitting here on your lovely terrace because a few weeks ago a girl whom I wouldn't know if I saw her looked at a brass plate in a Chinese wall in the city of Peking in the heart of China."

I told him the story. Like Shorty, he made me repeat the words: "Enjoy yourself: it is later than you think." During the rest of the afternoon he seemed a bit preoccupied.

The next morning I met him in the corridor of our hotel. "Doctor," he said, "please wait a moment. I have not slept well. It is strange, is it not, that a casual acquaintance, which you would say yourself you are, could change the current of a very busy life? I have thought long and hard since I saw you yesterday. I have cabled my wife that I am coming."

He put his hand on my shoulder. "It was a very long finger indeed," he said, "that wrote those words on the garden wall in China."

Many years have been added to the average expectation of life but each individual's fate is still a hazard. The most valuable people around us have lived largely for others. This seems the time to remind them that they will have more years, and happier ones, to do good for others if they start right now to do something for themselves; to go places and to do things which they have looked forward to for years; to give those who love them the happiness of seeing them enjoy some of the rewards which they have earned; to replace competition with a bit of contemplation."

The "Shorty" in this story lived only a few years more. I spent the last hours at his bedside. Over and over again he said, "Fred, I am so happy that we went to South America together. I thank God we did not wait too long."

Planning Parenthood

ONE enterprising mother solved the problem of getting her year-old infant to swallow a pill. She put first the pill, then the baby, on the playpen floor. True to the ways of small children, he promptly popped the pill into his mouth and gulped it down. —Contributed by Mrs. J. M. Eshleman

A YOUNG WOMAN with three youngsters under six was trying to keep track of them and shop at the same time. When she picked out one of those divided plates with a built-in space for hot water to keep food warm for dawdling youngsters, the clerk asked: "Wouldn't you like two more—one for each of the children?"

"They get the food while it's still hot," she answered grimly. "This one is for me!" —Contributed by Mrs. H. V. Davis

"SOME of us concocted a vacation plan last year that was so satisfactory we're repeating it this year," an acquaintance told my wife. "Four couples banded together and rented a country house for two months. Each couple spent their two-week vacation there, taking care of all 13 children."

"Good heavens!" exclaimed my wife. "I wouldn't call taking care of 13 children a 'vacation'—though it would be wonderful, of course, for the children."

"Oh, the two weeks were hell. The 'vacation' was the six weeks at home without the kids." —Contributed by G. H. Hennegar

"You are not one person but three — the one you think you are, the one other people think you are and the person you really are"

The Hardest Lesson

By Fulton Oursler   *Condensed from Cosmopolitan*

SOME PSYCHOLOGISTS believe that character is fixed in childhood and can never be changed. But my friend Dr. Edwin declares that any man who wants to can change himself at any age—if he has the courage. To illustrate, he tells about Frank Dudley.

Dudley, born poor, put himself and his younger brother through college. Then, on sheer nerve, he formed his own advertising agency in New York and earned a modest fortune. One day Dudley checked in at a Boston hotel, never dreaming that three brief telephone calls were about to change his life.

First he called his brother's home and asked his sister-in-law, Agnes, if she and his brother could have dinner with him.

"No, thanks," Agnes said briskly. "Eddie has a business appointment tonight, and I'm going to be busy, too. When he calls, though, I'll tell him to give you a ring."

Was there a faintly acrid undertone in her voice? Shrugging off the suspicion, Dudley called an old college friend and asked him to join him at dinner. His friend's answer made Dudley reel: "We're going to the party Eddie and Agnes are giving tonight. I'll see you there!"

Bewildered, Dudley had scarcely replaced the receiver when the telephone rang.

"Frank? This is Eddie. How are you? Sorry I'm tied up tonight.

How about lunch tomorrow?" Scarcely knowing what he said, the older man mumbled assent.

Since high school days, when both of their parents had died, Frank had been father and brother to Eddie. Naturally they had not been so close since Eddie's marriage. But never once had the older brother betrayed his disappointment in the match. Agnes could never be an intellectual companion for Eddie, who was a scholar, a teacher of history. Nevertheless, Frank had always treated his sister-in-law with tender gusto.

Why had they lied to him? After a sleepless night he drove to his brother's house.

When Agnes opened the door, he blurted out: "Why didn't you and Eddie invite me last night?"

"Frank, I'm terribly sorry. Eddie wanted to ask you, but I told him I'd rather not have the party. You'd have ruined everything."

"How can you say such a thing?"

"Because it's true, Frank. Why do you suppose we ever came to Boston except to get away by ourselves? You hurt Eddie every time you come around. You're the big successful man who has to impress everybody. You top everything Eddie says, every opinion he expresses, every story he tries to tell; you contradict him and make him look foolish. Well, last night the president of the college was coming to dinner. We hope Eddie's going to be promoted. Why should you take the spotlight and spoil everything? That's why I put my foot down. I've always known what you really think of me. But there's one thing I can tell you: I try to make Eddie happy and that's more than you ever do!"

"I'm not like that at all," Dudley cried.

"Aren't you, though?" Agnes said miserably. "You ought to get wise to yourself."

Eventually Dudley appeared in the office of his friend Dr. Edwin.

"I can't get this thing out of my mind, and can't decide what to do," said Dudley. "That woman is my mortal enemy. I won't let her separate Eddie and me. There must be a solution."

Dr. Edwin looked at his friend. "There is," he declared flatly. "But you won't like it. Your sister-in-law gave you the best possible advice when she told you to get wise to yourself. Like everybody else, you are not one person but three: the man you think you are, the man other people think you are—and the man you really are. Generally that last one is the man nobody knows. Why not make his acquaintance? It may change your whole life."

A gaunt look settled on Dudley's troubled face. "How do I start?" he asked finally.

"Why don't you play the game I call spiritual solitaire?" the doctor suggested. "Listen to yourself. Weigh your thoughts and impulses before speaking or acting."

That night Dudley went to dinner with several men he knew. Presently one of the group began to tell a joke. Dudley had heard the story before, and his eyes wandered away. He thought of another yarn, much funnier than this one, which he meant to tell the moment the narrator finished.

With a jolt, he remembered Dr. Edwin's game. And suddenly the words of Agnes resounded in his mind: *"You top everything Eddie says, every story he tries to tell."*

As a shout of laughter followed the story, Dudley blurted out, "Gosh, that's a good one! And how magnificently you told it!"

The storyteller turned to him with a grateful glance.

This little experience was the beginning of Dudley's adventure with himself. At lunch with a business associate the next day he learned that a certain man wanted to be elected vice-president of a trade association. "That won't be easy," Dudley objected.

"Why not?"

Dudley hesitated. He was learning to make hesitation a habit. He had intended to reveal how often the association's directors came to him for advice; he meant to hold forth, to expound—

Again Agnes's voice echoed in his memory: *"You're the big successful man who has to impress everybody."*

"That man," he stammered, "is too good for vice-president. He'd make a great president."

"Dudley," cried the other with joy, "you talk like a statesman! He's my closest friend, and with your help we can put him over."

Dudley was inwardly astonished at the meanness he had come so close to committing. And why? Simply because he wanted people to think how important he was.

There were many such discoveries. It startled him to detect the gossip with which he spiced conversation, the little detractions his tongue uttered against men whom he called friends. He found, to his horror, that he was capable of rejoicing over one man's misfortune and grieving over another's success. The more he learned about himself, the easier it was to forgive others.

Two weeks later he returned to Dr. Edwin, a package under one arm, and related his discoveries.

"What about your brother's wife? Are you still angry with her?"

"Doctor, I am so sore at myself I haven't room to be sore at anybody else. And I'm on my way to Boston. In this package is my young nephew's birthday present. I was going to buy him a $200 camera, until I realized that would be more expensive than anything his father could give him. This is something no money could buy for him."

At his brother's door Agnes looked at him uncertainly. Presently he sat with Eddie Jr., in the living room, the gift package opened on his knees. It was a stout black book; the worn cover had no title.

"This scrapbook," Dudley began, "is something I've been keeping for years. It's filled with things about your father: clippings from the sports pages when he was high school swimming champion; snapshots; and letters people wrote me when he was reported missing overseas. Here's a note about that from my second-best friend in the world: 'You,' he says, meaning me, 'have a brilliant mind, but your brother, Eddie, has splendor of the heart, and that's a lot more important.'"

In the silence, as the child read the letter, Agnes turned her back and went to the window.

"Who is your very best friend?" asked Eddie, Jr.

"The lady at the window," said Dudley. "A good friend tells you the truth. Your mother did that for me when I needed it most, and I can never thank her enough for it."

Agnes did something for the first time in her life—she put her arms around Dudley and gave him a sister's kiss.

An Open Letter to America's Students

By
Dwight D. Eisenhower

Then President of Columbia University

> *I receive many letters from young people. Mostly they ask a question that could be put like this:*
>
> *Shall I keep on with school? Or shall I plunge off into "life?"*
>
> *I try to answer these letters according to the circumstances of each case. But I sometimes feel that I would like to try to write a general answer to the whole general problem of "school" versus "life" in the minds of my correspondents. I think I would say:*

DEAR Jack—or Margaret: You say you wonder if it is worth-while for you to go on with high school. You particularly wonder if it is worth-while to enter and finish college. The tedium of study, nose buried in books, seems a waste of time compared with a job and the stimulus of productive work. You say you hate to bother me with this "trifling" problem of yours.

It is not a trifling problem at all. Your decision will affect your whole life; similar decisions by millions of other young Americans will affect the total life of our country. And I know how deeply it must worry you. It worried me and a lot of my schoolmates when I was your age.

In a small Kansas town, 40 years ago, a reasonably strong case could be put up in favor of leaving school early. Outside of those few who could afford to pick a profession, most of us knew our lives would be spent on the farm, or in one of the local stores, or at the creamery or elevator.

We could be good farmers, good storekeepers, good mill hands, without much book learning. The quickest road to practical knowledge was to *do*. That was the way we might have argued; and we would have been right if there were no more to successful living than plowing a straight furrow, wrapping a neat package, keeping a machine well oiled.

Fortunately, we came of stock that set the school on the same plane as the home and church. The value of education, above and beyond the immediate return in dollars and cents, had been bred into us. Our families stinted themselves to keep us in school a while longer; and most of us worked, and worked hard, to prolong that while.

Today the business of living is far more complex than it was in my boyhood. No one of us can hope to comprehend all its complexity in a lifetime of study. But each day profitably spent in schools will help you understand better your personal relationship to country and world. If your generation fails to understand that the human individual is still the center of the universe and is still the sole reason for the existence of all man-made institutions, then complexity will become chaos.

Consequently, I feel firmly that you should continue your schooling —if you can—right to the end of high school and right to the end of college. You say you are "not too good at books." But from books— under the guidance of your teachers—you can get a grasp on the thing that you most ought to understand before you go to work.

It is expressed in a moving letter I got the other day from a young girl halfway through high school. She said that in her studies she seemed to be a failure all along the line, always trailing everyone else. But then she ended by saying: "I still think I could learn to be a good American."

That's the vital point. School, of course, should train you in the two great basic tools of the mind: the use of words and the use of numbers. And school can properly give you a start toward the special skills you may need in the trade or business or profession you may plan to enter. But remember:

As soon as you enter it, you will be strongly tempted to fall into the rut and routine of it. You will be strongly tempted to become just a part of an occupation which is just one part of America. In school—from books—from teachers—from fellow students—you can get a view of the whole of America, how it started, how it grew, what it is, what it means. Each day will add breadth to your view and a sharper comprehension of your own role as an American.

I feel sure I am right when I tell you:

To develop fully your own character, you must know your country's character.

A plant partakes of the character of the soil in which it grows. You are a plant that is *conscious,* that *thinks.* You must study your soil—which is your country—in order that you may be able to draw its strength up into your own strength.

It will pay you to do so. You will understand your own problems better and solve them more easily, if you have studied America's problems and done something toward their solution.

Never forget that *self-interest and patriotism go together.* You have to look out for yourself, and you have to look out for your country. Self-interest and patriotism, rightly considered, are not contradictory ideas. They are partners.

The very earth of our country is gradually getting lost to us. One third of the fertile top layer of our soil has already been washed away into rivers and the sea. This must be stopped, or some day our country will be too barren to yield us a living. That is one national problem crying for solution; it affects you directly and decisively.

In our cities there are millions of people who have little between them and hunger except a daily job, which they may lose. They demand more "security." If they feel too insecure, their discontent might some day undermine *your* security, no matter how personally successful you might be in your own working life. That's another problem—and there are innumerable others—whose solution requires the thought and good will of every American.

I cannot put it to you too strongly—or too often—that it is to your *practical advantage* to learn America's character and problems, in the broadest possible way, and to help to bring those problems to their solutions.

It is dangerous to assume that our country's welfare belongs alone to that mysterious mechanism called "the government." Every time we allow or force the government, because of our own individual or local failures, to take over a question that properly belongs to us, by that much we surrender our individual responsibility, and with it a comparable amount of individual freedom. But the very core of what we mean by Americanism is individual liberty founded on individual responsibility, equality before the law, and a system of private enterprise that aims to reward according to merit.

These things are basic—your years in school will help you to apply these truths to the business of living in a free democracy.

Yours is a country of free men and women, where personal liberty is cherished as a fundamental right. But the price of its continued possession is untiring alertness. Liberty is easily lost. Witness the history of the past 20 years. Even the natural enthusiasm of warm youthful hearts for a leader can be a menace to liberty.

It was movements of misguided young people, under the influence of older and more cynical minds, that provided the physical force to make Mussolini the tyrant of Italy and Hitler the tyrant of Germany. Mussolini's street song was *"Giovinezza"*—"Youth." Hitler based his power most firmly on the *Hitler Jugend*—the Hitler Youth.

Never let yourself be persuaded that any one Great Man, any one leader, is necessary to the salvation of America. When America consists of one *leader* and 143,000,000 *followers,* it will no longer be America. Truly American leadership is not of any one man. It is of multitudes of men—and women.

Our last war was not won by one man or a few men. It was won by hundreds of thousands and millions of men and women of all ranks. Audacity, initiative, the will to try greatly and stubbornly characterized them. Great numbers of them, if for only a few minutes in some desperate crisis of battle, were leaders.

You will find it so in the fields of peace. America at work is not just a few "Great Men" at the head of government, of corporations, or of labor unions. It is millions and millions of men and women who on farms and in factories and in stores and offices and homes are leading this country—and the world—toward better and better ways of doing and of making things. America exceeds all other lands—by far

—in the number of its leaders. Any needless concentration of power is a menace to freedom.

We have the world's best machines, because we ourselves are not machines; because we have embraced the liberty of thinking for ourselves, of imagining for ourselves, and of acting for ourselves out of our own energies and inspirations. Our true strength is not in our machines, splendid as they are, but in the inquisitive, inventive, indomitable souls of our people.

To be that kind of soul is open to every American boy and girl; *and it is the one kind of career that America cannot live without.*

To be a good American—worthy of the heritage that is yours, eager to pass it on enhanced and enriched—is a lifetime career, stimulating, sometimes exhausting, always satisfying to those who do their best.

Start on it now; take part in America's affairs while you are still a student. There are responsibilities about your home, in your neighborhood, that you can assume. There are activities about your school, on your campus, that will be more productive of good by your contribution.

Don't think that you are too young. "Let no man despise thy youth," Paul the Apostle said to Timothy. These words apply to you as an American. Loyalty to principle, readiness to give of one's talents to the common good, acceptance of responsibility—these are the measure of a good American, not his age in years.

Alexander Hamilton—General Washington's aide in war, President Washington's Secretary of the Treasury in peace—was speaking before applauding crowds of his fellow New Yorkers on the political problems of the American Revolution when he was only 17 years old and still a student in King's College, now Columbia University. The same stuff of which Hamilton was made is in you and all American youth today.

But above all, while you are still at school, try to learn the "why" of your country. We Americans know "how" to produce things faster and better—on the whole—than any other people. But what will it profit us to produce *things* unless we know what we are producing them *for,* unless we know what purpose animates America?

To assure each citizen his inalienable right to life, liberty and the pursuit of happiness was the "why" behind the establishment of this

Republic and is today the "why" for its continued existence. What that means to you personally, what you must do toward its fulfillment, cannot be answered completely in a letter. But I repeat that the answer can be found in your school, if you seek it deliberately and conscientiously. You need neither genius nor vast learning for its comprehension.

To be a good American is the most important job that will ever confront you. But essentially it is nothing more than being a good member of your community, helping those who need your help, striving for a sympathetic understanding of those who oppose you, doing each new day's job a little better than the previous day's, placing the common good before personal profit. The American Republic was born to assure you the dignity and rights of a human individual. If the dignity and rights of your fellow men guide your daily conduct of life, you will be a good American.

Proverbial Nonsense

Too MANY ancient proverbs, masquerading as wisdom, have achieved a moral authority greater than that of the Ten Commandments.

I know a man who gave up golf because some ancient fool said, "Whatever is worth doing at all is worth doing well." He should have stood on his rights and pointed out the undebatable truth that the man who doesn't play golf well gets twice as much fun and exercise as the man who plays very well; he hits the ball twice as many times.

Is there any torture worse than to play contract bridge with three eager beavers who insist on doing it well? Can't a person relax playing bridge?

We see it in music, too. I forget who it was that said what America needed was "more poor music." He meant that we need more music in the home created on the spot for the sheer fun of it. More music made by Bill, Fred and Mabel, not by Decca, Victor and Columbia.

But because of an old wives' fable, we have traded all the bounce and gladness of *doing* something for the sodden inertia of looking at something or listening to something.   — Simeon Stylites *in The Christian Century*

How We Kept Mother's Day

By Stephen Leacock

Condensed from The Leacock Roundabout

ONE YEAR our family decided to have a special celebration of Mother's Day, as a token of appreciation for all the sacrifices that Mother had made for us. After breakfast we had arranged, as a surprise, to hire a car and take her for a beautiful drive in the country. Mother was rarely able to have a treat like that, because she was busy in the house nearly all the time.

But on the very morning of the day, we changed the plan a little, because it occurred to Father that it would be even better to take Mother fishing. As the car was hired and paid for, we might as well use it to drive up into the hills where the streams are. As Father said, if you just go driving you have a sense of aimlessness, but if you are going to fish there is a definite purpose that heightens the enjoyment.

So we all felt it would be nicer for Mother to have a definite purpose; and anyway, Father had just got a new rod the day before, which he said Mother could use if she wanted to; only Mother said she would much rather watch him fish than try to fish herself.

So we got her to make up a sandwich lunch in case we got hungry, though of course we were to come home again to a big festive dinner.

Well, when the car came to the door, it turned out that there wasn't as much room in it as we had supposed, because we hadn't reckoned on Father's fishing gear and the lunch, and it was plain that we couldn't all get in.

Father said not to mind him, that he could just as well stay home and put in the time working in the garden. He said that we were not to let the fact that he had not had a real holiday for three years stand in our way; he wanted us to go right ahead and not to mind him.

But of course we all felt that it would never do to let Father stay home, especially as we knew he would make trouble if he did. The two girls, Anna and Mary, would have stayed and gotten dinner, only it seemed such a pity to, on a lovely day like this, having their new hats. But they said that Mother had only to say the word and they'd gladly stay home and work. Will and I would have dropped out, but we wouldn't have been any use in getting the dinner.

So in the end it was decided that Mother would stay home and just have a lovely restful day around the house, and get the dinner. Also it turned out to be just a bit raw out-of-doors, and Father said he would never forgive himself if he dragged Mother round the country and let her take a severe cold. He said it was our duty to let Mother get all the rest and quiet she could, after all she had done for all of us, and that young people seldom realize how much quiet means to people who are getting old. He could still stand the racket, but he was glad to shelter Mother from it.

Well, we had the loveliest day up among the hills, and Father caught such big specimens that he felt sure that Mother couldn't have landed them anyway, if she had been fishing for them. Will and I fished too, and the two girls met some young men friends along the stream, and so we all had a splendid time.

We sat down to a roast turkey when we got back. Mother had to get up a good bit during the meal fetching things, but at the end Father said she simply mustn't do it, that he wanted her to spare herself, and he got up and fetched the walnuts from the sideboard himself.

The dinner was great fun, and when it was over all of us wanted to help clear the things up and wash the dishes, only Mother said that she would really much rather do it, and so we let her, because we wanted to humor her.

It was late when it was all over, and when we kissed Mother before going to bed, she said it had been the most wonderful day in her life, and I think there were tears in her eyes.

Copyright 1950 by The Reader's Digest Association, Inc. (May 1950 issue)
Condensed from the book, "The Leacock Roundabout," by Stephen Leacock,
published by Dodd, Mead & Co., New York 16, N.Y.

"In this area of human behavior, ignorance and shame can do as great harm in maturity as in adolescence"

SEX LIFE

AFTER MIDDLE AGE

By Margaret Culkin Banning

Author of "The Case for Chastity," "Mixed Marriage," "Letters to Susan"

THE YOUNG MAN taking his seat on the airplane noted carelessly that the motherly-looking woman by the window was deep in thought, and that the old fellow across the aisle—he was at least 60—looked half asleep. Well, said the young man to himself, when you get to be old, at least you don't have all this woman trouble *I* have.

He did not know that the woman was on her way to buy a trousseau for her wedding and was planning it with delight. He had no idea that the man across the aisle was dreaming with excitement of the coming reunion with his middle-aged wife, whom he had not seen for two lonesome weeks. If the young man had been told these things he probably would have said in derisive astonishment, "The old fools!"

But they were happier than he was. They had learned how to manage the problems of sex life which were bewildering and torturing him. They knew far more about the generosities and skills of love. They were aware of their own capacities, able to give happiness and to get it in return. They were far from being "old fools"; their desires and plans were both normal and sensible.

Today, as life expectancy has grown longer, the scientific study of the later years has become increasingly intensive. All kinds of ways to occupy the minds and abilities of those past middle age are being explored in an effort to prevent unhappiness. But too often the problem that interests people most deeply, their own human relations and the continuance of their sex life, is left to conjecture, wishful thinking or worry. Are the post-childbearing years also a postsexual period? Many people are unsure.

In this area of human behavior, ignorance and shame can do as great harm in maturity as in adolescence. It is constantly revealed to doctors that many women believe sex life is wrong, unhappy or shameful after the menopause; that many men believe their powers will fail before they attain normal life expectancy.

These two complete misconceptions have resulted in jealousy, cruelty and infidelity, and have wrecked many happy marriages. There is no reason why they should continue to do so, for a great deal of authoritative information is available that should destroy such worries and fears.

There is no sin, no wrong, no outrage in long-continued sex life in marriage. Says Dr. Leland Foster Wood, secretary for the Committee on Marriage and the Home of the Federal Council of Churches: "For both husbands and wives who fully understand the meaning of marriage and the interrelationships between the physical, emotional and spiritual factors, the sex relationship after the menopause can still be a rich and rewarding expression of love."

The Catholic religion concurs. A statement that is attributed to A. Ballerini, professor at the Catholic Gregorian University in Rome, says explicitly: "Married people are at liberty to make use of their marital rights even when the wife can no longer conceive because of age."

In *The Changing Years,* Madeline Gray writes: "For those of the Jewish faith, sex communion between husband and wife from the celebration of marriage until death is a ritual and a trust."

Woman's sex desire after the menopause is generally about the same as before, and in some cases actually increases. The late Dr. Frederic Loomis, in his book *Consultation Room,* stated, "There is a definite upward surge in the sexual lives of many women at 40, or 45 or even 50 —a recrudescence of the flame that has perhaps been dimmed by work or worry." With the fear of pregnancy removed, many women enjoy sex life more than at any other time during their marriage. Their families are complete, and they can offer their husbands love without the thought of the increased responsibility it can bring.

As for the man, his fears of losing his sex capacities are usually needless. Dr. Miriam Lincoln writes, "Nature has endowed the male with an almost lifetime possession of physical ability and emotional interest." Dr. Edmund Bergler, an authority in the field of impotence, says, "Sexual activity stabilizes itself in the late 30's or early 40's on a moderate level and remains more or less unchanged until the late 60's or early 70's, provided organic disease does not occur."

Nor do operations such as hysterectomies or removal of the prostate gland result in loss of either sex interest or enjoyment, medical authorities point out.

Men especially need these statements and reassurances. For with men the fear of growing old is, as a rule, inextricably and subtly tied up with reluctance to abandon, or to be thought incapable of, sexual activity. This last is a matter of the deepest masculine pride.

True sexual happiness is not to be found, however, merely because religious and medical authorities say it is possible. This happiness is an intangible and mysterious thing; it is based on physical unity but it must draw the physical aspect into mental and spiritual areas if it is to take root and grow. Too often a sense of unsuitability surrounds middle-aged love, particularly among women. That this is so is largely the fault of misunderstanding among older people themselves.

For physical love at its best has long been associated with youth and physical beauty. Young people have always believed that properly it belongs to them; poets and novelists have fostered the idea, and the claim has been generally conceded by older people. If the young man on the plane had called those elderly passengers old fools, it would have been only what he had been led to believe by the adults around him.

You've often heard a member of the older generation call another an old fool when a man of 60 married again or a grandmother took a new husband. In such mockery, however, there is usually a note of jealousy. "At her age . . ." they will say derisively—but a sharp ear can hear the envy.

Many older people *are,* in fact, fools in their attempts to retain the benefits and pleasures of continuing sex life. Because, secretly, they believe that these belong exclusively to youth, they try to falsify their own ages. They become absurd in appearance and in conduct. They deliberately fall out of their own generation and try to find room in a younger one. But they deceive nobody for long and only exhaust themselves trying to compete with the energies of youth. There are far better ways to achieve what they basically want, and mature men and women are beginning to find them out. F. Hugh Herbert says in his play *The Vintage Years:* "Aren't there lots of things that mellow and get better with the years? To the years ahead for us—the vintage years!"

Dr. Bergler has said: "There is no time limit on sex." This is what every one should be taught, and as early in life as possible.

On this foundation each person can fearlessly and honestly build his or her own sex life. The activity will vary with the passing of time, but it need never degenerate. For as sex accompanies later life, it becomes wiser, more informed, less selfish and less crude. It may be physically less beautiful at 60 but it can be even lovelier emotionally. It relates itself to philosophy as well as to poetry and therefore is less dependent on appearance and more dependent on character.

"Sex," wrote D. H. Lawrence, "means the whole relationship between men and women. The relationship is a lifelong change and a lifelong traveling. At periods sex desire itself departs completely. Yet the flow of the relationship goes on all the same, undying, and lasts a lifetime."

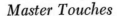

Master Touches

A FAMOUS headmaster of a school said that if he saw a boy in despair over his work he always gave him a higher mark than he deserved. The following week the boy always made a higher mark himself.

—Joseph Fort Newton, *Living Up to Life* (Harper)

A TEACHER who regularly makes a practice of hunting up the most unattractive child and whispering in her ear, "You're getting prettier every day," says it always works; almost at once the child begins to blossom into something close to beauty. —Marcelene Cox in *Ladies' Home Journal*

Turn Your Sickness into an Asset

By Louis E. Bisch, M.D. Author of "Be Glad You're Neurotic"

ONLY YESTERDAY you were marching in health and vigor; sickness was a far-off shadow. Then suddenly illness unhinged your knees, brought you limply to bed. And now you are a horizontal citizen of the sickroom, an unwilling initiate in the fellowship of pain.

Your reaction is to rail against fate, to resent bitterly such untimely interference with life's routine. Yet your illness can confer substantial benefits—and not just in the realm of Job-like piety, either. An enforced holiday in bed blamelessly releases us from a too-busy world, sharpens our mental and spiritual perceptions, and permits a clearer perspective on our lives. Any serious illness should be regarded as an opportunity to gather dividends and generate energies that mere health cannot possibly bestow.

I am not speaking of those chronic sufferers whose illness dooms them to a life of invalidism, and whose heroic readjustments lift them above the rank of ordinary men. The great American historian Francis Parkman is a triumphant prototype of all such conquerors of pain. During the greater part of his life, Parkman suffered so acutely that he could not work for more than five minutes at a time. His eyesight was so wretched that he could scrawl only a few gigantic words on a manuscript. He was racked by major digestive trouble, terrific rheumatism and agonizing headaches. Physically, almost *everything* was wrong with him, yet he contrived to write nearly 20 magnificent volumes of history.

But our interest here centers on the ordinary mortal stricken for the first time. These sick-chamber casuals rarely learn to make the most of illness, regarding it only as a visitation of bad luck. Yet thousands actually have found themselves for the first time during sickness. The "beloved physician," Dr. Edward Livingston Trudeau, was sent, as a young doctor, to the mountains where he expected to die of tuberculosis. But he did not die. As he lay in bed he had a vision of a great hospital where he could rebuild other sufferers. Flat on his back, he examined patients not as ill as himself. He raised money and labored until his dream became the great sanatorium at Saranac that helped thousands of tuberculosis patients. Trudeau's affliction turned an unknown doctor into a physician of world-wide fame.

Eugene O'Neill was an utter drifter with no plan of life until he was 25. A serious breakdown gave him the requisite leisure, he says, "to evaluate the impressions of many years in which experiences had crowded one upon the other, with never a second's reflection." It was in the hospital that he first began to write the plays that revolutionized American drama.

Like any major experience, illness actually changes us. How? Well, for one thing we are temporarily relieved from the terrible pressure of meeting the world head-on. Responsibility melts away like snow on an April roof; we don't have to catch trains, tend babies, or wind the clock. We enter a realm of introspection and self-analysis. We think soberly, perhaps for the first time, about our past and future. Former values are seen to be fallacious; habitual courses of action appear weak, foolish or stubborn. Illness, it seems, gives us that rarest thing in the world—a *second chance,* not only at health but at life itself!

Illness knocks a lot of nonsense out of us; it induces humility, cuts us down to our own size. It enables us to throw a searchlight upon our inner selves and to discover how often we have rationalized our failures and weaknesses, dodged vital issues and run skulkingly away. Mistakes made in our jobs, marriage and social contacts stand out clearly. Especially when we are a bit scared is the salutary effect of sickness particularly marked; typhoid and pneumonia have reformed drunkards, thieves, liars and wife-beaters. If a stiff bout of illness brings us near to death's door—perhaps so much the better. For only when the way straitens and the gate grows narrow, do some people discover their soul, their God, or their life work.

Florence Nightingale, too ill to move from her bed, reorganized the hospitals of England. Semi-paralyzed, and under the constant menace of apoplexy, Pasteur was tireless in his attack on disease. Innumerable illustrations might be cited. And the testimony from humbler sources is just as striking. A young man in a hospital for two weeks discovered that he had always wanted to be a research worker in chemistry. Till then he had been "too busy" as a drug salesman. Today he is making a splendid go of his new job. While recuperating from scarlet fever a woman in her 40's vanquished the terrors she had felt about approaching middle life. "I am not going to return to my former state of feeling superfluous," she resolved. "My children are married and can take care of themselves. I'm going to start a millinery shop and make them like it." She did, and needless to say, they do!

In talking with patients, I find that many who have sojourned in "the pleasant land of counterpane" say that for the first time they learned the true meaning of friendship, often undecipherable in the complex pattern of this modern world. They say also that they discovered secret depths of their own life-stream. "After a few days in bed," writes one of them, "time becomes an unimagined luxury. Time to think, time to enjoy, time to create, time at last to express the best and deepest part of human nature. Illness is one of the great privileges of life; it whispers that man's destiny is bound up with transcendental powers. Illness pares and lops off the outer parts of life and leaves one with the essence of it."

Even pain confers spiritual insight, a beauty of outlook, a philosophy of life, and understanding and forgiveness of humanity—in short, a quality of peace and serenity—that can scarcely be acquired by the "owner of pure horse flesh." Suffering is a cleansing fire that chars away much of the meanness, triviality and restlessness of so-called "health." Milton declared, "Who best can suffer, best can do." The proof is his *Paradise Lost* written after he was stricken blind.

In illness you discover that your imagination is more active than it ever has been; unshackled by petty details of existence, you daydream, build air castles, make plans. As your physical strength returns, your fantasies are not dulled; rather they become more practical, and you definitely decide upon the things you will put into action when you recover.

Your concentration improves tremendously. You are astonished to find how easily you can think a difficult problem through to its solution. Why? Because your instincts of self-preservation are speeded up, and all nonessentials are eliminated. It is interesting too that your reactions to what you see and hear are more acute. A robin at the window, a fleeting expression on a friend's face are delicately savored as memorable experiences. Illness *sensitizes* you; that is why you may be irritable. You may even weep at the least provocation. But this sensitivity should be turned to better uses. Now is an excellent time to develop yourself along a special line, to read widely, or to create original ideas. Contrary to an old belief, a sick body does not necessarily make a sick mind, except in those who try to make their illness an excuse for laziness. No one honestly can use his illness, whatever its nature, as an excuse for ineffectualness or failure.

If you have never been sick, never lost so much as a day in bed—then you have missed something! When your turn comes, don't be dismayed. Remind yourself that pain and suffering may teach you something valuable, something that you could not have learned otherwise. Possibly it may change for the better the entire course of your life. You and those around you will be happier if you can look upon any illness as a blessing in disguise, and wisely determine to make the most of it. You *can* turn your sickness into an asset.

»«

Traveler's Lament

A SIX-YEAR-OLD was motoring to the West Coast with his family. The weather had been bad, the traveling rough. After a particularly hard day they stopped in a Texas town, took the only available hotel rooms and sank wearily into their beds. Suddenly the silence was broken by the six-year-old. "Mommy," he wailed, "why don't we just go back home and live happily ever after?"   —Claire MacMurray in Cleveland *Plain Dealer*

The Art of
Paying a Compliment

By J. Donald Adams

ONE of the best ways to smooth relations with other people is to be adept at the art of paying a compliment. The sincere, appreciative remark helps the other fellow to realize his own inherent worth. And, what is more, the ability to pay a compliment bolsters our own ego—which is not a bad thing either.

We never forget a compliment that has deeply pleased us, nor do we forget the person who made it. Yet often the luster of praise is needlessly dimmed by awkwardness in the manner of its giving. Like all ventures in human relations, the art of paying a compliment takes thought and practice. We have all experienced the remorse of having our praise fall flat because we chose the wrong time to give it or the wrong language to couch it in.

· According to Leonard Lyons, a compliment of the right sort was paid Toscanini by Judith Anderson when she saw him after a concert.

"She didn't say I had conducted well," said the maestro. "I knew that. She said I looked handsome." It is human nature to enjoy praise for something we are not noted for. When someone calls attention to an unadvertised facet of our personality it makes him forever our friend.

We all pride ourselves on our individual distinctions. It is a gross misconception to think you are complimenting a person by telling him he looks exactly like So-and-So, even if So-and-So is a movie idol. I have noticed that nothing pleases us less than to have a double.

The best compliments are those which reinforce our sense of personal identity. A woman acquaintance of mine who is slender to the point of being skinny was sitting on the beach when a friend remarked, "You certainly have a flat stomach!" After the first shock wore off, she felt pleased by this frank tribute to her appearance.

One of the most satisfying kinds of compliment to give or receive is the double, or relayed, compliment—one passed on to you by someone who heard it. Recently, a correspondent enclosed a letter he had received from a friend who happens to be a man of eminence in his field. This man's opinion of a column I had written puffed me up considerably. Relayed to me by my friend, it was a compliment amplified —far more effective than if it had come direct.

The ingenuous compliment may touch us deeply, but it is probably the hardest to pay, for it depends on pure inspiration. I am reminded of an example that Margery Wilson cites in her book *Make Up Your Mind*. She once had a butler who knew a great deal about sculpture. His hero was Gutzon Borglum, the man who carved the massive portraits of Washington, Jefferson, Lincoln and Theodore Roosevelt on a mountainside in the Black Hills of South Dakota. Borglum came to tea and the butler, beside himself with excitement, spilled a glass of wine on him. Swabbing the sculptor desperately with a napkin, the butler said, "I could have served a lesser man perfectly."

To his embarrassed worshiper Borglum replied, "I was never so complimented in my life!"

Among the varieties of compliment is one with a particularly pleasing punch; I should call it a "bonus compliment of recall." It is indeed a heart-warming surprise when a person remembers something you said a long time ago that made a lasting impression on him. That it should have been hoarded and served up to you at an appropriate time is an experience bound to smooth out your kinks of self-doubt.

Urging me to go on a trip, a friend once said, "Memories are the best investment you can make." It was just as casual as that, yet it gave me courage to travel as I might not have, thinking I ought not to invest the money or the time. When I later reminded my friend of his remark, I found he had completely forgotten the incident. But my reminding him nourished his ego anew.

Compliments offered in the kidding vein hit home just as surely as those with a serious-minded approach. And they involve no responsibility on the part of the receiver for a mincing rejoinder. He can laugh with the crowd and happily accept his accolade.

I overheard a remark of this type in a restaurant recently. A group of businessmen were finishing lunch at the table next to mine. Said one of them, "Harry is the best computing machine here; he's a real mathemagician. So he gets stuck with figuring out the check!" They all chuckled; it was obviously a compliment.

A well-turned compliment is never unmindful of what are regarded as the distinguishing characteristics of the sexes. I think most men feel some measure of annoyance at being praised for individual features. Compliments on complexion or eyes, after all, border on what is most prized as a feminine attribute. But men will bask in the sunshine of being told how well built or how strong they are. Women, obviously enough, prefer to be saluted for their looks, their intuition, their capacity for understanding and sympathy.

Pushed to the point of flattery, the compliment is distasteful to most of us. We have all known people so vain that no syrup is too sweet for their taste, but they are in the minority. If we have any sense of proportion about ourselves, we are at once aware that we are being overpraised. This can be as painful as criticism.

Sometimes in a group of people we get so caught up in our own good words for a person that we overplay a tribute. When we finally stop, the recipient feels called upon to fill the sudden void in conversation with refutation equal in violence.

A compliment casually worked in, so that the threads of general conversation can easily be retrieved, makes less demands on the recipient—and leaves him with more glow than he would have gained from the spotlight. For example, as simple a thing as a question may become a compliment. If, instead of telling a neighbor that you think he has a wonderful garden, you ask him for advice about yours, you accomplish a number of things. You have indicated that you admire his gardening skill; you have singled him out from the crowd. He can give you advice without any to-do about acknowledging the compliment. And he's likely to feel you are a discerning guy.

When a man by virtue of success comes in for constant personal kudos, we face a dilemma when we want to get across to him our feelings of admiration. We know he must be tired of hearing the same things, of making the same perfunctory acknowledgment. Here is a place where we can use the indirect compliment to great advantage by telling him how much we admire his children, his house, his garden, a picture that hangs in his living room. In effect we are telling him that we admire what he admires. A man may question the truth of what we say about *him,* but he will not question a tribute to the things he loves.

One of the choicest indirect compliments I have heard was a husband's anniversary greeting to his wife: "I love you not only for what you are, but for what I am when I am with you." She prized those words more than the handsome present.

Compliments smooth the paths of social intercourse, help to dispel the recurrent dissatisfaction most of us have with ourselves and encourage us toward new achievement. "Appreciative words," says Dr. George W. Crane, "are the most powerful force for good will on earth."

Campus Hero

NEAR the university in Stockholm, I saw a mob of wildly shouting students surrounding a fair-haired lad. He was held high on their shoulders, his cheeks scarlet with excitement. There was a wreath of green leaves around his shoulders and he was being pelted with roses by the girls, while boys and girls alike shouted, "Rah, rah, Carl! Rah, rah, Carl!"

Football captain, I thought, and then inquired of a good-looking Swede: "Some brilliant athlete, I suppose?"

"No, madame. He is graduating and is the honor student of the year."

"Well, it's the first time I ever saw such wild excitement over scholarship," I commented.

There was a glint of amusement in the man's eyes as he asked, "For what purpose, then, does your country build schools?"

—Contributed by Montanye Perry

Sleep and How to Get More of It

By Robert Coughlan   *Condensed from Life*

A GALLUP POLL of eight North Atlantic nations in 1948 showed that Americans are the champion insomniacs: 52 percent said they had trouble part or all of the time going to sleep at night. They and their friends, the people who wake up in the night and the people who can't sleep past a fixed hour in the morning, are the sleeping-pill customers. In one recent year they bought 3,360,000,000 pills, an average of 24 for every American.

Insomnia has never killed anyone. But to the people who suffer from it, insomnia is as debilitating as anemia, as nagging as an ulcer, uncomfortable as a leg in a cast. And chronic insomnia has the peculiar distinction of being its own cause. The advanced insomniac approaches his bed in a state of anxiety and spends the next hours awake because he is fearful that he will do just that.

No one knows exactly what sleep is or exactly what causes it or exactly why it is needed. The process can only be described.

After a normal period of relaxation (up to 30 minutes) the prospective sleeper reaches a stage of semiconsciousness which is neither sleeping nor waking. It is a feeling of "floating" or being "disembodied." If all goes well, sensation ends and the subject floats over the borderline to unconsciousness. The passage takes only a few seconds and is marked at the end by an abrupt shift in the origin of brain waves (minute electrical charges) from the back part of the head to the front. This shift was discovered some years ago by Dr. Mary A. B. Brazier at the Massachusetts General Hospital, but there is no theory to explain why it takes place. It is a triumph to have discovered it, however, since heretofore sleep investigators have been handicapped by not knowing the exact dividing line between sleep and waking.

With the reversal in the source of brain waves sleep has come, bringing with it mysterious and rather alarming transformations. The sleeper breathes slowly. His eyeballs turn out and up. His fingers grow cold and his toes grow warm. His senses fade. The blood does not leave his brain, contrary to popular belief, but his blood pressure falls rapidly, becoming weakest about three hours after sleep begins. His heart rate also decreases, but often rises again to reach a peak in two or three hours, after which it slackens and becomes slowest about four hours later. His body temperature falls about one half a degree Fahrenheit. The sleeper has at first lain quietly, but soon he begins to move—an arm, a leg, now his whole body, shifting from side to side and front to back. In the morning he may declare with perfect honesty that he slept "like a log," but an observer would have recorded that he changed position between 20 and 60 times. It is possible to "sleep like a log" only if one is anesthetized or dead-drunk or feeble-minded.

After a certain time, depending on the sleeper's normal sleep span, the initial process is reversed. Sleep becomes lighter, consciousness flickers, fails, flickers, the brain charge is reversed—the sleeper is awake. Perhaps he yawns, thereby inhaling extra oxygen to lower the proportion of carbon dioxide that has accumulated in his body as a result of his muscular inactivity during sleep.

This, then, is normal sleep, "tired nature's sweet restorer," the insomniac's goal. Why is it so often so difficult to attain?

In general, insomnia is a price man pays for having become a man. Sleep is not a problem for earthworms, tadpoles, bears or even monkeys, and only rarely for young babies. These lower forms of life lack the intelligence required for insomnia—which means, physiologically, that they lack the highly developed cerebral cortex of the adult human.

Aside from purely physical causes such as disease and organic malfunctionings, it is one word—anxiety—in all its complexities of cause and effect, which explains most sleep aberrations. It usually is anxiety that causes nightmares and "night terrors" in children, and it is the most frequent cause of sleepwalking and sleeptalking. The cure therefore is obvious: stop worrying, especially at bedtime.

That, however, is easier urged than done. It is not enough, for example, to tell a battle-shocked soldier who relives his war experiences at night to forget them; obviously he would like nothing better. The same is true of the ordinary insomniac. Countless nights have reverberated to his ancient cry, "If I could only stop thinking!" In advanced cases the only cure may be psychotherapy, but for most of humanity there are techniques which can be applied in the privacy of one's own bedroom.

The first and obvious one is to direct the mind by an effort of will away from personal matters. If one must think, let it be about objective rather than subjective things: not about one's own love problems but about the bees and the flowers. Along with this must be a high degree of muscular relaxation. Complete relaxation is, of course, impossible (nor is it necessary; people go to sleep while driving, and exhausted soldiers fall asleep while actually on the march). But the insomniac should aim for as much of it as he can get, with special attention to the muscles of the head, neck and chest. The reason for this is simply that a greater area of the brain is devoted to the incoming and outgoing signals of these muscles than to those of all the others combined. After the eye muscles, the ones to discipline most firmly are the speech muscles. The ability to think is intimately connected with the ability to talk. It is, in fact, almost impossible to maintain coherent thought without activity (minute, to be sure, but present and measurable) in the voice muscles. It follows that if the muscles having to do with speech are relaxed, the mind, in bafflement, will at last give up. The best way to do this is to let the jaw and whole face go slack in an expression of complete stupidity.

Mental vacuity and physical inertness are thus the uncomely handmaidens of sleep. They can be acquired by practice, but not easily: sometimes a year of conscientious application is necessary. They can be helped along by various palliatives, which will be useful to the light and troubled sleepers as well as to the true insomniac.

There are no uniformly effective rules for the best way to sleep. Room temperature, bed coverings, ventilation are all matters of individual preference or habit. Most people sleep better alone. The admonition against lying on one's left, or "heart," side is pure superstition, since the heart is approximately in the middle of the upper body cavity and since, in any case, the normal turnings of the sleeper will inevitably land him on the left side several times during a night. Provided the sleeper enjoys normal digestion, a big meal helps rather than hinders sleep, and for some people the process may be helped along by a cup of good coffee to stimulate the digestive processes. And there is also much to be said for the "nightcap" as a soporific.

Other forms of bedtime nourishment seem to have little effect. Tests at the University of Chicago showed no significant differences whether the subjects did or did not take one or two sandwiches or hot or cold milk before retiring. If a snack, a bath and 15 minutes of music seem to form a satisfying pre-sleep ritual, then they are useful.

Women, on the average, get more sleep than men, partly because they carry around relatively fewer problems and partly also because of their custom of creaming their faces, brushing their hair and spending a good deal of time in similar pre-bed activities. The ritual itself comes to be associated with sleep and thus helps to bring it. The same associative value applies to the bed itself and speaks against making reading in bed a part of the ritual, especially the reading of mystery novels.

It is helpful to establish a regular time for going to bed and getting up. This can as well be late to bed and late to rise as the other way around, but it should be consistent. The reason lies in the workings of what Dr. Nathaniel Kleitman, University of Chicago physiologist who spent more than 30 years probing mysteries of sleep, calls "the diurnal sleep cycle." Everyone undergoes a rise and fall of body temperature over a 24-hour period. The average swing is a little over one degree, although swings of twice that are not uncommon. The drop in temperature brings with it a natural period for sleeping and this drop can be induced by repetition to arrive at a certain time.

Thus the problem sleeper, by going to bed at a regular hour, can establish a temperature cycle which automatically will make him sleepy at that time. He may choose any hour around the clock. Some persons can establish a cycle easily; others may take months and must count on a long period of nightly restlessness before the cycle clicks into place.

Temperature cycles differ. There is the kind that climbs steeply as its owner wakes up, causing him to jump out of bed eagerly. He is a "morning person"; his temperature keeps going up and reaches a peak around noontime, when he is at his most wide-awake. When it begins to fall soon after, he begins to feel less energetic. His temperature continues to fall, reaching the "drowsiness level" fairly early in the evening.

The "evening person's" temperature rises very slowly and does not reach its peak until late afternoon, when he feels at his best. He dislikes getting up, and feels groggy and out-of-sorts in the morning. By the time the "morning person" is looking forward to bed the "evening person" may be wound up and going strong. Dr. Kleitman is fond of the aphorism: "More marriages are broken up by temperature than by temperament."

Dr. Kleitman's tests show that in both mental and physical tasks performance and resistance to fatigue are best when temperature is high, worst when it is low. Consequently it is a good idea to arrange the most important affairs of the day so that they can be handled during the period of maximum temperature.

In the past many experimenters have supposed that fatigue created various "waste products" and "poisons" that numb the brain, and that sleep was needed to eliminate them from the body. There were several drawbacks to this theory. One was that no one could ever find any such poisons in the blood stream. Another was the evident truth of the familiar expression, "too tired to sleep"; there comes a stage when fatigue is a hindrance rather than a help to slumber. Also Dr. Kleitman discovered that people of all types usually are least efficient after a night's sleep; it was no longer possible to imagine sleep as a cleanser of poisons. Sleep can take place without fatigue. A completely rested person can fall asleep if he relaxes enough. On the other hand, "healthy fatigue" is an aid to relaxation.

The sleeping pill should be the last resort of an insomniac. The standard barbiturate drugs are not harmful in themselves if taken in medically prescribed doses. But, said Dr. Harris Isbell, director of research at the U.S. Public Health Service Hospital, Lexington, Ky., "taken regularly in large doses, they can be habit-forming, and the addiction can be much more painfully difficult to break and more dangerous than morphine addiction."

Suppose that the chronic insomniac has tried all the suggestions given here—in vain. What then?

He shouldn't lose any sleep over it. For it is certain that if he keeps at it he will learn the trick, and it is equally true that it will do him no serious harm if he takes a long time to do it. Chronic "undersleep-ing" is widely supposed to lead to mental and physical breakdown, but almost certainly it can do neither. Experiments show that protracted sleeplessness seems to have no pronounced effect on the fundamental physiological processes of the body. For tasks requiring short periods of physical or mental coördination, lack of sleep leaves performance as good as ever. In tasks calling for sustained effort, loss of sleep causes performance to fall off drastically. And it does increase sensitiveness to pain.

The common belief that one cannot "pay back" a sleep debt is un-true, and the debt, with interest, can be liquidated in one good long sleep.

There is no absolute answer to the question: "How much sleep should people get?" It depends on age, health and activity. Laboratory tests show that sleep needs tend to decline each year from birth to senil-ity. But a 50-year-old mathematician probably will need more sleep than a 25-year-old ditchdigger, for physical workers usually can get along on about two hours less a night than people who work with their brains. If Jones feels good on three hours' sleep, he needs no more; if Smith doesn't feel good on eight hours', the chances are that he needs nine or even ten.

Happily for the insomniac, rest can take place without sleep, and so long as he lies down and gets at least a measure of relaxation in mind and body, he can keep going almost indefinitely. He may not feel well; probably he will feel awful; but that will be the worst of it.

For Parents Only

» REASONING with a child is fine, if you can reach the child's reason without destroying your own.   —John Mason Brown

» WE LEARN from experience. A man never wakes up his second baby just to see it smile.

—Grace Williams, quoted by Frances Rodman in New York *Times Magazine*

We All Need PRAISE

Princess Alexandra Kropotkin

Condensed from Liberty

F PARENTS and bosses administered praise oftener, the psycho-analysts would get a rest from the overwhelming rush of patients suffering from inferiority complexes. For we must bask in the warmth of approval now and then; otherwise the health of our self-respect becomes seriously endangered.

As a rule, husbands are blinder than wives to this need in the home. A survey of rural life uncovered one general complaint made by women living on farms. As the wife of one prosperous Ohio farmer expressed it:

"Maybe when I'm a hundred years old I'll get used to having everything I do taken for granted. As it is, life comes pretty hard when you don't hear a word of thanks for your efforts. Sometimes I feel like copying the woman who served her menfolk cattle fodder one day for dinner, after waiting 20 years for a word of praise. 'I've never heard aught to make me think you'd know the difference,' she said when they declared she must be crazy."

Take the point of personal appearance. It is a curious thing how many men, who never fail to observe the looks of other women, let their own wives go year after year without a word of attention. Thereby is sown the seed for much jealousy.

Dr. Ira S. Wile, who had wide experience in dealing with difficult children, once told me of a particularly interesting case which made him realize the need of praise as a practical doctor's prescription.

"It was a case of twin boys," he said. "One was particularly bright; the other seemed mentally inferior. The father asked me to find the reason.

"When I had gained the child's confidence he told me the story children almost invariably tell in such cases.

"'Why don't people like me,' he asked, 'the same as they do my brother? When he does anything they smile. When I do anything they scowl. I can't ever seem to do anything as good as he does.'

"I separated those boys as much as possible," said Dr. Wile. "I had them placed in different classes in school. I told their parents to stop using comparisons as a goad upon the backward one, and to praise him for his own little accomplishments. He soon was standing on his own feet."

Lack of praise is evident in business offices, too. One New Year's Day a millionaire of my acquaintance, whose pride it was never to offer a tip for any service, faced an unforgettable tragedy. His chief accountant committed suicide. The books were found to be in perfect order, the affairs of the dead man—a modest bachelor—were prosperous and calm. The only letter left by the accountant was a brief note to his millionaire employer. It read: "In 30 years I have never had one word of encouragement. I'm fed up."

The Searching Question

At Columbia College they still remember the time the late Professor Raymond Weaver gave his first class in English literature their first quiz. A whistle of joy went up from the group, which had been trying to make things hard for the new instructor, when Weaver wrote on the blackboard, "Which of the books read so far has interested you least?"

But then Weaver wrote the second and last question: "To what defect in yourself do you attribute this lack of interest?"

—Joseph Wood Krutch in *The Nation*

Take Your Profits from Defeat

Condensed from The Forum

William Moulton Marston

F THERE IS any single factor that makes for success in living, it is the ability to draw dividends from defeat. Every success I know has been reached because the person was able to analyze defeat and actually profit by it in his next undertaking. If you confuse defeat with failure, then you are doomed indeed to failure. For it isn't defeat that makes you fail; it is your own refusal to see in defeat the guide and incentive to success.

Defeats are nothing to be ashamed of. They are routine incidents in the life of every man who achieves. But defeat is a dead loss unless you do face it without humiliation, analyze it and learn why you failed to make your objective. If you look upon defeat in the light of a friendly tipster, it ceases to be mortifying, and the task of analyzing its causes within yourself becomes both interesting and profitable.

Defeat, in other words, can help to cure its own cause. Hiram Kimball, a middle-aged New Englander, inherited his uncle's bookshop, which had been modestly successful for more than 20 years. Fired with ambition to modernize and expand the business, Hiram leased a new corner, put in a larger stock, advertised extensively and doubled his overhead. A couple of years later he was bankrupt.

Defeat left Kimball with the firsthand experience he had previously lacked and a lot of secondhand books the receivers had been unable to sell. He put defeat to work. He built a shack with his own hands on a much-traveled highway and spread his old books all over the place invitingly. Results came with surprising promptness. Secondhand books, as Hiram well knew, are gateways to mental adventure which few passers-by can refrain from exploring. In three seasons he made twice the money he had lost. His defeat equipped him for a satisfying and original success.

Not only does defeat prepare us for success, but nothing can arouse within us such a compelling desire to succeed. The desire to dominate is the first of four primary emotions to appear. If you let a baby grasp a rod and try to pull it away he will cling more and more tightly until his whole weight is suspended. It is this same reaction which should give you new and greater strength every time you are defeated. If you exploit the power which defeat gives, you can accomplish with it far more than you are capable of when all is serene.

John Paul Jones stood on the shot-torn deck of the *Bon Homme Richard*. The *Alliance* had deserted him. He was raked fore and aft by cruel fire from British men-o'-war. The *Richard* began to sink. John Paul was a beaten man. But when the British commander asked Jones to surrender, a fighting fury of defeat suddenly boiled over in the American. Said he, "I have not yet begun to fight." He rammed his waterlogged ship against the nearest British vessel, grappled and boarded her, and in no time at all the fight was over. From the bitterness of defeat, John Paul Jones drew a conqueror's spirit which assured him victory.

Heroes are often made in moments of defeat. Theodore Roosevelt, who insisted on finishing a political speech after a would-be assassin had pumped a revolver bullet into his breast, got that way by virtue of a good licking he took as a terrified boy. T. R. made up his exceedingly dominant mind that he would learn to box, to shoot, to play tough games with the best of them and to give more than he received. He carried out his resolution because he had the impetus of defeat behind him.

I know a man who suffered very unpleasant consequences from a love affair. The experience conditioned his whole life; it induced in him a fear of women which expresses itself in running away or turning in upon himself when they are present. To everybody but himself this fellow's phobia is amusing. But for him it is real and painful. Instead of facing his love defeat, analyzing its real causes and taking profits in future relationships, he is beaten by one reverse.

It will pay you to search your own behavior for stupidities of this type and get rid of them. There are people who have lost their jobs who are afraid to ask for work; people rebuffed when they sought a raise who are afraid now to speak to the boss; mothers whose children almost drowned who will not permit them to go into the water to learn to swim. Any fear of defeat which you do not possess will impress you as ridiculous. But the chances are you have a pet defeat of your own from which you run away with equal unreasonableness.

People try in many ways to disguise the fact that they are running away. The simplest trick is to tell yourself that you are not defeated, that you are making satisfactory progress when, as a matter of fact, you are completely blocked. I know a man who tries to keep his self-confidence by continually telling himself and his friends that he is about to get a promotion. His underconsciousness isn't fooled; he knows well enough that he long ago reached the limit of advancement in his present position. Actually he is losing confidence in himself with every pathetic attempt to cover up defeat.

Another trick some people play on themselves is to "forget" their defeats. There might be merit in this method if it were psychologically possible to amputate unpleasant memories. But it isn't. All you can do is repress them. Experiences thus buried throw off emotional poisons, fears, depressions, hatreds, antisocial feelings. They cause not only mental disorders but physical sicknesses. And instead of bolstering up your self-confidence, such a complex will in time destroy it completely.

If the shock of an imagined failure has numbed you for the moment so that you cannot think clearly, go out on a party, chop down a tree, punch a heavy bag; do something violent and unusual. Then sleep for a while. When you wake up you will find that your brain is thinking hard and fast. Now is the time to spot your profits and make your comeback. Note particularly the false values, the silly, futile desires which this temporary setback has stripped away. Then set your fundamental desires to work, free from the encumbrances which defeat has revealed to you. For this profit alone, defeat is worth while. Put all your resentment into a thrust toward your goal. If defeat releases inside of you an unbeatable dominance, nothing can keep you from success on your next attempt.

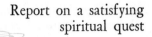

I Am For the Churches

By Roger William Riis

THERE WAS a time when I scoffed at the churches. Then one day during the last war, on a sudden whim, I attended a service—for the first time in 22 years. And what did the church offer me? A simple, reverent service, featured by a sermon on "Peter, the Rock," on the permanence and the beauty of the church.

I found that I was acutely interested in hearing about anything that had permanence, beauty and unselfish endeavor. It fell on my spirit like water on a desert, and I went out stirred and grateful.

A week later I took my curiosity to another church, and heard the minister—in a singularly lovely building—talk simply and beautifully on "The Ascending Life." Without a trace of sanctimonious heroics, he conversed informally about the insistent demand of life to rise, to grow, to improve itself. It was adult, it was spiritual; and to me personally it was helpful.

Since then I have made it a point to attend and study churches—all kinds. And I state with assurance that the critics of churches today don't know what they are talking about. True, a minority of churches still offer a dull, repellent form of salvation, some in ugly buildings, some with painful music, some with humdrum ministers. But you don't have to go to those churches, nor need you condemn all churches because some fail.

It is obvious that the assailants of churches do not go to church. They don't know what the churches are doing these days. They don't know that the average minister is a more interesting, better-informed man than most of the critics.

I am for the churches because they have something for me, and something for civilization. Dr. Ernest Fremont Tittle, the late great minister of First Methodist Church of Evanston, Ill., said: "Let God be thanked there is on earth an institution that has a high opinion of man, declaring that he is in some sense a son of God, who has within himself divine possibilities; an institution that transcends race, nation and class; an institution which is loyally undertaking to embody the spirit of Christ, and in His name to relieve human suffering, promote human welfare and carry on a ministry of reconciliation among men."

I find myself unable any longer to answer that kind of platform with "I'd rather go into the woods and worship alone. Many of the clergy are dull, concerned over trivial taboos. Sunday is my day for loafing."

Countless times I have found in church something which lifted my spirit. That, I now believe, was what I unconsciously sought. The churches' varied social activities mean little or nothing to me. But others find social outlets in church work. So much the better; they get what they seek, and so do I.

New York's beautiful Church of the Ascension has great wooden doors which open outward, but they are carved on the inside because they are never closed. Every year, 30,000 persons slip in for quiet meditation. They get what they seek.

The remote hamlet of Jonesville, Va., has been holding an annual four-day prayer meeting for more than a century. The day I was there 2000 people were in attendance. Men, women, children, earnest and devout. Revival stuff? No. Simple, direct Christianity. Love-thy-neighbor stuff. Good stuff. These people get what they seek.

The Dominican Sisters at Corpus Christi Church in New York conducted a "project" in tolerance in their church school. Not an attack on intolerance, but a positive, laboratory experiment in tolerance. This demonstration by Catholic, Jewish and Protestant children raised a wild flurry of hope in my heart; if human beings can do this sort of thing, we'll get this world fixed right yet!

When you go to church you should actively **seek** something. You must not go like an empty bucket, waiting passively to be filled. When you go to a movie you take at least a hopeful, sympathetic attitude. That's the least you should bring to a church. In many and many a church in every part of the country every Sunday you can see congregations of 1000 and 1500 people, obviously getting whatever values they seek. Church attendance, by the way, is bigger than skeptics think, and growing. Go see for yourself.

Why is one church a power in its community, while others are not?

The personality of the clergyman is the most important reason. Churches are human institutions, clergymen are human beings and they are not all great spiritual leaders. But when they are—and they are often—they manage to make your relations with God an astonishingly practical, useful, alluring thing.

The clergyman himself is the real factor in a church, much more important than architecture or music or furnishings. Most sermons are surprisingly good, and useful. It has been said that no one can deliver a vital address as often as a cleric must. But why miss the many vital addresses he does deliver? It is said that sermons are remote from world affairs. Yet half those I have heard interpreted world affairs from the Christian viewpoint. A third of them were concerned exclusively with Gospel teachings.

Successful churches are those whose clergymen set forth uncompromising Christianity, sticking closest to Christ's very difficult but challenging teaching. That is the great asset of the church. The more vigorously a church proclaims it, the more people respect and follow that church.

What I like most about going to church is that it turns one's attention, willy-nilly, to higher things for at least a little while each week. Man does *not* live by bread alone; he requires cultivation of his spirit. Even when I have wandered into a church where the minister was dull, the music bad, the interior ugly, I have been compelled by my very presence there to think about things loftier than my daily affairs. Even if you differ with what a minister says, you have to listen to him and organize your opposing reasons, and that's good for you. I know it is good for me.

In a world haunted by violence, churches do their very best to represent the spirit. I am warmly grateful for that. Significantly, the two nations which in my lifetime have been officially anti-church are the nations of Nazism and Communism. In nations where the spirit of man is free, churches flourish as men turn toward God.

It may be that the democratic way will not finally overcome the tyrannical way until and unless the democracies somehow crusade under the banner of the church. How can we defeat the destructive dynamics of Communism unless we employ the constructive dynamics of the spirit?

William Penn said, "Men must be governed by God or they will be ruled by tyrants." The world for a quarter century has been his witness.

"To love God," said a beloved minister, "is to believe, despite every appearance to the contrary, that slavery, war and crippling poverty can be banished from the earth, and that conditions favorable to the highest development of the human spirit can be created."

That is extraordinarily practical Christianity. In fact, I cannot distinguish it from the democratic ideal in action. Believing that, I can no longer say that I would rather do my worshiping alone, that Sunday is my day for loafing.

It is an exciting spiritual adventure, this going to church. Try it. Pay no attention to denomination while you investigate. Just out of the curiosity you owe your spiritual health, explore a little. You will almost certainly find, in every community, one church that will give you what *you* want, even though you cannot put that want into words.

Whether or not we realize it, each of us has a personal spiritual quest. It is the most important thing we should be about, and it is only ourselves we cheat if we ignore it. In this, of all ages, it is time we pushed that quest. I have found the churches a good place to pursue it. If they offered nothing but that, they should now be upheld by all men of intelligence and good will.

+-+-+-+-+-+-+-+-+-+-+

REPLYING to the tributes paid to him at a testimonial dinner, Herbert Bayard Swope said: "I cannot give you the formula for success, but I *can* give you the formula for failure—Try to please everybody."

—Leonard Lyons

It's More Fun

to Be Fit

By Gene Tunney
Commander, U. S. N. R.

PHYSICAL flabbiness has always seemed to me a criminal, even sacrilegious abuse of that wonderful instrument, the human body. Ever since boyhood I've made a religion of keeping in shape by regular, conscientious exercise. Adhering to a high ideal of stamina and endurance has paid me dividends not only in the prize ring but in the almost equally grueling struggle of everyday life.

To enjoy the glow of good health, you must exercise. I don't recommend that you develop bulging biceps or go in for exhausting roadwork and bag-punching. But I do say that, if you will regularly devote 15 minutes a day, preferably before breakfast, for 60 days to the simple set of exercises that I devised for conditioning men in the Navy, you will enjoy increased physical buoyancy and mental vigor. Perform them faithfully and you can take puffy inches off your waistline, recondition unused muscles, feel better, work better and live longer.

The man who has allowed his body to deteriorate cuts a pitiful figure—chest collapsed, stomach protruding. His sagging diaphragm forces his visceral apparatus out of place, hindering digestive and eliminative processes. He tires easily and complains that he feels like the breaking up of a hard winter.

The first thing this human mealsack must learn is proper posture, the basis of all physical conditioning. "Head up, chin in, chest out, stomach in." Proper body carriage conserves the energy that postural defects drain away.

The worst of these defects is the protruding paunch caused by abdominal muscles that have become flabby through disuse. There are broad bands of muscle-like cinch straps around your waistline, whose job is to hold the stomach, intestines and liver in place. When these muscles lose their firmness or "tone," they allow the intestines to sink down and become impaired in function. Indigestion, headache, constipation and chronic fatigue follow.

To toughen the abdominal muscles, I developed exercise No. 1. If you perform it 20 times every morning, gradually working up to 50, you'll get rid of that paunch and the evils that accompany it. Remember that it's never too late to start rehabilitating broken-down muscles. The material is there, waiting for you to begin working on it.

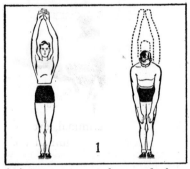

(A) Raise arms to front and above head, inhaling deeply. (B) Lower arms, keeping them stiff and straight, until hands touch knees, with head dropped until chin touches collarbone. Bend at diaphragm, not at waist. Draw stomach up. As hands touch knees, exhale. Do 20 times.

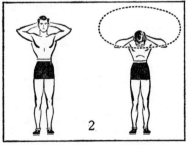

(A) Clasp hands behind head, heels 5 inches apart. (B) With diaphragm drawn up and shoulder muscles relaxed, swing upper body in circle, ending at original position. Exhale on way down, inhale on way up. Circle to left 10 times, then to right 10 times.

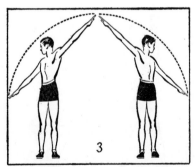

(A) Extend arms sidewise at shoulder level. Drop right hand 10 inches, raise left 10 inches. Draw stomach up; hold hips stationary. Swing right hand behind and down, the left going forward and up. Keep arms in straight line. Pivot from diaphragm, eyes and head following hand that goes back and down. Inhale as head comes up. (B) With stomach drawn up, exhale as head follows left hand around and down. Do 20 times to each side.

Another deformity of posture is the flat, sunken chest, which occurs when we persistently neglect to use full lung capacity. We can get along on only 20 percent of our lung capacity, but that dragging sort of existence is a poor substitute for the vitality we enjoy when the twin bellows of our lungs are taking in great drafts of oxygen. As Dr. George Crile said, "Oxidization is the only source of animal energy. We *live* in proportion to the oxygen we get into our lungs."

A concave chest means that your diaphragm is sagging. This elastic wall of muscle, the partition between your abdomen and chest, forms the major part of the bellows mechanism used in breathing. If the diaphragm sags, the bellows won't work properly and you don't get as much oxygen as

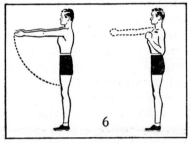

(A) Stand at attention; slowly raise arms straight to front, shoulder width apart. Inhale, filling lungs, and clench fists. (B) Move arms back and forward vigorously 6 times, holding breath. On 6th stroke, exhale and return to attention. Do this 6 times.

(A) Stand with your heels 15 inches apart. Inhale while rising on your toes and reaching arms overhead. (B) Bring the arms down stiff and straight between the legs, exhaling and bending knees and touching floor with the backs of your hands as far behind the heels as possible, to stretch back, hips and abdominal muscles. Repeat this exercise 20 times.

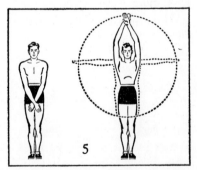

(A) Stand at attention; cross hands. (B) On count of 1, slowly raise arms in semicircle to front and overhead, rising on toes and inhaling steadily. Hands cross each other before reaching top position. On count 2, bring arms in semicircle slowly down to sides, holding breath until they reach original position. On count 3, exhale completely. Do 6 times vigorously.

you need. According to Dr. Herman N. Bundesen of Chicago, a sagging diaphragm may lead to a stroke of coronary thrombosis. He explains that an insufficient supply of oxygen slows down heart action; the blood flow becomes sluggish; a blood clot may form and clog the coronary artery of the heart, stoppering it like a cork.

Exercises Nos. 1, 2 and 3 will strengthen and put new resiliency into the diaphragm, and draw blood-purifying oxygen into every recess of the lungs. But the job isn't done when the exercise period is over. Keep your chest out and keep your stomach in, until it becomes a habit. At the end of a month you will have doubled your lung capacity, and thereby benefited every cell of your body.

Many people complain of a chronic weariness that sleep will not banish. Their trouble is that too little blood is pumped through the body per minute; this sluggishness, permitting poisonous waste matter to accumulate in every cell, clogs the channels of energy.

Sinking into an overstuffed armchair is not the cure. You must speed up your circulation. The only way to do this is to exercise. A brisk 20-minute walk will send 25 to 30 quarts of blood coursing vigorously through your arteries every 60 seconds—blood that contains four times more oxygen than when you loll in a chair.

While walking, inhale deeply for six paces, holding the breath, then exhale slowly. Do this ten or 15 times during your walk. Like a cleansing torrent, the increased circulation and fresh oxygen will sweep away stagnant, toxic impurities—and your tired feeling.

In youth, we get plenty of exercise through games and running around, but as middle life approaches, we settle down, literally and *figuratively*. Muscles that formerly were lean and resilient become slack and overlaid with fat. Fat is one of the chief enemies of the heart because it has to be plentifully supplied with blood and thus needlessly increases the pumping load that the heart must sustain. The less superfluous lard that you carry around with you, the easier job your heart has. The useless burden carried to a degree by every overweight man and woman is a principal factor in premature death.

If you are accumulating pads of fat around hips and abdomen, or if your once-lean arm and leg muscles are becoming suety, you must decrease your intake of starches and fats, and take regular exercise. Not violent week-ends of golf and tennis or sporadic outbursts of squash, but a daily drill that becomes as much a part of your life as brushing your teeth. The six exercises shown here, if performed every morning on rising, will not only strengthen the diaphragm and lungs but will also take off a pound a week.

Exercise should be regarded as tribute to the heart. This marvelous organ—which is a tough bundle of muscles—thrives on a good workout, and no person free of organic heart trouble need fear that exercise will strain it. More hearts have failed from flabby degeneration than from overexercise. If you're in doubt about the advisability of exercising regularly, see your family doctor and have him check you over.

You can buy substitutes for exercise in any drugstore—headache powders, antacids, laxatives, pick-me-ups—which promise to confer priceless blessings. But you need never buy them again. You will not need the false stimulation of benzedrine or the pain-killing effects of aspirin; you can shake off your dependence on habit-forming laxatives and overcome the acid torments of heartburn if you spend 15 minutes every day in exercise.

Today exercise is a voluntary effort that all civilized men and women should make toward physical perfection—a quickening, cleansing discipline that does for the body what prayer does for the spirit. Stimulated by it, our life-flame burns with a clearer ray; nothing seems hopeless or impossible, and we are charged with the joy of being wholly alive.

Sold!

» NOT long ago a Princeton student was very short of cash. Since it was only the third of the month, he didn't dare ask his parents for money. The only solution was to sell something. So the next issue of the *Princetonian* carried the following ad: "For sale: One good-looking sport coat. $25. Size 41. A superior coat, and I need money. Apply 312 Walker Hall."

Two days later a special delivery letter arrived from New York, containing the advertisement, a check for $25 and the terse comment: "I'll buy the dern coat. Love, Mother."   —Contributed by Charles T. Coyle

Even though you do the right thing, do you do it in the right way?

Have You

an Educated Heart?

By Gelett Burgess

Condensed from "The Bromide and Other Theories"

LAST OCTOBER I sent Crystabel a book. She acknowledged it, and promptly. But two months afterward she actually wrote me another letter, telling me what she thought of that book; and she proved, moreover, that she had read it. Now, I ask you, isn't that a strange and beautiful experience in this careless world? Crystabel had the educated heart. To such as possess the educated heart thanks are something like mortgages, to be paid in installments. Why, after five years Crystabel often refers to a gift that has pleased her. It is the motive for a gift she cares for, not its value; and hence her gratefulness.

Everything can be done beautifully by the educated heart, from the lacing of a shoe so that it won't come loose to passing the salt before it is asked for. If you say only "Good morning," it can be done pleasingly. Observe how the polished actor says it, with that cheerful rising inflection. But the ordinary American growls it out with surly downward emphasis. Merely to speak distinctly is a great kindness, I consider. You never have to ask, "What did you say?" of the educated heart. On the other hand, very few people ever really listen with kindly attention. They are usually merely waiting for a chance to pounce upon you with their own narrative. Or if they do listen, is your story heard with real sympathy? Does the face really glow?

Consider the usual birthday gift or Christmas present. By universal practice it is carefully wrapped in a pretty paper and tied with ribbon. That package is symbolical of what all friendly acts should be—kindness performed with style. Then what is style in giving? Ah, the educated heart makes it a business to know what his friend really wants. One friend I have to whom I can't express a taste that isn't treasured up against need. I said once that I loved watercress, and lightly wished that I might have it for every meal. Never a meal had I at his table since, without finding watercress bought specially for me.

Do you think it's easy, this business of giving? Verily, giving is as much an art as portrait painting or the making of glass flowers. And imagination can surely be brought to bear. Are you sailing for Brazil? It isn't the basket of fine fruits that brings the tears to your eyes, nor the flowers with trailing yards of red ribbon—all that's ordinary everyday kindness. It's that little purse full of Brazilian currency, bills and small change all ready for you when you go ashore at Rio.

There was old Wentrose—he understood the Fourth Dimension of kindness, all right. Never a friend of his wife's did he puffingly put aboard a streetcar, but he'd tuck apologetically into her hand the nickel to save her rummaging in her bag. Real elegance, the gesture of inherent nobility, I call that.

Is it sufficient simply to offer your seat in a streetcar to a woman? The merely kind person does that. But he does it rather sheepishly. Isn't your graciousness more cultured if you give it up with a bow, with a smile of willingness? Besides the quarter you give the beggar, can't you give a few cents' worth of yourself too? The behavior of the educated heart becomes automatic: you set it in the direction of true kindness and courtesy and after a while it will function without deliberate thought. Such thoughtfulness, such consideration is *not* merely decorative. It is the very essence and evidence of sincerity. Without it all so-called kindness is merely titular and perfunctory.

Suppose I submit your name for membership in a club. Have I done you (or my club) any real service unless I also do my best to see that you are elected? And so if I go to every member of the committee, if I urge all my friends to endorse you, that is merely the completion of my regard for you. It is like salt—"It's what makes potatoes taste bad, if you don't put it on."

Must you dance with all the wallflowers, then? I don't go so far as that, although it would prove that you had imagination enough to put yourself in another's place. All I ask is that when you try to do a favor you do it to the full length of the rope. Don't send your telegram in just ten carefully selected words. Economize elsewhere, but add those few extra phrases that make the reader perceive that you cared more for him than you did for the expense.

No one with the educated heart ever approached a clergyman, or a celebrity, or a long-absent visitor with the shocking greeting: "You don't remember me, do you?" No, he gives his name first. No one with the educated heart ever said, "Now do come and see me, sometime!" The educated heart's way of putting it is apt to be, "How about coming next Wednesday?" And strongly I doubt if the educated heart is ever tardy at an appointment. It knows that if only two minutes late a person has brought just that much less of himself.

You call once or twice at the hospital. Do you ever call again? Not unless you have the educated heart. Yet the patient is still perhaps quite ill. One there was who used to bring a scrapbook every morning, pasted in with funny items from the day's news.

Truly nothing is so rare as the educated heart. And if you wonder why, just show a kodak group picture—a banquet or a class photograph. What does every one of us first look at, talk about? Ourself. And that's the reason why most hearts are so unlearned in kindness.

If you want to enlarge that mystic organ whence flows true human kindness, you must cultivate your imagination. You must learn to put yourself in another's place, think his thoughts. The educated heart, remember, does kindness *with style*.

A wise woman once said to me: "There are only two lasting bequests we can hope to give our children. One of these is roots; the other, wings."   —Hodding Carter, *Where Main Street Meets the River* (Rinehart)

It's a great game—limbering up your imagination to solve
your more difficult problems

TURN YOUR

IMAGINATION LOOSE!

By J. P. McEvoy

FOR 40 years I have been cracked on the idea that all of us can learn how to think our way out of the booby traps of life," says Alex Osborn, advertising expert and author of a fascinating brain-dusting book, *Your Creative Power*.* "Imagination can be developed like a muscle and you can learn how to get ideas just as you learn how to swim." He has made his credo work successfully not only for himself but for thousands of others.

A chance remark started him on his career—that and being fired from a newspaper job in Buffalo. "I took a scrapbook of clippings around to another paper," he recalls. "The editor said, 'These are pretty amateurish but I'm going to give you a trial because each piece seems to have an idea.'

"The remark set me thinking! 'If ideas are so valuable, why don't I have more of them?' But soon I realized that while a good idea may come like an unexpected but welcome guest, most ideas must be trailed and trapped. They are around you all the time, disguised as the obvious and the commonplace.

"Each of us has a creative mind that thinks up ideas," Osborn points out, "and a judicial mind that criticizes them. The first trick is to keep these two minds from interfering with each other. This means you

*Published at $3 by Charles Scribner's Sons, New York 17, N. Y.

mustn't start pulling a new idea to pieces, trying to find all the reasons why it may not work. Use your energy to have another idea. And another. The more ideas you pile up, the more chances you have of getting good ones. Pay no attention to how wild they sound. It's easier to tone down than to think up. Ideas have a way of setting off other ideas if you don't interrupt the chain reaction with criticism. Later you can look over the litter with a critical eye, pick the most promising and drown the rest.

"The next-best trick is to pile up alternatives. Look at everything with a fresh eye. Ask questions like: *What* else? *How* else? Could it be longer? (King-size cigarettes.) Smaller? (The wrist watch.) A different color? Household-appliance manufacturers asked that one, and white kitchens and drab cooking utensils turned overnight into Technicolor profits. How about vice versa? The sewing machine was made possible when the inventor asked himself: 'Suppose I put the eye in the point of the needle instead of the conventional end?' That did it! How about 'more so'? Westclox gave Big Ben two alarms instead of one: a brief soft ringing to wake you gently, plus a loud alarm to blast you if you try to dog it.

"All of us don't want to be inventors, but we all want to be inventive. Someone suggested that telephone companies could give out the correct time and the latest weather report and charge for it. Result: The New York Telephone Company added two million dollars a year to its revenue."

Why not "let George do it"? Result: The cafeteria and self-help groceries, and the new self-help gasoline stations where the customer can save four cents a gallon by gassing up his own car, while girls on roller skates make change.

OSBORN is a fanatic about what he calls brainstorming.

"The conventional conference," he says, "puts a premium on criticizing ideas that come up—judicial thinking. It almost completely ignores creative thinking. When someone suggests an idea, he is usually pounced upon with all the reasons why it won't work. After that he just sits back and waits his turn to pin someone else's ears back. Instead of destroying an idea, suggest how it can be combined with a better one."

Osborn's technique is to bring a group of his bright young men and women together and throw a problem to them. "Come up with ideas," he says. "Never mind how impractical they sound. Think high, wild and handsome, everything goes—except criticism." A stenographer takes down the suggestions. The brainstorm group should be small—from five to ten people is ideal; they can be all men, all women, or mixed. All work equally well if there are a couple of self-starters in the group and the chairman keeps the ball in the air.

"Incurable critics of ideas will inevitably creep into these brainstorm sessions. When this happened in one of ours the leader blasted him with: 'No opinions, please! Think up or shut up!'

"Our Minneapolis office held seven 'brainstorms' in a single month. One meeting developed 45 suggestions for a home-appliance client; another produced 56 ideas for a money-raising campaign; a third, 124 ideas on how to sell more blankets. For a New York client we organized 150 of our people into 15 separate groups to brainstorm the same problem. Result: Over 800 ideas, 177 of which were submitted as concrete suggestions."

Osborn is proud that some of his most successful business "brainstormers" go home and apply what they have learned to their family problems. One who lives with his parents and five unmarried brothers says: "I have an explosive family but since I organized them into a discussion group we 'brainstorm' one family problem at a time. You'd be surprised how many of these ideas have worked out and improved the harmony of our home. Instead of getting mad at each other we have a lot of fun at these sessions."

Neighbors could get along better if they used their minds instead of their emotions to solve everyday problems. Osborn told me of a young couple whose three-year-old daughter was chased and knocked down by a neighbor's police dog. The mother frantically phoned her lawyer husband demanding he notify the police. Her husband argued that such a move would make it impossible for the two families to live side by side. Then he asked Osborn, "How do I think my way out of this one?"

"Exactly as if it were a case a client brought you," Osborn told him. "Write your problem down, mull over the facts. Then ask yourself, 'What can I do to make my neighbor realize that his dog might have killed my child?' "

Out of the many alternatives he selected one. In the files of the local newspaper he found the story of a child attacked and bitten by a dog of the same breed. He had a photostat made and sent it with a friendly letter to his neighbor. Soon afterward the neighbor was asked where his dog was. "Oh, Rex was too good to keep in the city. I sold him to my brother who has a big farm."

Osborn believes that parents are tragically guilty of not using their creative minds in bringing up youngsters. The parents' emotional reactions too often paralyze the resourcefulness they need. He tells the story of an old friend whose 16-year-old son sneaked the family's car out of the garage and crashed into a telephone pole.

Luckily the lad wasn't hurt, but his father and mother agreed that something drastic was in order. The boy was on his summer vacation, and the scheme his parents thought up was that he work in the local garage without pay in return for fixing the car. Day after day the lad helped tow in wrecks. By the time the kid had finished his six weeks of hard labor his teen-age pals were avoiding him for being such a bore on the subject of traffic safety.

MANY OF our civic problems could be solved if groups of citizens met regularly and "brainstormed"—instead of sitting back individually and criticizing. Just for the fun of it Osborn showed one group of women how to "brainstorm" a big charity affair. He organized ten squads of five women each and gave each squad a definite assignment. One was to come up with ten ideas on decorations; another, ten ideas on entertainment; another, ten ideas on refreshments, and so on. When they were through brainstorming, they had a hundred ideas to choose from and the affair was a rousing success.

In solving our personal problems, Osborn says, the basic rule is the Golden Rule itself. Only he rephrases it: "Put yourself in the other fellow's shoes." For example: Do you want a raise? Put yourself in the boss's shoes. Have you become more valuable to the company? Have you brought it any new ideas? Are you asking for a raise just because you need it? If you were the boss would you consider that a good enough reason?

A lot of labor troubles have been solved by bosses who asked themselves: "What would make me more satisfied if I were an employe?" Management has come up with such answers as recreation and rest rooms, safety engineering, rest periods, cafeterias providing food at cost, group health insurance, paid vacations, music while you work. Even so, management has done less fresh, original and dynamic thinking than the unions. Result: Management too often finds itself on the defensive, forced to make concessions which could have been anticipated by creative thinking in the other fellow's shoes.

"Jumping to conclusions," says Osborn, "is the only exercise some minds get, and that's not thinking. Yet creative thinking is not only good exercise but good fun. I like the story of the white-bearded New Hampshire native who sat with his cronies in front of the general store night after night, the silence broken only by the occasional splatter of tobacco juice. One day he was asked what they did, and he replied, 'We just think.'

"'But how can you possibly think that much?'"

"The old codger replied: 'I'll tell you, son, thinkin' is like sin. Them as don't do it is ascairt of it. But them as do it *enough* gets to like it.'

"Exercising one's imagination *is* fun. And few of us make it the asset it should be in our lives."

Why Were They Fired?

To LEARN what errors youngsters starting on their first jobs should be warned about, a group of vocational teachers wrote to several thousand employers asking them to look up the last three persons dismissed and tell why they had been let go. The teachers had expected a long catalogue of reasons. They were amazed that more than two thirds of the persons losing jobs had been fired for *one reason.* It was the same in every sort of business, for workers of all ages and both sexes. It amounted to this:

"They couldn't get along with other people." —Gwen Bristow in *This Week*

Live on What You Make!

A noted financial authority offers six rules for personal solvency

*By Sylvia Porter**
Condensed from The Atlanta Journal
and Constitution Magazine

Today you may be taking in the highest income you've ever earned. Yet, if you're like millions of others, never before have you fretted so much about making your income match your outgo, nor so eagerly sought financial peace of mind.

You won't attain these goals by trying to live according to a rigid plan, nor by trying to fit yourself into a ready-to-wear budget worked out for the "average family." You will be on your way to financing your bread and your dreams only when you work out your own plan designed to make your money buy things you want and need.

From my own experience and the studies of experts on money management, I've selected a half-dozen basic guides. They can help anyone whether he is earning $2500 a year or $25,000.

1. *Make your program a family project. Call the family together on a quiet evening and discuss what you're trying to do. Let the children become part of the team.*

This really is the only way to make any program work, for, if each member knows what is the family's aim, each will try to reach it. Early in our married life my husband and I sat down to discover why we were so persistently close to zero in our joint bank account: each of us, we found, was keeping a separate, "secret" budget, each buying and paying for things without the knowledge of the other. Right then we made our money management a family project.

*Sylvia Porter's *daily financial column, nationally syndicated, is read by millions.*

2. *Whatever records you keep, keep them simple. Never try to keep detailed records of where every penny goes—these only consume time and produce pain.*

Buy an inexpensive notebook. On one page jot down your monthly income; if you don't have an income 12 months a year, spread what you have into 12 "spending periods." On a second page jot down what you must put aside for major, unavoidable expenses—rent, taxes, debts, *savings*—and prorate them on a monthly basis. On a third page put down what you have left after you have substracted your unavoidable expenses from your gross income; this is the total you have with which to meet your day-to-day expenses. On a fourth page juggle your day-to-day expenses until you come out better than even and are satisfied that you're getting the maximum benefit and comfort from what you're spending.

If you have no past records, collect what receipts you can find and call on the family to supply what figures they can remember. Work along with trial records first and soon you'll adjust them so they fit your life.

3. *Deduct the money for your savings as an "unavoidable expense" BEFORE you start spending for the pleasant but unessential things of life. That's the secret of saving.*

You should have a rainy-day fund to take care of the unexpected bills that come up in every family's life. This fund should hold two months' income at least—six months' if you can manage it. If it doesn't, agree in your family conference on how much can be put aside each month until your nest egg is assured.

4. *Provide personal allowances for each member of the family, including the children. Then let each one decide what he wants to do with the amount allotted.*

No one should have to account for his allowance. If a husband wants to blow the entire sum on one evening with the boys, that's his affair. If a wife wants to spend it on what appears nonsense to everybody but her, it's her affair. Children learn to handle money surprisingly fast when they are given the chance.

5. *Don't be too arbitrary about your figures or set limits that are impossible to meet.*

You cannot anticipate an illness or an accident and its cost. If **you** set limits that are too tough for your family, your search for financial peace of mind will end in discouragement. If, after you've tried a plan for a few months, you find your limits are too stiff—change them. It's your budget and it's up to you to make it fit.

6. *Finally, if after all your efforts you still cannot make your income match your outgo, cut your spending or raise your income.*

That's the most fundamental rule of all. For if you cannot make ends meet even after the most careful budgeting, you are living beyond your means and you might as well face it. But there still are ways out.

You may think it impossible to increase your income now, yet many resourceful people have found ways of making their time produce more. One young mother takes care of small children along with her own when their mothers are at work or shopping. A man whose hobby is puttering in the workshop brings in respectable extra amounts by repairing and refinishing furniture.

You may suppose it is impossible to cut your spending; but, when you think it over, changes sweeping enough to reduce expenses all along the line may seem not only possible but desirable. You would not be lowering your fundamental standards, but maintaining your integrity and independence.

There they are—six guides which may seem deceptively simple but which actually are basic ways to financial peace of mind. Apply them and you'll discover how much they help you live on what you make.

Recipe for Romance

My brother put off telling his motherless daughter the facts of life as long as possible. But when she fell in love for the first time at 16, he realized that he had to talk to her. I overheard his concluding remark, "Jean, the best advice I can give you is written on the top of a mayonnaise jar." That night, when I mixed the salad for dinner, these words on the mayonnaise jar leapt up at me: "KEEP COOL BUT DON'T FREEZE."

—Contributed by Mrs. J. A. W.

Danger — GOSSIPS AT WORK

By Frederic Sondern, Jr.

IN A Midwestern town, not long ago, tongues began to wag about the teen-age daughter of a prominent citizen. Gloria had been seen, according to the gossips, getting out of a young man's car at seven in the morning, with her evening clothes askew, and staggering up the steps of her home. The story buzzed around town, gathering details as it went. There was talk of a wild week-end house party at a nearby college. The town drew the inevitable inference and treated Gloria accordingly—with stares and silence. A few weeks later the girl, her spirit broken, wrote in her diary: "I am not what they say. I would rather die." Then she took a lethal dose of sleeping pills.

The subsequent police investigation revealed the truth. Gloria had gone to a college dance with several other girls. They had missed the last bus back. With their parents' knowledge, all spent the night in a women's dormitory at the college. They were fetched early in the morning by the father of one of them and each was deposited at her home. It was weariness, not liquor, that had made Gloria stagger. The young man in the car, the disordered clothing, had been the imagining of a talkative woman who happened to see the girl's arrival and found it a juicy morsel for her round of morning telephone chats. When the police were through, the town felt sheepish. But Gloria was dead.

Every year countless lives are damaged and untold misery is caused by malicious gossip. Almost every one of us has suffered from it. And yet we continue to talk irresponsibly about other people.

Dr. Gordon Allport, professor of psychology at Harvard—who did brilliant work during the war tracking down and destroying dangerous enemy-inspired rumors—has devised an ingenious method of tracing in the classroom the development of a rumor. The first of a group of subjects is shown a picture flashed on a screen—the scene of an automobile accident, for example, or a street brawl. He then, in front of the class, describes the picture—which has now been blacked out —to a subject who has been waiting outside. Number two recounts what he has heard to a third, the third to a fourth, and so on until the description of the picture has gone through the ears, minds and mouths of half a dozen people in exactly the way that gossip travels.

The subject who tells the final version to the class—with his back to the picture which is now again flashed on the screen—usually gets a laugh from the students who have listened to the distortions injected by each reporter as he has passed the story along. The final version and the picture itself are rarely very similar. In one of Dr. Allport's experiments—the scene of a brawl in which a white man is threatening a Negro with a razor—the razor invariably winds up in the colored man's hand after the second or third telling.

By tests on several thousand people and the investigation of hundreds of individual cases of rumor, Dr. Allport, Dr. Hadley Cantril of Princeton and a number of other psychologists have been able to chart the behavior of various types of gossip. Most persons who start derogatory gossip, these investigators find, are motivated by hate, fear, envy, the desire to seem important, and sexual repression with a resulting vicious interest in the sex activities of others. Rarely does righteous indignation, which slanderers so often pretend, spark a derogatory rumor. Gloria was condemned not so much because of her "escapade" as for her good looks, prominence and wealth.

As a popular rumor develops, it usually goes through three stages— which the psychologists call "leveling," "sharpening" and "assimilation." During the leveling period the gossip takes the raw material of the story and chops off—either through malice, ignorance or simply a desire to entertain—any explanations which might decrease the effectiveness of the neat little news package that he or she has in mind. In Gloria's case the other girls in the car and the obvious middle age of the man who was driving were leveled out.

The next group of gossips then takes the leveled, easily told story and "sharpens" it, magnifying its salient points so that it becomes an attention-getter at the beauty parlor or the general store. Gloria's prom, for example, became a week-end house party at a fraternity.

In the "assimiliation" stage the story gets its final stature from the imagination, prejudices and emotional reactions of the whole community. Gloria's week-end had been so leveled and sharpened that it took the imagination of the strict, repressed little community by storm. The orgy at the college was a typical fabrication contributed by people who wished they could have attended one themselves.

All this happens with incredible speed. Dr. Hadley Cantril of Princeton ran a series of experiments to determine the velocity of gossip. In one he told six students in strict confidence that the Duke and Duchess of Windsor were coming to the next university dance. A survey one week later showed that the completely fictitious story had reached no less than 2000 students. Town officials had called the university demanding to know why they had not been informed of the forthcoming visit, and press agencies were frantically telephoning for details. "And that was a pleasant rumor," says Dr. Cantril. "A slanderous rumor travels even faster."

Gossip knows no distinction of educational level or income bracket. The country club produces slander as vicious as that of the corner drugstore and the bar and grill. A medical friend of mine who practices in a fashionable suburban district told me about one of his patients, a prosperous builder. After shooting a poor game of golf one day, this outspoken man unburdened himself to a friend in the locker room about various business worries and what he called his "high blood pressure." Tired and depressed, he made his financial position and his health sound far worse than they really were; both his business and his heart were actually in excellent condition.

Within the hour the card room had it that "poor old T.J." was broke and had a serious heart condition. A few days later he had trouble at his bank. "We think you're overexpanding, Tom," said a friendly but firm vice-president. "You ought to take it a bit easy. You're not looking too well, you know." Then a cold that laid him up for a few days was reported as a heart attack. "And so," explained the doctor, "they whispered him into it. When he came to me he was suffering from a general nervous condition and resulting heart strain.

He'll be all right; his heart and his business are doing fine. But he has suffered plenty."

The doctor's favorite example of the cruel twists that gossip can take is what he calls with a wry smile the Case of the Grecian Gown. "It would have been funny," he says, "if it hadn't nearly wrecked two very worth-while people." The young and attractive wife of a local minister had been seen, the country club had it, dancing in the moonlight on the Parish House lawn in a filmy Grecian gown. One of the club's social leaders had been the witness. While the story rocked the men's locker room with laughter, it did not amuse the club's ladies. A grievance committee was formed and a letter to the bishop drafted, relating the scandal.

At that point, fortunately, the doctor had a chance to interfere. The minister's wife was down with pneumonia. She had caught a chill when, on that moonlight night, she had suddenly discovered before going to bed that her cocker spaniel was missing. Pokey had a habit of wandering into a neighbor's property and worrying a big dog there. She had rushed out of the house in a white bathrobe. That had been the "Grecian gown." Her frantic efforts to find Pokey, and then to trap him, were the "dance" which the neighborhood had witnessed. The letter to the bishop, after the doctor was through with the ladies' grievance committee, was withdrawn. "But I hate to think," he says, "what might have happened."

The minister of a small New England farming community told me about a young physician, new in the township, who was called in the middle of the night to an outlying farm where an old lady lay dying after a heart attack. On the way the doctor drove off the road, smashed into a tree and was seriously injured. Before other medical help could be called, the woman was dead.

Gossip didn't take long to start. The stretch of road on which the doctor had been driving was straight, the night had been clear. "Must have been drunk," said somebody. Within a few hours that chance remark had become undisputed fact: The woman could have been saved, but the doctor had been drunk. The minister and the justice of the peace, among the few who refused to believe the gossip, investigated. They found that the doctor had been working without sleep for more than 24 hours. Sheer exhaustion had caused his accident. And no one, the county medical authorities agreed, could have saved the lady in any case. Although the doctor was cleared officially of any blame, it took two years for his practice to recover.

Almost all of us have been carriers, at one time or another, of such tales, often without thinking. It's fun to gossip, and we are inclined to forget the dividing line between the harmless and the malicious. We should give that dividing line a lot more thought. No psychologists are needed to establish it—just conscience.

Hannah More, the English writer, disliked gossip intensely. Whenever a visitor said something unpleasant about someone else or repeated a derogatory remark, Miss More had a disconcerting way of seizing the offender by the arm. "Come," she would say, "we will go and ask whether this is true." Nothing but a complete retraction would prevent the determined lady from dragging the slanderer to his or her victim. A more practical method for most of us was suggested a hundred years ago by an English pastor. "When you hear an ill report about someone, halve and quarter it," he said; "then say nothing about the rest."

Growing Pains

ON MY LIST of New Year's resolutions was: "Be more patient with my daughter, Janet. No matter how irritating she is, remember that, after all, she is only 15 and is going through the exasperating period of adolescence."

Imagine then my feeling when, quite by accident, I came across Janet's New Year's resolutions and saw at the head of her list: "Try and be more patient with Mother."   —Contributed by Mrs. C. R. Knowles

IT WAS the teen-aged daughter's first dance, and she desperately wanted an off-the-shoulder frock. Her mother felt she wasn't old enough to wear anything so sophisticated. There was a heated family discussion, and it was the father who finally settled the problem. "Well," he proposed, "let her try on one. If it stays up—she's old enough to wear it."   —Contributed by Margaret Helms

To Get Along with

Older People

By Julietta K. Arthur

Condensed from
Maclean's Magazine

EVEN the most saintly have asked at some time, "Why are so many old people difficult to get along with?" Dr. Erwin Ackerknecht of the University of Wisconsin believes he has the answer: "Two thirds of old persons feel unwanted, and many of them are right."

Psychologically, our society is geared to the young. Movies, sports, advertisements, fashions all stress the importance of youth, and we give the elderly less of a role to play than any other older generation ever had. At the same time the life span is increasing. This extra time can be years of tragedy unless younger people help their elders overcome the frustrations of old age.

The day when some older person's attitudes or actions conflict with your own, stop and ask: What do older people want to get out of life?

Years ago a member of the Society of Friends summed up the basic needs of the aged simply and succinctly: "Somewhere to live, something to do and someone to care."

How can you help your relatives fulfill these basic desires? You can do nothing at all unless you put yourself in an older person's place. To do so you must rid yourself of the misconceptions about age.

One misconception is that old age makes people different. Most of us assume that putting on grandmotherhood automatically assures a halo of sweetness and light. Or we take the opposite view: that old age makes people crabbed.

Any elderly person has taken a long time to get the way he is, and he is going to remain that way. The father who was a young autocrat at the breakfast table will remain so. The mother who was frivolous and vain in her younger years is not going to turn automatically into a self-effacing granny. And, of course, the man or woman who has always pulled his own oar is going to try to keep on doing it.

Another major misconception is that the old like to be in a safe and cozy nest. This probably accounts for more unhappy relationships than anything else. No older person likes to have his life planned for him, whether his children tuck him away in an old people's home or put him in a gilded cage.

Dr. Lillien J. Martin, who entered the field of old-age counseling when she herself was 69 and continued in it till she died at 91, used to say many older people are forced into loss of self-assurance by their offspring. "Children," she said, "may coddle aged parents not only out of concern for them but also because they really want their parents to live restricted lives so they will not interfere."

Most older people, Dr. Martin found, are remarkably tough and capable, even if they have physical limitations. In our anxiety to spare them worry and make them comfortable we underestimate their capacities and undermine their initiative. Plan with, not for, old people. To accept direction—very often correction—from those you used to have authority over in the diaper and romper stage is a soul-trying process.

When we say "tolerance must be mutual," we usually mean we expect older people to abandon some cherished activity which interferes with one of ours. Most of us can say of a teen-ager who has difficulty in adjusting to life: "It is because he is an adolescent. He'll get used to things." People of 70 or 80 are also entitled to have periods of adjustment: they have spent a lifetime accumulating habits and patterns.

If Grandfather refuses to stop smoking in bed, or Grandmother won't change the fashion of her clothes, neither one is doing it to annoy you. They may be biologically too old to change their ways, or they may be making an effort to adjust themselves and haven't yet succeeded.

If you force them, the result is likely to be a bitter, dejected individual.

There is no reason to feel guilty if you are apprehensive about sharing your home with your parents or in-laws. There are other ways of honoring your father and mother besides giving them a place at your fireside. Nor need you feel you must do for your older relatives what they did for theirs. Two or three generations had a much better chance, 50 years ago, of living amicably together. When households overflowed with children and space, there was always ample work and ample room for elderly relatives. Machine housekeeping has taken away much of that solace of the old.

If your older relative wants to cling to the living quarters where he's been content for so long, stand up for him. Older people value their own homes first, and privacy at all costs anywhere.

If you are the one on whose shoulders it will fall to make a decision there is only one safe rule to follow. If an aging individual doesn't *want* to live with you or someone else, it is more economical, in terms of the eventual strain that will develop on both sides, to help him stay where he wants to be, even if dollars-and-cents expenditure is greater.

Where an elderly person lives is not the major consideration. Making him know he is valued is all that counts. You can ask advice or confide your troubles to him. You can make such a simple gesture as asking a relative to write down his memories of family history or to preserve family heirlooms for the grandchildren. One woman stimulated her whole community when she asked people over 70 to talk before her club about their relics of pioneer days. This exhibition, now held annually, gives young people a chance to hear about local history and to respect their elders who shaped it.

If you want to get along with older people, whether they live in your home or not, discuss all grievances openly, even if there's danger of hurting their feelings. If you treat the elderly as if they were too eccentric or too old-fashioned to know what to do, you will only strengthen their conviction that they are being abused. If you bring pressure to bear through doctors, nurses or family counselors when they are facing a devastating break in long-established routine, they will feel you are persecuting them.

To prevent this, be candid. Older people can stand more shocks than younger ones think they can. What they can't bear is to feel baffled and helpless because well-meaning relatives too often act as if crises in family life ought not to be discussed with them.

Learning to live in amity with older people is a challenge that is worth more than passing study. For, even if it doesn't face you right now, remember that you are going to be "an older person" yourself someday.

I Demand Worse Weather!

THE WEATHER around my place isn't bad enough. I wish it would get worse, like on my neighbors' land where the elements constantly go berserk. Recently, for example, during a rugged cold snap, our thermometer registered ten below zero one morning. On the train I cited this figure to Thompson, my neighbor. "That all?" he asked. "You got off lucky. Fourteen below at my place."

"We had 19 below," chimed in Jameson, who, curiously, lives across the street from us. "Was up all night with an electric heater to keep our pipes from freezing."

It's always like that. If we get snowdrifts five feet high in our driveway, the man next door gets them eight feet high. Wind that blows my hat off blows people's coats off when it leaves our property.

Occasionally, of course, an erratic cloud wets us as much as it does the neighbors — above ground, that is. But not in our cellar. We're continually being humiliated by the puny floods we get there. If the water's up to our ankles, it's up to Jameson's knees. If mice are swimming around in ours, the Thompsons have beavers.

I'm beginning to suspect the trouble. We've got a leak somewhere that lets the water out. I'm going to locate that leak and plug it up with the best cement. Then, for the next cloudburst, I'm going to install a giant blower in the cellar.

Waves? Brother, we're going to have whitecaps!

—Parke Cummings in *This Week*

STOP WORRYING

By *A. J. Cronin*   Author of "The Citadel," "Beyond This Place," etc.

ILLIONS of people are beset by a secret enemy responsible for more casualties and greater suffering than almost any other scourge. Its name is Worry. As medical men know, worry can actually induce organic disease. And even when it does not, it can, by devouring our energy in unproductive ways, undermine health, render life intolerably miserable and shorten it by years.

Yet worry, against which the wonder drugs are useless, is quite curable *by the individual himself.* Worry lies in our minds, more often than not the result of simple misdirection of our imagination. By learning to control our processes of thought we can put worry in its proper place and make the world we live in cheerful instead of gloomy.

In setting out to achieve this control, the first popular fallacy of which we must rid ourselves is that worry is a peculiarity of the weak, the failures. On the contrary, worry may be a sign of potential strength, proof that a man cares about life and wants to make something worthwhile of his career. Men who have achieved the greatest heights, whose names are immortal, have been instinctive worriers. Yet they have nearly always had to contend, at some stage of their lives, with mental strain, and have taught themselves to overcome it.

Charles Spurgeon, celebrated 19th-century English preacher, confessed that when he was first obliged to speak in public he worried for weeks beforehand, even to the extent of hoping he would break a leg before the fateful occasion. The result was that when he entered the pulpit he was so exhausted by worry and tension that he made a poor showing.

Then one day Spurgeon faced up to the situation. "What is the worst thing that can happen to me during my sermon?" he asked himself. Whatever it might be, he decided, the heavens would not fall. He had been magnifying a personal problem into a world-shaking disaster. When he saw his worry in proper perspective, he found that he spoke much better, simply because he had not distracted his mind with empty fears. He eventually became the outstanding preacher of his time.

We should look on worry as a manifestation of nervous intensity, and therefore a potential source of good. Only when this latent force exhausts itself fruitlessly on unreal problems does it harm us. The remedy is to accept worries as part of our life and learn to handle them by redirecting the energy we are misusing into productive channels.

This is easier if we make a list of the tangible things that worry us. When they are down on paper we realize how many of them are vague, indefinite and futile. An estimate of what most people worry about runs as follows: Things that never happen: 40 percent. Things over and past that can't be changed by all the worry in the world: 30 percent. Needless health worries: 12 percent. Petty miscellaneous worries: ten percent. Real, legitimate worries: eight percent.

If we study our worries, keeping our sense of proportion, at least some of them should be eliminated. What we imagine most easily, for example, what we dread, in reality rarely comes to pass.

One evening at La Guardia airport I found myself next to a young man who was meeting his fiancée. Presently it was announced that the plane we were awaiting had been held up by bad weather. It was half an hour, then an hour overdue. The young man's agitation increased. It was not difficult to see that he was picturing some horrible disaster.

Finally I felt compelled to speak to him. I knew it was useless simply to tell him to stop worrying. Instead, I set up other pictures, asking whom he was expecting, what the girl was like, what she would be wearing. Soon he was telling me all about his fiancée, how they had met, and so on. In a few minutes his mind was so full of other things that he had crowded worry out—indeed, the plane came in before he realized it.

Financial worries, on the other hand, are real enough and constitute a considerable part of all human anxieties. I believe there is only one way to solve them—provided we are already using our resources to the best advantage. That is to apply Thoreau's famous exhortation: "Simplify, simplify." Thoreau found that by cutting down his needs to the minimum he was able to savor life to the full, undistracted by cares consequent upon trying to satisfy superfluous desires. With Socrates, who had applied the same remedy 2000 years earlier, Thoreau could exult: "How many things I can do without!" Yet few men have led fuller, richer lives.

One of the most contented men I know is an old Maine fisherman whose sole possessions are a battered scow and his little shack on the clam flats. Completely at the mercy of wind and weather, indifferent to money, cherishing only his independence and his freedom, he manifests always a serene, sublime tranquillity—a perfect example for those of us who worry ourselves to death seeking material possessions, striving desperately to insulate ourselves against the hardships and misfortunes that may lie ahead. For worry never robs tomorrow of its sorrow; it only saps today of its strength.

Self-pity is the root of many of our worries. When I was practicing medicine in London one of my patients, a young married woman, was stricken with infantile paralysis. She was sent to a good hospital, where it soon became apparent that she was responding to treatment and would eventually recover. Some weeks later I received a visit from her husband. In a state of intense nervous upset, he complained of sleeplessness and inability to concentrate. After a checkup I found nothing whatever the matter with him. But when I suggested that he get back to his job he turned on me furiously. "My wife is seriously ill. And you expect me to go on as though nothing had happened. Haven't you any feeling *for me?*" The basic cause of his worry was self-pity, masquerading as concern for his wife.

For self-commiseration there is only one answer. We must effect a revolution in our lives by which, instead of seeing ourselves as the center of existence, we turn our thoughts toward others and come thus to realize our true place, as members of a family, community and nation. There are many ways by which we can come to see our difficulties in true perspective. André Gide played the piano: he found that his worries became insignificant in the harmony of great music. Tolstoy, contemplating the sunsets on the steppes, felt ashamed to concentrate on his own obsessions when there was so much beauty in the world. Winston Churchill, burdened with the cares of the free world, took time off from war to paint a landscape for a Christmas card!

But the finest antidote to worry is work. Lawrence of Arabia was one of the most brilliant men of action this century has produced. His mother has descibed how, after his failure at the Peace Conference to fulfill his promises to the Arabs, he would sit entire mornings in the same position, without moving and with the same blank expression on his face. Worry over his defeat transformed him from a man of action into a brooding, lifeless shadow. His eventual self-cure was achieved by translating this wasting energy into creative effort. He set out to write *The Seven Pillars of Wisdom,* a masterpiece that changed the course of history.

"It is not work that kills men," wrote Henry Ward Beecher. "It is worry. Work is healthy; you can hardly put more upon a man than he can bear. Worry is rust upon the blade."

Lionel Barrymore, the distinguished actor, when past 70, gave as his prescription for a long and happy life: Keep busy. He said: "I go along getting the most out of life on a day-to-day basis. I don't worry about tomorrow, and I don't care what happened yesterday. Once you start thinking about life and its problems, and begin worrying over the future or regretting the past, you're likely to become confused. I figure if a person does his work well and extracts all he can from the present he'll have as happy a life as he's supposed to have." By idling away the hours or wasting them on unproductive time-fillers which do not fully occupy our attention or energies, we leave the door open for worry.

When troubles presented themselves, my old Scottish grandmother would remark with a shake of her head: "What cannot be cured must be endured." Then she would smile and add: "It's the Lord's will."

Worry, in the final analysis, is a form of atheism, a denial of the human need of God. It is like saying: "I shall never get the better of this, for there is no God to help me." The good Lord in His daily conversations was always warning His listeners against this particular lack of faith. After an enumeration of the various worries about the future with which men and women harass their minds, He said: "Take therefore no thought for the morrow."

No wiser philosophy could be evolved for a self-tormented humanity. If we follow it trustfully in all its prayerful implications, we shall raise ourselves beyond the reach of Private Enemy Number One and know true peace of mind.

Life with Father

NO AMOUNT of coaxing could persuade our 16-month-old son to take his medicine in any shape, form or fashion. In utter disgust I gave up and left the room. When I came back, I stared in amazement, for there stood my son gleefully opening his mouth for it.

My husband had solved the problem by mixing the medicine with orange juice, putting it into a water pistol and shooting it into him!
— Mrs. Hobby Stripling in Atlanta *Journal and Constitution Magazine*

EACH TIME I put our two-year-old on the closed front porch to play, he objected violently when I locked his gate to make sure he stayed there. Then one day my husband put the youngster in his "playroom" and locked the gate, and for once he didn't scream, but played happily.

My husband's explanation was simple. "I just told him I was locking the gate," he said, "so that you couldn't get in and bother him."
— Contributed by Lil Oswald Olsen

JOE LAURIE, JR., tells about a friend of his who made the mistake of leaving her baby daughter in her husband's care while she closeted herself in the library to pay bills. He buried himself behind his newspaper and forgot about the baby until he heard a series of thumps, followed by a horrendous wail. Clearly, baby had fallen down the stairs.

"Martha," called the father excitedly. "Come quick! Our little girl just took her first 24 steps!" — Bennett Cerf in *This Week*

How
I Learned to Conquer Grief

By Catherine Marshall

*Condensed from The Atlanta Journal
and Constitution Magazine*

WHEN Peter Marshall was pastor of the Westminster Presbyterian Church in Atlanta, we had a close friend who had known much sorrow. She used to look quizzically at Peter and me—young as we were, very much in love, fresh in the enthusiasm of our faith in the goodness of God.

"Neither of you has ever had any real trouble," she would say. "You're bound to have some sooner or later. I wonder if you will feel then as you do now?"

In the years which followed, we had our share of trouble—much illness, and finally my husband's premature death at 47. But today I still feel as we did then. In fact, I believe in God's love more firmly than ever, because now my faith has stood trial.

Trouble of some kind, especially bereavement, is the common experience of mankind. Since my husband's death, many people have written me to ask: How does one endure it? How does one keep one's faith and deal with it constructively? Let me quote one typical letter which reveals a number of quite human reactions to grief:

"My wife, Marie, died three years ago. I just don't know how I've gotten through the agony of separation since then. People are always saying, 'Time heals,' but in my case each day is worse than the last.

"I've tried plunging into work 16 hours a day. But everything seems futile without Marie. I try to pray, but my prayers just hit the ceiling and bounce back. What good purpose could God have had in taking Marie and leaving me here alone?"

First, let me say that I deeply sympathize with all who have suffered thus. Sorrow is a wound in the personality, as real as any physical mutilation. After a time, during busy hours, one can forget the pain. Then tiny things bring it back: opening a drawer and coming across a Christmas card written in a well-known hand; the sight of a distant figure reminiscent of a well-beloved form, wearing the same kind of slouch hat. And suddenly, the old pain is back with stabbing force.

But though I sympathize, I have learned that the first really helpful step to take is to face up to the fact that your grief is essentially selfish. Most of us grieve not for the interrupted happiness of the one who died but because of our own loneliness and need. Sorrow is usually interlaced with self-pity. Facing up to this squarely for the sin it is, is like opening a window to let a breath of fresh air into a fetid room. We must deal with this selfishness as we deal with all other sins: by confessing it to God and asking His forgiveness and release. Such a confession requires stern action at a time when the heart is sore, but it is more healing than all the expressions of sympathy from others.

Everyone bereaved goes through a period of sharp questioning and self-reproach: "I wasn't sympathetic and understanding enough. Why didn't I show more love and gratitude while he was alive?" There is one healthy road out of this self-reproach. If your conscience bothers you about any past mistakes or failures, deal with them as you dealt with self-pity. Confess them one by one to God, have them freely forgiven and forget them even as God has promised to do.

Few people avoid this merciless self-reproach. The only healthy road out of it is to face up to life as it is, not as we wish it might have been. For the God I know is a realist, and He expects us to be realists too.

I often wonder how those who during sunny days can't be bothered with God manage to survive sorrow. I have found, in time of trouble, that there is no substitute for Him. For grief is sickness of the spirit, and God alone is physician to the spirit.

But, my typical correspondent asked, "What good purpose could God have had in taking Marie and leaving me here alone?"

The problem of evil—why a good God lets good people suffer—is forever with us. I have no pat answer. But we must remember that this old earth is enemy-occupied territory. Disease and death are of the enemy—not of a loving Father. Yet I do believe that when Marie was stricken God had some plan by which He could bring good out of it.

Admittedly, it takes courage and no little faith to take the next constructive step: hunt for the open door, the new creative purpose, rather than stand weeping before the closed door of grief. But God is the Creator. It isn't possible for Him to be negative. If we are to coöperate with His purposes (the only way of getting our prayers answered) we too must be creative and positive. For God's way of binding up our broken hearts will be to give us worth-while work to do in the world.

At one time I did not think life worth living without my husband. Yet I can testify that today I am truly happy. That happiness by no means dishonors Peter; it is exactly as he would have it.

How did that come about? I took the steps of confession I have mentioned. Then I prayed that this tragedy which I did not understand would nonetheless "work together for good." God has answered that prayer in an astonishing way.

Once during a long illness I wrote in my journal, "One of my deepest dreams is to be a writer. Through my writing I would like to make a contribution to my time and generation." Less than a month after Peter's death, it was as if God put a pencil in my hand and said, "Go ahead and write. Make your contribution. I promise to bless what you write." And He has blessed every attempt, beyond all imagining.

Something else even more wonderful came of this new-found career. Peter and I were drawn closer together than ever before. And through a divine alchemy my writing has become the vehicle for continuing Peter's earthly ministry. Many people who have read what I have written about my husband say that they have been profoundly helped by his words and the example of his deeds. In so-called "death," his ministry has been widened, deepened, "multiplied by infinity."

And, as a final benediction, slowly, imperceptibly there has come into my life the definite feeling of still being loved, cherished and cared for. It has become the most comforting and sustaining force of my life.

I would not have you think that there is anything unique about my case. The help for which I prayed awaits your prayer. God's answer for you will not be the answer He had for me. It will be made to fit your needs, your own dreams, by a God who loves you personally.

"I Do Not Like Thee, Dr. Fell"

Dorothy Canfield *Author of "Hillsboro People,"*
"Raw Material," "The Deepening Stream," etc.

Condensed from The Christian Century

O NCE in the question-and-answer period after I had finished a talk at a woman's college, a girl asked me: "How do you stand it when some reviewer tears one of your books to pieces? It would just slay me to have such hateful things said about me."

Feeling that her question was easy to answer, I began with bland assurance: "Well, of course no writer would pretend it is pleasant to read a severely unfavorable criticism. But nobody can expect to be liked by everyone. The very same traits which make some people enjoy having you around will make other people hate the sight of you. Take your own personal life. You know well enough that not *everybody* who knows you likes you. You must have noticed—"

I was halted by a strange expression on her young face. Her eyes widened; she perceptibly paled. It was borne in on me, with a horrifying impact, that never before had it occurred to this 19-year-old child that anyone could dislike her—not *her!* For a moment I was far too embarrassed to speak. And as I looked from one sober young face to another I knew that I had broken dreadful news to them all.

Those girls should, for their own good, have learned that long ago. Yet the thought came to me that day, and I have had it many times since, that none of us really understands the phenomenon of personal likes and dislikes. It is ever present in our daily life, familiar to all adults, and yet it is an unsolved mystery.

The first day in school a new teacher faces a group of children, all unknown to her. The children face an adult they have never laid eyes on before. The teacher writes a few sentences on the board, gives a few directions, and then they all march off to the first school assembly. But already most of the children know whether they "like Teacher" or not. And already the teacher has thought, "That freckle-faced boy and the girl with very short hair in the back—I'm going to enjoy having them in the class."

Take the case of a person who has just undergone an operation. Even before the ether fumes are cleared from his head he likes some and dislikes others of the nurses coming and going in his sickroom. He has not seen them long enough to know anything about their qualities. He simply makes up his mind that he likes the sandy-haired one best. On the other hand, the man in the next room, fighting his way out of ether, may whisper to the doctor, "Keep that sandy-haired nurse away! She gives me the jitters. I'd rather have the little fat one."

As you look around you at people in streetcar or ferry or drugstore, why do you like some and dislike others?

These first-impression preferences often change as mysteriously as they appear. Only the most stubborn insist that they never modify a first like or dislike. But when one's likes and dislikes settle down to permanence, they are as inexplicable as ever. This fact is so disconcerting to logic and common sense that most people refuse to admit it. We bring up all sorts of things as reasons for our feelings. We say, sweepingly, "I like Pete because he's cheerful. I always like cheerful people." But even as we speak we remember (if we are honest) that So-and-So is cheerful and we have often wished he'd wipe that silly grin off his face. The simple point is that we like Pete and so we like his being cheerful; we don't like So-and-So and hence we dislike his cheerfulness.

And don't claim for one instant that you like anybody for his virtue, or dislike him for his faults. How many devotedly good people have rubbed you intolerably the wrong way? And how many times have you confessed, "Well, I know he doesn't pay his debts and is always getting out from under his responsibilities—but, darn it all, you can't help liking the fellow."

Moreover, our likes and dislikes are cheeringly free from the self-interest motive. The sick man who murmurs he'd rather have the sandy-haired nurse hasn't any idea that she can give him better nursing. The child who, gazing at the new teacher, finds mysteriously rising in his ignorant little heart a liking for her hasn't the least idea that she can teach him more geography and arithmetic than another. He doesn't like her because he can get more education out of her. Goodness gracious, no! He just likes her.

Is the phenomenon of personal liking and disliking so mysterious that nothing can be learned about the conduct of life from thoughtful consideration of it? Well, maybe one thing: the desirability of admitting to our minds without emotional protest the fact that each of us is bound to encounter some persons who dislike him, and that we might as well accept this universal phenomenon without making a fuss about it.

Much unhappiness, irritability and vain regret could be put out of our lives if we would but recognize that any universal phenomenon is bound to apply to us as well as to everybody else. It is childishness not to recognize this. Yet I have a notion that many a sensitive clergyman, many a lawyer, doctor, merchant, suffers from a shock not unlike that which paled the cheeks of my college girl when he sees dislike in the eyes of someone looking at him—even someone he secretly dislikes himself. If we could accept such shocks as philosophically as we accept the weather—and for the same reason, because there's nothing anybody can do about them—how much more inner peace we might have! We might learn to protect our self-respect by taking pains always to act with fairness and thoughtfulness to the occasional person who is so inhuman as to feel for us the dislike we feel once in a while for someone else. Beyond that, the best thing is just to take it as we take a wet day, aware that fussing about it only makes things worse.

Although this problem of likes and dislikes concerns us every minute we are in the presence of others, it is never seriously discussed by doctors, psychologists, clergymen, or anyone else among those who undertake to help us to understand life in order to manage it with intelligence. Did you ever see a reputable book on this subject? I never did. A few commercially minded people make money by teaching us tricks which will help us give an imitation of likability and hence perhaps sell more goods or more insurance. But that is about all.

The poets more than other human beings have here occasional deep divinations of truth. They have at least recognized the existence of this mystery. Elizabeth Barrett goes deep with the sonnet beginning:

> If thou must love me, let it be for naught
> Except for love's sake only. Do not say
> "I love her for her smile—her look—her way
> Of speaking gently—for a trick of thought."

Later she repeats with passionate insistence "love me for love's sake."

But it was no poet at all, only an irreverent student in a classroom a century or so ago, who produced a bit of doggerel so folk-perfect an expression for a universal human experience that his four lines bid fair to become immortal:

> I do not like thee, Dr. Fell,
> The reason why I cannot tell,
> But this I know and know full well—
> I do not like thee, Dr. Fell.

Request Performance

THE master of ceremonies on a Los Angeles radio program was interviewing engaged couples, asking for the details of their romances. When one couple came to the microphone, the bride-to-be explained that it was a second romance for both of them. They had both been married before—to each other—but extreme youth and the separation of war had broken their marriage.

"Just what made you two decide that you were meant for each other after all?" asked the M.C.

"Well," explained the lady, "our young daughter wrote a composition in school entitled, 'I wish my father would marry my mother.'"

—Contributed by Mrs. Martin Gordon

WHAT RELIGIOUS EXPERIENCE

CAN MEAN TO YOU

By
Norman Vincent Peale, D.D.   *Condensed from Guideposts*

ONE SUNDAY NIGHT in April 1912, Mrs. Archibald Gracie, wife of a retired Army colonel, felt strangely tired. Yet she could not sleep, and when she tried to read she felt a vague, unreasonable fear. As she reached out to a bedside table for the Episcopal Book of Common Prayer, the book fell to the floor and lay open at the prayer: "For Those at Sea."

Now Mrs. Gracie's apprehension had found an object: the Colonel was coming home, was even then in mid-ocean. Kneeling beside her bed, she prayed for the safety of her husband until five o'clock. Then peace came to her and she returned to bed and fell asleep.

A few hours later her sister roused her with the morning paper. The *Titanic* had struck an iceberg and had gone down. Colonel Gracie's name was not on the brief list of the rescued.

Mrs. Gracie then told her sister of her extraordinary experience during the night. Precisely how extraordinary it was she did not know until she learned later what had happened on the icy sea.

Dismissing hope for himself, Colonel Gracie had helped the crew lower lifeboats filled with women and children. When the last was launched, the old soldier began to pray that he might get a message through to his wife: *"Good-bye, my darling . . ."* Then, as the ship plunged to the bottom, a whirlpool engulfed him. Despite freezing water and the deadly pull of suction, he began swimming under water, with still but one thought: *Good-bye, my darling, until we meet again. . . .*

Suddenly he rose to the surface of the starlit waters. Looking around, he saw a capsized boat on which some men balanced perilously. Gracie swam toward it and clambered aboard. A lifeboat found them—at just about the time peace came to his praying wife back home.

Prayer is the greatest force known for grappling with everyday problems and for serenity of the soul. More than that, true prayer is a spiritual experience.

Conversation with God should be a constant habit, not a maddened plea when one is at wits' end. And it is to a Father and not to a Santa Claus that we must learn to speak, in trust and obedience. The supreme model was given in the Gethsemane prayer: "Not my will but Thine be done."

The first great benefit of prayer is its power to calm our minds, heal heartache and give us clear vision to act for ourselves.

A friend of mine who for ten years had been vice-president of a wholesale house thought when the president died that he would succeed to the job. But an outsider was chosen. My friend was polite to the newcomer and tried scrupulously to attend to his job, but deep in his soul he despaired—and his work suffered. Then one evening he ran across an old prayer by an unknown author: "Teach me, my Lord, to be gentle in all events, especially in disappointments. Let me put myself aside, to hide my little pains and heartaches so that I may be the only one to suffer from them. Let me use the suffering that comes across my path that it may mellow, not embitter me; that it may make me patient, not irritable; that it may make me broad in my forgiveness, not narrow, haughty and overbearing."

As he entered the office next morning he saw the new president. "Hello, John!" boomed my friend—before he even realized what he was doing. His voice was hearty with a new friendliness.

"Morning, Tom!" replied the surprised boss. "Come inside, will you? I need your help on a problem."

With the destruction of resentment inside himself, my friend found peace, which he has never lost.

If you are angry, anxious, vindictive, envious, you cannot think properly or act wisely. But in prayer, your emotions come under control, and your intellectual force drives into a problem, penetrates its essence for the right answer.

Many businessmen use prayer as a deliberate and reliable aid in their affairs. Walter Hoving, one of the nation's leading department-store executives, communes with God for 15 minutes each morning after breakfast. Both he and his wife firmly believe in the promise: "Where two or three are gathered together in my name, there I am also." They find that, afterward, decisions and resolutions often come to them with compelling force.

An industrialist uses his car as a chapel: "I conceive of Jesus Christ as driving to the plant with me. After all, He did say that He would be with us always. And I have got in the habit of talking problems over with Him. Instead of desperately expecting a prayer to pull me out of a mess, I now condition my mind in advance, so that no matter what comes up I am prepared to make calm and rational decisions."

Early Palm Sunday morning in 1937 several clergymen in Detroit were asked to come to the YMCA for a conference about the Chrysler sit-down strike, then at its inflammatory worst. The ministers were told that the unionists were organizing a mass meeting for four o'clock on Tuesday afternoon in traffic-jammed Cadillac Square. The mayor was out of town; the chief of police had refused a permit for the meeting; there was the smell of coming bloodshed.

At the conference with the acting mayor and representatives of the union, it seemed impossible to mediate the differences. The city was willing to permit a meeting in some other area, but not in downtown Detroit; the union was determined to meet in Cadillac Square, with or without a permit. After an hour of getting nowhere, one preacher suggested they all kneel and pray. To his astonishment, no one objected. Some prayed aloud, others silently; but each in his own way asked for help. Fifteen minutes later they sat again at the conference table.

The acting mayor cleared his throat. "How will it do if the meeting is held in Cadillac Square, but at six o'clock instead of four?"

"Suppose we hold our meeting only at one end of the square, so as not to tie up traffic?" the union leader countered.

The huge mass meeting at 6 p.m. that Tuesday afternoon was a completely peaceful affair.

"Because I believe in God," said Mahatma Gandhi, "I believe in prayer. It is the surest means of becoming conscious of His presence; that is the real meaning of prayer, its strength and its reward."

AN OLD WAY TO NEW LIFE

By Fulton Oursler

Condensed from Christian Herald

IN THE cemetery office a uniformed chauffeur approached the clerk at the desk. "The lady is too ill to walk," he explained. "Would you mind coming out with me?"

Waiting in the car was a frail, elderly woman whose sunken eyes could not hide some deep, long-lasting hurt.

"I am Mrs. Adams," she said. "Every week for the last two years I have been sending you a five-dollar bill for flowers to be laid on the grave of my son. I came here today because the doctors have let me know I have only a few weeks left. I wanted to drive here for one last look, and to thank you."

The clerk blinked at her irresolutely. Then, with a wry smile, he spoke: "You know, ma'am, I was sorry you kept sending the money for the flowers."

"Sorry?"

"Yes—flowers last such a little while! And nobody ever sees them."

"Do you realize what you are saying?"

"Oh, indeed I do. I belong to a visiting society. State hospitals. Insane asylums. People in places like that dearly love flowers—and they can see them and smell them. Lady, there are living people in places like that."

Some months later the clerk was astonished to receive another visit; doubly astonished because this time the woman was driving the car.

"I take the flowers to the people myself," she announced, with a friendly smile. "You were right; it does make them happy. And it makes me happy. The doctors don't know what is making me well—but I do! I have something to live for."

A physician friend of mine seems to possess miraculous healing power. Without drugs or knives he makes many of his patients well and happy; difficult cases, too, people suffering not only from personality difficulties but from heart trouble, alcoholism or paralysis. His colleagues are often mystified but he insists it is childishly simple:

"My patients make themselves well by using a prescription given long ago in Galilee. I wonder what would happen if the Sermon on the Mount were taken literally by the medical profession? Certainly Jesus gave us dependable keys for mental and physical well-being. Unselfishness is the greatest safeguard against self-pity, hate and fear; therefore it is a kind of specific against many forms of insanity."

One day a girl named Emily came to Prof. Ernest M. Ligon, head of the psychology department of Union College. She wanted to know what she could do with her life. She was a hapless, chapfallen figure, too tall and bony, and instinctively awkward. When Emily shook hands the professor winced—her palms and fingers were nervously cold and moist. And she had poor taste; her clothes, he declares in unacademic language, "were a mess!"

He said to her, "Emily, I want you to go out and buy yourself a new dinner dress—but remember, just ask the saleswoman to select a dress that she thinks becomes you. Then I want you to get a new hair-do—but again, just ask the hairdresser to do what he thinks is best for you. Then I want you to come to the church social next Tuesday night."

Emily shook her head. "I'll get my hair fixed and I'll buy the dress, but I won't come to the party."

"And I know why!" exclaimed the professor. "You think you won't have a good time. When you arrive don't look around with a sickly smile, hoping to heaven somebody will be polite to you. Just stand composedly and as soon as you see some man standing alone go over and ask his name and then inquire if he has a hobby. Then come and tell me. If he collects stamps I'll introduce him to another collector; if he likes to fish, I'll bring him a fisherman. Meanwhile, you go looking for another candidate. Keep yourself busy as if you were hired for the evening to look out for everybody's comfort. And promise me you will stay till the party is over."

Now, such are the unsearchable ways of life, Emily had a fine time. She was actually popular that evening. The professor could never make her lovely—but she was making herself lovable.

My doctor friend is a famous New York neurologist, and many dipsomaniacs come to him after having been pronounced incurable by other specialists.

"Know what I do with them?" he asked me. "I'll tell you about a man we'll call Bill Wilkins."

Bill Wilkins, Wall Street broker, woke up one morning in a hospital for drunkards. Despondently he peered up at the house physician and groaned:

"Doc, how many times have I been in this joint?"

"Fifty! You're now our half-century plant."

"I suppose liquor is going to kill me?"

"Bill," replied the doctor solemnly. "It won't be long now."

"Then," said Bill, "how about a little snifter to straighten me out?"

"I guess that would be all right," agreed the doctor. "But I'll make a bargain with you. There's a young fellow in the next room in a pretty bad way. He's here for the first time. Maybe if you showed yourself as a horrible example, you might scare him into staying sober for the rest of his life."

Instead of resentment, Bill showed a flicker of interest.

"Okay," he said. "But don't forget that drink when I come back."

The boy was certain that he was doomed, and Bill, who considered himself an agnostic, incredibly heard himself pleading with the lad to turn to some higher power.

"Liquor is a power outside yourself that has overcome you," he urged. "Only another outside power can save you. If you don't want to call it God, call it truth. The name isn't important."

Whatever the effect on the boy, Bill greatly impressed *himself*. Back in his own room, he forgot his bargain with the doctor. He still hasn't had that drink. Thinking of someone else at long last, he had given the law of unselfishness a chance to work on him; and through him it worked so well that he became a founder of a highly effective movement in healing faith—Alcoholics Anonymous.

*"Whither goest thou?" a famous author
asks himself and his fellow men*

QUO VADIS?   *By A. J. Cronin*

W E WERE in Rome with Italian friends whose one desire was to
make our stay a festival. Gay excursions to Tivoli and Hadrian's
Villa, parties at the Palazzo Doria and on the terrace of the
Casino Borghese. The Via Veneto throbbed with color and excitement
—sleek cars in slow procession, cafés filled with a fashionable throng,
flower stalls riotous with blossoms.

And then one golden afternoon as I drove back alone from a protracted luncheon in a garden near Albano I lost my way, found myself, to my annoyance, in a poor, dusty and deserted quarter holding
nothing of that elegant sophistication to which I had grown accustomed. I drew up. Across the empty street was a small square building
of gray stone. At a casual glance it suggested a branch administrative
bureau where I could obtain information as to my whereabouts. I left
the car, pushed open the door and went inside. Then, confronted suddenly by the dim and silent interior, I realized that I had stumbled
upon an ancient church.

I had seen the famous churches of Rome—St. Peter's and the Lat-
eran, the basilicas of St. Paul and St. Clement. But this small sanctuary
was wholly different—bare, simple, empty, yet filled with a strange and

reverent recollection of the past. As my gaze became adjusted to the inner twilight it fell upon a plaque set into the worn stone floor. Slowly deciphering the bronze inscription, almost obliterated by the years, I discovered where chance had brought me.

This was the chapel of Quo Vadis! Here on this exact spot, according to the legend, the apostle Peter, terrorized by Nero's threats and fleeing from pagan Rome, had been confronted in a vision by his reproachful Lord. And here, opening the mystical interview which sent the fugitive back with courage and faith renewed, were spoken those memorable words: *"Quo vadis? . . . Whither goest thou?"*

Under a queer compulsion I seated myself upon a low wooden bench, all my senses strained and intent. The moments passed, time lost its meaning, the silence echoed in my ears. And then from the cloistered shadows, through the overpowering stillness of that hallowed place, it seemed as though a whisper reached me, faint yet accusing, across the centuries. *"Quo vadis?* Whither art thou going?"

Was not this a question which I, or any man, might ask himself today? The thought of those past weeks of pleasure stung me. There came upon me an extraordinary sense of emptiness and dissatisfaction, an awareness, sharp as sudden pain, of how fatally I—and others like me—had become absorbed in worldly affairs. We had forgotten, or ignored, the kingdom of the spirit.

In the somber nave, barely illumined by a shaft of light stealing through the transept, I saw this, suddenly, as the blight which lay upon mankind. Throughout the modern world men had become oblivious to the purpose of their being; they sought only for temporal honor and material grandeur. The dominant cry today was no longer: "How much can I do?" but only "How much can I get?"

The standards of personal morality had become debased. Current events, reported in the daily press, revealed endless infractions of the moral law which might well chill the heart. Once men had ruled their conduct by the Ten Commandments. But how many in their daily round now gave thought to God? What did God matter when we had the best houses, the best automobiles, the best of everything?

How proud were the great democracies to call themselves Christian nations! Yet how few professing that code of ethics gave more than a passing thought to its heavenly Founder. Many, indeed, had written

God off as a pious fable; they never went to church, never spoke a word in prayer. Others temporized smugly in their belief, accepting Christ only as a great man, perhaps a prophet, rationalizing His miracle in terms of popular science, using every convenient device to evade what was most demanded of them. Most pitiful of all were those who, believing in their hearts and drawn to the path of faith, nevertheless through weakness or worldliness failed to follow it.

Yet now, more than ever before, Christendom was in danger, confronted by forces more barbaric than those of the pagan emperors— forces which sought to destroy belief in God, to bury the truth, wrung out of sacrifice and enlightenment, in the darkness of the abyss. How under heaven could we meet this challenge unless we stood firm, sustained by our own faith, twice-armed by our own integrity?

Today a global struggle was being waged for the minds, hearts and souls of millions of young people, a deadly struggle between the forces of evil and the forces of good. The enemy, by every trick of propaganda, subversion and deceit, was bent on annihilating forever in the rising generation and in generations to come the very concept of man's relationship with his divine source.

Like it or not, America had become the leader of the world, the champion of freedom and of right. Could we win through if we not only failed to show the way by our example but stood, instead, convicted as mere self-seekers, oblivious to the stern necessity of self-discipline, exhibiting our vaunted Christianity as a mockery and a sham?

A shiver passed over me as I sat in this shrine made hallowed by the apostle Peter. I thought of that great saint's martyrdom, and of the dark alcoves of the catacombs where lay the bones of the early Christians who, scorning the ways of ease, had dedicated themselves to their ideal. And I longed with all my soul that we might recover something of that shining faith, constant in life, steadfast in death. Then indeed would mankind, lost in the modern labyrinth, find itself in a spiritual revival, a surging wave of good will which would sweep across the world, wiping out malice and manufactured hatreds, reaching beyond despotic rulers and reuniting the masses of the people—making that hope forever cherished, the brotherhood of man, a firm reality at last.

This was the gleam upon the dark horizon. Yet such a change in the heart of the world could begin only in the heart of the individual, could

succeed only if we would—every one of us—put in practice the fundamental precepts of the great moral laws, fill our churches to overflow-
ing, unite our voices in common prayer, mobilize our spiritual resources
and loose a fervent new crusade by word and deed to all the corners
of the earth. Could we but give effect to the Sermon on the Mount, all
the difficulties, apparently insuperable, which confront us would melt
like mist before the rising sun.

Was such an idea naïve and unpractical in our modern age? No! To
follow this sublime teaching was the supreme goal of our existence.
How better could we fulfill the destiny for which we were created than
by practicing these eternal precepts: by casting out hatred, pride and
greed; fostering justice, kindness and charity?

No matter the creed into which we had been born, this was the
essence of true religion. And now religion should be the main concern
of our lives, not hidden apologetically in the background as if it were
something obsolete, no longer credited by advanced and intelligent
people. Religion was the only remedy for that sense of futility which
haunts so many of us today, a way of life which, apart from its
spiritual rewards, worked miracles in human relationships and brought
immense dividends in happiness and peace of mind.

Should we not pause, therefore, amid the rush and racket of our
daily lives and give heed to that inner voice which urges us to stop,
look and listen, which forever whispers in our ear those two momentous words: *"Quo vadis?"* Then perhaps our eyes would open to the
folly of misguided striving and the need of these things that are everlasting. Then indeed would we heed where we were going and make
our destination, and the destination of all humanity, eternally secure.

As I came slowly out of that little church the setting sun cast a
radiance upon the rooftops, upon the domes and pinnacles of the city.
And in that glow my spirits lifted. Despite the cruelties which men
inflicted upon one another, despite the blindness and indifference, the
threats of war and the destroyings and dispersings which afflict the
nations, I felt there still was hope for the peoples of the earth. The road
that we should travel still lay open, if only we would take it.

Unquenchable Spirit:

The Mark of a Man

By Dale Carnegie
Author of "How to Win Friends and Influence People"

Condensed from "How to Stop Worrying and Start Living"

O NE DAY when I was a boy, I was playing in an abandoned house in northwest Missouri. I rested my feet on a window sill for a moment—and then jumped. I had a ring on my left forefinger and the ring caught on a nailhead and tore off my finger.

I was terrified. I was positive I was going to die. But after the hand healed, I never worried about it. Now, I seldom think about the fact that I have only three fingers and a thumb on my left hand.

A few years ago, I met a man who was running a freight elevator in a New York office building. I noticed that his left hand had been cut off at the wrist. I asked him if that loss bothered him. He said, "Oh, no. Only when I try to thread a needle."

It is astonishing how quickly we can accept almost any situation—if we have to—and adjust ourselves to it. George V of England had these words framed on the wall of his library: "Teach me neither to cry for the moon nor over spilt milk." The same thought is expressed by Schopenhauer: "A good supply of resignation is of the first importance in providing for the journey of life."

Obviously, circumstances alone do not make us happy or unhappy. Our feelings are determined by the way we react to them. We can all endure disaster and triumph over it—if we have to. We may not think we can, but we have inner resources that will see us through if we only make use of them. We are stronger than we think.

The late Booth Tarkington had always believed that he could take anything that life could force upon him except one thing—blindness. Then when he was along in his 60's, he began losing his sight.

When total darkness closed in, Tarkington said, "I found I could take the loss of my eyesight, just as a man can take anything else. If I lost *all five* of my senses, I know I could live on inside my mind. For it is in the mind we see, and live."

Am I advocating that we simply bow down to all adversities? Not by a long shot! As long as there is a chance that we can save a situation, let's fight! But when common sense tells us that we are up against something that cannot be otherwise, then, in the name of our sanity, let's not pine for what is not.

Sarah Bernhardt was an illustrious example of a woman who knew how to coöperate with the inevitable. After half a century as the reigning queen of the theater on four continents, at 71 she found herself broke in Paris. Worse than that, while crossing the Atlantic, she had fallen during a storm and injured her leg so severely that phlebitis developed. The pain became so intense that the doctor finally concluded that the leg must be amputated, but he was almost afraid to tell the stormy, tempestuous Sarah what had to be done for fear the news would set off an explosion of hysteria. But he was wrong. Sarah looked at him a moment, and said quietly, "If it has to be, it has to be."

No one has enough emotion and vigor to fight the inevitable and, at the same time, enough left over to create a new life. Choose one or the other. You can either bend with the inevitable storms of life—or you can resist them and break!

Why do you think your automobile tires stand up on the road and take so much punishment? At first, manufacturers tried to make a tire that would resist the shocks of the road. It was soon cut to ribbons. Then they made a tire that would absorb the shocks of the road. That tire could "take it." You and I will last longer, and enjoy smoother riding, if we learn to do the same.

How to Make an Exit

By Luther Conant   Condensed from McCall's

HAVE you ever wondered why otherwise normal people say good-bye to their hostess and promptly stand at the front door for another ten minutes saying it all over again?

"If leave-taking is awkward for you," says Mrs. Agnes Rogers Allen, author of the recent best-seller *Women Are Here to Stay,* "wait for a pause and start a little story. As you tell it, rise from your chair. Come to the climax standing by your hostess. Put out your hand, thank her, say good-bye and *leave.*"

For married couples, Mrs. Allen suggests a quiet prearranged high sign. Otherwise the wife should take the initiative—walk over to her husband's group and make the most of that first pause when they turn toward her. Any little sentence: "John would like to talk all night, but we must go now." The secret is fast timing. If she joins the conversation, she'll be there another half hour.

Never make any excuses for leaving. "I'm afraid I have to go now" is nonsense. A good excuse only makes your hosts feel unimportant, and a weak excuse merely strands you at the door explaining inanely.

When you do have to leave well ahead of the others tell your hostess this as soon as you arrive, not when you're leaving. If it's a large party, just say good-bye to your hosts and people near you. Once you've said good-bye, don't bring up any new topic of conversation. We all have that impulse to say something interesting on the way out. Save it for next time and spare your hostess one of those prolonged hallway farewells.

Just when is the right time to go? Mrs. Audrey Winston, noted New York social authority, suggests:

A dinner party — two hours after coffee is served.

An after-dinner party — about two and a half hours.

A luncheon — 30 to 40 minutes after dessert.

A cocktail party — an hour and a half is ample.

An afternoon call — not more than an hour.

"If you've made up your mind about the right time to leave," says Mrs. Winston, "your exit can be much more relaxed." All you need do is glance at your watch, say a pleasant and *brief* farewell and put one foot in front of the other until you're out the door.

Copyright 1950 by The Reader's Digest Association, Inc. (September 1950 issue)
Condensed from McCall's, June 1950

Mother's Day

THE PHONE shrilled in the middle of the night, and I groggily picked up the receiver. It was a long-distance call. My heart hammering, I heard, "Is that you, Son?"

"Mom! What's wrong?"

"Nothing's wrong." I could hear Mother chuckle. "It's your birthday."

"Holy smokes! You didn't get me out of bed at 3 a.m. just to say Happy Birthday, did you?"

"Well, you made *me* get out of bed at 3 a.m. 30 years ago tonight — and it is high time I paid you back!"   —Contributed by Philip A. Lincoln

PRAYER IS POWER

By *Alexis Carrel, M.D.*

RAYER is not only worship; it is also an invisible emanation of man's worshiping spirit—the most powerful form of energy that one can generate. The influence of prayer on the human mind and body is as demonstrable as that of secreting glands. Its results can be measured in terms of increased physical buoyancy, greater intellectual vigor, moral stamina, and a deeper understanding of the realities underlying human relationships.

If you make a habit of sincere prayer, your life will be very noticeably and profoundly altered. Prayer stamps with its indelible mark our actions and demeanor. A tranquillity of bearing, a facial and bodily repose, are observed in those whose inner lives are thus enriched. Within the depths of consciousness a flame kindles. And man sees himself. He discovers his selfishness, his silly pride, his fears, his greeds, his blunders. He develops a sense of moral obligation, intellectual humility. Thus begins a journey of the soul toward the realm of grace.

Prayer is a force as real as terrestrial gravity. As a physician, I have seen men, after all other therapy had failed, lifted out of disease and melancholy by the serene effort of prayer. It is the only power in the world that seems to overcome the so-called "laws of nature"; the occasions on which prayer has dramatically done this have been termed "miracles." But a constant, quieter miracle takes place hourly in the hearts of men and women who have discovered that prayer supplies them with a steady flow of sustaining power in their daily lives.

Too many people regard prayer as a formalized routine of words, a refuge for weaklings, or a childish petition for material things. We sadly undervalue prayer when we conceive it in these terms, just as we should underestimate rain by describing it as something that fills the birdbath in our garden. Properly understood, prayer is a mature activity indispensable to the fullest development of personality—the ultimate integration of man's highest faculties. Only in prayer do we achieve that complete and harmonious assembly of body, mind and spirit which gives the frail human reed its unshakable strength.

The words, "Ask and it shall be given to you," have been verified by the experience of humanity. True, prayer may not restore the dead child to life or bring relief from physical pain. But prayer, like radium, is a source of luminous, self-generating energy.

How does prayer fortify us with so much dynamic power? To answer this question (admittedly outside the jurisdiction of science) I must point out that all prayers have one thing in common. The triumphant hosannas of a great oratorio, or the humble supplication of an Iroquois hunter begging for luck in the chase, demonstrate the same truth: that human beings seek to augment their finite energy by addressing themselves to the Infinite Source of all energy. When we pray, we link ourselves with the inexhaustible motive power that spins the universe. We ask that a part of this power be apportioned to our needs. Even in asking, our human deficiencies are filled and we arise strengthened and repaired.

But we must never summon God merely for the gratification of our whims. We derive most power from prayer when we use it, not as a petition, but as a supplication that we may become more like Him. Prayer should be regarded as practice of the Presence of God. An old peasant was seated alone in the last pew of the village church. "What are you waiting for?" he was asked; and he answered, "I am looking at Him and He is looking at me." Man prays not only that God should remember him, but also that he should remember God.

How can prayer be defined? Prayer is the effort of man to reach God, to commune with an invisible being, creator of all things, supreme wisdom, truth, beauty, and strength, father and redeemer of each man. This goal of prayer always remains hidden to intelligence. For both language and thought fail when we attempt to describe God.

We do know, however, that whenever we address God in fervent prayer we change both soul and body for the better. It could not happen that any man or woman could pray for a single moment without some good result. "No man ever prayed," said Emerson, "without learning something."

One can pray everywhere. In the streets, the subway, the office, the shop, the school, as well as in the solitude of one's room or among the crowd in a church. There is no prescribed posture, time or place.

"Think of God more often than you breathe," said Epictetus the Stoic. In order really to mold personality, prayer must become a habit. It is meaningless to pray in the morning and to live like a barbarian the remainder of the day. True prayer is a way of life; the truest life is literally a way of prayer.

The best prayers are like the improvisations of gifted lovers, always about the same thing yet never twice the same. We cannot all be as creative in prayer as Saint Theresa or Bernard of Clairvaux, both of whom poured their adoration into words of mystical beauty. Fortunately, we do not need their eloquence; our slightest impulse to prayer is recognized by God. Even if we are pitifully dumb, or if our tongues are overlaid with vanity or deceit, our meager syllables of praise are acceptable to Him, and He showers us with strengthening manifestations of His love.

Today, as never before, prayer is a binding necessity in the lives of men and nations. The lack of emphasis on the religious sense has brought the world to the edge of destruction. Our deepest source of power and perfection has been left miserably undeveloped. Prayer, the basic exercise of the spirit, must be actively practiced in our private lives. The neglected soul of man must be made strong enough to assert itself once more. For if the power of prayer is again released and used in the lives of common men and women; if the spirit declares its aims clearly and boldly, there is yet hope that our prayers for a better world will be answered.

The Knack of Intelligent Travel

By Leland Stowe

Distinguished foreign correspondent, Pulitzer Prize-winner

OFFICIALS estimate that a fantastic total of 750,000 Americans travel abroad in a single year. In addition, State Department records show that an all-time high of approximately 440,000 Americans reside and work outside the United States, an increase of some 25 percent over pre-World War II. These million-and-more human beings today constitute America's most important export.

Why most important? Because of the power that traveling Americans hold in their grasp: to kindle genuine friendship or to appear as resentment-breeding intruders.

This poses a significant question: *How exportable are we Americans?* As a State Department information booklet which is issued with each passport says:

"Travelers who assume an air of arrogance or who transcend the common bounds of decency can do more in an hour to break down a friendly approach between peoples than our government can do in a year of trying to stimulate friendly relations. As we act so are we judged. . . ."

In 26 years of travel on five continents as a newspaper correspondent, I've encountered many fellow countrymen who carried with them that priceless passport, the passport to the human heart. Unfortunately they were a select minority of the Americans I met.

"Monsieur, have you any books on understanding American tourists?"

Today the personal obligations of an American to represent his country well abroad are much greater than ever before. With few exceptions, Americans are recognizable wherever they go. Nothing in our make-up or experience enables us to blend easily into foreign landscapes. All too often we are singled out because of our bad manners.

We have had little education on how to get the most out of foreign travel. We are victims of miseducation. I went through school and college convinced that almost anything American was automatically best. When I first tasted French bread I found it so superior to ours it was almost an affront to my patriotism. I soon learned that the world's best-equipped kitchens seldom produce the best cooking—and a lot more.

I learned that relatively few things are strictly American, that we owe a huge debt to foreign cultures and peoples—to Scandinavian and Slavic industriousness, to British self-government and law, to German and Italian music, to African laughter.

Finally I grasped the wonderful fact—pregnant with potentialities for the good of mankind—that we Americans are directly related to almost every people on earth. This is one of the greatest but least-exploited assets which America possesses in a Communist-menaced world. We should embrace this hidden asset with gratitude and pride.

No experience in life can be more incessantly stimulating, more instructive or more gratifying than discovering what people are like in other parts of the world. This is an endless, magnificent adventure in living. First comes the superficial impression that people from country to country are very different. Then you gradually realize that, underneath, we are all quite alike. In the process you discover, with an elation born of sharing, that there are no geographical boundaries to the human heart. You can be a patriotic American, or Englishman, or Frenchman, yet the world and its peoples belong to you, just as you belong to the world. To be close to people of different traditions and customs is to rediscover your own self, to become a citizen of the world.

Here are suggestions for anyone who really wants to make travel a constant exploration in human relations:

Remember that you are a guest. Don't throw your weight around. In any café or public place bear in mind that you are already conspicuous because you are "foreign." Try not to attract further attention. The well-mannered visitor creates his welcome simply by meriting it.

Don't make a fuss about petty annoyances. If you forgot to declare several cartons of cigarettes, it's not the customs official's fault. The visitor who loudly proclaims that "these people don't know how to make coffee" is really telling the world that he hasn't been around much. If a taxi driver overcharges you, remember that this has been known to happen at home. If you can't get orange juice or ham and eggs for breakfast, well—why leave home? There is no substitute for that ancient adage, "When in Rome—."

Don't criticize foreign peoples because they do things differently; they have very good reasons for doing things their way. Why do the Basques wear broad berets in their hot climate instead of straw hats? Because they grow their own wool, do not have straw, and the beret protects both their heads and their eyes. Why do Normandy farmers strip the limbs from their trees? Because firewood is scarce, and when you cut off only the lower limbs you've still got the trunk—to grow more firewood.

Don't confine your social contacts to persons of your own occupational or educational level; meet as many kinds of citizens as you can. I know an American professor who spent a year in Paris. He met almost no one except a few French intellectuals, and saw only a few parts of that incomparable city. He almost never ate the world's most delicious cuisine in restaurants. He was saving money to buy a car when he got home. I wonder if he ever knew how much that car cost him! He went home knowing as little about France and the French as could be managed. You find Americans like that in every country, living in their self-insulated cells. They might be enriching their lives, from day to day, by new knowledge and new types of friends.

Treat people as your equals. In wartime Karachi a hotel manager remarked of the British: "They don't know how to treat people as equals." This has been true of most colonizers; was notoriously true of the German Nazis; has proved the case all too frequently of Americans abroad in recent years. In Prague (1946) a cultured young Czech woman, employed in the U.S. Embassy, said to me: "We thought only the Germans acted like the master race. We expected much better of your countrymen, but most of them look down on us merely because we are a small country. Some are as arrogant as the Nazis were. We have been sadly deceived in the Americans who came here."

Nothing wounds so deeply as an attitude of superiority shown by visitors. Americans are in danger of being universally regarded as chief offenders in this respect. The fact that the attitude is usually unconscious—that it stems from an over-awareness of America's position and power, or from thoughtlessness or ignorance—does not diminish the resentments which inevitably result.

I have an intense affection for the Spanish peasant because, as the philosopher Unamuno said, "Spain's peasants are its only true aristocrats." They receive every person as an equal but not more! In dealing with human beings that is exactly enough. It is perhaps the first key to open the door to a stranger's heart.

Be interested in everything that is typical or unusual wherever you go. On his first visit to America Sweden's present King, then the Crown Prince, rode in our subways, inspected factory assembly lines, visited museums and universities, went to a baseball game. Americans immediately decided that Sweden's royal visitor was a fine fellow and a real democrat—which he was and is.

You might not enjoy your first bullfight, but you can't begin to understand the Spaniards or the Mexicans unless you go to a few. You may think you won't like a Hungarian gypsy orchestra, but unless you are moved by a people's music you can't begin to feel close to them.

When you really know and appreciate any country's food, its music and favorite sports, you'll not only find much that you like about its people. You'll find that most of them also like you. The traveler to be most pitied is one of whom his foreign hosts say: "He doesn't like our food, nor even our music." What they mean is: "He doesn't try to like us."

Every nation is like a surprise package: its wrappings are yours to untie. And there are no people on earth who are not gratified and flattered when a stranger wants to know about *them*, about any aspect of *their* lives and *their* country.

Be willing to admit that Americans have their faults and limitations, and that you have some of your own. Speaking before Winston Churchill and London's governing elite in 1951, General Eisenhower said: "There are men in this room with whom, during World War II, I had arguments hotly sustained and of long duration." He then confessed publicly to "a later conclusion that my own position was not always right." Such an admission is the kind of honest, gracious humility which every American, as a citizen of the world's most powerful nation, can well afford to practice wherever he goes.

People respond instinctively to those who frankly recognize and admit their own failings. Americans abroad are bound to hear sharp criticisms of their country or its policies (as we do at home). Any traveler who claims infallibility for himself or his country becomes a bore or a public affront.

To any American traveler I would say: "You were brought up under the principle that 'all men are created equal.' You have only to *live* that. You come of a young and venturesome race, a people of much ingenuity and flexibility. Of all people, you should be able to take abroad with you the three Big T's—Tolerance, Tact and Teamwork."

→⟫ ⟪←

Progress Notes

REPLACING the old-time small-town hotel near the depot, where the trains kept you awake all night, with the modern highway motel where the big trucks do the same is, we guess, progress of a sort.
—Detroit *News*

THE NEWEST dream kitchen has a lounge with TV, bookcase and fireplace, but most women would chuck the whole thing for a good old-fashioned hired girl. —*Changing Times, The Kiplinger Magazine*

WE'RE NOT going to consider any of these models the real dream car of tomorrow until one of them includes a disposal unit built into the ledge behind the back seat to chew up all the comic books, graham cracker boxes, youngsters' mittens and road maps. —Bill Vaughan, NANA

GRACIOUS LIVING is when you have the house air conditioned, and then load the yard with chairs, lounges and an outdoor oven so you can spend all your time in the hot sun. —Detroit *News*

TYPICAL of man's genius is the way he develops a bomb designed to drive us into the cellar about the time he starts building homes without any cellars. —Homer King in Hemet, Calif., *News*

Let's Help Them Marry Young

By Howard Whitman

Condensed from Better Homes & Gardens

I'D HATE to be 22, and in love, these days. How could I support a bride? How could I find a place to live? How could I train for a profession—in a day when more and more training is essential?

Without financial help I couldn't.

That is precisely the spot thousands of young Americans find themselves in today.

"I'll have a gray beard by the time I'm able to marry," says Hal Smith. Hal makes $30 a week in a gas station.

"Marriage is a luxury we can't afford," remarks Jean Foster, whose boy friend is a medical student.

The case for making marriage available to hundreds of thousands of the blocked generation is not built on sentiment: it is a serious business of saving young people from frustration, of preserving the American home, of stemming the tidal waves of promiscuity, delinquency and divorce.

We surround boys and girls in their late teens and early 20's with ideals of marriage and home building. We admit that our Hal Smiths and Jean Fosters are biologically mature, that they possess growing and compelling urges toward mating and parenthood. We lure them toward marriage in our movies, our fiction, in the whole romantic gloss with which we daub youthful life. Then we snatch away this illusion with: "Don't be a fool, Alice. It's ridiculous to marry a boy who's making only $30 a week!" Or, "Out of the question, Ned. You can't marry until you've finished your internship!"

The result is a sexual dilemma. Psychiatrists' offices teem with men and women suffering from guilt complexes because they indulged in premarital sex relations, and with equal numbers who are frigid or impotent because they were too long repressed.

From the files of Dr. Janet Fowler Nelson come these case histories:

Tom and Lillian were in love and wanted to marry, but couldn't because Tom, an architect, was working out his apprenticeship at $28 a week. Faced with a wait of five years or more, Tom and Lillian realized that they had to make a decision. Either they would (1) have extramarital relations, thus breaking the rules of society, or (2) stifle their emotional and physical drives, with the resultant frustration. They chose the first alternative.

When they finally married, Lillian was oppressed with the fear that "Tom only married me because he thought he *ought* to," and Tom unhappily remarked, "If she was that way with me, maybe she'd be the same with any man."

Equally bitter is the case of conscientious Arthur and Margaret, who chose the second alternative. Margaret's parents refused to allow her to marry until she had a college diploma and had taught school for at least a year. She and Arthur "went steady" from the time she was 19 until she was 23. Then they were married. A few years later Margaret was in Dr. Nelson's office relating a sorrowful story of their failure to reach mature sexual adjustment.

"You see," Margaret said, "we ruled out all petting before we were married. We knew that was the only way to keep out of difficulty. I suppose it was puritanical, but anyway we prided ourselves on never showing any signs of physical affection."

Arthur and Margaret had fallen into a familiar trap. They had reined in their impulses by labeling them evil and tawdry. "This carried over into their married life and completely blocked a happy adjustment," Dr. Nelson explains.

If we gave young people hope that they could marry at 20 or 22, they could cope with their growing urges. "Early marriage," declares Dr. James F. Bender, director of the National Institute for Human Relations, "leads to far better marriage adjustment both physically and psychologically. The cases of incompatibility which come to my office are not the couples who married early but the late-marrieds who are crippled by stunted and repressed emotions or by previous, furtive experiences."

Promiscuity, sociologists agree, is the greatest foe of successful marriage. But a YMCA poll among men in their early 20's indicated not only that extramarital relations were "greatly increasing" but that 80 percent of the young men blamed financial bars against early marriage for the upward trend.

Our communities, up to their necks in delinquency, scream alarm at the numbers of wayward girls, young sex offenders, unmarried mothers. "Yet what is this," asks Will C. Turnbladh, of the National Probation Association, "but an indication of the stone wall many young people are up against?"

Early marriage is not merely a check against evils. It has plentiful assets of its own. In a veterans' housing project in New York City, I visited a number of young couples. Isaac Bardavid, a veteran of three years in the Pacific, and his wife, Charlotte, were married four years ago when she was 18 and he 21. "It's given us a chance to grow up and develop together," Charlotte said. "We feel we understand each other much better than we would if we had married four or five years later."

"And I can tell you this," Isaac put in. "Together we've got more courage to face the future than we'd ever have separately. Being a married man — with one child already and another on the way — I'm sure I'm a much better citizen than if I were single. I work harder. I have a bank account for the first time in my life. I plan for the future. I know if I were single today, I'd be running around, staying up until all hours, getting nowhere fast."

A neighbor, Paul Melone, didn't marry until he was 33, two years ago. "But I didn't wait through choice," he said. "I was stopped twice, once by the depression, once by the war." He glanced at six-month-old Billy, playing on the floor. "The trouble is, I'll be 50 by the time he's 15. It's much better for kids to have young parents. If I had my own choice in the matter, believe me, I'd marry young!"

But do young marriages stick?

In New York's Home Term Court, where hundreds of problems in family living come before Magistrate Anna M. Kross, cases repeatedly bear out the strength of early marriage. "I often advise young people to get married," Judge Kross declares. "The idea of waiting for 'better jobs' or 'money in the bank' is strictly materialistic. As a matter of fact, the hardship of starting out in life does not destroy marriage. It makes it stronger. The thing which really weakens our social structure is that family life starts too late!"

What can we do about it? The answer is simply a return to an idea which is as old as America—*family aid to young married couples.*

In the America which conquered a wilderness, it was unthinkable that a young couple should marry without being given a few acres of land, a team and wagon, or a plow, or a cow barn, or the old house by the meadow. Only in up-to-date, citified America have we come by the idea that a boy and girl must marry in the full armor of independence, forgetting the "hidden subsidies" of the 1800's which parents provided as part of the business of getting young people on their feet.

"We must substitute our own form of subsidy," declares Dr. Benjamin Gruenberg, eminent sociologist and educator. "In cities, this usually means assisting young couples financially until they are established. Family aid ought to be an accepted custom—in fact an obligation—just as it used to be."

We ought to revive, too, the sadly neglected customs of the dowry and the bride's chest. In France, where the family unit is probably stronger than anywhere else in the world, no family would think of turning out a *jeune fille* without enough francs to keep her going for a year or two. And fathers consider it their duty to give sons a part of their business, their shop, or farm.

Finally, we need a major refocusing of our views on marriage and higher education. Thousands of parents support their unmarried sons and daughters through college, yet threaten to cut them off without a penny if they marry while at school. Thanks to the GI Bill of Rights, we are learning how surprisingly well marriage and education go together. At many of our universities one third of the students are married. And the brilliant fact is that these students, particularly the ones with children, are getting the most out of education because they can and do apply their energies more completely. At the University of Wisconsin the married veterans received significantly higher marks than the unmarried ones—and those who had children did the best of all!

From the dean's office of the University of Iowa comes the statement: "Marriage has a settling influence on students. They have someone to make good for, someone who is pleased when their record is high, someone to encourage them when things go wrong."

The GI bill has shown us the light. It will be all to the good if—through parents' aid, scholarship grants, and campus housing plans—we continue to let marriage and higher education march forward hand in hand.

Any investment we make in early marriage is, after all, an investment in the future families of America. There is nothing more gilt-edged than that.

Two-Word Recipe

My YOUNGER BROTHER, Jim, has achieved business success at the age of 46 without a line of worry on his face.

His unruffled serenity is the more noticeable because of the daily pressures and harassing details connected with his position. Yet the busiest day finds him taking a few minutes out to relax—over coffee, in conversation, sometimes merely leaning back in his chair and looking out over the city. The rougher the going, the more complete his relaxation.

Knowing this was not his boyhood temperament, I asked him one day what magic formula had raised him spiritually above the stress of workaday affairs.

"Two words," he said. "They were spoken to me in the middle of a lake, when I was 19 years old."

He told me what had happened. He was with a girl who was a champion swimmer, and when she suggested that they swim across the lake he was ashamed to admit that he was afraid to attempt it.

They started out, but by the time they reached the middle of the lake Jim was certain he was done for. He was panicky and completely exhausted. He gasped to the girl that he could go no farther.

But the girl, unruffled, gave him just two words of advice.

"And I followed them," Jim said. "I've followed them ever since—except that I've learned to apply them before I'm completely exhausted. It works spiritually as well as physically. And it was so simple! All she did was smile at me and say, 'Float, Jim.'"

—Robert Ormond Case in *This Week Magazine*

HOW TO STOP SMOKING

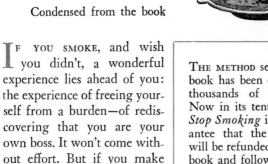

By Herbert Brean

Condensed from the book

IF YOU SMOKE, and wish you didn't, a wonderful experience lies ahead of you: the experience of freeing yourself from a burden—of rediscovering that you are your own boss. It won't come without effort. But if you make the effort you will win.

Why do people smoke? Medically speaking, tobacco is not habit-forming; it does not

THE METHOD set forth in this small book has been of enormous help to thousands of unwilling smokers. Now in its tenth printing, *How to Stop Smoking* is sold with the guarantee that the purchaser's money will be refunded if, after reading the book and following the author's advice, he is unable to break the habit. In the first three years fewer than 20 copies were returned.

worm its way into your physique and psyche, as opium or cocaine does. But it *is* habit-forming in the same way that three meals a day, or eight hours' sleep, or wearing clothes, are habit-forming. If you go without any one of them for a while you become uncomfortable.

But how comfortable are you with tobacco? Smoke a cigarette. Does it really satisfy you—in the way that a big meal does when you're hungry, or a warm coat when you're cold? You know better.

Light it, smoke it, taste its bitterness, put it out. Even as you do, you know that you'll soon want another. Not that you enjoy it. You simply want it.

Why? When you smoke, nicotine, carbon monoxide, small amounts of hydrocyanic acid, pyridine and various phenols and aldehydes are absorbed into your lungs and mouth, and then various things begin to happen. Your nervous system is momentarily stimulated. You start to salivate. Your blood pressure goes up. Your pulse rate increases. Tremors may appear in your hands and arms, and your extremities usually show a drop in temperature. (You notice none of these things, of course, though they are plainly detectable in the laboratory.)

Most important of all, your blood vessels undergo a constriction. The effect on them is like putting a flowing garden hose in a vise and tightening the vise a few turns. It "slows you down."

That is, after the momentary stimulation, smoking depresses, for a far longer period, both the sympathetic and the central nervous systems of the human body, as well as the endings of the motor nerves which activate the voluntary muscles.

This means that when you smoke you are artificially slowing down your body's normal activities. Now, suppose you are suddenly confronted with an emotional or psychological emergency: adrenalin is pumped into your blood stream, your muscles tense, you breathe faster and get edgy, jittery—"nervous." Tobacco smoke retards these natural processes by constricting your arteries, slowing down the blood circulation and thus "calming you down." You find a smoke is "good for your nerves."

If that were as far as it went there would be no occasion for worry. In fact, if you smoked only at times of real emotional stress it might be a good thing for you. But smoking goes much further than that.

If you smoke a pack and a half of cigarettes a day, you smoke an average of one cigarette every 32 minutes of your waking hours. That many crises don't arise every day. You need cigarettes simply because your body has come to expect this depressant effect every so often. If it doesn't get it you begin consciously to want a cigarette. When your body becomes habituated to tobacco you want a smoke fairly regularly. You are unhappy if you *don't* have it.

There is little pleasure in smoking—until you so inure your body to it that it puts up with the harsh taste, the hot dryness, the mouth bite, for the sake of tobacco's mild narcotic effect. If it were possible for you to go without cigarettes for the next 24 hours, and then light one, you would find out how distasteful and noxious tobacco smoke really is. After two deep inhalations of the first cigarette your head would be swimming, your legs and arms shaky. You might even feel faint and have to sit down. If you think that is an exaggeration, try it.

Or think back to the time many years ago when you smoked your first cigarette. Divorced from all the glamour and excitement of your first smoke, how did it *taste?* Gaseous, strong, biting, wasn't it?

Yet this is the experience that you give your system 30 to 60 times a day. You are able to do it because the human mechanism is a marvelously adjustable piece of machinery which can get used to living amid coal dust, or 110-degree heat, or doing the work of a truck horse. You can get used to almost anything.

Very well, you say, smoking is a bad habit. We've heard that before. What do we do about it?

It ought to encourage you to know that you have already taken one big step toward giving up smoking. For you have already read this far—which means that, for that long at least, you have been *thinking* about smoking and about giving it up. And that is an important rule. If you want to stop smoking, *think about giving it up.*

Think of it coolly and calmly, without fear or hopelessness. Many others have done it. You can, too. Consider the whole idea objectively for a little while. If you are not smoking at this minute, maybe it would be a good idea to take out a cigarette or pipe and light up. Analyze what you do and what you taste and smell. Drag the smoke into your lungs slowly and slowly exhale it. Just how good is it, really? Does it have the fragrance and goodness the copywriters claim?

Think for a moment of how much you get out of it, of how pleasurable it really is—aside from the negative pleasure of easing an otherwise painful craving. Then think of what it would be like not ever to *have* to smoke.

For giving up smoking isn't all asceticism and self-denial; there are compensations. In fact, there are so many that when you give yourself a chance to appreciate them you will never want to go back to nicotine.

When you give up smoking, your food will taste much better. Your nose and throat and lungs will not be continuously permeated with smoke and smoke's residue, soot. You will begin to *smell* the world around you. When you walk into a garden you will *smell* as well as *see* flowers; as you come home at night your nose will tell you what's for dinner.

Your teeth will look cleaner because they *are* cleaner, and they will not require a dentist's cleaning so often. The yellow stain on your fingers will disappear in a few days or a week. When you get up in the morning you won't find your throat clogged with phlegm, and you won't cough or clear your throat so often.

You will actually feel far less nervous. That's hard to believe—and during the first days of nonsmoking you *will* be nervous. The depressant effect smoking has exerted on your body for years suddenly ends, and the unfamiliar effect is almost overwhelming. You will possibly be more emotional, laughing at trivial things, and, for a while, tense, jumpy. But gradually the nervousness diminishes. When you are over it, you will be surprised what experiences you can meet and live through without reaching for a cigarette.

You'll be calmer, more poised, and you may well find that there now are more hours in the day. For, when you stop slowing down your body and cutting your energy with tobacco, you will find that you have much more energy; you sleep better and feel better adjusted. So there seems to be more time to get things done.

A word of caution here. It is generally believed that a reformed smoker gains weight. If you are of normal weight or underweight, there is nothing to worry about. If you have trouble with your waist-line, remember this: When you stop smoking you will probably gain. Don't worry about it—face it! Actually you will not gain more than a few pounds. For when you stop smoking you will have a great increase in *energy;* and in using up that *energy* you will burn away a lot of the weight that you put on.

If you have read this far you probably think you are about ready to swear off. But don't do it. Think about it—during the day and just a moment as you go to bed at night. Tentatively, like this: *One of these days, when I feel like it, maybe I'll try going without smoking and see what happens.* Just as an experiment, as a little change of pace in my regular routine.

Watch and wait until some time when your life is on a fairly even keel. Don't try it when you are leaving on an important business trip or preparing to give a big party, or when you are facing some personal emergency. Don't postpone it too long, either, or you will lose the momentum you are gradually building up.

But some morning—maybe on a week-end—you will wake up feeling especially good. You will have had a good night's sleep; you feel fit for anything, and the sun is shining sweetly. The idea of stopping smoking will pop into your head.

Why foul up a swell morning with the noxious fumes of burning nicotine? Why shoulder for another day the burden you've been carrying for years? Somehow it will not seem quite so impossible as it might at other times. Maybe this is the day.

Decide, then and there, quietly and firmly, that you're through with it! This is the moment, intelligently selected and properly prepared for, when you can get off with the running start of feeling good!

Now that we're on our way, let's take along some advice by a great psychologist, William James, whose observations on habits and their making and breaking are of extraordinary value to us right now.

James formulated several principles to get rid of habits. We can apply three of them to smoking.

One: Start yourself off on the new way of life with as much momentum as you can.

Tell your friends that you have given up smoking. Don't be smug or complacent or boastful, but let people know what you are doing. At some point when you are seriously tempted to smoke, the thought of all the derisive laughter you'll get for giving in may well carry you over the crises, which is the reason to tell others about what you are doing.

Most smokers have fixed ideas about the occasions when a smoke tastes best. The first cigarette after breakfast, or the one with a cocktail before dinner. If such associations are likely to tempt you to smoke, try to avoid them for a few days. If that is impossible, brace yourself in advance for such temptations; tell yourself that such an occasion is coming, and you must be prepared to want to smoke badly yet not give in to that want. If you hold out only for a moment, that sudden strong temptation will die almost as quickly as it arose.

Two: Don't permit yourself to make a single exception to your new rule until the nonsmoking habit is firmly implanted (and that will be a long time).

If a habit is not fed, it dies relatively quickly, but it can subsist for a long time on the slightest food. If you occasionally let yourself have one cigarette or pipe on the ground that "just one won't hurt," you will keep alive the desire to smoke. Just as one drink is too many for an alcoholic, one cigarette is too many for the heavy smoker who is trying to reform. Every time you say no to the temptation to smoke, you are making the next "no" easier.

The tough moments come only one at a time, and they get easier as you defeat them one at a time. Win the battle of the moment, and forget about an hour from now, or a day from now, or a week from now. Defeat one temptation, and the next one won't be quite so tempting.

Three: Deliberately expose yourself to small temptations and conquer them.

Just as a fighter conditions himself for a major fight by road work and sparring, you can develop your determination by deliberate "workouts." Go out of your way at least once every day to demonstrate how you have forsworn tobacco. Carry matches and light cigarettes for your friends. If you are accustomed to riding in the smoking car, continue to do so, and look at all the people around you who are riding there by necessity and not choice, as you are doing. They can't give up smoking. You have!

If you thus deliberately try to make it tough, it will seem far less so, and you will much sooner get over the worst of it, which usually lasts about a week.

Baby yourself in everything else. Most of us are inclined to launch sudden, widely ambitious programs of self-improvement which defeat their own purpose. We try to do more than we can reasonably expect of ourselves. Don't increase the difficulties of stopping smoking by simultaneously adding others. On the contrary, indulge yourself. Eat what you want and enjoy it. Have an occasional cup of coffee or soft drink when you feel the desire to smoke. Make it a habit to carry mints, gum and salted nuts.

This is especially important. Don't worry about getting the gum or candy habit. As the desire to smoke dies, so will the desire for a substitute. But during the first few weeks keep such substitutes on hand—and pop one into your mouth whenever you feel the urge to smoke.

Let your sleep work for you. On the night of the first day that you give up smoking, go to bed as usual and think for a moment of how today you did not smoke. Think of the various times during the day when you were tempted to, yet did not give in. Then tell yourself, "Tomorrow I am not going to smoke." Repeat it as you get drowsy. This will be the last thing in your mind as you drop off to sleep.

When you wake in the morning, remind yourself that you are going to get through this day, too, without smoking. Don't clench your teeth or tense your muscles or make a big issue of it. Just—briefly—say: "This day I don't smoke." And see what happens. Even if you don't follow the other rules set down here, this exercise in "controlled sleep" could get you over the hump.

We have scarcely touched on one great help in giving up the smoking habit: the knowledge, which you will gain as you go along, that you *can* do it. Added to all the physical pleasures which nonsmoking brings is the sudden sense of freedom, and independence, and self-assurance that results from simply going a half day, and then a day, and then two days without tobacco. That is a sharp and continuing pleasure, and every minute you live with it helps to strengthen you against the next minute's temptation.

And above and beyond that pleasant, heartening knowledge is the awareness that you are doing something which you will be proud of— not to mention healthier and happier for—during the rest of your life. Six months or six years from now, when someone offers you a cigarette, you will refuse it, but not weakly or defensively. You will say, "Thanks—I used to smoke, but I gave it up." And you will be looked at with a glimpse of wistful envy, like a freshman looking at a senior who has been through the mill.

A FRIEND of Clara Barton, founder of the American Red Cross, once reminded her of an especially cruel thing that had been done to her years before. But Miss Barton seemed not to recall it.

"Don't you remember it?" her friend asked.

"No," came the reply. "I distinctly remember forgetting it."

—*Think*

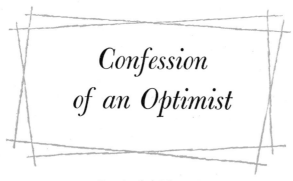

Confession
of an Optimist

By André Maurois

Y WIFE, my children, my friends tell me that I am an optimist. "Too much of an optimist" is what they say. "If you fell off a cliff," one of them told me, "you'd be thinking that the bottom was cushioned, and until you landed you'd be quite serene."

I am, I admit, an optimist; but I do not believe, like Voltaire's Pangloss, that all is for the best in this best of all possible worlds. I know the horrors and difficulties of life: I have had my share of them. But I refuse to regard humanity's condition as terrible. True, we are spinning on a lump of dirt in illimitable space, without being too sure why; true, we will surely die. To me this is a set of facts, a situation to be accepted courageously. The only problem is: What can we do, and what ought we to do, while we are here?

I am optimistic in the sense that I believe it is possible to better our own lives and, in a general way, humanity's life. I believe that tremendous progress has been made in this direction. Man has, to a large extent, overcome nature. His command of things is far greater than it used to be. The Pessimist replies: "Yes, but these marvelous inventions are used only for war, and humanity is on the road to self-destruction."

I do not believe that this is necessarily so. It depends upon ourselves, and my optimism is largely a product of my faith in human nature. I know that human nature also has its greatnesses.

My natural reaction to a circumstance is to seek what good there may be in it rather than what evil it may bring. For example, let us say that I am ill and condemned to a month in bed. The Pessimist would think: "What a disaster!" I am more likely to think: "What luck! Of course it's a nuisance, interfering with my work, and it may be painful; but 30 days of peace! At last I'm going to have time to think as much as I like."

That is the nature of my optimism. I believe that it has its origin in a happy childhood. I had the finest parents a boy could have; they always treated me with love and justice; and that gave me, in those first formative years, a robust confidence in human nature. School might have marred my innocent faith, because children are only too willing to give one another a foretaste of harshness. But it was there, in my philosophy class, that I had the good fortune of meeting Alain, the greatest of my teachers. He too was reproached by some, as I am, for his "blind confidence."

Alain and I after him pledged ourselves to be optimists because if one does not adopt invincible optimism as a standard, pessimism will be justified. For despair engenders misfortune and failure. If I believe that I am going to fall, I will· fall. If I believe that there is nothing I can do about my country's affairs, then there is nothing I can do. In the human tribe I make the fair weather and the tempest, primarily within myself. Pessimism is contagious. If I believe my neighbor to be dishonest and show my distrust, I make him distrustful and dishonest.

"Look here," says the Pessimist. "Do you really believe that this confidence in mankind, in life, is wisdom? Hasn't it brought you some frightful disappointments?" Yes, I confess that I have had some great disappointments. These past ten years—particularly with the horrors of Nazism, with exile, my family arrested, my home pillaged, with the dangerous defection of certain friends—have given me strong reason for doubting the perfection of this universe and the people in it.

But after all, I have always known that wicked people existed; I have always known that in times of disaster crowds can become stupid and bestial. My optimism consisted, and still consists, solely in this: We can have a certain influence upon events, and even if we must suffer misfortune we can overcome it by our manner of enduring it.

To love the fine people about me, to avoid the wicked, to rejoice in good, endure evil—and to remember to forget: this is my optimism. It has helped me to live.

Be an Intelligent Patient

By J. C. Furnas

Condensed from Your Life

IT TAKES two to get satisfactory results from modern medicine: a good doctor and an intelligent patient. Even the ablest medical man is badly handicapped unless the patient contributes his share toward solving the problem of healing.

The primary job of the patient is to find a good family doctor, then stick to him. Only by long acquaintance with your individual physical and mental personality can your doctor give maximum help. "Tramp patients" defraud themselves of efficient medical care.

You must be willing to "tell all" when you consult your doctor. And only by sharp self-observation can you give the necessary information —the exact location of your pain, its frequency and severity, what brings it on, what seems to relieve it. Have you been eating injudiciously? Tell the doctor. Tell him, too, about any medicine you may have taken —it may be disguising your true condition. For instance, accurate diagnosis of a gall-bladder condition is difficult if you fail to mention a recent dose of sedative which may mask the very pain the doctor is looking for.

Don't obscure your ailment with false shame. Tragic self-sabotage often results when patients conceal previous venereal infections, for example. Your doctor is not concerned with moral judgments; his sole interest is to cure you.

Skipping something crucial is especially risky when an operation is in prospect. Do you bruise easily? That indicates a blood condition essential for the surgeon to know about. Does morphine stimulate instead of quiet you? Do members of your family bleed excessively? Most of us veer from the norm in some way and it may escape even the most skillful examination.

Doctors prize the common-sense "early call." Waiting until 3 a.m., when you've had cramps since dinnertime, is unforgivable. It isn't a matter of saving the doctor's sleep. The delay can be fatal, especially when a stomach upset turns out to be a ruptured appendix. Streptococcus infections—of the throat, or even following a "mere scratch"—should also be caught early. A neglected hernia may have grave consequences. Postponing a checkup on breast lumps or abnormalities in the genital tract often prevents successful treatment of cancer.

Anything newly troublesome about your body demands attention. Bleeding from any cause. Shortness of breath. A mysterious rash, sores that won't heal, noticeable growths. Recurrent gastric upsets, diarrhea, or constipation. Sudden ups or downs in weight. Persistent headaches, colds, jumpiness, faintness. All these are premonitory symptoms of serious diseases. Do something about them.

But don't do it yourself. Remedies casually self-administered—a salve for the rash, a pill for the cold or headache—often amount to criminal negligence. When you take a cathartic for an abdominal pain, you risk peritonitis and death.

Sometimes the victim of a chronic ailment who follows the medical news in responsible periodicals can make fertile suggestions about his case. As any good physician admits, no one man can possibly keep up with all medical development. Recently I suggested to my doctor a new toxoid for chronic boils; it worked splendidly. I know a person who probably saved her sister from dying of pneumonia by showing the doctor a newspaper story on the first experimental successes of sulfapyridine.

But no patient is worse than the one who, hearing of diathermy or sulfanilamide, demands their use in and out of season; or who drags quack diets and cures into the doctor's office and gets annoyed when they are rejected.

If you suffer from a recurrent malady, you can sometimes help the doctor by keeping a copy of a prescription which hit your ailment right on the button. This as it stands, or with minor changes at his discretion, may be just what you need. But it is dangerous to get an old prescription refilled without consulting your doctor. Your condition may have changed; and the cumulative effect of some medicine is definitely injurious.

When you summon a physician be prepared for him. Have on hand hot-water bottle, ice bag, atomizer, enema outfit. Have the address and telephone number of the nearest all-night drugstore, in case you need an emergency prescription in the small hours.

Public schools ought to teach everyone how to report symptoms intelligently over the phone. The busy doctor appreciates crisp information about temperature, pulse, headache, nausea. This enables him to judge whether an ambulance is needed or merely good advice. Take a few moments to organize pertinent information before phoning your doctor.

Nothing exasperates a doctor more than to hear: "Come right away; I feel feverish." The urgency of your case will be better demonstrated if you can say: "I have a temperature of 102.8." Your physician will cheerfully show you how to use a thermometer.

Surprisingly enough, many patients fail even to execute accurately the doctor's orders in such simple matters as quantity and times of dosage. A little thought should make it plain that there is a reason for such orders and that they are important to the patient.

The good physician appreciates the patient who knows how to suggest the delicate matter of a "consultation." He may hesitate to mention consultation himself, for fear of alarming the patient or because of the extra expense. It is no reflection on his skill if you say: "Maybe I'm not getting on as well as you'd like, Doctor. Isn't there somebody you have confidence in, who could give us some help?" Honesty features the intelligent relationship of doctor and patient.

Suggesting consultation is one thing; running to specialists on your own is another. You have, let us say, a headache; you think it is due to sinus trouble. But to dash off to a nose-and-throat specialist before consulting your family doctor is to disregard the fact that headache may come from pituitary disturbance, high blood pressure or one of a score of other things. Let your general practitioner decide which specialist you should consult. In many cases he can save you money by handling the ailment ably himself.

The intelligent patient gets money matters clearly understood beforehand, particularly when surgery or special treatments are needed. Close relations between patient and family doctor help. He knows your financial postion, can talk it over with the surgeon behind your embarrassed back, may even arrange for installments. Or if Dr. Elder feels unable to operate for what you can pay, he may send you to Dr. Younger who, he knows, will do a good job for what you can afford.

Most of us know that periodic dental inspection is necessary, but we overlook the greater importance of a regular annual medical checkup — particularly as we approach the period of slackening vitality. The bill for examination of heart, lungs, nervous reactions — for blood tests, urinalyses and basal metabolisms — may look large. But it is cheap insurance against bills ten times larger. Heart disease, tuberculosis and diabetes are only a few of the grim ailments that may be checked or cured if discovered in time.

The doctor can't force you and no law requires you to be an intelligent patient. If you don't wan't to bother ... well, it's your own funeral.

My Father's Legacy

From an Elsa Maxwell CBS Broadcast

I HAD a wonderful father. I was his only child. In 1907 my father sent for me and said, "I'm going to die and I've nothing to leave you. You've got to go out into the world and make your own living. How are you going to do it? You're nothing much to look at, never will be. You have no name. You haven't any money. But I'm going to leave you a legacy. It's three simple rules.

"First, never be afraid of 'they.' People are more afraid of 'they' than anything else in the world. Strong generals with great armies will face courageously the most outrageous foes yet be terrified of what 'they' might say, 'they' might do, 'they' mightn't like.

"The second rule," he said, "is even more important. Never collect inanimate objects. You can't do it, for they collect you." So I thought the more you own the more you are possessed; therefore I own nothing but essentials. I'm free as air, and it's wonderful.

And the third one, which suited me rather well, he said was, "Always laugh at yourself first. Everybody has a ridiculous side and the whole world loves to laugh at somebody else. You laugh at yourself first, and the laughter of others falls off harmlessly as if you were in golden armor." I have always followed that, too.   —*Talks*

DON'T GROWL—KICK

By James H. Collins

Condensed from McClure's Magazine

A DOZEN passengers boarded a New York surface car, presenting transfers. "Not good on this side," the conductor declared to each one. "You'd ought-a got on over on the other crossing. Fare, please!"

Each passenger growled, and some of them tried to argue; but the conductor listened only in amusement. "It's a rule of the company" was his retort. In the end they all paid another fare, and as the conductor took the money, triumphantly, it was clear that this rule afforded him much diversion—he liked to watch its infallible workings.

One of those passengers wrote to the Public Service Commission the next day asking why a mere difference in sides of a street made transfers worthless at that crossing. The facts were set down without anger. A couple of weeks later the Commission wrote that the street-car company had modified its rule, making transfers good on both sides of that street.

Nobody knows how long people had been growling about that rule, yet doing nothing further. The Public Service Commission had never had a complaint before and the street-car company was probably astonished to learn that its rule, made originally for some sound traffic reason, was not giving the public pleasure.

Talk with anybody in the management of a business that serves the public, and you will find that the average American will growl, but seldom complains when something is wrong in his daily life. He will likely argue with a ticket-seller, or a meter-reader, or a city employe. They have no authority to set things right. But he will not go to the trouble of sending an orderly complaint to officials, with names, dates, facts. Least of all does he suspect that he owes a duty to the community in such matters.

An editor could not get to sleep in his New York apartment because some fellow across the area was busy hammering at a night job of home carpentry. In desperation he telephoned to the police with very little hope of relief. To his astonishment the police were interested, and thanked him. Within a few minutes a patrolman appeared and told the disturber he was violating a city ordinance, forbidding unnecessary noise after a certain hour at night.

It really pays to stop growling, and kick!

But before kicking, get all the facts. Just assume that you were going to be called into court, and have facts upon which you can testify. Then the next best step is—forget to grow angry. Most of the irritation over such happenings comes from your own assumption that it will not be much use to complain, that corporations are soulless and greedy, public officials indifferent, that nobody will do anything about it anyway.

Usually, this is a false assumption. Corporations really have souls, public officials actually try to serve, the system is much better than the average fellow knows, and somebody is probably waiting to attend him in this very matter.

When you are ready to write your letter, it is good policy, if nothing else, to be courteous—even a little smooth! Say that you believe the company is trying to give good service. Say you realize that there are many chances every day for details to go wrong in a big business, and that you believe they will be glad to hear of your experience, and have an opportunity to improve the service.

A letter like that will bring better results than a sarcastic one. So don't suffer silently. It pays to kick!

P<small>AIN</small> makes man think.
Thinking makes man wise.
Wisdom makes life endurable.
—From John Patrick's play, *The Teahouse of the August Moon* (Putnam)

Have you ever considered the danger
of having your prayers answered?

The Calculated Risks of Prayer

By Frank Halliday Ferris   Condensed from "Standing Up to Life"
Pastor Emeritus, Fairmount Presbyterian
Church, Cleveland Heights, Ohio

IN THIS tumultuous world, teachers of religion encourage people to seek comfort and assurance in prayer. They give practical suggestions about how to pray; point out the essential elements of thanksgiving, confession, petition. Yet there is one aspect about which they seldom speak: the serious risks to which prayer exposes us.

The first is the risk of *seeing ourselves as we are*. "Know thyself" was graven over the entrance of the temple of Delphi. But it is not easy to know ourselves, nor is it entirely pleasant. What we think of ourselves is often what we want to be, not what we are. The dodges of self-deception, the devices we use to escape admitting the truth about ourselves, are legion.

We tend to repress anything which conflicts with self-esteem. We give ourselves plausible excuses for doing what we have already done or made up our minds to do. We see virtues in ourselves which are not there. If anything strips us of our illusions, forcing us to face the truth about ourselves, it is likely to make us desperately unhappy.

That is why prayer is a healthful, if humbling, practice. In prayer we voluntarily face the truth about ourselves. The man who prays must ask himself: What are my motives, my dominant desires? What is my attitude toward others? What are my weaknesses? Am I trying to overcome them? Do I judge myself by the standard of those about me, or do I judge myself by an ideal standard?

In our dealings with God we have to come clean. All our subter-
fuges, the flimsy excuses we contrive to hide our inner poverty from
ourselves, must come down. We face the truth about ourselves when
we ask God to take us as we are and make us as we ought to be. This
is the prerequisite to moral progress—but it is hard on our pride.

The second risk of prayer is the danger of *becoming more like Christ*
in a world which worships the deity Success.

There is nothing reprehensible about success. The fact that a man is
successful doesn't prove him a rogue any more than the fact he is a
failure proves him a saint. The qualities that produce success are often
admirable ones. But there come times in the life of every man when
he has to choose between doing the advantageous thing or the right
thing and, if he chooses the right thing, taking the consequences.

Christ was faced by this choice at the outset of His career. The
tempter came to Him with three temptations which had this in common: all were temptations to use His unique personal power in such
a way as to win worldly success. We do not know how severe the
struggle was, for we have never been subjected to temptation on the
same scale. We do know that He saw it as a temptation, conquered
it, chose not to be smart but to be right. His integrity brought Him
not fame and fortune but loneliness and a felon's death.

He foresaw His impending fate, and He shrank from it as any normal, healthy man in his early 30's would. He prayed in agony to be
delivered from it; He had to screw His courage to the sticking place to
go through with it. But when it came to a choice between going back
on His ideals and winning what the world calls success, or being true
to His ideals and taking the consequence in ignominious failure, His
choice was made. The second risk of prayer, then, is the danger of
becoming more like Christ in a world which crucified Him.

A third risk is the danger of *having our prayers answered*. I believe
that God answers prayer; sometimes that belief comforts me and sometimes it frightens me. Beware, then, for what you pray; your prayer
may be answered.

We pray for the brotherhood of man, not insincerely. All of us have
an amiable wish that men would treat one another better. But suppose
God should answer that prayer? It would mean that I should have to
treat all men—including people whom I find it hard to like—not with

condescending politeness but as I treat my own brother whom I love and for whom I would do anything under heaven. Do I really want God to answer my prayer for the brotherhood of man?

We pray to God to make us honest. Most of us are honest up to a point. We pay our bills. We seldom tell a lie unnecessarily. Yet all of us who try to face the truth about ourselves are aware of how much insincerity and deceit there is in our natures. We say things we do not mean, express emotions we do not feel, praise when we secretly condemn, try to make people think we are other than we are.

"God, make me honest." But wait a minute—do I really want to give up my pet pretensions? Do I really want to do what an honest man must do, be what an honest man must be?

"Create in me a clean heart, O God." But think what it means giving up! Do I really want to get rid of the unclean images and imaginings with which I tease myself, the secret lusts I hanker for? Or am I like St. Augustine, who tells in his *Confessions* that he prayed, "God make me pure—but not yet"?

"Calculated risk," an expression we learned during war, is an element in effective living. Anyone who has ever become sufficiently dissatisfied with his moral status to want to do something about it, anyone who has seriously tried to improve his character, change his habit pattern, knows that it is not kid-glove undertaking. One has to take hold of it with the rough hand of a man who is in earnest, who is undeterred by the prospect of blood, sweat and tears.

God give us courage to run the calculated risks of prayer: of seeing ourselves as we are, of having to become more like Christ, of having our prayers answered.

FINDING Phillips Brooks, the noted New England divine, irritably pacing his study, a friend asked, "What is the trouble?"

"The trouble is," answered Dr. Brooks, "that I'm in a hurry—but God isn't."   —*Ladies' Home Journal*

HOW TO RELAX

By Joseph A. Kennedy

Condensed from "Relax and Live"

Most of us, in practically all our everyday activities, are driving with the brake on. That brake is unconscious tension. We have worked and played in a tense condition for so long that we regard it as more or less normal. We do not notice the clenched jaw, the tight abdomen, the constricted muscles. Yet the resulting fatigue burns up our energy, impairs our skills and even dulls our appreciation of the world about us.

Tension is excess effort: trying too hard to do things that should be done automatically. It causes muscles to jam and contract. Make a conscious effort to speak correctly and you stutter or become tongue-tied. Let the accomplished pianist think about his fingers and he is likely to make a mistake.

Most of us put forth too much effort for the task at hand. Our muscles work better when we speak our orders quietly than when we shout them. In order to see perfectly, for example, the eyes must make numerous minute movements, scanning the object under observation. This scanning is an automatic reflex; it is no more subject to your will than is your heartbeat. But when you stare—make a conscious effort to see—the eyes become tense. They do not scan as they should and sight suffers.

Nor is the damage done by tension limited to the body. When muscles are tense, contracting without purpose, a feeling of confusion is relayed back to the brain. Why is it that a poised man whose ideas reel out effortlessly when he is in his own study suddenly finds his mind a blank when he is attending an important board meeting? Because tenseness, resulting from making too much effort, has jammed his psychomotor mechanisms.

Tension tends to become an unconscious habit; muscles tend to stay constricted. How, then, can you become conscious of unconscious tension? How can you relax?

First, by locating the tension in your muscles. For example, you are probably unaware of any tension in your forehead at this moment, but there is a good chance that some is there. In order to recognize it, consciously produce more tension: wrinkle your forehead into a frown and notice the feeling in the muscles. Practice sensing the tension that you thus consciously produce. Then, tomorrow, stop working for a moment and ask yourself, "Am I aware of any tension in my forehead?" You can probably detect the faint sensation already there. One student told me, "When I started to relax, I discovered layer after layer of tension of which I had been totally unaware."

Once you learn to recognize tension, you can learn to relax. The way to do this is first to produce *more* tension in your muscles. Don't *try* to relax! A muscle tends to relax itself. Consciously tense a particular muscle; then stop. The muscle relaxes and will continue to relax automatically if it is not interfered with.

The muscles of the brow and forehead need special attention, for they are closely associated with anxiety and confusion. With the brow relaxed it is practically impossible to feel worried. The next time you have a problem to solve, make it a point to keep your brow relaxed and see if the problem does not seem less difficult.

The jaw is one of the most expressive parts of the human body. We grit our teeth in rage, clench our jaws in determination. When your jaw is tensed, your brain, which is constantly receiving nerve messages from your muscles, reasons something like this: "We must be in difficulty, we must have a terrible job to do." You then become conscious of a feeling of pressure.

As soon as you relax your jaw muscles, however, your brain says, "Ah, we are out of difficulty now," and you get a feeling of confidence. So, every time you feel anxious or experience self-doubt, notice that you are contracting your jaws. Then stop.

The hands are the main executive instrument of the body. They are involved in almost everything we do or feel. We throw up our hands in hopelessness, shake our fist when we are angry. When hands are kept tense, the whole body is geared for action. Learn to relax your hands when you find yourself in a tight spot or when something irritates you. It will take the pressure off and give you a feeling that you are master of the situation.

If you were expecting a blow in the pit of the stomach, you would instinctively tense the abdominal muscles for defense. And if you habitually live on the defensive, your subconscious keeps your stomach muscles continually tensed. Thus, another vicious circle is set up. The brain receives defensive messages from the abdominal muscles and this keeps you feeling insecure. Learn to break the circle. When you feel anxious or worried, stop and relax your abdomen.

If you try to control your anxieties mentally, you will probably only make yourself more nervous. But you *can* control your key muscles.

Learn to relax your muscles quickly at midmorning, just before lunch and in midafternoon. Sit down and "jelly" yourself into the most comfortable position. Or lie on your back on a bed with your arms at your sides. Then check your key points for tension: brow, abdomen, jaw, hands, and so on. Tighten each, and then let go, allowing the muscle to relax by itself.

Breathing furnishes a valuable control for toning down the degree of excitement throughout the entire body. When we are emotionally tense, we say we have something on our chest. When a crisis is past, we say that we can breathe easier. But it works both ways. If we can learn to breathe easier in the first place, we won't get so tense.

It will help you to learn to breathe correctly if you recognize that the body has two separate breathing patterns. Nervous breathers breathe high in the chest by expanding and contracting the rib box. They also breathe too fast and too deeply. This particular breathing pattern was engineered for emergencies. It is the way you breathe when you are out of breath from running a race. Your chest heaves as you take in great gulps of air. Your muscles need oxygen fast, and this is the way to get it. Nervous people are so used to reacting with emergency behavior to simple, ordinary tasks that they use this emergency-breathing mechanism all the time.

Non-emergency breathing is belly breathing. It is done more from the diaphragm; most of the movement is in the lower chest wall and the upper abdomen. As the diaphragm smoothly contracts and lets go, a gentle massage is applied to the whole abdominal area. The abdominal muscles relax. It is virtually impossible to feel tense when you breathe habitually from your belly.

If you find yourself breathing nervously and fast, keep right on—but breathe that way because you *want* to. Take as many as 50 to 100 of these deliberate nervous breaths, thus bringing your breathing under the control of your will. This conscious control will in itself cause the feeling of nervousness to diminish. After a time you will find that it is an effort to keep breathing fast, and a relief to let yourself breathe more slowly.

One of the most malicious causes of tension is hurry. You can hurry while sitting down, apparently doing nothing, or while waiting for a bus. Many people feel hurried because they think there just isn't enough time. They would do well to heed Sir William Osler's advice to his students when he told them to think of how much time there is to use, rather than of how little.

Whenever you feel a sense of hurry, deliberately slow down. Everyone has his own best pace or tempo for doing things, and when we give in to hurry we allow external things and situations to set our pace for us. The great Finnish runner, Paavo Nurmi, always carried a watch with him in his races. He referred to it, not to the other runners. He never hurried but insisted on running his own race, keeping his own tempo, regardless of competition.

A basic cause of tension is putting too much emphasis on the ultimate goal, trying too hard to win. It is good to have a clear mental picture of your objective; but your attention should be concentrated on the specific job at hand.

And when that job is done, remember there will be something else to do tomorrow. So relax! Life is not a 100-yard dash, but more in the nature of a cross-country run. If we sprint all the time, we not only fail to win the race but we may not last long enough to reach the goal.

Three Steps to Personal Peace

By *Norman Vincent Peale, D. D.*

Pastor of Marble Collegiate Church, New York City

Condensed from "The Power of Positive Thinking"

MERICANS are so keyed up nowadays that I, a minister, must report that it is almost impossible to put them to sleep with a sermon. It has been years since I have seen anyone asleep in church. And that is a sad situation.

Most of us don't realize how accelerated the rate of our lives has become, or the speed at which we are driving ourselves. Men and women are destroying their bodies by this pace—and, what is even more tragic, their minds and souls as well. For constant overstimulation produces poisons in the body and creates fatigue and emotional illness.

There are times when the only way to check this headlong pace is to stop—abruptly. I went to a certain city on a lecture date and was met at the train by a committee. I was rushed to a bookstore for one autographing party and then on to another. After that I rushed to a luncheon, rushed through it, and on to a meeting. After the meeting I rushed back to the hotel, where I was told I had 20 minutes to dress for dinner. While I was dressing, the telephone rang. "Hurry," the voice said, "we must get down to dinner."

"I'll be right down," I said.

I was about to rush from the room when suddenly I stopped. "What is this all about?" I asked myself.

I telephoned downstairs and said, "If you want to eat, go ahead. I'll be down after a while."

I took off my shoes, put my feet up on the table and just sat. Then I opened the Bible to the 121st Psalm: "I will lift up mine eyes unto the hills, from whence cometh my help." I read it very slowly, aloud. Then I had a little talk with myself: "Come on now, slow down. God is here and His peace is touching you."

I shall never forget the sense of peace and personal mastery I had when I walked out of that room 15 minutes later. I had the glorious feeling of having overcome something, of having taken control of myself emotionally. And all I had missed was the soup.

Everyone should insist upon not less than a quarter of an hour of absolute quiet every 24 hours. As Thomas Carlyle said: "Silence is the element in which great things fashion themselves." Go alone into the quietest place available and sit or lie down for 15 minutes. Do not talk to anyone. Do not read. Think as little as possible. This may be difficult at first because thoughts are stirring up your mind, but practice will make it easier. Conceive of your mind as the surface of a body of water and see how nearly unruffled you can make it. Then try to listen for the deeper sounds of harmony and beauty and of God that are to be found in the essence of silence.

Go out some warm day and lie down on the earth. You will hear all manner of sounds, the wind in the trees and the murmur of insects; presently you will discover a well-regulated tempo. You can find it in church, and you can also find it in a factory. An industrialist in a large plant in Ohio told me that his best workmen are those who get into harmony with the rhythm of the machine on which they are working; they are less tired at the end of the day. To avoid tiredness and to have energy, feel your way into the essential rhythm that is in all things.

By the very words we use and the tone in which we use them we can talk ourselves into being nervous, high-strung, upset. Other words produce a tranquil state. The words of the Bible have a particularly therapeutic value. Drop them into your mind and allow them to "dissolve"; they will spread a healing balm over your spirit.

A salesman told me that on a business trip he had gone to his hotel room, terribly nervous. "I tried to write some letters, but couldn't get my mind on them," he said. "I paced the room, tried to read the paper —anything to get away from myself.

"Then I noticed the Bible on the dresser. I hadn't read one in years, but something impelled me—I opened the book to a Psalm. I remember I read that one standing up, then sat down and read another.

"Soon I came to the 23rd Psalm. I had learned it as a boy in Sunday school and was surprised that I still knew most of it by heart. I tried saying it over: 'He leadeth me beside the still waters. He restoreth my soul. . . .' I sat there repeating the words—and the next thing I knew I woke up.

"Apparently I had dropped off to sleep. Only about 15 minutes had passed, but I was as refreshed as if I'd had a good night's sleep. Then I realized that for the first time in a long while I felt at peace."

Emotional control cannot, however, be developed by merely reading a book, although that is often helpful. The only sure method is by working at it regularly and persistently. The secret is to keep the mind quiet, avoid all hasty reactions, keep the tempo down.

Capt. Eddie Rickenbacker is a very busy man, but he manages to handle his responsibilities in a manner indicating reserves of power. I found one element of his secret quite by accident.

I was filming a program for television with him. We had been assured that the work could be done quickly, but the filming was delayed long beyond the time anticipated. The Captain showed no signs of agitation. He did not pace up and down or put in frantic calls to his office. He sat down in an old rocking chair, completely calm.

"I know how busy you are," I said. "How can you be so relaxed?"

"Oh, I just practice what *you* preach," he replied. "Come, sit down beside me." I pulled up another rocking chair and did a little relaxing on my own. Then Eddie gave me his formula to attain serenity. I now use it myself several times a day and find it effective.

First, collapse physically. Let go every muscle in the body. Form a mental picture of a huge burlap bag of potatoes. Then mentally cut the bag, allowing the potatoes to roll out. Think of yourself as the bag. What is more relaxed than an empty burlap bag?

The second element in the formula is to drain the mind of all irritation, resentment, disappointment, frustration, annoyance. To do this, think of the most beautiful and peaceful scenes you know—a mountain at sunset, a valley filled with the hush of early morning, a forest at noonday, a lake by moonlight.

Third, turn the mind to God. At least three times a day "lift up your eyes unto the hills." This keeps you in tune with God's harmony. It refills you with peace.

Don't put it off too long!

"Charlie Would Have Loved This"

By J. P. McEvoy

S HE was sitting beside me on the beach at Waikiki. Sounds romantic, doesn't it? But it wasn't really. There were many ladies just like her—tourists from everywhere—white-haired, restless, lonely. On a small stage, flaming with tropical flowers, a colorful group of Hawaiian singers and dancers were broadcasting their weekly sun-kissed program of synthetic romance to the frostbitten unfortunates on the Mainland.

"This is your Isle of Golden Dreams, calling to you from across the sea," crooned the announcer. His assistant ran a few yards down to the lapping waves with a microphone.

"Listen, folks! The waves of Waikiki. Can't you see the surfboard riders? Can't you just picture those hula girls swaying under the palms?"

The white-haired lady beside me said, "Charlie would have loved this. It's just like we used to hear it on the radio back in Illinois. Saturday nights when Charlie came in from the fields, he'd turn on this program 'Hawaii Calls' and we'd listen, and Charlie would say, 'Mary, we're going there someday,' and I'd say, 'When?' and he'd say, 'Soon as we've saved up some money and get some time,' and I'd say, 'You've been saying that for years, Charlie, but every time we get a little money ahead you buy another 40 acres. Are you trying to buy up the whole state of Illinois?' That was a joke we had, and Charlie would laugh and say, 'No, I just want the piece next to me.' So Charlie never did get out here."

"You are listening to the Singing Surfriders," purred the announcer, "but unfortunately you cannot see the lovely Lani dancing her famous hula under the palms. She is wearing a green ti-leaf skirt and a red hibiscus in her long black hair."

The little white-haired lady said, "We had such good times together. If only Charlie was here with me now."

Every Sunday night, in the High Talking Chief's Long House on Waikiki Beach, Don the Beachcomber puts on a luau for the tourists. This is a Polynesian-type clambake where only the barbecued pig comes fully dressed, while the guests sit on the floor, kick off their shoes, drape leis of white gardenias or pink carnations around their necks, and the ladies stick a red hibiscus over their ear—the right ear if they have a man, the left if they want one.

Tourists milled around the bar, carrying bamboo tubes filled with rum concoctions playfully labeled Missionary's Downfall, Cobra's Fang and the Vicious Virgin. I spotted my white-haired friend, timid and alone, but bravely sporting a man's aloha shirt that looked like an explosion in a paint factory. But the conventional black skirt and high-heeled shoes were definitely out of place in this technicolor jungle of muumuus, holokuus, sarongs, bare torsos and coconut hats.

I walked over and said, "Are you with anyone?"

"No," she said. "Is it all right to come alone?"

"You're not alone," I told her and hung a flower lei around her neck and kissed her cheek. "Let's go sit down. They're bringing in the barbecued pig."

I introduced her to my party and they moved over to make room for her as she looked around a bit helplessly. "But everybody's sitting on the floor."

"That's right," I said. "Those creaking noises you hear are just old Mainland joints like yours and mine." She sat down on the floor beside me. "Now kick off your shoes and dive in," I told her.

Wooden platters were set before each guest but no knives or forks. My friend watched as we old-timers dug in with bare hands and licked our fingers. Then she followed suit, embarrassed at first, but quickly getting into the spirit of the occasion.

"What are we eating?" she asked. "Not that I care," she added quickly.

"This is pig baked underground with heated rocks. And this is lau-lau—butterfish wrapped in ti leaf. And this," I said, dipping it up with my fingers, "is the poi they sing about. It looks and tastes like paper hanger's paste. If you can scoop it up with one finger, it's one-finger poi. If you need two fingers, it's two-finger poi."

Don came over and tucked a red hibiscus into my friend's white hair over her right ear. I explained the difference and she moved it to her left ear.

"Charlie would have loved this," she said.

And then the jungle drums started and a beautiful young Poly-nesian typhoon, wearing a crown of plumeria blossoms and a grass skirt, exploded into a dance.

"Wouldn't it be wonderful if people could live like this all the time," she said. "Kick off your shoes and sit on the floor and eat with your fingers and wear flowers in your hair and listen to music like that and watch dancers like what's-her-name there."

"Johnny," I said. "She comes from Pukapuka in the South Seas."

"Charlie always wanted to go there," she said. "There was a book, *White Shadows in the South Seas*. He used to read it aloud to me and once we saw a movie by the same name and he said, 'Someday I'll take you there.' But he kept putting it off. And when he died I wouldn't have been able to make this trip if it hadn't been for the insurance money he left."

A troupe from Samoa took the floor and did a dazzling fire dance. My friend sighed.

"I guess we waited too long." She shook her head a little, be-wildered. "There's something wrong somewhere. What's the use of working yourself to death if you don't live to enjoy it?"

"Maybe we don't have to," I said. "When we want homes we don't wait until we're too old to get them. We borrow the money and live in the houses while we pay it off. Lots of us do the same about cars. We don't walk our legs off until we need wheel chairs. We get the cars and manage somehow to pay for them. Suppose Charlie had added a few hundred more to the mortgage and brought you out here while you both could enjoy it. Wouldn't that have made a lot more sense than buying another 40 acres? Practical people would be a lot more practical if they were just a little more dreamy. Then they wouldn't put off living until they were dead. Someday we may even be practical enough to invest in our dreams first."

"Aloha!" cried Don the Beachcomber. "Let's sing the song we all know—

> *"One fond embrace*
> *Before we now depart,*
> *Until we meet again. . . ."*

There's no sweeter, sadder song. Even in broad daylight you feel like crying like a baby when perfect strangers sing "Aloha" and wave farewell to you from Honolulu piers and airports. As the party ended we started out into the street in our bare feet.

The little white-haired lady from Illinois had forgotten her shoes under the table, but her red hibiscus dangled jauntily over her left ear, and there was a brave swing to the flower lei around her neck.

"You know what?" she said.

"Yes," I said. "Charlie would have loved this."

"That's for sure," she said, and she walked across the street to her lonely hotel room.

Children—Seen and Heard

AN EIGHT-YEAR-OLD taken to the hospital to see a new baby was asked what she thought of him. Disappointed but polite, she stammered, "He's—he's—just my favorite shade of red!"

—Contributed by Laura Rountree

THE COCKTAIL PARTY was in full swing, when the host's small daughter pulled at her father's sleeve. "Daddy," asked the puzzled youngster, "haven't we had this party before?"

—Bob Considine, King Features

A man may be reasonably happy and successful
in a job for which he has small aptitude but not
in one for which he is not suited in temperament

HOW TO BE AN EMPLOYE

By Peter F. Drucker
Noted economist; author of "The Future of Industrial
Man," "The New Society," etc.

Condensed from Fortune

MOST OF US are employes. Yet you will find little if anything written on how to be a good employe.

You can find a great deal of very dubious advice on how to get a job or a promotion. You can also find a good deal on work in a chosen field: metallurgy, salesmanship, bookkeeping. Each trade requires different skills, sets different standards. Yet all have employeship in common. And certainly more people fail because they do not know the requirements of being an employe than because they do not adequately possess the skills of their trade.

What kind of employe should you be? This involves four choices you alone can make, and cannot easily duck.

The first question: Is "security" for you? Do you belong in a job calling primarily for faithfulness in performance of routine and promising security? Or do you belong in a job that offers a challenge to imagination and ingenuity—with the attendant penalty for failure? This decision is the one most people find easiest to make.

The difference is one of basic personality. In practically everybody I have ever met there is a leaning one way or the other. And the choice is important. A man might be happy and quite successful in work for which he has little aptitude. But he can be neither happy nor successful in work for which he is temperamentally unfitted.

Inside jobs in banking or insurance normally offer great job security but not rapid promotion or large pay. The same is true of most government work, and of most clerical, bookkeeping and accounting positions.

At the other extreme are such areas as buying, selling and advertising, in which the emphasis is on adaptability, imagination and a desire to do new and different things. In these, by and large, there is little security. The rewards, however, are high and come more rapidly. Major premium on imagination—though coupled with dogged persistence on details—prevails in most research and engineering work. Jobs in production, as supervisor or executive, also demand much adaptability and imagination.

Second question: Do you belong in a large or in a small organization? In a small enterprise you operate primarily through personal contacts. In the large enterprise you have established "channels" of organization and fairly rigid procedures. In a small enterprise you can see the effect of your work and decisions right away, once you are a bit above the ground floor. In a large company even the man at the top is only a cog in a big machine. In a small or middle-sized business you are exposed to all kinds of experiences, and expected to do many things without much help or guidance. In a large organization you are normally taught one thing thoroughly. In the small one the danger is of becoming a jack-of-all-trades and master of none; in the large one it is of becoming the man who knows more and more about less and less.

Third: Should you start on the lowest rung of the promotional ladder, with its safe footing but also with a long climb ahead, or should you try to start near the top?

I do not mean that you have any choice between a beginner's job and a vice-presidency at General Electric. But in every organization there are "management trainees" or positions that, while subordinate, modestly paid and usually filled with beginners, nonetheless are in view of the top. There are positions as assistant to one of the bosses, as private secretary or as liaison for various departments. Each of these gives a view of the whole rather than of only one small area. Each brings the holder into the deliberations and discussions of people at the top.

In such a job you may have real power and influence. But for that reason everybody has his eye on you. You are a youngster who has been admitted to the company of his betters and is therefore expected to show unusual ability. Good performance is often the key to rapid advancement. To fall down may mean the end of all hopes of getting anywhere within the organization.

On the other hand the great majority of beginners' jobs are at the bottom, where you begin in a department or in a line of work in the lowest-paid and simplest function, and where you are expected to work your way up as you acquire more skill and more judgment. Here there are few opportunities for making serious mistakes. One has to fall down in a rather spectacular fashion for it to be noticed by anyone but one's immediate superior.

Fourth: Are you going to be more effective and happy as a specialist or as a "generalist"?

There are many careers in which the emphasis is on specialization—engineering, accounting, production, statistical work, teaching. But there is an increasing demand, particularly in administrative positions, for people who are able to take in a large area at a glance, who are capable of seeing the forest rather than the trees.

The specialist understands one field; his concern is with technique, tools, media. The generalist deals with people; his concern is with leadership, planning, direction-giving and coördination. It is your job to find out into which of those two job categories you fit, and to plan your career accordingly.

Your first job may turn out to be the right job for you—but, if so, this is pure accident. Certainly you should not change jobs constantly or people will become suspicious—rightly—of your ability to hold any job. At the same time you must not look upon the first job as the final job; it is primarily a training job, an opportunity to analyze your fitness for being an employe.

There is much to be said for being fired from the first job! It is the least painful way to learn how to take a setback. And whom the Lord loveth He teacheth early how to take a setback.

Nobody has ever lived, I dare say, who has not gone through a period when everything seemed to have collapsed and when years of life and work seemed to have gone up in smoke. No one can be spared this experience, but one can be prepared for it. The man who has been through early setbacks has learned that the world does not come to an end because he has lost his job.

Obviously you cannot contrive to get yourself fired. But you can quit. And it is perhaps even more important to have quit once than to have been fired once. The man who walks out acquires an inner independence that he will never lose.

One should quit when self-analysis shows that the job is the wrong job, in the light of any of the decisions I have outlined. One should also quit if the job does not offer the training one needs. The beginner not only has a right to expect training from his first few years in a job: more, he has an obligation to get as much training as possible. But he should remember that promotion is not the essence of a job.

There is no surer way to kill a job and one's usefulness than to consider it as but one rung in the promotional ladder rather than as a job in itself that deserves serious effort.

The schools teach a great many things of value to the future accountant, the future doctor or the future electrician. Do they also teach anything of value to the future employe? The answer is yes. They teach the one thing that it is perhaps most valuable for the future employe to know: the ability to organize and express ideas in writing and in speaking. Yet few students bother to learn this basic skill.

As an employe you work with and through other people. This means that your success will depend on your ability to communicate with people and to present your thoughts and ideas to them. The letter, the report or memorandum, the ten-minute spoken "presentation" are basic tools of the employe. And the further away your job is from manual labor or the larger the organization for which you work, the more important it will be that you know how to convey your thoughts in writing or speaking.

Therefore, the most useful vocational courses in the typical college curriculum are the writing of poetry and the writing of short stories. These courses force one to organize thought. They demand of one that he give meaning to every word. They train the ear for language, its meaning, precision—and pitfalls.

The typical employer does not understand this yet, and may look with suspicion on a young graduate who has majored in short-story writing. But the same employer will complain that young men out of college do not know how to write a simple report.

To be an employe it is not enough that the job be right and that you be right for the job. It is also necessary that you have a meaningful life outside the job, a genuine interest in which you can use your capabilities and impose your own standards of performance. This can be a permanent source of self-respect and standing in the community outside and beyond your job; an area in which you will find recognition and acceptance.

This is heretical philosophy these days in many companies which believe that the best employe is the man who lives and sleeps job and company. But our large companies are beginning to understand that the man who will make the greatest contribution to his company is the mature person—and you cannot have maturity if you have no life or interest outside the job.

Being an employe means working with people. Intelligence, in the last analysis, is therefore not the most important quality. What is decisive is character and integrity. If you work on your own, intelligence and ability may be sufficient. If you work with people, you are going to fail unless you also have integrity.

The one quality demanded of you will not be skill, knowledge or talent, but character.

Recipes for Refreshment

» Dr. Lillian Gilbreth, professor of management at Purdue University, studied women in the rest room of a dress factory. Some of them were limp with fatigue; some bright-eyed and wide awake. Yet all the women had been working the same number of hours. Dr. Gilbreth found that most of the wide-awake ones had plans for the evening—a party or a date—and were anticipating a good time. The tired ones were those who had nothing to look forward to.

—Amy Selwyn in *Coronet*

» Human beings find less rest in idleness than in a change of occupation. If you scoff at the idea, just try it. Instead of collapsing in an easy chair, try tackling your hobby. Or write that neglected letter, or help Johnny to build that radio receiving set. Activity—especially creative activity—is far better recreation than loafing.

—Gardner Hunting in *Weekly Unity*

Why Do We Get So Tired?

By Albert Q. Maisel   Condensed from Today's Health

D o YOU seem to tire too easily? Do you often feel all in for no clear reason? Do you sometimes wake up more tired than when you went to bed?

If you are wearily nodding "Yes" to these questions, you are far from alone. Most of us, at times, feel the same sort of puzzling fatigue.

What causes that tired feeling? Most experts agree that fatigue is a protective reaction against stress, a warning that strains upon our bodies, our minds or our emotions are approaching a dangerous level.

Nature uses the same red lights whether our weariness is caused by physical exertion, mental work or emotional frustration. Brain-fag, for example, may bring on the physical reactions—sweating, heart palpitations, shortness of breath—that come with hard labor. Emotional frustration frequently masquerades as fatigue. Mental performance falls off sharply as physical exhaustion sets in.

How does hard work make us tired? It was long widely believed that our muscles threw off some sort of "tiredness toxin." Then scientists began studying the body's fuel supply. They found surprisingly small reserves of oxygen and blood sugar. As these become depleted, muscles starve and stall, the way an auto engine falters when you cut down its air supply or dilute its gas.

At rest, we require barely a cupful of oxygen a minute. But as soon as we do any work, oxygen consumption skyrockets. It may mount as high as six and a half *gallons* a minute. Yet our lungs can step up the supply of new oxygen to barely one gallon a minute. We must "borrow" the rest of the oxygen we burn from the reserves stored in our red blood corpuscles. This totals only four to five gallons.

Our oxygen reserve enables us to spend our energies at an enormous rate—for a short time. When we run to catch a train or play a fast game of tennis, we may drain off nearly one third of this reserve. However, try as we may, it is almost impossible to drive ourselves to the point of utter exhaustion. All sorts of lifesaving discomforts force us to slow down. Muscles ache. We get a "stitch" around our heart. Lungs beg painfully for a chance to catch up with their work.

In moderate physical work, supply and demand of oxygen are more nearly in balance. But here another limiting factor comes into play. Our reserves of energy-giving blood sugar are small. Ordinary walking doubles the rate at which we burn up blood sugar. Heavy labor uses it up five to 15 times as fast.

Brain and nerves are particularly sensitive to lack of sugar and oxygen. Long before our blood is deeply drained of its reserves, they protect us by slowing down and cutting off the nerve impulses that spark muscle movements. Tiredness—the "normal" tiredness of physical exertion—sets in to keep us from destroying ourselves.

Why does mental work make us physically tired? The brain comprises only two percent of the body's weight. But even though it performs no mechanical work, it requires 14 percent of the total blood flow and consumes 23 percent of our entire oxygen intake. Its sugar consumption is also large.

We don't know exactly why the brain needs so much fuel. We do know that it converts the chemical energy of oxygen and sugar into electrical brain waves and nerve impulses. Having no oxygen or sugar reserves of its own, it must get a constant supply from the circulating blood. Cut that supply for a few minutes and the brain goes into coma. In barely eight minutes irreversible damage occurs and the brain cells die.

Since life and death hang so delicately in the balance, the brain must protect itself against even a slight decrease in oxygen or sugar. It flashes on the red lights of physical fatigue to slow down our other organs so that fuel can be shunted toward the endangered brain. Thus brain-fag and the physical feeling of tiredness go together.

How do emotions affect fatigue? Primitive man often had to mobilize all his strength to fight or flee from his enemies. His adrenal glands provided a device to tap energy reserves. Emotions like rage or fear sent a charge of adrenalin coursing through his blood to deepen his breathing and make his heart beat more rapidly. Blood was shunted toward the heart, the muscles and the brain, bringing them extra oxygen. Sugar was freed from the reserve in his liver. After the struggle was over and the adrenalin stopped flowing, he felt all in.

You and I have inherited this vital protective mechanism. It helps us to survive sharp, short-term crises. But unlike primitive man, we often face situations that cannot be solved by energetic action. We may dislike our work, but we fear the economic penalty of quitting. We may be constantly irritated by a nagging spouse or a noisy neighbor, but few of us express our anger physically. As long as conflicting emotions oppose each other, our energy-mobilizing machinery is jammed and we may suffer chronic fatigue.

Is chronic tiredness often a sign of physical disease? When we're sick, the fatigue mechanism discourages unnecessary exertion and channels all our energies into fighting the disease. Thus tiredness is a common symptom of most illnesses.

When persistent tiredness is the *only* obvious symptom, however, physicians have a hard time deciding whether they're dealing with a subtle physical disease or a neurotic, emotional tiredness. Recent research warns against too readily branding persistent tiredness as just a neurotic symptom. Without a thorough medical checkup, a serious physical cause may be overlooked.

Can frequent snacks ward off fatigue? Yes. At Yale, Physiology Professors Howard W. Haggard and Leon A. Greenberg studied workers who ate three meals a day. Their blood sugar and muscular efficiency rose to a peak one hour after each meal, then fell off rapidly. But when the workers switched to four and five smaller meals a day, both blood sugar and muscular efficiency stayed at a higher, more constant level. Fatigue was greatly reduced.

Can dieting cause persistent tiredness? Yes. Few people who diet are content to burn off fat slowly. Many eliminate all sugar, slash other carbohydrates and cut down to a mere 800 or 1000 calories a day instead of the normal 2400 to 3000. As a result, physical effort becomes intensely fatiguing and mental work suffers. The only way to avoid this is to plan a slower reducing regimen with the aid of a physician.

Can tiredness be caused by lack of exercise? Since we become tired after strenuous work or play, we blame exertion for our fatigue. But recent research indicates that our susceptibility to fatigue may often trace back to a lack of consistent exercise.

At Harvard, Professor Ross McFarland put athletes and sedentary students through identical exercises, then compared their pulse rates. The hearts of the athletes pumped more blood in fewer beats. In another Harvard study, Professor D. B. Dill found that people who exercised regularly required less oxygen to perform the same amount of work. Consistent exercise increased both the capacity and the efficiency of their lungs.

Other research has shown that sudden vigorous exercise taken by previously sedentary individuals may destroy from 12 to 30 percent of their red blood cells. This sharply lowers the ability of the blood to transport oxygen to the muscles and brain. That's why the man who sits at a desk all week may find himself peaked for days after a week-end of strenuous tennis or lawn-mowing.

Why do we sometimes wake up tired? During sleep our energy-spending organs slow down much more than the processes that create energy reserves. Normally, in seven or eight hours, these reserves become replenished and we wake refreshed.

Let your blankets slip off in a cold room, however, and the body's work in fighting the cold will slow down the energy-restoring process. In a too-hot bedroom, lungs and heart have to work harder than usual to dissipate body heat.

Where deep-seated emotional conflicts are bringing on fatigue, sleep often fails to provide relief. The frustrations that haunted us at bedtime may remain quite as frustrating when morning rolls around.

Does coffee really prevent fatigue? Caffeine does stimulate the brain and facilitate muscle contraction. Coffee, tea or cola drinks can help us push exertion somewhat further before tiredness makes itself felt. But this is postponing fatigue rather than preventing it. When we finally *feel* our tiredness, we then need more rest to restore our more deeply drained reserves.

Are pep pills effective? Many people take amphetamine or closely related drugs to fight off fatigue. Even more than caffeine, they stimulate the brain and thus postpone the feeling of tiredness. But their undesirable effects are greater. They can be habit-forming. They depress the appetite. An overdose can bring on dizziness, headaches, insomnia, even death. Useful in the hands of a skilled physician, *they should never be taken except on a doctor's prescription.*

Does drinking relieve tiredness? Alcohol is a depressant rather than a stimulant. In small quantities it relieves tension and can temporarily suppress the feeling of fatigue.

Heavy drinkers, however, become more than normally susceptible to fatigue. Getting much of their calorie supply from alcohol, they lack other nutrients. Their blood sugar is usually low, their vitamin-starved nerves and muscles ache, their mood is depressed. They're half-tired before they exert themselves and fully fatigued when others are just getting into their stride.

Can smoking give you a lift? The nicotine in tobacco smoke increases the pulse rate and steps up blood flow. This may at first increase the brain's blood supply, bring it more blood sugar and thus relieve fatigue. But smoke also contains carbon monoxide which excludes oxygen from the red blood cells. The chain smoker who inhales soon accumulates enough carbon monoxide to counterbalance the lift he gets from nicotine.

Drugs, pick-me-ups and other devices that postpone fatigue may be useful, but only if used wisely, to get us through a short-term emergency. They can never replace rest and sleep, nature's method of curing fatigue.

Energy Unlimited

"You HAVE more energy than anyone I know," Edna Ferber once said to Eleanor Roosevelt.

"It isn't that I have so much energy," replied Mrs. Roosevelt, "it's just that I have never wasted any of it on indecision or regret."

—Leonard Lyons

The Faith of
Chaplain Kapaun

By
First Lt. Ray M. (Mike) Dowe, Jr.

As told to Harold H. Martin

Condensed from The Saturday Evening Post

H E WORE the cross of the Corps of Chaplains instead of the crossed rifles of the infantry, but he was the best foot soldier I ever knew, and the bravest man, and the kindest. His name was Emil Joseph Kapaun, and he was a Roman Catholic priest. To the men he served in the prison camps of Korea—Catholic, Protestant and Jew alike—he was simply "Father," and each of them, when trouble came, drew courage and hope and strength from him. Because of his sermons and the food he stole for us and the care he gave us when we were sick, many of us came back who never would have survived without him.

He wore his piety in his heart. Outwardly he was all GI, tough of body, rough of speech sometimes, full of the wry humor of the combat soldier. When the Communists tried to brainwash him he had the guts to tell them they lied.

In the prison camp I once came upon him sitting in the sunshine, a look of happiness in his eyes. "What are you thinking of, Father?" I asked.

"Of that happy day," he said, "when the first American tank rolls down that road. Then I'm going to catch that little so-and-so, Comrade

Sun, and kick his butt right over the compound fence." He was the son of a Kansas farmer and he had a farmer's flair for down-to-earth, homely talk.

He had become a legend among the troops long before the Chinese captured him. When his outfit, the Eighth Cavalry Regiment of the First Cavalry Division, was fighting along the Naktong, he would stuff his pockets with apples and peaches he had scrounged from Korean orchards and ride a ramshackle bicycle over rocky paths and through the paddy fields to the forward outposts. There he'd drop into a shallow hole beside a nervous rifleman, crack a joke or two, hand him a peach, say a prayer and move on to the next hole.

He always stayed close to the fighting. He'd set up his altar on a litter stretched across two ammunition boxes and, with mortar fire coming in and the enemy massing for a counterattack, he'd hear confessions, celebrate Mass and administer Holy Communion. He seemed to have no fear that he himself might be killed. At Kumchon early in the war, when word came back that there was a wounded man in a position so exposed that the litter men could not reach him, Father Kapaun and another officer went after him and brought him back, crawling through fire so thick that the chaplain's pipe was shot out of his mouth.

It was his devotion to the wounded which finally cost him his freedom, and his life. At Unsan, in November 1950, for 36 hours the Eighth Cavalry had been beating off a fanatical attack. Finally, at dusk, the order came for every man who could still walk to try a breakout through the surrounding enemy. Father Kapaun, who was unwounded, might have escaped but he stayed on, helping Capt. Clarence L. Anderson, the regimental surgeon, take care of the wounded. And there, at dark, the Chinese took him as he said the last prayers over a dying man.

The Chinese allowed us prisoners a starvation ration of 450 grams of millet or cracked corn per man per day. It was obvious, Father said, that we must either steal food or starve, so he said a prayer to St. Dismas, the Good Thief, asking for his aid.

I'll never doubt the power of prayer again. Father, it seemed, could not fail. He'd sneak at night into the little fields around the compound and find where the enemy had hidden potatoes and grain beneath the corn shocks. Or at mealtimes, while the rest of us started a row with the Chinese who were doling out the rations, he'd sneak into the supply shed, snatch up a sack of cracked corn and scurry off into the bushes.

Some of the other men who stole squirreled their stolen food away for themselves. Father never said a word to them, but he'd say a prayer of thanks to God for providing food "which all can equally share." That seemed to shame them, and soon the private hoarding stopped.

When the wounded in the sick house—only the Chinese called it the hospital—began to die by dozens, poisoned by their untended wounds, the Chinese finally allowed Dr. Anderson to go to their aid, though he had nothing but the skill of his hands to help them. Father asked permission to go with the doctor.

"What these men need is medicine, not prayer," the Chinese told him.

"Since they aren't getting any medicine," Father answered, "a little prayer won't hurt."

"No," the Chinese said, "you will not be permitted to spread your poisonous Christian propaganda here."

Then began Father's most hazardous exploits. With his pockets full of stolen food, he'd creep over to the house where the wounded were, ducking under the bushes to keep out of sight of the guards. He took their old bandages, foul with corruption, sneaked them out and washed them and sneaked them back again. He picked the lice from their bodies. He let them smoke his pipe, loaded with dry cotton leaves; he joked with them, said prayers for them, and held them in his arms like children as delirium came upon them. But the main thing he did for them was to put into their hearts the will to live. For when you are wounded and sick and starving, it's easy to give up and quietly die.

Somehow, as it says in the Testament, "power came forth from him and healed them." In the compound where Father Kapaun was kept, conditions were the same as in the camp known as Death Valley, yet in Death Valley the death rate was ten times higher.

When he had done all he could for the wounded and helped to bury the dead he would conduct services for the rest of us. He'd urge us not to lose hope of freedom and, above all, not to fall for the lying doctrines the Reds were trying to pound into our heads.

"Be not afraid of them who kill the body," he'd quote from the Scriptures. To Father, the man who accepted the Communist teachings —and a small group did out of ignorance or opportunism—was selling his immortal soul.

He did a thousand little things to keep us going. He traded his watch for a blanket, which he cut up to make warm socks for men whose feet were freezing. All one day, in a freezing wind, with a sharp stick and his bare hands he cut steps in the steep, ice-covered path that led down to the stream, so that the men carrying water would not fall.

By mid-March we were in desperate condition, boiling weeds in our effort to get vitamins. Pellagra and beriberi robbed us of our strength, and the hideous swelling of the body that is the first mark of approaching death by starvation was showing up on more and more of us. As our bodies weakened, the Reds stepped up the pace of their propaganda assault upon our minds. Hour after hour we sat in lectures while Comrade Sun, a fanatic little Chinese, assailed our "rotten, capitalistic Wall Street civilization." Then we'd have to comment upon the truths he revealed.

A few bold men, in reckless despair, commented in unprintable words of contempt and were thrown into a freezing hole or subjected to other severe tortures that sometimes resulted in death. Some veiled their ridicule: "According to the great doctrines taught us by the noble Stalin, Lenin, Marx, Engels, Amos and Andy—"

Father was not openly arrogant, nor did he use subterfuge. Without raising his voice he'd answer the lecturer with a calm logic that set Comrade Sun screaming and leaping on the platform like an angry ape.

"When our Lord told us to love our enemies," Father once said, "I'm sure He did not have Comrade Sun in mind."

Strangely, they never punished him except by threats and ominous warnings, but two officers who knew him well were taken away and tortured. With their hands tied behind them they were lifted by ropes until their wrist joints pulled apart. They then were brought back to accuse him publicly of slandering the Chinese. They said he advocated resistance to the Reds' study program, which was true. They said he threatened men with courts-martial on their return if they went along with the Chinese, which was not true. Father never threatened anybody.

When the two men came back after their ordeal Father was the first to greet them. Looking at their twisted hands, he said, "You never should have suffered a moment, trying to protect me."

We expected that the public accusation would bring Father a farcical trial. Instead, the Chinese merely called him in and threatened him. We realized then what we had half known all along: they were afraid of him. They recognized in him a strength they could not break.

On Easter Sunday, 1951, he openly flouted their law against religious services. In the yard of a burned-out church, at sunrise, he read the Easter service. All his Mass equipment had been lost at the time of his capture but he still had the purple ribbon, called a stole, which he wore round his neck as a badge of his priesthood, the gold ciborium in which the Host had been carried for Holy Communion, and the little bottles of holy oil used to administer the last sacraments. He fashioned a cross out of two rough pieces of wood, and a rosary of barbed wire cut from the prison fence.

As we watched him it was clear to us that Father himself had at last begun to fail in strength. For months he had been sharing his meager rations with sick and dying men. For weeks, we knew, he had been suffering the terrible bone-aches—a by-product of hunger—that came upon men at night with such fearful pain that they would scream and beat the ground in agony. The Sunday after Easter, as he read in the Epistle, "And this is the victory that overcomes the world—our Faith," his voice faltered, and we caught him as he fell.

Beneath his tattered uniform his right leg was dreadfully swollen, a mass of purple, blue and yellow flesh. Dr. Anderson applied hot packs, and slowly the swelling began to subside. Soon Father could walk again.

Then one day he came down with pneumonia, and soon was in delirium. But he passed this crisis, too.

The Chinese, however, did not intend that he should live. He was sitting up, eating and joking, when the guards came with a litter. We knew then that he was doomed, for in the "hospital" men were left to lie untended in filth and freezing cold until merciful death took them.

Father himself made no protest. He looked around the room at all of us, and smiled. He held in his hands the ciborium, the little covered cup in which, long ago, he had carried the blessed bread. "Tell them back home that I died happy."

As they loaded him on the litter he turned to Lieutenant Nardella. "You know the prayers, Ralph," he said. "Keep holding the services."

He turned to another officer, who, before his capture, had been having trouble at home. "When you get back to Jersey, get that marriage straightened out," he told him, "or I'll come down from Heaven and kick you in the tail."

Then he turned to me. "Don't take it hard, Mike," he said. "I'm going where I've always wanted to go. And when I get up there, I'll say a prayer for all of you." I stood there crying, unashamed, as they took him down the road.

A few days later Father Kapaun was dead.

On His Own

NOT LONG after our youngsters and the children from the neighboring farm went off to the woods to pick huckleberries, a sudden summer shower came up. It really poured, and soon all the children came back—with dripping wet clothes and very few berries. All except my son, Byron Lee. It wasn't until much later, after the shower was over, that he came around the corner of the barn. His face was beaming as he proudly held up his bucket full of berries, and to our amazement his clothes were as dry as a powder horn.

Asked how he'd kept dry, Byron Lee said, "Oh, I heard that rain a-comin' so I pulled my clothes off and stuffed them in a hollow log and kept on picking berries. By the time the sun came out I had my bucket full, so I put my clothes on and came home."

With Byron Lee's Yankee ingenuity and habitual good luck, we were confident he would return safely from World War II. Our son didn't come back—but we are certain that these rare qualities made him a good soldier as long as he lived.   —Contributed by Mrs. R. B. Johnson

Your Voice Is Your Fortune

By Paul D. Green and Cliff Cochrane

Condensed from This Week Magazine

HEN Billy Rose listened to a transcription of his first radio script he cried, "Take it away! That's an impostor. It sounds like a nail file rubbing a cheese grater!"

His reaction was one common to most people hearing a recording of their own voices for the first time. For, as Pat Kelly, supervisor of announcers for NBC, says, "Only five persons out of a hundred are born with good voices. The rest of us have to work for one."

The important thing is, you *can* work for a good voice. And it's well worth doing. Bad speech may adversely affect your career, your social life, even your family life. High school and college graduates with clear, intelligent-sounding voices have a much better chance of landing good jobs than those with harsh or hard-to-understand voices. A college survey proved it last summer.

An example of the relationship between voice and career was given us by the vice-president of a Chicago bank. "A fellow we'll call Jenkins was behind a teller's cage in this bank for 20 years. He couldn't figure out why he never got advanced. Family obligations finally prompted him to ask for a promotion to the New Business Department.

" 'Jenkins,' the president told him, 'in this job you have to see a lot of important customers; you have to interview executives and owners of large businesses. Frankly, you sound so flat and dispirited we're afraid to give you the chance. But if you can learn to put some snap into your voice, so that it really carries conviction, we'll talk about it again.'

"Jenkins went to work on his voice. Within a few months he had what amounted to a new personality. He got the promotion, and before long was made an officer of the bank.

"I know how much that man owes to his voice improvement," the vice-president finished, "because, you see, I'm that man."

An illustration of a different type is furnished by the middle-aged widow who had a timid, meek voice and made few friends. Largely to have something to do she took a speech course evenings at the local high school. Suddenly her voice gained new authority; people were interested when she talked. She joined a couple of organizations, became head of one, and found herself making many new friends. She even found a new husband.

Of all speech defects, the commonest, according to the New York Telephone Company, is the slurring of words. "J'eat yet?" "Whyncha c'mover?" and so on. Such sloppy speech grates on an employer's ears, even if your friends may not mind it. Other speech sins, according to a survey of business firms made by Dr. James F. Bender of the National Institute for Human Relations, include these:

Among men—mumbling, a rasp, tonal monotony, overloudness, stilted accents. Among women—a whine, shrillness, nasal tones, baby talk, affected accents.

An employer may take exception to a voice that he fears may annoy subordinates. A former Navy officer found this out when he sought a position with a large shipbuilding firm.

"Mr. Anderson," the personnel director told him, "you have the training and experience necessary. But your harsh manner of speaking would irritate our employes and, I'm afraid, lead to inefficiency."

The man decided to do something about it and enrolled in a speech-improvement course. In three months the steel wool was combed out of his voice. He applied for a similar position in another shipyard, and is now yard superintendent.

How can you check up on your own voice deficiencies? A good way is to have a transcription made. There are other, more simple means. Stand in an enclosed space—a stall shower is good—and talk. Don't be misled by resonance; tune your ears for whiny, nasal and unpleasant tones, for slurred syllables and unclear consonants. Or stand close to a wall and talk through a paper cone; the sound of your voice will bounce off the wall and back to your ear. Singers and radio announcers cup their hands behind their ears in order to get a truer idea of what their voices sound like. Try reading aloud to the family and ask for criticism.

Once you have taken the measure of your voice, here are steps to improve it, according to voice experts:

1. Pick a model to imitate. Men should choose a person whose voice hits a good average, like Lowell Thomas, for example, rather than one with a distinctive accent or intonation, like Basil Rathbone or H. V. Kaltenborn. Women would do well to pick someone like Loretta Young or Irene Dunne rather than Katharine Hepburn or Tallulah Bankhead. Study your model's diction, style of delivery, pausing technique and tonal quality, but don't go overboard in imitation. Keep your own personality.

2. Take regular breathing exercises to develop your lung power, remembering to push your diaphragm out when breathing in.

3. Make an effort to improve your speaking personality by pumping enthusiasm into your tones.

4. Have a complete medical checkup on your speech apparatus, including adenoids, tonsils, larynx, teeth and sinuses.

5. Try lowering the pitch of your voice. It's usually an improvement.

If your voice problem is extreme you should go to a good speech school or to a private instructor. The American Speech and Hearing Association, whose offices are at the State University of Iowa, Iowa City, and at Purdue University, Lafayette, Ind., can give you a list of approved schools.

Copyright 1950 by The Reader's Digest Association, Inc. (April 1950 issue)
Condensed from This Week Magazine, January 15, 1950

The best bridge between despair and hope is a good night's sleep.

—Harry Ruby in *Variety*

New help for childless couples

The Problem of Infertility

By Grace Naismith

Condensed from Today's Health

IT IS a distressing fact that at least one out of every ten married couples in this country who want children are unable to have them. Yet such great strides have been made in the study of infertility in recent years that today, with treatment, nearly a third of these cases can achieve parenthood. Some 100 fertility clinics, many connected with university medical schools, now offer aid, and a growing number of doctors are becoming better trained in diagnosis and treatment.

One of the oldest clinics of this kind was started 28 years ago by Dr. John Rock at the Free Hospital for Women in Brookline, a suburb of Boston. Since then, chances of helping childless couples, at this clinic and elsewhere, have increased from one in ten to almost three times that number.

A typical patient at Dr. Rock's clinic is the young wife who came after four years of childlessness. She was shy and hesitant as she gave her medical history to the secretary. "My husband and I can't understand why we don't have a baby," she said. "We both want one, terribly."

The secretary was quietly reassuring as she escorted the young woman to one of the doctors for an explanation of the clinic's procedure.

"It will help," the doctor began, "if you understand fully the human reproductive system, and what tests we use to see if each part is working properly." He showed her diagrams of the male and female organs. Appallingly few men and women know even the simplest facts about conception. "Normally each month one of a woman's two ovaries produces a single egg. This egg, or ovum, about one tenth as large as this period"—the doctor penciled a dot on his desk pad—"passes downward from the ovary into the uterus.

"If conception is to occur, the male seed, or sperm, which has been ejaculated into the woman's vagina, must proceed up through the uterus and into the Fallopian tube to meet the egg and fertilize it. Only one sperm out of the millions that start this short journey enters the ovum.

"Sometimes the Fallopian tubes are blocked. To find out, we do a Rubin test, which means passing carbon dioxide into the tubes under pressure. Any well-trained doctor can make this test quickly and safely. If this gas cannot go through, we know the egg or sperm could not pass either. Then we take an X-ray picture—we call it a 'tubogram'— which will show where the obstruction lies.

"We make another examination to determine the condition of the lining of the uterus, for the fertilized egg must find a proper bed on the uterine wall on which to grow. We study a tissue sample in our laboratory to see if there is anything about it that might interfere with the egg's development.

"We must also find out if the sperm can get into the tubes. A mucous fluid is produced in the cervix, the neck of the uterus, through which the sperm must pass. This may have qualities which will destroy the sperm. To determine this, we examine mucus removed after intercourse. So we ask you to have intercourse the night before your next appointment here.

"This simple, painless postcoital test also throws light on your husband's fertility. For you to conceive, your husband must be able to produce active and sufficiently numerous sperm. There are from 200 to 500 million sperm in an average ejaculation, and doctors believe it takes between 50 and 125 million to make conception probable. Since husbands are at least partly the cause of childlessness in fully 40 percent of the cases, we have a special clinic for husbands."

The doctor then asked the young wife to take her temperature each morning directly on awakening, and to record it on a chart. There was a possibility that she and her husband had never had intercourse at the right time for conception—which can occur only at the time of ovulation, when the ovary has released the egg into the Fallopian tube.

Usually this occurs 14 to 16 days before the beginning of a woman's next expected menstrual period. The "waking temperature" is lowest before ovulation. Then it goes up about a degree, presumably at the time the ovary discharges the egg, and levels off until menstruation.

Since normal sperm remain active for approximately 48 hours, and the egg is thought to stay alive an even shorter time, it is important to determine as nearly as possible the time of ovulation. Temperature records are not infallible tests. Even a slight cold, indigestion or an emotional shock may upset temperature. But most specialists find such records a helpful guide.

The operation to open a blocked tube, when other treatments have failed, may take two or three hours, and requires about eight days of hospitalization. Scar tissue tends to close the canal again. But surgeons at the Free Hospital for Women have found that a tiny tube of harmless, nonirritating polyethylene plastic can be left in the canal at the time of the operation. It is removed after healing is complete.

Failure to produce an egg is another cause of infertility. For this, hormone treatment is sometimes effective. Tumors may be a cause. Frequently they can be removed. Inflammatory condition of the uterus can be treated with antibiotics.

Only couples who have tried unsuccessfully for at least a year to have a baby are considered by Dr. Rock's clinic. Thereafter, four or five visits to the clinic, over a period of several months, may be required. Sometimes pregnancy occurs before a diagnosis has even been made. Some doctors believe that anxiety and tension are often the culprits in preventing conception, and that they can be relieved merely by a better understanding of the problems involved.

"It is not news," the clinic psychiatrist points out, "that a severe shock or great fear or excitement can interrupt menstruation or ovulation—or bring them on at irregular intervals." Emotional stress may even cause a muscle spasm of the Fallopian tube and bar the passage of the egg or the sperm, or bring on excessive secretion in the cervix which may hinder or harm the sperm.

One frequently hears that a couple, childless for years, have adopted a baby and then soon afterward conceived one of their own. Many investigators believe that the frustrated desire for a child, or the unconscious fear that they may not be able to care for a child properly, may have made a couple temporarily infertile. At the Free Hospital, any connection between adoption and fertility is considered speculative. A survey made by Dr. Rock and Dr. Frederick M. Hanson of 202 couples who adopted children revealed that eight percent of the wives subsequently became pregnant. But conception without any treatment is considered likely in ten percent of apparently infertile couples.

Treatment of infertile husbands is usually less involved and less expensive than that of women. Sometimes nothing is needed but improvement of the general physical condition by means of diet, rest, exercise and, if possible, the removal of emotional tension.

At the clinic for husbands a specialist gives private examination and counsel. Frequently the cause is failure of effective intercourse or of proper placement of semen in the vagina. More often the number of sperm is insufficient—sometimes a vigorous he-man, quite without his knowledge, may produce none at all.

The reputed high cost of tests and treatment for infertility has prevented many couples from embarking on the sometimes long procedure. At Dr. Rock's clinic, which is restricted to those in the lower-income brackets, charges for basic tests seldom exceed $25. To those who cannot afford to pay, only a memorandum of the hospital charge is given, and if at some future date they can pay they may do so. Research at the clinic is partly supported by foundations and pharmaceutical companies.

The clinic's doctors follow each new line of research. What about enzymes, hormones, vitamins? Will X-ray treatments of the pituitary gland improve fertility? Will they harm future generations? Are there better ways to determine the time of ovulation? When should artificial insemination be recommended?

Meanwhile, to the ten percent of married couples in the United States to whom infertility is a direct personal problem, it is hopeful news that for nearly a third of them their tragedy can now be righted.

The name and address of the fertility clinic nearest your home may be obtained by writing to Planned Parenthood Federation of America, 501 Madison Ave., New York, N. Y.

EAT A BIGGER BREAKFAST

AND BE THIN
By *Fredrick J. Stare, M.D.*
of the Harvard School of Public Health
and Julia A. Shea

Condensed from Collier's

SKIMPY BREAKFASTS may be one cause of the shocking number of overweight adults in the United States—a total set by public-health authorities at 15 million.

The key to this seeming paradox lies in the discovery of what nutritionists believe to be a trigger control of appetite. According to a theory evolved by Dr. Jean Mayer and his associates in the Department of Nutrition at Harvard's School of Public Health, proteins seem to control this trigger mechanism: the higher the protein content of our food intake, the longer we can keep the mechanism in the off, or not-hungry, position.

Breakfast is the most important meal. Fruit juice, cereal with milk, an egg and bacon, toast and coffee will add fewer pounds in the long run than a breakfast of only coffee with sweet rolls. While the larger breakfast contains roughly 200 more calories, it will carry you over with no midmorning snack and less desire to tackle too big a lunch or dinner. Protein content is the answer: 17 grams in the larger meal, and only four in the other. Thus, with no loss of energy, we can lose weight safely while rarely feeling hungry.

It was formerly believed that hunger was caused by an increase in stomach contractions; when the stomach was full, contractions slowed down and hunger disappeared. Followers of this theory advocated reducing diets high in bulk but negligible in food value, such as special cellulose products. The scheme was to keep something, anything, in the stomach so long as it was low in calories. But this theory was exploded when it was found that surgical patients complained of hunger even after their stomachs had been removed.

It was known that appetite centers exist in the lower part of the brain, the hypothalamus. So Dr. Mayer reasoned that changes in make-up of the blood passing through these centers might trigger the appetite.

Earlier investigators had found that amounts of sugar in the blood fluctuate abruptly after eating. Mayer began a series of experiments which showed that the sugar level, like heat acting on a thermostat, did control the appetite centers.

We feel hungry, we eat, and part of our food turns to sugar. When the sugar level of our blood rises to a certain point, click! the control shuts off and we no longer feel hungry. (This control has been nick-named the "appestat" by Dr. Norman Jolliffe of the New York City Health Department.) As we expend energy, the sugar level drops, the appestat snaps on and we are hungry.

One implication of this discovery was: If sugar levels could be maintained for longer periods above the appetite line with fewer calories, we could eat less without feeling hungry. Overweight persons could diet without suffering from hunger pangs.

Our food consists mainly of carbohydrates, proteins and fats. Coffee with cream and sugar, and rolls are mainly carbohydrate foods. Cereals with milk, as well as eggs and meat, are good sources of protein.

Carbohydrates raise the blood-sugar level abruptly; they are "quick energy" foods. But this energy is soon used up and the hunger signal flashes on again. Proteins also raise the sugar level, but they hold it above the hunger mark far longer. Since fats slow down the rate at which carbohydrates and proteins are digested, they too help maintain a more constant blood-sugar level.

The man who starts off his workday with only coffee and rolls is going to feel hungry by midmorning; he will want to slip out for "doughnuts and coffee" to tide him over until lunch. Hungry again, he will eat a larger lunch than if he had had a substantial, high-protein breakfast. By the end of the day, he will have consumed far more calories than if he had eaten the heartier breakfast.

The housewife who skimps breakfast with the desire to keep her figure will usually more than make up for her morning calorie loss by eating large snacks throughout the day.

Everyone should eat at least a quarter of the day's total calories and proteins at breakfast. No one can say how much an average person—if one exists—should eat during the day, but let's say 2500 calories is about right for you if you get normal exercise. You could eat quite a large breakfast—fruit juice, cereal and milk, poached egg on toast, toast and butter, milk and coffee—and still have no trouble eating regular, moderate amounts at the next two meals.

If you are one of those who can't face a big breakfast, get up a few minutes early and take a moderate amount of exercise. You'll be surprised how hungry it will make you.

Make a Mistake!

*To err is human—and sometimes it's
the best thing that could happen to you*

How OFTEN we intend one thing and it turns into another! There is a joke in the Greek Anthology about a man who invented a stove that didn't work but served excellently as a wine cooler in summer. The New England eccentric, "Lord" Timothy Dexter of Newburyport, Mass., sent a strange cargo of warming pans to the West Indies and made his fortune when the natives discovered that the pans, with their long handles, were perfect for cooking in a hot climate. Columbus aimed at India and found America. The experience has become proverbial: We aim for the goose and hit the gander.

The same thing happens with cheerful frequency in daily life. A job is lost which, if it had been taken, would have prevented the acceptance of a better one. The wrong book comes home from the library and opens a whole new field of interest. I know of a student in college who wandered into the wrong classroom and was so interested in the subject discussed there that he pursued it and made it his career. I need scarcely add that, being so absent-minded, he became a professor.

It should take the edge off disappointment to remember that half the things that go wrong surprise us by turning out all right.

—Robert Hillyer, Pulitzer Prize Poet, in *This Week*

The story of a retarded child, told by her mother,
an article of incalculable comfort to parents
facing a similar problem

The Child Who Never Grew

By Pearl S. Buck
Author of "The Good Earth," "Pavilion of Women," "Kinfolk," etc.

Condensed from Ladies' Home Journal

THIS STORY is a true one, and that makes it hard to tell. The many letters which I have received over the years from parents with a child like mine have helped me finally resolve that the time has come for it to be told. The letters ask two things: what shall they do for their children and how shall they bear the sorrow of having such a child?

I answer the first question by telling them what I have done; but the second is difficult indeed, for endurance of inescapable sorrow is something one must learn alone. And only to endure is not enough. Endurance can be harsh and bitter, destroying other lives. There must be acceptance, the knowledge that sorrow fully accepted brings its own gifts. For there is an alchemy in sorrow. It can be transmuted into wisdom, which can bring happiness.

The final reason for setting down this story is that I want my child's life to be of use in her generation. There is afoot in our country today a great new movement to help all children like her. Wise men and women are beginning to accept the mentally retarded person as part of the human family, and to educate him in the things he can do, so that he may be happy in himself and useful to society. That this may be done, the primary work of research must progress as it never has. In this work the facts of my child's condition may be of use. It is too late, of course, for her to be helped—she is now a grown woman, physically. But it is not too late for many little ones, and surely for others yet to be born.

My child was born in China, at the height of my young womanhood. I had always wanted children, and I remember so well my boundless joy when the Chinese nurse held my baby up for me to see for the first time. Her features were clear; her eyes, it seemed to me, wise and calm. I said to the nurse, "Doesn't she look very wise for her age?" She was then less than an hour old.

"She does, indeed," the nurse declared. "And she is beautiful, too. There is a special purpose for this child."

How often have I thought of those words! Proudly at first, as the child grew, always healthy, always good. I remember when she was two months old that an old friend saw her for the first time. The child had never seen a man with a black mustache before and she stared for a moment and then drew down her little mouth to weep.

"Extraordinary," my friend said. "She knows already what is strange to her."

I do not know when her mental growth stopped, nor to this day do we know why it did. There was nothing in her ancestry to make me fear that my child might be defective. No young mother could have been less prepared than I for what was to come. I think I was the last to perceive that something was wrong. She was three years old when I first began to wonder; for she did not yet talk. I remember voicing anxiety to my friends. Their replies were comforting, too comforting. They spoke all the empty words of assurance that friends, meaning well, will use, and I believed them.

My child was nearly four years old before I discovered that her mind had stopped growing. She had now begun to talk a little, and could feed herself, and put on her clothes. She liked to look at picture books and she understood much more than she could say. I read meaning into her gestures and into the few broken words.

Then I went one day to hear an American pediatrician lecture and as I listened I realized that something was very wrong indeed with my child. The doctor pointed out danger signs: the slowness to walk, the slowness to talk, and then when the child could walk, the incessant restlessness—all were danger signs.

After the meeting was over I asked the doctor to come and see her. She came the next day and sat a long time watching, then shook her head. "Something is wrong," she said. "I do not know what it is. You must have a consultation of doctors."

She pointed out to me the danger signs I had not seen, or would not see. The child's span of attention was very short indeed. Much of her fleet running had no purpose—it was merely motion. Her eyes, so pure in their blue, were blank when one gazed into their depths. They did not hold, or respond.

The doctors met the next day and, after studying the child, said, "You must take her to America. There the doctors may know what is wrong. We can only say there is something wrong."

Then began that long journey which parents of such children know so well. Driven by the conviction that there must be someone who could cure, I took my child over the surface of the whole earth, gradually losing hope.

The end of the journey came at the Mayo Clinic in Rochester, Minn. Day after day we had spent in meticulous examination, and my confidence had grown. Surely so much study, so much knowledge, would tell me the truth and what to do with it.

At last the head of the children's department collected all the reports and made his diagnosis. Much of it was good. My child had certain remarkable abilities, especially in music. There were signs of an unusual personality struggling against some sort of handicap. But—the mind was severely retarded. Why, he didn't know. "Somewhere along the way, growth stopped."

"Is it hopeless?"

Kind man—perhaps he was not really sure. "I think I would not give up trying," was what he finally said.

And now came the moment for which I shall be grateful as long as I live. As my child and I walked down the hall, a small, inconspicuous person came quietly out of an empty room and beckoned to me. I had seen him before, when he brought the reports to the head doctor.

"Did he tell you the child might be cured?" he asked.

"He—he didn't say she could not," I stammered.

"Listen to what I tell you!" he commanded. "You will wear out your life and beggar your family unless you face the truth. She will never be normal—do you hear me? I know—I have seen these children. She will never be able to speak properly, or read or write. Do not deceive yourself. This child will be a burden on you all your life. Get ready to bear that burden! Above all, do not let her absorb you. Find a place where she can be happy and leave her there, and live your own life. I tell you the truth for your own sake."

I remember that he looked cruel, but I know he was not. I know now that he suffered while he spoke. I shall forever be grateful to him, who cut the wound deep, but clean and quick.

I took my child home again to China.

Mine is no unique experience. Almost one person in every hundred is or will be mentally retarded—the majority from noninherited causes. And every retarded child means a stricken, heartsick family. I meet often nowadays with parents' organizations, parents of mentally deficient children who are coming together in their deep need for mutual comfort and support. How my heart aches for them! I know every step of their road to Calvary.

To learn how to bear inescapable sorrow is not easily done. Death would be far easier to face, for death is final. How often did I cry out in my heart that it would be better if my child died! If that shocks you who have not known, it will not shock those who do know. I would have welcomed death for my child and would still welcome it, for then she would be finally safe.

Yet I know that the parents one reads about occasionally who end the physical lives of their children do wrong. Society decrees death for certain crimes, but the innocent may not be killed, and there is none more innocent than these children who never grow up. Were the right to kill any innocent person assumed by society, the effect would be monstrous. For first it might be only the helpless children who were killed, but then it might seem right to kill the helpless old.

My common sense, my convictions of duty, all told me that I must not let the disaster spoil my life. But common sense and duty cannot always prevail when the heart is broken. I tried to act as much like my usual self as possible, to talk, to laugh, to take an interest in what went on. Underneath, the rebellion burned, yet I tried to conceal my weeping from my child because she stared at me and laughed. It was this uncomprehending laughter which crushed my heart.

I do not know when the turn came, but finally the process of accommodation began. The first step was acceptance—a step which had to be taken over and over again. The sight of a neighbor's normal little daughter doing the things my child could never do was enough to send me down into the morass of despair. But I learned to come up again, and necessity finally drove me to think what I ought to do about the child's future.

Had there been security in her life with me, I would have felt it best to keep her with me, for I did not believe that anyone could understand her as well as I did, or do for her what I could. But if I should die too young, what would become of her? The world is not shaped for the helpless. The best that could be expected was that she would be taken to our country, the United States, and put into an institution. There, alone, she would have to make the adjustment of being without all that had meant home to her. She would not understand why, and the puzzle and grief might disturb her beyond control.

It came to me then that it would be best for her to make the adjustment while I could help. She could gradually change her roots from this home to a new one, knowing that I was near and would come to see her again and again.

An incident, very slight in itself, crystallized my thinking. One of our American neighbors had a little girl just the age of mine. They had always gone to each other's parties. One day, however, the other little girl was prattling as little girls will, and she said, "My mamma says I can't have your poor little girl to my party next time."

Next time, indeed, the invitation did not come. The great separation had begun. I realized then that I must find another world for my child, one where she would not be despised and rejected, one where she could find friends on her own level, and function within her capacities.

I felt, however, that before I let my child leave me I ought to test her abilities thoroughly, so that I could make the best possible choice of her future home. I decided to take a year, during which I would try to teach her to read, to write, and, since she loved music, to learn notes and to sing little songs.

I found that my child could learn to read simple sentences, that she was able, with much effort, to write her name, and that she was able to sing simple songs. I think she might have been able to proceed further, but one day, when I took her little hand to guide it in writing a word, I noticed that it was wet with perspiration. I realized then that the child was under intense strain, submitting to something she did not in the least understand, with an angelic wish to please me. She was not really learning anything.

It seemed my heart broke all over again. When I could control myself I got up and put away the books forever. "Let's go outside and play with the kitties," I said.

Her little face took on a look of incredulous joy, and that was my reward.

I gave up all ambition for her, all pride, and accepted her exactly as she was. And I have learned, as the years passed, to be intensely grateful for the fact that the difficulties of ordinary existence would never be hers. Instead, the joys and irresponsibilities of childhood are hers forever. She loves to skate and ride a tricycle, she finds pleasure in dolls and toy dishes and a sand pile. Above all is her never-failing joy in music. She has a large collection of records, and by some instinct—since she cannot read—she can distinguish one from the other. The gift that is hidden in her shows itself in the still ecstasy with which she listens to the great symphonies hour after hour, her lips smiling, her eyes gazing off into what distance I do not know.

This is one of the compensations. I want parents of other children like her to know that there are such compensations for these little children.

I kept my child with me until she was nine years old, and then we came to the United States to search for her final home.

Since I was not resident in my own country, state institutions were not easily open to me. Moreover, most of them were overcrowded and the children lived in strict routine. Oh, how my heart suffered for those big rooms of children sitting dully on benches, waiting, waiting!

"What are they waiting for?" I asked my guide one day.

"They aren't waiting for anything," he replied in surprise. "They're just sitting. That's all they want to do."

But I know the children were really waiting for something pleasant to happen to them. Perhaps they did not know they were waiting, but they were. I know now that there is no mind so dim that it does not feel pain and pleasure.

My search for a suitable home ended at an institution whose head was sympathetic, but not eager to receive my child. He said diffidently that he did not know whether I would be satisfied with his school, but we might look around. I saw that every child's face lit when he came into the cottages, and there was a clamor of voices to greet him—Uncle Ed, they called him. He took time to play with them and he let them hug his knees and look in his pockets for chocolates—very tiny ones, not enough to spoil a child's appetite. He knew every child, and he greeted the attendants with courtesy. And when he made a suggestion the attendant was quick to agree.

The buildings were pleasant and adequate, and I saw children playing around the yards as though they were at home. I saw a certain motto repeated again and again on the walls, on the stationery, hanging above the head's own desk: "Happiness first and all else follows."

"That's not just sentimentality," the head said. "It is the fruit of experience. We've found that the only child who can learn is the happy child."

Upon a September day I brought my little girl to the place I had found. We walked about to accustom her to the new playgrounds and I went with her to the corner where her bed stood. We met the woman who was to be her attendant, and the superintendent of girls. The child clung to my hand. What went on in her little mind I do not know, but I think some foreboding was there. We had never been separated, and the time for separation was coming.

In the afternoon of that day which was so dreadful in its passing, the head talked to me gently and gravely. I have never forgotten his words. "You must remember," he said, "that these are happy children. They are safe here. They will never know distress or want, nor will sorrow ever touch them. No demands are made upon them which they cannot meet. The joys which they can appreciate they have. Your child will escape all suffering. Will you remember that and let it be a comfort to you?

"Of course it is not possible for your child to live here exactly as she has in your house," he continued. "She will be individually cared for and watched and taught, it is true, but here she is one of many. This will mean some loss of freedom to her. This loss you must weigh against the gain. For you cannot shield her from everything. She is a human creature and she must bear her little share, too, of what is common to all human life. When she learns to fall in with the others in the small routines that are necessary in any big family, she will even enjoy the sense of being with the crowd."

When he finished speaking, I knew that he had done what he meant to do—he had helped me to find strength to think of the child's larger good. So I left her there. But I shall never forget as long as I live that I had to pull her little arms from around my neck and that I dared not look back. I knew the matron was holding her fast and I knew I must not see it, lest my courage fail.

Years have passed since that day. I visit her often, and she is used now to my coming and going, and yet even now there is a brief clinging when I leave. "I want to go home," she whispers again and again. She comes home sometimes, too, and is filled with joy for a few days. But after she has been at home a week or so she begins to miss the other home. She inquires after "the girls," and asks for some toy or record that she left behind. At last almost willingly she goes back again, after making sure that I am coming soon to see her. The long struggle is over. The adjustment has been made.

In the years which have passed since I led my child into her own world, again and again I have been able to find comfort in the fact that her life, with others, has been of use in enlarging the whole body of our knowledge. No child ought to be merely something to be cared for and preserved from harm. He has something to contribute, even though he is helpless. There are reasons for his condition, and if they can be discovered, others may be born whole because of him.

Psychologists working with mentally retarded children at The Training School at Vineland, New Jersey, have found that while the IQ may be very low indeed a retarded child actually may function a good deal higher because of his social sense, his feeling of how he ought to behave, his wish to be liked. Acting upon this observation, they developed the Social Maturity Scale, widely used in the armed forces, schools and colleges. We have to thank the helpless children for teaching us that mere intelligence is not enough.

They have taught us, too, how people learn. The minds of retarded children are sane minds, normal except that the processes are slowed. Psychologists, observing the slower processes, have been able to discover, exactly as though in a slow-motion picture, the way the human creature acquires new knowledge and new habits. Our educational techniques for normal children have been vastly improved by what the retarded children have taught us.

Research has taught us how to cure many ills, and is being carried on for those we still do not know how to heal. People must not die of cancer or polio. Neither should they be mentally deficient if it can be prevented.

We know some of the reasons for injury to the brain, both prenatal and postnatal, but we do not know enough. We know, for example, that if a woman has German measles in the first three months of pregnancy her child may be born mentally defective, but we do not know why. We must know why. The Mongoloid child can appear in any family. We must find out what conditions cause this child.

The need is more pressing than the public knows. Our state institutions are dangerously overcrowded and, unless research is hastened, millions of dollars must go into more institutions for children whose care must be paid for by public funds. How much wiser it would be to pay for scientific research which would make such care unnecessary!

Something, of course, has already been done. We know that at least 50 percent of the mentally deficient children now in the United States can be educated to be productive members of society. Education alone would relieve our overcrowded public institutions. Studies have shown that there are 19 types of jobs that can be done by an adult whose mentality is no more than that of a six-year-old child. Twenty percent of all work in the United States is done by the unskilled worker.

All this is grounds for hope, and hope is essential for activity. More than half the children now mentally deficient need not have been so. More than half now mentally deficient can, with proper education, live and work in normal society.

It is too late for some of our children, but if their plight can make people realize how unnecessary much of the tragedy is, their lives will not have been meaningless.

There Is *Magic in a Word of Praise*

By Fulton Oursler

A BROADWAY COMEDIAN once had an excruciating nightmare: he dreamed he was telling stories and singing songs in a crowded theater, with thousands of people watching him—but no one laughed or clapped.

"Even at $100,000 a week," he says, "that would be hell on earth."

It is not only the actor who has need for applause. Without encouragement any one of us can lose confidence. Thus we all have a double necessity: to be commended and to know *how* to commend.

There is a technique in giving a compliment, a right way to go about it. It is no real compliment, for instance, to praise a man for some obvious attainment. Use discernment and originality. "That was a wonderfully convincing speech you made tonight," a gracious woman once said to a businessman. "I could not help thinking what a fine lawyer you would have made." The merchant flushed like a schoolboy at the *unexpected* character of the tribute. As André Maurois once remarked: "The general did not thank me when I talked to him of his victories, but his gratitude was unbounded when a lady mentioned the twinkle in his eye."

No one, great or obscure, is untouched by genuine appreciation. Yale's renowned English professor, the late William Lyon Phelps, relates: "One hot summer day I went into a crowded railroad dining car for lunch. When the steward handed me the menu, I said, 'The boys in the kitchen certainly must be suffering today!' The steward looked at me in surprise. 'People come in here and complain about the food, kick about the service and growl about the heat. In 19 years you are the first person who has ever expressed any sympathy for the cooks back there in the kitchen.' What people want," Mr. Phelps concluded, "is a little attention as human beings."

In that attention, sincerity is essential. For it is sincerity—unmixed with the possibility of flattery—which gives potency to a compliment. The man coming home after a hard day's work, who sees the faces of his children pressed against the windowpane, waiting and watching for him, may water his soul with their silent but golden opinion.

The simple principles of the art of praise—to realize the human need for it, to compliment sincerely, and to train ourselves to look for the praiseworthy—help rub off the sharp edges of daily contact. And nowhere is this more true than in marriage. The wife or husband who is alert to say the heartening thing at the right moment has taken out valuable marriage insurance.

Women seem to have an instinct for such things; they look at life, so to speak, through their hearts. Lyon Mearson, the author, and Rose, his wife, were married on February 23. "Well," remarked Lyon, "I will never forget our wedding anniversary. It will always be the day after Washington's Birthday." "And I," his bride answered, "will never forget Washington's Birthday. It will always be the day before we were married."

One night Sir Max Beerbohm went with his aging wife to a theatrical party in London. As they entered the room he was ambushed by a horde of stage and film beauties, all eager to impress the great critic and caricaturist. Beerbohm turned to the lady on his arm: "My dear, let's find a quiet corner. You are looking so charming tonight that I want to talk to you alone."

Children especially are hungry for reassurance, and the want of kindly appreciation in childhood can be a lifetime calamity. A young mother told the Rev. A. W. Beaven of a heartaching incident:

"My little daughter often misbehaves and I have to rebuke her. But one day she had been an especially good girl, hadn't done a single thing that called for reprimand. That night, after I tucked her in bed and started down the stairs, I heard her sobbing. Turning back, I found her head buried in the pillow. Between sobs she asked, 'Haven't I been a *pretty* good girl today?'

"That question," said the mother, "went through me like a knife. I had been quick enough to correct her when she did wrong, but when she had tried to behave I had not noticed it. I had put her to bed without one word of appreciation."

The same principle—using the kind word—is potent in all human relationships. In my boyhood in Baltimore, a new drugstore opened in the neighborhood, and old Pyke Barlow, our skilled and long-established pharmacist, was outraged. He accused his young rival of selling cheap drugs and of being inexperienced in compounding prescriptions. Finally the injured newcomer, contemplating a suit for slander, consulted a wise lawyer, Thomas G. Hays. "Don't make an issue of it," Hays advised. "Try kindness."

Next day, when customers reported his rival's attacks, the new druggist said there must be a mistake somewhere. "Pyke Barlow," he told them, "is one of the finest pharmacists in this town. He'll mix an emergency prescription any hour, day or night, and the care he takes with them sets an example for all of us. This neighborhood has grown —there's plenty of room for both of us. I'm taking Doc's store as the pattern for mine."

When the older man heard these remarks—because compliments fly on the winds of gossip quite as fast as scandal—he could not wait to meet the young fellow face to face and give him some helpful advice. The feud had been wiped out by sincere and truthful praise.

Wherever human beings gather, thoughtfulness is needed. In a group conversation the kind person will help everyone to feel a part of the discussion. A friend once paid this tribute to Prime Minister Balfour as a dinner host: "He would take the hesitating remark of a shy man and discover in it unexpected possibilities, would expand it until its author felt he had really made some contribution to human wisdom. Guests would leave, walking on air, convinced that they were bigger men than they had thought."

Why must most of us leave unuttered some pleasant truths that would make others happy? It would help if we remembered more often that "a rose to the living is more than sumptuous wreaths to the dead." A charming old gentleman used to drop in occasionally at an antique shop near Conway, N. H., to sell merchandise. One day after he left, the antique dealer's wife said she wished they had told him how much they enjoyed his visits. The husband replied, "Next time let's tell him so." The following summer a young woman came in and introduced herself as the daughter of the salesman. Her father, she said, had died. Then the wife told her of the conversation she and her husband had had after her father's last visit. The visitor's eyes filled with tears. "How much good that would have done my father!" she exclaimed. "He was a man who needed to be reassured that he was liked."

"Since that day," says the shop-owner, "whenever I think something particularly nice about a person, I tell him. I might never have another chance."

As the painter, the musician and all other artists find joy in giving beauty to others, so anyone who masters the art of praising will find that it blesses the giver quite as much as the receiver. It brings warmth and pleasure into commonplaces and turns the noisy rattle of the world into music.

Something good can be said about everyone. We have only to say it.

Dearly Beloved

Mark Twain's courtship of his beloved "Livy" by no means ended with their marriage. He wrote her love letters almost every day when he was separated from her, sometimes four letters in a single day. And even when he was home he wrote to her—little notes, to be put on her breakfast tray, or longer missives slipped into her hand. This is what he wrote on November 27, 1885, her 40th birthday and the 17th anniversary of their becoming engaged:

"We have reached another milestone, my darling, and a very, very remote one from the place whence we started; but we look back over a pleasant landscape—valleys that are still green, plains that still bear flowers, hills that still sleep in the soft light of that far morning of blessed memory. And here we have company on the journey—ah, such precious company, such inspiring, such lovely, and gracious company! And how they lighten the march! Our faces are toward the sunset, now, but these are with us, to hold our hands, and stay our feet, and while they abide, and our old love grows and never diminishes, our march shall still be through flowers and green fields, and the evening light as pleasant as that old soft morning glow yonder behind.   YOUR HUSBAND"

— The Love Letters of Mark Twain,
edited by Dixon Wecter, as quoted in *The Atlantic Monthly*

Do the Thing You Fear

By Henry C. Link, Ph.D.

Director of the Psychological Service Center, New York City,
and author of "The Return to Religion"

*I*T IS with some hesitancy that I write on the subject of fears because, unquestionably, many of the fears from which people now suffer are due to the voluminous writings on this subject. I wish, for example, that the term *inferiority complex* had never been printed, because then millions of people would not even know they had an inferiority complex. There would be one less idea for them to fear.

Most fears are actually generated by too much reading, thinking and talking. They do not, as a rule, just happen. We nurse them and feed them until, from an inconsequential trifle, they have grown to monstrous proportions. The mother who avidly reads the extensive literature on bringing up children becomes increasingly fearful of how to deal with them, and well she may. The young woman too fussy about her appearance soon worries too much over what people will think of her. Groups of people who learnedly discuss the state of the country often turn pessimism into fear.

Before me as I write is a letter from a young woman, beginning: "Ever since I was 16 years old I have been afraid to converse in a strange group." The letter goes on to enumerate other fears—fear of her employer, fear of losing her job, a fear of men, fear of driving a car, fear to make a report at a girls' club, and others to the total of 11. All of them are fears on a common level, experienced by millions of people. In almost every case, the result of these fears is the same— a sort of creeping paralysis, a feeling of misery, of suffocation, of panic, of defeat.

A young man told me that he could not sleep. He gave me a long psychological explanation of how this had come about. "Can you help me get rid of this obsession?" he asked. "No," was my reply. "Then what can I do?" he implored. "Run around the block at night until you are ready to drop. What you need is exertion. You have put too much of your physical energies into imagining things. If you run hard enough, you will automatically relax and go to sleep. You have thought yourself into this fear with your mind, you can run yourself out of it with your legs"—and he did.

A mother not long ago gave this significant summary of her life: "As a young woman I was troubled with many fears, one of which was the fear of insanity. After my marriage these fears still persisted. However, we soon had a child, and ended by having six. Whenever I started to worry, the baby would cry or the children would quarrel and I would have to straighten them out. Or I would suddenly remember that it was time to start dinner, or that the ironing had to be done. My fears about myself were being continually interrupted by family duties, and gradually they disappeared. Now I look back on them with amusement."

The moral of this episode may not be to have six children, but it is true that the smaller families and increased leisure of our time are conducive to the generation of fears. It is equally true that many people who are obsessed by nagging fears might find a new interest in life if they became concerned *about other people* through participation in community activities.

You don't like such activities? Then you must remember that every step in the conquest of fear requires, at the outset, an act of will. Those who have learned to dive remember the process. You got yourself poised, then leaned forward, hesitated, and drew back in fear. Again you made the attempt and withdrew. With each hesitation your fears mounted. Finally, in angry disgust with yourself, you plunged in, arms and legs askew, and with a terrific flop. You came up chagrined and embarrassed, the laughter of your friends making you feel still worse. If, at this point, your fears had prevented you from making further attempts, you might never have learned to dive; your fears might have become insurmountable. If, however, you persisted, and continued to make awkward and painful dives, you finally went in smoothly and came up feeling pleased. You were on the way to becoming an expert.

This is the basic psychology of overcoming fear and gaining confidence in every phase of life, *and there is no escape from this process.* Again and again we must plunge into the stream of life, adding one conquest to another, overcoming first this fear and then that. As Emerson said, do the thing you fear and the death of fear is certain. Actually our fears are the forces that make us, when dealt with by decisive action, or that break us if dealt with by indecision, procrastination and ratiocination.

A young man not long ago asked me to suggest some difficult things for him to do. "Your book recommends," he said, "such activities as dancing, basketball or some competitive sport, bridge, parties and games. It says a person should do such things even though he dislikes them. I not only disliked but was afraid to do these things. However, I made up my mind to try them. For a while I had a terrible time, I was miserable. But before long I lost my fears and actually began to like these new activities. In fact, I am enjoying my new life so much that I am in danger of getting soft. I wish you would tell me some things to do which I would really find difficult."

This young man had learned the lesson of using his fears as a means to conquest and livelier enjoyment. He was headed for a fuller and more effective life, both socially and intellectually.

The first step in overcoming fear is sometimes a very elementary process. I remember a certain young man so overwhelmed with various fears that he could scarcely talk audibly. He worked in a large bank and knew a dozen men in his department, but as he went to his desk in the morning he greeted no one. We suggested that he begin by saying a hearty "Good morning, Frank! Hello, Keating! Good morning, Mr. Eaton," to the men as he passed. He tried it with such gratifying results that he was encouraged to try more difficult tasks, one conquest leading to another.

The more general fears—of insanity, of persecution, of strangers, of inferiority, are usually the result of one's failure to conquer enough minor fears by such practice. Sometimes, however, they are due to the fact that a person for some reason—disappointment in love, the death of a dear relative, financial reverses, loss of a job—withdraws from his accustomed activities. After a catastrophe, especially, one should not only keep up old activities but bend his will and energies toward beginning some new and preferably strenuous pursuit. After losing his position, a man of 56 who had been with one company for 30 years began to mope and to withdraw from all contacts with his former friends. Within six months he had become a bundle of fears, both small and great. Finally he was persuaded to visit a relative living on a farm. Soon he was drawn into the routine of the establishment. In six months he was himself again.

Although generalizations are dangerous, I venture to say that at the bottom of most fears, both mild and severe, will be found an overactive mind and an underactive body. Hence, I have advised many people to use their heads less and their arms and legs more—in useful work or play. We generate fears while we sit; we overcome them by action. Fear is nature's warning signal to get busy.

In its mild and initial stages, fear takes the form of aversion to, or criticism of, certain activities and people, constituting an alibi by which the individual justifies his continued inaction. The world is full of malcontents, parlor communists and social theorists who, because they will not change themselves, talk about changing the entire system. Many of them do not seem to realize that in any social order whatsoever there would still be misfits. Through conversation they rationalize their anger with the world, instead of becoming enraged with themselves and flying into worth-while action.

Father Knows Best

WHEN the last guest had gone after the wedding of my youngest daughter, I sat down in the living room and wept bitterly. I felt utterly bereft. For 25 years my three girls—their health, education, clothes, friends and pleasures—had completely absorbed my time, energy and thought.

My husband, whistling softly, strolled in. "Oh, Tom," I sobbed, "what am I going to do? All three of the children gone!"

There was a moment's silence, then my husband asked, "Has it ever occurred to you that you might try getting married?"

—Contributed by Elizabeth Williams Cosgrove

One of the world's eminent men challenges
us to seek adventures for the soul

Your Second Job

By Dr. Albert Schweitzer

As told to Fulton Oursler

OFTEN people say: I would like to do some good in the world. But with so many responsibilities at home and in business, my nose is always to the grindstone. I am sunk in my own petty affairs, and there is no chance for my life to mean anything."

This is a common and dangerous error. In helpfulness to others, every man can find on his own doorstep adventures for the soul—our surest source of true peace and lifelong satisfaction. To know this happiness, one does not have to neglect duties or do spectacular things.

This career for the spirit I call "your second job." In this there is no pay except the privilege of doing it. In it you will encounter noble chances and find deep strength. Here all your reserve power can be put to work, for what the world lacks most today is men who occupy themselves with the needs of other men. In this unselfish labor a blessing falls on both the helper and the helped.

Without such spiritual adventures the man or woman of today walks in darkness. In the pressures of modern society we tend to lose our individuality. Our craving for creation and self-expression is stifled; true civilization is to that extent retarded.

What is the remedy? No matter how busy one is, any human being can assert his personality by seizing every opportunity for spiritual activity. How? By his second job: by means of personal action, on however small a scale, for the good of his fellow men. He will not have to look far for opportunities.

Our greatest mistake, as individuals, is that we walk through our life with closed eyes and do not notice our chances. As soon as we open our eyes and deliberately search we see many who need help, not in big things but in the littlest things. Wherever a man turns he can find someone who needs him.

One day I was traveling through Germany in a third-class railway carriage beside an eager youth who sat as if looking for something unseen. Facing him was a fretful and plainly worried old man. Presently the lad remarked that it would be dark before we reached the nearest large city.

"I don't know what I shall do when we get there," said the old man anxiously. "My only son is in the hospital, very ill. I had a telegram to come at once. I must see him before he dies. But I am from the country and I'm afraid I shall get lost in the city."

To which the young man replied, "I know the city well. I will get off with you and take you to your son. Then I will catch a later train."

As they left the compartment they walked together like brothers.

Who can assay the effect of that small kind deed? You, too, can watch for the little things that need to be done.

During the First World War a cockney cab driver was declared too old for military service. From one bureau to another he went, offering to make himself useful in spare time and always being turned away. Finally he gave himself his own commission. Soldiers from out-of-town camps were being allowed leave in the city before going to the front. So at eight o'clock the old cabby appeared at a railroad station and looked for puzzled troopers. Four or five times every night, right up to demobilization, he served as a volunteer guide through the maze of London streets.

From a feeling of embarrassment, we hesitate to approach a stranger. The fear of being repulsed is the cause of a great deal of coldness in the world; when we seem indifferent we are often merely timid. The adventurous soul must break that barrier, resolving in advance not to mind a rebuff. If we dare with wisdom, always maintaining a certain

reserve in our ap-
proach, we find that
when we open our-
selves we open doors
in others.

Especially in great
cities do the doors of
the heart need to be
opened. Love is always
lonely in crowds.
Country and village
people know each
other and realize some
common dependence,
but the inhabitants of

> Dr. Albert Schweitzer achieved fame in diverse fields—as one of the best of modern biographers, as the first concert organist of Europe, and as the most eminent Protestant Bible scholar in the world. His books on philosophy profoundly influenced university teaching everywhere. Yet Schweitzer, musician, philosopher, biographer and theologian, has also become one of the world's great surgeons as well as the pre-eminent Christian missionary of his time. In the midst of his European career, he renounced fame and income in order to study medicine and devote his life to helping the natives of Africa.

cities are strangers who pass without salute—so isolated, so separate, often so lost and despairing. What a stupendous opportunity is waiting there for men and women who are willing to be simply human!

Begin anywhere—in office, factory, subway. There may have been smiles across a streetcar aisle that stayed the purpose of a suicide. Often a friendly glance is like a single ray of sunshine, piercing a darkness we ourselves may not dream is there.

As I look back upon my youth I realize how important to me were the help, understanding and courage, the gentleness and wisdom so many people gave me. These men and women entered into my life and became powers within me. But they never knew it. Nor did I perceive the real significance of their help at the time.

We all owe so much to others; and we may well ask ourselves, what will others owe to *us*? The complete answer must remain hidden from us, although we are often allowed to see some little fraction of it so that we may not lose courage. You may be sure, however, that the effect of your own life on those around you is—or can be—great indeed.

Whatever you have received more than others—in health, in talents, in ability, in success, in a pleasant childhood, in harmonious conditions of home life—all this you must not take to yourself as a matter of course. In gratitude for your good fortune, you must render in return some sacrifice of your own life for other life.

For those who have suffered in special ways there are special opportunities. For example, there is the fellowship of those who bear the mark of pain. If you have been delivered from bodily anguish, you must not think you are free. From that moment on, you feel bound to help to bring others to deliverance. If an operation has saved you from death or torture, do your part to make it possible for medical science to reach some other place where death and agony still rule unhindered. So with the mother whose child has been saved, and the children whose father's last torment was made tolerable by a doctor's skill; all must join in seeing to it that others may know those blessings also.

In renunciation and sacrifice we must give, most of all, of ourselves. To hand ten dollars to someone who needs it is not a sacrifice if you can well afford the money. The widow's mite was worth more than all the rich men's donations because her mite was her all. In our own ways we must give something that it is a wrench to part with, if it is only time from the cinema, from favorite games or from our other pleasures.

I hear people say: "Oh, if I were only rich, I would do great things to help people." But we all *can* be rich in love and generosity. Moreover, if we give with care, if we find out the exact wants of those who need our help most, we are giving our own loving interest and concern, which is worth more than all the money in the world.

Organized welfare work is, of course, necessary; but the gaps in it must be filled by personal service, performed with loving kindness. A charitable organization is a complex affair; like an automobile, it needs a broad highway to run on. It cannot penetrate the little bypaths; those are for men and women to walk through, with open eyes and hearts full of comprehension.

We cannot abdicate our conscience to an organization, nor to a government. "Am I my brother's keeper?" Most certainly I am! I cannot escape my responsibility by saying the State will do all that is necessary. It is a tragedy that nowadays so many think otherwise.

Even in family life children are coming to believe they do not have to take care of the old folks. But old-age pensions do not relieve children of their duties. To dehumanize such care is wrong because it abolishes the principle of love, which is the foundation in upbuilding human beings and civilization itself.

Tenderness toward those weaker than ourselves strengthens the heart toward life itself. We do terrible things to each other because we do not have comprehension and pity. The moment we understand and feel sorry for the next man and forgive him, we wash ourselves, and it is a cleaner world.

But why must I forgive my fellow man?

Because, if I do not forgive everyone, I shall be untrue to myself. I shall then be acting as if I were innocent of the same offenses, and I am not. I must forgive lies directed against me because so many times my own conduct has been blotted by lies. I must forgive the loveless-ness, the hatred, the slander, the fraud, the arrogance which I encounter, since I myself have so often lacked love, and have hated, slandered, de-frauded and been arrogant. And I must forgive without noise or fuss. In general, I do not succeed in forgiving fully; I do not even get as far as being always just. But he who tries to live by this principle will know the real adventures and triumphs of the soul.

A man has done us a wrong. Are we to wait for him to ask our for-giveness? No! He may never ask pardon and then we shall never forgive, which is evil. No, let us simply say: "It does not exist!"

In a railway station I watch a man with dustpan and broom sweeping up refuse in the waiting room. He cleans up a portion, then moves on to the next. But let him look back over his shoulder and he will behold a man throwing a cigar stump on the floor, a child scattering paper around—more litter accumulating where a moment before he had it all swept clean. Yet he has to go right on with his work and feel no rage. So must we all! In my personal relations with people I must never be without my pan and broom. I must continually clean up the litter. I must rid myself of useless things. If the leaves do not drop off the trees in autumn, there will be no room for new leaves in the spring.

You may think it is a wonderful life my wife and I have in the equa-torial jungle. But you can have a still more wonderful life by staying where you happen to be and putting your soul to the test in a thousand little trials, and winning triumphs of love. Such a career of the spirit demands patience, devotion, daring. It calls for strength of will and the determination to love: the greatest test of a man. But in this hard "second job" is to be found the only true happiness.

Learn to Live with Your Nerves

By Walter C. Alvarez, M.D.

A condensation from the book

To LIVE easily with your nerves, the first thing is to get acquainted with the ways in which they play tricks on you. Often I must say to a worried patient, "There is nothing seriously wrong with you; your symptoms are all produced by your erratic nerves." And the patient will ask, "But why do they play such tricks?"

Often the most distressing spells follow a trying experience, a sleepless night, a tiring day. For instance, a businessman began to suffer severe heart palpitation the day he had to face the unpleasant task of dismissing an old employe. A woman who woke one night with the feeling that she was strangling had spent the evening arguing angrily with a relative over money. One can easily see why the nerves of these persons were on edge and ready to go on a rampage.

Many times, however, the storm seems to come out of a clear sky. A highly nervous woman tells me that her life is easy—she has a loving husband, a comfortable home, good children, no worries. Why, then, should she have spells in which she is jittery, terribly tired, apprehensive or depressed? Usually in such cases I find marked nervousness in the family. Let us say that you have inherited your father's quick temper or your mother's tendency to worry. You cannot entirely get rid of these tendencies, but you can learn to control them and to live with them better.

When, as a young man, I faced failure and poor health because of my inheritance of my mother's bad nerves, I resolved that I would do the many wise things she did, but I would struggle hard never to do the foolish things she did, such as worrying and fretting and living life the hard way. I decided I would hoard my energies. And when I did, I found I had enough for two jobs: one earning a living and the other doing research, writing, teaching and lecturing. I even had enough left over for hobbies. Someone once said our relatives are given us to show us what we shouldn't do and be!

Learn to keep your nervous system as fit as possible with the help of good mental hygiene. By this I mean living sensibly—getting the proper amount of sleep and rest and recreation. People forget that the brain is a delicate and complicated bit of apparatus, and that it should be given care and consideration. Today many of us work too long hours, then stay up much too late. We would be much healthier if we were always in bed by 10 p. m. Our vacations may be so strenuous that we get no real rest or recreation and do not store up energy. Many people, also, abuse their nerves by smoking and drinking too much.

Many nervous persons wear themselves out on nonessential activities. They put too much energy and thought into doing things that another person does almost automatically. That is why they get so little done and become so terribly tired doing it. Dr. W. J. Mayo, carrying on a huge surgical and consultant practice, administering and building up a huge institution, lecturing and writing and serving on many boards, never seemed hurried or impatient. As he once told me, he tried never to waste energy or emotion on things that did not count.

Years ago a woman gave me the key to nervous breakdowns. I asked her why she, who had wealth and little to do, was so worn out. She said, "I wear *myself* out." She wore herself out with petty worries.

Often I find people wasting energy on needless conflicts—especially with themselves. They are full of resentments, animosities, hates, jealousies, envies. Blessed is the man or woman who goes through life easily—not irritable, touchy, impatient, irascible. It is wonderful how helpful this way of life is to the nervous system; and it is wonderful how much energy it leaves free for useful work.

I admire my sensible daughter who is never ruffled by the ceaseless activity of her two little boys. She says, "I would much rather have them active and into everything than sickly or apathetic." One day when she left a can of paint within reach of the baby, and he spilled it on the floor, her only comment was that she should have had more sense than to leave it where he could reach it. As a result of such serenity, she always has energy to spare to run a house, play tennis, swim and engage in civic affairs.

If we want calm nerves we must not nurse resentments and jealousies or indulge in envy. In every business one can find envious men who spend more time trying to hold back the leaders among their associates than they spend in studying and working to advance themselves. How much energy they waste and how bad it is for their nerves! I have seen envy of this type wreck a man's health.

One of the greatest curses of life today, and one of the greatest breeders of nervousness, is working under tension. The late Stewart Edward White once built himself a cabin in the California Sierras. An old mountaineer used to come and watch him. One day, as White was sawing violently at a log, the mountaineer remarked that White sawed like all city fellows, going as fast as he could to get the log sawed. "Now," said the old man, "when *I* saw, I just saws."

All of us with tense nerves could almost cure ourselves by learning to "just saw." We must learn to tackle just the job in hand and stay with it quietly. I often have said to my secretary, if she could see in one pile all the letters she is going to write in the next ten years, she might want to jump out the window. But by writing them one at a time, the job is bearable.

When Will Rogers was asked what he'd do if he had only five days to live, he said he'd live each day one at a time. All of us would do well to learn to live each day in a sort of compartment, not weeping over the mistakes of the past or holding constant post-mortems over them, and not worrying about the morrow. A man can work efficiently in this way. All he needs then is to do quickly and as well as possible the work that lies right at hand. It is helpful, also, to learn to tackle a difficult job without hesitation and get it done. Many nervous persons break down after putting off work that must be done.

The same goes for indecision. Nervous persons could save themselves worlds of now-wasted energy if they would only learn to make decisions quickly—and make them stick. Mayor LaGuardia used to call after a man who had just gotten a decision from him about a matter, "And don't bring that back to me!"

A wonderful saver of energy is Sir William Osler's trick which he called "burning one's own smoke." He meant that we should not indulge in the miserable habit of taking out on others our discomforts, griefs and annoyances.

I belong to the Sierra Club of California, which each year takes 200 members into the high mountains. Their most important but unwritten bylaw goes something like this: "Thou shalt never utter the least word of complaint if it rains all day and all night, or if the pack train is late and thy food does not arrive until 10 p.m." Many a night I have seen the party wet, cold, hungry and without shelter, but always there was fun and good humor and never any grousing. Among those people to "crab" is the unpardonable sin.

There is another hint that we can take from the teachings of Osler, and that is to cultivate equanimity and serenity. As he said, we must learn not to be too upset by the pinpricks—and even the big shocks—of life. We must learn to take them in our stride. As one writer said so wisely and well: "O Lord, grant me the serenity to accept the things I cannot change; the courage to change the things I can; and the wisdom to know the difference."

What's Luck?

J. J. LERNER, owner of the stores bearing his name, met an admirer of his playwright son, Alan Jay, who authored such delights as *Brigadoon* and *Love Life*. "Isn't it wonderful how lucky your boy is?" said the man.

"Yes," replied Lerner, "isn't it wonderful? The harder he works the luckier he gets." — Walter Winchell

---

The Human Robot

AT A RECENT meeting of air scientists and pilots, the scientists made it clear that they would like to replace the pilot in the aircraft with instruments and servo-mechanisms. Scott Crossfield, a U. S. test pilot who has flown the Douglas Skyrocket at 1327 m.p.h., rejoined by asking:

"Where can you find another non-linear servo-mechanism weighing only 150 pounds and having great adaptability that can be produced so cheaply by completely unskilled labor?"

—New York *Times*, quoted in *Business Week*

How to Write a Letter

By Cameron Shipp

Condensed from The Christian Science Monitor

ᴇᴄᴇɴᴛʟʏ a man I know scrawled on the back of his bank statement: "We are eating three times a day. How are you?" and mailed it to me.

Not many of us have the nerve or the wit to send our bank statement to a friend instead of the letter we have been putting off for weeks. But this man could not have written a more interesting letter if he had polished phrases for hours. My family and I put in an evening trying to figure out his income and how he spent his money — which was precisely what he had intended.

Why is it so difficult for us to write a few short words on a piece of paper? Why is it that a man who is interesting when you meet him becomes as inarticulate as a fish the moment he takes pen in hand? And why does the brightest, friendliest woman you know swear she'd rather slave in a salt mine than write a letter? Why do *you* hate to write letters?

I think I know. We have been taught that letter writing is a formal thing, like drawing up one's will; that letters must be written on proper paper, with stately salutations and false-modest endings. We have been made to feel that a letter — even to an old friend or relative — has to be a *society* gesture, else the person who receives it will conclude that we don't know the rules of polite social behavior.

Two other reasons, I believe, why we shudder at the thought of writing a letter are: (1) I can't think of anything to say. (2) Who stole my pen? Nonsense!

Consider Richard Armour, who heads a department at Scripps College; he is one of our most prolific writers of light verse, is active in the military reserves and travels widely as a lecturer. Busy man, obviously. Yet he is a faithful, constant correspondent who turns out an average of a dozen written messages a day to friends and business acquaintances.

I said "written messages" because Armour seldom writes letters. He has discovered the postcard. He knows he seldom has anything to say that can't be put in less than 100 words, and he generally stays within 20. No salutation, no closing. Just:

"Good to see you last week. Kathleen and I leaving for San Francisco tomorrow. Agent likes my new book. Call you Monday when we return. Dick."

No literary pretensions. Just 25 words typed on a postcard, but how effective! He recalled a pleasant meeting, gave me two pieces of news, made an appointment. Most important, he kept in touch, let me know he had me in mind. This cost Armour two cents in money and perhaps one minute of time. If he can get away with this sort of thing, why not you?

One of the most famous letter writers in America today is the novelist and humorist, Homer Croy. It was he who sent me his bank statement. His letters seldom run more than a dozen words.

Homer understands the fundamental fact of friendship: you must share your experiences. He often types or scrawls his lines on the backs of letters that people have written him. A recent example: "Cam—I saw Dale yesterday and we mentioned your name. Favorably, too. H. C." Just 12 words. He had seen an old friend and they had talked about me. He knew that I could read between the lines of this casual, un-newsworthy hail much that he did not need to say.

I turned the letter over. There was a note from a magazine editor accepting a story Croy had written. Mentioned the price, too. Croy had let me look over his shoulder, had shared an experience with me. Anybody can do the same.

My Aunt Margaret in North Carolina once sent me a receipted bill for her new hat which had cost $28.75. On the reverse side she wrote "Whee!"

How much more eloquent and exciting that one word than eight or nine pages about Aunt Margaret's sinus, her recalcitrant tulips or her reasons for not having written sooner. I got a job, once, through a one-word letter. I had called several times on the late W. C. Dowd, Jr., publisher of the Charlotte *News*, but he had no opening. Three months later, from another city, I wrote him:

> Dear Mr. Dowd:
> Yes?
> Sincerely,
> Cameron Shipp.

Mr. Dowd hired me, apparently believing that brevity might be a good thing in a reporter.

One friend of mine is a newspaper clipper. My name seldom appears in newspapers, but if it does and he sees it, he clips and mails it to me. But he is more likely to send along something about my home state, North Carolina, or about fruit trees in which I once had a disastrously expensive interest. It's surely one of the shortest and happiest ways to get around writing a letter.

Business letters are a special department, and a big one. Experts are cleaning up the correspondence of many corporations, eliminating hackneyed phrases, encouraging informality. There is even a movement afoot to delete the absurd "dear." Why, indeed, call a man "dear" when you are about to complain that his company has been negligent with your order? Why call anybody "dear" except your own sweetie-pie?

One type of letter which troubles everybody is the letter of condolence. It is the hardest of all to write, but here especially the rule of brevity applies. Don't try to write a "beautiful" letter, or inscribe a "tribute" or an epitaph. Don't describe your own shock and amazement. And don't go overboard about religion. If your friend is religious he already has that best of all comforts; if not, his clergyman can express it better than you can.

The best letter of condolence I ever received said merely: "You know how sorry I am. Is there anything I can do?" There's not much more that anybody can say.

To sum it all up, here are a few simple rules about letter writing:

First: Be brief.

Second: Offer a piece of news or enclose something, such as a clipping, that will interest your friend.

Third: Don't try to show off your literary ability. Literary people seldom write "literary" letters.

Fourth: Forget the book of etiquette. Be informal, spontaneous, even unconventional. Be funny if you can, but don't try too hard.

Fifth: Write at least a few lines every day. There's always a pencil in the house. (There's no law requiring you to use pen and ink.)

Sixth: Use postcards liberally. They are the greatest advance in cheap communication since the smoke signal.

Seventh: Start now.

→⫸ ⫷←

That's My Pop!

Hundreds of children sent in letters for the Milwaukee *Sentinel's* "My Pop's Tops" contest. Here are quotations from some of them:

"We have such good fun with my daddy that I wisht I had knew him sooner."

"My Pop's Tops because he always takes good care of us children when my mother is in the hospital getting another. I have eight brothers and four sisters and know from experience."

"He taked me fishin he taked me hunting, once he even taked me to the burlest show. It was wonderful."

"I don't have no real father because he went away when I was young, but now I have got two fathers, both very good."

"He wants me to learn. Once he took me to Fence Lake and thrun me in to see if I could swim and I couldn't. He saved me, too."

"All Pops are tops. If we didn't have Pops where would we be?"

"He is a farmer. He smells like a cow and when I smell that cow in the house I know Pop is home and I am glad."

"My Pop is tops because every time I ast him for a knickel he will start preaching that when he was a boy he had to earn his kenickls and at the same time he is putting his hand in his pocket and pulls out a kinckel, saying this is the last kinkel I have."

"My Pop's tops because he was a brave soldier. He didn't see me until I was three years old yet he is just as good to me as if he knew me all my life."

—Charles House in Milwaukee *Sentinel*

A LITTLE PIECE OF LIGHT

By *Thomas Sugrue*

Condensed from Christian Herald

WHEN I was of bicycle age I knew a woman who had more troubles than anyone else in town. Her children were a laboratory for accident and disease; her own health teetered continuously on the edge; her husband was an inept man who could stumble over his own feet and believe he had been tripped. Yet none of this misery seemed to afflict her disposition. Her hair turned white and her face became thin, but her eyes stayed bright and when she smiled the air around her filled with something that felt like a warm sweater on a cold day.

I often carried medicines to her from the drugstore. One day after I had expressed sympathy for her latest misfortune, I said, before I could stop myself, "Gosh, ma'am, how do you stand it?"

She turned her smile on me. "I have a secret helper," she said. "I was raised on a farm, with three younger brothers. My mother had the care of all of us, and lots of farm work besides. When I was seven, on a freezing winter afternoon things got worse than ever. A cow was ailing, the water in the pump froze, and two of my brothers were sick. I was frantic with worry for my mother, and determined to help her. I came into the kitchen carrying a pail which I had filled with snow to melt for water to wash the dishes.

"My mother looked at the pail of snow and began to laugh. Then she cried a little. Then she kissed me, took me by the hand and said, 'You and I are going to sit down and have a cup of tea together.'

"She made tea from the snow water, and we sat at the kitchen table and drank it. It was my first cup of tea.

"That is my secret helper—that scene in the kitchen. Whenever I feel discouraged or very tired, I think of it, and I begin to laugh, and then to cry a little—it's good to cry now and then—and I sit down and make myself a cup of tea. When it's finished I'm ready to pull my apron tight and get on with what needs to be done."

She turned from the door. "Come in. We'll have a cup together right now." When I left she pushed her fingers through my hair and said, "A happy memory is the most valuable thing in the world."

Memory has always been man's true friend. Yet in our age of psychology, memory is regarded as a hiding place for the hurts of childhood, a jungle in which the psychologist hunts for wolves of fear and snakes of anxiety.

Actually, most of any man's memory is a record of his mediocre efforts to be a better and more admirable human being. There are painful incidents he does not want to face; but there are also, if he looks for them, happy memories—moments when time's aperture is widened suddenly and the full sweep of life's plan comes into view.

These moments occur most often when we are doing casual, routine things. We see a taxi driver helping an old lady, a child talking rapidly to herself as she walks home from school, a flight of geese on the way south, the passage of summer wind through a field of wheat. It is never an unusual thing; it is an ordinary scene in an ordinary day, which, in an instant when the mind is open to impressions, strikes through to the screen of the soul and leaves its image.

Too often we disdain such memories because they are "sentimental." We should honor them because they are true. In each of us there is at least one of these happy memories—waiting to give joy and confidence to us again and again, if we will accept it.

Mine came to me 13 years ago, in the spring of 1940. We were living in Virginia, on the coast. I was very ill; I could not get out of bed or do anything at all to help myself. In mind and spirit I was desolate. I lay in a bedroom which overlooked the sea. Across the street was a small Catholic chapel, and early each morning I heard, through my open window, the voice of Father Brennan saying Mass in his strong, musical brogue. One afternoon he visited me and I asked if he would bring me Communion after Mass on the following day. He said he would, and early next morning my wife covered my bedside table with a linen cloth and placed on it a lighted candle.

It was a dark morning, filled with mist. As I watched the flame of the candle the door to my room opened, slowly and very softly, and my little daughter, Patsy, let herself in. I watched her as she looked at the candle. She had never seen one before and the sight transfixed her.

She was then two years and four months old. Her hair was the color of corn silk. Her mother had dressed her in corduroy overalls and a sweat shirt; on the back of her head was a cut-down freshman cap from the university nearby. As the flame of the candle paddled back and forth against the darkness of the room, light and shadow played on her cheeks and over the white wall of her forehead.

She stared for what seemed a long time, then whispered, as if to herself, "Oh! It's a little piece of light!"

She turned to me and scrambled up on the bed. She pointed to the candle. "What is that?"

"It is a candle." Because I wanted her to know that she was right, I added, "A candle is a little piece of light."

We both watched the candle flame until I heard the chapel door slam and the sound of Father Brennan's footsteps across the road.

"Father Brennan is coming to bring you the Dear Lord?" she asked.

"Yes," I said.

She slid off the bed, leaving the room as quietly as she had come. In a minute Father Brennan's hand was on the doorknob.

"An Irish morning," he said. "The mist is like a prayer."

He was not with me long. He had blown the flame of the candle out, and now the mist began to fall away and some of the morning light came into my room. In a little while Patsy returned. She closed the door, then climbed quickly up on the bed.

"Where is the Dear Lord?" she asked.

"He is here," I said, "in my heart."

She put her head on my chest and moved it about until she found the sound of my heart. Her freshman cap fell off and her golden hair splashed over me. After a while she lifted her head.

"Do you hear Him?" I asked.

"Yes," she said. "What does He say?"

There was no time to think: the flicker of a pause would inform her that I was making up something.

"He says He hopes you are happy, and He didn't mean to get you wet in that shower yesterday. He wanted to wait until you got home, but the violets were so thirsty they would not be patient.

"He says there is a lot for Him to do in spring, with the grass and the gardens to be watered, and the farms drink so much He doesn't really know what to do about it. He says He can usually find enough water for the world, though, and enough sunshine, but what He is short of sometimes is love. He wants you to help Him, so if you will love the world He will thank you.

"He wants me to love the world, too. And He is going to see if He can find out what is making me ill, and if He does He will fix it. But I am all right, He says, so long as I have you to look after me."

She gave me a nod of understanding and smiled with that look of motherly tenderness which is natural to all women from birth. The room was filled with light now, and the brilliance attracted her. She slid off the bed and went to a rocking chair that had its back to the window overlooking the sea. She climbed up and stood with her chin and arms on the back, rocking slowly and looking out. The last of the mist fell away.

"The sun is here," she said.

The words made her think of something. "The sun is the Dear Lord's candle?" she asked.

"Yes," I said. "The sun is the Dear Lord's candle."

I watched her as she slowly rocked, and that is the way the memory returns to me now, whenever I have need of it. I see her golden head rocking in the sun, and my mind and spirit are no longer desolate.

There is no time when this happiest of memories is not available to me; I have summoned it while lying in hospital beds, while flying over oceans, while rolling through storms at sea, while facing the afflictions of flesh and mind and emotion which fall on everyone.

THOMAS SUGRUE was smitten by a crippling disease and spent 15 of his 45 years in bed or a wheel chair. Despite this, he traveled through Europe and the Near East in his wheel chair, wrote seven books, gave many lectures. This article, the last he wrote before his death in January, 1953, reveals one source of his strength.

JOURNEY

BEYOND FEAR

By William D. Blair, Jr.

While serving as a war correspondent in Korea for the Baltimore "Sunpapers,"
the author was shot through the lung during a battle for Seoul. After recovery he
was assigned to report activities of U.S. forces in Germany for the same papers.

Condensed from V.F.W. Magazine

A FEW HOURS after arrival in Korea we were on a train, jerking toward the west and the enemy. There had been word of guerrilla activity, and on every flatcar men kept watch on the hills, ready to fire. Sometime during this five-hour journey war came home to us all —war and fear.

It came first to some as they faced the reality of being shot at, of having someone actually trying to kill them. Others felt it first when we passed a hospital train returning from the unknown with its load of silent, bandaged figures; others when they saw two rigid bodies floating slowly down the river which ran close to the tracks. It was only a dull fear, this first feeling, hardly more than an uneasiness. But we were realizing reluctantly that whatever control we had over our destinies was now slipping from us.

Arrival in the combat area did nothing to reassure us. Some wounded soldiers were playing cards on the road near our debarkation point. One of our newly arrived Marines, mustering his self-confidence, jeered:

"Is that the way you people fight a war?"

"This isn't the movies, Marine." The card players were tired but superior. "You'll be goddam lucky to do as well as the 27th!" That was the unit the newcomers were to relieve.

"You the 27th?"

"We're what's left of it."

It was a sobering remark, and with it came, for all of us, the beginning, but only the beginning, of real fear.

There had been hard fighting at Chindong-ni for over a week. A company of the 27th had been cut off and was still surrounded, desperately short of ammunition, water and rations. A number of Marine units were dispatched to effect a rescue. As they set out along a dusty track under a malicious sun there was no conversation. Dungarees grew dark with sweat, and you settled into an automatic slouching pace. Instead of excitement there was lethargy as you plodded past the ruins of Chindong-ni. Past dead, swollen cattle, their legs jutting stiffly in air. Past an ammunition bearer who had fainted from heat exhaustion. And forward into fear, as two hidden machine guns opened fire from the flank.

We stared, ignorantly amazed; then leaped for cover, feeling the sudden singe of terror as we saw the bullets splash dust in the road. This was a deeper fear than before; it wiped out the past and the future—everything except the utter and immediate necessity for safety. Until we found cover we were animals—wild with fear and moving by instinct alone. Once we were in ditches or behind rocks our fear somewhat subsided. But then the officers, swearing, exhorting, brandishing carbines, stood exposed on the road and ordered us up and on.

It is one thing to lie in a snug trench while you listen to the bullets ricocheting from the stones over your head or smacking the turf just beyond; there you are calmly, almost pleasurably, afraid. It is another thing to stand where you can receive a bullet in your stomach—which is now bottomless and sick. The fear that comes then is a frenzied pounding in the breast, a feeling of nakedness, a frantic attempt to blot out everything but the sight of the ground directly ahead and the sound of the voice of command, and to go on and on and on until it's done. In days, or weeks, a fear like that becomes either grim determination, or it festers into panic, hysteria and collapse. It makes man of boy, or child of man.

It's a wonderful thing to discover that you're not as afraid as you thought you'd be. It gives green youths an immeasurable lift in their first days of fire. After these initiations they look at each other and smile; they've shown themselves, maybe for the first time, that they aren't cowards. They can do their duty in spite of their dread. Unfortunately, the discovery loses its potency in repetition: fire fights, patrols, assaults, barrages follow one another in meaningless order, and simple courage isn't enough. Mind and body are worn thin; the last drop of will power is wrung out, and you need something more. Providentially, it comes. A strange emotion, a truly marvelous exhilaration, takes over. Born of the endless fear, it sweeps the endangered along heedless, even fiercely jubilant, to whatever end of the road. For the survivor, the memory of this experience often lingers and wields a powerful influence. It is like a remembered orgy, which exerts a fascination and arouses a craving for more indulgence. Men inflamed by the ecstasy will go back from safety to the battle when for them there is no call.

I think it must be this driving intoxication which inspires heroes, the men who hug grenades to their chests to save their fellows, or dash singly against impregnable enemy positions. It must be the thing that makes warriors—for there are some who enjoy war. There was a young lieutenant, possibly still living, in command of a platoon at the bank of the Nam. Communist raiders were slipping by night into the no-man's-land village on the other side, setting up mortars and machine guns to harass our outposts. The lieutenant crawled out to the village and, alone in a maze of rubble, lay in wait for the raider band. He killed 20 Reds before they could turn and run, and came grinning back to his lines. I think he was as happy at his work as any man I've known.

But the danger-lust is more remarkable in ordinary men, doing their job as best they can and finding no pleasure in it. These the fever can transform into something wholly foreign to their natures. One company of soldiers stayed five days on a ridge surrounded by ten times their number. At night the enemy would slink into their midst, and in the morning crumpled bodies of their comrades would be found with knife wounds in their hearts. Finally a rescue force cut its way through, and the soldiers could fall back. But they seemed to take no joy in their salvation. "They were so doggone mad they didn't care if they *ever* came back!" marveled a member of the relief. The unit to which that company belonged became famous for its ruthless efficiency. Its schooling had been complete.

Green, scared troops approach their first test by fire, and begin to realize how dependent they are on each other. They reappraise each other, and pray fervently every other will turn out true. One man's laxity or weakness can kill all the rest. Afterward the survivors feel a hot pride in their collective achievement and a glow of gratitude and trust for each other. In very little time a bond is forged in a platoon or a company—a bond which is stronger than most family ties, for the price of its dissolution is often death. Transfer a soldier out of a unit like that and he will be acutely unhappy and afraid; in his new place he can't be sure that the men on his right and left will still be there when the assault waves come. Many soldiers, comfortably convalescing from wounds, plead to be sent back to their company. They would rather go back and fight beside their friends than take their full measure of rest, and then risk being sent to a different unit.

The fraternity of such soldiers is infectious; it spreads over a whole combat area. Every man who does his job under fire becomes the brother of every other who is in the same fix. A man passing by my hole may be a stranger, but he's my friend; he is here, being shot at, rained on, deprived of food, water and comfort, and today may be his last as well as mine. After a while you love just about every man you see—each one is suffering for you.

It is a common remark among soldiers that the farther back you go, the less sympathetic are the people. The less hardship the man knows, the less he is driven into the arms of his neighbor, and the more he is just what he was in his peaceful home—self-centered, unfeeling.

Many fears go into being afraid for your life. Perhaps it is all other fears violently mixed in one: Fear that a wife will be a widow, that children will be fatherless. Fear that all the pleasures and joys you find in your life will be felt no more. Fear that you will be judged by your errors; that you will never demonstrate your beliefs.

Sometimes fear becomes so intense that it breeds unaccustomed courage. In the dense fog near Seoul a young soldier found himself alone. The order to pull back somehow never had reached him. He tried, frantically, to follow his comrades, but the mist was like a blindfold. After every brief desperate rush he stopped, uncertain, staring at the little space he could see around him. As panic mounted he heard the scratches of feet against stone, the metallic snick of metal on metal and metal on rock. He had been a soldier long enough, and he knew by the sounds that it wasn't his platoon. The impulse to scream was almost too strong to control, but he bit it down. Miraculously, right there in front of him, loomed a huge boulder. He leaped around it and crouched in the shelter it afforded.

Suddenly two pairs of soft-shoed feet stepped onto the flat rock above his head. Two voices murmured—not in English. His heart was like a pneumatic drill, crashing and blasting its way through his frame; his eyes blurred with stinging tears. Time became meaningless. But the human being can stand no more than so much, and he relaxed slowly. It didn't matter, now, once you knew, and it was so peaceful. Life had seldom given him a sweeter moment than this acceptance of its limit. The young soldier stood up. Careless, and yet strangely confident that his step in the dark would sound like any other, he walked down the hill and through the fields and back to the arms of his brothers.

That, in the end, is how a soldier is made: through fear. Fear for your life—until you are so afraid that you can be afraid no more.

Circumstantial

PEOPLE ARE always blaming their circumstances for what they are. I don't believe in circumstances. The people who get on in this world are the people who look for the circumstances they want, and if they can't find them, make them. —George Bernard Shaw

THERE ARE no circumstances, no matter how unfortunate, that clever people do not extract some advantage from; and none, no matter how fortunate, that the unwise cannot turn to their own disadvantage. —La Rochefoucauld

The "average" man has no physical and mental idiosyncrasies—
but there is no such person

We're All Peculiar

By Roger J. Williams *Director of the Biochemical Institute, University of Texas*

Condensed from "The Human Frontier"

IN OUR APPROACH to various human problems we tend to think of society as composed of average individuals, all more or less alike. But society is composed mostly of abnormal people. For each of us may be regarded as abnormal in one or several respects. And we will come much closer to understanding problems of human relationship if we are aware of the many deep-seated physiological differences that make each of us act, think and feel differently from everyone else.

Take the matter of taste, for example. A large group of scientists tasted phenyl thiocarbimide. It was bitter to some, while many insisted that it was really tasteless. Each group suspected the other either of untruth or of some gross physical abnormality. One man to whom it was tasteless tried to get his wife (to whom it was very bitter) to taste it again and again to convince her of her error. Since such differences are common, and occur in *all* our senses, the incident showed how easily human conflict may arise from physical differences we cannot help.

I know of three people who have a normal sense of smell in most respects but are not able to detect the odor of skunk. And variations in the reaction to color are very wide. Red may accelerate the pulse rate and raise blood pressure while blue may have the opposite effect. Some individuals are unusually sensitive to these stimuli and others relatively indifferent. Thus one man may be thrilled with delight at a colorful sunset while another may not give it a second's thought.

The variations in our eyes give rise to many differences in vision besides the common ones the ordinary oculist observes. The person with poor peripheral vision cannot see anything unless he is looking almost directly at it. If two persons, one with good peripheral vision, one with poor, are looking for an item in the newspaper, the former will be able to find it in a fraction of the time that the other takes. But if they play golf together, the one who has excellent peripheral vision may see *too much* and be distracted. Poor peripheral vision on the part of either pedestrians or drivers is probably an important factor in accidents.

People vary widely in their reactions to drugs. Morphine puts most individuals to sleep, but an occasional individual is stimulated in such a manner that thoughts race through his mind pell-mell, causing great distress. Reactions to caffeine vary so widely that some can sleep soundly after having drunk several cups of strong coffee while others may be kept awake for hours by a portion of a cup. Similarly with nicotine: some people can smoke all day long without becoming ill while others, pharmacologists say, can never get adapted to the free use of tobacco.

For each of us the nervous system functions differently with respect to waking and sleeping rhythms. When we have probed more deeply into the nature of sleep we shall probably find reasonably satisfying answers to the problem which will enable us to make more efficient use of our waking and sleeping hours. But meantime we can cease regarding people who need a great deal of sleep or seem to need almost none as freakish or abnormal.

Sexual patterns also show a wide range of variance. One man in his 30's suffers exhaustion for several days as a result of sexual indulgence. At the other extreme, a man past 70 consults his doctor in fear of impotence because of his inability to perform the sexual act more than twice daily. The many factors involved in a successful marriage and the wide differences already known to exist between individuals make it rather surprising that so many marriages work out as well as they do! But recognition of natural variability and its physiological basis should tend to make members of the partnership more tolerant.

Just as we have tended to judge men and women as "normal" or "subnormal" in physical respects instead of recognizing how variable physical characteristics are, so we have been wide of the mark in judging their relative intelligence. To classify members of the human family as either intelligent or dumb may be convenient for some purposes, but it is not justified by the scientific facts.

Men we rate as brilliant are not necessarily brilliant in every respect. There is no reason for thinking that Albert Einstein's mind is in *every* respect phenomenal. There are plenty of good mathematicians who are relatively poor in mental arithmetic and from stories told of Einstein's boyhood it would appear that he belongs in this group. In fact, as a child he was so slow in learning to talk, his parents feared he might be abnormal.

We can rate individuals on their mental ability at certain specific tasks—their ability as spellers, their ability to memorize, the facility with which they handle numbers. But when it comes to total intelligence we human beings cannot be rated 1, 2, 3, etc., any more than we could rate in the same classification Shetland ponies, race horses and draft horses.

If we wish to be intelligent on the subject of intelligence we must face the fact that each human mind is a mixture of many (perhaps as many as 300) distinct mental abilities, tendencies and traits, any of which we may have in either high or low degree.

Consider the "idiot-savants"—individuals who according to ordinary tests and educational standards are feeble-minded or even idiots. Some of them have remarkable mental powers.

One man of 21 was found by intelligence test to be a low-grade moron. In some phases of intelligence, particularly those which are indispensable for book learning, he had the mental age of a small child. It was observed, however, that he could repair door locks, bicycle bells, almost any mechanical contrivance. He was given the Stenquist Mechanical Aptitude Test; it showed that in mechanical aptitude he was a superior adult. There are records of a considerable number of such people; some of them have developed into highly skilled wood carvers.

A school principal took a feeble-minded youth to a special clinic for examination. Among the tests applied was a structural visualization test involving fitting together irregularly cut segments of a block. It took the principal "18 minutes of unhappy fumbling." The feeble-minded boy did it in one minute.

The "feeble-minded" often have outstanding memories. A feeble-minded boy in an Ohio town memorized the telephone directory and the automobile license numbers of many of the citizens and would call them off on request. A Texas imbecile would ask any man he met the date of his birth, his father's and mother's dates, his wife's maiden name, and so on. Years later he could recite the complete details. His memory was so perfect that he was consulted when the county records were found not to be clear.

These instances demonstrate the independence of the different kinds of mental abilities. Idiot-savants are simply extreme caricatures of you and me and our neighbors and friends—strong in some traits and weak in others. As psychological testing is usually carried out these ups and downs are overlooked. Too much is lumped together and called general intelligence. For purposes of predicting school behavior, conventional tests are generally successful. But they still overlook the significant fact that *individuals possess different mental abilities in highly variable degrees.*

Our failure to pay more attention to individual children in schools has been due in part to the idea of carrying out education on a mass-production basis and attempting to reduce everything to statistics. There are articles and books galore dealing with educating "the child," but the importance of recognizing each child as an individual with widely different aptitudes has rarely been stressed.

One of the functions of education is to help the student find his place in the world. We could start on this problem much earlier than we do. Students go all the way through college without learning what their aptitudes are or what they might be fitted for. I know of one who found out his aptitudes for the first time after college graduation, in an Army examination. If he had been tested in grade school, he could have been saved four years of misdirected study and a good deal of unhappiness.

The need for better understanding of individual differences is great in all activities directed toward improvement of our physical and mental health. But the need is even greater in our management of public affairs.

One of the inevitable results of an increasing knowledge of human beings, I believe, will be an appreciation of the fact that no man is by nature equipped to be *the* leader in every avenue of life.

Society needs leaders badly; leaders in industry, in science, education, government, every other line of human activity. But it doesn't need universal leaders—those who lead, or rather dominate, in every field. No one is able to qualify for such leadership.

Actually dictatorships and unwarranted dominance by individuals arise partly because of our general ignorance of individual limitations. When a human being shows unusual prowess or ability along one line, and thus possibly qualifies for leadership in that field, we can often be led to imagine that these abilities carry over into other fields.

The abuse of power has often come about in this fashion—the individual demonstrates some special ability, often as a maker of speeches, whereupon other virtues and abilities are attributed to him and gradually he becomes an authority and finally *the* authority on all subjects. A better knowledge of the nature of human abilities and of human frailties would make this impossible. It is difficult to imagine a dictatorship arising in a country well informed about the attributes of individual human beings.

Satchel's Secret

IN *Collier's*, Satchel Paige, the St. Louis Browns' pitcher of indeterminate age, gave his six rules for staying young:

1. Avoid fried meats which angry up the blood.

2. If your stomach disputes you, lie down and pacify it with cool thoughts.

3. Keep the juices flowing by jangling around gently as you move.

4. Go very light on the vices, such as carrying on in society. The social ramble ain't restful.

5. Avoid running at all times.

6. Don't look back. Something might be gaining on you.

It's a wise parent who knows how
to encourage a child's hidden talent

Every Child Has a Gift

By Hughes Mearns
Author of "Creative Youth" and "The Creative Adult"

IT WAS over 50 years ago, and I was not much more
than a boy myself when I faced my first class.
I went into teaching simply because the job paid
enough to keep me until I could find something bet-
ter. But those boys and girls captured me at the start. What I began
to learn from them kept me in teaching for the remainder of my
active life.

To relieve their tension at meeting a new teacher, I joked with them
about my own ignorance. They laughed, but not too loud. I asked
them what I was supposed to teach them, and they named some of the
subjects. "Oh, yes, and physiology," one small girl piped up.

"What's that?" I asked.

Laughter, but pleasant and friendly. "It's about the bones," she reported rapidly, "and the blood and the intestines and the stomach."

"Ugh!" I interrupted. That amused them immensely. I pondered,
"Physiology? I don't believe I could even spell the word." Then they
did laugh, a roar and a scream of laughter.

A teacher thrust her head into the room. "Any trouble?" she asked.

"Why, no," I replied.

"I heard a laugh," she snapped.

Later the children told me about whippings at home whenever they
got a low mark in "conduct"—a common practice in the late '90's.

"From now on," I said, "each of you will get the highest mark in
conduct." This had the eventual effect of making that class the best-
behaved in the school. To bring out the best in a child, I was discover-

ing, one must be on his side, a defender against adult-imposed customs aimed at suppressing his good natural instincts.

After school those boys and girls gathered around my desk and stayed until the janitor's sweeping drove them home. In those after-school meetings I came upon a treasure of unsuspected gifts. I found a boy who had invented quick ways of adding. He could add up a column of figures as fast as one could call out the numbers. There was a girl who drew continuously in her beloved sketchbook. I am glad that I did not order her to stop that nonsense and attend to me! The famous William Chase later opened to her a career as a portrait painter. Here, too, I came upon the boy with absolute pitch. With his back to the piano he could name any note struck on the instrument.

Though few children are geniuses, all children, I discovered, possess gifts which may become their special distinction. A thousand talents await recognition! In the able ones who decline to push into first place; in the slow worker who eventually does a superior job; in those with special interests beyond school demands, like entomology or stamp collecting; in those with a flair for decoration or design; in the natural housekeeper. The young inventor may be so absorbed in his work that he neglects important studies; the skillful user of tools may need adult appreciation to protect him from the snobbishness of the book learners, including teachers.

I became convinced that someone should stand by in the early years to watch for and foster these natural endowments. It is not enough to discern a native gift; it must be enticed out again and again. Above all it must be protected against the annihilating effect of social condemnation. The fair-minded boy may be called "softie" by his mates; the polite girl be accused of posing for adult favors; the budding scholar may be discouraged by the epithet "bookworm." All too often adults encourage only a limited range of traits, those commonly believed to be essential for success, to the detriment of the whole vast range of gifts which children possess.

Often it is the seemingly unimportant gift which is most useful in life. The ability to communicate confidence may at times serve a doctor better than his medical skill; a passionate love of justice, discouraged as forwardness in a child, may one day contribute more to a lawyer's success than the ability to prepare a brief.

This discovery opened for me a way into the secret hopes and delights of childhood. With like-minded teachers, I helped to found a private school which specialized in discovering and encouraging hidden abilities. We watched the children in their recess periods—not for the bad traits, which we noted, but for the good traits that show up best in free play.

A fifth-grade boy who was uncommunicative in class had been labeled stupid by his teacher. I watched him as the catcher in a sand-lot ball game where his vocabulary was profuse, strident and authoritative. He kept his team together and won the game by continuous invective behind the plate. I asked him to write me an account of that game, but insisted he do it in his own colorful language.

Here was a naturally fluent lad who had been driven into silence by unsympathetic correction. Now I made him feel that his rough way of telling a story had merit. After a year or two his lapses into slang were eliminated. Later that "stupid" boy had no difficulty with college-entrance examinations. Approval is a powerful stimulant to the forces of self-education.

"But how," I am constantly asked, "can parents go about discovering unsuspected gifts in their children?"

By cool observation. Stop trying to make children what they eventually ought to be, and see what they really are now. Set aside the reproving eye and the authoritative command, and substitute impersonal observation as if these were some other person's children.

Once I told a mother that her boy had given me a long, stumbling lecture on insects. He had made a considerable collection of beetles and had read a lot about them. She asked me why I had let him bother me. "Oh," I said, "he *was* boring, but it is most important that someone should share his interest just now in order to keep it alive." I watched that boy on into high school. There he shone as a high-ranking member of the science club.

The author of some distinguished books writes to me that I was an inspiration in his boyhood. All I did that I now remember was to accept from him a daily outpouring of his writings. His intense desire to produce seemed to me an important gift. I never stopped his early effusions with a word of instruction. There would be time enough for that later. What he needed at the moment was encouragement.

The best time for watching children is when they are off guard: on picnics, at sand-lot games, during visits to places of public interest, at young people's parties, in the informal hours of home life. Here the often-overlooked gifts are exposed: wholehearted sharing, grit to contest against odds, natural leadership, care for the younger and the weak, cheerfulness, an interest in planning.

I think that parents should be as interested in having their children become members of the Scouts, the Campfire Girls and the like as in their getting high grades in school. The important thing is to expose children to a multiplicity of activities and interests, so that their inherent gifts will have as many chances as possible to show themselves.

The best time for achieving good communication in the home will vary with the children. If breakfast or dinner is a relaxed period, and if at that time children's views, wishes and hopes are really given consideration, superior qualities in thinking and in feeling may be revealed. Many mothers have found that a propitious hour for confidences is just before bedtime. Children become more expansive then, often are more willing to share the hopes and the imaginative fancies that spring from their secret hearts.

Besides the discovery and encouragement of an aptitude, it goes without saying that opportunities for its exercise should be made convenient. The wise parent will see that the raw materials are at hand. Parents who take a childish interest to heart will go out of their way (and even stop the car) to aid a quest. It may be for rocks or for snakes or for words; it may involve a house-wrecking search for some secret in chemistry. Whatever it is, let it develop.

For some adults, discovering hidden gifts in children will demand a change in personality; for self-effacement in an adult is what draws the child out. Children think about the world, and come to worthy conclusions—their own. They think about themselves and those around them, and come to worthy conclusions—their own. The parent who values these judgments as steppingstones to higher judgments will have the enjoyment of seeing unsuspected gifts appear and grow. It is hard to learn to listen, even to one's own children, but the fascination of the game is worth every effort.

THE WAY BACK

By Fred Raymond Gilpatric

THE MAN at the iron-barred window closed the book. As he watched the sun going down, he repeated the words he had just memorized: "Whatever else life may give or deny, one thing is absolutely indispensable—that a man should not break faith with himself; that he should keep his honor bright in his own eyes."

Once life had given this prisoner everything he wanted, but now, beyond the closed door of his room, he could hear the bedlam of the asylum. Life had taken away everything it had given; doctors had decided that he must be kept in this state hospital until he died.

How, then, could he hope for another chance?

More than a year has passed since the inmate at the darkening window asked that question. Tonight the same man sits at home, writing these words.

The doctors cannot explain the change of my personality that led them to set me free. This is the first time I ever told of that miracle of renewal.

When I was young, I believed a man could plan his life as definitely as a sailor charts a voyage. From the day I was graduated at Amherst, I knew my ultimate goal would be an executive post in some manufacturing business. I would marry a good-looking girl with brains, and we would raise a family and be leaders of our community.

Before many years had passed, these blueprints became realities. I did marry a girl with both intellect and beauty. I became manager of sales promotion in the large Stanley Works in New Britain, Conn. I was busy in town affairs and popular at our country club. Our two sons, one at Deerfield, the other in Amherst, promised to make the later years richest and finest of all.

But one day in 1940, my older son took his own life. Why he did it is still a mystery.

Not to run away from grief but to get back to ourselves, my wife and I took a long trip. When at last we came home it was with the resolve to make the best of the years to come. We both tried hard to keep that pact, but I was aware of my wife's silent, unceasing battle against despondency. I thought she was winning the struggle, but one winter day she took her own way to join our dead son.

After that second tragedy, I was like an injured man who walks away from an accident, not knowing how badly he is hurt. Gradually I yielded to an overpowering feeling that somehow I must have been the real cause of those tragedies. I began to avoid friends. I was alone now, my son Randall having enlisted for military training. Before long no one could induce me to leave my bedroom.

Then began a weary circuit of private hospitals and treatments that finally exhausted my savings. In November 1944 I entered State Hospital, my last stop, I felt sure.

My only request was to be left alone. I was fed up with psychoanalysis, occupational therapy and electric-shock treatments. Most of the day I sat in a chair and stared out the window into the courtyard. Apathy became more and more like a fog in the mind; all sounds seemed a little farther off and what I saw, I saw dimly.

For two years I remained in a state of living death. I refused to talk, would not reply to the simplest question. When letters came from my son I let them fall from my lap unopened; nor did I write to him. One day a guard slapped me on the shoulder.

"Mr. Gilpatric, there's a bomber pilot of a B-29 who wants to see you. He's straight from Okinawa."

Behind him stood my son. As he strode forward, arms out to embrace me, I turned my face to the wall and refused to say a word. But I could hear the doctor talking as he led Randall away:

"Captain, it is a fine thing for you to want to take your father home —but the poor man is never going to get well. Leave him here where he can be looked after until the end."

Any effort to draw me back into the treacherous world of reality made me tremble. That was why I resented a new doctor, Gabriel Sutch, who came to my chair one day and said: "I must ask you to do a little chore. For years people have been sending books here for the patients to read, but nobody has ever done anything about them. I am having some shelves built, and I've got to have those books separated into three simple piles—detective stories, other kinds of fiction and nonfiction. You don't have to say a word while you're sorting. Are you ready?"

I stood up sullenly. At least I would be working alone. And alone I was left with great disorderly mounds of books in the basement.

All day, without a flicker of interest, I stacked the books. It was almost time to quit when I spied a volume that bore a name familiar to me in bygone years. I can see the faded gilt letters now—"by Harry Emerson Fosdick."

My mind raced back to long ago when my brother had owned a place near the Fosdick summer home in Maine. As if by evocation, I stood again on a dock. The green waters of Boothbay Harbor were lapping the mossy pilings. Sputtering to the little Juniper Point wharf came a rickety old motorboat, at the wheel of which stood a fuzzy-haired, sunbaked pilot—Harry Fosdick! My brother shouted a good-natured, jesting welcome.

And over the magic bridge of years I remembered the little burst of laughter. Here in the moldy basement I even chuckled at that vivid recollection. Then an icy shiver ran through me. At the thought of my brother, my family, my personal life, all the old darkness came rolling back. Against that returning nightmare I lifted the book again and looked to see its title—*The Power to See It Through*.

I hid the book under my coat and carried it back to my room. There I turned the pages to the chapter called "Staying Power":

"Staying power is always associated with a certain integrity of conscience. Whatever else life may give or deny, one thing is absolutely indispensable—that a man should not break faith with himself; that he should keep his honor bright in his own eyes."

These words struck me with accusing force. Psychiatrists had said I was suffering from a mistaken conviction of guilt. I blamed myself for the fate of my son and wife, feeling sure that others also blamed me, including even my younger son. Thus I ran away from them, escaping a challenge I felt I could not meet. But mere diagnosis of what was wrong did me no good, because the doctors did not hold me morally accountable. They considered me a victim; now I began to see I was a culprit.

Dr. Fosdick's words cut through that dead diagnosis and made it clear that I was to blame for what had happened, not to my loved ones but *to myself!* When I quit life before the game was over, simply because events had gone against me, I had broken faith. A poor sport, I was sorry for myself. I was drowning in my own tears.

The charge implicit in Dr. Fosdick's words stung like an astringent on a wound. Yet I had to read more: "Staying power is always associated with something greater than oneself, to which one gives loyalty —an object of devotion."

My thoughts turned to my son, Randall. He had lost more than I— mother and brother by death, and father by illness—and yet, because of something greater than himself, his devotion to his duty, he had shown the staying power to see it through. He had refused to marry the girl he loved, because he felt I would need him.

"I salute you, my son," I thought miserably.

What was there, beyond myself, that I could hitch on to and be loyal to? Until that instant I had not wanted to get well. I still did not want to get well. But this much I knew: at last I wanted to want to get well.

Again I read: "A vital faith in God gives a man internal power, a spiritual vision from which divine companionship he draws replenished strength."

Could I make myself believe that there was present with me here and now, by a madhouse window, the actual companionship of God? I remembered that Abraham Lincoln once said: "I have been driven many times to my knees by the overwhelming conviction that I had nowhere else to go."

The yearning that welled up in me then was like a prayer, passionate and confused. I saw that only by going back into the game and playing my part could I restore my self-respect. In my heart I pleaded for another chance, for an object of devotion. And as if in answer I presently became aware that there was something to which I could give my loyalty. The library for the hospital patients!

I exulted in the sudden conviction that this was a new birthday in my life. I was experiencing the bliss of rebirth, the renewal of my soul, which gave me the strength to know that I did not stand alone, that in God's safekeeping I could face the world unafraid. That faith has never left me. It is in my heart now as it was when I went stalking down through a concourse of unhappy and distracted patients to seek out Dr. Sutch and tell him the news that I was a man born again in faith and purpose—that I was well.

For a long time Dr. Sutch studied me with enigmatic eyes. Then he asked: "What is it you propose?"

"I want you to have faith that I am completely well. I ask you to transfer me from the ward to the parole section. I would like to have the privilege of going in and out of the institution without permission at all times."

"And what would you do on the outside?"

"I want to go to a good barber first. Also buy myself a new suit of clothes. Then I want to go to the public library. For the next few weeks I intend to read everything I can find about modern library methods. Then I would like to stack those books the best way they can be stacked—to make them a real library for the patients."

"I believe you *are* well!" grinned the doctor.

When my son came to see me again he pleaded that I come home. But I shook my head: "I can't leave here until the job is done. I must have the staying power to finish it."

When the job was completed, six weeks later, I walked out with exciting work awaiting me: I had been able to obtain a beginner's appointment as reference assistant in the Springfield, Mass., public library. Many have asked me why I did not go back to the work in which I had been so successful. My reason was that, since I had no further need to make a lot of money, I wanted to do work which I believed would help my fellow man. Every day I guide students to sources of knowledge, and that makes me feel that I am serving something beyond myself. My work, my son and my new daughter-in-law —these are the objects of my devotion.

Sometimes people ask me if I am not afraid that my cure may prove only temporary. I am not afraid, because God is with me and I shall keep faith with myself and my honor bright in my own eyes.

Shangri-La on a Shoestring

By Barbara Cloud   *As told to Robert Froman*

IT WAS in 1948 that my husband and I contracted island fever—a virulent malady from which, happily, we've never recovered. John, a commercial photographer in Boston, had been asked to make aerial photographs of a factory in Portland, Maine. On the way up in the client's plane we saw more lakes with more islands than we had ever thought existed. (We learned later that Maine has 2400 lakes and ponds with an appropriate number of islands to go with them.)

I suppose that like lots of others we may have dreamed of owning an island some day—if we ever got rich. But since we knew we'd never be rich, we labeled it a dream and nothing more. Now we were beside ourselves. Islands passed under the wings in all shapes and sizes, most of them apparently uninhabited! We hardly spoke—but we both knew we had to have an island, an island all our own.

John got his pictures, and we stayed on to do some prospecting. After several futile earth-bound efforts we hired a pontoon-equipped plane and told the pilot what we wanted. Apparently he had met all kinds of people, so if a couple of offset characters wanted to go island shopping it was all right with him.

Within a matter of hours we found our gem, an unoccupied, beautifully wooded isle in Lake Sebago. There were several little peninsulas, two of them sheltering a pleasant cove. Our pilot dipped down and landed on the lake. We climbed out of the plane and waded ashore.

It was love at first meeting. The island looked as though it had been lying there waiting for us since the dawn of time. The cove faced the mainland a half mile away. On the far side was a gorgeous ten-mile sweep of sparkling water with a view of snow-capped Mt. Washington in the distant background.

As we wandered over the island John paced it off: 800 feet long and half that wide—about eight acres in all, most of it covered with a dense stand of pine, beech, hemlock and maple. Great masses of blueberries were turning deep purple in sunny clearings. Occasionally we stopped our excited talk and listened to the gentle lapping of water along the shore, the sigh of wind in the trees, the sounds of great activity from the birds.

Eventually we tore ourselves away and taxied across to the mainland to inquire about "our" island. We learned that it was Inner Green, one of the Dingley islands, only 25 miles from Portland. The owner allowed he would sell for $1500. And we allowed we could afford to pay $500—*maximum*. (In the end, of course, we paid the $1500, which we got by borrowing against John's accounts receivable and by working evenings and week-ends on extra photographic jobs.)

After weeks of eager waiting, our deed to paradise arrived. We were the sole owners of "eight acres more or less of island known as Inner Green, including all the land exposed at low water, plus all rocks, reefs and peninsulas between Inner Green and neighboring islands."

We loaded the car with simple camping equipment and set off for our shoestring Shangri-La.

When we stepped ashore from a borrowed rowboat on July 14 we were royalty surveying a new empire. We spent the day in a trance of exploring and planning. John caught two landlocked salmon, and we cooked them over our campfire for supper.

In the following weeks we built a wood platform and topped it with a 16-foot-square Army-surplus tent. John improvised a rough fireplace for cooking. Fortunately the lake, which is a part of Portland's water supply, provided abundant fresh water, so we didn't have to dig a well.

Aside from boating, swimming, fishing, most of the first two years —that is, long week-ends from early spring to late fall—went into clearing and building. Because we had gone in over our heads in buying Inner Green we couldn't afford professional help. But gradually we acquired skill with hammer and saw, and our happiness deepened.

Our first architectural endeavor was somewhat hastily conceived. The owner of a Boston parking lot that was going out of business offered us an all-metal prefabricated hut that had served as the office. The hut was imbedded in concrete and the assembly bolts were thoroughly rusted. By the time John got it disassembled the side panels were somewhat mangled. But he trucked the pieces to the lake, got them astride a pair of borrowed rowboats and with a helper towed them out to the island. By fall the little building was re-erected. It had a list there and a sag here, but it was weather-tight and it was home.

Our first privy had only a large beach umbrella for weather protection. Later John built an appropriate structure which I painted with an off-white interior and blue trim. From the privy the long view to the west is particularly lovely at sunset.

The following year we were planning a substantial cottage when the tale of our struggles reached the students at a Boston building-trades school. Six of them offered to help us start the cottage in return for a two-week vacation on the island.

The boys were as good as their word. They enjoyed themselves immensely, and left us with the foundation and frame of a three-room house plus detailed plans for finishing it. At a lumber mill up the lake we bought inexpensive odd-length boards for a shake roof. We got the roof on in one terrific day of sawing and hammering, finishing by lantern light. Working week-ends, we completed the cottage, walls and all, before the fall freeze-up.

The cost, including a secondhand refrigerator and stove that run on bottled gas, was a shade over $1000. We were broke but happy. Our entire kingdom—island, hut (now a guesthouse), cottage and a rowboat with a small outboard motor—came to less than $3000.

By now the drive to and from Boston had grown increasingly irksome. Even in light traffic it took three hours. Our route lay past a seaplane base and we thought how wonderful it would be to fly back and forth. The lake was perfect for landing, our cove an ideal place to moor a plane. But flying, of course, was not for the likes of us.

One day, however, we stopped to watch the planes and fell to questioning a friendly mechanic. The result, I guess, was foregone. By spring we had learned to fly, our lessons costing us a little over $100 apiece. A rebuilt 65-horse Piper float plane set us back $1500. We got $1100 for a second car John had used in his business and put up $400 cash. Later we sold the Piper to buy an all-metal Luscombe for an additional $300.

Now we make the trip from Boston in an hour and at less cost than travel by car. Occasional aerial-photography jobs have paid insurance and operating costs, plus the price of a two-way radio.

During the week, after a hard day's work, we sometimes fly up to Inner Green just for an evening of being monarchs of all we survey. The moment we cut the throttle and glide to a landing at the island our city cares drop away and our hearts fill with special joy.

The plane has greatly simplified our housekeeping problems. Formerly it was a long trip by boat and car to the nearest store. If we forgot something we just did without. Now we hop over to Naples on Long Lake, seven crow-flight miles away. Whenever we have a yearning for seafood the plane lifts us over to the lobstermen on the coast; 30 minutes later we have lobsters on the stove at Inner Green.

The plane also has brought us friends. Seaplane owners are a tight-knit fraternity and are likely to take to one another on sight. For a number of them our island has become a rendezvous and they occasionally drop down just for a chat and a cup of coffee.

We fish right off our doorstep for salmon, trout and bass. In the fall there are deer on the mainland, and on our island pheasant and partridge. And the wild rice and coontail we've planted along our shore attract ducks and geese.

Inner Green keeps us busy. John has built a small but substantial dock so we no longer have to wade ashore from the plane. This past summer he finished the fieldstone fireplace and chimney for the main cottage. Though we like the soft light of our kerosene lamps, he has also wired the cottage against the day when we can have electricity from a generator.

I began a flower garden our second summer and last summer we got enough ground cleared to add a small vegetable patch—for fun and self-sufficiency.

Mind you, we have no special theories about how to live. Our way of life has evolved by accident. All we can say is that island fever is a heady thing. If a man's home is his castle, his island is almost a world in itself.

Including the plane, our island represents an investment of something over $5000, plus hours of work we have never bothered to count. Occasionally someone asks us what we would sell for. Our stock answer is a million dollars.

And what would we do with the million? The only way we know to get as much fun as we've had would be to buy another island.

Doctor's Dilemma

"Doctor, you remember I consulted you two years ago about a patient?" a much younger colleague once said to a famous New Haven physician. "I followed your advice, and the patient got well. Later another patient had the same symptoms, and I followed the same treatment—but the patient died. Now how do you explain that?"

"You remind me of my mare, Sally," said the old doctor.

"How's that?"

"Well, I had to drive into the country one night after a storm, and came to a place where the bridge had been washed away. Sally stopped. Slapping the reins, I shouted, 'Sally, get across!' She hunched herself, gave a great leap and was across. Months later, Sally and I again faced the same crossing, the stream now flowing under the repaired bridge. Sally stopped, hunched herself and leaped to the other side."

"But what connection has that with my case?" asked the man.

"Well," replied the old doctor, "I'd say Sally had a wonderful memory, but damned poor judgment!"   —Contributed by Alice C. Johnson

"Not more than one in 20 marriage problems springs from actual adultery"

This, Too, Is Infidelity

By *Margaret Blair Johnstone*

Pastor of the Union Congregational Church, Groton, Mass.

HE DICTIONARY has been required reading for all couples I marry, ever since the night Joan came to me about David.

She was upset about her husband's late working hours. She said he didn't answer his office phone at night, that his office was dark, and that he had not brought home any overtime pay. In spite of my arguments that there could be a good reason for these facts, Joan was convinced David was being unfaithful to her.

"I'm having it out with him tonight!" she cried.

Later, a frantic Joan and a white and shaken David came to my study. "Apparently you have more faith in me than my wife has," David declared. "What's left to a man when he finds out that his wife is faithless?" ·

"*I*—faithless?" Joan bridled.

"Yes. Faithless," repeated David. "Without faith. Look it up in the dictionary!"

"But how did I know your phone was disconnected at the switchboard, or that you worked in the back file room at night, or that you were saving your overtime pay for my birthday?" Here Joan broke down and sobbed.

"Faith is what you have when you *don't* know, isn't it?" David asked quietly. Turning to me, he said, "Everybody harps too much on the adultery angle of infidelity. This is infidelity too, isn't it—this doubt?"

I reached for the dictionary. David was right:

"*Infidelity:* Want of faith or belief; atheism or disbelief in God or religion; unfaithfulness in married persons; adultery; unfaithfulness to a charge or to moral obligation; treachery; deceit."

It is significant, I think, that one word expresses both marital faithlessness and lack of religious faith. For a successful marriage must be built on the same strong, unswerving faith that is found in religion.

Sometimes infidelity in wedlock demonstrates itself in adultery. Far more often it is nonadulterous faithlessness, as in Joan's case, which undermines marriage.

Another common infidelity is, as the dictionary's definition states, "unfaithfulness to a moral obligation." How many of us renege on our wedding vows?

Women promise to honor their husbands "for richer for poorer." If you nag your husband about his earning power, you are being unfaithful to your vow.

Have you neglected the moral obligation you assumed when you promised your husband that he was getting a "wedded wife to have and to hold"? Are you a responsive mate? Or don't you consider that the satisfying of sex needs is a moral obligation? If not, you may be guilty of another type of infidelity mentioned in the dictionary: deceit. Over and over again as a counselor I find some form of conscious or unconscious fraud underlying marital tensions.

Most women before marriage think they will be capable of meeting their husbands' sexual needs. Rather than admit later that they have overestimated their inclination, some women start what may be a completely unconscious process of deception. Instead of frankly working through the adjustments every marriage requires, they develop an illness or a fatigued or nervous state which excuses them from marital duty.

Wives are not the only ones who commit the infidelity of deceit, nor is sex the only area in which it appears. Consider financial matters. "I should have realized that his reluctance to discuss money matters before we were married meant trouble," one woman explained. "But he always seemed to have money and he kept talking about our future family. Now I find that he is dead set against children because it would mean giving up my job and my salary."

Cultural interests and leisure activities are frequent subjects of deceit. "You used to be wild about bowling and ball games," Bill accuses Sarah.

"Was I?" she answers. "You once enjoyed going to plays and concerts."

"Well, we're married now," Bill replies. "I don't have to keep up with that highbrow stuff any longer."

Yet another type of infidelity is treachery. This involves betrayal; in it we humiliate our loved one, in the eyes of others or in his own eyes.

The marks of this marital treachery can be detected in everyday conversation. At a party recently a husband, speaking about his wife, said: "You want Carol to run for president of the club? That's a laugh. Why, she doesn't have any more executive sense than a rabbit." And a wife, in the presence of her husband, said to her daughter: "Why should I go to the PTA fashion show? On your father's salary I couldn't afford a new hankie!"

Add to these the personality foibles, in-law tangles and business secrets you have heard married people reveal about each other, and then ask yourself: Do I commit the treachery of personality exposure? To get sympathy do I demolish the pride and self-confidence of the one I have promised "to love, cherish, honor and keep"?

However deep the subsequent remorse, nothing can restore the intimacy killed by exposure of personal affairs. No attempt to make up for it can quite replace the rapport riddled by public disparagement.

A vow in the marriage covenant says: "Forsaking all others, keep thee only unto him." You don't have to have an affair to adulterate the emotional relationship between you and your mate. You can displace your fidelity just as thoroughly by continuing to cling to your mother, for instance.

It happened to be a woman, but it is just as often a man, who complained to me, "Sunday is the only day we have together. Yet every Sunday we go to his family's house. If we don't he's in a tizzy all day wondering how to pacify his folks, and he blames me for hurting their feelings."

"There's no reason why she can't take this trip with me," a husband complained bitterly. "Our son would get excellent care at my sister's. But that child takes all of my wife's affection and time."

Occupational interests can also discourage adherence to the person to whom you owe first loyalty. Many husbands are guilty of displaced fidelity through overdevotion to their jobs. And working wives are frequently unwise in the management of their careers. "She got so wound up in that job of hers that she just didn't have time for the rest of us."

In my experience as a counselor, not more than one in 20 marriage problems stems from actual adultery. Well over half the cases, however, involve some other form of unfaithfulness. In one instance I remember, it was a child who accurately diagnosed his parents' marital ills.

"Mother," he asked, "what does 'married' mean?"

"Why, it means mothers and fathers promise to love and honor each other all the rest of their lives," that mother answered.

"Then you and Daddy aren't always married, are you?" he countered.

Forgotten Failures

HE STRUCK OUT 1330 times, a record in futility unapproached by any other player in the history of baseball. But that isn't what we remember about Babe Ruth. His 714 home runs completely obliterated the 1330 strike-outs.

Cy Young, perhaps the greatest pitcher of all time, accumulated 511 victories, a mark that never has been threatened. But what is generally forgotten is that Young actually lost almost as many games as he won.

One of the failingest men who ever lived was always trying experiments that were unsuccessful. Yet we never think of Thomas Edison as a failure.

At Fort Necessity, during the French and Indian War, a young American officer capitulated to the enemy. But George Washington is never thought of as the man who surrendered to the French.

People would feel a lot less sensitive about failure if they remembered it just doesn't matter, except as a guidepost for oneself. Success is a bright sun that obscures and makes ridiculously unimportant all the little shadowy flecks of failure. —Harold Helfer in *The Kiwanis Magazine*

A Faith
for Tough Times

By Harry Emerson Fosdick, D.D.   Condensed from the book

SAMUEL GOLDWYN once remarked that he wanted "a film which begins with an earthquake and works up to a climax." He rightly assessed the popular attractiveness of the colossal. If, however, one's thinking is dominated by the gigantic events of our time, one can hardly avoid despair. The world's spectacular doings are in turmoil. As George Bernard Shaw said, if the other planets are inhabited they must be using this earth as their insane asylum.

Christian faith maintains its assurance, despite the world's disorder, by centering attention not on the vast or noisy things but on the quiet, the unobtrusive, the inconspicuous, the vital. Every Christmas we celebrate this truth. How irrelevant to the vast affairs of the Roman world seemed the birth of a baby at the inn! Gigantic affairs were afoot then. Yet empires fell, the Caesars are dust, and that diminutive bit of vitality has proved more enduring than them all.

No wonder that William James, impatient with the worship of size, exclaimed: "I am against bigness and greatness in all their forms, and *with* the invisible, molecular moral forces that work from individual to individual, stealing in through the crannies of the world like so many soft rootlets . . . and yet rending the hardest monuments of man's pride, if you give them time."

If this seems sentimental, imagine yourself back some millions of years ago on this planet, facing two factors: on one side a vast turbulence — volcanos, huge, terrific, from the inexhaustible fires of the earth's core; on the other side protoplasm, microscopic, invisible along the water's edge, fragile, quiet, vital. On which would you bet—volcanos or protoplasm? Protoplasm had no credible chance to mean anything against the violent forces of volcano and earthquake. Yet see what came of it at last: life, spirit, art, music, prophets, apostles, martyrs, scientists and saints! Vitality *is* mightier than size.

This creative power of the vital is a momentous fact in human history. It explains, at least in part, the striking contrast between the estimates of stormy generations by their contemporaries and by posterity. In retrospect the 18th century, with its American and French Revolutions, appears to us one of the most creative in history; but many who lived then never guessed that posterity would so regard it. Even Rousseau called it "this great rottenness amidst which we live."

In those stormy eras something momentous was afoot, not easily discernible amid the noise, but germinative, creative, decisive. So today many look on our generation with hopeless eyes, but if we have anything like the faith and character of our forefathers at their best our posterity will sometimes wonder why we, who had the privilege of living now, did not better understand that we were "dwelling in a grand and awful time."

Of course our generation is in turmoil. Not long ago nations, races and religions, fairly well capsuled by geographical isolation, could live each for itself, so that the idea of one world was a dream; but now suddenly we have all been poured into one container, distance conquered, so that what happens anywhere happens everywhere. Optimists foresaw world brotherhood as the immediate result of this new propinquity. This didn't come to pass—instead came friction, turmoil, confusion, misunderstanding, hatred, war! We shall not get out of this mess in a hurry.

However, the abiding, creative factors in this revolutionary time are its vitalities: man's ideals, his just demands for life, liberty and the pursuit of happiness, his endeavors to better his condition. Not serene generations but times of tumult have always been the creative epochs in human history. Our generation will yet be seen by our progeny as one world painfully in the making.

The history of mankind is pretty much the story of dough into which the leaven of personality is introduced, with consequences none could have foreseen. Here was the dull, sodden mass of man's thinking, and then a person came, unknown, unrecognized, often derided, but vital. Men denied his truth and fought against it. The dough said it would have none of the leaven, but at last Copernicus, Galileo, Darwin won.

This is the way the world runs. Always the new beginnings to which the future belongs are born, as it were, in a manger, their prophetic import seen by none save three wise men, it may be, a few shepherds. If, therefore, we believe the noisy and ostentatious to be the determining factors, we miss the most important truth about any era. The wise men believed in a baby. They did not believe in Herod, in Caesar's legions, in the imperial power that loomed large in their generation. They believed in something newborn and vital.

As for us as individuals, often seeming powerless in a mad world, the Christian story brings a message, challenging even when it seems incredible. Vital persons count. Men and women of integrity and rectitude are "the strong nails that hold the world together." We never see the truth in history or in contemporary life until we pierce behind the mass of huge affairs and recognize the importance of individuals. The world's destiny is ultimately determined inside personality.

We are not saying that the large matters of the world—its politics, economic systems, national and international affairs—are unimportant. They are important.

But it is the dismaying aspect of the world's large affairs that makes all the more important the vital groups—homes, friendships, neighborhoods, churches—where the leaven of decency, kindness, good will, love has got its start. Small they are, but they are like hothouses, where slender growths begin which can be transplanted to the wider field.

One of the tragedies of our time is that so many people, obsessed by size, dispirited by the world's chaos, lose heart and relax their loyalty to such vital groups.

Stop being obsessed by size; stop worshiping the colossal or letting the colossal frighten you. Your hope is in vital persons, ideas, groups. In the long run the future belongs to them. The solution of every gigantic problem is already here, almost imperceptible it may be, in some inspired person, some germinative idea, some leavening group.

Common-sense advice for everybody

Teach Your Wife
to Be a Widow

By Donald I. Rogers   *Condensed from the book*
Financial Editor, New York Herald Tribune

TOO MANY HUSBANDS fail to comprehend one significant and binding pledge in the marriage vow: "With all my worldly goods I thee endow." In a worldly sense that's the backbone of the contract, and the "until death do us part" is no escape clause. Even after death a man should guard the welfare of the girl he married.

The American husband, in seven cases out of ten, passes to his reward before his wife does, frequently leaving only an insurance policy and a mortgaged home. Seldom is this enough to provide the skimpiest existence for his survivors. It's the rare wife, moreover, who knows all she should about her husband's business, income, investments, debts and budget. Yet she may have the whole problem dumped in her lap without an hour's notice.

Not until their joints begin to creak do most men think in earnest about what will happen to their wives after they are gone. But a man of 30 should be more concerned than a man of 60. If *he* dies, his wife may face up to 40 years of widowhood. She has to make the insurance money stretch farther, and is more likely to have a home to pay for and a family to raise. A husband should start teaching his wife to be a widow as soon as he can. It's not morbid; rather, it's sensible and kind. And if the problem is approached sensibly it may in the end contribute substantially to a longer life for the husband, since few things are more destructive of health than worry.

The first step in the wife's education can be taken right after the honeymoon. The groom should then put the management of household finance in her hands. After all, he will be busy enough working to earn the family's income. The wife might undertake to pay all the bills, manage the budget, figure out how much insurance can be carried, work out the income taxes. She should keep track of deductible expenses, charting the entire tax program.

In this way she'll have to be acutely aware of her husband's business, expenses and investments. She will, through the years, acquire some knowledge of the business world. She may soon be asking why hubby allows $200 to lie idle in the checking account when it could be earning interest at a savings bank. Women have a penchant for details that men seldom possess. Once she's inoculated with the business bug, a wife will be the best business partner a man ever had. And he'll know that if she comes into a sum of money—say, from his insurance—she'll not be stampeded into squandering it.

The next step is insurance. Any man's a fool to be without all the insurance he can afford. It's a good investment, sound planning and the easiest way to build an estate. If a man has a mortgage he should take out enough insurance to cover it, so that the survivors will have their home free and clear.

How should the benefits be paid? It depends on the wife's business sense. If you're an average earner your insurance money will be more than she is accustomed to handle. Will she get the illusion that she is rich, buy that good coat and other things she's always wanted, forgetting that there'll be no further income? Insurance companies have long been aware that an overwhelming majority of widows spend their lump-sum insurance within a year after receiving it. To meet this situation they have worked out scores of different programs which call for staggered monthly or annual payments to beneficiaries. In other words, instead of getting $15,000 cash, you can arrange for your wife to get, say, $200 a month for a specified period.

If you can teach your wife to be a sound business manager, however, it's sensible to leave the money in a lump sum and let it work for her. Insurance companies pay some interest for the use of money left in their possession, but it doesn't approach the earnings a widow could realize by investing in stocks and bonds through a good broker.

Furthermore, money invested in most common stocks will keep pace with inflation.

I'm teaching my own wife to handle her investments herself. The "education" costs a few pennies a day—the daily newspapers. We study the financial pages and pretend to buy some selected stocks. We've learned something by trial and error without risking a cent. All wives should acquire some elementary knowledge of stocks and the stock market in case they want to—or have to—invest their husbands' insurance money or manage their estates.

Another step in teaching your wife to be a widow is to prepare her for some gainful occupation so that she could, if necessary, be self-supporting. A friend of mine told me that his wife could get along if anything happened to him—she was a secretary before their marriage and she could earn her living again if necessary.

I felt it my duty to point out that they have been married 15 years and during that entire time the wife has never so much as typed a letter. She's rusty at her trade and a great many younger and more proficient gals have come along since. Perhaps she could become secretary to a church committee and take down the minutes of the meetings in shorthand, just for the practice. Maybe she could help her husband with some of his correspondence. The same kind of career planning might be a wise safeguard for other wives.

Every husband needs a will. You can't take it with you, but you can't leave it all behind either. Both federal and state governments will want part of the accumulation of your life time in estate taxes. These will be affected to some extent by the provisions of the will.

For some reason the practice of drawing wills seems to be confined to the rich and the near-rich, though a simple will costs as little as $10. Yet it is the widow of moderate means, whose husband leaves an estate of diminutive proportions, who most needs the clear, red-tape-cutting help of a will. In many states, if the husband doesn't leave a will, the wife gets only one third of the estate and the children get two thirds. If the children are minors, the wife may have to wait for the probate court to give her permission to spend her children's money for their own necessities!

No matter how little he has to leave, a man has not only the right but also the obligation to dispose of his worldly goods by means of a will. It's his duty to name an executor—whether his wife or an outsider—who will carry out his last wishes to the family's best advantage.

It's a good idea for the wife to meet her husband's banker and lawyer, so that when she has to consult these men she will not be dealing with total strangers. She ought, indeed, to learn the basic facts about banking. There is a startling ignorance of the bank laws as they affect widows.

A man's bank account is frozen when he dies. In some states the death of one of the joint-checking-account depositors results in the immediate freezing of half the account until taxes are settled. It is well, therefore, for a wife to keep some emergency money in her own savings account to tide her over the expensive days after her husband's departure.

Some states where there is an inheritance tax (as in New York) insist that banks seal a safe-deposit box upon the death of its renter. The box may not be opened until a state tax appraiser is present. This applies even if the box is jointly owned by husband and wife. For all this, a safe-deposit box is an ideally safe place for policies, deeds and other important papers. However, it is advisable to have records of the insurance policy at home: name of company, amount of the policy, its number, date of execution and beneficiary.

A sensible precaution is to prepare a letter of final instructions and leave it in a handy place for your wife. The letter should cover the many things a widow ought to know about her husband's insurance, investments, debts and what others owe him. It should give her the essential practical details about his estate and other taxes, what to do about every item of his property and his ideas of a budget tailored to her new income.

The most important thing for a husband and wife to realize is that there will be less money for a woman as a widow than she had as a wife, despite insurance. This simple and logical fact is rarely faced squarely. Having faced it, a man will recognize the urgency of preparing his wife to be a widow.

When You Talk to a Child

By Emily Rautman and Arthur Rautman

*Condensed from
Mental Hygiene*

WHEN introduced to a five-year-old child, many adults show the uneasiness observable otherwise only when a well-fed man is confronted with a tiger on half rations. Time and again we have been amazed to see how inept many otherwise competent people become when they encounter a live child.

Some of our acquaintances, for instance, are struck speechless when we introduce our young nephew. But far more of a problem are the garrulous adults who insist upon taking over the whole show from the moment they cast their eyes upon "the little darling," leaving us with a youngster who requires an hour of heavy handling before he becomes a reasonably civilized creature once more.

It is no unusual experience for us to be sitting in a restaurant with everything quite under control, only to have some well-meaning stranger walk up, ruffle the child's hair with a loving hand, make sundry remarks as to where he got his lovely curly hair, what beautiful brown eyes he has, and so on—with half of the people in the room beaming approval—and then, well satisfied with her work of destruction, walk out. Before this session of appreciation, we were enjoying our food and each other's company. Now the well-behaved boy has been transformed into a show-off, and the rest of the day is on precarious ground.

Some of our friends carry a liberal supply of candy or gum in their pockets to give to the youngster the moment they see him. "Go on and eat it. Your aunt won't mind!" They seem to assume it is possible to gain a child's affection by training him, like a horse, to come for a lump of sugar.

What, then, *should* an adult do when he meets a youngster? Above all, remember that a child is an individual, not a toy or a thing, and address him as a person. Don't stick your thumbs into his ribs to make him hysterical. This kind of romping, although it has its place, is difficult for it usually is impossible for the excited child to recognize where the socially acceptable boundary of such activity lies. He becomes quite unable to stop. What you started as innocent fun almost invariably changes the youngster into an irritating nuisance who persists in interrupting your conversation with his parents. The end is usually punishment for the child.

Don't talk baby talk! In spite of the fact that you know better you probably do it more often than you think. It is an insult to anyone to be taunted with his own imperfect speech. The child wants to learn *your* way of speaking, not to see how well you can imitate and mock his infantile pronunciation.

Don't try to be silly. When confronted with a child, most adults are silly enough, without deliberately using silliness as a form of entertainment to cover their inability to deal with the situation. Say what you have to say to the youngster, and then stop.

When you meet an adult with a child, it is probably best to address your first remarks to the adult. Then turn to the child, say a few words of greeting and, if you wish, ask about some activity of interest to him. Do not try to carry on a parallel conversation with both adult and child at the same time. But whatever you do, don't try to ignore the child. It is discourteous, and with most children it simply can't be done. A child will go through his entire repertoire of tricks to gain at least some little attention.

No matter what your relationship with the child, never forget that he is under the care of the parent or other guardian, who is responsible for his behavior and for his routine. It is a gross unkindness to subject a child to divided authority. "Never mind what your mother says. Here in my house you may do so and so." Never have words caused more ill will between adults, particularly between parents and grandparents. And never have they been more disturbing to the child, since he now no longer knows which voice to obey. It is easy to say, "Ask your mother if you may," and it pays dividends in parental good will. What seems to you an unreasonable prohibition may have been proven to them by bitter experience to be an essential safeguard.

Don't talk down to a child. Speak to him about things that interest him and in terms that he can comprehend. Particularly, in commenting upon his drawings or coloring, his efforts at carpentry, his attempts at writing, or the music that he has played or sung for you, focus his attention upon *what* has been done, not upon how well *he* has done it. An honest piece of work, at any level of accomplishment, deserves honest appreciation; comments upon the work leave the child free to participate in the conversation, instead of forcing him into bashful and self-conscious silence.

Do not embarrass a child by criticizing him for something beyond his control. "Why didn't you come to visit me as you promised?"—when the visit or non-visit was not of the child's choosing—is an unkind question that can have no answer.

Even though the child seems to be absorbed in his play, don't think that you can talk about him, even in a foreign language, without his realizing that he is the subject. He probably will understand the tenor of the conversation. Even worse, he may not *quite* understand your meaning, and will then fill in details from his own vivid imagination and fears. Half-understood ideas and misinterpreted terms have been a source of serious worry to many a child, particularly since even the most fortunate youngster usually has some phase of life in which he feels dangerously insecure.

When a child has been hurt, it is important to keep conversation on a matter-of-fact basis, sympathetic but casual. Because of his limited experience, the child evaluates his injury primarily by watching and copying the reactions of those about him; and hence by poorly chosen expressions of sympathy or by inviting him to recite and relive all the sad details of his trouble, you actually increase his pain. How often one hears, "Oh, dear! How did you bang up my little sweetheart like that? Tell me. How *did* you do it?" How seldom, "Well, you had a little bump, didn't you?" And rare, indeed, is the adult who has the good sense to drop the subject at this point and casually introduce some more absorbing topic.

Children can be fun, a pleasure to themselves and to all they meet. They can also be a source of embarrassment and annoyance, of humiliation and man's deepest grief. They want, earnestly, to learn to live in an adult world; they look up to all grownups, therefore, to teach them how to achieve this goal. It is the inescapable responsibility of every adult to do all that he can to help each child he meets in his effort to achieve maturity.

The Understanding Heart

Sɪʀ Wɪʟʟɪᴀᴍ Oꜱʟᴇʀ, visiting one of London's leading children's hospitals, noticed that in a convalescent ward all the children were clustered at one end of the room dressing their dolls, playing games and playing in the sandbox—all except one little girl, who sat forlornly on the edge of her high, narrow bed, hungrily clutching a cheap doll.

The great physician looked at the lonely little figure, then at the ward nurse. "We've tried to get Susan to play," the nurse whispered, "but the other children just won't have anything to do with her. You see, no one comes to see her. Her mother is dead, and her father has been here just once—he brought her that doll. The children have a strange code. Visitors mean so much. If you don't have any visitors, you are ignored."

Sir William walked over to the child's bed and asked, in a voice loud enough for the others to hear, "May I sit down, please?" The little girl's eyes lit up. "I can't stay very long this visit," Osler went on, "but I have wanted to see you so badly." For five minutes he sat talking with her, even inquiring about her doll's health and solemnly pulling out his stethoscope to listen to the doll's chest. And as he left, he turned to the youngster and said in a carrying voice, "You won't forget our secret, will you? And mind, don't tell anyone."

At the door he looked back. His new friend was now the center of a curious and admiring throng. —Contributed by John P. Eaton

DON'T CALL ME BROAD-MINDED

By

Elizabeth Massey Hill   *Condensed from Woman's Home Companion*

*T*O BE broad-minded seems to be the most desirable trait possible today. Beat your wife if you like; steal if you must; but never deviate from the path of broad-mindedness. It amounts to a fetish and I for one am sick of it.

I cannot discover a single thing—except Communism, of course—which we are not supposed to tolerate. Did your neighbor cheat his brother's widow out of her inheritance? Poor thing, he must have been the victim of some childhood insecurity which left him with a pathological craving for money.

Has your best friend run off with your husband? You must realize that monogamy is an unnatural state for the male animal and most likely your friend's mother didn't teach her when she was small that it is rude to grab. You must just get a divorce on polite grounds, give a party for the happy pair when they return from their flight, and teach Junior to call the lady "aunt."

Every undesirable trait must be excused on the ground of improper upbringing (or too proper, which is apparently even worse) or some mental or physical maladjustment. Never suggest that just possibly a mature individual should be held responsible for his own acts, that he is given a brain with which to reason and control his desires, and that living entirely to please oneself is not always the ideal of life.

Almost anything can be blamed on poor old Mom if you try hard enough; an inhibition is more to be feared than a thousand devils and duty is the last reason for any act.

Well, I am now through being tolerant. It seems to me that a bit of insistence on the old-fashioned virtues might be a healthy change. If my son should write home that he is flunking college because he has discovered that he has a mother fixation and must free himself of the desire to please me, I would arrange things so that he would have to spend more time earning his way and less dreaming up fixations to make himself more interesting.

I think psychologists should make it quite clear that inhibition — that bugaboo of modern life — means not the conscious control of undesirable impulses but the abnormal fear of them. This fear is what causes the inhibited person to push such impulses out of the conscious mind altogether, down into the subconscious to fester and infect the whole mind and body. Resisting a conscious desire is quite different and never did anyone any harm.

Even in smaller matters I am quitting the broad-minded group. I shall not force a lenient smile when someone in my presence uses words which wouldn't have been tolerated in a well-run saloon a generation ago. I shall do my bit to put discussions of marital relations back into the privacy they should never have left. When guests at my parties drink themselves into an objectionable state, I shall never again invite them. There is a line, and I am going to draw it.

I fail to see that our vaunted modern tolerance and easy philosophy have made either society or individuals better or happier. Our parents and grandparents may not always have been as saintly as they pretended, but they did have definite standards which they insisted on and lived by in large part. Religion was large in their lives. And they weren't afraid of inhibiting their children by teaching them to do their duty and strive after goodness, and by smacking their little bottoms when they didn't.

Yet the degree of stability and of human happiness generally was greater then, I think; and certainly our present appalling increase in crime and in neurotic and psychiatric cases is scarcely an argument for our modern way. We are trying to steer a course without a compass and it appears to me we are foundering.

It sifts down to the fact that broad-mindedness has come to mean moral apathy—either a complete lack of any principles or standards of decency or, at best, the lack of any convictions strong enough to fight for. Nothing worth building was ever founded on quicksand; no statue carved from putty; no enduring society or satisfactory life built on laziness, selfishness and irresponsibility.

So from now on, call me anything else you like, but don't call me broad-minded! Those are fighting words!

The Great Discovery

I was a born worrier. If through the years I have acquired any aptitude for "rolling with the punches," it is due to the advice of three friends. Clarence S. Funk, manager of a big Chicago company, was one. I was just 22. The little business that employed me suddenly went busted, and I was out of a job. Funk called and said: "I get my exercise by walking after supper. Come over tonight and join me." I accepted eagerly, expecting sympathy, encouragement, perhaps a job. To my surprise, he said: "You are a very fortunate young man."

"Fortunate!" I exclaimed. "I've lost two years of my life and $1600 in unpaid salary."

"Any man is fortunate," he continued, "who gets his disappointments *early* in life. He learns to start over again. He learns not to be afraid. The man to be pitied is the one who, at 45 or 50, after getting all the breaks, has disaster suddenly descend on him. He has no iron in his soul, no inner strength born of previous struggles. He has never learned how to make a fresh start, and he is too old to learn."

My second counselor, Robert Updegraff, the business consultant, wrote: "Never complain about your troubles; they are responsible for more than half of your income." How true. Millions of jobs involve no responsibility and present no troubles. But they are never more than modestly rewarding. Only the jobs with big problems command big pay.

My third friend was an Irishman named George Buckley. "How old are you?" he asked one day. "Forty," I answered.

"Then you have five years before you make the Great Discovery—that trouble is not spasmodic. Trouble is chronic. Trouble is not an interruption in the normal processes of life. Trouble *is* life."

A Sensible Way

to

Lessen Tooth Decay

By Charles W. Freeman, D.D.S.   *As told to William F. McDermott*
Dean, Northwestern University Dental School

SEVERAL years ago the Dental School at Northwestern University launched one of the most extensive, costly and practical experiments in dental history. The results indicate that *tooth decay can be reduced 50 to 60 percent* by the simple process of brushing or rinsing the teeth *right after eating.*

The experiment was directed by Dr. Leonard S. Fosdick, professor of chemistry at the Dental School, and was conducted among 946 men and women students at five colleges in the Midwest and South. For two years a test group of 523 students brushed their teeth with a neutral paste within ten minutes after eating; or, if brushing was inconvenient, they rinsed their mouths thoroughly with water. The other 423 students continued their regular habit of brushing their teeth night and morning.

Examinations by X ray and visual means at the end of the first year showed the latter group developed new cavities at a rate which made an average of 2.2 each, while the test group had an average of only .8, a reduction of 63 percent. At the end of the second year the test group had 53 percent fewer cavities than the control group.

Back of these experiments lay a good deal of careful observation. Dental caries appears to be a "disease of civilization," for primitive peoples have little of it and prehistoric skulls show a remarkable preservation of the teeth.

The principal trouble lies in our tremendous consumption of sugar and other carbohydrates. The yearly intake of sugar has increased from nine pounds per person in 1824 to 96 pounds in 1948. And it is now definitely known that tooth decay roots mainly in fermentable sugars in food, candy and soft drinks. Some of the sugar lodges between the teeth and in crevices or hollows in the teeth. Bacteria, always present in the mouth, rapidly transform it into acid which attacks the teeth. Nature has provided a measure of defense in saliva, which tends to neutralize acid; among people using little sugar it suffices, but for those who indulge in quantities of sweets as we do, it is woefully inadequate.

Tooth decay is not a steady wearing-away process like water dripping on stone. It is the result of a series of violent and rapid acid attacks on the teeth, each attack being like a chisel blow, nicking away a tiny speck of enamel. Assaults often start within three minutes after the ingestion of sugar; they reach their peak of damage within 20 or 30 minutes. The destruction goes on until the saliva counterattacks.

The speed of the acid action on the teeth varies with people—likewise the saliva reaction. Where the acid acts swiftly and the saliva slowly, the person is constantly troubled with new cavities; where the acid is slow and the saliva fast, you have the rare individual—one out of 50—who can eat anything and is seldom or never bothered by tooth decay. Most of us are between the two extremes.

Brushing the teeth just before retiring at night and right after arising in the morning cleanses the teeth, sweetens the breath, and leaves a pleasant taste in the mouth, but does little to eliminate tooth decay.

Many dentists years ago began brushing their teeth or rinsing their mouths right after each meal and right after taking sugar in any form, and urged their patients to do likewise. The result was a marked reduction in new cavities.

Dr. Fosdick, who previously had constant trouble with caries, has not had a single tooth decay since 1937. His three children, aged 11, 13 and 16, have so far averaged but one or two cavities each, far fewer than most children of their ages.

For 20 years I have practiced brushing my teeth vigorously after every meal and sugar intake. Before that time I had frequent cavities; since then I have had only three. I have also materially reduced my sugar ingestion, which is partly responsible for the improvement.

Most of the students in both groups participating in our study had soft drinks and candy available during the day. Those who did not have ready access to these sweets developed fewer caries. Whenever a water fountain was close to the soft-drink and candy dispensers, fewer carious surfaces were found than where water was not readily available. While the two-year experiment is not conclusive, it is impressively significant; other smaller experiments have yielded substantially the same results. It is not unreasonable to believe that brushing the teeth or rinsing the mouth immediately after eating would result in the prevention of 25 to 50 million cavities a year in the teeth of the American people. The main preventive agent is simply water.

According to figures of the American Dental Association, there are 500 million untreated cavities in the teeth of our population — at least three decayed teeth per person. It would take our 84,000 dentists three years to catch up with this backlog of afflicted teeth.

Clearly, the only program of dental care that can be truly successful is one of prevention. Extensive research in the past 20 years has made remarkable progress, and some practical means of prevention may soon be available. Several agents are now being used, such as fluorine, ammoniated dentifrices, Vitamin K and others; but, while some results are encouraging, research is still in the experimental stage.

We recommend simple rules, based on our experiment:

1. Brush your teeth night and morning as usual; then brush them *immediately* after every meal whenever convenient, using a dentifrice or even plain water.

2. At all other times after eating, or indulging in candy or soft drinks, take a drink of water and before swallowing it swish it around in your mouth. This can be done without inconvenience or embarrassment. It will dissolve most, if not all, of the sugar remaining in the mouth, also wash away the acid that already may have formed.

I know some men who carry miniature toothbrushes in their pockets and women who keep them in their handbags, ready for use at any favorable opportunity. This is a wise health provision. There is substantial reason to believe the oral hygiene recommended here will cut tooth decay in half for those who earnestly and persistently practice it.

How long has it been since you've had ice cream for breakfast?

The Art of
Being a Nobody

By Eric Manners

Condensed from The American Mercury

F YOU ASKED why I respect our old family doctor so highly, I might dredge up such sensible reasons as his medical skill or his work in research. They'd be true enough, but I rather think the real reason for my respect lies in what he eats for breakfast: a bowl of cereal on which he places a dollop of ice cream.

Mind you, he doesn't boast about this as an impressive affectation. He just eats that because it's what he likes for breakfast. He's been doing it for years, and I found out about it only when I made an unexpected early-morning call on him.

We are fond of a notion nowadays that we lead independent lives, that we think things out for ourselves and are not ruled by "Authority." Unfortunately, this isn't true.

Actually we are handed (and accept) more advice as to what is right and wrong, more urgings to a docile conformity, more authoritarian They-Says, than any creatures calling themselves free should dream of bearing.

Does that seem to be pitching it too strong? Tell me: What did you think of the doctor's breakfast? Absurd, affected, "wrong"? There isn't anything wrong about it. It is merely an example of an almost lost art that used to be called "being oneself." And there's nothing wrong with the doctor. It's the rest of us who are in danger—of letting ourselves be persuaded into a confining and endless conformity that is bad for the human spirit.

There is no counting the publications today devoted entirely to "How-To" directives for forming our characters—rules for dressing right and eating right and speaking right and rightly getting ahead in the world. Just follow these rules and you too can join a standardized populace in one great gray goo of bumpless similarity.

I think the time is at hand for a sublime burst of putting ice cream on our cereal. This is the hour for our finding, in a flash of ancient glory revived, the art of being ourselves. You don't "form character" or "get ahead" or even "become more attractive to others" by following a set of instructions. You do it by being yourself. All you can learn by listening to rules and sedulously conforming your life to them is the hideous art of how to be nobody at all.

Think of the people you have known who have most memorably seemed to possess "character," who have seemed most interesting, most truly "adjusted" to the adventure of being a free-willed, creative, ideal-harboring human being. How many of these have been bound to the everlasting orthodoxies of How-To?

How-To says that the right way to get rested is to sleep eight hours a night. Thomas Edison, listening to the inner voice of his personal self and its needs, slept four. A friend of mine sleeps 11; that's the natural sleep-way for him.

You're *you*. If it's truly a part of the youness of you, sleep in a tree. (Charles Waterton, the grand old English naturalist and grander individualist, used to do that every now and then. He said it gave him the right tuning for feeling like a piece of God's creation, along with the chimpanzee and the owl.)

How-To would have you polish your way of speaking so that no infinitive ever gets split and no participle ever dangles and the sound of you becomes indistinguishable from the sound of every radio announcer. Henry Ward Beecher didn't do anything like that. He spoke *his* way, and it made him the greatest orator of his day. Sometimes he used words in an unconventional way, or bent formalities of grammar to his purpose. Once, when he'd done so, a woman reproved him after the sermon. "Madam," he said, "I am Henry Ward Beecher. If the English language gets in my way, God help it."

Is your native personality of a shy sort? How-To says you must overcome that. You must conform, so to speak, to standard brass. Young Charles Darwin didn't. He was so shy that he became almost sick when he had to mix in gatherings of important people. But he just went on being Charles Darwin, a nonmixer who followed his star into long, lonely contemplations; and he came up with the Theory of Evolution.

Do those exercises? Surely, if we really think they're right for us. But, if we've decided they're not . . . there was once a nonexerciser who got as fat as a buttertub. It didn't prevent his being a worth-while personality. His name was Thomas Aquinas.

Budget your time? If that's best for you, do it by all means. But if you find it's better to live in a furious blaze of activity for 20 hours at a stretch—if the light you need for your personal vision comes best from burning a candle at both ends—well, an old friend of mine lived that way, and the self that came of it was a self worth being. She was Edna St. Vincent Millay.

There is a dangerous threat in the air these days—the threat of our being thought for, ruled, regulated, pushed around, made into Things. There is only one weapon against that. The weapon is the Self—the unique and incalculable reality that is a human soul.

Man of Few Words

WHEN anyone asked my grandfather the secret of his 50 years of serene married life, he always told this story:

Right after our wedding, we started out to my ranch, with Jenny up behind me on the mare. Suddenly the mare stumbled. "That's once," I said. After a while she stumbled again. "That's twice," I said. And a few miles later on she stumbled the third time. "That's three times," I said, and pulled out my gun and shot the mare dead.

Jenny got sore because I had killed a perfectly good horse, and she read the riot act, real mad.

I waited until she was completely unwound. Then I said, "That's once." —Helen Peters in *True*

By Joshua Loth Liebman   A condensation from the book

ONCE, as a young man, I undertook to draw up a catalogue of the acknowledged "goods" of life. I set down my inventory of earthly desirables: *health, love, talent, power, riches* and *fame*. Then I proudly showed it to a wise elder.

"An excellent list," said my old friend, "and set down in not unreasonable order. But it appears that you have omitted the one important ingredient lacking which your list becomes an intolerable burden."

He crossed out my entire schedule. Then he wrote down three syllables: *peace of mind*.

"This is the gift that God reserves for His special protégés," he said. "Talent and health He gives to many. Wealth is commonplace, fame not rare. But peace of mind He bestows charily."

"This is no private opinion of mine," he explained. "I am merely paraphrasing from the Psalmists, Marcus Aurelius, Lao-tse. 'God, Lord of the universe,' say these wise ones, 'heap worldly gifts at the feet of foolish men. Give me the gift of the Untroubled Mind.'"

I found that difficult to accept; but now, after a quarter of a century of personal experience and professional observation, I have come to understand that peace of mind is the true goal of the considered life. I know now that the sum of all other possessions does not necessarily add up to peace of mind; on the other hand, I have seen this inner tranquillity flourish without the material supports of property or even the buttress of physical health. Peace of mind can transform a cottage into a spacious manor hall; the want of it can make a regal residence an imprisoning shell.

Analyze the prayers of mankind of all creeds, in every age—and their petitions come down to the common denominators of daily bread and inward peace. Such pleas for spiritual serenity must not be identified with ivory-tower escapism from the hurlyburly of life. Rather, they seek an inner equilibrium which enables us to overcome life's buffetings.

Peace of mind cannot be won by any brief or superficial effort. Association with noble works—literary, musical, artistic—helps to promote inward peace, but these alone cannot wholly satisfy the dimensions of the soul. Certainly we shall not find peace in the furious pursuit of wealth which slips like quicksilver through our grasping fingers. And finally, not even in the sublime sharings of human love—that emotion which most powerfully conveys the illusion of perfect happiness—is peace of mind reliably to be found.

Where then shall we look for it? The key to the problem is to be found in Matthew Arnold's lines:

> *We would have inward peace*
> *But will not look within . . .*

But will not look within! Here, in a single phrase, our willfulness is bared.

It is a striking irony that, while religious teaching emphasizes man's obligations to others, it says little about his obligation to himself. One of the great discoveries of modern psychology is that our attitudes toward ourselves are even more complicated than our attitudes toward others. The great commandment of religion, "Thou shalt love thy neighbor as thyself," might now be better interpreted to mean, "Thou shalt love thyself properly, and *then* thou wilt love thy neighbor."

A prominent social worker received a letter from a society woman who wanted to join in his crusade to help the poor of New York. She spoke at some length of her imperfections and ended by saying that perhaps her zeal for *his* cause would make up for her shortcomings. He wrote a brief reply: "Dear Madam, your truly magnificent shortcomings are too great. Nothing could prevent you from visiting them on victims of your humility. I advise that you love yourself more before you squander any love on others."

Some will argue that this is a dangerous doctrine. "Human beings love themselves too much already," they will say. "The true goal of life is the rejection of self in the service of others." There are errors in this estimate of human nature. Is it *true* that we are spontaneously good to ourselves? The evidence points in quite the opposite direction. We often treat ourselves more rigidly, more vengefully, than we do others. Suicide and more subtle forms of self-degradation such as alcoholism, drug addiction and promiscuity are extreme proofs of this. But all the streets of the world are teeming with everyday men and women who mutilate themselves spiritually by self-criticism; who go through life committing partial suicide—destroying their own talents, energies, creative qualities.

Such actions constitute a crime not only against ourselves but against society. He who does not have proper regard for his own capacities can have no respect for others. By loving oneself I do not mean coddling oneself, or indulging in self-glorification. I do, however, insist on the necessity of a proper self-regard as a prerequisite of the good and the moral life.

There are myriad ways in which we show contempt for ourselves rather than self-respect. Our feelings of inferiority, for instance: how often we attribute to our neighbors superior powers; we exaggerate their abilities, and sink into orgies of self-criticism. The fallacy here is that we see in others only the surface of assurance and poise. If we could look deeper and realize all men and women bear within themselves the scars of many a lost battle, we would judge our own failures less harshly.

To one who goes through life hypnotized by thoughts of inferiority, I would say: "In actuality, you are quite strong and wise and successful. You have done rather well in making a tolerable human existence out of the raw materials at your disposal. There are those who love and honor you for what you really are. Take off your dark-colored glasses, assume your place as an equal in the adult world, and realize that your strength is adequate to meet the problems of that world."

Another road to proper self-regard is the acceptance of our imperfections as well as our perfections. Most men have two pictures of their two selves in separate rooms. In one room is hung the portrait of their virtues, done in bright, splashing colors. In the other room hangs the canvas of self-condemnation, painted equally as unrealistically in dark and morbid shades.

Instead of keeping these two pictures separate, we must look at them together and gradually blend them into one. We must begin to know and accept ourselves for what we are—a combination of strengths and weaknesses. It is enough if we learn to respect ourselves with all our shortcomings and achievements; to know that true love of self neither exaggerates its powers nor minimizes its worth.

The great thing is that as long as we live we have the privilege of growing. We can learn new skills, engage in new kinds of work, devote ourselves to new causes, make new friends. Accepting, then, the truth that we are capable in some directions and limited in others, that genius is rare, that mediocrity is the portion of most of us, let us remember also that we can and must *change* ourselves. Until the day of our death we can grow, we can tap hidden resources in our make-up.

Every person who wishes to attain peace of mind must learn the art of renouncing many things in order to possess other things more fully. As young children, our wishes were sovereign; we had only to wail and the adult world hastened to fulfill our every desire. We knew, at that stage of development, very little about the postponement of satisfaction or the necessity of renunciation. But as we grow older we learn that every stage of human development calls upon us to weigh differing goods and to sacrifice some for the sake of others.

The philosopher Santayana pointed out that the great difficulty in life does not so much arise in the choice between good and evil as in the choice between good and good. In early life, however, we do not realize that one desire can be quite inconsistent with another. The young boy may vacillate between a dozen different plans for the future, but the mature man will have to renounce many careers in order to fulfill one. The same truth exists in the realm of emotions. It is fitting for the adolescent to transfer his love interest from one object of affection to another, but it is tragic when the grown man still plays the role of the adolescent. The man trying to wear youth's carefree clothing, the woman costuming her emotions in doll's dresses—these are pathetic figures. They have not yet learned that human growth means the closing of many doors before one great door can be opened—the door of mature love and of adult achievement.

The first fundamental truth about our individual lives is the indispensability of love to every human being. By "love" I mean relatedness to some treasured person or group, the feeling of belonging to a larger whole, of being of value to others.

Our interdependence with others is the most encompassing fact of human reality: our personalities are made by our contacts with others. A boy may catch the contagion of courage from his father, or receive the misery of fear from his mother. In a spiritual sense, we digest our heroes and heroines and make their way of life part of our own emotional substance. Thus every saint and every sinner affects those whom he will never see, because his words and his deeds stamp themselves upon the soft clay of human nature everywhere. There is, therefore, a duty which falls upon all of us—to become free, loving, warm, coöperative, affirmative personalities. If we understand this relatedness with others we shall get on noticeably better with our family, friends, business associates—and ourselves.

Next to bread, it is simple kindness that all mortals most hunger for. In times of catastrophe and disaster it finds a natural expression, good to contemplate in men's actions. But too often it is lacking in our daily lives. Many of us are dictatorial or bad-tempered toward others—employes, salespersons, domestic help. "I call no man charitable," said Thoreau, "who forgets that his barber, cook and hostler are made of the same human clay as himself." When we fail to be kind to all men, we destroy our own peace of mind. The jeweled pivot on which our lives must turn is the realization that every person we meet during the day is a dignified, essential human soul.

In the exchange of simple affection lies the true secret of marriage —which at its best is mutual encouragement. When we are accepted, approved, *needed* by those who know all about us and like us anyway, we have the first inkling of the peace that transcends understanding.

To love one's neighbors is to achieve an inner tolerance for the uniqueness of others, to resist the temptation to private imperialism. Among our renunciations we must renounce undue possessiveness in relation to friends, children—yes, even our loves. The world is full of private imperialists—the father who forces his artistic son into his business, or the mother who rivets her daughter to her service by chains of pity, subtly refusing the daughter a life of her own.

When we insist that others conform to our ideas of what is proper, good, acceptable, we show that we ourselves are not certain of the rightness of our inner pattern. He who is sure of himself is deeply willing to let others be themselves. He who is unstable in his own character must reassure himself by trying to compress others into his mold. We display true love when we cease to demand that our loved one become a revised edition of ourselves.

Every normal person experiences countless fears and worries. But it is possible to master these enemies of serenity.

It is true in a sense that man is blessed by his capacity to know fear. Fear is often the stimulus to growth, the goad to invention. Moreover, fear experienced in the presence of real danger is desirable. But are not most of our fears groundless? Scrutinize that large body of fears coming under the heading of "personal anxiety." Sometimes we are afraid about our health; we worry about our hearts, our lungs, our blood pressure, our insomnia. We begin to feel our pulse to find evidence of disease in every innocent or meaningless symptom. Or we become concerned about our personalities. We feel insecure, bemoan our failures, and imagine that others scorn or disapprove of us.

We must realize, of course, that our fears may disguise themselves. Some deep self-distrust may appear as an unreasoning fear of high places, of closed rooms. Again, our fears cunningly cloak themselves in the garments of physical pain. The new science of psychosomatic medicine has demonstrated that a whole gamut of illnesses, from the common cold to crippling arthritis, can often be traced to mental rather than physical troubles. It is so much easier to be sick than courageous! The ill health enjoyed by many chronic invalids is no more than an elaborate disguise for deep-seated fears.

Many such feelings of insecurity are hangovers from childhood when we really *were* inadequate and inferior, and knew that there was a vast difference between our weakness and the strength of the adult world. This difference disappears as we grow, but our childhood is a blackmailer that makes us pay over and over again for failures or mistakes that long ago have been outgrown.

Are we obsessed perhaps with a fear of death or the thought of punishment in an afterlife? Let us come to see that such fear is a projection from some early experience when we were punished by a parent, locked in a room, left alone. Are we continually haunted by the disapproval of others, frightened of social rejection? Let us look at these anxieties in the light of maturity, see that our neighbors are no less fallible than ourselves, and realize further that in the adult world we should not expect to be coddled as we were in childhood.

A source of hope lies also in the fact that our moods are temporary. This is a hard lesson to learn. When we are tired, every pinprick becomes the stab of a knife. But it is natural and normal to have depressed moods, and we should always remember that we will come out into the light again. We human beings are very tough organisms, able to withstand many shocks, to shed many tears, to live through many tragedies without breaking. Let us learn not to take the depression of the day or month as the permanent state of our life.

It is natural to experience fear concerning our economic and social future. Countless people are frightened of unemployment or the collapse of their careers. These fears are very real. But firmly attached to them are highly neurotic residues. Americans particularly are engaged in a marathon race in which the runners are extremely anxious about those panting at their heels and envious of those ahead. This relentless race for economic success is the source of many breakdowns and premature cardiac deaths.

A yearning for achievement is an admirable attribute of human nature. Where, then, do we go wrong? We err in the excessive energy that we devote not to real accomplishment but to neurotic combat. A man may have a home, possessions, a charming family, and yet find all these things ashy to his taste because he has been outstripped by some other runners in the race for material things. It is not that he does not possess enough for his own wants but that others possess more. It is the *more* that haunts him and makes him minimize his real achievements.

The time has come to say: "I am no longer going to be interested in how much power or wealth another man possesses so long as I can attain sufficient for the dignity and security of my family and myself. I am going to set my goals for myself rather than borrow them from others. I refuse any longer to destroy my peace of mind by striving only for money; I will also judge myself in the scale of goodness and culture."

We have learned that unexpressed emotions ultimately have their vengeance in the form of mental and physical illness. This truth illuminates for us the problem of achieving peace of mind in the face of bereavement and grief.

Dr. Erich Lindemann, in clinical work at the Massachusetts General Hospital with hundreds of grief patients, has uncovered the basic fact that to repress real feelings of grief may lead to morbid reactions later. Dr. Lindemann's patients included some who developed severe illness or depressions years after the loss of a loved one. Amazing cures of the mental and physical ills resulted when patients were persuaded to express the pain and sorrow that should normally have found outlet before.

How absurd is that notion which has gained currency in modern society that men and women must repress emotional outbursts. It is not those outbursts but the avoidance of them which scars the fabric of the soul.

The first law, then, which should be followed in the time of the loss of a loved one is: *give way to as much grief as you actually feel.* Do not be ashamed of your emotions; released now, they will be the instrument of your later healing.

The discoveries of psychiatry—of how essential it is to express rather than to repress grief, to talk about one's loss with friends and companions, to move step by step from inactivity to activity again— remind us that the ancient teachers of Judaism had an intuitive wisdom about human nature which our more sophisticated age has forgotten. The Bible records how open and unashamed was the expression of sorrow on the part of Abraham and Jacob and David. Our ancestors publicly wept, wore sackcloth, tore their garments, and fasted. It is unfortunate that in our time the expression of honest emotion has become taboo. Let us understand that the unrepressed experience of pain somehow has a curative function and that any evasive detour around normal sorrow will bring us later to a tragic abyss.

Armed with such knowledge, if we are courageous and resolute we can live as our lost loved ones would wish us to live—not empty, morose, self-centered and self-pitying but as brave and undismayed servants of the greater life.

It is not often that we are brave enough to come face to face with the thought of our own mortality. Yet man is not free in life unless he is also free from the fear of death.

As far as our own deaths are concerned, we should remember what science teaches about the process of dying. We needlessly frighten ourselves with anticipated horrors which never come to pass. As the famous physician, Sir William Osler, put it, "In my wide clinical experience, most human beings die really without pain or fear. There is as much oblivion about the last hours as about the first."

Montaigne said a wonderfully wise thing about this: "When I have been in perfect health, I have been much more afraid of sickness than when I have really felt the sickness. . . . Death is not to be feared. It is a friend."

No, death is not the enemy of life but its friend, for it is the knowledge that our years are limited which makes them so precious. Plato was right when he declared that infinite life on this earth would not be desirable, for a never-ending existence would be without heights or depths, without challenge or achievement. It is profoundly true that the joy of our striving and the zest of our aspirations would vanish if earthly immortality were our lot.

At the same time, we dare not ignore the hunger in the human heart for some kind of existence beyond this narrow span of life. There is an almost universal feeling that God could not shut the door completely upon our slowly developed talents—that there must be realms where we can use the powers achieved here. And one should not lightly dismiss the thoughts of the philosophers who insist that there is nothing inherently impossible about life in undreamed dimensions; that just as infrared rays are invisible to our eyes, so a creative, growing universe might well have hidden unsuspected continents beyond the perception of our senses.

Moreover, we should always remember that there are other forms of immortality besides personal survival. Man displays perhaps his most remarkable and his most unselfish genius when he turns from the thought of individual immortality and finds inspiration in the immortality of the human race. The more we concentrate upon the immortality of mankind, strangely enough, the richer becomes our own individual life. As we link ourselves to the heroes and sages and martyrs, the poets and thinkers of every race, we come to share the wisest thoughts, the noblest ideals, the imperishable music of the centuries. Poor, indeed, is the man who lives only in his own time. Rich is the man who participates in the riches of the past and the promises of the future.

Both science and religion teach us, at last, that the obstacles to serenity are not external. They lie within ourselves.

If we acquire the art of proper self-love; if, aided by religion, we free ourselves from shadow fears, and learn honestly to face grief and to transcend it; if we flee from immaturity and boldly shoulder adult responsibility; if we appraise and accept ourselves as we really are, how then can we fail to create a good life for ourselves? For then inward peace will be ours.

The Vague Specific

WOMEN HAVE a conversational peculiarity which I have named the Vague Specific. For example, I overheard a conversation between my wife and the maid.

"Here," my wife said, "you can put these out there somewhere."

"With the others?"

"No," said my wife, decisively. "Put them with those things behind the others."

The terrifying thing was that each knew exactly what the other meant.

I could make an indefinite list of Vague Specifics my wife pulls on me, such as: "Do you remember that time we were at the shore, and it rained?" (We've been to the shore 14 or 15 times, and it always rains.) Or, "What was the name of that couple we met that night?"

I come home from work and my wife greets me: "The men came today." Once I thought I had a system figured out to beat her at that one. I asked (craftily), "What did you tell them?" But that's where my system backfired, because she answered: "I told them to go ahead." The only satisfaction I got was that, whatever the men had gone ahead and done, it was going to cost me money.

—Richard B. Gehman in *Collier's*

Sudden Death

in the Home

By J. C. Furnas
Condensed from Ladies' Home Journal

As HE took out his key he noticed that Olive had taken down the Christmas wreath that hung outside the door during the holidays. The house was very quiet. Olive usually appeared when she heard the click of the door latch, to say an affectionate hello. He called softly and got no answer; then, after searching upstairs and down, he went to the cellar.

The floor was littered with artificial wreaths, tinseled stars and gaudy glass balls. And amid them lay Olive, dead of a fractured skull.

The story was easy to piece together. Olive had repacked all the Christmas doings and started for their storage spot in the cellar. Resting her chin on the stack of boxes to steady it, she could not see an empty pail on the top step. Her first step was her last.

That was one of over 30,000 deaths from home accidents that year. Each year the figure increases.

To leave a pail on the top step of a cellar stair is a foolish thing to do, as most people know when they stop to think. Yet an astounding proportion of the millions of home accidents annually come from just such foolishness.

"Don't stand on chairs to reach things — use an approved set of household steps" is something practically everybody knows. Yet:

A neighbor glimpsed faint smoke drifting out of Mrs. Arleen Callahan's kitchen window and went over to investigate. In another breath she was kneeling over Arleen's prostrate body. The smoke came from Arleen's new green house dress. Arleen had climbed on an elderly chair to reach some beeswax for her ironing. When the chair broke she knocked herself out and upset the ironing board; and the iron, still turned on, bit into her savagely. Only a very expensive plastic operation, which she cannot afford, would take away the red scar on her side. And she was lucky at that. Her dress might have burst into flame and burned her to death.

Good but unintelligent intentions can be hazardous, too. Tidy Mrs. Anderson, who always scalded out her empty milk bottles, set some outdoors on a very cold morning. The sudden difference in temperature, between 150 and 200 degrees, cracked a bottle in her hand and a long splinter of razor-sharp glass slashed her wrist artery. If she had been alone, her chances of bleeding to death would have been high.

Stoves often play a share in household tragedies. Little Frances Hirsch had on a lovely, fuzzy new sweater. When she started supper, Frances waited too long before applying the match to the oven and a gust of igniting gas turned the fuzzy sweater instantly into a seething shirt of flame.

Levelheaded even in her agony, she rolled in a bedspread to smother the fire. But by then she was a crimson statue of screaming pain from waist to throat. That much burned area can kill you. Frances survived — as have other housewives who nevertheless have lost eyebrows and front hair the same way.

Many a housewife has told many a daughter to turn pot handles toward the back of the stove. And many a daughter proceeds to forget it — like a certain mother last year whose apron string caught the handle of a large kettle of boiling water. Her small boy was tagging around after her in the kitchen. He got the full gush of the capsizing kettle, head to foot. His death was much less merciful than if his mother had dashed out his brains on top of the stove.

Risks like these are especially hazardous to children. Left alone for a few minutes, a small boy electrocutes himself by biting moistly into an electric cord, as innocently as he bites into a wooden toy. A small girl washing her doll clothes proceeds to feed her own arm into the electric wringer; her screams bring mother running, but it is too late for that blackening, swelling little arm. The loose window screen, the too widely spaced balustrade, even warm and protecting bedclothes — 1500 babies die yearly of accidental smothering — lie in wait for small fry.

Sometimes the devil exercises special ingenuity. A small-town house-wife, cleaning out the family medicine chest, dumped some 30 little boxes and bottles into an ash can. Two small boys found the collection and began to play doctor. Gravely one selected a dull blue pill for his patient's complaint and administered it. The pill was bichloride of mercury, once used for sterilizing during a family illness. The small boy died, to dramatize for his neighborhood that medicines are a hazard.

Every day people risk death by taking a pill in the dark or by failing to check the label before taking. It is only common sense to stick pins in the corks of poison bottles or tape their tops to call unmistakable attention to what is inside. As for leaving medicines within children's reach, actual poison is not the only risk. A youngster died not long ago from the consequences of eating most of a bottle of cascara pills.

Few engineers could devise a better killing device than stairs, particularly when they are supplemented by throw rugs, graceful curves and bad lighting. Slip on a level surface and you get only one blow from the floor. Slip at the top of a stair and the hard edge of every tread hammers your skull. A simple thing like an all-night dim light at the stairhead would keep many a drowsy person from taking the wrong turn.

The lovely white or pastel surfaces of bathrooms have often made a shocking contrast for blood and violent death. Tub, toilet and washstand are all made of porcelain or enamel baked over cold steel—sanitary but shatteringly dangerous to fall on. Add the slipperiness of soap and water on such surfaces, lack of proper handhold bars, and the prevalent habit of drying the feet while standing one-legged in the tub without a nonskid mat. Not long ago a girl who slipped in the tub knocked herself out face downward while the water was still running, and drowned. An elderly judge slipped in the tub, accidentally turning on the hot water, and scalded himself to death.

Bathrooms specialize in electrocutions, for human beings conduct electricity far better when in contact with water or a damp surface. Plenty of unimaginative people still insist, while in the tub, on turning lights on or off, or handling electric heaters, electric razors and electric curling irons. They are asking for trouble just as surely as those who smoke in bed alone or leave ice on walks and steps in winter.

A psychologist's recipe for the Elixir of Youth

Your Mind
Can Keep You Young

George Lawton

Condensed from The American Magazine

THE FEAR of growing old can strike you at almost any age. As a consulting psychologist, specializing in the problems of the aged, I find that a goodly percentage of my clients are still in their 30's—men and women who are already worried by the specter of approaching age. What I tell them can be read with profit by anyone from 17 to 70 who's interested in remaining young.

But before I give you my formula perhaps we'd best define our terms. Age can't be measured by the number of your birthdays. In the first place, biological time isn't at all the same thing as clock time. As the years pile up, biological time slows down; the older you are, the more slowly you age. Physically, you don't change as much from 30 to 40 as you did from 25 to 30; from 55 to 75 as from 40 to 55.

Another reason why the calendar furnishes a false clue to age is that different parts of you grow old at different rates. Your eyes began to age at ten; your hearing around 20. By 30 your muscular strength, reaction time and reproductive powers have all passed their peak.

On the other hand, your mind is still young and growing at 50; your brain doesn't reach its zenith until ten years after that. And from 60 on, mental efficiency declines very slowly to the age of 80.

At 80 you can be just as productive mentally as you were at 30—and you should know a lot more. Older people frequently suffer some loss of memory, but creative imagination is ageless. What's more, with age we develop insight and perspective. Our judgment and reasoning powers improve; so, thanks to a wealth of experience, does our strategy in tackling tough problems. In short, we acquire wisdom. That's why the old doctor, the veteran lawyer, the experienced craftsman, can usually hold his own against younger and more vigorous rivals.

Don't make the mistake of confusing emotional immaturity with true youthfulness. It takes a mature person to be really young. Men and women who refuse to grow up emotionally are usually the first ones to grow old; and the reason why, in later years, some people relapse into second childhood is that they never really emerged from their first. Masquerading as much younger than you are is a sure sign that you've not grown up emotionally.

My formula for staying young is simple: Concentrate on the part of you that's still young and growing—your brain. Keep your mind awake and you'll stay young all over. These are exciting times. Take an interest in the world around you. And make a point of learning at least one new thing every day.

Above all, don't "settle down." Psychologists are accustomed to seeing two contrasting personality types develop in the middle 30's. Some men and women, although keen about their families and jobs, are constantly broadening their other interests. They keep up with the newspapers and magazines; they busy themselves with creative hobbies, preferably ones that use their hands as well as their brains.

Another man begins, at 35, to slump into a dull but comfortable routine. Day after day he does his job, comes home, has dinner, glances at the comic strips or sporting page, fiddles with the radio and goes to bed. His wife does the housework, looks after the children, listens to soap operas, reads an occasional love story and attends a bridge club.

People of the first type grow younger with increasing years. Men and women of the second group have already hit the skids; if they don't change they'll be old at 45.

Regardless of your age it's not too late to make your life more interesting. I know a housewife who, at 50, with no previous experience made herself into an outstanding industrial designer. I know a retired electrical engineer who has become a highly paid ceramic artist. One of my clients—a woman of 70 whose children thought she should retire to the shelf—conducts a successful cooking school for brides.

Get over the notion that you're ever too old to go back to school. I know a man who entered medical college at 70. He got his degree with honors and became an eminent physician. Another man went to law school at 71 and is now an active lawyer. And a 91-year-old California woman has just gone back to college for a refresher course in American history. I know a woman who learned to paint at 77, held a "one-man" show at 80, and today, at 86, is still going strong. It's never too late to add another skill to those you now possess.

Irrespective of years, staying young is easy for those who live in the future. You can do it if you care enough to try. Keep your mind awake and active; that's the only youth elixir guaranteed to work.

Cross-Examination

A TEN-YEAR-OLD BOY, who presented his parents with a dreary report card, did not feel a bit chastened or inferior. Instead, he said, "I'd like to give the teacher an exam. I'll bet you I could ask her lots of things I'll bet she doesn't know." Whereupon he listed the questions he would ask his teacher. The long list included:

How can you tell a GMC or a Mack truck from a Ford truck from the rear?

What food can you put out at a bird-feeding station that even grosbeaks like?

What is the horsepower of a Caterpillar bulldozer, Model D-8?

Where is the best place in the neighborhood to catch frogs?

What do they use an 0-4-0 locomotive for?

What is a Phelps screwdriver?

What do you feed a pet garter snake?

What is the best way to start a car when the starter's stuck?

How do you tell grouse from pheasant tracks in the snow?

What is the difference between a Christie and a jump turn on skis?

Why do some trucks have dual rear wheels?

"There," said the young man, "is an exam I could pass easy."

— "Topics of The Times" in New York *Times*

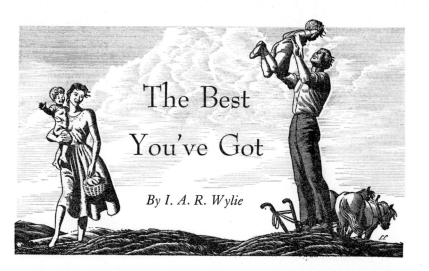

The Best You've Got

By I. A. R. Wylie

Decoration: Steele Savage, from International Telephone and Telegraph Co.

$\mathcal{I}$ HAD KNOWN him as a roughneck little boy when we played together in the back yards of a London suburb. Years later I met him again as a gangling adolescent who amazingly, overnight, became a trim, vigorous, resolute young man. I watched him fall in love with a charming girl, above him in education and social position, whom he wooed with all he had of imagination and ardor. For her sake he rubbed off his rough corners, literally made himself over to meet her on her own level. And in the end he won her.

He is now president of a large manufacturing company and on his way to bigger things. But he is divorced and sees his two children, whom he adores, only on those brief occasions prescribed by law.

"If I'd given my family half the intelligence I gave my business," he said to me once, "I shouldn't be the lonely, homeless man I am."

After marriage, the understanding, thoughtful lover had become a matter-of-fact husband, generous but casual and sometimes irascible. He wasn't really casual. He cared deeply. His irascibility was the explosion of pent-up irritations, carefully controlled in his day's work. It never occurred to him that they might work havoc in his home.

In all this he was like most of us who take for granted those nearest and dearest to us. Too often we treat the very essence of our lives—

getting on with one another in peace and happiness—with hit-or-miss methods which we would never dare apply to business or profession.

A scientist who knows that a millimeter of miscalculation may wreck his life's work, and himself with it, pays only rule-of-thumb attention to the no less delicate and potentially dangerous inner workings of his home. A clever businessman grouses over the breakfast table but becomes poised and well mannered as he enters his shop or office. He knows too well that it would be "bad business" to "be himself" with his boss or best customer or even with subordinates on whose loyal efficiency he depends. Back home again in the evening he can "let himself go" and give his moods full rein. His wife and children may accept and endure—up to a point. But one day, like my tycoon friend, he may wake up to find that what was once a warm and lovely sanctuary has become a deserted heap of rubble.

The truth is that a human relationship is the most delicate mechanism in the world, requiring for its successful maintenance an unceasing vigilance. It is easy to fall in love, but in order to stay in love each partner has to contribute all that he has of lovableness. It is an exacting task, not made up of occasional glamorous gestures but of a steady self-discipline, a sensitive awareness of what hurts, what irritates, what pleases.

Love, after all, must be sustained by liking, and we all know how we sometimes dislike those whom we love most—how often we wince at their ugly mannerisms, their displays of vanity, their tempers, their apparent disregard for us. And with that pitifully masked exasperation and dislike, love itself begins to fade into resigned indifference.

One day a famous composer got up from breakfast and left his wife forever because she had a trick of drumming with her fingers on the table—an apparently trivial cause for breaking up a partnership and yet not really trivial at all. It proved surely that the wife was too callously indifferent to her husband's sensitivity to spare him the nervous exasperation of a bad habit. Too many of us make the same tragic mistake of overburdening love with what seem to us trivia.

A friend of mine was a vivacious, well-groomed girl. During her engagement she showed wise concern for the tastes of the man she loved. But after her marriage, she let herself become slovenly, unpunctual, physically unattractive. When her husband finally left her she was broken-hearted and bewildered. "I was devoted to him," she wept to me. "I would have done anything on earth for him."

"Except powder your nose and be on time," was my unspoken comment. I know she would have stood by him in disaster, died for him if necessary. But daily life is not made up of disasters or spectacular acts of self-sacrifice. It is made up of small happinesses, small troubles, small opportunities to help or hurt. As another friend observed, "I wouldn't care so much if Jim failed me in a crisis, if only he would be pleasant when there wasn't one."

But surely, someone will argue, we ought to bear with each other. Surely I ought to be able, in my own home, to put off my best manners and rely on those who love me to understand.

The answer is that you do so most unfairly and at your peril. You didn't win love with your moods, weaknesses and foibles, and you cannot expect to keep it with them. And what do we get for ourselves out of thus letting-go? What do we derive from an explosion of home tantrums except jangled nerves and the weary necessity of picking up the pieces? (And whether we realize it or not, there is always one less piece to get back into the broken pattern.)

We are happiest when in spite of fret and discouragement we put up a good home front. Gratitude and tenderness reward us over the years when we keep our tempers at an even keel, when we put off an exasperating habit, when we rouse ourselves from our day's weariness to make those gestures of affection and understanding with which we first earned love for ourselves.

If at some time we feel overwhelmingly impelled to be devilish, why not do it for the benefit of outsiders—who don't care anyway and who can get out from under? The answer is, our vanity. We want to impress strangers. We should realize, however, that the love of our family and friends for us makes them more acutely aware of our shortcomings—and more vulnerable to the hurt of them.

This is a dangerous world we live in. There doesn't seem much that we as individuals can do to govern its course. But we are more important than we think. Each of us who makes his home a warm and happy citadel creates a core of strength in his community.

The dissolution of all previous civilizations has been marked by the weakening of human relations, the break-up of the home. Perhaps, therefore, the real heroes of our society are not the great soldiers, states-men and scientists, but the great lovers—not the flamboyant lovers, the Antonys and Cleopatras, but the Elizabeth and Robert Brownings, the old, happy pair in the frame house down your street whose life's devotion has been tended with daily care.

They fulfill ideals which we are sometimes too lazy or too thought-less to fulfill ourselves. They are the good citizens, the wise philoso-phers, the great artists in the art of living. They remind us of what we all know in our heart of hearts but forget too easily: that the love and friendship which is the basis of our lives, and of our way of life, needs the best we've got—all the time.

Not by Bread Alone

Mᴀɴ does not live by bread alone, but by beauty and harmony, truth and goodness, work and recreation, affection and friendship, aspira-tion and worship.

Not by bread alone, but by the splendor of the firmament at night, the glory of the heavens at dawn, the blending of colors at sunset, the loveliness of magnolia trees, the magnificence of mountains.

Not by bread alone, but by the majesty of ocean breakers, the shim-mer of moonlight on a calm lake, the flashing silver of a mountain tor-rent, the exquisite patterns of snow crystals, the creations of artists.

Not by bread alone, but by the sweet song of a mockingbird, the rustle of the wind in the trees, the magic of a violin, the sublimity of a softly lighted cathedral.

Not by bread alone, but by the fragrance of roses, the scent of orange blossoms, the smell of new-mown hay, the clasp of a friend's hand, the tenderness of a mother's kiss.

Not by bread alone, but by the lyrics of poets, the wisdom of sages, the holiness of saints, the biographies of great souls.

Not by bread alone, but by comradeship and high adventure, seek-ing and finding, serving and sharing, loving and being loved.

Man does not live by bread alone, but by being faithful in prayer, responding to the guidance of the Holy Spirit, finding and doing the loving will of God now and eternally.   —*The University Presbyterian*

What Men
Notice About Women

Condensed from Ladies' Home Journal
By Judith Chase Churchill

FIRST IMPRESSIONS are a whole lot more important than most of us realize. For it seems that men not only take note of surprising details but have devised some very special ways of their own for uncovering clues to feminine character.

Until we popped the question to various celebrities, we were under the delusion that the ways in which men were first impressed by women were pretty well standardized. But we had another guess coming. Men, we now discover, are far more alert than we had ever before suspected.

Sir Norman Angell: "I judge women by what they do *not* have. If they have the courage to wear the nails they were born with, be cautious with the lipstick and the cocktails—these negative signs indicate someone who may be worth knowing better."

Robert Taylor: "I notice her walk. I hate to see a little mincing walk on teetery heels just as much as I hate to see a girl striding along like a distance walker. You can tell a lot about a woman from a half block away just from her walk, before you ever see her face."

Bing Crosby: "The first thing I observe about a woman is her eyes: if they twinkle she has a sense of humor and can take a rib—and I dearly love to rib a dame."

Michael Arlen: "The first thing I notice about a woman is whether she is attractive or not. The next thing I *try* to notice is whether she thinks I am attractive or not."

Henry C. Link: "For me there are two ways of looking at a woman: either as a picture or as a personality. In a restaurant, on the street and in public places I look at women primarily as pictures. In social groups I look on them as personalities. Personality is measured by the extent to which a person has developed habits which interest and serve others. What a woman does to others is far more revealing than what she does to herself."

Guy Lombardo: "Mood is very important—sometimes a woman's attitude changes her entire appearance. I've seen women look so radiant you aren't aware of what kind of clothes they're wearing or whether they're blonde or brunette."

Budd Schulberg: "Very early in the game I divide those women whose role is being attractive from those who are more at peace with themselves and meet you as people rather than as manikins. The manikins are fine in their place, but an attractive woman who doesn't feel that she's entitled to a life pass to the ball park merely because she exists—she's a thing of beauty and a joy forever."

Hodding Carter: "I look first at a woman's eyes. They tell more of her character, intentions, and whether one would like to meet her."

Victor McLaglen: "I notice hands. Not the shape of them so much as the way a woman uses them."

Eddie Cantor: "A look into a woman's eyes has always been for me a sort of laborsaving device."

Victor Moore: "I always like to see them approaching and sometimes I like to look at them departing."

What Women Notice About Men

Condensed from Ladies' Home Journal
By Judith Chase Churchill

WATCH the way a man walks. Does he scurry along with quick, short steps, his shoulders hunched until they almost meet in front? Then he's a scared guy. Does he swagger until he almost pivots with every step? He's a blowhard and apt to be a bore. I warm most to an easy and free-swinging stride, a sign that a guy knows where he's going and how to get there.　　　　—*Betty Hutton*

THE CLUE to a man's personality lies in his voice. A quiet, well-modulated voice usually indicates a man of character and sureness; a raspy, squeaky or whispery voice usually belongs to a man who hasn't got a good enough grip on himself to control his own breathing. The person who can afford to relax within himself has a pleasing voice without even trying.　　　　—*Irene Dunne*

IF A MAN is quiet I am intrigued. I get a feeling that there is something of genuine worth under the quiet exterior. I do not care so much what the person inside really is if he is truly himself. I like to get the feeling of a genuine, sincere and self-contained personality which is not on parade. If this quality is there it is much more important to me than good looks or any of the more conspicuous trade-marks.
　　　　—*Margaret Bourke-White*

THE EYES, particularly the expression in them—let's be candid—with which he looks at me; that is, of course, provided he is fairly attractive.
　　　　—*Cornelia Otis Skinner*

THE FIRST THING I notice about a man is his self-possession. If he has this he is potentially all the other things: intelligent, handsome, successful and masterful. The worst thing that can happen to a man is to lose this belief in his powers. No barber, tailor or haberdasher can replace it. —*Bertita Harding*

A MAN'S WAY of arguing is to me his most revealing characteristic— his pace in speaking, his expression when he gropes for a word, and his technique: whether he drives his point home with a sledge- hammer blow, a gentle, slithering push, or the Chinese drop-torture method of infinite repetition. —*Felicia Lamport*

I NOTICE very much the way in which a man talks about women. I like a man who speaks with spontaneous affection and simplicity of either his mother or his wife. And I particularly notice whether he is interested in life for its own sake, apart from what he can get out of it. —*Elizabeth Bowen*

If he laughs, *how* he laughs, and *what about.* —*Mignon G. Eberhart*

ESPECIALLY I notice what he does with his hands. There are men whose hands speak of peace and calmness and good sense. They don't drum and patter. When these men have nothing to do with their hands, they keep still. When they have something to do, their hands move quietly and efficiently. —*Gwen Bristow*

THE EXPRESSION of the face. From his ancestors a man inherits the shape of his nose, the color of his hair, his stature. His mannerisms are often acquired in unconscious imitation of the people around him. But the *expression* is what has been brought to the person by his own way of life, his own attitude toward others, his own feeling about him- self. —*Dorothy Canfield Fisher*

WHAT ALL women from eight to 80 would answer if truthful, and that is whether or not he notices me. —*Faith Baldwin*

One of the secrets of good health is to escape the tyranny of
telephone, clock and calendar

Tension's Little Trigger Men

By Richard H. Hoffmann, M.D.
As told to Clarence W. Hall

Condensed from The American Weekly

I SAW Bill Jones's picture staring at me from the obituary columns
the other day. A highly successful executive in his early 40's, Jones
had come to me a few months before. He had the symptoms of
several diseases—headaches, insomnia, loss of appetite, rising blood
pressure. Yet examinations showed no organic disruption. A few days
later I dropped into his office, spent a half hour observing his work
habits. Then I said: "There's nothing wrong with you, Bill, that you
yourself can't cure. You're simply allowing yourself to be riddled by
three of today's most potent killers—the Telephone, the Clock and
the Calendar. They can be the trigger men of your death."

They were.

I volunteered the same warning to a harried housewife. When she
came to my office she was a museum of complaints for which careful
diagnosis could reveal no physical cause. From the description of her
average day, I got the picture of a civic do-gooder furiously dashing
about between kitchen stove, an ever-jangling telephone and endless
deeds of mercy. She somehow found time to fret constantly over her
limited household budget, worry over appointments and entertain an
almost paranoiac fear of the future.

"Right now," I told her, "you are nothing more than a victim of
your telephone, clock and calendar. As such, however, you have made
yourself a likely candidate for any of a number of real diseases."

She listened impatiently to my advice on how to revise her manner of stressful living, then flounced out, annoyed that I had not uncovered an interesting psychiatric condition or prescribed some glandular injection. Six months later she was taken with a severe—and fatal—kidney ailment.

Both she and Bill Jones, like many of the 300,000 other middle-aged Americans who this year will succumb to stroke, hypertension, angina pectoris and gastrointestinal diseases, were active accessories to their own killing.

More than half our hospitals are occupied by people with nervous troubles—most of them caused by such out-of-hand emotions as anxiety, despair, discontent, fear, frustration. By our own habits we heckle our nerves with minor irritations, reduce efficiency of body and mind, sour our dispositions and turn existence into a rat race.

After 40 years of general and psychiatric practice, I am convinced that tensive states, being self-induced, must be self-cured. I am further convinced that worriers would do well to start with those despots, the telephone, the clock and the calendar.

The telephone's peculiar tyranny is that of *interruption*. People in public life are not being arrogant when they refuse to have their phone numbers listed. They won't allow themselves to become victims of the telephone's conversational shrapnel.

Few of us can afford the luxury of a secretary who acts as a buffer, yet we can learn to live more calmly with the phone. Have the instrument placed as far from your usual base of operations as convenience will allow. Before answering, relax, take a few deep breaths, compose your suddenly aroused nerves. Don't run; *walk* toward it. When phoning others, ask: "Are you busy now? Will it be more convenient if I call back later?" Make your calls as brief as possible. The dawdlers and gossips who tie up a line indefinitely provoke needless resentment.

The clock's despotism is the tyranny of *appointment*. Safety experts estimate that nine tenths of the accidents on streets and in homes are caused by careless rushing. Bent on beating a deadline, tens of thousands of us every year jaywalk to our deaths, accelerate our cars into fatal smashups, fall down stairs or skid on skittery rugs.

Resolve to make your whole day less dominated by the ticking tyranny of clocks. Get into the habit of starting a few minutes earlier to work; the same in keeping an appointment. Avoid making your day's program too tight with successive engagements. Pad your time budget with little chunks of extra minutes to rediscover what Don Herold calls "the lost art of doing nothing." Leave some leeway for emergencies. You will be amazed how this increases your efficiency and conserves your vitality.

The tyranny the calendar exercises is that of *apprehension;* it gets in its most killing licks when we allow the morrow to saddle us with unreasoning fears. I have a patient who regularly goes into an emotional tailspin with the advent of each income-tax day. Other calendar dates produce repeated tensive states—such as the first of the month, a time for paying bills.

The fear of growing old is perhaps the calendar's sharpest thrust. Scores of people are plunged into mental and physical upset by fear of future insecurity, loneliness, failure, sickness. Our American cult of youth has created the silly concept that in youth alone is beauty and excitement and achievement. Now, happily, a host of individuals are demonstrating the fallacy of that notion.

Only a few years ago a star of stage and screen brought me her woes. She wailed that she was a has-been, with glamour gone, youth long past. I scoffed at her: "Why not be your age—and act your age?" She accepted the leading role in a dramatic production featuring a has-been, and rose to popular acclaim. Now, healthy in body and spirit, she boasts about grandchildren whose existence she had kept hidden before.

No better advice was ever given the calendar-cowed than that offered by Sir William Osler: "Waste of energy, mental distress, nervous worries dog the man who is anxious about the future. Cultivate the habit of a life of *day-tight compartments"*—with each day sufficient unto itself.

You will have taken one of the longest steps toward the achievement of serene living when you tackle these tyrannies of the telephone, the clock and the calendar. Three simple rules will start you:

Look *inside* yourself. The human body is a delicately adjusted mechanism. Whenever its even tenor is startled by some intruding emotion like sudden fright, anger or worry, the sympathetic nervous system flashes an emergency signal and the organs and glands spring into action. The adrenal glands shoot into the blood stream a surcharge of adrenalin which raises the blood sugar above normal needs. The pancreas then secretes insulin to burn the excessive fuel. But this bonfire burns not only the excess but the normal supply. The result is a blood sugar shortage and an underfeeding of all vital organs. So the adrenals supply another charge, the pancreas burns the fuel again, and the vicious cycle goes on. This battle of the glands brings on exhaustion.

The body can handle a reasonable number of emergency calls. But if they are repeated too often, your nerves and organs and glands, fatigued from trying to keep up with all those confusing false alarms, finally quit—and you're in for a nervous breakdown.

Look *at* yourself. If we who rush and worry needlessly could see ourselves as others see us, simple pride would stop us. Let any morbidly distraught woman consult her mirror when she is under the lash of our trinity of tyrants, her face ugly with frowns, her jaws clenched. Cosmetic tricks won't banish those beauty destroyers.

A candid survey of ourselves might also make us cease calling our stressful commotion by such flattering names as "diligence to duty . . . love of getting things done . . . wise provision for the future."

Look *away* from yourself. Practice lifting your mind, every now and again, above the rush and confusion around you. Take time out during your busiest day to think of something pleasant. Says Edwin Markham: "At the heart of the cyclone tearing the sky is a place of central calm." Each of us, in cyclonic situations, has his own place of "central calm." One secret of living above the tensions of the day is finding that place—and repairing to it often.

Paste a skull-and-crossbone label on your telephone, clock and calendar. Then sit back and say—as did the late Mahatma Gandhi— "There is more to life than increasing its speed."

---

*W*ives, like children, need to be loved most when they least deserve it.
—Quoted by Dr. Paul Popenoe, National Newspaper Syndicate

Love is not blind — it sees more, not less. But because it sees more, it is willing to see less.   —Rabbi Julius Gordon, *Your Sense of Humor* (Didier)

Obey That Impulse

William Moulton Marston

Author of "The Lie Detector Test," "Try Living," and "March On"

Condensed from a CBS Broadcast

FOR YEARS as a psychologist I have sought in the careers of great and of everyday people the inner springs that make for successful living. There are two which seem to me of prime importance: The first is hard work, governed by cool, logical thoughtfulness. The other is sudden, warm, impulsive action.

Admitting that I can't name a single person of true accomplishment who hasn't forged success out of brains and hard work, I still hazard the sweeping assertion that most of the high spots and many of the lesser successes in their careers stem from *impulses* promptly turned into action.

Most of us actually stifle enough good impulses during the course of a day to change the current of our lives. These inner flashes of impulse light up the mind for an instant; then, contented in their afterglow, we lapse back into routine, feeling vaguely that sometime we might do something about it or that at least our intentions were good. In this we sin against the inner self, for impulses set up the lines of communication between the unconscious mind and daily action. Said William James, "Every time a resolve or fine glow of feeling evaporates without bearing fruit, it is worse than a chance lost; it works to hinder future emotions from taking the normal path of discharge." Thus we fail to build up the power to act in a firm and prompt and definite way upon the principal emergencies of life.

Once, in Hollywood, where Walter B. Pitkin and I were retained by a motion-picture studio, a young promoter presented an ambitious production idea to us. The plan appealed to both of us. It was, I thought, distinctly worth considering; we could think it over, discuss it and decide later what to do. But even while I was fumbling with the idea, Pitkin abruptly reached for the phone and began dictating a telegram to a Wall Street man he knew. It presented the idea in the enthusiasm of the moment. (As delivered it was almost a yard long.) It cost money, but it carried conviction.

To my amazement, a ten-million-dollar underwriting of the picture project came as a result of that telegram. Had we delayed to talk it over we might have cautiously talked ourselves out of the whole idea. But Pitkin knew how to act on the spur of the moment. All his life he had learned to trust his impulses as the best confidential advisers he had.

Behind many an imposing executive desk sits a man who is there because he learned the same lesson. You've probably seen him in action more than once. Somebody is presenting to him a new idea, say in employe relations. It calls for extensive changes in office routine. And, deciding instantly, he calls an associate and gives instructions to make the change—then and there, not next week or next month.

We envy such men the ease with which they make up their minds and swing into action. But this ease is acquired over a long period of years. Rather than being, as we sometimes think, a privilege of their position, it is a practice that has led to their success. First in small matters and then in larger ones, they have acquired the do-it-now habit.

Calvin Coolidge remains an enigma to political commentators because the reasons for his actions were seldom apparent and the source of his astuteness could not be traced. No one could seem less impulsive than Coolidge, yet all his life he trained himself to rely on "hunches." He was not afraid of his impulses, and the celebrated Coolidge luck followed a pattern of action based on them. As a young attorney in a country law firm Coolidge was interviewing an important client one day when a telephone message informed him that the county political boss was in town. It occurred to Coolidge that he ought to see the local bigwig at once and propose himself as a candidate for the legislature. Without hesitation, this usually shy young lawyer cut his legal conference short, left the office and hunted up the county leader. That impulse bore fruit, and from then on the inner urges of Calvin Coolidge led him consistently on to political success.

It should be clear from Coolidge's case that the person who follows his impulses is not necessarily flighty. The timid soul, however, is fearful lest impulse lead him into all manner of mistakes. But mistakes are inevitable—we are bound to make them no matter which course we take. Some of the worst mistakes in history have followed consciously reasoned decisions. If we're right 51 percent of the time in our impulsive actions we aren't doing badly by any standard.

The mistakes of inaction, flanked by heavy reasoning, are likely to be worse than the mistakes of genuine impulse. For one thing, they make our inertia worse day by day. Not long ago a woman whose husband had left her came to seek my advice. The difficulty between them appeared to be one of temperament which could be easily adjusted. And the woman told me that what she really wanted to do was simply to call her husband up and talk with him. I told her to follow that inclination.

She left me somewhat at peace. But she didn't make the call; and in a few days she was back again. Once more she left with the impulse to call her husband. Unhappily, she never did. And a domestic rift that a few impulsive words on the phone might have healed finally ended in Reno. From childhood she had made time after time the mistake of letting her impulses die a-borning, and when the time came for a simple, direct decision in a situation that mattered, she was unable to act.

We all know people who go through agonies of indecision before taking any important step. There are always arguments for and against, and the more we think about them the more they seem to offset each other, until we wind up in a fretful state of paralysis. Impulsive action, which originates in a swift subconscious appraisal of the situation, might have saved all that worry. And when a painfully thought-out decision proves wrong, how often we remember an original hunch that would have been right!

The way to get things done is to bring mind and muscle and voice into play at the very second a good impulse starts within us. I know a writer. who was once engaged on a major project and was resolved that nothing could divert him from it. But he saw an announcement of a contest for the ten best rules for safe driving. The announcement flashed a light on the panel of his mind. Here was something he knew about. He interrupted his job long enough to get to a library and study up. He wrote 250 words. He turned in his entry in his own typing, not wanting to stop his stenographer from the bigger job. Months later that obeyed impulse netted him an award of $25,000. The project from which he turned aside for a moment finally brought him $600.

Or consider the young college instructor who sat listening one day to a commencement address by Woodrow Wilson, then governor of New Jersey. The instructor had written a book on political science, but had sought a publisher in vain. It embodied his innermost convictions and its apparent failure had caused him to despair of the future of his teaching.

Something Mr. Wilson said made the instructor feel that he ought to seek the governor's advice. He had heard that Wilson was cold and hard to approach; but at the end of the address he let his impulse carry him forward through the crowd; he grasped Mr. Wilson's hand, and said rapidly, "Your speech was wonderful! I've written a book maintaining that . . ." In a few pithy sentences he stated his theory.

Wilson shook his head. "No," he said. "You're wrong. I'll tell you why. See me after lunch at the Faculty Club." There for two hours Wilson talked earnestly. And under the inspiration Wilson gave him, the instructor wrote a new book. It sold more than 100,000 copies and launched him on a distinguished educational career. The first vital impulse, half-hesitantly obeyed, was the starting point.

The life stories of successful people are chock-full of such episodes that have marked major turning points in their careers. True impulses are intelligent. They show the path we can most successfully follow because they reveal the basic interests of the unconscious mind.

There is in all of us an unceasing urge toward self-fulfillment. We know the kind of person we want to be because our impulses, even when enfeebled by disuse, tell us. Impulsive action is not to be substituted for reason but used as a means of showing the direction reason is to take. Obviously the path is not without pitfalls. To start suddenly throwing ourselves around on impulse might be hazardous. But we can begin responding oftener to inner urges that we know we can trust.

We *know* that in the midst of reading we ought to stop and look up a word if the meaning is not clear. We know that we ought to speak more words of unpremeditated praise where they are due. We know that we ought to wriggle out of selfish routine and take part in civic activities, that we ought to contribute not merely money but time to the well-being of the neighborhood.

Such separate moments of achievement are cumulative and result in enriched living, a consciousness of daily adventure, a long-term sense that life is not blocked out and cut-and-dried but may be managed from within. The man whose philosophy is summed up in the feeble and indecisive motto, "Well, we'll see about it," misses the savory moments of experience, the bounce and gusto of life.

Thumb back over the pages of your own experience and note how many of your happiest moments and greatest successes have followed spur-of-the-moment actions and decisions. They are reminders that only from the depths of your inner self can you hope for an invincible urge toward accomplishment. So, obey your best impulses and watch yourself go!

DR. RANDOLPH RAY, rector of the Little Church Around the Corner, doesn't believe in giving young couples long-winded advice on marriage. His usual parting speech is a terse, nine-word affair. "Now," he tells them with a smile, "don't both get mad at the same time!"

—Robert Stein in *Collier's*

WE WERE discussing the philosophy of "Live each day as though it were your last."

"Well," said the sweetest old lady of the group, "that's a fine saying, but for 20 years I've been using a philosophy that's a little different. It's this: 'Treat all the people you meet each day as though it were *their* last day on earth.'"

—Contributed by Barbara Reid

Don't Teach
Your Youngster to Drive

By Amos E. Neyhart

Administrative Head of the Institute of Public Safety, Pennsylvania State College

Condensed from The American Magazine

NOT LONG AGO a 16-year-old high school student asked me if I thought it was all right for his father to teach him to drive. "No," I said. "Get an expert to do it."

A few days later the father indignantly said to me: "I've been driving for 20 years. Why shouldn't I teach my own youngster?"

"Because it's murder!" I replied.

Few parents ever had adequate driver education themselves, so they can't see anything dangerous about giving their children the same kind of hit-or-miss training. Yet in Pennsylvania a recent study of the driving records of 1500 youngsters who were taught to drive by their parents or other amateurs disclosed that they were involved in three times as many traffic accidents and violations as an equal number who learned about cars and driving in high school. After Massachusetts introduced driving training in its schools, personal-injury accidents involving 16- and 17-year-olds dropped from an average of 1206 to 642 per year. Other evidence gathered throughout the nation tells the same story.

It is dangerous for children to learn how to drive from their parents because the chances are that the grownups aren't very good drivers themselves, not nearly so good as they think they are. Experts, keeping score on the driving behavior of thousands of adults, have found that only seven percent are "excellent" drivers; only 24 percent rate as "good." The other 69 percent are "average," "poor" or "very poor." In other words, they have acquired habitual mistakes at the wheel. It is natural for their children to imitate these mistakes. The results may be grim.

Recently a young girl I knew was killed in a collision. An investigation showed she had been driving on the wrong side of the road while making a blind curve at 60 m.p.h. A truck swept around the curve and collided head-on with the girl's car.

Further investigation revealed she had been taught to drive by her mother, who made a practice of taking curves wide. Thanks to plain luck, or the skill of other drivers, the mother had escaped trouble for many years. She didn't realize what a dangerous habit it was and unintentionally taught it to her daughter.

In another recent case an 18-year-old boy stopped for a traffic light. When the light changed he gunned his motor for a fast start, but instead of going forward he rammed backward into a car behind him. A man in the other car was seriously hurt and is suing for $100,000 damages.

Why did the boy throw the car into reverse instead of low and thus go backward instead of forward?

Police discovered he had been taught to drive by his father, who made a practice of starting his car in second gear. When you are going from neutral to second it is all too easy to slip into reverse instead, as the boy did at the traffic light.

Other perilous practices which young men and women acquire from their parents include dangling arms out of windows, riding the clutch or the brake, weaving in traffic. Few fathers and mothers keep one car length behind the vehicle ahead for each ten m.p.h. they are traveling. Few observe the important rule that after passing another vehicle you should be able to see it in your mirror before cutting back in front of it.

Even parents with good driving habits are not usually fitted to teach their youngsters to drive. Teaching is a science in itself.

A friend who held a Ph.D. degree in automotive engineering felt perfectly capable of teaching his son to drive—until he got into his car with the boy. Then he suddenly found he didn't know what to teach him first. Should he start out by delivering a lecture on safety principles, the relation of speed to stopping distance? Or how to start the engine, or steer, or shift gears?

When I gave him a teaching manual he discovered there were so many things he didn't know about giving driving lessons that he wisely decided to let an expert instruct his son.

Teaching requires a great deal of patience. It is human nature for most of us to be less patient with our own flesh and blood than with strangers; that fact alone makes most parents ineligible as driving instructors. A calm and objective attitude is essential, and the boy or girl whose parent is exasperated can't be expected to learn to drive well.

Experience has shown that a youngster learning to drive should receive at least 30 hours of classroom instruction about automobiles, safe-driving practices and highway courtesy. This work employs textbooks, charts, blackboard diagrams and motion pictures.

When the student is ready for practice driving he should start in a car equipped with dual clutch and brake pedals which can be operated by the instructor if necessary. Other mechanical devices also help the professional do a better teaching job than a parent possibly can; these include detonators for measuring reaction time and braking distance.

A high percentage of otherwise good citizens violate traffic regulations, regard highway policemen as natural enemies and express low opinions of other drivers on the road. These attitudes are readily absorbed by their children, who frequently grow up to be traffic violators and discourteous drivers like their parents. Rudeness and smart-aleckism are responsible for an untold number of highway tragedies.

A man I once knew was forever cussing other drivers. Even when he took his five-year-old daughter for a spin in the country on Sunday afternoons he turned the air blue with his criticism of other motorists. Then one Sunday his wife took the child for her outing. When they returned, the little girl reported.

"We had a wonderful ride, Daddy," she said. "We saw cows and chickens and pigs and little lambs. And you know what?" she piped rapturously. "We didn't see a single bastard all afternoon!"

In thousands of the high schools which offer driver training today traffic experts explain local regulations to students. Police officials discuss their traffic-enforcement problems. From these authorities boys and girls will accept advice which they wouldn't take from their parents.

We have found that the word "safety" doesn't appeal to the student. He is sick of being told not to do things. Consequently we emphasize good sportsmanship. He is taught that driving, like any other game, requires fair play and adherence to the rules, respect for the traffic authorities, who are the referees, and courteous conduct toward other drivers, or "players."

If your high school doesn't offer a driving course, the chances are that you can interest the local educators in starting one. It costs comparatively little. In virtually every community auto dealers, encouraged by car manufacturers, will lend cars free for high school instruction. It costs only about $35 to equip a car with dual clutch and brake pedals; the only other money a school board has to spend is for insurance, classroom equipment and the expense of sending a high school teacher to take an authorized college course in driver training.

Anniversary Tale

A COUPLE on their Golden Wedding Anniversary were interviewed by a reporter.

"And tell me," he asked, pencil poised, "in all this time together did you ever consider divorce?"

"Oh, no, not divorce," the little old lady said, "but sometimes" —she paused and winked at her husband—"murder!"

—Helen Papashvily in *Good Housekeeping*

The Retort of the Native

A TOURIST spending the night in a small Vermont town joined several men sitting on the porch of the general store. They were a taciturn bunch and, after several vain attempts to start a conversation, he finally asked, "Is there a law against talking in this town?"

"No law against it," answered one of the men, "but there's an understanding no one's to speak unless he's sure he can improve on silence." —Margaret Schooley

If your emotions are boiling, don't drive!

SOREHEADS AT THE WHEEL

By Louis Gay Balsam   Condensed from The Kiwanis Magazine

Louis Balsam, Harvard Ph.D. in Sociology and formerly chief of personnel of the Norfolk Prison, Mass., was prompted to undertake the inquiry which led to this article by seeing a friend leave his home one afternoon "blind mad at his wife." The friend ended up badly smashed in a hospital. Dr. Balsam wondered if his friend's anger had anything to do with the accident and set out on a round of interviews that took six months to complete.

I HAVE interviewed more than 600 persons involved in major traffic accidents. In the vast majority of cases these people had two things in common: all were deeply unhappy before the accident and this unhappiness came to a head a few hours before the smashup.

Jim Robinson of Los Angeles (this name, like all others mentioned, is fictitious) had been heavily fined and given a suspended jail sentence of six months for ignoring a red light and plowing into a car driven by a woman taking two children home from school. "Do you remember anything unusual about your thoughts or feelings before the accident?" I asked him.

He nodded sadly. "Yes, I do. I'm a quiet sort of guy. But that day I had a fearful row with my foreman. He said I wasn't earning my salary. I felt he was rotten unfair. Blew my top. Got my hat and left.

"I was so burned up I don't even remember driving, let alone seeing the red light. All I could think of was how I hated that foreman. I'm lucky to be alive. I couldn't have explained about my blowup to the judge, now, could I?"

As a matter of fact, he could have. Several judges told me they realize that unhappiness or emotional unbalance is back of thousands of smashups. But, as one judge said, "we can't excuse anyone for that reason."

Ellen Wingate of Springfield, Mass., was convicted of knocking down an elderly man while doing 25 miles an hour in a 15-mile zone. He died two months later. "On the day of the accident," she told me, "I accused my husband of paying too much attention to another woman. He said some bitter things, all the more bitter because they were true. He told me I was getting sloppy and that my home was a mess. I tried to defend myself, but he walked out. I got in the car raging mad at him—and saw the man in the road too late."

Helen Sullivan of Seattle, Wash., was found guilty of hitting a man and a woman at an intersection, nearly killing both.

"I'll say there was something unusual about that day!" she responded to my question. "I was in love with my boss and I thought he was in love with me. One morning he phoned from out of town and asked me to wait for him at the office. He said he had something to tell me. I was sure he was going to ask me to marry him. When he arrived he told me the news. He was going to marry somebody else!

"When I left the office I didn't care whether I lived or died, or what happened. And I ran into that couple within an hour. No, I'm still not over it. But I know enough now to stay out of the car when I'm feeling bad."

My investigation of these 600 drivers proves that motor accidents and bruised egos go together. For a car is a most effective salve for emotional hurts. All day long, on the job, perhaps at home, you have been carrying out orders given by others; behind the wheel of your auto you are boss—you step on the gas and great power leaps to your command. You put distance between yourself and your unhappiness—temporarily. Your car never argues; it obeys, and you, like all the rest of us, crave being boss some of the time. All this is fine when things go well for you. But when you're emotionally upset, your car can instantly turn into a lethal weapon.

We must face the fact that cars are safe to drive only when our feelings are normal. Never otherwise. We have always known that most accidents are the result of carelessness. It's about time we asked ourselves the cause of this deadly carelessness. Take the case of Don Willett of Oklahoma City.

"I know now," he told me, "that an emotional upset was what really caused my smashing into that other car. I realized it a week after the accident when I caught myself doing some crazy driving again. My mind had been on my son, who was running around with a married woman. He'd as much as told me he was 21 and free. Told me to mind my own business. Finally I decided I'd quit nagging, and I asked his forgiveness for butting into his affairs. Inside of three weeks, he decided to drop that married woman. I was emotionally stable again. I haven't done any crazy driving since."

"This is my second accident," said a woman in Syracuse, N. Y. "I might have had a third, but I realized that my driving troubles always happened soon after I left my work. Then I tumbled to the fact that I hated my job in the mill. I had always wanted to be a stenographer, but my folks couldn't afford to send me to school.

"I told my ambition to the personnel manager, and he let me learn stenography. Then he gave me a secretarial job in the office. I'm a different person. I'll have no more accidents."

As a result of my investigation I'm convinced these suggestions are important to help you avoid accidents:

1. If you find yourself concentrating on unhappiness, that's a danger signal. If it leads you to "blow your top," *stop driving!*

2. If your job is making you deeply unhappy, get a new one. It may mean less money, but it is cheap life insurance. Many I interviewed traced their accidents to serious job worries.

3. If a family problem is troubling you, do what is necessary to correct it. Look first into your own heart. "To be wroth with one we love doth work like madness in the brain." Today that "madness" kills and maims.

In short: when your feelings boil, don't drive until you—not your unhappy feelings—are boss. Never allow your hurt ego and your car to get together.

How Your Prayers
Are Answered

By the Rev. Earl A. Blackman

Condensed from The American Magazine

A CHILD came to me with a dime in his hand. "Look what God gave me," he said.

"God doesn't give little boys dimes," I replied in reproof.

"Well," he said gravely, "He gave me this one. I asked God for a dime to buy food for my pet turtle, and kept on asking Him, until suddenly, as I was walking across the park, I saw a dime lying in the grass, right where God had dropped it." Frankly I was awed, the boy was so simple and convincing.

Everybody I have known has told me he prayed at some time or another. In frustration or danger or in the presence of a problem more formidable than we can overcome, we call back to the source of our being for renewed strength. But as they grow older, many persons are less inclined to pray because they do not see the immediate answer lying, like the little boy's dime, shining in the grass. One must be able to recognize the answer to a prayer.

A parishioner of mine almost went mad when the doctors told him his wife was dying of cancer. He came to my house every night and together we prayed for her recovery even though her condition was too serious for any hope.

The poor woman died. Later I asked him whether the death of his wife in the face of our prayers had weakened his faith.

"Certainly not," he said. "It strengthened my faith. I thought I could not bear to lose her, but God gave me strength to accept the inevitable. My prayer was answered in a larger way than I asked it."

The way to get your prayers answered is to pray for strength to answer them yourself.

People have asked me whether there is any prescribed attitude of prayer more efficacious than another. I do not think so. One of my most devout friends told me he did most of his praying while driving his car. I told him that, considering the way he drove, it probably was the best time to pray. But he was quite serious about the matter. He said there was something about driving that brought from the subconscious the half-articulated desires and the forgotten sins.

I have always done most of my private praying at night in bed, between waking and sleeping. Airplane pilots have told me that they feel most prayerful when in flight, poised between heaven and earth, and intensely aware of their own insignificance. Any setting or attitude that relaxes tense minds and muscles seems to me most desirable.

I know one man who writes letters to God on the typewriter. He is not conventionally religious and looks upon prayer as a kind of mental hygiene. He thinks that by writing out his prayers he is better able to define his half-formed desires and, even as he defines them, so does he analyze his faults and his sins.

While it is most efficacious to talk to God in prayer, it is very important that we listen to Him, too. If you talk all the time, you can't learn anything, and so the calm silences, fraught with childlike faith, are as necessary in prayer as is a continued beseeching.

When I am in trouble, and pray for a long period, guidance never fails to come—usually in the form of some self-decision. The decision may be extremely painful, but ultimately I find that it is the best thing.

A prayer need not be uttered to be said. Many of my friends feel that their ineffable yearnings, their sense of beauty, rightness and hope are themselves prayers. Pearl Buck, the novelist, and the late George Washington Carver, the famous Negro chemist and educator, have both told me that their prayers were seldom, if ever, articulated. Yet both had their unuttered prayers richly answered. Donald W. Douglas, of the Douglas Aircraft Company, says that his idea of prayer is a constant attitude of the individual toward the world in which he lives.

"This attitude should be one of expectancy of good, free of personal judgment or criticism," he says. "It should strive to be continuously friendly and helpful. It should have enough faith in the plan under which we live to be thankful for triumphs, yet to embrace disaster calmly with a wish to make the bitter lesson a stairway to happy surroundings, rather than a decline into hopelessness and despair."

My favorite prayer was written by St. Francis of Assisi:

"Lord, where there is hatred, let me sow love; where there is doubt, faith; where there is despair, hope; where there is darkness, light; and where there is sadness, joy.

"O Divine Master, grant that I do not so much seek to be consoled as to console, to be understood as to understand, to be loved as to love; for it is in giving that we receive, it is in pardoning that we are pardoned, and it is in dying that we are born to everlasting life."

I like this prayer because it places full responsibility for its answer upon him who says it. We may pray for friendship when we are lonely, but we receive friendship only when we give it.

Once formed, the habit of prayer becomes as natural as breathing.

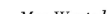

Men Wanted

Good PROSE has been pretty near clubbed to death by advertising. As a reminder of the incomparable power of the properly chosen word, let me recommend this, perhaps the greatest of all advertisements. Signed by a famous Antarctic explorer, it appeared in a little box in the London *Times* of 1900. A few lines of type, no pictures, no women, no coupons, no gimmicks, no rhymes, no tinsel. It pulled answers from all over England:

> Men wanted for Hazardous Journey. Small wages, bitter cold, long months of complete darkness, constant danger, safe return doubtful. Honor and recognition in case of success.—*Sir Ernest Shackleton*

—Robert L. Heilbroner in *Harper's Magazine*

So You're In Love!

By Paul Popenoe
Director of the American Institute of Family Relations, Los Angeles

Condensed from Your Life

A YOUNG stenographer wrote me recently that she has been going for a year with a young man whom she would like to marry. He has proposed to her, conditionally: "He says the most important thing in marriage is satisfactory sexual adjustment. He insists that we find out beforehand if we are so adapted to each other. If so, we'll get married. If not, we'll avert a tragedy. I wasn't brought up this way, but I want to do the scientific thing. What is your opinion?"

This common idea shows a complete misconception of what sexual adjustment in marriage really means. It presupposes that sexual adjustment is something fatalistic; that it exists or it doesn't; and if it doesn't there is nothing you can do about it. This is merely part of the ultra-romantic view of marriage which assumes that two people may be "meant for each other" and that if they are, they will sail along in effortless bliss; if they aren't, the only thing to do is to get a divorce. This ignorant view is fostered by the widespread delusion that sexual adjustment depends on some physical condition.

Actually, sexual maladjustments are almost always psychological in origin. Those based on anatomical incompatibilities are practically unknown.

This experimental scheme also ignores the fact that sexual adjustment is *normally* not perfect at the outset of marriage. The husband often finds, on first trial, that he is impotent because of nervousness; in still more cases the wife derives no satisfaction.

Making a study of 1000 educated married women, Katherine Bement Davis was told by 250 that they were repelled by the first sexual experience of married life. The Institute of Family Relations, in questioning hundreds of wives, discovered that only 51 percent found the first experience enjoyable; 44 percent "merely tolerated" it; the remainder were distressed.

Complete satisfaction may not be reached by the wife for some time. Of 658 women who reported on this point, a normal climax was attained as follows: first time, 25 percent; after days or weeks, 27 percent; after 1-11 months, 26 percent; after one year or more, 16 percent; never, 6 percent.

It is significant that there was no difference in the average marital happiness in the first three groups.

Normally, sexual adjustment improves steadily, under favorable psychological and social conditions. These conditions include feelings of confidence and trust, of permanence and security; they include freedom from fears.

Obviously, then, sexual adjustment is something to be attained, *not* predetermined. The conditions of attainment are not likely to be present in premarital experiments, which are unrealistic and encounter many obstacles:

Impossibly high standards. Often young people have read books on sex that set up fictitious ideals of perfection. When their experiments do not measure up, they are convinced they are "not made for each other."

Overanxiety because of the importance attached to the outcome. Anxiety is an enemy of sexual adjustment; when people are staking so much on the experiment, they are doubly likely to fail.

Unfavorable or unromantic surroundings. Haste. Necessity for secrecy or fear of discovery. Fear of premature pregnancy. Fear on the girl's part that the man will care for her less afterward. Fear that the man is merely taking advantage of her and has no intention of marrying; it is easy for him to say they are not meant for each other.

With all these difficulties, it is not surprising that marriages are often prejudiced by ill-advised attempts to determine their prospects. The results are various:

A serious inferiority complex may be created. The man has staked his future on this experiment and finds that he is apparently abnormal—when actually there is nothing the matter with him.

Each is likely to blame the other for failure. The more the two are emotionally involved, the greater is this unconscious tendency. The result is that a desirable marriage may be abandoned. In that case, the individual has certainly not been helped to make a happy marriage later on.

What shall people do to make sure they will have successful sexual adjustment in marriage?

They should possess normal emotional makeup and attitudes. They should possess knowledge and understanding. This calls for a realistic sex education—now becoming widely available through scientific sources—not one based on erotic fantasies turned out by pathological novelists. They should have a psychology of permanence—a recognition on the part of each that this relationship is part of a lifelong sharing, without reservations. With such a foundation no one need worry about attaining satisfactory adjustment in marriage.

How to Enjoy the Happiest Day of Your Life

Joseph Fort Newton in Philadelphia Evening Bulletin

WE CAN DO anything for one day. So, just for today, let us be unafraid of life, unafraid of death which is the shadow of life; unafraid to be happy, to enjoy the beautiful, to believe the best.

Just for today let us live one day only, forgetting yesterday and tomorrow, and not trying to solve the whole problem of life at once. Lincoln said that a man is just as happy as he makes up his mind to be. Suppose we make up our mind to be happy just for today, to adjust ourselves to what is—our family, our business, our luck. To try to make the world over to suit us is a large order. If we cannot have what we like, maybe be can like what we have.

So, just for today, let us be agreeable, responsive, cheerful, charitable; be our best, dress our best, walk softly, praise people for what they do, not criticize them for what they cannot do. And if we find fault, let us forgive it and forget.

It has its uses, but has anyone seen it in action lately?

WHAT'S HAPPENED
TO
COMMON SENSE?

By Mary Ellen Chase
Professor of English, Smith College; author of "A Goodly Heritage,"
"The Bible and the Common Readers," etc.

Condensed from Coronet

WHENEVER I return to the isolated Maine village where I spend every summer, I am pleasantly impressed by the way in which my neighbors there hold on to certain old terms.

One of these is *grit*, with its companion, *gumption;* another is *get up and get,* which in Maine means to depend on oneself; yet another is *common sense.* These words describe the human qualities which my neighbors, fishermen and their wives, extoll above all others. For fishing is a hard calling. It demands gumption or, in more polite terms, self-reliance, the power of decision and the determination not to be downed by adverse circumstances.

My neighbors are frankly suspicious of anyone who lacks these old American virtues. They voiced their common judgment of a man who had lost his lobster traps in a northeast gale and had been bewailing his fate with too little reserve.

"Why don't he shut his mouth and pick up his feet?" they said. "You can't sail straight by takin' time to bawl about bad luck."

They and I stem from the same rural background. In the country school of my childhood, precepts were written on the blackboard each Monday morning by "old-fashioned" teachers who knew it to be their duty to instill iron in our souls as well as common fractions in our minds. Through the years those precepts have proved salutary to me in moments of indecision and anxiety. Usually they were in terse prose:

It takes a live fish to swim upstream, but any old log can float down.
Don't expect others to bear your troubles; they have their own.
Life isn't all you want, but it's all you have; so have it.

Occasionally a rhyme enlivened us. One I recall as a favorite:

> *The mind of man has no defense*
> *To equal plain, old common sense.*
> *This homely virtue don't despise,*
> *If you would be happy as well as wise.*

Parents, too, 50 years ago dealt out such robust aphorisms liberally, sometimes even sternly, in the upbringing of children. I was taught early by both precept and example that *a job once undertaken has to be completed whatever the cost,* and that *no one but the maker of them ought to be expected to pay for mistakes.*

At the age of ten I undertook the job of driving our family cow to pasture every morning and fetching her at night from May to October for $5. In spite of her name, Constancy, she was unpredictable.

Whimsical by nature and agile of movement, Constancy was given to hiding in thickets and swamps at the close of day and bounding away once I had discovered her. I shall never forget the exasperations of that interminable summer, the terrors which lurked in gathering darkness, the mosquitoes and the black flies, the countless tears shed in secret. But no one came to my assistance. The job was mine alone, as was the hard-earned $5 bill in October.

During my life as a teacher I have often questioned whether we have discovered any worthy substitutes for those precepts and teachings which, outmoded as they seem, are rooted deeply in our history and our ways of life.

In place of the old sayings we use today new words and terms to describe our states of mind and our meeting of those difficulties and questions which will always beset us. We are now *insecure,* or *ill-adjusted,* or *frustrated,* or made ineffective by a *sense of inferiority.* These new words lack the optimism of the old. Implicit in them is the notion that we are surrounded by foes difficult to defeat.

The new vocabulary comes into use early. We hesitate to look upon our children as simply ill-mannered or spoiled. We fear that they are *problem* children who need expert care lest they become *neurotics* or *uncontributive members of society.*

In high school and college they are surrounded by advisers on what they would best study, what work in life they are best fitted for. They are too seldom encouraged to face problems by themselves, to make their own decisions and to pay the consequences of their own mistakes.

Nor are adults free from waves of anxiety. Too many of us are looking about for some panacea which will ease the burdens of our past and present errors in judgment and lighten our fears of the future. Something, we feel, is wrong somewhere, and, without making any stout attempt on our own to discover what it is, we turn to professional advice which guarantees to show us how to understand ourselves.

Even a cursory reading of such books reveals nothing but what we used to call plain old common sense. They urge upon us a calm and objective weighing of ourselves; a frank and even merciless recognition of our weaknesses and failures; a determination to oust at any cost oversensitiveness, which is but a form of self-indulgence; a sense of personal responsibility for the well-being of our families and communities; a fresh start; in short, reliance on our own powers of self-discipline.

No one in his senses would suggest that such books are not often helpful to the anxious mind. But the assumption that most of us have somehow acquired emotional conflicts which we cannot cope with by ourselves surely has its dangers.

We Americans have since our beginnings been known for our self-reliance, for our gumption and common sense. We are, or at least we *were,* adventurers, and our history is the story of a game played against tremendous odds and gloriously won. Why not recall the tough moral fiber which made the winning possible? Isn't it about time that we return as individuals to those values and practices which we have not so much forgotten as neglected? Shouldn't we stop dumping our ash-cans on our families, our friends, our physicians—save our self-respect, make our own decisions, and attempt to work out our own problems?

Life may not be all we want, but it's all we have, as my old school precept said, and it's high time that we *have* it. We shall not find its secrets or its possible riches in the advice of others, however wise, unless we complete that counsel with our own grit, gumption and common sense.

Selling an Idea

By Elmer Wheeler

Condensed from Your Life

HAVE you ever approached your boss with a red-hot idea for increasing efficiency—only to have him become resentful instead of enthusiastic? Have you ever offered your wife or the neighbors "good advice"? If you have, you know what I mean when I say that people resent having other people's ideas forced on them.

When someone approaches us with a new idea, our instinctive re-action is to put up a defense against it. We feel that we must protect our individuality; and most of us are egotistical enough to think that our ideas are better than anyone else's.

There are three tested rules for putting your ideas across to other people so as to arouse their enthusiasm. Here they are:

Rule One: Use a fly rod—not a feeding tube. Others won't accept *your* idea until they can accept it as *their* idea.

It was said during World War I that Colonel House was the most powerful man in the world because he controlled the most powerful man in the world—Woodrow Wilson. "I learned that the best way to convert him to an idea," explained House, "was to plant it in his mind casually, to get him thinking about it on his own account."

When you want to sell someone an idea, take a lesson from the fisherman who casts his fly temptingly near the trout. He could never ram the hook into the trout's mouth. But he can entice the trout to come to the hook.

Don't appear too anxious to have your ideas accepted. Just bring them out where they can be seen.

"Have you considered this?" is better than "This is the way." "Do you think this would work?" is better than "Here's what we should do." Let the other fellow sell himself your idea. Then he'll stay sold.

Rule Two: Let the other fellow argue your case. He instinctively feels called upon to raise some objection to save his face. Give him a chance to disagree with you—by presenting your own objections!

"The way to convince another," said wise old Ben Franklin, "is to state your case moderately and accurately. Then say that of course you may be mistaken about it; which causes your listener to receive what you have to say and, like as not, turn about and convince you of it, since you are in doubt. But if you go at him in a tone of positiveness and arrogance you only make an opponent of him."

Franklin used this technique, against great opposition, in his sale of the idea of adopting the Constitution of the United States.

"I confess," he began, "that I do not entirely approve of this Constitution; but, Sir, I am not sure I shall never approve it; for having lived long, I have experienced many instances of being obliged by better information or fuller consideration to change opinions, even on important subjects, which I first thought right. I cannot help expressing a wish that every member of the convention who may still have objections to it would with me on this occasion doubt a little of his own infallibility, and, to make manifest our unanimity, put his name to this instrument."

Abraham Lincoln used the same technique in selling his ideas to a jury. He argued both sides of the case—but there was always the subtle suggestion that his side was the logical one. An opposing lawyer said of him: "He made a better statement of my case to the jury than I could have made myself."

Another technique is to sell the other fellow the idea as his, not yours. "You gave me an idea the other day that started me thinking," you begin.

Tom Reed, for many years Speaker of the House, was an adroit persuader. At a committee hearing he would remain silent until everyone had had his say, making notes of all objections. Then, when everyone else was argued out, Reed would say, "Gentlemen, it seems to me that what has been said here can be summarized as follows. . . ." Reed would then present *his* ideas—and sell them.

Once Dudley Nichols, the movie director, wasn't satisfied with a scene in one of his pictures. To remedy the situation, he said to Rosalind Russell, the star, "Wonderful, wonderful, but I could see, Miss Russell, when you hesitated that brief instant, that you were thinking about the possibility of playing the scene down just a trifle more. Shall we try it once the way you were thinking?"

Rule Three: Ask—don't tell. Patrick Henry, another famous idea salesman, was a political unknown when first elected to Virginia's House of Burgesses—but every resolution he introduced was passed. Listen to him in his famous "Liberty or Death" speech and see how he uses questions to get his ideas across:

"Our brethren are already in the field—why stand we here idle?"

"Shall we lie supinely on our backs?"

"What is it that gentlemen wish? What would they have? Is life so dear or peace so sweet as to be purchased at the price of chains and slavery?"

Try saying the same thing in positive statements and see how much antagonism it would invoke.

When you put your ideas across with questions, you give the other fellow a share in the idea. You don't tell him—you ask him for the answer. You're giving him a chance to sell himself.

Try these rules the next time you want to put an idea across to your boss, your family or the neighbors.

At Jan Struther's funeral the minister read an epitaph which the author wrote for herself some years earlier:

One day my life will end; and lest
    Some whim should prompt you to review it,
Let her who knows the subject best
    Tell you the shortest way to do it:
Then say, "Here lies one doubly blest."
    Say, "She was happy." Say, "She knew it."

—Margaret Fishback in a letter to the New York *Herald Tribune*

YOU WON'T BE SNUBBED

By

Henry Morton Robinson

AROUND ME, a bright-mufflered throng of winter-sports enthusiasts loafed in the white Adirondack sunshine. Lean ski jumpers puffed at blunt brown pipes; bobsledders tossed challenges and snowballs at each other; wind-burned debutantes basked in deck chairs. The thin northern air crackled with frost and gaiety; everyone was having fun.

That is, everyone but me. The deck chair beside me was vacant, yet no one sat down in it. For years, no one ever *did* sit down by me voluntarily. For some reason I had always been unable to draw other human beings into warm personal contacts.

But the whole picture changed on that snow-brilliant day when David Jessup sat down in the deck chair beside me. I had particularly observed this man; it was a joy to watch him approach a stranger and melt the icy cellophane that most human beings come wrapped in. I envied him his easy approach to others, yet I would have gone to my grave (so stern were the proprieties of my New England upbringing) before speaking to him or any stranger first.

But evidently my high-fenced reserve was no barrier to Jessup, for he turned his friendly gray eyes on me, and smiled with genuine good nature. There were no inanities about the weather, no self-conscious preliminaries. Like a man imparting news of interest to an old friend, he said without tension or embarrassment: "I saw you watching that bronzed chap mending his snowshoes. He's the Rhodes Scholar from New York. He stroked the Cornell crew last year and was president of the debating club besides. Don't you think he's a splendid type to represent American youth at Oxford?"

Jessup's opening remarks led us at once into a discussion of Cecil Rhodes' dream of cementing Anglo-American friendship. From that take-off, our talk continued through many fields of common interest and special information. When we stopped an hour later we were friends. It was something of a miracle, and I asked Jessup point-blank how he did it.

"Your happy knack of speaking to strangers—how do you manage it? Personally, I'm limited in my human acquaintance, which is confined to a small circle of friends, all of the same type. All my life I've wanted to mingle with strangers who could widen my interests and quicken my sense of being alive, yet I've always hung back, afraid of a rebuff. How does one overcome this fear of being snubbed?"

Jessup waved his hand inclusively at the throng around us. "My fear of being snubbed," he said, "completely disappears when I remember that the dearest friends I have were once strangers. So when I see a young woman arranging a cluster of holly boughs, or a group of men tinkering with a bobsled, they needn't belong to my private collection of acquaintances before I speak to them. If I speak, perhaps they *will* belong to that collection, and I shall be the richer for knowing them."

"But," I persisted, "how about being misunderstood?"

"If you approach your fellow man with honest sympathy and a desire to be humanly friendly," said Jessup, "he is not likely to misread your motive. I have met men of the most formidable self-importance, and found them all responsive, eager to visit with me. Rarely have I encountered even the slightest hint of a snub. No, my friend, you mustn't let fear be the basis of your seclusion. The new, the unusual, is no more dangerous than the familiar, and it has the advantage of being decidedly more exciting."

Subsequent experiences with David Jessup proved how right he was. Wherever he went, he would enter into conversation with all manner of people, and was forever turning up strange new types and odd, stimulating information. On one of our trips together we passed a granite quarry in which a number of men were walking about on tiptoe, carrying red flags and acting like advance messengers of doom. Instead of hurrying past, Jessup spoke to one of the flag-carriers, and in a few moments the man was telling us a hair-curling story. It seems that many years ago, engineers had drilled 50 holes in this quarry, packed the holes with dynamite, then wired them up for a blast. But some of the wiring was defective, and as a result only half of the dynamite exploded! For 20 years workmen could not be persuaded to go near the quarry; it had to be abandoned, and was now being re-opened by men who received double pay because of the attendant danger.

Another time, on the shores of a beautiful lake in a state park, Jessup noticed a man making sketches. Skillfully engaging the man in conversation, Jessup discovered that he was a marine horticulturist with a new idea called "pond-scaping." "On the lakes surrounding the ancient Aztec capital," said the sketcher, "were many floating islands covered with feathery trees and rare flowers. I believe that I have rediscovered how such islands can be constructed and kept in motion, and am now making some sketches to interest the park commission in my idea."

On the way home I remarked, "That was one of the most interesting things that ever happened to me. Both the man and his drawings were fascinating."

Jessup agreed, then added slyly: "And you wouldn't have met him in a thousand years if you had waited for an introduction, would you?"

"Don't rub it in, please. I've always known that I was missing a great deal, but I never knew how to get people started."

"To talk to a stranger," advised Jessup, "begin with a remark that penetrates to the core of his interest. Usually it will be something that applies to his work. Inane general remarks or fussy little questions only irk the busy man. One must be genuinely interested in what the stranger is doing, make an intelligent comment, then wait for him to respond. And he *will* respond, for the simple reason that most human beings are overjoyed when another person shows interest in their work. Take that floating-garden chap for instance: if we had seemed bored he wouldn't even have begun to talk, for no man likes to expose his treasures to the indifferent. But when he saw that we were really deriving pleasure from his conversation, he tried to reward our interest and prolong our pleasure. Why should he do this? Simply because no one has ever yet discovered a keener happiness than giving pleasure to others."

I was always expecting Jessup to be snubbed, but the snub never came. Once while touring with him, a trio of noisy roughs boarded our bus and began to annoy the passengers with a display of downright coarseness. Dignified, serious, Jessup got up and went back to them. "Here," thought I, "my friend is riding for a fall." But I was wrong. What Jessup said to those fellows I never knew, but within five minutes he had engaged them in an earnest discussion of labor conditions throughout the country and their own chances of employment.

I've seen Jessup address women bred in the strictest code of convention, and wondered how he avoided being cut by them. He explained it in this way: "If in speaking to a woman you reveal that you are primarily interested in her personally or as a member of the opposite sex, she will instantly resent it, as she has every right to do. In effect, you are insulting her by the assumption that her attention may be so cheaply won. But speak to her as one human being to another, as one interested in the same scenery, the same music, or the same social problems, and she will extend her ready fellowship. Both men and women love to use their minds, and women especially regard it as a distinct compliment to be met on the intellectual plane common to both sexes."

Since knowing David Jessup, the stranger at my elbow has become the most interesting and approachable thing in life. And I know if I approach him unaffectedly there is no danger of being snubbed.

For ultimately we are not so different from one another. Training and tradition may have cast us in dissimilar molds, but the basic stuff of our humanity is pathetically the same. It is this realization that now makes every stranger accessible to me. He may be a barber or a banknote-engraver, but it is almost certain that he can tell me something that will heighten my mental stature or increase my spiritual gauge. I may like him or I may not; if he bores me, I can be off. But the thing that constantly surprises me is the scarcity of people who are really boresome or offensive. By far the larger part of our human race is composed of interesting and friendly members, all eager to know each other. And I have yet to see the person who did not become more attractive and more *alive* for laying aside his too-prized reserve and mingling on equal terms with other members of our common, struggling, hungering human family.

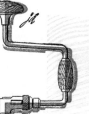

We Found a Substitute for Income

By Darrell Huff Condensed from Harper's Magazine

IT'S A GOOD THING I'm not a mayor or a cop who might find himself on the sticky end of a graft investigation. For my income and my scale of living do not jibe.

How, an investigator might ask, do I keep a wife and four children in something like country-estate style on an income so small that the tax people can hardly afford to open my annual envelope? What about the house and land I have acquired—clear—in seven years? They are worth more than half my total income for that period plus the small savings on hand at the beginning.

Actually, questions like these apply to a surprisingly large number of families. And the answer is quite simple: It is all done with the hands. A lot of us are doing for ourselves things that most Americans in clean-hands jobs used to pay others to do. The area in which this is happening most clearly is in building and maintaining the home. And since this item is about one fourth of the usual budget any change in it is important.

Money is probably the primary cause of this do-it-yourself trend that has been sweeping the country. A Chicago lumber dealer, quoted in *Time*, sums it up: "It's a simple economic fact that a $75-a-week book-keeper can't buy the services of a $150 carpenter." Convenience also favors the man who does his own work. He is almost always able to put in an odd hour or less. He can do a 20-minute job in 20 minutes; with coming and going, the professional may put in a couple of hours —at quite a bit per hour. Technology is in it, too: new tools and machinery made especially for home use put the amateur artisan on an equal basis of efficiency with the building tradesman.

We can gain insight into all this by looking at the paint industry, which is thriving, and the painter's trade, which is not. Professional painters are no more numerous today, yet paint sales have grown by nearly 50 percent. Somebody is slapping on all that paint and the people in the business have no doubt who it is: the householders themselves.

The amateur painter often gets started when he finds that doing the job himself is actually easier than hiring it done. To have your bathroom ceiling painted you must first call a painter and arrange to choose a color and a time (which may be a month from next Wednesday) and then you must get the place ready for him. You or your wife will probably have to watch him while he works to be sure he does what you want. In the end you're likely to find it simpler to buy supplies and put on the paint yourself.

Certainly it will be cheaper that way. It isn't so much what the man gets for doing your work—he isn't getting richer either—as what you pay for nothing. What brings the bill up to more than you may ever hope to earn per hour is overhead and his boss's office expense and advertising and a truck tied up and time coming and going.

The multiplying of the amateur artisan has led manufacturers to bring out more and more products especially intended for home use by nonexperts. Painting is just one field that has been particularly adapted for the homeowner. Big sellers in resilient floorings now are those in tile form: small squares of asphalt, plastic, linoleum, cork, rubber or wood. The big sheets were hard for the beginner to handle. There is even carpeting in tile form.

What happens when the amateur puts up wallpaper has long been a humorist's favorite. It is easier now. Some wallpaper comes pretrimmed and some has the adhesive already applied. Recently appearing on the market is a paste that dries so slowly that the user can slide the paper about until he gets it where he wants it.

And so it goes with many other products. Plastic pipe for wells, yard sprinkling and all cold-water plumbing can be connected with the use of a single common tool: a pocketknife with a screwdriver blade. A new gypsum-board system eliminates all filling and taping. Plywood comes in "handy panels." There are gutters that can be put together without soldering.

Sales literature that used to be devoted entirely to telling what and how good the product was now most often carries the words "how to" in its title. Advertisers who used to boost their building products mainly in trade publications now use general magazines to address the householder. The Kimberly-Clark Corp. describes its building insulation as the "ideal do-it-yourself insulation" and encourages lumber yards to install "do-it-yourself self-selling centers" for this and other products, including tools. The same company is authority for the figure that homeowners are now buying ten power saws and construction tools for every one bought by the professionals.

The recent success of multiple tools is another indication of the importance of the home user. The professional has never cared much for these things; he doesn't want to take time to change over the tool. The amateur loves them because they give him more versatility per dollar and take up less space. In one case juggling various parts of the tool converts it from table saw to lathe to sander to drill. More than 10,000 such devices have been sold since 1947 at around $200 apiece.

What are all these people doing with these tools? They are not electrified whittlers with time to kill. The people I know want something more than umbrella stands or whatnot shelves to show for their time and money.

One young couple, for example, after the war set up housekeeping in a house in Palo Alto. With the down payment taken care of, they had just about $200 left for furniture. They spent the money on power tools and lumber and built their own—a houseful of distinctive and, in the best sense, functional furniture. Now they are contemplating selling the house, at a good profit, and putting their tools and skills to work at building a new home.

And when I say building, I mean just that. More and more, the hand that used to sign the checks is now holding the hammer as well. Nobody knows just how many Americans are personally raising their roofs these days, but there are some good bases for guesses. One is in the behavior of such building-trade magazines as the *American Builder.*

A few years ago it ignored these people. By last year it was worrying about them, editorially wondering how "builders can capture this market."

A Bureau of Labor Statistics survey one year indicated that owner-builts made up 29 percent of the new homes in Atlanta, 25 percent in Boston, 20 percent in Chicago, 29 percent in Seattle, 40 percent in Pittsburgh. Alarmed carpenters and plumbers should keep in mind that not all these builders did all the work themselves; some may have merely handled their own contracting or hired their own help.

American Builder estimates that the cost of these homemade homes runs between $5000 and $10,000. Since this is usually cost of materials only, the builder who does his own work normally gets between two and three times as much house as he pays for. The owner-built home is no shack; by *American Builder's* figures it runs well above the national average in size and quality.

Amateur builders seem to spend about two thirds as much money as they would if buying in a tract and to get about 50 percent more house. For example, I have spent about $10,000 (including cost of land and well) to get a place that should be worth $25,000. I figure my gain three ways (time and calluses aside): a cash saving of perhaps $5000; a property worth an extra $10,000 if I should wish to sell it; and meanwhile a larger and more comfortable home than I could otherwise afford to give my family.

If the home has become a major hobby, then actually building that home from the ground up is the greatest hobby of them all. It is likely to be a never-ending process. We began with kitchen-dining-living room, a couple of half bathrooms and two bedrooms. Two children became four and we added a separate building to give the two older girls a bedroom and sitting room of their own. We turned the double garage into another bedroom and a parents' sitting room plus laundry and darkroom. And now I must put up a car shelter to take the place of the lost garage.

Like so many of the people who have learned to do things for themselves, we are both individualistic and given to coöperative endeavor. Together with the family on the adjoining acres, we have built a woodworking shop, an office in which to work and a swimming pool.

A home-magazine editor has remarked that possibly some of this do-it-yourself is at the expense of cultural activities. I think not. There is little cultural loss in driving nails instead of selling more insurance or dry goods in order to earn the money with which to hire a carpenter. Taking part in so many kinds of work impresses me as a gain in itself; my children know that a house or a chair or a sidewalk is made of something besides money and hired labor.

I Never Saw a Fat Woman in Bali

How do the women of Bali keep their lovely, graceful figures? An important factor is the custom of frequent nibbling rather than eating three meals a day. Breakfast is a cup of coffee with a good deal of sugar at six or so in the morning. An hour later the Balinese will take a *mouthful* of cold boiled rice packaged in a banana leaf. In another hour they will eat a piece of fruit. Throughout the day they nibble on fermented soybean cake, beans, a piece of fish, coconut meat, cassava, more rice, or sweetened colored water. The quantities are very small—any solid food is only a tablespoon or two wrapped in a banana leaf.

This custom of keeping lean by eating several small meals a day supports Dr. Jean Mayer's theory, developed in our laboratory, that the level of sugar in the blood is important in regulating those cells in the brain that regulate appetite. When the sugar in the blood is below a certain level, the "appestat"—as Dr. Norman Jolliffe terms those cells—is turned on and you are hungry. As soon as the blood sugar rises above this level, your appestat shuts off and you are not hungry. By their frequent nibbling, the Balinese keep their blood sugar at a level that minimizes the desire for eating and thus reduces food intake.

Eat three moderate meals a day, with emphasis on breakfast. Save part of what you would normally eat at lunch or dinner for snacks. Then you can nibble without adding more calories.

—Frederick J. Stare, M.D., in *McCall's*

Great men in all the ages have turned to God for help;
prayer brings harmony to the life of the humblest

WHAT PRAYER CAN DO

Fulton Oursler
Author of "The Greatest Story Ever Told"

Condensed from Guideposts

ONE SPRING MORNING when I was a small boy, my mother dressed me
up in my Sunday best and warned me not to leave the front steps.
"We'll be walking over to see your aunt," she promised.

I waited obediently until the baker's son from the corner shop came
along and called me a sissy. Then I sprang from the steps and
whammed him on the ear. He shoved me into a mud puddle, splotch-
ing my white blouse with slime and leaving my stocking with a bloody
hole at the knee. Hopelessly I began to bawl.

But my grief was stilled at a sudden tinkle of bells. Down the street
came a peddler, pushing his jingling green cart—"Hokey-pokey ice
cream, one cent apiece." Forgetting my disobedience, I ran into the
house and begged my mother for a penny. Never can I forget her
answer:

"Look at yourself! You're in no condition to ask for anything."

Many a harum-scarum year went by before it dawned on me that
often, when we ask for help from God, we need to take a look at ourselves; we may be in no condition to ask Him for anything.

Believers admit no limits to what the power of prayer can do, and
even skeptics who study the results with an open mind become im-

pressed with the potency of faith. But if his prayers are to be answered, a man has to meet his Maker halfway.

"The trouble is that most prayers are not honest to God," declares a psychologist, a man of no religious faith. "People have the ungracious audacity to ask for heavenly handouts although they are not on speaking terms with their next-door neighbor; they have forbidden relatives their house; they are spreaders of gossip and envious detractors of their best friends.

"To feel free of bitterness one must be rid of malice, resentment, envy, jealousy and greed, which are certain causes of mental illness and even physical disease. Simply by obeying the scriptural rule to be reconciled to our brother before prayer, we can wash away these breeding germs of neuroses and psychoses. Honest-to-God prayer is a kind of mental-health insurance."

In his *Self-Improvement Handbook* Norman Vincent Peale gives two hints on how to forgive.

1. "Repeat the Lord's Prayer inserting your offender's name: 'Forgive me my trespasses as I forgive Henry Jones.'

2. "Speak to others in a kindly manner about the person against whom you harbor antagonism."

The more we can free our hearts of grudges and enmities, the closer we come to the supreme goal of inner peace. Then we begin to realize that prayer is infinitely more than an appeal for personal favors. It is itself the greatest of all gifts; an ever-richer experience, a continuous feeling of being in harmony with the constructive forces of the universe. It brings the wonders of "visiting with God" to the life of the humblest man of faith. And that sense of divine companionship will powerfully influence his thoughts and actions.

A young American Indian left his Huron tribe in northern Wisconsin to be educated in city schools. He became a lawyer and the green forests saw him no more, until in middle life he returned for a hunting and fishing vacation. Presently his woodsman guide noticed that at every sundown the Indian vanished for an hour. One day, beset with curiosity, the guide trailed him.

From behind the low spread of a hemlock tree, he watched the Indian build a fire in an open clearing; saw him balance a log across two stones on one side of the fire and place another such bench on the opposite side, then seat himself on one of the logs and stare into the blaze.

The guide started to walk toward the fire, when the Indian, seeing him, held up restraining hands. Without a word he arranged another log and invited the guide, by a gesture, to join in his vigil. For a half-hour the two remained together in complete silence.

After they had returned to camp and eaten supper, the Indian explained the mystery:

"When I was a child my mother taught me to go off by myself at the end of each day and make a place for a visit of the Great Spirit. I was to think back over my actions and thoughts of the day. If there was anything of which I was ashamed, I must tell the Great Spirit I was sorry and ask for strength to avoid the same mistake again. Then I would sleep better that night. I had forgotten all about it, but here, among these tall trees where I played as a boy, I have found my lost faith. I have not known such peace since I was a child. And from now on I shall somehow manage to visit with the Great Spirit every day."

Ezio Pinza, who starred in *South Pacific,* has his own story about the pathway to peace. It is reported by Ed Sullivan in his famous syndicated column:

"On the night before *South Pacific* opened," said Pinza, "I told Mary Martin if she could not sleep because of nervousness to do what I'd found best—get up, dress and go to the nearest church. 'Just sit there in church,' I said, 'and soon all your nervousness will vanish, as if it had been smoothed away.' God has been so good to me and my career has been so crowded with great luck that I turn to Him all the time. Others may fail; God never. When I explained this to Mary she started to cry, and it was on this note that our friendship was founded."

Communion with the infinite is of solid value in our most practical affairs. I know of a manufacturer who likes to drive back and forth to work so that he can think about business problems without interruption.

"One morning," he relates, "I suddenly realized that problems were always coming up that I had not anticipated. How could I think about crises before they ever happened? Only by prayer. Right there I began to pray that I might meet wisely and well the problems of the day ahead. I arrived at my office feeling refreshed and confident, and I had one of my best days. I soon realized that I had hit upon a wonderful technique. Instead of praying to get pulled out of troubles, I was now conditioning myself in advance to make calm, rational and sound decisions on any problem that came up."

The divine promise "Ask and ye shall receive" does not guarantee that you will receive exactly what you ask for. Often we do not know what is good for us; the old Greeks had a proverb that when the gods were angry with a man they gave him what he wanted. Many of us have lived to be thankful that our prayers were denied. The wise person adds a proviso to every request: "Nevertheless, not my will but Thine be done."

There was Rosalie, the daughter of a poor Parisian, who showed early promise of becoming a great artist. But an artist needs more than promise. Rosalie wanted to draw from life and her father had no money to pay for a model. Very earnestly the girl prayed for enough francs to pay a model's hire, but no shower of money rained down on her back yard.

One day, as she was taking a walk, she had a sudden feeling that everything was going to be all right. Near a crowded market place she noticed a farmer's dray horse hitched for the day behind a vegetable stall. He would not object to being her model—not if Rosa did not mind drawing a horse! In the Metropolitan Museum of Art in New York City there now hangs a world-known canvas, *The Horse Fair*. It was painted by Rosa Bonheur, imperishably famed for her masterpieces of horses.

As horizons broaden, we learn to ask less for ourselves and to re-remember the needs of others, both friends *and* enemies—healing for the sick, comfort for the grieving, help for the jobless, mercy for all. "God make thee beautiful within," was Plato's prayer for those he loved.

When the late Laurette Taylor was starring in her last Broadway play, *The Glass Menagerie,* her friends knew that she was in poor health. They knew also that she had quarreled with her co-star, Eddie Dowling.

One midsummer matinee, in the course of a scene near a table at which Dowling was seated, Miss Taylor suddenly swayed and grabbed a chair for support. The company manager, fearing that she had been about to faint, rushed back to her dressing room as soon as the curtain fell.

"I'm all right," Laurette assured him. "It was just that something happened on stage that nearly knocked me off my pins. We were playing the part where Eddie is supposed to be trying to write something while I am scolding him. I happened to look over his shoulder and saw that he really was writing—and what he was writing was a prayer *'Dear God—please make Laurette well and strong, and help us to be friends again.'*"

That prayer broke a black spell between the rival stars. Later I learned that for months at every performance Eddie Dowling had been writing prayers for friends and foes during that same scene. "It kept my mind sweet—which it badly needed," Eddie told me.

Even the old hostility of science is beginning to be tempered by a respect for the incomprehensible mysteries of faith. Three years before he died, Dr. Robert A. Millikan, 82-year-old Nobel Prize winner, and head of the California Institute of Technology, told the country's leading physicists that a lifetime of scientific research had convinced him that there is a Divinity that is shaping the destiny of man. No scientist had delved more deeply into the mechanisms of matter than Millikan. It was he who first determined the charge and mass of the electron, the smallest particle in the universe. In his speech he said:

"Just how we fit into the plans of the Great Architect and how much He has assigned us to do, we do not know, but if we fail in our assignment it is pretty certain that part of the job will be left undone.

"But fit in we certainly do somehow, else we would not have a sense of our own responsibility. A purely materialistic philosophy is to me the height of unintelligence."

As by an infallible instinct, great men of all ages turn to God for help. They seem to by-pass intellectual doubt, finding a short cut to universal truth. No one has ever expressed it better than Abraham Lincoln: "I have had so many evidences of His direction, so many instances when I have been controlled by some other power than my own will, that I cannot doubt that this power comes from above. I frequently see my way clear to a decision when I am conscious that I have not sufficient facts upon which to found it. . . . I am satisfied that when the Almighty wants me to do, or not to do, a particular thing He finds a way of letting me know it. . . . I am a full believer that God knows what He wants men to do, that which pleases Him. It is never well with the man who heeds it not.

"I talk to God," Lincoln went on to say. "My mind seems relieved when I do, and a way is suggested. . . . I should be the veriest shallow and self-conceited blockhead, in my discharge of the duties that are put upon me in this place, if I should hope to get along without the wisdom that comes from God and not from man."

The hardest-headed skeptic can, through prayer, test this guidance for himself. Let him try it as Lincoln did. He may undertake the experiment as an unbeliever, but with an open mind, seeking to learn what prayer can do. I predict for him a series of happy surprises.

Modern Inconveniences

Howard Maxwell of Los Angeles is a man in tune with his times. So when his four-year-old daughter Melinda acquired a fixation for "The Three Little Pigs" and demanded that he read it to her night after night Mr. Maxwell, very pleased with himself, tape-recorded the story. When Melinda next asked for it, he simply switched on the playback. This worked for a couple of nights, but then one evening Melinda pushed the storybook at her father. "Now, honey," he said, "you know how to turn on the recorder."

"Yes," said Melinda, "but I can't sit on its lap."

—Gene Sherman in Los Angeles *Times*

An old friend was living in solitary grandeur in her three-story mansion, surrounded by hundreds of new one-story houses. When her grandchildren from the West Coast came to visit her she decided to give a party and invite the children from the development. The next day I asked her how the party had gone. I knew she had planned it in the grand manner with a magician and ventriloquist.

"Times have changed even more than I ever dreamed," she said. "The children said they were sick of looking at magicians and ventriloquists on television. All they wanted to do all afternoon was slide down my banisters!"   —Contributed by Margaret B. Link

THE CASE AGAINST
MARITAL INFIDELITY

By Abraham Stone, M.D.
Director of the Marriage Consultation Center of the
Community Church of New York

"*S*UPPOSE it was like one of those secretary-boss affairs. She was working in my laboratory. Often we worked side by side late into the evening, and even on week-ends. I had no special feeling for her, nor she for me, I am sure; but gradually we drifted into a physical relationship. Last week my wife surprised us in the laboratory —and now I just don't know what to do."

The man was a scientist who had made notable contributions to his special field of research. He was highly respected in his community, and was the father of three children. Now he was bewildered, and felt that his home and family life—everything he had built and valued—were in danger. "How did I ever get into this situation?" he asked. "Does it happen often?"

Infidelity in marriage is more common than most people wish to believe. The most disturbing fact in the Kinsey reports was its high incidence—among some 10,000 persons interviewed, one out of every two married men and one out of every four married women up to the age of 40 admitted extramarital relations.

There are societies in which men are permitted by law and custom to have more than one wife, or to have concubines if they can afford them. Our culture, however, maintains that marriage shall be monogamous: when a man and woman marry, they are required by law, religion and social custom to remain faithful to each other.

In early America adultery was regarded as a crime subject to severe punishment. Today it is still punishable by law, but prosecution is rare.

However, it remains the one offense that is legal ground for divorce in every state. Moreover, in a study of 148 different societies, Dr. George P. Murdock, Yale anthropologist, has found that in only five are adulterous relationships condoned. "Marital fidelity," he states, "is one of the main buttresses of any social structure."

Why, then, is infidelity so widespread?

Some of those who have studied the problem hold that man, like other animals, is promiscuous by nature. "Most of the male's extramarital activity," says Dr. Kinsey, "is undoubtedly a product of his interest in a variety of experience." Most males, he states, would agree that variety is attractive per se, whether it be in music, recreation, literature, food or sexual partners. If there were no social restrictions, he concludes, man would be promiscuous throughout his life.

Women are less interested in sexual experience with more than one man. But how much of this difference in attitude is due to basic differences in biological and psychological needs, and how much to training from childhood on? Some authorities say that under certain cultural conditions women, too, would be interested in varied experience. Clellan S. Ford and Frank A. Beach, in their book *Patterns of Sexual Behavior,* state: "In societies in which a variety of sexual liaisons is permitted, women avail themselves of their opportunity as eagerly as do men."

But does the desire for variety justify the extramarital affair? There is an important difference between seeking variety in food, music or recreation and seeking it in sexual partners. A husband's extramarital sexual relations cause involvement of others—the wife, the other woman, the children.

Many psychiatrists regard infidelity as an emotional disturbance or a neurotic tendency. "Psychiatrists feel that immaturity and frigidity are the basic causes of infidelity," says Dr. Edward A. Strecker. And Dr. Frank Caprio, in his book *Marital Infidelity,* writes: "Infidelity, like alcoholism or drug addiction, is an expression of a deep basic disorder of character which has its roots in childhood experiences."

This theory can explain only certain forms of infidelity. It may apply to the compulsive philanderer, the one who has an irresistible urge for new romantic conquests. But not all men or all women who stray from the marital bed are immature, neurotic or have a character disorder.

A major cause of infidelity is marriage without mutual understanding, without an awareness of the partner's physical and emotional needs, without love. "Where there is marriage without love," wrote Benjamin Franklin, "there will be love without marriage."

A wayward husband entangled in an extramarital affair recently said to me: "I could have been perfectly happy with my wife, but I never got from her what I wanted most in our marriage—affection, approval, occasional praise. I wanted her to want me, to need me, but she constantly rejected me. Eventually I sought those satisfactions elsewhere. When I met the other woman I thought I had found the warmth I needed."

This was not mere rationalization on his part. When I talked with the wife later, she too was able to recognize the degree to which her coolness toward her husband's needs had been a cause of his affair. "As I see it now," she said sadly, "I think I drove him into her arms."

Under the same conditions a wife may become susceptible to an outside affair. Not long ago a woman told me that her marriage was, in the main, successful: she had two children, she was interested in her home, in her husband's work and in the social activities of the community. But her husband was phlegmatic and undemonstrative.

"Evenings," she complained, "he wants only his dinner and his newspaper. If I make any affectionate gesture he just pats me on the head, as if I were a child or a pet. If he would only make his touch mean something! I know he loves me, but I need to be loved with some passion."

Here the soil was ready for outside romance, and romance sprouted rapidly when she met another man during a summer vacation with the children at a beach resort. The marriage probably would have broken up if she had not realized in time the dangers involved. She, and later her husband, sought professional aid. In time she came to realize how much deeper and more meaningful her husband's love and loyalty were than a casual physical attraction, and he how necessary it was for him to be more attentive and expressive if he was to hold his wife's interest.

Some psychiatrists claim that a casual extramarital affair may serve as a safety valve and preserve a marriage which might otherwise break up. Yet from my quarter century of counseling on marital problems I cannot recall a single case where infidelity has strengthened the marital bond. Seldom does either husband or wife find lasting emotional satisfaction in an extramarital relationship. In fact, it usually leads to deep personal conflicts and family disruption.

Even if it is unknown to the other mate, an act of infidelity is still a disintegrating force. There is always a feeling of guilt and the fear of detection, a need for inventing excuses and complex explanations. With the effort to deceive, a wedge is driven between husband and wife.

When the affair is known, there is emotional injury that often leads to a broken home. It is rare for a wife to accept her husband's unfaithfulness openly, and even rarer for a husband to be tolerant of his wife's infidelity. Few men or women can fail to feel deep resentment and deeper hurt when faced with the fact that the mate has preferred, even transiently, another sexual partner.

And what of the effect upon the children within a family? The bewilderment, the sense of insecurity, of shame, of grief which children feel when they learn of their father's or mother's extramarital affair frequently lead to emotional injury that may leave lasting scars. A 27-year-old patient told me that at the age of 11 she had found her mother in the embrace of another man. The episode had haunted her for 16 years and profoundly shaken her own attitude toward marriage.

The primary purposes of marriage are to satisfy three basic human needs: the need for the security of affection, companionship, "belonging"; the need for the gratification of the sexual urge; the need for reproduction. The family provides a socially and morally sanctioned unit for the fulfillment of these needs. Families cannot, however, be held together merely by the pressures of law, religion and society. Marital stability depends on the cohesive power of an inner harmony between husband and wife which is built on mutual love and comradeship. Such unity cannot be achieved without fidelity.

The solution, then, to the extramarital problem is to make marriage and family life so satisfying, so fulfilling that neither partner will want to stray. By cultivating sound attitudes toward sex and marriage and by realizing the values of a happy family, fidelity can be maintained.

Successful marriage requires character and effort, an adherence to basic social values and to the precepts of the Golden Rule. Often it requires self-discipline. Is a good marriage worth it? I believe it is.

What Is a Boy?

BOYS COME in assorted sizes, weights and colors. They are found everywhere — on top of, underneath, inside of, climbing on, swinging from, running around or jumping to. Mothers love them, little girls hate them, older sisters and brothers tolerate them, adults ignore them and Heaven protects them. A boy is Truth with dirt on its face, Wisdom with bubble gum in its hair and the Hope of the future with a frog in its pocket.

A boy has the appetite of a horse, the digestion of a sword swallower, the energy of a pocket-size atomic bomb, the curiosity of a cat, the lungs of a dictator, the imagination of a Paul Bunyan, the shyness of a violet, the audacity of a steel trap, the enthusiasm of a firecracker, and when he makes something he has five thumbs on each hand.

He likes ice cream, knives, saws, Christmas, comic books, the boy across the street, woods, water (in its natural habitat), large animals, Dad, trains, Saturday mornings and fire engines. He is not much for Sunday school, company, schools, books without pictures, music lessons, neckties, barbers, girls, overcoats, adults or bedtime.

Nobody else is so early to rise or so late to supper. Nobody else can cram into one pocket a rusty knife, a half-eaten apple, three feet of string, an empty Bull Durham sack, two gumdrops, six cents, a slingshot, a chunk of unknown substance and a genuine supersonic code ring with a secret compartment.

A boy is a magical creature — you can lock him out of your workshop, but you can't lock him out of your heart. You can get him out of your study, but you can't get him out of your mind. Might as well give up — he is your captor, your jailer, your boss and your master — a freckle-faced, pint-sized bundle of noise. But when you come home at night with only the shattered pieces of your hopes and dreams, he can mend them with two magic words — "Hi Dad!"

— Alan Beck in New England Mutual Life Insurance house magazine (copyright 1949)
Reader's Digest (January 1950 issue)

Making Habits Work for You

By William James

Condensed from "Psychology: Briefer Course"

"HABIT a second nature? Habit is ten times nature," the Duke of Wellington exclaimed; and the degree to which this is true no one can appreciate as well as a veteran soldier. Daily drill and years of discipline make a man over in most of his conduct.

Habit is the flywheel of society, its most precious conserving agent. The great thing, then, is to make our nervous system our ally instead of our enemy. We must make automatic and habitual, as early as possible, as many useful actions as we can, and guard against growing into ways that are disadvantageous as we guard against the plague. The more of the details of our daily life we can hand over to the effortless custody of automatism, the more our higher powers of mind will be set free for their proper work. There is no more miserable person than one in whom nothing is habitual but indecision, and for whom the lighting of every cigar, the drinking of every cup, the time of rising and going to bed every day, and the beginning of every bit of work are subjects of deliberation. Half the time of such a man goes to deciding or regretting matters which ought to be so ingrained in him as practically not to exist for his consciousness at all.

In the acquisition of a new habit, or the leaving off of an old one, there are four great maxims to remember: First, *we must take care to launch ourselves with as strong an initiative as possible.* Accumulate all possible circumstances which reinforce the right motives; make engagements incompatible with the old way; take a public pledge, if the case allows; in short, envelop your resolution with every aid you know. This will give your new beginning such momentum that the temptation to break down will not occur as soon as it otherwise might; and every day a breakdown is postponed adds to the chances of its not occurring at all.

Second, *never suffer an exception to occur till the new habit is securely rooted in your life.* Each lapse is like letting fall a ball of string which one is carefully winding up; a single slip undoes more than a great many turns will wind up again. Continuity of training is the great means of making the nervous system act infallibly right.

Success at the outset is imperative. Failure is apt to dampen the energy of all future attempts, whereas past successes nerve one to future vigor. Goethe says to a man who consulted him about an enterprise but mistrusted his own powers: *"Ach!* You need only blow on your hands!" And the remark illustrates the effect on Goethe's spirits of his own habitually successful career.

The question of tapering off in abandoning such habits as drink comes under this head, and is a question about which experts differ in individual cases. In the main, however, all expert opinion would agree that abrupt acquisition of the new habit is the best way, *if there be a real possibility of carrying it out.* We must be careful not to give the will so stiff a task as to insure its defeat at the outset; but *provided one can stand it,* a sharp period of suffering and then a free time is the best thing to aim at, whether in giving up a habit like drinking, or in simply changing one's hours of rising or of work. It is surprising how soon a desire will die if it be *never* fed.

"One must first learn to proceed firmly before one can begin to make oneself over again," writes Dr. Bahnsen. "He who every day makes a fresh resolve is like one who, arriving at the edge of the ditch he is to leap, forever stops and returns for a fresh run. Without *unbroken* advance there is no such thing as *accumulation* of positive forces."

The third maxim is: *Seize the first possible opportunity to act on every resolution you make.* It is not in the moment of their forming, but in the moment of their producing *motor effects* that resolutions communicate the new "set" to the brain. No matter how full a reservoir of *maxims* one may possess, and no matter how good one's *sentiments* may be, if one has not taken advantage of every concrete opportunity to *act,* one's character may remain entirely unaffected for the better. With mere good intentions hell is proverbially paved. And this is an obvious consequence of the principles we have laid down. A "character," as John Stuart Mill says, "is a completely fashioned will";

and a will, in the sense in which he means it, is an aggregate of tendencies to act in a firm, prompt and definite way upon all the principal emergencies of life.

A tendency to act becomes effectively ingrained in us only in proportion to the frequency with which the actions actually occur, and the brain "grows" to their use. When a resolve or a fine glow of feeling is allowed to evaporate without bearing practical fruit it is worse than a chance lost; it works so as positively to hinder the discharge of future resolutions and emotions. There is no more contemptible human character than that of the nerveless sentimentalist and dreamer, who spends his life in a weltering sea of sensibility and emotion, but who never does a manly concrete deed. Never should we suffer ourselves to have an emotion at a play, concert, or upon reading a book, without expressing it afterward in some active way. Let the expression be the least thing in the world—speaking genially to one's grandmother, or giving up one's seat in a car, if nothing more heroic offers—but let it not fail to take place.

If we let our emotions evaporate, they get into a way of evaporating. Similarly, if we often flinch from making an effort, before we know it the effort-making capacity is gone; and if we suffer the wandering of our attention, presently it will wander all the time. As the fourth practical maxim, we may, then, offer something like this: *Keep the faculty of effort alive in you by a little gratuitous exercise every day.* That is, be systematically ascetic or heroic in little unnecessary points, do every day or two something for no other reason than that you would rather not do it, so that when the hour of dire need draws nigh it may find you nerved and trained to stand the test. Asceticism of this sort is like the insurance a man pays on his house. The tax does him no good at the time and possibly may never bring him a return. But if the fire does come, his having paid it will be his salvation from ruin. So with the man who has daily inured himself to habits of concentrated attention, energetic volition, and self-denial in unnecessary things. He will stand like a tower when everything rocks around him, and when his softer fellow mortals are winnowed like chaff in the blast.

The hell to be endured hereafter, of which theology tells, is no worse than the hell we make for ourselves in this world by habitually fashioning our characters in the wrong way. If we realize the extent to which we are mere walking bundles of habits, we would give more heed to their formation. We are spinning our own fates, good or evil, and never to be undone. Every smallest stroke of virtue or of vice leaves its never so little scar. The drunken Rip van Winkle in Jefferson's play excuses himself for every fresh dereliction by saying, "I won't count this time!" Well! he may not count it, and a kind Heaven may not count it; but it is being counted none the less. Down among his nerve cells and fibers the molecules are counting it, registering it and storing it up to be used against him when the next temptation comes. Nothing we ever do is, in strict scientific literalness, wiped out. Of course this has its good side as well as its bad one. As we become permanent drunkards by so many separate drinks, so we become saints in the moral, and experts in the practical and scientific spheres, by so many separate acts and hours of work. Let no one have anxiety about the upshot of his education, whatever its line may be. If he keep faithfully busy each hour of the working day, he may safely leave the final result to itself. He can with perfect certainty count on waking up some fine morning, to find himself one of the competent ones of his generation, in whatever pursuit he may have singled out.

The Perfect Tribute

On her frequent trips on foot to Temuco, Chile, an old Araucanian Indian woman used always to bring my mother a few partridge eggs or a handful of berries. My mother spoke no Araucanian beyond the greeting *"Mai-mai,"* and the old woman knew no Spanish, but she drank tea and ate cake with many an appreciative giggle. We girls stared fascinated at her layers of colorful hand-woven clothing, her bracelets and necklaces, and we vied with each other in trying to memorize the singsong phrase she always spoke on rising to leave.

At last we learned the words by heart and repeated them to the missionary, who translated them for us. They have stayed in my mind as the nicest compliment ever uttered:

"I shall come again, for *I like myself* when I'm near you."

—Contributed by Elizabeth Mauske

"There is no burden that is not lightened by the sharing of it"

Keeping
the Heart's Door Open

By I. A. R. Wylie

ANY YEARS AGO a friend whom I knew fairly well but not intimately came unexpectedly to see me. I sensed at once that she was in serious trouble, but being young, shy and afraid of seeming intrusive, I made no effort to help her unburden herself. I held her at arm's length. We talked of the weather, mutual friends, the news. We drifted further and further away from what was so vitally concerning her. That night she tried— fortunately unsuccessfully—to commit suicide. I realized then that at a critical moment I had shut the door in the face of a desperate need for sympathy and help.

This near tragedy brought me up sharp against a problem that confronts us all: we often realize that behind the calm façade of a friend's life are griefs and anxieties we shrink from touching, which are only revealed to us by chance flashes of self-betrayal. This knowledge creates in us a sense of helplessness and insufficiency. And it compels us, in our turn, to keep our own silence, to make ourselves little islands of loneliness surrounded by seas of reserve and so-called pride.

I think we have made too much of this tight-lipped endurance. I am not decrying silent courage, but I think that the silence has been overvalued. It may be, to some extent, the cause for the alarming increase in mental breakdowns. Our burdens, unshared, become too heavy to be borne.

True, we must be neither self-pitiers nor wailing walls for the self-pitiers to weep against. But the people who lock their doors most securely against us are often the most in need of being reached. There are times when we need the courage to batter at the locked door and demand admittance even at the risk of rebuff.

I had a friend once who was truly afflicted with misfortune. She had a sick husband; she herself was ill. There was no money. But she wore a bright and smiling countenance that became in time almost a distorted mask. Her friends fell back from her inaccessibility as from a high stone wall. I cared deeply for her and one day I took my courage in both hands and told her, "I know you are in desperate straits. If you want to talk about them please prove that we are friends and talk. If I can, I shall be proud to help. I shall be prouder still that you trusted me."

She was silent for a moment, fighting herself. Then she began, for the first time, I suspect, in years, to cry her heart out. It was like the bursting of a pent-up river. All the concealed fears and perplexities and griefs poured over its banks. And when the flood tide had passed, her strained, make-believe cheerfulness had given place to an open-hearted serenity. We talked for hours. Her story is not mine to tell. I can only say that just by talking freely she was able to work out the worst of her difficulties.

Long afterward she confided that she had felt herself to be on the verge of a mental breakdown. My seemingly brash disregard for what she had considered her pride, her obligation to live out her tragedy in silence, had pulled her back from the abyss.

There is another approach which, though indirect, sometimes leads to the heart of the matter. When I feel in my bones that someone I know is very unhappy but doesn't know how to unburden herself or thinks that to do so would impose upon her friends, I go to *her* for help and advice. I confide my troubles to her. She recognizes that I have trusted her and returns the confidence.

The highest walls that people build around their troubles seem to be those constructed around financial misfortune. Money can be wonderful to have. It is cruel-hard to be without it. But that men should be proud of having it or ashamed of not having it is silly. I brush aside the defenses of friends who believe that though they can accept my time and strength—so much more valuable—they would be forever humiliated if they confided their financial troubles to me or accepted financial help from me. To one protesting friend I retorted, "You mean that if I accepted help from *you, I* ought to feel humiliated."

After a moment's thought, she laughed. And the false pride which she had built around herself melted like a mist in sunshine.

Sometimes delicacy can be a form of crudity. To be "delicate" in your sympathy with someone in financial straits is, to my mind, to be clumsy and heavy-handed. It creates the impression that something as simple and natural as giving what you happen to have to someone who happens to be in need of it is in itself an indelicacy. Try forthrightness with a friend in need. You will find tight-lipped reticence breaking down before your matter-of-fact assumption that where money is concerned pride and reticence are out of place.

I suppose marital troubles are among the hardest to hear, certainly the most dangerous to the well-intentioned sympathizer. It is a case of intruding "where angels fear to tread." And yet, referring back to the instance in my first paragraph, it was my failure to intrude that allowed my friend to drift to the brink of suicide.

In that case, I was a friend of both husband and wife; I sympathized with both. I realized they were the victims of an incurable circumstance rather than of wrongdoing. There seemed little I could do. But I could have given her time. She was crushed breathless under her unhappiness. I could have persuaded her to talk her heart out; perhaps then she might have faced her disaster with more judgment.

I failed her, partly from youth and diffidence but also because of a subconscious reluctance to take my share of another's burden. For the moment we become aware of another's troubles we become automatically responsible. The friend's troubles are ours until we have done our best to relieve them. So it appears much easier not to see, not to intrude.

Sick people—especially the chronically sick—are hard to approach. Sympathy can become a real intrusion, a cause of exasperation and finally in itself perfunctory. And yet it was from an invalid that I once learned a great lesson.

"I don't want sympathy," she said. "I want to feel you need me."

She had given me the key not only to her own citadel but to many other grimly defended citadels. From those who need us we can accept anything.

When we are perplexed as to what part we should play in our friends' troubles, it is our motive which should be our guide. And motives are tricky things. Are we seeking the gratification of mere curiosity? Do we want to make ourselves interesting by purveying gossip, by passing on, under the guise of sympathy, what has been entrusted to us?

When we are sure that we seek nothing but the relief of another's distress then I think we have the right and duty to risk the dangerous adventure of interference. We may fail. It may cost us dearly. But it is better to seem tactless than to be heartless, better to risk intrusion than to be indifferent. By intruding we may set someone who is on the verge of disaster back onto the road to rehabilitation.

If we give freely we must also accept freely. If we lock our own doors against sympathy we cannot expect other doors to open to us. We should remember that there is nothing that makes a good friend happier than to be trusted with his friend's troubles. There is no burden that is not lightened by the sharing of it.

Above all, we must keep our own doors open, so that grief can feel instinctively that with us it can find shelter and so that happiness can be sure of welcome.

Applied Psychology

Seeking counsel from Dr. George W. Crane, the psychologist, a woman confided that she hated her husband and intended to divorce him. "I want to hurt him all I can," she said.

"In that case," said Dr. Crane, "I advise you to start showering him with compliments. When you have become indispensable to him —when he thinks you love him devotedly—then start the divorce action. That's the way to hurt him."

Some months later the wife returned to report that she had followed the suggested course. "Good," said Crane. "Now's the time to file for divorce."

"Divorce!" exclaimed the woman indignantly. "Never! I've fallen in love with him."   —William F. McDermott in *The Rotarian*

"The spark from heaven falls. Who picks it up?
The crowd? Never. The individual? Always."

The Source of All Our Strength

By A. Whitney Griswold President, Yale University

Condensed from an address

SINCE that moment, lost in the mists of time, when man first looked upon himself and saw the image of God, he has struggled against the powers of nature and the supernatural, and against the tyrannies of his fellow men, to fulfill the promise in that image. He has lived to the full the gregarious life to which half of his instincts committed him. And, in response to the other half, he has striven in every element on earth, in the skies above the earth and in the waters under the earth, to express himself as an individual.

Philosophers have long recognized this conflict in the bosom of man and we, like every generation before us, have been witnesses to its political manifestations. Our world is divided by political philosophies which proclaim man's mechanistic fate as a species, and those which proclaim his creative destiny as an individual. At the moment the mechanistic idea seems to be in the ascendant. It is propagated at the point of the sword by dictatorships now governing nearly half the peoples of the world and seeking to extend their dominion over the rest. Perhaps never in history has the individual had to defend his birthright against such formidable odds.

This is a dark outlook for a country like ours which by tradition and temperament looks to the individual for the salvation of the race. We may be thankful that it is only an outlook and not a reality. We do not know our strength; and we do not know our strength because we do not know our history. Time and again we have seen the individual apparently ready to exit from the stage, only to return with fresh and more dynamic lines.

We had Communism in the Plymouth Colony in 1620, two centuries before Marx wrote his *Manifesto* and three before the Russians ever heard of it; and we gave it up, after a pragmatic test, because, as Governor Bradford wrote in his diary, "the experience that was had in this commone course and condition, tried sundrie years, and that amongst godly and sober men, may well evince the vanitie of that conceite of Platos and other ancients, applauded by some of later times —that the taking away of propertie, and bringing in communitie into a commone wealth would make them happy and flourishing; as if they were wiser than God. For this communitie (so farr as it was) was found to breed much confusion and discontent, and retard much imployment that would have been to their benefite and comforte."

We had totalitarianism, complete with purges and secret police, in the Massachusetts Bay Colony, three centuries before Hitler, Stalin and Mussolini; we gave it up in revulsion.

In our traffic with foreign nations we have always looked out on a world full of despotisms. As colonies we were their pawns. As a young republic we were surrounded by them. And if the airplane had been invented a century earlier than it was, the chances are we would still be their pawn. Democracy is a very new thing in the world. Our knowledge of man in society goes back to the Neolithic Age, 9000 years ago. Over that span of time man has seen and suffered despotisms of every conceivable variety.

Democracy, the hopeful philosophy, attuned to man's instincts as an individual and addressed to their cultivation for the benefit of society, first appeared in Athens about 500 B.C. It saw fitful revival in the Italian City States of the 11th and 12th centuries, and later in the Swiss cantons, but it did not make its modern appearance until the Puritan revolution in England in the middle years of the 17th century. It did not attain the form in which we know it until the 19th century. Compared with despotism it is but a few minutes old. The remarkable fact is not that it is still opposed by despotism but that it has survived that opposition as vigorously as it has.

It has survived because time and again it has proved, under stress, its ability to harmonize and make productive, in every sphere of thought and action, the individual and the social instincts innate in man. In these respects it has demonstrated its superiority over all other political philosophies. All try to draw the line between the opportunities and responsibilities of the individual and those of society, but none draws it so subtly in accordance with reality as democracy.

And what is that reality? It is that for 9000 years society has depended upon its members as individuals for those creative achievements of mind and spirit that have guided it along the path of civilization. The spark from heaven falls. Who picks it up? The crowd? Never. The individual? Always. It is he, and he alone, as artist, inventor, explorer, scholar, scientist, spiritual leader or statesman, who stands nearest to the source of life and transmits its essence to his fellow men. Let them tie his hands or stop his mouth or dragoon him in the name of uniformity, and they cut themselves off from that source.

Wisdom and virtue cannot be forced from a crowd as eggs from chickens under electric lights. There is no such thing as general intelligence. There is only individual intelligence communicating itself to other individual intelligences.

And there is no such thing as public morality; there is only a composite of private morality. The Athenian statesman Pericles perceived these truths when he said of democracy in its earliest phase that it trusted "less in system and policy than to the native spirit of our citizens." And so did Thomas Jefferson, when he wrote, "It is the manners and spirit of a people which preserve a republic in vigor." The same could be said of all forms of government, but of none so truly as that in which the voice of the people is the voice of God.

This is another way of saying that democracy is fundamentally a moral philosophy, a fact which, more than any other in its nature and history, has enabled it to survive all of its previous incarnations. This is as true now in the atomic age as it was in the age of Pericles.

We have the means for achieving democracy's promise in the most far-reaching system of education any free people has ever known, a system developed expressly for this purpose. We have the material resources to enable this system to fulfill its purpose without diverting a penny from the essential needs of our armed forces or from any other national interest of comparable importance. The problem is to create the will, not the resources.

In the solution of this problem hangs the fate of our nation and our civilization. For the very scientific progress that some think spells the doom of democracy depends for its continuation on two things: first, the continued discoveries of individuals in the realm of pure science, hence the continuation of an educational process that produces those individuals; and second, a social philosophy that converts human energy, newly rescued from drudgery by technological advances, to social uses consistent with this purpose.

This vast store of energy, exceeding in human terms our greatest accomplishment in the conservation of natural resources, in military and political terms equivalent to the enlistment of a powerful new ally in the defense of democracy, is at hand and ready to use. How shall we use it? Shall we abandon it to the entertainment industry? Shall we neglect it while we accuse one another of treason, like the farmer in the Bible who spent so much time pulling up tares that he harvested no ripe wheat? Shall we forget it in our fear of the ideas of a group of Russian doctrinaires, isolated even from their own people, whose conception of the world is not as sound as Columbus's nor as courageous as Ferdinand and Isabella's?

If we do these things we shall have to answer for them, as have all bodies politic that held their individual members in contempt. For "every tree that bringeth not forth good fruit is hewn down, and cast into the fire."

Capsule Course in Human Relations

Five most important words: I AM PROUD OF YOU.
Four most important words: WHAT IS YOUR OPINION?
Three most important words: IF YOU PLEASE.
Two most important words: THANK YOU.
Least important word: I.   —*Forbes Magazine*

TIME:

Our Greatest Benefactor

By Dorothy Dix

Condensed from
New Orleans Times-Picayune

WE ALL think of Time as our enemy. Especially do women regard it as their most malevolent foe, for does not Time steal the roses from their cheeks and dull the luster of their hair and fade the color from their eyes and take from their forms their lissome grace? Would not most women rather be accused of a scandal than of growing old? Is it not against Time that we fight a ceaseless battle in which we are always vanquished in the end?

How foolish! For, in reality, Time is not our enemy but our friend. It is an anodyne for our suffering. It is a philosopher's staff on which to lean. It is the magic that lifts the crushing burden from our shoulders and makes smooth the rough places in life.

Even to women Time is kinder than they think. It offers itself to them as an ally instead of an adversary if they will meet it in the right spirit, and if it takes from them the fleeting beauty of youth it will give them instead a charm that will never fade. For no women are so fascinating as those whom age and experience have ripened and perfected and given sophistication and taught every art of pleasing. Compared to them, the prettiest teen-ager is as a hard and knotty little bud to the full-blown rose.

And age gives beauty to many women who never had it in their youth. Time is a sculptor that chisels the rough features of many a girl into symmetry. It hardens many a flabby girl's figure into flowing lines of grace. It gives poise and dignity to the overgrown hobbledehoy. Many an old woman's face is luminous with the goodness of her soul that shines through like light through an alabaster vase.

Time is the greatest solver of all our problems, if only we had intelligence enough to trust it. All of us have difficulties we cannot settle. We lie awake at night and worry over them, wondering, if this or that contingency happened, what should be the best way to act. We cannot tell because we do not know what lies behind the veil of the future. How much anxiety, how much sleeplessness we might spare ourselves, if only we would lay our problems on the knees of Time. For when the hour comes, we find that Time has solved it all and our course is perfectly obvious. There is only one thing to do, and we do it.

Time is the strengthener. Sometimes we are confronted with conditions that turn our very souls sick with loathing. Sometimes the tasks appointed us seem more onerous than we can perform. At first our courage ebbs to the last drop and we feel that we must curse God and die.

Then Time begins somehow mysteriously to blur the harsh outlines of the background against which we must live, to strengthen our backs to bear the burdens that have been laid upon them, and to breathe into us new hope and spirit that enables us to carry on.

Time brings with it the blessing of forgetfulness. It turns the memory of hardships we have endured into piquant reminiscences. It makes our mistakes and blunders something to laugh over instead of cry over, and makes our fellow creatures condone our faults because our transgressions were committed so long ago.

And Time is the great peacemaker. Time robs old feuds of their enmity and old hatreds of their bitterness and makes us forgive those who have wronged us; those who have cheated, misused and betrayed us; those we had stored up anger against and had thought to be revenged upon. Time teaches us how senseless it is to sour our own lives with a grudge, and so our enemies gradually fade out of the picture.

Best of all, Time is the great consoler. When we lose those we love, we feel that the sun has set for us and that forevermore the earth will be shrouded in blackness. We find no cheer in anything, no interest in anything. Our horizon ends in a grave. No words, no sympathy, no philosophy can lighten our sorrow. Nothing can help us but Time.

For it has been mercifully ordained that the wound must heal and the ache and the pain grow less poignant, so slowly and insidiously that we do not realize it. Time brings us fresh interests, other joys; it thrusts our duties to other people upon us; it gives us work that absorbs us, and so by degrees it turns the grief that rended us into a sorrow that can be borne.

Blessed be Time that heals us.

ARE YOU LISTENING?

By Stuart Chase   Condensed from "The Power of Words"

LISTENING is the other half of talking. If people stop listening it is useless to talk—a point not always appreciated by talkers.

Listening isn't the simple thing it seems to be. It involves interpretation of both the literal meaning of the words and the intention of the speaker. If someone says, "Why, Jim, you old horse thief!" the words are technically an insult; but the tone of voice probably indicates affection.

Americans are not very good listeners. In general they talk more than they listen. Competition in our culture puts a premium on self-expression, even if the individual has nothing to express. What he lacks in knowledge he tries to make up for by talking fast or pounding the table. And many of us while ostensibly listening are inwardly preparing a statement to stun the company when we get the floor. Yet it really is not difficult to learn to listen—just unusual.

Listening is regarded as a passive thing, but it can be a very active process—something to challenge our intelligence. A stream of messages is coming in to be decoded: how close can we come to their real meaning? What is the speaker trying to say? . . . How does he know it? . . . What has he left out? . . . What are his motives?

Sometimes only about a quarter of an audience understands clearly what a speaker has said. To sharpen the ears of its members, the New York Adult Education Council has inaugurated "listening clinics." One member reads aloud while the others around the table concentrate on what he is saying. Later they summarize what they have heard and compare notes—often to find that the accounts differ widely. Gradually the listeners improve; often they find themselves transferring the skill to business and home affairs. As one member said:

"I became aware of a new attitude. I found myself attempting to understand and interpret the remarks of my friends and associates from *their* viewpoint, and not from my own as I had done previously."

Some years ago Major Charles T. Estes of the Federal Conciliation Service was called in to help settle a long-term dispute between a corporation and its unions. The Major proceeded to invent a technique for listening that has since had wide application in the labor field. He asked delegates from both union and management to read aloud the annual contract which was in dispute. Each man read a section in his turn; then all discussed it. If a dispute began to develop, the clause was put aside for later examination.

In two days the delegates really knew what was in the contract, and were competent to go back and tell their fellow managers or fellow workers what it contained. "We had conditioned them to communicate," said the Major. The contract was not rewritten but has continued in force with very few changes for ten years. Good listening had transformed bad labor relations into good ones.

Carl R. Rogers, University of Chicago psychologist, suggests a game to be played at a party. Suppose a general discussion—say on the French elections—becomes acrimonious. At this point Rogers asks the company to try an experiment: Before Jones, who is on the edge of his chair, can reply to the statement just made by Smith, he must summarize what Smith has said in such a way that Smith accepts it. Any attempt to slant or distort is instantly corrected by the original speaker. This means careful listening, during which emotion is likely to cool.

The result is that everyone in the circle, by listening and rephrasing, acquires a working knowledge of the other fellow's point of view, even if he does not agree with it. The players are quite likely to increase their knowledge of the subject—something that rarely happens in the usual slam-bang argument. The experiment takes courage, says Rogers, because in restating the other man's position one runs the risk of changing one's own.

F. J. Roethlisberger of the Harvard Business School, in a recent study of training courses for supervisors, describes a significant contrast in listening. An executive calls foreman Bill to his office to tell him about a change in Bill's department. A casting will be substituted for a hand-forged job, and the executive tells Bill how to do it.

"Oh yeah?" says Bill.

Let us follow two steps which the boss might take at this point. First, suppose he assumes that "Oh yeah" means Bill does not see how to do the new job, and it is up to the boss to tell Bill. This he proceeds to do clearly and logically. Nevertheless, Bill is obviously freezing up, and presently things begin to happen inside the boss. "Can it be," he asks himself, "that I have lost my power to speak clearly? No, Bill just doesn't understand plain English; he's really pretty dumb." The look which accompanies this unspoken idea makes Bill freeze up even harder. The interview ends on a note of total misunderstanding.

But, says Roethlisberger, suppose the boss sees from the "Oh yeah" that Bill is disturbed, and he tries to find out why. He says: "What's your idea about how the change-over ought to be made, Bill? You've been in the department a long time. Let's have it. I'm listening."

Things now begin to happen inside Bill. The boss is not laying it on the line, he's willing to listen. So ideas come out, slowly at first, then faster. Some are excellent ideas and the boss becomes really interested in Bill's approach—"Smarter man than I thought!" A spiral reaction is set up, as Bill begins to realize that he never appreciated the boss before. The interview ends on a note of close harmony.

In the first case, the boss did not listen to Bill, he *told* Bill; and though the telling was clear enough the goal moved farther away. In the second case, the boss listened until he had located what was worrying Bill; then they went along together.

So far, we have been talking about sympathetic listening in face-to-face situations, to make sure we grasp the speaker's full meaning. But critical listening, too, is needed in a world full of propaganda and high-pressure advertisers. Here are some techniques which help to develop critical listening to a speech or a conversation, a sales talk at your door or the testimony of a witness before a jury:

Look for motives behind the words. Is the speaker talking chiefly in accepted, appealing symbols—Home, Mother, the Founding Fathers, Our Glorious Heritage, and so on—avoiding the need for thought, or is he really trying to think? Speeches are often solidly larded with symbols, and the well-trained ear can identify them a long way off.

Is the speaker dealing in facts or inferences? With practice you can train your ear to find this distinction in political and economic talk, and to follow the shifts from one level to the next.

The listener should also consider his own attitude toward the speaker. Is he prejudiced for or against him? Is he being fair, objective, sympathetic?

The sum of careful listening is to work actively to discover how the speaker feels about events, what his needs and drives appear to be, what kind of person he is. The appraisal can only be rough, but it can be a decided help in dealing with him, in giving him a fair answer.

One other thing: I find that careful listening also helps me to keep quiet rather than sound off foolishly. The best listeners listen alertly, expecting to learn something and to help create new ideas.

Are you listening?

Food for Thought

A DOCTOR in Berkeley, Calif., is making a name for himself by his success in reducing overweight women. Asked his secret, he replied, "I get a head start on a case, that's all. On the patient's first call I spend only a few minutes with her, just long enough to weigh her and instruct her to keep a complete written record of every bite she eats during the two weeks until her second appointment. And," he smiled, "by the end of those two weeks most patients have already lost about ten pounds!"

—Contributed by John C. Sergeant

What Friendship Means to Me

By
Grove Patterson,
Editor of the Toledo Blade

Condensed from The Rotarian

A PANHANDLER stopped me on the street and said: "Grove, tomorrow is Easter, and I haven't got an egg in the house." Such vagrants as we have in our town usually call me by my first name. So I bought him an egg. The other day at a downtown corner an especially seedy fellow caught my eye. "Can you let me have a dime for a cup of coffee?" he almost whispered.

"Brother," I said, "you don't want a cup of coffee. You want a drink." I smiled right into his unhappy eyes. Contrary to popular practice, a smile brings out the truth much faster than a stern look.

"Yes," he said, "I sure do."

Hazlitt, the 19th-century British essayist, wrote: "One cannot expect people to be other than they are." That idea has guided me on the greatest adventure of my life—the adventure of friendship. With those vagrants, I tried to put myself in the place of each one, and acted as I hoped some understanding person might have acted toward me. You do not choose your friends from the dreary ranks of beggars; neither do I, but it seems to me these simple instances are illustrative of the pervasive spirit of friendship.

For to be a friend you have to care about people, what they think, what they feel, what they suffer. If you just don't like people, you may still be cordial to acquaintances, but friendship is no go. You must try to understand people, their hopes and fears and aspirations. At least a remnant of dignity shines through the rags of the tramp who craves a drink and the one who needs an egg for Easter.

Friendship stumbles most often on the rock of inconvenience. Most of us have an abundance of good impulses which we either forget or find inconvenient to translate into actuality. In my experience I have found most men kindhearted. They are usually willing to do generous things, if they can do them without much personal inconvenience. They are thoughtful of the sorrow and the needs of others—if they have time and the occasion is not too difficult.

Take the story of the Good Samaritan, on the road that led from Jerusalem down to Jericho. There were many who traveled it. Among them was one who was deep in trouble and lay helpless at the roadside. Two prominent citizens hurried by—good, average men, probably, generous in impulse, accustomed to going to church on a Sunday morning. Perhaps they were members of the Jericho Lions or Kiwanis or Rotary Club.

But this day on the Jericho road it was getting late. They were bound for supper and an evening at home. Perhaps good old So-and-So was coming in, and it would be nice to open a bottle of the older wine and be warm. Too bad about the poor fellow across the road. Probably a drunk. He did look a bit sad with that black eye, but, then, somebody would doubtless pick him up.

Now I have a hunch the Good Samaritan was much the same kind of chap as the two prominent citizens. Probably he, too, was thinking of a pleasant evening soon to come. It was just as late for him as for the other two. Yet he reached down into the gutter, set the poor devil on his beast and took him to the inn. And he gave a bit of money to the landlord and said: "Take care of him, and whatsoever thou spendest more, when I come again I will repay thee."

You see, the Samaritan had a kind heart *plus,* and it's only the kind heart plus that goes all the way. Every morning each one of us goes out on the Jericho road. Yet no matter what a good-natured, well-meaning citizen you or I may be, no matter what a hearty, hand-shaking member of the luncheon-every-Thursday service club, if we haven't the plus which makes us humbly willing to take inconvenient action, we are only jolly good fellows and the Jericho road will never be smoother because we walked that way.

Friendship is a plant that has to be cultivated; it must be watered and tended if it is to produce sweet and wholesome fruit. Just for example, I am an inveterate note-taker. When it occurs to me, day or night, that someone I know has done a particularly nice piece of work, and could use a word of appreciation, or is sick and needs an inquiry, I write it down as something to do. I realize, of course, that I am selfish about it, because I enjoy doing it.

The more I pursue my favorite study, the study of human nature, the more I wonder that so many people care to spend so much time and thought and worry about other people's business. Often men come to me and say: "I know you are close to Jones and I think you ought to tell him that he is making a mistake to do the things he is doing, or failing to do the things he is not doing."

This leaves me cold. I shall not put my hand into the wheels and cogs of my friends' lives and try to make them run the other way. I find there are barely enough hours in the day in which to correct some of my own faults and mistakes, and I invariably have a lot left over at sundown.

Friendship, to me, is an intangible thing, a kind of circle which completely surrounds another person, taking him in with all his good points and all his bad, enveloping him in his entirety. If I come to like a man and a friendship is formed, it is because I have discerned something likable and lovable deep within him, something of character and fineness, although from time to time he may, as we all do, violate that which is fine and which is customarily a part of him. If he is my friend, there are two things which I shall not think of doing: First, I shall not hurt him, and second, I shall not cross him off my list because he was drunk or disorderly or thoughtless. To me it is cruel to criticize a friend in other than a light way. I prefer to leave criticism to his mere acquaintances. Inasmuch as they are not his friends they cannot hurt him.

My mind goes back to a young man in a bank, long ago, who on one or two occasions had been careless in his habits, although those who knew him best realized that he was a man of sound ability and good character. A group of associates went to the president of the bank and suggested that the young man be dismissed. Whereupon the president, who was old and kind and had seen a great deal of life, called a meeting. And when the executives were gathered, he said gently: "Now let him who is without sin cast the first stone."

In the midst of a deafening silence the meeting adjourned.

To be a friend, in the deeper sense, may sometimes mean that you will be set down as an easy mark, a push-over. Most of the easy marks I have known have been a great deal happier than the smart little people who fooled them. The fullest life is one which has contained the richest experiences, even though some of those experiences may have eventually led to disillusionment and to disappointment. Once I heard my friend Raymond Swing say: "I should rather believe in something and be wrong than not believe in it and be right." So with the man who has my friendship.

Friendship inevitably affects the body as well as the spirit. I doubt if it is possible to hate anybody and be completely healthy. Physicians agree that resentment fosters poison in the human system. It is not possible to love everybody, or even to like everybody, but at least, when there is no friendly response, the robe of tolerant indifference can be put on. I have in mind a man who lived on a level above the mean resentments of life, and in nearly 80 years I don't believe he was ever ill enough to require the services of a physician. He was my father.

I am sure there are more good friends and good friendships in the world than we realize. From close observation of human beings I have come to the conclusion that the average person is better, not worse, than he seems to be. I have more than once discovered that men whom their fellows call selfish, ungenerous, hard, are almost daily engaged in the odds and ends of a thousand little kind and thoughtful acts. I have found many a soft conscience in a hard coat and many of the deeper qualities of friendship in an inarticulate man.

One who is genuinely friendly ought not to be too critical of his acquaintances who are tactless, undiplomatic, and rarely express thanks or show gratitude. So many feel deeply, but do not have the gift of expression. Some who seem rude are only shy. Some who seem ungrateful are only timid. On the other side, there are people who find it easier to talk than feel. These unfortunates lack the master quality of sincerity. Insincerity may have a pleasant sound but rings no silver bells of truth. Insincerity is the tinkling cymbal of human relationship.

Above all, friendship means to me the immeasurable capacity for forgiveness. It means the ability to check off resentment, rather than let it persist and poison the spirit. Robert Louis Stevenson wrote: "He is a green hand at life who cannot forgive any mortal thing." There is no more enduring thing in life than real friendship. If it is not enduring, then it is not real, and has never quite found its way from the far-flung fields of acquaintance to the inner circle of devotion.

You're Not Feeling Well?

THERE IS a legend at Harvard that the late Le Baron Russell Briggs, beloved dean of the College, once asked a student why he had failed to complete an assignment.

"I wasn't feeling very well, sir," said the student.

"Mr. Smith," said the Dean, "I think that in time you may perhaps find that most of the work of the world is done by people who aren't feeling very well."

I have often thought of this remark and wondered whether Dean Briggs, a man of none too robust health, may not have been feeling a little seedy himself when he uttered it; whether he may not have dragged himself to the office that morning only because he put his responsibilities ahead of his comforts.

The Dean knew that there is such a thing as a sensibly prudent attitude toward one's health. But he also knew that the symptoms of fatigue and of laziness are practically identical; that it is hard to tell the difference between not feeling well and not feeling like doing a hard job. He knew, too, that the wise man who has an assignment to complete by Friday has done so much of it on Tuesday and Wednesday that a headache Thursday won't matter much.

He knew the difference between the fellow who plans his jobs and fits his pleasures into the chinks between them and the fellow who plans his pleasures and then begins to think of his responsibilities.

Again and again Dean Briggs' remark comes back to me on those dismal mornings when it seems outrageous that anybody should have to settle down to work at nine o'clock. And I start laughing at myself, and presently I feel more like buckling down and doing the thing that has to be done.

—Frederick Lewis Allen in *This Week*

How I Found Freedom from Fear

By Margaret Lee Runbeck

Condensed from Independent Woman

WHEN I was graduating from high school I was a very self-conscious and awkward child. But by reason of sheer brute scholarship I found myself on the platform during the earth-shaking commencement exercises with the valedictory speech seething in my frightened little head.

Our class was ranged along the stage of the auditorium, and down below us in a dizzy, blurred sea of drowning faces were our parents. Among them were mine, my mother's blessed forefinger still pricked from the thousands of tiny hand stitches she had put into my graduating dress, my father spending one of his precious day's leaves in order to witness the great event. If I disgraced them today—as I most likely should—I couldn't possibly forgive myself.

It had been arranged that we four dry-mouthed performers—the class prophet, the valedictorian, the class poet and the grind who was to be given a university scholarship—were to sit in conspicuous segregation in the center of the stage. Having to mumble a speech was horror enough, but having to sit there where all could gaze upon my plumpness and the fever blister which had popped out from sheer terror was agony unbearable.

To make the whole thing worse, next to me was an empty chair for the invited speaker who was to deliver our Commencement Address. My English teacher had said firmly that I must chat cordially with him during the few minutes before the exercises started. It would show the audience how completely at ease everyone was, she said. This, of course, was the final ordeal, for what could I possibly find to say to a strange grownup?

When he came swinging gracefully onto the stage, while the high school orchestra was scraping through *The Blue Danube,* my despair reached its climax. But my English teacher nodded imperatively at me, so I smiled deliriously at our speaker and tried to give a pantomime impression that all was well.

"I'm supposed to talk wittily to you," I gulped in a breathless croak, "but . . . but . . . I haven't a thing to say. I'm scared to death."

"I'm scared, too," he said. "I've got a speech written down, but I don't think it's much good, and besides—"

"But *you* don't have to be afraid," I said in amazement.

He looked at me carefully, not as a man looking at a child but as one human being measuring another to see where help might be given.

"Neither do you," he said. "I'll tell you a secret; then you'll never need to be scared again. Everyone on earth is shy, self-conscious and unsure of himself. Everybody's timid about meeting strangers. So if you'll just spend the first minute you're in the presence of a stranger trying to help *him* feel comfortable, you'll never suffer from self-consciousness again. Try it."

In his handsome face I saw a kindness that made me suddenly aware of what a fine thing a man with sympathy and insight in his soul can be.

"I *will* try it," I said, very loudly, from the bottom of my heart.

Then suddenly, to my horror, I realized that *The Blue Danube* had come to its end, and that my voice had blazed out like a bullet in the silence. Our principal, a stern narrow-faced little man, was staring at me, and all my classmates were gazing open-mouthed. It was a moment which easily could have toppled into neighborhood disgrace.

But the man beside me laughed with assurance, and reached out and patted my shoulder in such a friendly way that everyone in the hall felt good, and pleased, and friendly. In spite of myself, I had done exactly what my English teacher had said I must do—I had talked pleasantly with our guest, so that everyone would feel at ease.

I don't remember how the speeches went off, either his or mine. But I do remember how happy I was, and how wonderful the whole occasion seemed. Most of all I remember the advice of the man who generously gave a frightened, unattractive child his secret for getting over discomfort by losing self in helping a stranger.

I've used his secret thousands of times; I've watched it work with all kinds of strangers; and increasingly I've been grateful to the man who gave it to me. I often wished I could remember who he was so that I could tell him of my gratitude.

Recently I had to dispose of an atticful of valueless treasures and trivia hoarded through the years. In a box with a few old letters I found the Commencement Day Program of Eastern High School, Washington, D. C. It has a blue-and-silver seal on the front, and a line which says:

Commencement Address, by the Honorable Franklin D. Roosevelt, Assistant Secretary of the Navy.

It is too late now for me to tell him of my gratitude. But I can pass along his secret to help others, as he passed it along to me.

The Summing Up

In *A Few Buttons Missing: The Case Book of a Psychiatrist,* Dr. James T. Fisher, one of the country's foremost psychiatrists, writes:

If you were to take the sum total of all the authoritative articles ever written by the most qualified of psychologists and psychiatrists on the subject of mental hygiene, if you were to combine them and refine them and cleave out the excess verbiage, if you were to take the whole of the meat and none of the parsley, and if you were to have these unadulterated bits of pure scientific knowledge concisely expressed by the most capable of living poets, you would have an awkward and incomplete summation of the Sermon on the Mount. —Written in collaboration with Lowell S. Hawley and published by Lippincott

*A simple yet neglected antidote for tension
and a tonic for well-balanced living*

STOP—And Meditate

By
Austen Fox Riggs, M. D.   Condensed from the book "Play"

L IVING at a sustained pitch of high tension is injurious to both physical and mental health. Yet most of us can think of only two ways to use the leisure time we all have: we either work or play—and in either case, do it hard. It rarely occurs to any of us that there is another valuable use for the pauses in everyday life: namely, meditation.

What would most of us think if we saw a man sitting quietly in a hotel lobby or in the living room of his house—neither reading, nor writing, nor working, nor playing—just sitting, apparently doing nothing? Our first thought would be that he was waiting for someone, and probably we would feel a bit sorry for the boredom he must be suffering. It would never enter our minds that he was actually doing something both important and delightful—allowing his mind to wander and to wonder, to disconnect itself entirely from the immediate surroundings and spread its wings in meditation.

Meditation holds refreshment and rest, conserves energy for future needs, and helps to keep life balanced and elastic. Through it we often arrive at a revision of values which helps inward development.

No special or definite technique is required. It is simply a matter of freeing one's mind and allowing it to wander in peace beyond the objectives and so-called "practical" things of the present. It is no more than deliberately bidding one's thoughts to take a holiday and leave the lesser realities of everyday life, and thus purposely producing the same state of mind which one automatically falls into when listening to beautiful music or looking into a sunset or gazing at great mountains. The attitude is one of wonder without expectancy, of contemplation without planning or striving.

No physical aids are required save a reasonably comfortable place to sit. Neither are surroundings important. Quiet and beautiful surroundings do help, however, to induce the proper state of mind.

The great psychologist, William James, recommended frequent attendance of chapel to his philosophy students. He told us that the practice of going to a quiet place which was suggestive of contemplative thought aided in keeping one's point of view right side up. He said that going to chapel was much like the experience of a person who, being jostled about in a crowd, climbs up on a nearby doorstep, looks over the heads of the people, sees what the crowd as a whole is doing, and is then able to descend again into the jam and push in the right direction. He might have used the same simile in speaking of meditation. Meditation raises us above petty considerations so that we may distinguish the important from the unimportant.

To start the process of meditation one needs only to "shove the mind off" on the right track. This preliminary direction should aim the mind upward and outward in the direction of the universal and impersonal, rather than downward and inward toward the specific egocentric.

Tired of practical planning and fed up on specific thinking, the mind leaves all such narrow thoughts with surprising ease. The best way to initiate the process is through short periods of concentration on some general and abstract idea, such as the nature of beauty, the meaning of truth, the spirit of courage, the destiny of the human race, the quality of immortality, or any one of the eternal verities of religion. Or take some inspiring quotation and let the actual quotation or the idea derived from it rest in your mind. Perhaps a new interpretation may occur to you.

In time of trouble, when one is harried by anxiety or under some other emotional stress, there is no more reliable method of attaining comparative calm. Nor do I know of any which is so economical of time and energy in helping one regain control of reason and judgment. Meditation is an important part of living wisely.

The Delightful Game

of Conversation

By Gelett Burgess

Condensed from Your Life

I N SAN FRANCISCO once I belonged to a small group which met weekly for the purpose of reviving the lost art of conversation. We realized that there is a fundamental principle underlying good talk. This principle—the basis of all good manners—is the avoidance of friction in social contacts, emotional friction caused by irritation, boredom, envy, egotism or ridicule. Here are some of the rules we finally adopted to guide our conversation and make it a delightful game.

1. *Avoid all purely subjective talk*. Don't dilate on your health, troubles, domestic matters; and never, never discuss your wife or husband. Streams of personal gossip and egotism destroy all objective discussion —of art, science, history, the day's news, sport, or whatever. Such chatter bores the listener, and the talker, repeating only what he already knows, learns nothing from others.

2. *Don't monopolize the conversation*. One of my friends was a laughing, attractive person, who told stories well—but too many of them. You roared with laughter, but after a while you grew restless and yearned for more quiet, comfortable talk with plenty of give and take. You couldn't help remembering what John Dryden said about those "who think too little, and who talk too much." Or what Sydney Smith wrote of Macaulay: "He has occasional flashes of silence, that make his conversation perfectly delightful."

3. *Don't contradict*. You may say, "I don't quite agree with that," but flat contradiction is a conversation-stopper. One should seek to find

points of agreement. In that way the subject develops in interest with each one's contribution. "That is the happiest conversation," said Samuel Johnson, "where there is no competition, but a calm quiet interchange of sentiments."

4. *Don't interrupt.* Of course when you throw a few grace notes into the talk, such as, "How wonderful!" or, "You mean she didn't know?" it doesn't put the train of conversation off the track. But to interpolate views of your own often leaves the speaker hanging uncomfortably in mid-sentence.

One perfect conversational dinner party is still alive in my memory. It was given in Boston by Mrs. James T. Fields, and there were six present—the ideal number for an intimate dinner; if you have more the conversation is apt to break up into separate side dialogues. Each of us talked and each of us listened. No one interrupted, no one contradicted, no one monologued. The affair had the charm and pleasing restfulness of music.

5. *Don't abruptly change the subject.* Some people, after patiently— and painfully—waiting for a talker to pause a moment, jump into the conversation with a totally new subject. In our Conversation Club it was an unwritten rule that after a person stopped talking there should be a brief silence in which to reflect, digest and appreciate what had been said. It is the proper tribute to anyone who has offered an idea for consideration.

6. *Show an active interest in what is said.* This brings out the best in a speaker. You need not only your ears to listen well, but your eyes, hands and even posture. I have often tested an article I have written by reading it aloud to friends. What they said about it never helped much, since one often liked what another didn't. But if their eyes went to a picture on the wall, if their fingers fiddled, I knew that the manuscript wasn't holding their interest and I marked the dull spots for revision.

There is no surer way to make people like you than to pay them the compliment of interest and sympathy. Prolong their subject, ask more about it, and they expand like flowers in the sun. Yet what usually happens is that, should you venture to describe some misfortune that has happened to you, others immediately narrate a similar mischance that they have suffered.

7. *After a diversion, bring back the subject.* Often while a subject is not yet fully considered it is lost in some conversational detour. There is no surer test of being able to converse well than to reintroduce this forgotten topic. This is not only polite and gracious, but it is the best evidence of real interest.

Of course, if it is your own story it is futile for you to bring it back to persons who have bypassed it. Let it go, but see that you don't commit their error.

8. *Don't make dogmatic statements of opinion.* The Japanese tea ceremony is perhaps the most refined social form ever practiced. It is a cult of self-effacement. One of the rules concerns conversation. It is considered vulgar to make any definite, decisive statement. One may speak of anything, but never with an expression of finality. The remark is left up in the air, for the next guest to enlarge upon, so that no one is guilty of forcing any personal opinion upon the others.

It is a good game, but difficult; try it some time with your friends. You may state facts as facts; but your application of them should be tentative, with such qualifications as "It seems to me," or "Isn't it possible that—" Those who really know things usually speak thus, "with meekness of wisdom," as St. James says, while the ignoramus is always for cut-and-dried pronouncements.

9. *Speak distinctly.* While I was a member of the executive committee of the Authors' League I was fascinated by the fact that those who spoke slowly and clearly dominated our meetings. High, hurried voices simply couldn't compete with Ellis Parker Butler's deliberate words, and his voice maintained his leadership for years. If you observe a group talking you'll find that the one with a low, controlled voice always gets the most respect. The eager, temperamental contenders dash up against it like waves against a rock, and the rock always wins.

10. *Avoid destructive talk.* We are all likely to make many unnecessary derogatory remarks. Evil, of course, must be condemned. But try to avoid the unnecessary criticism, the desire to raise a laugh through ridicule, the tendency to look on the unpleasant side of life. Cynical comments may sound clever, but they make others uncomfortable.

So much for the negative side of conversational rules. How can you create an agreeable conversation?

The secret is simple. To talk well one must think well. You must think underneath the subject, above it and all around it.

This kind of thinking is well illustrated in the conversation of baseball enthusiasts. Are they content with telling the score, the number of hits and runs? Not at all. They discuss a team's potentialities, the characteristics of the different players, the technique of the game. The same principle applies to all conversation. *Anyone who finds it hard to talk should learn to think about what he sees and hears and reads.* As you ponder, associate the subject with your own experience and observation.

To avoid falling into the rut of shop talk, enlarge your interests by making acquaintances engaged in pursuits other than your own. Develop a curiosity about what has so far been outside your range of knowledge. Read up on subjects that have interested you, that have been outside your field of view.

If you fertilize and enrich your thinking in such ways you need not worry about being able to converse well. Every new experience will make your talk more interesting and more valuable.

Time for the Soul

A FRIEND OF MINE, a distinguished explorer who spent a couple of years among the savages of the upper Amazon, once attempted a forced march through the jungle. The party made extraordinary speed for the first two days, but on the third morning, when it was time to start, my friend found all the natives sitting on their haunches, looking very solemn and making no preparation to leave.

"They are waiting," the chief explained to my friend. "They cannot move farther until their souls have caught up with their bodies."

I can think of no better illustration of our own plight today. Is there no way of letting our souls, so to say, catch up with our bodies? If one thinks over the sort of life led in innumerable homes a generation ago, our immense speeding up in the process of living today is clear. People then, as we say, "had time." Now, no one "has time."

—James Truslow Adams, *The Tempo of Modern Life* (Boni)

Stupidity and humidity are related, after all

WATCH OUT FOR THE WEATHER

By Jacqueline Berke and Vivian Wilson

A condensation from the book

ALL OF US have days when everything we do seems to go wrong. At such times don't blame yourself; there's impressive evidence that off days are more apt to occur when the barometric pressure is low and falling than at any other time. These are the times when people tend to be on edge, irritable, nervous.

The deportment records of more than 2000 school children showed that they misbehaved most often on muggy days preceding a storm. Bank of England officials discovered that there was a higher percentage of clerical errors on foggy days.

Nobody has established exactly how barometric-pressure changes act on the organs of our bodies; but experiments have shown that pressure influences the water content of our tissues. This may account for the mysterious knowledge of the arthritic weather prophet. When the barometer falls, the water content of the tissues is increased and the tissues swell. Normally healthy people will not have any sharp discomfort at these times, but since an arthritic has sensitive joints he will feel pain and be able to predict stormy weather. On low-pressure days, the tissues of the brain are also taking up more water. Any such change will show up in our emotions.

Edwin Grant Dexter, author of *Weather Influences,* showed that children behave best on cold, calm and clear days; they misbehave when it is muggy, hot and windy. He found that girls are less affected by weather conditions than boys.

Every time temperature or barometric pressure changes, the body has to make an adjustment. Usually it adjusts easily; but at other times the weather makes drastic demands on both mind and body.

There are times when weather is the stimulus that makes you perform at a superior level that you'd never dreamed you could achieve. At other times weather bogs you down; instead of thinking clearly, you become confused.

When the weather is cool and invigorating you feel optimistic, invulnerable. In a temperate climate you do your best mental work in late winter, early spring and fall; your worst in the summer.

Figures collected in the state of Massachusetts show that 75 percent of the people who take educational tests for civil-service jobs pass in April. November is almost as good: 73 percent make it. But in August only 58 percent come through.

Constant, unrelieved heat saps physical vitality and cripples mental ability; it breaks down moral judgment, too. Crime rates soar in the spring, reach their peak in the summer. More murders are committed in the hot months of July and August than at any other time. There are also more acts of violence, more crimes of passion. One criminologist studied the incidence of crime in France and Italy; he found that in the warm southern sections of both countries crimes of violence and sex were twice as numerous as in the cool north. And they always reached peak proportions in the hottest, most oppressive summer months.

Edwin Dexter studied 40,000 cases of assault and battery in New York City: every year for eight years the incidence of this crime increased from the coldest month, January, to the hottest month, July. In fact, the monthly crime curve and the monthly temperature curve were practically identical.

Ellsworth Huntington, one of the first men to approach weather and man scientifically, established that the ideal temperature for health and work is an average of 64 degrees for day and night.

But, strangely enough, there is such a thing as weather that is too good. Monotonous weather has a depressing effect on the health and mentality of people. It doesn't matter too much what the change is; change in itself is good if it is not too sudden or too severe.

Man's constant body temperature does not change with the weather —but it must adjust itself to it. One of the most familiar responses to weather is spring fever. You wake up some spring morning feeling as if you haven't slept at all. As the day goes on, you try to work, but you can't keep your thoughts in line. The reason you're tired and let down is that when the temperature of the air rises your body has to get rid of heat. The blood vessels dilate so that they can carry blood to the surface and thus throw off the heat. As the vessels expand, your body keeps up with them by increasing the blood volume.

Plasma, the watery substance in the blood, is increased before the other substances are released into the bloodstream. This means that, for a short time after the cooling-off process starts, your blood will be more diluted than usual. So, even though grandma did not know the physiology of it, she was right when she said the blood "thins out" in the spring. This process is a lot of work for your body and it accounts for that enervated feeling you experience every spring, particularly if you are already fatigued after a winter of rough weather.

Our new-found understanding of the power of weather can help us, but we have not nearly caught up with the latest discoveries. We still live as if weather were as mysterious in its workings and effects as it was to medieval soothsayers.

The Time to Buy

Bᴇʀɴᴀʀᴅ Bᴀʀᴜᴄʜ, who made millions on the market, tells how easy it is: "If you are ready and able to give up everything else, and will study the market and every stock listed there as carefully as a medical student studies anatomy, and will glue your nose to the ticker tape at the opening of every day of the year and never take it off till night; if you can do all that, and in addition have the cool nerve of a gambler, the sixth sense of a clairvoyant and the courage of a lion—you have a Chinaman's chance." —Clayton Rand, Publishers Syndicate

Your Mind Can Keep You Well

By John A. Schindler, M.D.
Chief Physician of the Monroe, Wis., Clinic

Condensed from a radio broadcast

HAT ONE THING contributes more than anything else to unhappiness? As a doctor I can answer that: a long period of illness. It is a little frightening, when you think of it, because there are a thousand different ailments that this human clay is heir to, and one of them is as common as the other 999 put together. Fifty per cent of all the people going to doctors in the United States today are victims of this one disease. Many would put the figure higher. At the Ochsner Clinic in New Orleans a report was published reviewing 500 consecutive admissions to that institution; of those, 386—or 77 percent—were sick with this one disease. Persons of any age, in any walk of life, can contract it. Furthermore it is a terrifically expensive disease to diagnose and treat.

I hesitate to give you its name because immediately you will get a lot of misconceptions. The first will be that it is not a real disease. But don't kid yourself. It used to be called psychoneurosis. Now it is known as psychosomatic illness. And it is *not* a disease in which the patient just *thinks* he is sick. The pain you get is often just as severe as the pain you get with a gall-bladder colic.

Psychosomatic illness isn't produced by a bacterium, or by a virus, or by a new growth. It is produced by the circumstances of daily living. I have tried to find one word for it, but it takes three, each one of them meaning about the same thing but in different degrees. They are: *cares, difficulties, troubles*. Whenever one has such a thick, impenetrable layer of c.d.t. that he can't get up above it into a realm of joy and pleasure occasionally, he gets a psychosomatic illness.

There are three general groupings of people who suffer from c.d.t. In the first group are the people who are habitually crabby. A friend of mine has a beautiful farm. I drove past his farm one summer day and I thought to myself, "Those oats ought to make Sam happy." So I drove in, and I said, "Sam, that's a wonderful field of oats," and Sam said, "Yes, but the wind will blow it down before I get it cut." He got it cut all right, he got it threshed, and he got a good price for it. Well, I saw him one day and I said, "Sam, how did the oats turn out?" And he said, "Oh, it was a good crop, and I guess the price was all right, but you know a crop like that sure takes a lot out of the soil."

People like Sam invariably get a psychosomatic illness, and when they get it they get it hard. As a rule they are invalids for the rest of their lives. There is nothing you can do about it.

The second group, where most of us belong, are the people who all day long manage to be concerned, to be anxious, to be worrying about something. If there's nothing around home or the business, they worry about Mrs. Smith down the street. Why doesn't she get her daughter in before 11 o'clock at night? Something is going to happen to her!

The third group is made up of those who have an acute case of c.d.t. Maybe they have gotten themselves into some kind of mess— financial ruin or domestic trouble, perhaps. They are usually easier to treat than those in the second group. And those in the second group are certainly easier to treat than those in the first group.

How does this c.d.t. bring on illness? To understand that, we must consider what thinking is and what emotion is. Thinking, we ordinarily suppose, is something that goes on solely in the brain, but that is quite wrong. Thinking involves the entire body in a series of correlated nerve impulses that center in the brain. Particularly is this true when an emotion colors our thinking. The psychologist William James gave us the best definition that we have of emotion when he said that it is the state of mind that manifests itself by a perceptible change in the body.

One emotion we all recognize is anger. You don't have to be told when a man is angry. His face either gets white or it gets red; his eyes widen; his muscles tighten up so that he trembles. That is the state of mind manifesting itself by a perceptible change in the body.

Another emotion is embarrassment. A person who blushes certainly doesn't have a disease of the skin. In his case embarrassment produces a dilation of the blood vessels in the face.

A third example in the group of unpleasant emotions is the man or woman who vomits or faints at the sight of blood. The sight of blood leads to such painfully disagreeable thinking that the stomach does the things that result in vomiting. Or the heart and the blood vessels leading to the brain do the things that result in fainting.

Now, how does all this bring about a disease? Very simply. Most of our disagreeable emotions produce muscle tightness. Suppose that all day long your thinking is acutely disagreeable. You are tightening up muscles. Take your fist and hold it loosely; it doesn't hurt; but hold it tight for a long time and it begins to hurt. The squeeze produces pain.

One of the first places to show tension is the group of muscles at the back of the neck. Another group that come into play very early are the muscles at the upper end of the esophagus. When they squeeze down you feel a lump. It is difficult to swallow. If the muscles in the lower esophagus contract, then it's more serious. Much more commonly the stomach is involved. And when the muscles of the stomach begin to squeeze down you are conscious of a heavy, disagreeable pressure inside. When the muscles squeeze down hard, then it hurts. And it hurts just as bad as any ulcer. In our town we had a grocer who had a pain exactly like that of an ulcer. He had plenty of trouble —a competitive business, a nagging wife, a wayward son—and he had this pain most of the time. Doctors assured him he had no ulcer. He finally began to believe them when he noticed that every time he went fishing the pain disappeared. And it didn't come back again until he was almost home.

This same kind of muscle spasm can occur in any part of the colon. Many persons who complain of a pain exactly like gall-bladder pain don't have gall-bladder trouble at all. They're dissatisfied, and the upper colon is squeezing down. And their suffering is real. If the pain happens to be lower down in the colon, it will seem just like appendicitis. And then it takes a very smart doctor not to open that abdomen.

Other muscles besides those in the intestinal tract respond to emotional stimuli, particularly the muscles of the blood vessels. A good many of the people who have a headache severe enough to cause them to go to a doctor have that headache because some blood vessel inside or outside the skull is squeezing down so hard from nervous excitation that it produces pain.

And a third of all skin diseases treated by dermatologists are produced by blood vessels in the skin reacting to anxiety, worry, disgust, and so on. Each time certain individuals become upset or irritated or peeved, serum is actually squeezed out through the wall of the blood vessel and into the skin. The tissue becomes thickened with serum. Finally the serum is pushed up through the surface of the skin where it becomes scaly, crusty and itchy, and the patient has a neurodermatitis.

One favorite place for nervous tension is the muscles in the upper left part of the thorax. People rarely come to see us doctors because they have a pain on the right side. It's almost always on the left. If it's on the right—pshaw!—it doesn't amount to anything. If it's on the left —ah!—could be heart trouble! Then they start watching for it. And merely watching for it can bring the pain on.

Muscle tension is just one way in which the symptoms are produced in a psychosomatic illness. One of the other ways is the effect that the emotion has on the endocrine system. Most of you have driven down a street in an automobile too fast when suddenly somebody has backed out from a side road. You started to breathe deeply, your heart started to pound and you got a little faint. Acute fear in your mind produces these bodily changes. An impulse is sent to the adrenal glands, which squeeze adrenaline into the blood stream. When that adrenaline hits the heart, the heart starts to thump. When it hits the respiratory center in the brain, you start to gasp. When it hits the blood vessels going into the brain, they narrow down and you feel woozy.

There are other organic effects of psychosomatic illness. If it happens to be the blood vessels on your heart that squeeze down every time you get excited or angry, it is serious. John Hunter, the English physiologist, had that kind of heart, and he always said, "The first scoundrel that gets me angry will kill me." And that's exactly what happened. He got up in a medical meeting one time to refute something that he didn't like, and in a fit of anger produced such a contraction of the blood vessels on his heart that he fell dead.

Many victims of psychosomatic illness are up and around. Many are in hospitals. Thousands have been in bed at home for years. To avoid psychosomatic illness, you must learn to think right. There ought to be in every university a course called "The Art of Human Living." It should teach us how to make our attitude and thinking as pleasant and cheerful as possible. It would be idiotic for me to tell you that you can be pleasant and cheerful all the time. Of course you can't. But I can offer certain suggestions which will help you to think right about yourself.

First, quit looking for a knock in your motor. Don't be analyzing your feelings all the time, looking for trouble.

Second, learn to like to work. To get any place in this world you've got to work. One of the things you will escape, if you learn to like to work, is work tension, the tension that comes to those who look upon work as something to be gotten over with.

Third, have a hobby. A hobby is an important element in getting your mind off work tension. During the day when you are hurrying and worrying, just relax for 30 seconds by thinking briefly about that thing you're making in the basement, that community project you're interested in or that fishing trip you're taking next week-end.

Fourth, learn to like people. Carrying a grudge or dislike can have disastrous bodily effects. We had a man in the hospital who got there because he had to work in an office with a man he didn't like. He said, "I don't like the way he combs his hair; I don't like the way he whistles through his teeth; I don't like the way he always starts a sentence with 'Listen!'" On questioning the patient I found that he never liked anybody—his mother or his father or any member of his family. But you have to meet people. You've got to live with them, so learn to like them.

Fifth, learn to be satisfied when the situation is such that you can't easily change it. A young lady was in a hospital with a psychosomatic illness because she had become dissatisfied with her life. She had been a secretary, had held a war job in Washington. There she married an Army captain. After the war she found herself living in a trailer, raising three children. She didn't like to live in a trailer, didn't like to raise children in a trailer, wasn't sure that she liked to live with her husband in a trailer. She wanted to be a secretary, back in Washington. I didn't tell her what her trouble was. I just advised her to send to the library and get the four Pollyanna books and read them. She did, and she returned to live in the trailer and like it. She had learned that it is just as easy under most conditions to be satisfied as it is to be dissatisfied, and it is much more pleasurable.

Sixth, learn to accept adversity. In this life you're going to meet some adversity. You may meet a lot, but don't let it bowl you over. I had a patient who hadn't worked for a year. Then his wife died. A month later his son was killed. And he sat around thinking "How unfortunate I am—why did this have to happen to *me!*" He became very sick. He hadn't learned to accept adversity. A lot of people start a psychosomatic illness after an adversity.

Seventh, learn to say the cheerful, humorous thing. Never say the mean thing, even if you feel like doing so. In the morning, look at your wife or your husband and, even if it isn't so, say, "My dear, you look good this morning." It will make her (or him) feel better, and it will make you feel better.

Finally, learn to meet your problems with decision. About the worst thing to do is to have a problem and to mull it over and over in your mind. If you have a problem, decide what you are going to do about it and then quit thinking about it.

These are some of the things that you have to learn if you want to escape the most common disease of all. The key is: *I'm going to keep my attitude and my thinking as pleasant and as cheerful as possible.* There isn't any better definition for happiness.

Letter Perfect

A FRIEND, away from home on a long visit one summer, kept receiving from her husband and daughters such bright accounts of their doings that she began to wonder if she were missed at all. Then a letter from her ten-year-old son removed all doubt. "Dear Mom," he wrote, "this is the biggest house I ever saw since you went away."

—Contributed by Elizabeth Mills

*The job-seeker with an idea and the initiative to put
it into practice sets himself apart from
99 percent of applicants*

MAKE YOUR OWN JOB

By James D. Woolf   Former vice-president of J. Walter Thompson Co.

Condensed from Forbes

U NLESS an employer has a definite job to offer an applicant, he is likely to turn him away with the response, "I'm sorry, but we don't need anyone right now."

If this happens to you, don't forget that the employer may be mistaken. For often there is a job just waiting for somebody with imagination to come along and create it.

This is a lesson I learned as a boy. Anxious to earn extra money, I asked all three drugstores in my town for a job—any kind of job. There were no openings. But a week later one of these stores had taken on a new boy. Screwing up my courage, I asked the owner why.

"Well, I'll tell you, son," he said. "I didn't *think* I had a job open when you asked for one. But then Freddie came in with an idea. He owns a bicycle, and he suggested that I start a delivery service, meaning himself. That's a new notion for this town. It's going to make a hit."

Well, I had a bicycle, too, but Freddie had something I didn't have —an idea.

A friend of mine, for many years the successful sports editor of a big Pennsylvania daily, also *thought* himself into his first job. He wanted to be a newspaperman, but the only paper in his small town turned him down. So he started to study the paper for weak spots. Presently he settled on its almost total lack of sporting news and its meager coverage of farm happenings.

Seven days later the young fellow went back with two ideas—and a fistful of copy to back them up. It had been a busy sports week: two high school ball games, an amusing horseshoe pitching contest, and horse races at the county fair. He handed the editor a brisk account of these events as the pattern for a sports column. Then he suggested another column, "Farm Doings," a collection of items he had picked up from farmers. He was hired on the spot.

Recently a lad in Iowa, back from war work in California, got his start by *making* it. A good mechanic, he tackled the owner of a garage. No job! But the youngster didn't give up: he had an idea. He offered to help around the place without pay. The owner said he didn't mind.

The garage had only one repair truck; hence many calls from stranded motorists were turned down. The unpaid helper fixed up a broken-down motorcycle with a sidecar and loaded it with tools for emergency repair jobs. The owner, pleased, gave this returned war worker a well-paying job.

Simple ideas? Maybe so. But consider this fact: During more than 30 years as an advertising agency executive I have interviewed at least 5000 job hunters—and not more than 50 of them came up with even the simplest idea that applied to problems we were talking about.

When scouting for ideas, make a habit of observing *critically* jobs that are being poorly done. The indifference of others may spell opportunity for you. Take, for instance, the case of a man who started life carrying newspapers in Paterson, N. J. He noticed that boys who distributed handbills for stores threw them around so carelessly that most of them were wasted.

"How much more profitable it would be," the lad thought, "if each circular were handed to the housewife at the door." He took this idea to the owner of a new store about to open in Paterson, and got the job of distributing his announcements.

The youngster spent four days distributing fliers that another boy would have handled in one day. But on the morning of the opening, there was such a rush of business that the store nearly had to close its doors. The newsboy was hired. Four months later, at the age of 16 (believe it or not!) he was asked to manage another store in the chain. In time that newsboy, T. J. Grassey, became president of Great Eastern Stores—63 of them.

Make it a habit also to keep on the lookout for unusual ideas that others are already using successfully. Your idea needs to be original only in its application to your prospective employer's business. Watch the advertising in your local newspapers for new angles in store service. Study, too, the classified sections of the big telephone books. You will find many ads of specialized businesses with a novel twist, and you may have some talent or experience that fits right into one of these slots.

Every field of human activity is covered by America's 1700 trade journals, whose business is to report new ideas and developments. They're full of better ways of doing things. Employers and managers are often so busy they cannot search their trade magazines for ideas. The job-seeker who shows he has the energy to root them out, and the initiative to put them into practice, is sure to get an interested hearing.

The rapid growth of new developments—television and other electronic devices, air conditioning, civilian aviation, food freezing, and many others—will furnish a fertile field for imagination and initiative. Today's job-seeker will find about him on every side fresh problems to be solved, and better solutions of old problems to be thought out. The ever-changing needs of postwar America are calling to him—and it's up to him to hear and heed that call.

One of Those Days

DURING a week when her husband and all three children were sick at home, the harassed young wife commented: "The toughest thing about being a housewife is that you have no place to stay home from."
—Contributed by Patricia C. Beaudouin

AFTER a period when our younger daughter had been particularly trying, my husband turned to me and asked: "Do you think we should take her to a psychologist to find out what's wrong with us?"
—Contributed by Helen M. Coombe

"ACT AS IF—"

The First Step Toward Faith

By Samuel M. Shoemaker, D.D.

Rector, Calvary Episcopal Church, Pittsburgh

Condensed from **Christian Herald**

SOME YEARS AGO I found myself talking with a congenital skeptic. He had made a fortune and lost it, made another and lost that. Now, he told me, he couldn't pay his rent, and was taking pills in order to sleep. I think he doubted if there was any way out of his predicament.

"Want to try an experiment?" I asked.

He answered, "I don't even believe in God, you know."

"Well," I said, "there is Something that seems to help people who do. And I believe that Something will help you if you will let It."

"How can I let It if I don't even believe in It?" he asked.

I said, "Suppose we try telling the truth about your situation, and the way you feel about it, to whatever is the ultimate Truth and Reality in this universe—and honestly ask that Power for help and guidance."

"How would you do that?" he asked.

I suggested that we kneel down out of reverence toward the Unknown, and then that he say exactly what he was feeling—not pretending he believed anything he didn't believe but exposing himself to whatever creative force runs through existence.

"Well," he mused, "I certainly am in a jam. I'll try anything once."

He got down on his knees, half laughing at himself, and said, "O God, if there be a God, send me help now, because I need it."

It was a good, honest, selfish prayer. Climbing back into his chair somewhat sheepishly, he said, "I don't feel any different."

I told him I didn't especially care how he felt but that I was interested in what he was going to do. I suggested that he read a chapter in the Bible that night before he went to bed—perhaps the third chapter of St. John; and another when he woke up next day—maybe the 12th chapter of St. Luke. I suggested that he come to church Sunday and see whether he could catch anything from the faith of other people. Also that he keep praying. "Keep saying whatever is honest about yourself and your situation to whatever is the Truth behind all creation. I think you'll feel you are being answered."

He tried it—intermittently at first, fighting almost every step of the way. But he kept on with the experiment. His own need prodded him. The faith of other people gave him a helpful atmosphere. And at last he had to admit that *something* was helping him, for he began sleeping without barbiturates, and his business slowly began to come back.

The skeptic was baptized and confirmed, and later became a vestryman of my church.

How did this man "get religion"? *By acting as if he had faith*—until, indeed, there was an opening for God to come through. Faith is primarily a kind of expectant loyalty toward God, life and the universe, and only secondarily an intellectual conviction. It is much more like falling in love than like adopting a philosophy.

In its earlier stages, the finding of faith may be much like a scientific experiment. You take a hypothesis, you test it, you confirm or disprove it. Science and religion can be quite close together in the all-important matter of method of approach. As Lowell phrased it, "Science was faith once."

Some will say, "But isn't it hypocrisy to 'act as if' when you really don't believe at all?" My answer is that it is not hypocrisy for a scientist to regard a hypothesis as true long enough to prove that it is or is not. A real experiment, entered into with an honest and open mind, is an avenue to truth.

One day a young doctor with a warm heart, who was experiencing the tragedy of pain and illness in children for the first time, met a minister whom he knew and said, "I guess I need to talk to you. Instead of believing more in God, sometimes I feel like shaking my fist in His face and saying, 'D—— you for letting little children suffer like this!' "

Instead of being shocked, the minister said, "Probably that is the first real prayer you ever said."

The young doctor was surprised that the clergyman would liken what sounded like pure blasphemy to prayer. He was told that if he would pursue this further, and really tell God all that he was thinking and feeling—say *to* God whatever he had felt like saying *about* Him—it might be the first step in an experiment of faith.

It was also suggested to the doctor that prayer is a two-way proposition. After talking to God, why not listen to Him a little while? He did. No great illumination came—only a strong conviction that his job was to alleviate as much pain and suffering as he could, and that somehow God was interested in that. This experimental approach afforded him an avenue to faith.

Last year some ideas of experimental faith were tried out by a group of young married people in Pittsburgh. They began by acknowledging the fact that Christianity had a primary place in the emergence of our western ways of freedom and democracy. They went on to ask, "How do you find this faith?" I pointed out that what we call faith is as evident and real a power in this universe as the power of electricity or the atom, but that samples of faith do far more good than sales talks about it. So these couples began praying to find God's will, not trying to get Him to change it in favor of their own. They put unselfish prayer and love and faith to work in daily business situations.

One of these young men told me: "For years I tried to find God by reason and logic. I could find reasons for believing in God, but I could also find reasons for not believing. Then someone told me to act as if God *were*, and see what would happen. I did—and prayer has become a real, life-giving force to me. I live under less pressure, sleep better, make sounder decisions in business, give more time to my family, and am generally a much happier, and I hope, more useful, member of society."

He has joined the church, is teaching a class of boys on Sunday, and has found a new source of inner power. None of this has come by swallowing something he could not digest intellectually, but by exploring in a field where he did not know exploration was possible.

The leap of faith is not the admission of credulity but of a kind of courage. We really believe only when we have found sufficient evidence. The first steps of faith consist of looking for the evidence. And the greatest evidence of all is a firsthand experience of God. That is why we must seek to come into His presence.

So long as we merely talk *about* God, we can indulge a great deal of doubt. But when we walk right into His presence, and talk *to* Him, doubt comes to seem curiously out of place, irrational, silly. I'll wager that what you will get back from Him will not be a blinding light or a gush of sentimental feeling but rather a sense of added strength, some insight about a problem or a person, a realization that you are in touch with more Power than ever before in your life.

In faith, as in every other experiment, there is a point where the experiment turns into an experience. You want to learn to swim. You get in and splash around. Somebody tells you what to do with your arms and legs. After a while you find that the water, plus your own efforts, is holding you up and moving you forward. It is the same with faith. Mrs. Thomas A. Edison told me that her husband worked for five years to create the electric-light bulb. He had faith that such a thing could be made, and had ideas about how it might be done. He tried one after another until he struck the right one. The world takes the incandescent bulb for granted, but it was one man's faith plus years of trial and error that led to the discovery. Should we begrudge the hours or months or years it may take us to find God?

We need not expect that all hidden meanings will become immediately clear if we make the experimental approach to religion. But we can, as Thomas Huxley enjoins us, exhibit the true scientific spirit by sitting down before the facts as a little child, prepared to give up our preconceived notions.

We need merely to start on our way, and remember the truth of the ancient Chinese proverb: the longest journey begins with a single step.

Even for a moderate drinker, alcohol can be a costly bargain

WHY I GAVE UP LIQUOR

By Channing Brewster

I AM no alcoholic. I was what is called a moderate drinker—that is, a blend of the social drinker and the serious drinker, with a dash of bitters. And I finally gave it up. The results have been all to the good. I am not a saver of other people's souls, but if anyone else can benefit enough from my experience to try it for himself—well, it's a free country.

In my business, drinking during office hours is frowned on—unless you can think up a good excuse, such as Christmas or somebody's birthday. Like most moderate drinkers, I began my potations after five o'clock. But unlike the majority I have never found drinking at a crowded bar or in a cocktail lounge tolerable. And if I tarried in such places, people might say there must be trouble between Charlotte and me. So, after work I would grab the first bus home.

I would find Charlotte in the kitchen. Jeremy, our seven-year-old, would beg me to play with him. Somehow, the kitchen clatter and my son's begging might rub me the wrong way. What I needed was a cocktail. So I would shake up a few.

"Pour me one, and I'll be out in a minute," Charlotte would say— and always she would end up sipping her dispirited affair all through dinner.

Meanwhile I would settle down with the newspaper and the shaker. By the time dinner was on the table I would have emptied the shaker. Charlotte would invariably say something scathing about my drinking too much. I would answer in kind. What were a couple of cocktails?

Of course, it was hard to say exactly how many a couple were—having downed my share of the shaker and what was left of Charlotte's share (I always counted her in for half).

But it would be inaccurate to say that I was drunk. I could talk coherently, though with more than normal animation. I could eat with gusto, though with little sense of taste. After dinner my head would grow heavy. Whatever I attempted to do—read, play with Jeremy, go to the movies with Charlotte—was ruined by a dull desire for rest.

If we went to a party, it was the same only more so. I would swallow enough pre-party drinks to get in the mood to face it. At the party, after I had had a couple more, strangers would look familiar, and some neighbor's wife would assume an exotic strangeness. After that I would be so impressed by the new-found human qualities of the guests and by my own wit that there would be no time for counting drinks. The fog would roll in.

What happened later depended on a number of variables—mainly solid food, fresh air and more drink. The hangover might wait for its morning-after or begin operations in the middle of the night. But its visitation was as certain as death and taxes, and just as funny.

If a Sunday followed the party, the hangover would be hugged to my bosom in the privacy of my bedroom. If a workday followed, the shaking hand, the blinding headache, the effort of concentration and the fear of making errors made the hangover twice as nerve-racking.

Such were my drinking habits. I should add that there were many days when I had only one or two drinks.

Then one day I quit drinking. And since that day I have done without alcohol. I have known no craving for liquor, no envy of those who quaff highballs while I guzzle orange juice. Twice I have deliberately broken my abstinence. These tests strengthened my resolve. It was like trying to reopen a canceled love affair.

My abstinence was self-imposed. No public disgrace drove me to repentance. I took no pledge. I simply considered the problem in its totality and made my decision. The decision, like most of the important ones we make in life, was merely the culmination of a sort of ripening process. It was the same procedure I have followed in all my adult dealings—entering a new field of business, getting married, buying a home.

Considering the over-all picture, I had to admit that drinking, as a contribution to the enjoyment of life, was for me a bust. It cost a lot of money, even though I was no big operator. But I was spending at least a dollar a day for drink, even though I had an aversion to bars and night clubs were nonexistent in our town. Thirty dollars a month is a very substantial fraction of a middle-bracket income. That much saved for ten years—and just as Jeremy was ready for college I would be ready with cash instead of alibis.

On a level of greater significance, I said thumbs down to liquor because I was kidding myself about it. I lacked the classic excuse of the alcoholic—I was not escaping from anything. My life contains no deep maladjustments. I love my wife, my wife loves me. I like people, people like me. My job keeps me on my toes. My excuse was the usual defense of the moderate drinker: that I was tired and tense. Of course, by the end of a busy day I suffered a bit from office fatigue. But I have found during the past year that I am not so tired that a brisk walk or an hour's workout on the school grounds with Jeremy's four-man baseball team won't un-tire me. Alcohol gave me a lift and then let go, and I was tired-er and duller than before.

No doubt alcohol removed my tension. But it acted like a spot remover that takes the cloth with it. I came to see that I should do something more intelligent about the tension than to pour jiggers of rum over it.

It was a myth I was embracing when I thought alcohol was going to turn a party of my townsfolk into a gathering as witty as a Noel Coward first act. My neighbor's wife, tight or sober, is neither wit nor wanton. Nor are the rest of the people of our town. Nor am I. Whatever capacity to amuse my conversation may possess is drawn forth not by alcohol but by the stimulation of imaginative minds.

If I fortify myself by reading a book that has some meat in it, and then seek out a friend who is not allergic to ideas, a brilliant conversation may not necessarily ensue, but at least I return home with a clear head and the feeling that I have not wasted time in utter stupidity.

For the true enjoyment of life, I find, a muddled head is no asset. I want to grasp the quality of an experience or the meaning of an idea in its natural state, not refracted through the obfuscating haze of a pint of gin and vermouth.

Why did I give up drink? Above all because I resented its power over me. Yes, I was a moderate drinker. I did not crave drink. Yet liquor was my master. One or two drinks could make me see the world as the world is not. Several could convince me that I could dance the *rumba* and drive a car exceedingly fast with the greatest of care.

I guess it was really pride that put me on the wagon. I have the reputation of being "independent." I resist vigorously even fancied attempts to boss me around. Yet liquor was acting as my boss. I didn't like the idea of not being my own master.

So I went dry. And as the saying goes, I am suffering no pain. I have felt constantly a wonderful sense of freedom—the way I used to feel when school let out and I took off my shoes and went barefoot. The pay-off came when a big organization took over my company and for three months I was out of a job. Those were tough days, but I blessed my new-found freedom and full reliance on my own self without the danger of treachery from a glass crutch that might skid out from under me. I weathered the crisis and am now doing better than before.

I have no desire to persuade anyone else to discontinue the use of alcohol. But I do believe that anyone who wants freedom from a great deal of expense, headaches and lost time, freedom from one more thing that complicates life, may have it simply by doing what I did.

Numbers Game

» ALTHOUGH a couple we know have been married for years, they never seem to sink into that glum silence at restaurants and public places that so many long-married couples fall into. Finally someone asked the wife how they found so much to say to each other.

"The truth is," she replied, "that we decided a long time ago that we'd look and act animated when we're out. So, if I feel one of those silences coming, I say to my husband, with an interested expression: '1, 2, 3, 4, 5,' and he answers, '6, 7, 8, 9, 10.' That at least starts us laughing, and soon we find something real to talk about."

—"The Woman Who Sees" in New York *Sun*

Our children have too much to see and hear,
not enough to do

Teach Them to Open Doors

By T. E. Murphy

I**F NATURE** continues faithful to her trust we shall have, in the future, saucer eyes, ears like loving cups and double-spread bottoms—the better to see, hear and sit. Our arms and legs will shrink to sausagelike appendages; the head will atrophy to a tiny thread connecting the used senses of eyes and ears. For we are fast becoming a nation of watchers and listeners; we have too much to see and hear, not enough to do.

A process that began four decades ago is now reaching its logical conclusion with the advent of television. We watch other men fight, make love, play baseball or football, even attend religious services. (Catholics have had to be warned that hearing Mass by television does not fulfill the requirements of Catholic doctrine.) We listen avidly to a dreary procession of stale jokes and songs about dream houses and faraway places. Because of these diversions we are giving up a good part of our heritage. We are robbing our children, too. The classics of childhood—*Huck Finn, Tom Sawyer, Alice, Treasure Island, The Wind in the Willows*—are unopened books, unexplored lands. We have supplanted them with the Lone Ranger and Gorgeous George.

Living is more than watching and listening. It is *doing*. I believe in the heresy that it's more fun to kiss a pretty girl myself than to watch some shadowy figment go through the motion on a screen. I would rather bat a ball to a bunch of kids than watch Joe DiMaggio hit a homer. Evenings, I would rather paint a picture or bake a cherry pie than to sit on my calluses listening to timeworn allusions to Jack Benny's miserliness or Bob Hope's nose.

Oh, I don't dislike spectator sports. Some of my best friends are spectators. In the course of a year I'm likely to see a couple of fights, some baseball and college football. I like them all in small doses. I refuse to let them dominate my life.

A few years ago I walked into the office of a distinguished elderly lawyer and found him reading a book of verse by an obscure 19th-century poet. Behind him were volumes on astronomy, botany and geology. When I expressed surprise at the range of his reading, he said: "Life is a corridor with many doors. I am hurrying to open as many as I can before the ultimate one is opened."

I thought of that next day when I tried in vain to hire a carpenter to screen a porch. At the library I got a book telling how to do it, and for the first time in my life I built something with my own hands. It wasn't an expert job. But I learned the thrill of doing something I'd always thought beyond me. It was a small door I opened then, but it was the first of many.

An important thing to remember is that, no matter what strange new door we plan to open, there are experts to guide us—*for free*. Want to paint a picture? There are hundreds of books to tell you how—books in which the great masters have spread out their own hard-earned knowledge. Want to build a swimming pool or a kitchen table? Want to be a sculptor in your spare time? Want to learn French or Italian? You can learn if you have enough curiosity to open a door.

One of my favorite doors opens into the world of gardening. A lot of jokes have been told about the "book" farmer. I'm a book farmer and don't care who knows it.

A neighbor of mine who had planted the same strain of corn for 50 years was inclined to look down his nose at book farmers. One day I gave him a handful of hybrid seed.

A few weeks later I stopped by. "It's the only corn that's any danged good," said my friend. Then, in reluctant capitulation, "I'd like to learn some more about them seeds."

Some people are timid about trying new things. I know one chap who'd been taking photographs for 20 years. One day, after a big local event, I asked him how his pictures came out. He looked surprised. "I won't have them back for a couple of days."

"Do you mean you don't develop and print your own pictures?"

He shook his head. "I'm afraid that's a little too technical for me."

I led him to the nearest drugstore. "Look at the label on this developer can," I said. "You can read, can't you? The manufacturer has been writing all these things for you."

He took the plunge and is now an excellent all-round photographer.

A woman I know was discouraged by the high prices of clothing during the war years. A complete novice at sewing, she found all the information she needed in manuals and pattern guides. Today, though dresses are cheaper, she continues to make her own. "Now I'm *doing* something while I listen to the radio," she explains.

I believe that doing things for yourself is the vital component for a sound personality and an exciting life. In the past two years I have done 50 or more oil paintings, most of them bad. I have written a little poetry and read a great deal more. I have baked everything from a loaf of bread to a mince pie. I have studied Spanish and geology. And because I have four children I have also fished, skated, played baseball, made snowmen, played badminton. Meanwhile I have held down a full-time newspaper job.

I believe fervently in the idea that the hallmark distinguishing man from beast is his creative instinct. It is one of the anomalies of our civilization that the most intensive efforts to satisfy man's creative needs are made in mental hospitals.

Creative expression is not confined to "making" something. I know one middle-aged woman with a grown family who refurnished her cellar as a club for teen-agers. In a few years thousands of young boys and girls had come under her warm and pleasurable influence. Another middle-aged childless couple acted as foster parents to state wards. They kept none of the board money but put it aside for the education of these homeless waifs. They've raised dozens of children and had fun doing it.

An industrialist friend of mine started out as a song writer and then went into a factory. He has made a lot of machinery and some money. But only when he organized a neighborhood singing club did he fulfill his ambitions. "Sometimes," he says proudly, "they even sing some of the songs I wrote."

These are doors to new worlds. They are tiny declarations of independence against being made into the faceless mass man who sits, listens and watches.

A philosopher once observed that man lives in a prison cell lined with mirrors. Today that prison cell is lined with loudspeakers and screens. All very fine, to a degree. But for a really full life we've got to burst out of the cell—and our children with us. For them the danger of growing into a race of super-robots is greater because the conditioning has begun earlier.

Teach them, by example, to open doors. Show them the value of a wide range of interests in contrast with the narrowly grooved life, the difference between apathetic acceptance of things as they are and inquiry. The result? It is the difference between man the intelligent, creative creature and man the village videot.

Dwight D. Eisenhower, awarding the Medal of Merit to a group of war correspondents at ceremonies in the National Press Club, said he regretted he was not enough of an orator to do justice to the medal's recipients.

"It reminds me of my boyhood days on a Kansas farm," Ike related. "An old farmer had a cow that we wanted to buy. We went over to visit him and asked about the cow's pedigree. The old farmer didn't know what pedigree meant, so we asked him about the cow's butterfat production. He told us that he hadn't any idea what it was. Finally we asked him how many pounds of milk the cow produced each year.

"The farmer shook his head and said: 'I don't know. But she's an honest old cow and she'll give you all the milk she has!'

"Well," Eisenhower concluded, "I'm like the cow; I'll give you everything I have."

—Gerry Robichaud in Pasadena *Independent*

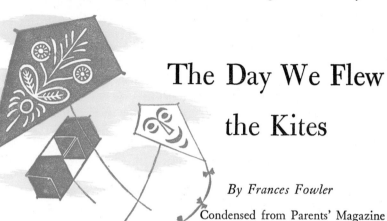

The Day We Flew

the Kites

By Frances Fowler

Condensed from Parents' Magazine

"STRING!" shouted Brother, bursting into the kitchen. "We need lots more string."

It was Saturday. As always, it was a busy one, for "Six days shalt thou labor and do all thy work" was taken seriously then. Outside, Father and Mr. Patrick next door were doing chores.

Inside the two houses, Mother and Mrs. Patrick were engaged in spring cleaning. Such a windy March day was ideal for "turning out" clothes closets. Already woolens flapped on back-yard clotheslines.

Somehow the boys had slipped away to the back lot with their kites. Now, even at the risk of having Brother impounded to beat carpets, they had sent him for more string. Apparently there was no limit to the heights to which kites would soar today.

My mother looked out the window. The sky was piercingly blue; the breeze fresh and exciting. Up in all that blueness sailed great puffy billows of clouds. It had been a long, hard winter, but today was Spring.

Mother looked at the sitting room, its furniture disordered for a Spartan sweeping. Again her eyes wavered toward the window. "Come on, girls! Let's take string to the boys and watch them fly the kites a minute." On the way we met Mrs. Patrick, laughing guiltily, escorted by her girls.

There never was such a day for flying kites! God doesn't make two such days in a century. We played all our fresh twine into the boys' kites and still they soared. We could hardly distinguish the tiny, orange-colored specks. Now and then we slowly reeled one in, finally bringing it dipping and tugging to earth, for the sheer joy of sending it up again. What a thrill to run with them, to the right, to the left, and see our poor, earth-bound movements reflected minutes later in the majestic sky-dance of the kites! We wrote wishes on slips of paper and slipped them over the string. Slowly, irresistibly, they climbed up until they reached the kites. Surely all such wishes would be granted!

Even our fathers dropped hoe and hammer and joined us. Our mothers took their turn, laughing like schoolgirls. Their hair blew out of their pompadours and curled loose about their cheeks; their gingham aprons whipped about their legs. Mingled with our fun was something akin to awe. The grownups were really playing with us! Once I looked at Mother and thought she looked actually pretty. And her over forty!

We never knew where the hours went on that hilltop day. There were no hours, just a golden, breezy Now. I think we were all a little beyond ourselves. Parents forgot their duty and their dignity; children forgot their combativeness and small spites. "Perhaps it's like this in the Kingdom of Heaven," I thought confusedly.

It was growing dark before, drunk with sun and air, we all stumbled sleepily back to the houses. I suppose we had some sort of supper. I suppose there must have been a surface tidying-up, for the house on Sunday looked decorous enough.

The strange thing was, we didn't mention that day afterward. I felt a little embarrassed. Surely none of the others had thrilled to it as deeply as I. I locked the memory up in that deepest part of me where we keep "the things that cannot be and yet are."

The years went on, then one day I was scurrying about my own kitchen in a city apartment, trying to get some work out of the way while my three-year-old insistently cried her desire to "go park and see ducks."

"I *can't* go!" I said. "I have this and this to do, and when I'm through I'll be too tired to walk that far."

My mother, who was visiting us, looked up from the peas she was shelling. "It's a wonderful day," she offered; "really warm, yet there's a fine, fresh breeze. It reminds me of that day we flew the kites."

I stopped in my dash between stove and sink. The locked door flew open, and with it a gush of memories. I pulled off my apron. "Come on," I told my little girl. "You're right, it's too good a day to miss."

Another decade passed. We were in the aftermath of a great war. All evening we had been asking our returned soldier, the youngest Patrick boy, about his experiences as a prisoner of war. He had talked freely, but now for a long time he had been silent. What was he thinking of—what dark and dreadful things?

"Say!" A smile twitched his lips. "Do you remember . . . no, of course you wouldn't. It probably didn't make the impression on you it did on me."

I hardly dared speak. "Remember what?"

"I used to think of that day a lot in PW camp, when things weren't too good. Do you remember the day we flew the kites?"

Winter came, and the sad duty of a call of condolence on Mrs. Patrick, recently widowed. I dreaded the call. I couldn't imagine how Mrs. Patrick would face life alone.

We talked a little of my family and her grandchildren and the changes in the town. Then she was silent, looking down at her lap. I cleared my throat. Now I must say something about her loss, and she would begin to cry.

When she looked up, Mrs. Patrick was smiling. "I was just sitting here thinking," she said. "Henry had such fun that day. Frances, do you remember the day we flew the kites?"

Because of the housing shortage near the military base where he was stationed, a young doctor and his wife and three children had to live in cramped quarters in a hotel. A friend said to the doctor's six-year-old daughter, "Isn't it too bad that you don't have a home?"

"Oh, we have a home," the youngster replied quickly. "We just don't have a house to put it in." —Contributed by M. Elizabeth Lynch

ADD YEARS TO

YOUR LIFE

By Francis and Katharine Drake

Condensed from The American Mercury

JUST HOW YOUNG you will be at 70 depends largely on how well your health has been preserved between 40 and 60. Almost all of us begin slowing down, physically, after 40—despite the fact that our bodies are capable of reaching 100 without wearing out in any vital part. Now, thanks to geriatrics—that branch of medicine concerned with the body's aging process—we have an excellent chance of advancing vigorously into the 70's and 80's.

This depends on two things: the guidance of an experienced geriatrician and initiative on the part of the "patient" in having regular health checkups and following instructions.

The importance of this simple program is shown by the physical condition of most Americans passing the 60-year milestone. Twenty-eight percent are far overweight, and 99 percent of such overweight is due to injudicious eating. At any age, overweight people die at the rate of nearly two for one by comparison with persons of normal weight. Most people of 60 have from one to eight diseases or deficiencies; three out of four lack minimum healthful amounts of calcium, protein, iron or vitamins; 25 percent of those over 65 are anemic.

By contrast, the record of those who have had regular health check-ups is outstanding. In a pioneer geriatric clinic in Rhode Island, less than one percent of the patients have required hospitalization in the past ten years. In a Connecticut insurance center, over a five-year test period, there were 44 percent fewer deaths among medically supervised employes than among those who refused the service. When surgery is unavoidable, geriatric patients have been found to be incomparably better risks.

After 40 our illnesses generally come from many causes, and seldom give definite warning of arrival. Before they reach the "symptom" stage—pain, fever, nausea, etc.—disorders of middle-life may already have sabotaged a perfectly sound organ far removed from the original trouble site. For example, that heart attack which hospitalized Mrs. Jones for months was not due to a faulty heart; it was caused by a steadily increasing traffic-jam of fat in her arteries, which forced the heart to increase its pumping load so far above the legal limit that it revolted. In common with countless "heart" sufferers, Mrs. Jones had long been taking too many sweets and fats with her daily fare.

The aging of human organs is a highly individual thing. As Dr. C. Ward Crampton, Chairman of the Sub-Committee on Geriatrics of the Medical Society of New York County, says, "a 60-year-old man may have a 40-year-old heart, 50-year-old kidneys and an 80-year-old liver and be trying to live a 30-year-old life."

The geriatrician's first job is to establish the top health potential of each patient. This he determines by a complete physical examination and by informing himself of his patient's background, family, work, worries, responsibilities and the like. If the over-all picture is good, the patient can go his way rejoicing for another year. But if anything is functioning poorly, the geriatrician brings into play every art of medical science to lift the patient's over-all condition as near maximum efficiency as possible—and keep it there.

Although it is prudent to conserve health by checking up at 40 rather than at 60, much can be done at any age, even in cases of chronic illness. For instance, if the heart is organically weak, the geriatrician also checks the other organs and the nutritional resources of the patient. Vitality may be stepped up with iodine or iron, resistance fortified with proteins, skin and tissues refreshed with selected vitamins, arteries relieved by diet, blood enriched with liver extract. Improving the whole system automatically reduces the strain on the heart.

The big saboteurs of health after 40 are our pet theories of what, and how much, we should eat. In this country we are surrounded by excellent food in endless variety, yet clinical records show that about 75 percent of the senior half of the population suffers from malnutrition. Doctors find as many dietary deficiencies among the well-to-do as among the lower-income groups. One geriatrician cites the case of a 60-year-old millionaire, half starved by his belief that proteins, especially meat, were "bad for anyone over 40."

What, then, should men and women over 40 eat, and how much? Nutritional needs vary, but some basic food rules hold good for everybody. Calcium, iron and protein head the list of needs—without an abundance of each, the body withers. Calcium poverty keeps bones from knitting properly after a break; iron poverty—the most frequent health impairment found in adults—brings anemia and that exhausted feeling; protein poverty may make us a setup for ulcers of the stomach.

Calcium, which nourishes the blood, bones and tissues, is in leafy green vegetables, cheese, milk. Iron, which helps to make blood, is in lean meat, liver, green vegetables, eggs, oysters, dried peas and beans, apricots, raisins. Rich in proteins, which furnish energy, restore tissues and repel disease, are lean meat, eggs, lima beans, peanuts, poultry, fish, milk and cheese.

Raw fruit and vegetables are right for everyone, with qualifications: (a) if you chop them to pieces, you reduce their vitamin values, (b) if they contain seeds or fibers, they can irritate delicate intestines. Liquids are indispensable to proper body balance—between one and two quarts a day after 40, in such forms as water, milk, tea, coffee, soup.

Here is a doctor's table of basic daily food that will take care of a person's minimum needs after 40:

Milk: 1 pint (may be in soups, cooking, etc.).

Orange, grapefruit or tomato juice: 1 liberal serving.

Green vegetable: 1 serving.

Other vegetable: 1 serving.

Eggs: one or more.

Meat or fish: 1 serving.

Butter or margarine: two or three pats.

This list must be supplemented in accordance with each person's daily requirements, and it is here, in calorie mathematics, that the unsupervised majority make the dangerous mistakes. A man of 60 needs 35 percent fewer calories than a man of 30, even if both are performing identical work. After 40, the gradually slowing down human power-plant cannot keep up its former pace of converting calories into energy. Result: unconverted calories begin to get dumped—around the waistline or, worse still, around arteries and organs. Many people who eat light meals fall into the insidious "snack" habit. One geriatrician traced the mounting avoirdupois of a matron with a "birdlike appetite" to the salted nuts she had nibbled evening after evening for years.

Not to begin cutting down on fats, sugars and starches after 40 is to invite disaster. These are the snipers that end so many lives prematurely by a stroke, a blinding stab of angina, hardening of the arteries and coronary artery disease. Life-insurance figures show that fat people with high blood pressure are 12 times as susceptible to heart disease as people of normal weight. Doctors deny the popular belief it is "natural" to gain weight during the middle years—the potbelly and the middle-aged spread in virtually every case come from improper diet.

Other important controls on the geriatric health program may include a switch from too strenuous exercise to safer routines, instructions for rest or massage or different shoes. Medical records show that after geriatric care the vast majority of people become more vigorous than they were before, their aging processes definitely retarded.

Typical is the history of the Smiths, a couple who might pass for 50 but are actually 62 and 60. Some years ago Smith sought medical help because colds, digestive and kidney distresses and heaviness in the chest were causing him to lose more and more workdays. "Nothing the matter except age, I guess," he told the geriatrician. But examination showed high blood pressure, a faint whisper over the heart, neglected infections in both sinuses, one kidney damaged by a long-congested prostate and insufficient acid in his stomach juices for proper digestion.

Mrs. Smith, height five feet four, weight 152 pounds, breathing heavily after the short walk to the doctor's office, was pretty well, she thought. It was just that she hadn't any pep, caught colds easily, found things getting on her nerves. The geriatric analysis showed that almost all of her troubles stemmed from faulty diet—not enough liquids, too many starches and a dangerous shortage of thiamine, the age-fighting vitamin which the nervous system needs increasingly after 40.

Nowadays the couple's friends exclaim, "What *have* you been doing to yourselves?" Smith has not lost a day's work in a year, his infections, knocked out by penicillin, have not returned, he digests whatever he eats, his blood pressure is down to 143. Mrs. Smith is buying the size 14's she wore at 30; her metabolism rate, thanks to iodine, is back to normal; and she feels as gay as she looks. Both are grateful to medical science for a totally unlooked-for revival of vigor and interests. In reply to their friends' questions, the Smiths say: "Eat less, drink more, get a calorie chart, a good pair of scales—and leave the rest up to the doctor. That's the way to forget about birthdays."

A Little Happiness

In *Under Whatever Sky,* Irwin Edman wrote:

I recently saw in France—over a little shop selling miscellaneous gifts and souvenirs—the sign "Au Petit Bonheur."

How suggestive a phrase, I found myself thinking. The little happiness, the minor felicity, the modest joy. . . . Moralists are always talking of the grand and comprehensive happiness. And to the romantic imagination, joy is conceived of as a great joy, an altitude, an ecstasy, a forever. But the French specialize in the *petit bonheur:* the small omelette, the little wine, the intimate foyer of enjoyment.

Is it sour grapes to settle for the little happiness, to aim to make happiness out of the most modest ingredients: little things lovingly collected, simple meals in modest surroundings with unpretentious friends, discoursing, perhaps, on not too grand ideas? Do we tell ourselves the unspectacular moments satisfy only because all moments are threatened, because even gentle goods—like honey for tea in England—cannot be taken for granted any longer? How many millions in the world would now compound for the *petit bonheur!*

Maybe the "closed" economic field
offers a really soft touch

NO FRONTIERS?

Condensed from Life

JACK KAPP, president of Decca Records before his death in 1948, was interested in talking to college students. On every campus, said Mr. Kapp, he was asked, "What chance have I got in this system?" The students added such wistful remarks as, "Everything is in the hands of a few people."

Well, college students have always been skeptical before diving into the somewhat disconcerting whirlpool of that first job hunt. But today the disbelief is part of a world-weariness that afflicts even those who have good jobs and secure niches in adult society. Undergraduates can hardly be blamed for reflecting a philosophical attitude that is cultivated not merely by the young but by practically everybody, even some of the professors.

There was a peculiar irony, however, when disbelieving questions were addressed to Jack Kapp, of all people! For Mr. Kapp was proof that no man in America is destined by circumstances to spend his life behind a large and immovable eight ball. Mr. Kapp was born in Chicago in 1901, the son of a house-to-house canvasser for the old Columbia Phonograph Co. He worked his way through high school as an errand boy. In 1926 he was in charge of the Brunswick Co.'s "race record division"—meaning that his business was to go around the country making recordings by Negro talent.

In 1934 Mr. Kapp decided the time had come to strike out on his own. "What chance did he have?" The record business was near the all-time low. Radio had forced the bankruptcy of hundreds of record companies; only two remained. "Everything was in the hands of a few people."

Mr. Kapp proceeded to prove that a "closed" field is the softest of touches. As he himself put it, any company which casts itself in the role of "custodian of the *status quo*" is destined to die. With the record business on the rocks because of *status quo* custodians, Mr. Kapp hived up in the public library for a week to study old record catalogues. He discovered that the business was oriented toward Europe; there were 1200 recordings of Chopin to few of Irving Berlin. You could get plenty of foreign voices, but U. S. singers such as Bing Crosby were considered *infra dig.*

All of this gave Mr. Kapp an idea. Bucking the rest of the industry, which considered it foolish to put entire musical-comedy scores into album form, Mr. Kapp made thousands of dollars by selling Gershwin scores complete. He made Bing Crosby a rich man.

Mr. Kapp liked to repeat the words from Emerson's *The American Scholar:* "We will walk on our own feet; we will work with our own hands; we will speak our own minds." Emerson isn't much favored these days, and the modern American scholar might insist that Mr. Kapp had a monopoly in four-leaf clovers.

But the college student who has spent winter week-ends riding up a few of America's 1000 ski tows might reflect on the fact that in 1932 there wasn't a single ski tow in the whole United States. Maybe it is impossible to start a new automobile company today, but General Motors is going to need a new president in a few years, and it is certainly going to need new production men. According to a recent survey this country needs to train 15,000 new doctors; indeed, if present trends continue, we may be faced with a doctor shortage of 30,000 to 50,000 by 1960.

"What chance have I got?" In the light of the world's hunger for services and moving ideas, the chances would seem to be as manifold as the inside of the human skull can make them.

SUCCESS in dealing with other people is like making rhubarb pie — use all the sugar you can, and then double it.   — *Banking*

Spare the discipline and spoil the child

Don't Be Afraid of "Don't"

By Donald A. Bloch, M.D.
U. S. Dept. of Health, Education and Welfare

Condensed from National Parent-Teacher

PARENTS today have rightly turned their backs on the old, stern, arbitrary type of discipline which enforced continual unquestioning obedience on their children. But many have wheeled around too far; statements like "It's time to go to bed" or "That's enough dessert" have become take-offs for a small fry's arguments about why it isn't time or why it isn't enough.

This overtolerant attitude is an effort to save the little ones from "frustration"—a fate considered worse than death. As a child psychiatrist I am strongly opposed to frustrating children. But children are not nearly as thwarted by controls suited to their age and to the occasion as they are by lack of the right kind of direction and discipline.

I don't advocate putting Ming vases and a hammer in a baby's playpen, but I do maintain that a toddler can be taught that he must not go near fragile objects in the living room. Instead of keeping the room stripped like a barracks, parents need simply to say, "Don't touch!" A child who never encounters opposition for sound reasons is being shielded from situations he may have a hard time facing later on.

Children are not born with a sense of right and wrong. It is something gradually absorbed as one grows up until, as a full-fledged adult conscience, it becomes an automatic inner signal that regulates behavior. While children are little they need to be provided with a conscience just as they need to be provided with food and shelter. A child will become a more agreeable, likable person and therefore a happier one if, long before he is able to grasp such abstractions as justice and fair play, his mother simply makes him give Johnny a turn on the swing.

As a matter of fact, most youngsters are happy to obey parents who are fair, gentle and loving—unless self-esteem is endangered, as when a boy is asked to do some chore that keeps him from playing outdoors with his friends, or when a teen-age girl is forbidden lipstick although the rest of her friends use it.

Every parent has definite ideas of how his children should behave, and youngsters are bound to be aware of them. For example, Mother may tell Junior, when he wants to explore her desk, to go ahead, but her tone of voice betrays the fact that she doesn't really want him to. So Junior, hearing permission yet sensing objection, doesn't know what to do. Despite the fleeting disappointment, he would be much better off knowing exactly where he stands with her by hearing her say clearly: "Desks are for grownups and I don't want you to get into mine."

Lack of direction, even in little things, may lead to a confused state of mind. Going to bed, if not consistently regulated, can become a dilemma to a child. He is weary, but he does not want to miss any fun. A firm "Time for bed!" solves the problem he can't solve for himself.

A small child has to depend upon the decisiveness of an adult to keep himself in hand. Practically every normal child, at one time or another, will scream, "I'll kill you," hitting out at his mother or father. If you give the youngster a whack or react to his outburst by shouting, "Don't you dare talk to me like that!" you show him that you, too, are unable to control your emotions. If you ignore the outburst or cajole or bribe him into calming down, he fails to learn the limits of acceptable behavior and also gets an exaggerated sense of his power.

If you calmly say something like: "I'm sorry you feel that way; now tell me what you're so angry about," you show him that he is not all-powerful, for you have not withered under his fury, and you have set the line beyond which he may not go. Kindly and strong, respecting his right to have feelings but firmly disapproving of the way he acts, you have not frustrated him—you have brought him relief.

Loving direction had been missing in the life of a delinquent boy I once treated, and when he was seven he had announced, suitcase in hand, "I'm going to run away." His mother had merely said, "Go ahead." She didn't really love him, he felt, for she didn't care what he did.

The incident is unhappily typical. When a child threatens to leave home he is really pleading, "Stop me! Please love me enough to stop me!" A casual reaction to a runaway threat takes the wind out of a child's sails, but the dangerous forlorn feeling persists in his mind.

The ironic thing about overpermissiveness in rearing children is the fact that we don't set up a similar complete freedom of action as an ideal for ourselves; we don't advocate anarchy as our way of life. We defend speed limits and other restrictions of law, and would feel insecure without them.

For children, the feeling that they are being wisely guided tells them that they are precious objects, loved and cared for. The other day I overheard Mary and Jeanne, two little girls in my neighborhood. Mary asked, "Does *your* mother let you play in the street?" "She never says anything," Jeanne answered. "*Mine* won't let me," Mary said, with obvious pride. "She's afraid I might get run over."

Even adolescents, although they would be the last to admit it, crave a measure of adult control. It's a striking fact that teen-agers, in their clubs and societies, usually make more elaborate regulations for themselves than adults would make for them.

Another way adult authority bolsters children is that often it bails them out of situations from which they can't escape by themselves without losing face. If a grownup makes two youngsters quit fighting, neither has the disgrace of losing. When I was a boy in New Jersey I used to climb the Palisades, the steep cliffs on the shore of the Hudson River, and more than once I got myself into a spot where I couldn't go higher without fright or descend without ignominy. I made a great show of objecting when my father finally forbade Palisade climbing, but his interdiction was secretly welcome.

Overpermissive parents, in their zealous desire to make their children's lives more pleasant, actually make them harder. If a child gets explicit instructions about what to do when his parents have company, he is poised in the assurance that he's doing what is expected. He may even come to enjoy greeting the grownups and passing refreshments. A child given no idea how to behave in such situations is confused and a pest to the family and guests. Reasonable rules, which include wholehearted go-aheads as well as definite hold-backs, are more like guidelines than strait jackets.

As a child grows older, parental authority should gradually be relinquished. The scope of what a youngster may or may not do and also the manner of directing him need to be changed. Small children can't understand that too much candy is bad for teeth and digestion, and attempts to reason with them are ridiculous; but for older children you should add an explanation. And at mid-teens level you no longer tell them—you suggest. By that time a youngster is able to reason and general guiding principles that were laid down through years of thoughtful discipline are well established.

Ask yourself, "Is what I am allowing—or prohibiting—helping my child toward self-mastery and the ability to get along with others?" To do away with proper discipline is throwing out the baby with the bath water.

Where There's a Wile

WHILE I was working in the credit department of a department store, a young woman came in one day with some charge slips and asked me to send them to her husband. "We had a tiff," she explained, "and he moved out. When he sees these, I'm sure he'll come back."

"Sending your bills to him doesn't seem exactly the way to make him forgive and forget," I said dubiously.

"Oh, it isn't the bills," she replied, with a smile. "It's what I bought."

I looked at the slips a second time and read:

> 2 Old-Fashioned glasses
> 2 steak knives
> 1 perfume
> 1 bra and panty set
> 1 nylon nightgown

There was a reconciliation, I learned later.

—Contributed by Loretta Allen

A true and moving story of how our much-maligned public schools perform the job they were created for

I Was a Hobo Kid

By Billie Davis

Condensed from The Saturday Evening Post

NOT so long ago I was a small ragged hobo sitting beside a campfire, hungrily licking the fishy oil from the lid of a sardine can. Today I am a citizen, clean and educated, equal to other citizens. Perhaps more than most persons I am a product of the public-school system. That is why I am surprised and disturbed at the lack of appreciation for our schools today. I want to tell the American people something they must have forgotten—or maybe never recognized—about the relationship between public education and personal liberty. I can show them plainly by telling my story.

I was born into that unique clan of American gypsies—gypsies by manner of living rather than by blood. You used to find them camped under the bridge or down at the dump or out by the stockyards of any small southern town. A vagabond people, they sometimes picked cotton or fruit, sometimes shucked corn. But mostly they traveled from town to town peddling novelties, trading horses, sharpening scissors, making keys.

Mine was a "rustic-furniture" family—Dad made willow chairs, tables and novelties from the young willows which grew by the rivers. Mornings I would set out to peddle the small willow baskets, complete with crepe-paper roses. Up one side of the street and down the other I went, praying the next house would have a doorbell, hating screened porches through which no one could hear my knock, anxiously watching for dogs and dreading more than anything else to meet another child.

The children who lived in houses looked so clean and cared for—so smooth, I used to think. My hair was a mass of snarls; my dress was usually dirty and never ironed. I wanted to be like the children who played in the pretty yards. *How can I ever be like people who live in houses?* I asked myself desperately. I would hurry by school buildings —there were so many children around them. They stared and laughed and pointed at my high-laced canvas shoes. (School kids wore nice Oxfords or shiny black shoes with straps.)

School! Was that the secret? Perhaps school made the difference between bums like us and people who lived in houses. The idea became an obsession. Anybody, I thought, can be clean and smooth and live in a nice house if he is smart. And school can make you smart.

Schools, I had learned, were free, and every child was supposed to go. But school meant staying awhile in one place, and that was not good for the rustic business. So for two years after I was old enough to begin school I lived in a state of longing and frustration. I would peek into schoolroom windows, and sometimes after hours I would slip inside, touch a book or a desk wonderingly and stare fascinated at a blackboard.

Then one September we were camped with some carnival people on the grounds of an old fort in Wyoming. There was to be a pioneer celebration, and my folks were to make rustic novelties for prizes. It looked as though we would be there for several weeks.

"I'm going to send my children to the consolidated school," one of the women told my mother. "There's a school bus comes right by here. Why don't you send yours?"

Somehow like a miracle there was a new dress. There was a long red pencil, a fat yellow tablet and a little lunch pail. And then I was standing with a group of children, waiting ecstatically for the school bus.

Soon I had a room and a teacher and, most wonderful of all, a desk. When I sat there I was equal to anyone else. Outside, they could jeer at my clothes and laugh because I lived in a tent and peddled on the streets. But so long as I sat at the desk and learned my lessons well I could be free of sickening inferiority. Some of the clean, smooth children did not do as well as I in school. Next time they called me a dirty gypsy it would not hurt so.

There were many schools as the years went by. There were proud new consolidated schools of yellow brick. There were sand-scratched wooden cubes along Nebraska lanes, and powdery crumbling red brick cubes in little square towns of Kansas.

In each town I would walk to the school, find a teacher and say, "I would like to go to school here, please."

Without exception, I was greeted with kindness. Usually there was a bustling off to an office to answer questions: "No address? No transfer from previous school? No report card? Have you studied long division?"

"No, sir, but I belong in the fourth grade. Just put me in the class and let me try it. If I can't do the work, you can put me back a grade, can't you?" In the end my questioner would smile and show me to a room and a teacher.

There was Miss Williams, kind and motherly, who had found me hiding at recess so the children could not tease me. After that she let me stay in at recess and water her plants.

There was Miss Euland, quick and proficient, who noticed one day that I was squinting. She took me to an eye doctor, bought me the glasses he prescribed. I could pay for them someday, Miss Euland said, by doing for some other child what she had done for me. It was the nicest thing anyone had ever told me, because it meant that Miss Euland knew I would not be a camper all my life.

That was what made me love teachers. They believed in me. Even my parents mocked my "highfalutin' ways," but the teachers could see the spirit flickering within that tattered caricature of childhood.

At last there came that torrid, shimmering afternoon when our old Model A Ford puffed and steamed across a little valley in southern California. Should we pick dates? Green beans? Carrots? Should we go on to Bakersfield and maybe hit some fruit on up the San Joaquin? Or try our luck peddling over the coast way?

Then I saw the school building. It was sprawled yellow stucco, surrounded by date palms and backdropped with a row of dusky hills. I caught my breath sharply.

Dad grinned sardonically. "Billie sees a schoolhouse," he said.

"After all, Dad," I said, "it is October, and this is the year I should be in high school."

Two hours later we were pitching our tent beside a row of tamarack trees, and the next morning I went to register at the school. Several other new pupils were seated at a table filling out forms. Evidently the school was accustomed to registering transients, and the process had been carefully planned — so well, in fact, that the same course of study was offered to all. As I read my schedule my heart sank: cooking, general math, clothing, English, hygiene.

"Do we have no choice of subjects?" I asked the teacher.

Often I have thought how easily she could have brushed me aside. Instead she came and sat by me.

"There are electives," she explained. "But this is a basic course which we are sure you will find profitable and enjoyable while you are here."

"But I can't spend all that time on cooking and sewing," I said. "Already I am older than most pupils in my grade."

She suggested then that we talk with the principal.

"What subjects do you have in mind?" the principal asked.

"History, dramatics, English and Spanish," I said.

"Dramatics is an upper-division elective, and it seems a little late to start a foreign language." The principal looked at the teacher.

"Well, if her English grades have been good and she works hard . . ." They called in the Spanish teacher to ask me a few questions. Then two other teachers came to see me, and the result was that I was enrolled in all four courses.

Five months we camped under the trees and I went to the yellow high school. We (all eight of us) picked dates or beans or carrots; I peddled my baskets from door to door in the surrounding towns. We cooked on the campfire and slept in a row on one long pallet in the tent. At night, after the others had settled on the family bed, I did my homework by an ancient kerosene lantern.

Somehow I did not think of myself as a hobo now. I was the freshman who had the leading part in a play at Valley High!

The next fall I found another high school in another town, and its spirit was the same. Finally in my cherished blue cap and gown as I spoke at the commencement exercises, I found freedom and equality which gave me faith and inspired me.

As I sat on the platform that night of graduation, I thought of all the tents and wagons and campgrounds and worn-out autos. I thought of the canvas shoes. I looked down at the neat blue-and-white pumps I was wearing. Then I looked at the rows of commencement gowns. Young people from wealthy and prominent families were wearing blue gowns like mine. I knew then what was meant by "democracy" and "the American way."

It was not sentimental thinking. It was logical. I, an unkempt hobo from nowhere, had in this high school of considerable size and reputation become editor of the school paper, served on the varsity debate team, been president of the scholarship federation.

I looked at the row of solemn teachers and wondered if they realized their power to shape a life, to change a destiny, to free a world. How unlimited could be the effects of proper education! I glanced at the notes of my speech: "What East High Has Meant to Me." Childish. So inadequate. Someday I would write a real tribute to the teachers and to the public schools of the United States of America.

Many times since that night I have tried to think of a fitting tribute. But proper words have never come. There is so little I can say—except that I am not a hobo now. I am a citizen, equal to other citizens. And I live in a house.

Marriage Matters

WHEN General Mark Clark was asked what was the best advice he ever got, he answered, "To marry the girl I did."

"Who gave you that advice, General?"

"She did." —Tex McCrary and Jinx Falkenburg in New York *Herald Tribune*

AGATHA CHRISTIE, the detective-story writer, lives most of the time in Bagdad, where her archaeologist husband is working on important excavations. "An archaeologist," she says with conviction, "is the best husband any woman can have. The older she gets, the more he is interested in her."

—*Gothenburg Trade and Shipping Journal*, quoted by Alec de Montmorency, NANA

We Keep a Family Log

By John Kord Lagemann

RECENTLY the whole family tried to figure out where Kord, our
ten-year-old son, had lost his wrist watch. Then we remembered
a possible clue — and we located the watch hanging on a fence in
a friend's back yard. What gave us the clue? Kord had duly noted a
neighborhood baseball game in the family log.

Our log is just an ordinary loose-leaf notebook, crammed with a
varied assortment of letters, mementos, pictures and jotted entries. But
actually it's much more than that. It tells us what our family life is
all about. It reminds us of that epoch when the youngsters were too
little to eat without spilling, when they found it hard to comb their
hair. The small exciting gossip of the first day of school comes back,
the problems of early married life, a forgotten face, the joyous details
of family Christmases. Little events become bigger when they're written down.

The log started on that day in the hospital when I saw our first-
born son through the door of the delivery room. On the back of an

envelop I jotted down a note to him: "We're calling you Kord. You're well formed, bigger than most babies, healthy as spring water and unmistakably male. And your mother is more beautiful than ever."

This penciled scrawl turned up later in a folder of letters my wife and I wrote each other during the war. We kept the folder on a handy bookshelf, and from then on our log just grew. By means of it we slow the onrush of time: last year or ten years ago seems as real to us as yesterday—and it's all a part of today. And, going back to written entries, we're often surprised how rich in detail they seem when compared with our unaided memories.

Our log has helped every member of the family take his own measure in relation to the events around him. Kord, criticizing his younger brother, Jay, for "making faces with his voice," discovers in the log that he himself did the same thing a few years back. Now, when Jay does something to annoy him, Kord may tell him: "It's just a phase you're going through."

Also, my wife, Betzy, and I can laugh at earlier mistakes and apply to present problems the lessons that somehow escaped us while we were experiencing them. How often the log has pulled us out of a fit of depression by reminding us of other occasions when our fears proved groundless, when seemingly irreconcilable differences turned out to be trifles!

For most persons the first decade of life is a fog of forgetfulness lit up by occasional flashes of memory. The parents of our childhood do not emerge as distinct, three-dimensional human beings until after our adolescence—when we are busy declaring our independence of them. So, to our log we have added such things as photographs of Betzy and myself in our youngster days, and some reminiscent letters our mothers wrote. "I'm not sure I would have liked you two as children," Kord told me after reading some of these letters the other day. Well, neither my wife nor I was a model child, but we feel that we have lost none of our boys' respect in letting them know this. We think they'll understand *themselves* better because the log gives them a chance to share *our* childhood years.

The log is a wonderful reminder of something grownups often forget—that every age, day and hour of life has its own immediate value. "Wait till you're older," we keep telling children, as if life didn't really begin till 18 or 21 or 40. Actually children are not, as Jay once put it, "living on approval." For their part, swapping experiences and keeping the log with grownups makes them feel understood and appreciated. When two generations meet on common ground in this way, both reap a profit.

It is easy to start a family log and fun to keep it. The simplest way is to gather together in a sturdy binder or loose-leaf notebook the records which have already accumulated and then add to them whenever the spirit moves you. Don't make a chore of it. It's the spontaneous contributions which make it a living family story. The children will want to get in all kinds of trivialities and irrelevancies—let them do it. Many of these entries bring back the flavor of past times as more sensible things never could.

My wife has found that the log is a space-saver. Instead of having letters, photographs and notes scattered about in drawers and closet shelves, they're clamped neatly into binders—in chronological order. This filing of family data serves another practical purpose in any household. Out in the country last summer, for instance, Jay stepped on a rusty nail. When did the children have their last anti-tetanus shots? The log's answer saved the unpleasantness of another injection.

"Here's one for the book" has become a family expression. Each of us, we find, is on the lookout for fresh observations on the world about us. And they're all recorded exactly as they come out—family words and phrases which would doubtless have been lost if we hadn't written them down.

A good deal of the history of our times creeps into the log—history as experienced in the everyday lives of a family. Inflation, taxes, the atom bomb, Communism, the threat of World War III—all these turn up in stories about school drills, clothes drives, civil-defense classes, the business of making ends meet.

One of the best things our log has done for our children is to give them a feeling of confidence. By putting them in touch with the past, it gives them faith in the future. Their sense of security in belonging to a going concern has been strengthened by the stories we have written down about their grandparents and great-grandparents—personalities who are very real to them despite the fact that some of them died long before Kord and Jay were born.

Life today is very different from the past when children grew up in a kind of kinship community, a world of grandparents and uncles and aunts, a world reduced to an intimate scale in which children could orient themselves to all the great experiences of life—birth, death, work, marriage. Now American families are often isolated by half a continent from their nearest kinsfolk.

What will our children have to look back on as symbols of home? Certainly not the rented apartment or the rapidly changing suburban neighborhood where they are growing up. If they are to "go home again" it will not be to the old homestead but to the family log and the memories it keeps alive. Yes, if our home ever caught fire, you can guess what we would all think of saving first: our family log.

Who Helped You Most?

"OUR CHIEF WANT in life is somebody who shall make us do what we can." Finding those words of Emerson's not long ago seemed to crystallize something I had always sensed but never fully grasped: the astonishing fact that we don't begin to live up to our potentialities so long as we are trying merely to please ourselves.

All of us need someone who wants us to achieve, someone who expects the utmost from us, someone who gives us a reason outside of ourselves for succeeding. It can be an inspiring teacher, a loved parent, a boss who gets the best from you because he expects it.

Selfishness, Emerson seems to be saying, will carry us so far but no farther. There must be somebody who cares whether or not we go farther still. Somebody to work for, live for, sometimes even die for....

You can argue that the improved performance comes only because human vanity craves an audience. I think it goes much deeper. I think we respond to this outside challenge mainly because it establishes contact—warm, tangible contact—with another human being. And that contact banishes the most paralyzing of all fears: the fear of loneliness.

Read Emerson one sentence farther: "Our chief want in life is somebody who shall make us do what we can." And he added, "This is the service of a friend." —Arthur Gordon in *This Week*

Lecomte du Noüy, renowned biologist,
finds religious faith behind the drama of evolution

GOD'S NEWEST WITNESS

By Fulton Oursler

E VER SINCE Darwin advanced his theory of evolution, disbelief in many of the fundamental doctrines of Christianity has been spreading. It became popular to look upon man as a mere biological accident, to deny the existence of the human soul and its free will to choose between good and evil; to regard life as without purpose and meaning. Skeptics insist that the death blow to faith was given by science.

But now we hear a fresh voice—a scientific one—declaring all the old beliefs to be true. God's new prophet is a biologist, Dr. Lecomte du Noüy, formerly of the Rockefeller Institute and the Pasteur Institute. In his extraordinary book, *Human Destiny,** he reveals a new theory of evolution. By means of science and reason, Dr. du Noüy seeks to turn into realities those old, disputed hopes of mankind—free will, a meaning for life, the importance of the individual, immortality and God.

As a biologist, du Noüy begins by confessing the fallibility of science. Nothing in this world can be absolutely known. Our five senses are imperfect; our technical instruments never precise enough.

Nor can we ever perceive reality. Flour and soot mixed together form a powder that looks gray. But a microscopic insect moving among the grains of that powder will see white and black boulders. On the insect's scale of observation there is no such thing as a gray powder. All our ideas of truth must be relative, in a universe whose very scale is beyond our grasp.

---

*Published at $3.50 by Longmans, Green & Co., 55 Fifth Ave., New York 3, N. Y.

In this mighty cosmos, science toys with tiny fractions of knowledge but the chasms separating known facts are vast and deep. We are living on a globe which is about 2000 million years old. On this vast stage was played the drama of evolution. But how did the curtain go up? So far it has been impossible to ascertain how life began. No one has even explained the origin of vertebrates to which you and I belong.

The whole history of evolution is spotted with improbable mysteries. Every great step forward was made against the most rigid scientific laws of probability; each advance an unlikely conquest from a lower to a higher level.

For example, there is that moment when life changed its technique of begetting. For millions of years, protoplasmic cells just kept on multiplying and separating, breaking apart and renewing—seeming to possess immortal life. Suddenly, mysteriously, there came into life a singular new mode of begetting—sexual generation. And how odd it does seem that, as in the story of Adam and Eve, when sex came into life, death came with it.

Again and again du Noüy, a most courageous biologist, points out symbolical parallels between the early chapters of Genesis and the known facts of evolution. It is as if the writer of the first book of the Bible intuitively knew the grand program of life prepared for the world by its Creator. Often truth comes to man through intuition, while knowledge is acquired by intelligence, and both sources must be respected.

Five basic facts about evolution are undeniable: (1) the beginning of life in extremely simple forms; (2) evolution into more and more complex forms; (3) the result of this age-long process—man with a human brain; (4) the birth in man of abstract thought; (5) the spontaneous growth of moral and spiritual ideas in different parts of the world. Not one of these five facts can be explained scientifically. We must bridge the gaps by setting up an hypothesis.

Often an hypothesis is a necessity. In working out his theory of relativity Einstein used more than a dozen unprovable postulates—yet, thanks to his work, we released the energy of the atom. Du Noüy's hypothesis sees a pattern, a moral purpose, in evolution. It is based on the impossibility of attributing to the simple play of chance the beginning of life and its ascent to the wonders of the human brain.

For years materialists have been telling us that chance held an absolute despotism over all things mortal. But du Noüy replies, "Man is free either to follow his animal instincts, which give him physical pleasure, or to seek another kind of goal. To reach that different goal he has to struggle against powerful animal instincts in himself. Often the fight means agony to him. Yet some men do make that fight, in spite of pain. Such a choice exists for man alone."

Many men choose one path, very few the other. But it is the few who have always played the great role in evolution. This nonconforming minority has followed an irresistible but invisible leadership; it has obeyed a great compelling Final Cause that drew it on.

The melting snows on a mountaintop become brooks and mighty rivers as they flow downward toward the sea. They flow downward, of course, in obedience to a law of finality called gravitation. In evolution, life flowed upward, drawn by a law of equal finality.

Has orthodox science been blind to these clues of pattern and design in evolution? Not at all. In life's continuous ascent, the rigid laws of chance have been so frequently flouted that the most hardheaded materialists have had to admit the presence of some unknown factor.

To deal with this unknown factor the materialists had to give it a name. Cherishing some deep antipathy to the revered name of God they called it "anti-chance." How little it matters whether you call it anti-chance or call it God!

For a thousand million years—until man began to think—life was governed by the one basic motive of survival. Then certain human beings appeared who were ruled by a new motive, by an idea of right and wrong for the sake of which they would willingly *lose* their lives.

Du Noüy says it was as if the voice of some Final Power spoke to the human soul:

"So far you have been concerned only with living and breeding. You could kill, you could steal food or mates, and go to sleep peacefully. But from this day on, you shall combat your instincts. You shall not kill! You shall not steal! You shall not covet!

"And you shall sleep peacefully only if you have mastered yourself. You shall be ready to suffer and to give your life rather than abandon your ideals. No longer are your principal aims to live and eat. For noble ends you will endure hunger and death. And you must be noble, for that is the will of the new being who has risen in you. You must accept him as master even though he curbs your desires."

Man does not represent the end of evolution but only a middle stage between the past with all the memories of the beast, and the future rich in the promise of the soul. From now on, our progress will be not physical but spiritual. The man of the future will be completely liberated from destructive human passions—egotism, greed, lust for power. Though he will enjoy the pleasures of the body, he will not be ruled by them.

Clearly the evolution of the future will lie with the good people of the world. But what is good and what is evil? The materialists deny the very existence of good and evil; du Noüy not only affirms their existence but seeks to define them.

All through evolution, he argues, there have been just two kinds of living creatures—you can call them good and bad, or evolvers and adapters. The bad kind, the adapter, has always done the expedient thing. It has conformed and appeased. It adapts itself to environment and circumstances—and then stops progressing. The other kind of creature is rebellious. Refusing to conform, it chooses rather to surpass itself, and so evolves into something better. In the clash of these two motives du Noüy finds his difference between wrong and right.

The criterion of the adapter is usefulness; of the evolver, freedom— liberation from all destructive restriction. Ever since the first rudiments, this test has singled out the rising scale. It was the creatures who sought freedom who carried life upward. As du Noüy puts it: "Evolution progresses from instability to instability. It would perish if it encountered only perfectly adapted stable systems."

What is important is that man has changed his master. Once he was a slave to physiochemical biological laws. Now he can think for himself. All his ancestors were irresponsible actors in a play which they did not understand. Now man wants to comprehend the play.

He has become capable of perfecting himself. Ideas of the beautiful come to him, esthetic visions born in him can be materialized by his hands. He invents and learns. No longer does the satisfaction of any appetite seem enough. Yet he is still largely animal and that makes him a confused and bewildered fellow.

The voice of his newborn conscience contradicts old orders and gives him new ones. Is it any wonder that he revolts? Like a wild horse he rages against the bit—but he differs from the horse for he himself imposes the check while remaining free to accept or reject it. Because mastery of self is based on the liberty to choose between good and evil, it gives birth to human dignity that is the goal of evolution.

Once we understand this enormous fact we see a further refinement of the definition of right and wrong: *Good must be also the respect of human personality; evil is the contempt of this personality.*

Here is the most important event so far in all evolution. Henceforth, in order to evolve, man must disobey his own nature. Now it is the individual who counts and no longer the species!

We should not despair because there are so few good people in the world. As in billions of past years, growth will still be carried on by the few. Those few will prove to be the forerunners of the future race, ancestors of the spiritually perfect man of which Christ was the ageless example.

Will it take another two billion years to reach this goal? Du Noüy says no. The whole process can be hurried along because of man's greatest tool, his brain. While it took ages for animals to develop wings, man conquered the air in only three generations. Thanks to the human brain the range of our senses has been increased beyond all dreams. We can see the infinitely small and the infinitely remote. We have dwarfed distance and put time in chains.

But this facile power of thought increases our responsibility. We are free either to forge ahead or to destroy ourselves. Too many look upon our inventions as symbols of true civilization. Not human comfort and convenience but human dignity must be our ideal. Intelligence, unless governed by conscience, will generally influence man adversely in the choice between good and evil. It will counsel him to conform, to appease, to adapt. It will never advise him to rebel, to resist, to evolve. Common sense has yet to make its first hero or martyr. That is why intelligence alone is dangerous. Alone it made the atomic bomb. Suddenly people realized that a triumph of science brutally challenged their security; the conflict between pure intelligence and moral values had become a matter of life and death.

Unhappily, there are still many who insist that man is a glorified animal, and nothing more. They can see only an animal solution of our problems. In the field of politics they want to regiment people like insects. In a large part of the world dictators have already done so, denying to the individual any role except that of the drone. Yet the will of "anti-chance" or God, the grand design of evolution, is that man be not regimented but remain free to evolve.

We must respect human personality because it is a worker for evolution and a collaborator with God. Here many persons ask: If there is a God, how can He permit all the evil that is in the world? This question shows a misunderstanding of the new theory. In the beginning of evolution, progress depended solely on God. Now it no longer depends solely on Him but also on the effort made by man individually. By giving man conscience and free will, God abdicated a part of omnipotence in favor of His creature. Thus He breathed a spark of Himself into man.

This liberty is so real, so actual, that God Himself refuses to interfere with it. If we accept the fact that a Supreme Power has created the laws of life then we must know that the Creating Power will not prevent these laws from operating. It is not nature that is incoherent but man who is ignorant—he still has a long way to go.

Again the intelligent man bogs down, because he cannot think of God sensibly. What does God look like? A giant with a beard, conceived in the image of man? In these scientific times the answer should be clear. Imagine God? Who can visualize even an electron? Any scientist will tell you that the electron is inconceivable. You cannot diagram its shape. No man has ever seen one. Neither the unseen electron nor the unseen God can be visualized, but they exist.

The law of evolution is and always has been to struggle upward, and the fight has lost none of its violence because the battlefield has changed from the material to the spiritual plane. The divine spark is in us. We are free to disregard it, to kill it, or to come closer to God by showing our eagerness to work with Him.

It is not for true believers that du Noüy has written his book. Instead he addresses himself to doubters and skeptics; to increasing millions whose despair makes them wonder whether life is worth living.

To them the author of *Human Destiny* offers courage and hope.

You Can Change the World

World

By James Keller

Founder, in 1945, of the Christophers

A condensation from the book

"Better to light one candle than to curse the darkness" — so goes an old Chinese proverb.

I

N a small California town a young Negro, studying to be a teacher, took a part-time job at a filling station to help support himself and his wife until he got his degree. But some customers objected; they wanted to buy gasoline only from white men. The owner was about to fire the boy when a woman neighbor asked:

"How many customers will you lose if you stand by this fellow?"

"About 18. Maybe 20."

"If I get you 20 new customers, you will keep him on?"

"You bet I will."

Not only did this aroused woman bring 20 new customers, but five more for good measure. She was a Christopher, one of a growing band of men and women united in the purpose to help change the world into a better place.

What is a Christopher? He is one who believes in individual responsibility for the common good of all and sets himself a specific job to do; an average man or woman ready to work and make personal sacrifices. It is literally astounding to learn the results that are being achieved singlehanded by little people of faith and zeal.

Although under Catholic auspices, the movement embraces all faiths among its followers. The movement has no chapters, no committees, no meetings; there are no membership lists and no dues. From a central office in New York occasional bulletins are mailed out to almost a million interested persons; that is the sole unifying contact. Each believes that alone and unaided he has a post of his own in the war between good and evil. And he must believe in the power of himself, as an individual, to change the world.

How singlehanded efforts multiply into power was symbolized at a patriotic meeting of 100,000 citizens jammed into the Los Angeles Coliseum one starless night. Suddenly the chairman startled the throng:

"Don't be afraid now. All the lights are going out."

In complete darkness he struck a match.

"All who can see this little light say 'Yes!'"

A deafening roar came from the audience.

"So shines a good deed in a naughty world. *But suppose now every one of us here strikes a light!*"

Faster than it takes to tell, nearly 100,000 pinpricks of flame flooded the arena with light—the result of 100,000 individuals, each doing his own part. That is how the Christopher movement works.

No matter who you are, or what you are, or where you may be, you can do something to change the world for the better. You, as an individual, are important. You count!

Remember the gigantic letter-writing campaign which helped to smash the radical forces in the Italian elections a few years ago. Millions of letters went out from people of Italian descent in the United States encouraging relatives in the old country to vote against totalitarianism. One of the men who fostered that dazzling campaign was a barber in Southampton, Long Island.

Irritated by Old World criticisms and lies about our American ways, he was also exasperated that people who resented such attacks did nothing to counteract them.

He decided to do something about it personally.

First he wrote to relatives in St. Catherine, Sicily, describing his happy life here. Next he wrote his wife's relatives. Then he persuaded his son, a doctor, and his daughter, a dietitian, to write. Meanwhile he appealed to newspaper editors and even to President Truman to help enlist the nation. All agreed it was a good idea but too unwieldy. Various organizations wished him well, but that was all.

But the barber, enraptured with his cause, refused to quit. He kept on asking for help. Slowly the idea burned with its own fire. Businessmen, young GI brides from overseas, housewives, veterans' groups, civic societies and religious leaders joined in. A steady trickle of letters to Italy swelled to a torrent; the democratic victory heartened all Europe.

One man helped start this, because he lifted himself out of his own narrow, selfish sphere and into the larger world with all its breathtaking potentialities.

Not spectacularly, but in countless ways, tens of thousands of Christophers are busy and never before in history were such efforts needed so desperately. For today the world is ill of the disease of the soul called materialism. If the trend toward paganism continues, it is only a matter of time before our nation will collapse from within. That is what happened in Germany.

Millions of decent Americans have long forgotten the basic truth that every human being gets his fundamental rights from God—*not from the State!* That, in fact, the chief purpose of the State—as the Founding Fathers repeatedly affirmed in the Declaration of Independence—is to *protect* those God-given rights.

To believe that these rights are safe today is to embrace illusion.

The stockbroker who, forsaking Wall Street, lowered his entire family's living standards to take a government job and fight for good principles is a Christopher. So is the Baptist lawyer down in Texas who spends all his leisure time making speeches on the brotherhood of man. And so is a girl epileptic, bed-bound in a small California hospital, who started writing a column that would "concentrate on the good in life around us, instead of just the opposite." A little newspaper printed her words; fan letters poured in—and, believe it or not, this girl is now almost completely recovered from epilepsy. Her doctors understand why; she got out of herself and out of her own narrow world, gave herself a purpose in life and so did away with mental and emotional frustration.

It is estimated that subversives who are trying to undermine the United States compose less than one percent of the people of our country. Christophers believe that one percent of the normal, decent citizens of America can be found ready and willing to work just as hard to restore divine truth and human integrity to American life.

The story of one American wife shows the inestimable power of a woman, working behind the scenes in her own home. Her husband told her the Reds were taking over his union. "Keep out of that!" she advised him. "It'll only mean trouble."

But a Christopher explained how getting decent people to stay away from union meetings was just what the Reds wanted. From then on, she urged her husband to attend every meeting, she induced him to urge others, finally she egged him on to run for president of the union. In substance, that is the history of how a large union was taken away from an organized leftist minority. One woman with a Christopher purpose was all that was needed to start the fire!

In the home, in all our personal relationships, we must practice love and we must pass on the message of the good life. As you grow in love for others, you will find your own power increasing. You will learn how to disagree without being disagreeable. You will become more approachable. You will better understand why *all people* want to be truly loved and not just tolerated. You will emphasize more and more the good side of even the worst people. You will develop an inner warmth, an abiding sense of humor; naturally you will make mistakes, but you will always be able to laugh at yourself. Your never-say-die spirit will give courage to everyone you meet.

Life itself will take on a new and exhilarating meaning, because you will be fulfilling the purpose for which you were created: to love God above all things and your neighbor as yourself.

"We hate Christianity and Christians," proclaimed Anatole Luna-charsky, Soviet Commissar of Education. "Even the best of them must be considered our worst enemies. They preach love of one's neighbor and mercy, which is contrary to our principles. What we want is hate. . . . Only then will we conquer the Universe." (Quoted in *Izvestia*.)

The only thing that terrifies the godless the world over is the fear that some day all those who believe in Christ will wake up—*and start acting their beliefs.*

Once that happens, most of the great problems which plague mankind will disappear overnight.

Should Persons

of Different Faiths Marry?

By **David R.** Mace   *Professor of Human Relations, Drew University*

Condensed from Woman's Home Companion

N ANXIOUS mother recently wrote me that her daughter was engaged to a man of different religious faith from her own.

"When Violet and Harold first met," the letter said, "they were not aware of the difference. Now they do not consider it important. They are in love. Harold takes his religion seriously; so does Violet. My husband and I are afraid that after the glamour of romance has worn off disharmony and unhappiness will be inevitable. Are we worrying without cause?"

Thousands of parents could have written such a letter. In a democratic nation in which young people of different cultural backgrounds and religious faiths are wisely given every opportunity to meet and mingle, it is natural that some of the friendships thus formed should deepen into love and the desire to marry.

It is good that men and women of Catholic, Jewish and Protestant faiths should be friends. But is it also good that they should marry?

Almost with one voice the official leaders of these faiths say no. The Roman Catholic attitude is expressed in the Code of Canon Law: "Everywhere and with the greatest strictness the Church forbids marriages between baptized persons, one of whom is a Catholic and the other a member of a schismatical or heretical sect; and if there is added to this the danger of the falling away of the Catholic party and the perversion of the children, such a marriage is forbidden also by the divine law."

Sometimes a dispensation may be granted for a Roman Catholic to marry a non-Catholic. This requires the non-Catholic party to make a solemn promise that the Catholic party shall be entirely free to practice his or her religion, that all children shall be "baptized and educated in the Catholic faith" (even if the Catholic parent should die), that the teaching of the Catholic Church concerning birth control and divorce shall be adhered to. In addition the Catholic party promises to strive "to bring about the conversion of my consort."

Religious leaders agree that inter-faith marriages are almost invariably a source of trouble to the individuals concerned and to their religious communities. Three major studies show that the chances of divorce and separation are two and a half times greater in an interfaith marriage than in a marriage between partners of the same faith. Other researches indicate that in marriages which do not break up disagreement on religious matters is a definite cause of unhappiness.

Dr. Murray H. Leiffer, professor of sociology at Garrett Biblical Institute in Evanston, Ill., in a study made with the coöperation of 22 churches and the partners of 743 mixed marriages, found that the "adjustment" of religious tensions most frequently resorted to was for one or both partners to give up religious practices altogether. As parents give up their religion, an increasing number of children are brought up without any kind of church attachment.

A survey made by the YMCA found that where both parents were Catholic 92 percent of their sons were also practicing Catholics; where both parents were Protestants 68 percent of their sons were also practicing Protestants. But where one parent was Catholic and the other Protestant only 34 percent of their sons were practicing members of either faith.

What we know about the way these marriages work out seems to indicate that it is in the best interests of parents and pastors to give careful teaching to their young people on the subject—preferably during early and middle adolescence. Such teaching should not be based merely upon pronouncements by religious leaders or statistical surveys of mixed marriages. It will be necessary to discuss just why interfaith marriages are hazardous. Here are some important reasons:

1. Differences in religious attitudes are fundamental differences. Young people strongly attracted to each other may feel an emotional harmony which seems to make their differing faiths unimportant. This is quite deceptive. Friendships can be maintained across barriers of faith. But marriage is a relationship in which spiritual unity is so essential that the fullest union between husband and wife is unattainable without it.

2. Religious differences always imply wider areas of conflict. Even those who no longer practice the faith in which they were reared still have been molded by their early training. Cultural patterns and personal values differ deeply from faith to faith. Orthodox Judaism calls for the observance of detailed regulations in daily living. Catholicism involves a basic submission to the authority of the Church. Protestantism stresses individual freedom and personal religious experience. The attitudes based on these differences reach down to the very roots of married life. Conflict is almost certain to arise in an area far wider than that of specific religious belief and observance.

3. Church loyalties and family loyalties will usually clash. Every church asks of its members a portion of their time, money and interest. When the allegiance of husband and wife differs there will be times when both want to be free at once, there will be money which each wants to allocate to a different purpose, there will be arrangements made by one partner which will inconvenience and displease the other.

4. The upbringing of the children presents constant problems. This is generally considered the most serious cause of trouble. It can be deeply distressing to a parent to see his or her child brought up in an alien faith. Nor is it merely a question of religious beliefs. The child will inevitably form friendships and cultivate values and standards which one parent may view with deep disapproval. In these circumstances it is impossible to achieve the warm family fellowship enjoyed by those who on all essential matters are of one heart and mind.

These are formidable obstacles to happiness in marriage. Young people who are taught these facts will recognize the wisdom of avoiding emotional entanglements which might lead to a mixed marriage.

But what of those who are already deeply in love and quite determined to marry?

The best assurance that a marriage will be successful comes when both unite in the same faith. That is not easy, and Dr. Judson Landis, associate professor of family sociology at the University of California, found that in two out of three cases the necessary sacrifice could not be made. Where one spouse did change to the faith of the other the concession was made as often by the Catholic as by the Protestant, despite the stricter rules binding the former. The divorce rate for these couples was decidedly lower than the rate for mixed marriages as a whole, although it was not nearly so low as for couples with the same religious background.

If neither of the young people will embrace the other's faith, at least they can study each other's beliefs with understanding and sympathy. Thus they will find it easier to be tolerant when the tension becomes severe. It is a wise plan, also, for them to try to arrive *before marriage* at a clear mutual agreement about the policy to be adopted on all controversial points.

There are married couples of different religions who, despite every obstacle, win through to deep and lasting happiness. But our young men and women, whose chief concern is to create peaceful homes and to raise happy families, should know that they stand a much better chance of doing so if they choose life partners whose spiritual background is the same as their own.

What's Wrong With Grownups?

*W*hen the ten-year-olds in Mrs. Imogene Frost's class at the Brookside, N. J., Community Sunday School expressed their views on "What's wrong with grownups?" they came up with these complaints:

1. Grownups make promises, then they forget all about them, or else they say it wasn't really a promise, just a maybe.

2. **Grownups don't do the things they're always telling the children to do—like pick up their things, or be neat, or always tell the truth.**

3. Grownups won't let their children dress the way they want to—but they never ask a child's opinion about how they should dress. If they're going out to a party, grownups wear just exactly what they want to wear—even if it looks terrible, even if it isn't warm enough.

4. Grownups never really listen to what children have to say. They always decide ahead of time what they're going to answer.

5. Grownups make mistakes but they won't admit them. They always pretend that they weren't mistakes at all—or that somebody else made them.

6. Grownups interrupt children all the time and think nothing of it. If a child interrupts a grownup, he gets a scolding or something worse.

7. Grownups never understand how much children want a certain thing—a certain color or shape or size. If it's something they don't admire—even if the children have spent their own money for it—they always say, "I can't imagine what you want with that old thing!"

8. Sometimes grownups punish children unfairly. It isn't right if you've done just some little thing wrong and grownups take away something that means an awful lot to you. Other times you can do something really bad and they say they're going to punish you, but they don't. You never know, and you ought to know.

9. Grownups talk about money too much, and bills, and things like that, so that it scares you. They say money isn't very important, but the way they talk about it, it sounds like the most important thing in the world.

10. Grownups gossip a lot—but if children do the very same thing and say the same words about the same people they're being disrespectful.

11. Grownups pry into children's secrets. They always think it's going to be something bad. They never think it might be a nice surprise.

12. Grownups are always talking about what they did and what they knew when they were ten years old—but they *never* try to think what it's like to be ten years old *right now*.

Don't Let Your Illness Go to Your Head

By Clinton P. Anderson
U. S. Senator from New Mexico; former Secretary of Agriculture

I T WAS the lowest moment of my life. I was only 21. A few weeks before, I had been well on my way in the newspaper business in my home town in South Dakota, and was eagerly anticipating getting married. Now, confined to bed in a tuberculosis sanatorium in New Mexico, I had nothing to look forward to, I thought, but death.

The doctor had wired my father to come within five days if he wanted to see me alive. All through the night—my first in the sanatorium—a boy in the room next had cried for his mother, then died at daybreak. I looked at the bottle of poisonous rubbing alcohol on the table by my bed and vaguely considered drinking it to end my misery.

Then I realized that someone was standing beside me. It was Joe Maas, an old "lunger." The words he spoke literally saved my life. They have come back repeatedly in moments of crisis and helped pull me through.

"Remember this, son," Joe said in the husky whisper of the advanced TB case. "What you got will never kill you if you keep it in your chest. But if you let it get up here," and he tapped his temple significantly, "it's fatal. Worrying kills more patients than TB itself ever did."

The veteran's words made my young heart leap. I determined to keep thoughts of my illness out of my head. I would seize this opportunity to do the writing I had hoped to do.

I sent for my typewriter and had it suspended from the ceiling on a pulley. Each morning, propped up on a pillow, I lowered the machine onto my lap. Throughout my eight months in bed I laboriously pecked out sketches, poems and short stories. I could have plastered my wall with rejection slips. Occasionally, however, came a tonic sentence like one from *Harper's Magazine* saying, "You almost got it!" That made up for a hundred replies starting, "We regret. . ." And every day for four years I wrote a letter to the girl I was going to marry, and received a letter from her. I never doubted that I'd get well.

As my weight and health slowly improved, I worked on the weekly hospital newspaper, writing short features about new patients. To every one, I passed on Joe Maas's warning against letting TB go from the lungs to the head. I noted in my diary the mental attitude of 2000 patients I interviewed. In nearly every instance those with a cheerful outlook survived.

Three years ago I was in the office of a Washington, D. C., heart specialist.

"Do you depend upon your salary for a living?" he asked me.

"No."

"Then resign from the Senate, pack up and go home. You've got a bad heart."

His diagnosis was confirmed by three other doctors. Added to the fact that I am diabetic, kept alive by daily shots of insulin, this made me panicky for a moment. Then Joe Maas's advice came to my rescue.

I stopped acting as if the entire legislative structure of the United States would collapse unless I personally propped it up every day. No longer did I work in my office until after midnight to clear off the last piece of paper on my desk. I quit taking exhausting trips to keep tiring speaking engagements. For an entire year I did not make a single strength-sapping speech on the Senate floor. I studied bills conscientiously, did my committee work and quietly voted my convictions.

The pains across my chest disappeared. The last time I had a checkup the doctor laid down his stethoscope and said, "That heart's in pretty good shape."

That, I thought, is because Joe Maas taught me to keep my physical illness where it belonged—and not let it go to my head. His advice saved my life more than once. It can bring peace of mind to anyone who will use it.

I'd Pick More Daisies

By Don Herold

O<small>F COURSE,</small> you can't unfry an egg, but there is no law against thinking about it.

If I had my life to live over, I would try to make more mistakes. I would relax. I would be sillier than I have been this trip. I know of very few things that I would take seriously. I would be less hygienic. I would go more places. I would climb more mountains and swim more rivers. I would eat more ice cream and less bran.

I would have more actual troubles and fewer imaginary troubles.

You see, I have been one of those fellows who live prudently and sanely, hour after hour, day after day. Oh, I have had my moments. But if I had it to do over again, I would have more of them—a lot more. I never go anywhere without a thermometer, a gargle, a raincoat and a parachute. If I had it to do over, I would travel lighter.

It may be too late to unteach an old dog old tricks, but perhaps a word from the unwise may be of benefit to a coming generation. It may help them to fall into some of the pitfalls I have avoided.

If I had my life to live over, I would pay less attention to people who teach tension. In a world of specialization we naturally have a superabundance of individuals who cry at us to be serious about their individual specialty. They tell us we *must* learn Latin or History; otherwise we will be disgraced and ruined and flunked and failed. After a dozen or so of these protagonists have worked on a young mind, they are apt to leave it in hard knots for life. I wish they had sold me Latin and History as a lark.

I would seek out more teachers who inspire relaxation and fun. I had a few of them, fortunately, and I figure it was they who kept me from going entirely to the dogs. From them I learned how to gather what few scraggly daisies I have gathered along life's cindery pathway.

If I had my life to live over, I would start barefooted a little earlier in the spring and stay that way a little later in the fall. I would play hooky more. I would shoot more paper wads at my teachers. I would have more dogs. I would keep later hours. I'd have more sweethearts.

I would fish more. I would go to more circuses. I would go to more dances. I would ride on more merry-go-rounds. I would be carefree as long as I could, or at least until I got some care—instead of having my cares in advance.

More errors are made solemnly than in fun. The rubs of family life come in moments of intense seriousness rather than in moments of light-heartedness. If nations—to magnify my point—declared international carnivals instead of international war, how much better that would be!

G. K. Chesterton once said, "A characteristic of the great saints is their power of levity. Angels can fly because they can take themselves lightly. One 'settles down' into a sort of selfish seriousness; but one has to rise to a gay self-forgetfulness. A man falls into a 'brown study'; he reaches up at a blue sky."

In a world in which practically everybody else seems to be consecrated to the gravity of the situation, I would rise to glorify the levity of the situation. For I agree with Will Durant that "gaiety is wiser than wisdom."

I doubt, however, that I'll do much damage with my creed. The opposition is too strong. There are too many serious people trying to get everybody else to be too darned serious.

AN OLD NURSEMAID once made a comment to me that I've never forgotten: "I finds, Miss Evie, that your luck is how you treats people."   —Contributed by Evelyn A. Benson

WHY DIDN'T YOU
GET THAT PROMOTION?

By Howard Whitman   *Condensed from Collier's*

T HE WAY to get ahead in the world is changing. With psychological tests and "evaluation interviews," big companies are now determining not only how good a man is at his job but how good he is *as a person*—and what he can develop into. Fitting square pegs into square holes is no longer enough. The trick is to find out what kind of wood the peg is made of, what quality, how durable.

"We are looking beyond the old idea of promotion," says Dr. Walter D. Woodward, psychiatrist at the American Cyanamid Co. "We are looking toward a man's long-term progress. We want to develop men who can fit into future vacancies, take jobs which don't even exist yet."

This new approach is based not so much on how well a man or woman can do a particular job but on how mature and well integrated he or she is. After all, the mainsprings of personality supply the incentive, integrity, vigor and enthusiasm a person brings to his work.

A study by Chandler Hunt covering 80,000 clerical and office workers in 76 companies analyzes the reasons why people are not promoted. Lack of skill accounts for only 24 percent of the trouble. Personality failings—lack of initiative and ambition, carelessness, noncoöperation, laziness—account for 76 percent.

These personality failings can be observed in surface behavior. But today's personnel experts listen also for deeper rumblings. Let's say the management is considering Mr. A for promotion to foreman. To find out what kind of director of other men Mr. A will be the personnel expert asks a "revealing situation" question:

"Suppose one of your men has been late twice in the past ten days. Each time you spoke to him about it and received his assurance that he would be on time in the future. This morning he is late again, and an important job has been held up. What would you do about this man?"

"I'd fire him" or "I'd give him another chance" is the wrong answer. "I'd find out why he was late" is the right answer.

The man may have been late because his wife was suddenly taken to the hospital or for another emergency reason. To ask him about it shows an even, judicial temperament in a provoking situation. The man can be fired or forgiven after the facts are known.

Dozens of questions in today's personality tests have no right or wrong answers, but each answer adds another brush stroke to a person's portrait. Examples:

On meeting someone, do you wait for the other fellow to say hello first? (*hostility*)

Are you hurt if someone fails to return your call? (*inferiority feelings*)

Would you rather make a decision yourself or have someone help you make it? (*sense of adequacy, confidence*)

Would you speak up or let the incident pass if someone pushed ahead of you in line? (*aggressiveness, assertiveness*)

Is it hard for you to say no to a salesman? (*suggestibility*)

If a man says it is not hard for him to say no to a salesman he may not make a good salesman himself. Checking with control groups has shown that 90 percent of successful salesmen find it hard to say no to another salesman.

After the batteries of tests comes the evaluation interview—heart of the scientific approach to promotion. This is just talk, but extremely skilled talk.

In Cleveland, at Western Reserve University's Personnel Research Institute, I sat in at an interview held for the Solar Steel Corp. The interviewers were two psychologists, Dr. Erwin K. Taylor, director of the institute, and Theodore Kunin. The subject was a Solar Steel employe, Mr. X. Dr. Taylor had said to me in advance, "I intentionally will not introduce you. This is to be a 'stress interview,' and your unexplained presence will add to the stress." After half a dozen questions the stress was turned on. Dr. Taylor said, "Mr. X, I'll play the role of a customer, who for some reason has stopped doing business with your company. You have to win the business back."

Mr. X: I haven't had an order from you for some time. Is anything wrong?

Dr. Taylor: No, nothing's wrong.

Mr. X: Well—We took care of you when steel was short, didn't we?

Dr. Taylor: Do you think I'm under obligation to you?

Mr. X: I wouldn't say that. I just mean we took good care of you.

Dr. Taylor: You made a profit on every ton, didn't you?

Mr. X: All I mean is, I'd like to be fair about this thing.

Dr. Taylor: Oh, then you think I'm being unfair!

Mr. X: Oh, no. That's not what I meant. I just thought—well, steel might be short again sometime.

Dr. Taylor: Are you threatening me?

Poor Mr. X had considerable color in his cheeks by now, and just when I thought he'd blow his top Kunin came to the rescue by taking the interview up another path.

The interview lasted two hours and covered everything from life history and job history to hobbies and ambitions. There were no answers to many of the "stress" questions; they were framed expressly, as Dr. Taylor put it, "to get Mr. X in deep—and then get him in deeper."

The purpose of the stress test is to evaluate the man's resourcefulness, to see how much it takes to throw him off balance, to see what his quitting point is, to test his adroitness in handling people in impossible situations.

When the results of the tests and the interview have been collated recommendation is made for or against the man's promotion. Sure to be mentioned are the same traits of character which interested employers in grandpa's day—but evaluated scientifically.

Take the trait of thoughtfulness versus interest in overt activity. Psychologists find that the man who is a bit on the introvert side makes a better supervisor than the extrovert, because the extrovert "is so busy interacting with his environment that he is a poor observer of others and of himself. He is probably not subtle and may be lacking in tact. He dislikes reflection and planning."

The trait of aggressiveness has long figured in getting a man to the top of the ladder. A company chairman tells the board, "We want men who will tackle the job aggressively." Yet we condemn aggressiveness in such common remarks as "Don't push other people around" and "Don't try to get ahead by stepping on other people's toes." An aggressive person often finds himself disliked.

The personnel psychologist comes up with the answer to this apparent clash. Sheer aggressiveness he regards as a negative character trait. For most jobs it is undesirable. But "unobtrusive aggressiveness"—power, drive and alertness without offense or disregard for others—marks the socially mature go-getter.

Ola C. Cool, veteran management counselor and director of the Labor Relations Institute, said, "The men and women who know best how to get along with people—these are the ones who get the promotions." Cool told of a brilliant engineer, an MIT graduate, who was tops technically but missed out on promotion to a $25,000-a-year job. Cool explained, "This man was so good technically that he lost respect for the others around him, and he showed it. Result—he couldn't get good work out of his men."

One industrial firm, before promoting a machine operator to supervisor, always makes him a machine fixer for three months. Why? "A machine fixer gets around. He has to deal with fellows all over the plant. He doesn't know it, but in three months we have a full-length portrait of his social adaptability."

The importance of human relations goes up the scale with the importance of the job. In most jobs the initial promotions, during the first two to five years, are based on skill. But when a man gets up to supervisory levels—when he stops handling tools and starts handling people—an almost total reversal of qualifications begins.

Know-how is 90 percent for a rank-and-file worker. For promotion to foreman know-how is 50 percent and human relations 50 percent. For promotion to executive know-how is 20 percent and human relations 80 percent.

In one company the personnel manager named a man for promotion to a job for which he had no previous training. When asked why, he said, "We can teach that man all the know-how he needs in six weeks—but it has taken him 32 years to become the person he is."

HOW TO SAY NO

By Vance Packard   Condensed from Future

ANY OF US are harassed in daily life by an inability to utter a firm but gracious no. Often our difficulty is caused by a desire to be a good fellow.

A relative of mine, Edgar Wright, is a small-town businessman. Edgar is serving on 17 committees, mostly because he just can't say no. He goes to bridge parties which bore him. When his hostess offers him chocolate cake, for which he has an allergy, he eats it politely and is sorry later.

Edgar's wife, Ella, is just as bad. A few weeks ago an acquaintance who sells cosmetics by home demonstration asked her to sponsor a "cosmetic party." Ella tried to say no, but the woman kept coaxing until she said yes. Ella persuaded 20 of her friends to come; they couldn't say no either. Edgar estimates that the "party" cost him and the other husbands $148.

Almost every day many of us are caught in positions where we should logically say no, but don't. However, there are several reasonable and friendly ways of saying no. You may find one of them useful the next time you are faced with the problem.

Put it on an impersonal basis.

One of the most serene housewives I know says she achieved her serenity when she licked the problem of saying no. She explained: "I go by rules."

When an acquaintance asks her to wrap packages for unfortunates in Mozambique she says simply: "Sorry, I can't. This year I'm confining myself to two things, the Girl Scouts and the polio drive, and trying to do them right."

When a salesman knocks at her door, she is polite but firm: "My husband won't let me buy anything at the door."

Make it clear that you would like to say yes.

Tim Gammon, at the Liberty Mutual Insurance Co., is in charge of adjusting claims made against clients the company has insured. Though his office approves millions of dollars in payments each year, Gammon often has to say no. However, he always shows sympathy for the claimant. He explains that morally he may agree with him, but legally his hands are tied. In this case the company's legal department has ruled that the insured has no liability. He adds, regretfully, "We are unable to make a voluntary payment."

"People usually go away," he says, "feeling that at least we would like to be helpful."

Show that you have given the request real thought.

And *do* give it real thought. It is the brush-off that causes resentment. As Clarence Lyons, at the Industrial Bank of Commerce of New York, explains: "You must make the person see that you understand his problem, even if you have to say no."

Joe Stauffer, of N. W. Ayer & Son advertising agency, has to turn down many amateur ideas submitted for radio and television programs. He observes, however, that "most of the people seem satisfied if they simply get a chance to tell their story."

Congressman Jacob Javits, a durable Republican from Democratic New York City, says he receives about 75 requests a week, many of them utterly unreasonable. Once a mother appealed to him to get her fighting son out of Korea on the ground that it was dangerous there. Javits explained that the request was beyond his powers, but that he was sending along a welfare report on her son which showed that he was in good health.

Say no by helping the person say no to himself.

One of my neighbors is an interior decorator. He never says no to clients when they want to incorporate impractical ideas into their homes. Instead he educates them to say yes to what he wants them to do.

He told me about a couple who built a modern home with floor-to-ceiling windows and open layout. The day came when the wife was to pick curtain material. She preferred flowery chintz — most inappropriate to the house.

The decorator suggested: "Let's go through the house and see just what you want your curtains to do." As they walked he talked about the functions the curtains would serve in each room, and what fabrics would harmonize best with the modern *décor*. By the time they were through, the woman had forgotten her enthusiasm for chintz.

In saying no, show what needs to be done to get a yes.

Should you try to cash a check at a Statler Hotel without sufficient identification, the clerks will not merely say no. They will helpfully suggest some way that you can obtain identification locally.

Dr. William Reilly, author of *Successful Human Relations,* is a management consultant. Here is how he advises business executives to handle the man who wants a raise but doesn't deserve it.

"Yes, George, I understand your need for a raise. However, to give it to you we will have to make you more valuable to the company. Now let's see what we need to do. . . ."

Say no by showing that the request isn't reasonable.

By asking questions you may turn up circumstances which give you a legitimate excuse for saying no. Asking questions also gives you time to think up a graceful refusal.

Here is how a smart executive will say no, gently, to a poor idea without discouraging future ideas: "John, your suggestion has merit, but what would you decide if you were in my place?" He then weighs the pros and cons to show why the answer must be no.

Most important, say your no in the nicest, warmest way you can.

I learned one of my best lessons in the art of saying no nicely from my four-year-old daughter, Cindy. A few days ago a rather effusive elderly woman decided to become Cindy's pal. After fussing over the child a while she asked: "Cindy, would you like to come up to my house and play tomorrow?"

I held my breath as Cindy considered the proposal. I would have stumbled all over myself trying to reject such an invitation. Cindy's face broke into a big warm grin as she gave her one-word answer. She said, "No."

Her no was friendly and appreciative and good-humored. But it was so unmistakably firm that the woman did not pursue the matter.

Why do husbands so often die early?

Stop Killing Your Husband!

By Louis I. Dublin *Condensed from Lifetime Living*

IN 40 YEARS as the statistician of a large life-insurance company, I
have come to the conclusion that many men who die before their
time could have been saved if their wives had taken more seriously
a wife's responsibility to watch over her man.

Life-insurance statistics are proof of the axiom: The shorter the
waistline, the longer the lifeline. The effort to maintain a fashionable
silhouette keeps women watching their weight and diet. The result has
aided their health as well as their appearance. Unfortunately, fashion
has failed to have a similar effect on men. And the little woman, taking
pride in providing her husband with luscious pies, cakes and hot breads,
goes on contributing to his overweight.

Excessive weight goes hand in hand with many diseases, especially
heart and circulatory disorders: high blood pressure, hardening of the
arteries, coronary disease. Overweight persons are prone to chronic
diseases of the kidneys, liver and gall bladder; diabetes; arthritis;
hernia.

Obesity is not inherited. Not fat but the habit of overeating runs in
families. Where all members of a family are overweight, all usually
are eating more than they can use, and generally of the sweet or
starchy foods.

The typical husband tends to put on weight as he grows older because he needs less food and often eats more. With the years his metabolism rate slows; his body does not require as much fuel, chiefly because

he is less active physically. If he tends to become overweight there should be a *permanent* change in his dietary habits. The wife might start dinner with an appetite-cheating, low-calorie, vitamin-rich salad, and try to win her husband away from Boston cream pie to a simple dessert of fruit. She can also stop keeping snacks in the icebox and throw away the cookie jar.

Frequently obesity is indirectly caused by a state of mind. "People often take to eating," points out Cornell University's Dr. Harry Gold, "when they are unhappy, or for release from depression or tension." (Some, for similar reasons, take to drink, which also adds calories.) The wife of a man who overeats because he is tense should help him relax. If she feeds his emotional hunger with love and admiration, he may be more willing to relinquish the dollop of cream on his dessert.

High food prices have caused an increased intake of carbohydrates in bread, potatoes, noodles and pastries—all taboo in reducing diets, most of which call for steaks and fat-free chops, now beyond most budgets. I suggest, instead, eggs, cheese or fish. The average portion of seafood has fewer calories than the average portion of meat; it is a fine protein that equally satisfies hunger.

A man who has taken ten years accumulating 20 or more extra pounds cannot lose them in ten days. Not only must his way of life be changed but a new way of thinking developed—by the wife as well as the husband.

Between 70 and 80 percent more men than women die in their early 50's, usually from some form of heart or circulatory disease, to which years of too much strain, too much food and too little rest have contributed. Typical is the following true story (the names are fictitious):

John Edwards, 35, is a brilliant executive with a big future—if he lives. He leaves the house daily at 7:30, returns about seven, and puts in another hour or two at office work he has brought home with him.

His wife, Jane, is ambitious for him. A little while ago she proudly told an observant friend of the family that John had been offered a better job—a wonderful opportunity for a young man.

"Shorter hours, less strain?" asked the friend.

"No, but more money," Jane said.

"This is suicide or murder," said the friend bluntly. He pointed out the result of cumulative strain, bad eating habits and violent week-end exercise, all of which characterized John's way of life.

"At least," he advised, "don't let him take this new job until he's had a checkup."

Jane agreed, fortunately. The doctor found early signs of wear and tear, including heightened blood pressure. He advised John to slow down, and gave him a diet which eliminated many of the rich foods that Jane, in wifely solicitude, prepared.

Many wives feel that it is part of their responsibility to encourage their men to keep up with the Joneses. But a man will probably live longer if his wife encourages a spirit of contentment with modest achievement, and creates an atmosphere of peace and enjoyment of simple pleasures.

Statistics show an excessive accident mortality among fat men— possibly because they are not spry, or because of other physical impairments which go with overweight. Recently I ran across the case of a man in his 40's who was killed by a fall from the roof he was mending. To save money, his wife had permitted him to endanger himself.

Accidents, like many diseases, are sometimes due to emotional tensions. A man constantly frustrated, harried, becomes accident prone. Anger may readily cause him to become a danger on the highway. Or it may seethe inside him until he becomes a hazard at his job and gets in the way of machinery. These risks may be averted by an understanding wife.

What, then, should a wife do in order to keep her man sound, healthy and alive?

Watch his weight as carefully as she does her own, and patiently reform his eating habits if these are causing overweight.

Insist on an annual medical checkup. If indications of a disorder are discovered, help him follow all his doctor's instructions.

Encourage him to be happy in his work and to preserve reasonable ambition without grueling overdrive.

See to it that his home is one of security, rest and quiet happiness. Help him to be relaxed.

It's nice to have a man about the house. Keep him there.

His Own Built-In
Social Security
By Booton Herndon

DO YOU THINK you work too hard? That you haven't time to do all the things you want to do? Or that the Government ought to give you a little more security? If so, you ought to meet Bill Stoneburner.

Bill is skinny, tall, 40 years old and lives in my home town, Charlottesville, Va. Bill not only gets more work done but has more fun than anyone I know. Further, he and his wife have solved family problems that would send most people running helplessly to a psychiatrist—or to Reno.

Last summer my house needed painting. Bill gave a reasonable estimate so I hired him. But he didn't limit his job to painting. He fixed a screen door, took a stuck window apart and made it work, drove my wife into town shopping one day when I had the car, and answered approximately 100,000 questions put to him by my nine-year-old son— none of which showed up on the bill. When it was all over, as a matter of fact, he apologized for taking so long.

"I had two other inside jobs I was finishing up at night," he said. "And we've had some fires, too."

Bill's real job, you see, is with the fire department, where he is on duty 24 hours alternate days. He paints on his days off. His salary as a fireman is about $200 a month, which, with a wife and two children, doesn't go far.

"Why don't you quit the fire department and be a paint contractor?" my wife asked him one day.

Bill squirmed a little. "Somebody's got to put out the fires," he answered. "I don't want my own house to burn down."

"Then you ought to ask for more money from the city," said my wife, who comes from New York.

"Why, gosh," Bill said, scratching his head, "I don't think the city's *got* any more money. Taxes are high enough as they are."

My wife went back into the house and sat down. "That man's crazy," she announced.

Bill's wife, Bertha, a frail-looking creature—who actually has the stamina of a marathon runner—is an expert seamstress. Take her a clipping from a fashion magazine and, without a pattern, she'll make a garment just like it. Her price, with your material, is $10 for a dress, $20 for a tailored suit. "Where'd you say she lives?" my wife asked, reaching for the keys to the car.

So all right, I said to myself, the Stoneburners work like horses. But do they ever have any fun? I got my answer the next Sunday, on the Shenandoah River. A friend and I were out in my canoe. When our wives and children pleaded to come along we told them we wanted to do some *serious* fishing. Our fancy equipment impressed the daylights out of everybody but the fish.

And then down the river in a homemade boat loaded down with Bertha, the two kids and a dog, came Bill Stoneburner. They were using everything from a fly rod to a pole, but they were dragging in fish. Bill is actually an ardent fly fisherman who hasn't missed the opening day of the trout season for years, but he doesn't let it interfere with having a good time with his family.

We finally did get some fish that day. Bill gave them to us.

How would you be at living with your in-laws? Bill and Bertha live in a 12-room house populated by ten persons of four generations—not to mention five dogs, a cat and a bird. There are Bill's grandfather; his parents; his unmarried brother; Bill, Bertha and their two children, Billy and Cookie. Bill's sister is divorced and her two kids live there too.

That isn't all. A construction engineer and his wife were here on a job last year, and their son fitted in just right at the high school. When his parents moved on he stayed. Bill built him a little shack in the woods back of the Stoneburner house. He sleeps there and takes his meals with the family. "There's always room for one more in a family like this," Bill says.

Once Bill and Bertha had a home of their own, a little dream house, just right for them because Bill designed and built it himself. But he sold it to pay the mortgage on his parents' home, so they would have no worries in their old age. I know few husbands who would have made that sacrifice and no wives who would have let them.

As parents, Bill and Bertha have had two widely diverse problems. The older child, Billy, suffered an attack of polio which impairs his walk.

Did you ever see parents get impatient with their children when they lag behind, walking? Well, I'll never forget the first time I saw Bill Stoneburner and Billy, together. It was at a baseball game. The stands were located a long way from the entrance, and in the eighth inning I saw Bill, Bertha and Billy get up and start the long walk early, so that Billy could beat the crowd.

It was a pretty exciting inning, but I found myself devoting all my attention to the little family making its way around the field. That night energetic Bill Stoneburner was the darnedest slowpoke I ever saw. He stopped to talk, to pick up a blade of grass, to brush imaginary burs off his pant leg. Billy all the time was walking at his own gait. Never once did he have to hurry to catch up. As a matter of fact, when they were nearing the gate, I saw *Billy* look back impatiently. I guess it was then that I was proudest of all that I know Bill Stoneburner.

Cookie, the Stoneburner's nine-year-old daughter, is talented—and talented children can be as much of a problem as crippled ones; they can be spoiled brats. Says Alice Amory, an experienced dancing teacher, "I've seen a lot of budding dancers, but Cookie has more talent than any child I have ever seen. She can be as great as she wants to be."

Despite this, Cookie is one of the sweetest, best-mannered children you ever saw—a nice tribute to the way Bill and Bertha Stoneburner have kept their feet on the ground. But how about the expense of developing her talent?

Alice says, "Cookie wouldn't have to pay me a cent. I consider it my duty to develop such talent. But Bertha and Bill won't let me give her one minute of instruction free. They insist on working for it."

"Bill painted our house," Alice's husband, O. T. Amory, said to me. "Look at these interiors. Perfect. Three coats."

"Bertha makes my clothes," Alice said. "And Bill laid this tile in the studio. We give our recitals at the high school auditorium, so Bill measured the stage, then marked off the exact dimensions here on the studio floor. It was his idea. Now when a student steps over the line, I say, 'Oh, you just fell in the orchestra.' It's wonderful!"

"I had to do something for Bill," said O. T., "so I gave him the lumber that had been left over when the house was finished. All I asked was that he leave enough for a couple of benches for the studio. He took it all—which I thought was unlike Bill. A week later he brought us a beautiful bench, all sanded, varnished and waxed. 'I'll bring you the other one next week,' he said. And he did." O. T. shook his head. "What can you do with a guy like that?"

In the course of any painting job Bill does lots of extra touching-up and patching that he doesn't charge for. People come to him, he figures, because they want a good job, but can't afford a contractor. If he charged for every little thing his customers might not be able to afford him. "What I really want," he says, "is for people to like my work. I guess I'm selfish, really. I want appreciation."

Bertha feels the same way. She makes costumes for the dance recitals, for instance. Five dollars is her top for a costume, even if it takes her three working days. "I couldn't charge any more," she says. "The children's mothers couldn't afford it and they'd try to do it themselves and the costumes would look terrible, especially beside Cookie's. Then they'd feel bad. I want them to feel good.

How many mothers do you know who knock themselves out so other people's daughters will look as well as their own?

The other night Bill, Bertha and I were lounging in Bill's hobby shop, each of us holding a sleeping dog. Bill had been painting eight or ten hours a day half that week, and laying tile at night, and there'd been a few fires, too.

"I guess I'm lazy," Bill said, "but I just don't like to work in a garden. Of course," he added after a pause, "things like corn and tomatoes and pole beans—they don't take much time. We plant some every spring. Outside of a few things like that, though, when it comes to gardening I guess I'm just plain lazy."

With rather poor humor, I asked Bill what he did in his spare time. I never saw a man come alert so fast in my life. He showed me, with great enthusiasm, what he is doing in his spare time: he is making a four-poster bed, every post reeded and carved by hand. He got the walnut at a sawmill way out in the country, and had it kiln-dried. Each leg has taken about 25 hours' work (in his spare time); soon he will be able to put the sides on. When that is done he will sand it four times, water-stain it, sand it again, apply sealer, sand it lightly, then apply seven coats of lacquer. Then he will polish it with pumice and oil, and wax it.

"Only trouble is," Bill said, "the room Bertha and I have isn't big enough to take the bed. So, after I finish the bed, I've got to tear out the wall between our room and the next one and then replaster and paper it. Then we'll have a room to put the bed in."

It was 11 o'clock. Bill had been working since seven and had to be at the firehouse early the next morning. Yet there he was, talking about what he was going to do in his spare time. Bertha gently went over to him and brushed his shirt collar. She didn't say anything, but she didn't have to. It was there in her eyes for all the world to see.

And so I left them and went home to my own bed, the one I bought from the furniture store.

As I said, if you ever feel that you work too hard, or that you haven't enough time to do all the things you want to do, or if you think the Government ought to give you a little more social security, come on down to Charlottesville. I'll introduce you to Bill Stoneburner. He'll be glad to talk to you. He's got plenty of time.

The best cosmetic in the world is an active mind that is always finding something new.   —Mary Meek Atkeson

In marriage there is security in numbers

Love, Marriage, Children
—and Security

By Henry C. Link   *Author of "The Return to Religion," etc.*

Condensed from "The Way to Security"

IF YOU had to choose one of the following—an interesting job, an independent income of $100 a week, a happy family and home life —which would you choose? That question was asked recently of a cross section of husbands and wives. Eighty percent answered: a happy family and home life.

A happy family life is probably the principal factor in the security of adults—as it is in the security of children. Much has been written about marital security. Yet most discussions of what makes a happy marriage place little emphasis on the necessity of having children. Wars can come, jobs can go, money can run out, but if father, mother and children stand by each other, hope and happiness may survive.

Recently I was talking with a father who expressed concern about the approaching arrival of a fifth child. "And yet," he remarked, "in spite of the trouble and expense, my wife and I are convinced that a large family is better than a small one. There is a certain security in numbers."

He was right, of course.

In my experience with unhappy couples, the one most apparent cause of unhappiness is their unwillingness to have children, or their prolonged postponement of parenthood. They do not want children until they can afford them, or the wife wants to keep on working until they can buy a home. In their quest for security before having children they risk the chance of not having any security at all.

The case of one young husband who was worried about his marriage is not uncommon. "We seem to be drifting apart," he told us, "and for no reason that we can see." He and his wife had agreed before marriage, six years ago, that she would keep her job until his salary was up to $5000 a year. He was still short of the mark by $400. He was now 31 and she 28.

For six years they had defied their natural desire to have children. For six years they had said, in effect: "We can live without the risks of children until we can have children without risk." They did not realize that meanwhile they had probably lost the very security they were working toward.

Man has concocted many theories and notions about marriage, among them the theory that each couple has the right to decide whether to have children. Regardless of theories, the chief purpose of sex and marriage is children. This is a law of human nature which cannot be defied with impunity. A couple who enter marriage without planning to have children soon are courting disaster from the beginning.

Having children is a physical process but the experience is a spiritual one as well. It involves continuous self-sacrifice of many kinds, possibly even the sacrifice of immediate financial security. It is through the choice of spiritual values, where they conflict with material values, that true security is to be found.

Probably the most popular as well as the most dangerous theory about love is that it is something one falls out of as well as into. This ignores the truth that love, no matter how it starts, is something that must be consciously created. Lasting love depends on permanent sex compatibility, and this in turn depends heavily on having children. When the experience of sex is subordinated to the birth and care of children it takes on a new spiritual significance. This is the basis for true and lasting love, a continuous process of creation and self-sacrifice centered around raising a family.

One of the most important studies of marriage is that by the psychologist, Lewis M. Terman, at Stanford University. The results have been published in his book *Psychological Factors in Marital Happiness*. Of all the influences that determine a happy marriage probably the four most important are:

Being eager to have children.

Having parents who are happily married.

Having a mature character and effective personality.

Being religious and of religious parents.

Sexual compatibility alone is not regarded by psychologists and sociologists as a major factor. The reason is that such compatibility is something that has to be achieved, and its achievement depends on the four factors just mentioned.

Lack of money has often been given as a principal cause of marital unhappiness and divorce. And yet the higher the income, the higher the divorce rate. Obviously, people without sufficient money to indulge their whims, their impulses, their selfish desires, must of necessity make greater efforts to overcome their difficulties. These difficulties often prove temporary and so the couple remain united and regain their happiness. Thus financial *insecurity* may be a help in achieving marital *security*.

Having a child is the final and strongest pledge of a couple's love for each other. It is an eloquent testimony that their marriage is a complete one. It lifts their marriage from the level of selfish love and physical pleasure to that of devotion centered around a new life. It makes self-sacrifice rather than self-indulgence their guiding principle. It represents the husband's faith in his ability to provide the necessary security, and it demonstrates the wife's confidence in his ability to do so. The net result is a spiritual security which, more than any other power, helps to create material security as well.

WHEN Major Gen. William F. Dean was released by his Communist captors, a newsman asked him what most upheld him during those three years of misery. "I never felt sorry for myself," replied the General, "and that's what licked it. Self-pity whips more people than anything else." — Erich Brandeis, King Features

Stay Put, Young Man! By Arthur Gordon

Condensed from The Rotarian

WHEN I was a young fellow raring to go places, I didn't hesitate—
I went. I left the town that had produced me and several generations of ancestors. I headed straight for the biggest city that I
could find.

The bigger the city, I reasoned happily, the bigger the opportunities.
My native state was run-down, decrepit, half-paralyzed with poverty.
I was energetic, ambitious and no doubt quite insufferable. I was sure
I could twist a couple of skyscrapers around my little finger. So off I
went.

But now, years later, the uneasy feeling is creeping over me that
maybe I made a gigantic mistake.

The first inkling came when I went home about a year ago. I had
been back on short trips, but this time I really looked around. I was
astounded by what I saw. The apathy and inertia were gone. Towns
that had been stagnant pools of unemployment were humming with
new industries. Shiny new tractors combed the red earth. The bank-
failure rate was the lowest in the nation.

Clearly, while I had been chasing my gilded rainbows, prosperity
had come to the area I had so blithely left. More significant, I found
myself feeling that I had missed out on something spiritually im-

portant. The people at home had something that I had not. You could see it in their faces. Comparing them with those who had uprooted themselves, as I had, to go east or west or north or wherever opportunity seemed to beckon, I found that in almost no case could I point to an individual who was better adjusted or basically happier because he had moved away.

It was a disturbing discovery—so disturbing that I began to talk to people about it. And what I learned from these conversations adds up to the conclusion that the average American is happier and more successful if he digs in and does a lifetime job right in his own back yard.

This seems like a startling notion for a frontier-minded people. But the frontier is no longer a receding line in the wilderness; it's in the average American town. That is where the best opportunities exist. Not for making money, necessarily. For making contributions to life itself.

That, I'm afraid, is a distinction I failed utterly to grasp when I had completed my so-called education. Success to me meant money, and job prestige, and maybe even fame—and I still think those are pleasant properties to own. But the lasting satisfactions seem to come from other sources.

I'll give you a simple example. I know a man in Manhattan who writes a $2000 check every year for the Greater New York Fund. I also know a doctor in a tiny town near Atlanta who donated eight acres of land for a children's playground. The first gentleman, no doubt, gets a momentary glow of satisfaction from his generosity. But the doctor, whose gift has much less dollar value, will go on drawing spiritual dividends from it the rest of his life. He can *see* it. It's *there*.

It was this kind of satisfaction that I could discern—and envy—in the lives of my contemporaries who had had the good sense, or the good luck, to stay put. They would be the last to think of themselves as pioneers, but that's what they are. They don't have to battle Indians or wolves, but poverty, disease, ignorance, prejudice, all these old enemies of mankind are still with us. They can only be attacked locally, and the best attackers are those who are literally at home in their environment.

There are sound psychological reasons why this should be so. Every industrialist knows that happy people are the most productive people. Happy people, by and large, are those who are adjusted to their surroundings. Insecure people, on the other hand, have little time or energy to spend helping others; they are too busy trying to find help for themselves. And nothing fosters a sense of insecurity like being an outsider.

"I left home," said a girl who works in a New York bank, "because I was convinced that no real opportunities existed there. I wasn't going to be just another stick-in-the-mud—not me! So what did I gain? The doubtful pleasure of being an almost invisible frog in a tremendous puddle. And what did I lose? A lot of intangibles that were far more important than I thought. At home, people were really interested in what I did, in what happened to me. Here—let's face it —nobody gives a damn. I'm independent, sure. But sometimes independence is just a fancy name for loneliness."

A man who had moved his family away for a time, then moved back, said: "Oh, people were nice to us, friendly enough. But we always felt like outsiders. We *were* outsiders! So we were always knocking ourselves out trying to prove that we were acceptable.

"Here"—he swept his arm in an affectionate semicircle—"we don't have to prove anything to anybody. Friends are real friends because— well, friendship is largely shared experience, isn't it? We've been sharing experience with these people ever since we could walk.

"My wife and I are willing to get out and work for this town the way our parents did because it's *ours*. It's better for the kids, too. They have a standard of decency to live up to—do you know what I'm talking about?"

I knew what he was talking about, all right. He was talking about roots. It's an American custom, and probably a good one, to discourage ancestor worship. But the sense of obligation that comes from a family tradition of community service and good citizenship is something worth keeping and passing on.

"We were lucky," he added thoughtfully. "We came back in time. If you wait too long, you pass the point of no return. That's the point where you become a stranger in your own home town."

Some people, I found, had moved successfully. One was an executive solidly established in a big Pennsylvania manufacturing city. "We're all right," he said. "At least, we're all right now. But it took us years to feel that we belonged here. I made money, sure, but sometimes I think I'd have made it just as fast at home.

"The point is this: When you migrate to a place, it's invariably to see what you can get out of it. You don't think in terms of what you can put in—not until you've been there a long, long time. Some people never do learn to think that way. And yet"—he looked pensively out the window—"it's the secret of successful living in any community."

Others had put down new roots with less conscious effort. For some, the specialized careers they wanted simply did not exist at home. For others, family difficulties or emotional problems existed that made them happier elsewhere. As for those who had stayed at home, I didn't find any who regretted it.

"I'll tell you what we have that you don't," said one of them with a grin. "We have local pride."

I recalled the conversation I had had with another of the stay-at-homes, the vice-president of a power company. We were talking about the spectacular improvements I had noticed throughout the state.

"Well," he said, "we had to do something. Too many of our young people were leaving the way you did. So we decided to pull up our socks, make our towns clean and attractive, persuade industry to settle here—and incidentally use our electricity!

"We did it by reminding people that their home town was the most important place on earth—to them. We worked like the dickens, and it was a lot of fun. And it paid off! The youngsters aren't leaving home much any more. In fact, the smart ones are coming back."

The smart ones are coming back. They are the ones, no doubt, who have learned ruefully that distant pastures are not always so green as they look, that the brighter financial prospects, if any, are not worth the emotional strain, social dislocation and diminished opportunities for service that breaking new ground usually entails.

But what about the young people—and there are still many, I'm sure—who feel cramped at home, who yearn to plant their flags along new frontiers?

To them I can only say, somewhat wryly, that I had the same decision to make, and I'm pretty sure now that I made the wrong one.

The real opportunities then were precisely, in my case, the poverty and apathy and wasted human resources that I was running away from. I really owed it to myself to stay and help mend fences which needed mending. I could not see this at 19, but I can see it at 39, and I would like to pass it along for what it may be worth.

Think it over, you young people. If you have your hearts set on conducting a symphony orchestra or discovering a cure for cancer, you will have to go where the opportunities exist, of course. But if you simply want to be a good doctor, lawyer, merchant or fire chief, chances are you'll function best in the surroundings you know best, where you know and like the people, and they know and like you.

In short, stay where you've got some roots. For through those roots will come the strength to do a good job in the best of all possible surroundings for you—your own home town.

And No Popcorn

M ULLING over the timeworn excuses people give for not going to church, the Rev. Grant H. Elford of Lake Crystal, Minn., and Dr. Ronald Meredith of Fresno, Calif., on a trip together, compiled this list of reasons "Why I Do Not Attend the Movies":

1. The manager of the theater never called on me.

2. I did go a few times, but no one spoke to me. Those who go there aren't very friendly.

3. Every time I go they ask me for money.

4. Not all folks live up to the high moral standards of the films.

5. I went so much as a child, I've decided I've had all the entertainment I need.

6. The performance lasts too long; I can't sit still for an hour and three quarters.

7. I don't always agree with what I hear and see.

8. I don't think they have very good music.

9. The shows are held in the evenings, and that's the only time I am able to be at home with the family.   *—Newsweek*

ARE YOU ACCIDENT-PRONE?

By Lawrence Galton

Condensed from Nation's Business

OR YEARS it has been said that industrial accidents can be prevented, that all you need are such devices as nonskid floors, guards on the machines, caution signs on the walls. It sounds good—until you run up against Mary Jones.

In five years at a big New Jersey factory, Mary averaged 16 accidents a year. Other workers doing the same job had no trouble. Finally she became the subject of an intensive investigation. Turned out that Mary, quick-tempered herself, was the daughter of an equally hotheaded father. The two clashed frequently.

When the management convinced her that the cause of her accidents might be emotional instability due to her home life, Mary took a drastic step. She moved into an apartment of her own—and hasn't had an accident since.

Several years ago young Bill King worked for a large railroad. No matter what job he held, his accident record was alarming; it culminated in the loss of an eye. There wasn't a thing physically wrong with Bill. But he had one incessant worry. When he married, Bill had borrowed $100 from a loan shark. Although more than the hundred had been paid back, another hundred had mounted in interest. He just couldn't seem to get clear.

After a company lawyer talked forcefully to the loan shark, the obligation was canceled. Bill hasn't had an accident since.

Both Mary Jones and Bill King were emotionally sick—sick enough to cause accidents, even if not sick enough to visit a doctor. In recent years many such cases have been discovered. Here is a basic cause of the accidents which annually kill 17,500 workers and injure 1,800,000.

Worry is a prolific source of occupational injuries. "No worker," declared Dr. Lydia G. Giberson, industrial psychiatrist, "ceases to be parent, or lover, or dreamer, or hater merely because he dons overalls. There is more connection between the size of a grocer's bill and a broken leg than the average industrialist realizes." A death in the family, a broken engagement, or a fire at home may temporarily daze a man. Hence it's often better for an employe not to have to carry on his job for a few days while suffering from such shocks.

Evidence that certain people are overly susceptible to accidents started accumulating at least as far back as 1929 when a large mid-western railway company discovered that 30 percent of its employes had been involved in 44 percent of all accidents reported.

Some years ago four large utility companies, trying to reduce accidents, could find nothing to explain why certain of their truck drivers had repeated mishaps. Finally the men with heavy accident records were shifted to other work: immediately truck accidents were sizably reduced. But the shifted drivers all went through a series of accidents at their new jobs.

Recently a large financial institution put on a safety drive in its office. A list was made of the 100 people who had had the most accidents. Many of them had had at least three accidents within a year; some had had more than five. The list was then sent to the consulting psychiatrist. Every person on the list was known to the psychiatrist because of emotional upset.

To detect accident-proneness, more careful entrance interviewing is needed. "Employment interviewers," said William H. Hollis, of New York University's Center for Safety Education, "ought to be trained to recognize obvious personality difficulties."

Study of near-accident records may also reveal the accident-prone individual who tends to have many minor injuries, before he has the costly major one. He can then be put in a nonhazardous position.

When a young woman worker kept reporting minor injuries to the medical department of an electrical manufacturing plant, she was found to be suffering from rheumatism, bad eyes and extreme nervousness. The girl was placed in a position offering little hazard and periodically given special safety instructons. So far she's done well.

Better training of supervisors would pay off. Personal worries such as financial problems have a way of lessening considerably after they're talked over with a sympathetic supervisor who can at least lend moral support and who may be able to offer clearheaded advice.

However, one of the most important single aids in the accident-prone situation is employment of a competent psychiatrist to help employes solve emotional problems. After one plant had checked its records and found that a few people in one department were having an undue number of accidents, the company psychiatrist discovered that the basic cause lay in a maladjusted supervisor who provoked nervousness. The psychiatrist's work with the supervisor soon halted the accidents.

When the case of one young woman with a record of many minor accidents was studied, it was found that she had had an undue number of injuries all her life. As a child at home, whenever she hurt herself she had received sympathetic attention, and she continued to have accidents because unconsciously she still believed that was the best way to achieve sympathy. When the psychiatrist pointed out these facts, the girl was astounded—but finally convinced. Soon she was as free of accidents as any other employe.

Recognition of the accident-prone problem is growing rapidly among large corporations. When it is solved, there will be benefits not only of reduced accidents in industry but also off the job, for more workers are killed and injured every year by accidents at home, on the street and elsewhere than at work.

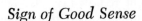

Sign of Good Sense

WHILE touring through New Mexico I stopped at a gas station long enough to step into the ladies' rest room. I was delighted to find it immaculately clean and neat. Then I noticed the sign tacked above the wash basin: "Have you an imagination? Won't you please pretend this is the bathroom in your own home and your mother-in-law is coming for a visit?"   —Contributed by Mrs. E. F. Guingona

Get in There and Paint!

By
Joseph Alger

Condensed from Recreation

"To HAVE reached the age of 40 without ever handling a brush or fiddling with a pencil, and then suddenly to find oneself plunged in the middle of a new and intense form of interest and action with paints and palettes and canvases, and not to be discouraged by results, is an astonishing and enriching experience. I hope it may be shared by others."

Thus wrote Winston Churchill, many years ago. He became so enthusiastic an amateur that he even took his brushes to Casablanca and after that historic conference stole a day to go painting.

Mr. Churchill wasn't talking through his cigar! Painting pictures is fun. You can do it. Anybody can do it. And if you mistake this for one of those now-even-*you*-can-play-the-saxophone claims, you will ban yourself from a hobby that guarantees huge dividends in ecstasy. It is the only hobby that is wholly insulated against the intrusion of worry. It is an authentic passport to delightful new powers of observation by which you will really appreciate for the first time everything from the

Taj Mahal to a tin cup. And the pictures you paint will always remain heartening reminders of the happiest moments of your life.

The best thing about painting as a hobby is that it is so easy. You don't have to be able to draw. *Painting in oils is the easiest form of art.*

"What about water colors?" you ask.

Glad you brought that up. It leads us to a very important point: water colors must go!

We give children little tin water-color boxes because water colors are cheaper than oils and (most important) they are far more tidy. The picture of a six-year-old set loose with a palette of oils is a horrible one. But those little tin boxes have done more to stifle interest in painting than the competition of all other hobbies combined.

Water colors in amateur hands are feeble things, pale imitations of the bright glories of nature. And hard to handle: they run, they streak, they blur. You paint in the sky and quickly realize it is much too dark. Too late! You can't correct it. So no matter how much you like the experts' water colors, avoid trying to make your own.

Let's get some oils and start painting. You will find people in artists'-supplies stores friendly and helpful, and quite used to beginners and their questions. You can get all the materials you'll need for less than $10. Probably you would feel self-conscious in a smock, but do wear old clothes and have plenty of rags at hand. A blob of vermilion doesn't look so good on a new gray suit.

Remember, you don't have to draw to paint. The effect of a painting is produced largely by color; all you need are a few lines to indicate general shape.

You're going to paint that picturesque old barn. All right. One vertical line (better use charcoal) will place the corner of the barn, another line the base. A couple of lines for the trunk of the tree and maybe a branch or two. Then a line for the horizon. That's all! No leaves, doorknobs, cats, mice or daffodils. It's the painting that's fun, and any time wasted on a mess of little details is to be deplored.

The great moment is upon you. Soon you will reach that ecstatic state of self-confidence which takes advice from nobody. So before it's too late, one word: Plaster it on! These are no flimsy, treacherous water colors. These are lusty, pliable, coöperative oils. There is nothing you can do that cannot be undone at the next stroke of the brush. One other thing. Keep everything big! If it's too small for a good-sized brush it shouldn't be in the picture.

Now squeeze out little blobs of color on your palette, and a big blob of white. Take a look at that sky. It is, let us say, cloudless. And it really is blue. Still not as blue as Uncle Ed's shirt. Take a half of a butter ball of white on your palette knife and plaster it on the front of your palette. Careful now! Just a pinch of blue and mix with the white until there are no streaks. Not blue enough? All right, just a tiny bit more. Satisfied? Dip your brush in the turpentine, then in the paint and slap it on! Boldly—never mind if you slop over the barn a bit.

The barn is red: vermilion and white seem to mix the right tone for the sunny side. A very little black and blue darken it for the shady side. The grass in direct sunlight is golden green—yellow with a little blue and some white. In the shade it's a deeper green, so we add a lot of blue.

By now you have painted over some of the trunk of the tree. But don't let that worry you. Corrections are a cinch and a joy in oil painting. You just scrape your mistakes off with the palette knife, wipe with the rag. Or you can let the whole thing dry (it takes one to three days) and paint right over what you've done.

Back off now, five or six paces, and take a look. Begins to shape up like something, doesn't it? And yet this is your very first try! You're on your own, from now on. Squint, make up your mind what color you see, and experiment until you get it. As you paint, forget all the traditional color associations, such as "roses are red." That distant hill is purple now, but two hours ago it was a bright light green, and it may be brown or blue soon. Paint what you see *at the moment.*

After the barn, what else shall we paint? Something outdoors on a sunny day is perhaps the easiest. But if it's a gloomy or cold day, and you want to paint in the house, try a still life. The still life is the show-off of the professionals. It proves that they can take humdrum subjects and do fine painting for painting's sake. But it's great sport for amateurs. So group your pipe, bottle, book and orange to please your own taste and paint away. Again, keep it big. Make your objects fill up most of the canvas. You will also enjoy doing the corner of a room with a chair, a table and a lamp. And you will get happier results if

Aunt Susan is not sitting in the chair. Portraits are for professionals.

Snow is a painting pushover, a sure-fire subject for the amateur. Snow, as advertised, is white. Water is whatever color it reflects, and sky is or is not blue, as happens. But snow is right there in your tube of white. Sometimes it will catch glints of yellow or pink, and its shadows are blue, not black. Still, snow is white, and a great comfort. Snowdrifts, a red barn, the bare limbs of an apple tree, a cold blue sky —there's a picture. Corny? Sure—so what?

The painter is master of all he surveys. If you think your picture would be more interesting with that tree moved over beyond the shed, put it there, and apologize to nobody. If there is a dull and complicated wheelbarrow in front of you, ignore it. Omission is no sin in painting, it is the road to good results. What you want is a picture, not a real-estate chart.

You will learn that many "pretty" things are not especially good for painting. Flowers, for example. Their bright colors are bait, but their delicate and demanding details are pitfalls. A few blobs of red, showing poppies in a field—that's one thing; but a spray of gladioli is quite another. And skip sunsets. They have been the inspiration for more bad pictures than any other subject.

Ugliness, curiously, is often turned to beauty in painting. Try a picture sometime when you happen on a parched field with decayed tree stumps and a tumble-down shack. Or see what happens when you paint such a mundane object as a filling station or a railroad depot.

Notice how your interest in everything around you picks up after you take up oil painting. You will be delighted to find that you have gained another sense, the sense of observation as contrasted with mere sight. Brambles on the beach take on remarkable beauty as they bow to the wind. Giant squashes posing majestically under the panoply of their elephantine leaves assume an intricate grace. Your piano, which you have seen 50 times a day since you made the first down payment, suddenly has a stately beauty.

Your newly acquired sense will make you conscious, too, of the discords of sight. You will become aware that many things in the house are ill-proportioned, many colors sickly and vulgar. For painting raises the curtain on a new world full of beautiful and comical and ugly and breath-taking sights.

You will feel a new fellowship with artists. You admire the way Corot does foliage, and feel he would give you a pat on the back for the way you handled that picket fence. You begin to refer to artists as "We"—and that does more for your soul than a free trip to Paris. The fact that professional artists have no profound respect for amateurs should cause you no discomfort at all.

You can find triumphant solace in the large number of your fellow amateurs. The country is riddled with painters, although usually you discover them only through some chance remark. You may hear of one of the many painting clubs, such as the Chicago doctors' or the self-deprecatory Awful Arts Club in New York, which have been daubing away happily for years.

One of the pleasures of painting lies in the memories your picture collection evokes. The still life of oranges and guitar brings back a rainy afternoon when several friends dropped in, and you gave them all paints and brushes to try their hands.

That picture of the small side-street house brings back a smile. All the morning you had been painting it in the comfortable tall grass and spring shade. A boy came whistling home from school, and, of course, stopped to inspect. After fully five minutes of silent observation he exclaimed, "Why, that's *my* house!" Such inevitable insults are more than atoned for by words of praise. One "Gee, I wish I could paint!" is worth a dozen art-school diplomas. You may even get "Gee, I wish I could paint like that!" which is a sort of Phi Beta Kappa award.

So go and get paints and a handful of brushes, palette and canvas and easel. Or use a makeshift palette and one brush and no easel at all. The thing is: Get in there and paint!

≫ ≫ ≪ ≪

DAVID SARNOFF, reminiscing about his early years in the radio industry, mentioned the strong competition he had had to face. "But I'm grateful to my enemies," he said. "In the long-range movement toward progress, a kick in the pants sends you further along than a friendly handshake."   —Leonard Lyons

If you want the world to take stock in you —

Don't Sell Yourself Short

By Gelett Burgess

Condensed from Ladies' Home Journal

A T A PARTY I was much attracted to a pretty girl with a charming personality. A fellow I know — doing publicity for a big diamond firm — sauntered up to her, spoke of her graceful posture and told her she was pretty. After a while he said he'd like to use her as a model for photographs to advertise some jewels. She could pose with a half-million dollars' worth of necklaces and bracelets, he said.

She laughed and said she'd love to. "But my hands are awful," she added, and sprawled them out to him, with her fingers wide apart.

Up to that moment I hadn't noticed her hands — which were a bit red and rather large. But after that uncalled-for remark I almost forgot her hair, that I had thought so fetching, and her lovely violet eyes and engaging smile. And as we went on talking I saw nothing but hands. She seemed to have so many hands. . . .

I don't say that you ought to wave flags and ring bells in an attempt to advertise your own excellence and importance. There are enough boasters, heaven knows. But if you're too modest to throw bouquets at yourself, must you throw brickbats? Why call attention to your deficiencies?

Let me tell you of a wise and a foolish virgin I met at that same party.

One of them, Alice, pulled off one of her earrings and showed it to her friend. "Pretty, aren't they?" she asked. "And just think, Eloise, I got them at a ten-cent store. Oh, they're not so nice as yours, I know. But then of course yours are expensive."

Eloise the wise virgin smiled and said nothing. But she also, I happened to know, was wearing inexpensive earrings.

You think she should have told her friend? Why? It was nobody's affair but her own where she got her things. It would have been dishonest to lie about the matter if she had been asked, but she wasn't asked. She didn't have much money but did have excellent taste. Why shouldn't she benefit by her superior judgment and allow people to think what they pleased?

What was the result of Alice's indiscretion? Well, as I was leaving the party I heard one lady say to another, "No, not the dark girl with Harry—I mean the one with the ten-cent earrings."

This incident illustrates the almost inevitable effect on hearers of any self-dispraise. When you open that personal door of familiarity, those who rush in can often be very disagreeable.

To illustrate how ill-advised most self-disparagement is, just imagine that those slurring remarks are made by someone else. You say, perhaps, "Oh, I don't care how I put on my hat. I'm too old now. Nobody notices me any more." But suppose some personal demon followed you about saying, "Oh, shove it on any which way, old gal. You're far too old to bother about your looks." How would you like it? Isn't it just as bad when you say it yourself?

If you spotlight the bad feature, all the good ones are apt to fall into a shadow. If that woman had kept her pretty mouth shut about her wrinkles and long nose and paid more attention to her dress and deportment, if she had been careful of her posture and cultivated her voice, she might easily have acquired a name for having style—and style is a kind of beauty accessible to all.

Many people make themselves unmagnetic—if not actively disliked —by always making a play for sympathy. Your mother or your sweetheart may care, but to everyone else the recital of your troubles and illnesses is usually a bore.

If, when you try to account for not looking well, you say, "I didn't shut my eyes all night; I must look awful," you've just injured yourself uselessly. Nobody is interested in the reason you're seedy, and nobody believes you anyway. If you exerted yourself to be animated and charming, if you complimented others and thought of something kind to do or interesting to say, perhaps they wouldn't notice your haggard face.

Why do so many people voluntarily disparage themselves, and reveal failings and deficiencies better left untold? For several reasons, perhaps—all mistaken. Some say, "I'm afraid this dress is awful," merely in hopes that you may say, "Why no, Ida, I think it's very pretty, and most becoming." They are merely fishing for compliments. With some it's a sort of chronic self-pity. Saying things like "I'm broke —I don't see how I'll make out till payday," or "My husband made a terrible fuss about the household bills today," reveals a definite inferiority complex.

But most of these voluntary confessions are due to simple thoughtlessness, or an inordinate tendency to talk. For when one talks too much, you know, one is apt to talk of oneself. Some people indulge an irresistible urge, upon meeting a friend—any friend at all, a stranger, even—to pour out a sort of oral diary, telling everything that has happened to them and everything that is in their minds. And it is in the midst of such uncontrolled chatter that these little derogatory confessions slip out.

Quite apart from the practical benefits in guarding against self-depreciation, a discreet repression improves your morale. Just as a boiler that has no outlet compresses the steam and makes it more powerful, so a certain amount of reticence gives you more power. It lifts you to a higher plane of self-respect. The boy who is deformed and doesn't complain or mention it; the girl who is handicapped in beauty and is silent about it, and seeks to excel in other lines; the woman who suffers pain and never betrays it; the man who is disappointed and carries on with a smile—all are acting with a more effective mental and moral force than the one who lets his tongue wag over his troubles. They are building character; they are making themselves more valuable; they are growing in power, in wisdom and in influence.

Stories of the fortitude of actors under suffering and misfortune are classic—and mostly true. When the curtain is up, private trials must be forgotten.

I once called on a well-known star who was suffering from such an excruciating attack of arthritis that he had to remain in his dressing room at the theater night and day for almost a month. But not only did he go onto the stage at every performance and act his part so well that no one in the audience suspected his agony—that was nerve—but he positively forbade every member of his company to speak about his condition—that was intelligence.

"The show must go on!" That's the rule of the theater: it should be the rule in life as well. We, too, owe it to our friends to play our parts without apologies.

A World of Challenge

DURING a discussion of "The World We Want" at the New York Herald Tribune Youth Forum, Johnny B. Antillon, 18-year-old delegate from the Philippines, made the following contribution:

"Usually, when I discuss with people the kind of world we want, they astonish me by describing a Utopia without cares. As for me, I like this world we have. I like living in this century—so full of strivings and plans that I feel part of a wonderful and exciting experiment. I like the suspense which gives to life its only true zest. Let me have this world, with dreams for me to dream and problems for me to solve.

"If I had lived before the A- and H-bombs I might be less optimistic of the future. But today I have great hope that we shall enjoy peace, for I feel deeply that no nation will start a war which none can possibly survive.

"I believe that this world we have deserves a vote of confidence. With its dirt and cleanness, its ups and downs and its total unexpectedness, it has given, through variety, more pleasure than pain. Whatever else it may be, this particular century is still the broadest, the most exciting, the most promising of all.

"May this world always be as challenging as it is. May it always have something to be solved, patched or mended. But above all, may this world never be a soft place for soft people with soft heads. For I want a world where a man, by facing his troubles, can prove his manhood. With a world of such challenge and scope, our lives will never be complacent, but they will certainly be worth living."

A plan to relieve you of the drudgery of an uncongenial job

How to Avoid Work

By William J. Reilly, Ph.D.
Career Consultant

Condensed from The American Magazine

Is YOUR job work or fun? If it is work, you would probably be wise to get out of it before another month ends. Work is doing something you don't enjoy doing. Your life is too short and too valuable to fritter away on a job that bores you, or forces you to be with people you don't like, or calls for a knack you haven't got.

Yet all my studies indicate that a majority of Americans are dissatisfied with their jobs and wish they were doing something else. I see accountants who wish they were teachers or explorers, and salesmen who wish they were cabinetmakers. I recently talked with the son of a wealthy lawyer who was grimly studying law. He said: "Oh, I'll plow through these courses somehow." Deep in his heart he wanted to be a geologist.

A person in a job he dislikes reacts by being moody and nervous. He becomes tired easily and is a victim of indigestion and insomnia. As he continues to feel frustrated he becomes rebellious, grows sour on the world.

Recently I counseled a young newspaperman who had been advised to go into newspaper work because he had definite writing abilities. He hated his work. Noncompetitive by nature, he moved at a slow tempo. The newspaper pace distressed him. He had always yearned to teach.

I persuaded him to take a teaching job in a boys' school and he is now writing in his leisure hours. For the first time in his life he feels whole and adequate.

Often it is not necessary to change to a completely new line of activity. Some months ago I counseled the business manager of a manufacturing firm who was approaching a nervous collapse. Our diagnosis was that in his present business he was dealing with *things,* whereas his yearnings were to deal with *people.* My recommendation was that he stay in the field of business management but find a job where he could more directly serve people. A month later he wrote that he had become business manager of a hospital.

In many cases it may be impracticable to make an abrupt change of jobs. But it is always possible to test your desire out first by studying and experimenting in another field during your spare time. Then draw up a plan whereby you can shift the emphasis from one career to the other over a period of time. When Herbert Hoover decided he wanted to become an engineer, he took a job as a typist so that he could work somehow in an engineering firm.

The main thing is to stick to the plan. When you start making excuses for postponing action you are doomed to stay where you are. I've heard a thousand people make such excuses. It is always one of these:

"I don't have the money." Some time ago I talked with a man nearly 50 who was hunched over a draftsman's board. He mentioned he had wanted to paint landscapes ever since he was in high school. "May I see some of your work?" I asked. "Oh, I've never painted," he replied. "I've never had the money to support myself while painting."

"I don't have the time." A gas-station attendant who wanted to be an accountant told me he had been forced to give up a correspondence course in accounting because he didn't have the time. But in the past week he had bowled, gone to the movies, played poker, and spent two hours at a bar.

"My family won't let me." Frequently wives try to restrain a husband from any "rash" change that would make undue demands on his time, involve low pay, or not add to the social prestige of the family. But most wives can be won over if the husbands are persistent and explain how much the proposed change means to them.

I know a man, 38, who became bored with his work as a factory foreman. He decided he wanted to be a country doctor, back in the Kansas village where he had spent his youth. Today he works as a garage mechanic at night and is studying medicine by day. This man is no longer bored. He's learning the feeling of achievement.

I have found that three factors are paramount in deciding your success in any job:

Your ability to do the job. Your capacity for getting along well with the people you work with. Your actual desire to do the job.

Of the three, ability is normally the least important and desire is overwhelmingly the most important in determining your success. One large corporation that began considering the actual desires of its salesmen, along with the other two factors, cut its turnover of salesmen in half. And in a factory where two thirds of its line workers had been quitting or washing out every year, the turnover was likewise cut in half.

Thomas Edison worked out a simple plan for discovering the interests of new employes. He sent beginners around the laboratories and shops on tours of inspection. Each day they were to make reports, with suggestions and criticisms. One lad who had majored in chemistry in college had applied for a chemist's job. His reports, however, showed no constructive suggestions in that field, but many on production and layout. Obviously, these subjects were closer to his real interests, and he was assigned to production.

A few corporations expose new employes to a variety of jobs for the first few weeks and then ask them which they like best. I believe this is a shrewd investment; yet industry almost universally ignores the desire factor in hiring men.

Millions of people are held back by their failure at the human-relations level. If you are continually in conflict with associates your job is work of the worst sort. But when a person is careful about his human relations, almost any job is a pleasure. Lord Chesterfield revealed one clue for getting on congenially with others when he wrote his son: "Make other people like themselves a little better, my son, and I promise you they will like you very well."

Any job can also be made more interesting if you seek ways to improve upon what you are doing. Look for some phase of it that challenges your ingenuity.

However, the best way to achieve true happiness is to express yourself with all your skill and enthusiasm in a career that appeals to you more than any other. In such a career you feel a sense of purpose, a sense of achievement. It is not work. A doctor who has felt the pulse of life does not feel he is working when he must leave a party to deliver a baby.

Altogether too much emphasis has been placed on what we ought to do rather than what we want to do. Amelia Earhart once wrote: "I flew the Atlantic because I wanted to. If that be what they call 'a woman's reason,' make the most of it. It isn't, I think, a reason to be apologized for by man or woman.

"Whether you are flying the Atlantic or selling sausages or building a skyscraper or driving a truck, your greatest power comes from the fact that you want tremendously to do that very thing, and do it well."

The Tie That Binds

Waiting for the pediatrician to give my husky three their tetanus shots, I was attracted by the shy smile of a tiny girl with a crutch beside her chair. "I'm going to walk pretty soon," she confided. "The doctor just promised me!"

The door of the inner office opened and her mother came out leading a little boy whose arm was shriveled.

I was shocked. "The mother of those two has a really hard row to hoe," I said to the doctor when they had gone.

"She's one of the happiest people I know," he replied. "Interesting thing. She had a sorry childhood—her father in a mental hospital, her mother obsessed by the fear that his illness would be transmitted to the daughter. She met her husband on a train as she was going to visit her dad. His mother was a patient there, too. Later, when they wanted to be married, they came to me. I told them what I knew— darned little—and they decided to go ahead but never to have children. However, they asked me to help them adopt a baby—'Not a picture-book one, guaranteed perfect, but one with the cards stacked against it.'

"So I found Pete for them. A fine lad. When he was four, they found Meg. And they're going to have another child soon."

I stared at him. "You mean—?"

"As soon as Meg is walking, a kid who's been battling rheumatic fever all his life is joining them. They're raising the finest family in my whole practice."   —Contributed by Mrs. William Wallace

A LITTLE AT A TIME

By John Erskine

I MUST have been about 14 then, and I dismissed the incident with the easy carelessness of youth. But the words Carl Walter spoke that day came back to me years later, and ever since have been of inestimable value to me.

Carl Walter was my piano teacher. During one of my lessons he asked how much practicing I was doing. I said three or four hours a day.

"Do you practice in long stretches, an hour at a time?"

"I try to."

"Well, don't!" he exclaimed. "When you grow up, time won't come in long stretches. Practice in minutes, whenever you can find them — five or ten before school, after lunch, between chores. Spread the practice through the day, and piano-playing will become a part of your life."

WHEN I was teaching at Columbia, I wanted to write, but recitations, theme-reading and committee meetings filled my days and evenings. For two years I got practically nothing down on paper, and my excuse was that I had no time. Then I recalled what Carl Walter had said.

During the next week I conducted an experiment. Whenever I had five unoccupied minutes, I sat down and wrote a hundred words or so. To my astonishment, at the end of the week I had a sizable manuscript ready for revision.

Later on I wrote novels by the same piecemeal method. Though my teaching schedule had become heavier than ever, in every day there were idle moments which could be caught and put to use. I even took up piano-playing again, finding that the small intervals of the day provided sufficient time for both writing and piano practice.

There is an important trick in this time-using formula: you must get into your work quickly. If you have but five minutes for writing, you can't afford to waste four chewing your pencil. You must make your mental preparations beforehand, and concentrate on your task almost instantly when the time comes. Fortunately, rapid concentration is easier than most of us realize.

I confess I have never learned how to let go easily at the end of the five or ten minutes. But life can be counted on to supply interruptions. Carl Walter has had a tremendous influence on my life. To him I owe the discovery that even very short periods of time add up to all the useful hours I need, if I plunge in without delay.

Mortified Mothers

A MOTHER I know had spent the whole summer in the company of her children, thinking only of their needs. On her return in the fall she went for the first time in months to an adult dinner party. To her horror she discovered that, to start conversation with the distinguished man next to her, she said automatically: "I bet I can finish my soup sooner than you can." —John Mason Brown in *McCall's*

As THE middle-aged mother of a 13-year-old daughter, I should have known better. But the girls seemed to be having such a wonderful time riding the waves on their surfboards that I decided to try. However, I caught the breaker too late, and was swept to the bottom and turned over and over. I struggled to my feet, glad to find that the water came only to my waist. But I found that my suit had slipped to an indecent low and was bunched around my middle. I hastily adjusted it, hoping that no one on the beach had seen me. But as I came out of the water my daughter greeted me: "Mother, if you're going to make a spectacle of yourself, you could at least wear lipstick!" —Contributed by Jane Christenson

Suburbia: Of Thee I Sing

By Phyllis McGinley   *Condensed from Harper's Magazine*

TWENTY MILES east of New York City as the New Haven Railroad flies sits a village I shall call Spruce Manor. It is a commuters' town, and the epitome of Suburbia. By day, with the children pent in schools, it is a village of women. They trundle baskets at the A & P, they sit under driers at the hairdressers', they sweep their porches and set out bulbs and stitch up slip covers.

On one side of Main Street are the grocery stores and the drugstores and the Village Spa where teen-agers gather of an afternoon to drink their Cokes and speak their curious confidences. There one finds the shoe repairers and the drycleaners and the secondhand stores which sell "antiques," and the stationery stores which dispense comic books to ten-year-olds and greeting cards and lending-library masterpieces to their mothers. On the opposite side stand the bank, the firehouse, the public library.

Spruce Manor in the spring and summer and fall is a pretty town full of gardens and old elms. In the winter the houses reveal themselves as comfortable, well kept, architecturally insignificant. The population is perhaps four or five thousand. No one is very poor here and not many families are rich enough to be awesome. There is not much to distinguish Spruce Manor from any other of a thousand suburbs outside of New York City or San Francisco or Detroit or Chicago, or even Stockholm for that matter.

But, for some reason, Spruce Manor has become a sort of symbol to writers, a symbol of all that is middle-class in the worst sense, of smug and prosperous mediocrity. I have yet to read a book in which the suburban life was pictured as the good life or the commuter as a sympathetic figure. He is a stock character: the man who "spends his life riding to and from his wife," the eternal Babbitt whose sanctuary is the club locker room, whose ideas spring ready-made from the illiberal newspapers. His wife plays politics at the PTA and keeps up with the Joneses. Or—if the scene is more gilded—the commuter is the high-powered advertising executive with a station wagon and an eye for the ladies, his wife a restless baggage given to too many afternoon cocktails.

These clichés I challenge. I have lived in the country, I have lived in the city. I have lived in a middle-western small town. But for the best 11 years of my life I have lived in Suburbia and I like it.

We came here from an expensive, inconvenient, moderately fashionable tenement in Manhattan. Our friends were aghast that we could find anything appealing in a middle-class house on a middle-class street in a middle-class village full of middle-class people. To this day they cannot understand us. You see, they read the books. They even write them.

As for being middle-class, what is wrong with acknowledging one's roots? And how free we are! Free of the city's noise, of its ubiquitous doormen, of the soot on the window sill and the radio in the next apartment. We have released ourselves from the seasonal hegira to the mountains or the seashore. We have only one address, one house to keep. I do not insist that we are typical. There is nothing really typical about any of our friends and neighbors here, and therein lies my point.

We could not keep up with the Joneses even if we wanted to, for we know many Joneses and they are all quite different people. The Albert Joneses spend their week-ends sailing, the Bertram Joneses cultivate their delphinium, the Clarence Joneses are enthusiastic about amateur chamber music. The David Joneses dote on bridge but the Ernest Joneses prefer staying home of an evening so that Ernest can carve his witty caricatures out of pieces of old fruit wood. We admire each other's gardens but we are too busy to compete. So long as our clapboards are painted and our hedges decently trimmed, we have fulfilled our community obligations.

On our half acre we can raise enough tomatoes and assassinate enough beetles to satisfy the gardening urge. Or we can put the whole place to lawn. We can have privacy and shade and the changing of the seasons and also the Joneses next door from whom to borrow a cup of sugar or a stepladder. Few of us expect to be wealthy or world-famous or divorced. What we do expect is to pay off the mortgage and send healthy children to good colleges.

For when I refer to life here, I think, of course, of living with children. The adjacent waters of Long Island Sound are full of them in summer, gamboling like dolphins. The lanes are alive with them, the yards overflow with them, they possess the tennis courts and the skating pond and the vacant lots. Their roller skates wear down the asphalt and their bicycles make necessary the 25-mile speed limit. They converse interminably on the telephones and make rich the dentist and the pediatrician.

Spruce Manor seems designed for the happiness of children. Better designed than the city; better, I say defiantly, than the country. Country mothers must be constantly arranging and contriving for their children's leisure time. There is no neighbor child next door for play-mate, no school within walking distance. An extra acre or two gives a fine sense of possession to an adult; it does not compensate children for the give-and-take of our village where there is always a contempo-rary to help swing the skipping rope or put on the catcher's mitt.

Of course, our taxes are higher than we like and there is always that 8:11 in the morning to be caught. But the taxes pay for our excellent schools and for our garbage collections and for our water supply. As for the 8:11, it is rather a pleasant train, say the husbands; it gets them to work in 34 minutes and they read the papers restfully on the way.

"But the suburban mind!" cry the die-hards. "The suburban conver-sation! The monotony!" They imply that they and I must scintillate or we perish. So far as I know, not one of my friends is doing any of the things that suburban ladies are popularly supposed to be doing. Some, undoubtedly, are ferociously busy in the garden. One lady is on her way to Ellis Island, bearing comfort and gifts to a Polish boy—a stowaway who did slave labor in Germany and was liberated by a cousin of hers during the war—who is being held for attempting to attain the land of which her cousin told him. Twice a week she takes this tedious journey, meanwhile besieging courts and immigration authorities on his behalf. This lady has a large house, a part-time maid and five children.

My friend around the corner is finishing her third novel. The village dancing school is run by another neighbor, as it has been for 20 years. Some of the ladies are no doubt painting their kitchen or a nursery; one of them is painting the portrait, on assignment, of a distinguished personage. Some of them are nurse's aides and Red Cross workers and supporters of good causes. But all find time to be friends with their families and to meet the 5:32 five nights a week. They read something besides the newest historical novel and their conversation is for the most part as agreeable as the tables they set. The tireless bridge players, the gossips, the women bored by their husbands live perhaps in our suburb too. Let them. Our orbits need not cross.

And what of the husbands? Do they spend their evenings and their week-ends in gaudy bars? Or are their lives a dreary round of taking down screens and mending drains? Well, screens they have always with them, and a man who is good around the house can spend happy hours with the plumbing even on a South Sea island. Some of them cut their own lawns and some of them try to break par and some of them sail little boats all summer with their families for crew. Some of them are village trustees for nothing a year and some listen to symphonies and some think Milton Berle ought to be President. Some are passionate hedge-clippers and some read Plutarch for fun. But I do not know many who either kiss their neighbors' wives behind doors or whose idea of sprightly talk is to tell you the plot of an old movie.

This afternoon my daughters will come home from school with a crowd of their peers at their heels. They will eat up the cookies and drink up the ginger ale. Presently it will be time for us to climb into our very old Studebaker—we are not car-proud in Spruce Manor—and meet the 5:32. There is something delightfully ritualistic about the moment when the train pulls in and the men swing off. The less sophisticated children run squealing to meet them. The women move over from the driver's seat and receive an absent-minded kiss. Deluded people that we are, we do not realize how mediocre it all seems. We will eat our undistinguished meal, probably without even a cocktail to enliven it. We will drink our coffee at the table, not carry it into the living room. If a husband changes for dinner here it is into old trousers and more comfortable shoes. The children will then go through the childhood routine—complain about their homework, grumble about going to bed, and finally accomplish both ordeals. Perhaps later the Gerard Joneses will drop in. We will talk a great deal of unimportant chatter and compare notes on food prices; we will discuss the headlines and disagree. We will all have one highball and the Joneses will leave early. Tomorrow and tomorrow and tomorrow the pattern will be repeated. This is Suburbia.

But I think that someday people will look back on our Spruce Manor way of life with nostalgia and respect. Suburbia, of thee I sing!

New Horizons

THE utter dreariness of the night that held the plane in rain-drenched darkness was reflected in the face of the young man bound South, where his wife had been killed in a motor accident that day. Neither I (the flight steward) nor a priest who happened to be aboard could penetrate the shell of his misery and self-pity. I told the captain about him when I took up his coffee. For a moment the pilot looked into the blackness ahead, then said, "Go back and fasten the passengers' seat belts. Perhaps I can help."

I felt the plane begin to climb. For a long time we bored upward, and at last we were flying between towering cloud castles and great peaks. These, too, dropped below us and we were alone in an ethereal world on which the moon shone in splendor.

The young man turned to the window and looked long on the eternity of unlimited space. When we descended again into the darkness of the earth and the storm, his face was composed. And I thanked God for a captain who understood—and who must sometime also have sought the hope that lies above the darkness of earth.

—Contributed by Belvin Horres

What Became of the Man I Married?

Anonymous

Condensed from Better Homes & Gardens

THERE is one luxury that any man, rich or poor, can give his wife. It costs him nothing, yet it is, curiously enough, the one thing that his wife wants more than anything under heaven. But, by some perverse force of fate, it is also the one thing the average American male puts the least stock in.

The American husband has many virtues. He is a good provider. He works faithfully and hard. He buys more insurance against illness, accident, old age and his own demise than any man anywhere in the world. What's more, he is fundamentally loyal. When the telephone rings and a husband sighs, "I won't be home for dinner, dear, I've got to work late," 99 women out of 100 can believe him implicitly.

He can be counted on not only because he's basically decent but also because he's simply too unromantic to kick up his heels. Give him a comfortable home, a place to pursue his hobby, a wife who feeds him well, sympathizes with his problems and takes good care of the children—and home is the one place he'd rather be than anywhere else. And he's usually too busy reading the newspaper or puttering about the basement to notice or care whether or not his dream girl still wears that cute curl and is a svelte size 12. She's with him and he's with her. And that, to him, is proof positive of love.

That this attitude is the direct opposite of every phase of courting never bothers him. As Dorothy Dix said, "When you've caught your streetcar, you don't go on chasing it." Relieved of the frantic need to rush after his heart's desire, he settles down to the business of her support, not even suspecting that he's neglecting her nearest and dearest desire—romantic love.

Yet romantic love is, to every normal woman, quite as important as material security and faithfulness. It is, in most cases, the reason a woman marries in the first place. What man ever won fair maiden by promising, "I will hoe the garden, pay the bills on time and take out life insurance"? No. He pleads, "Darling, I can't live without you. I want you forever in my arms." And she believes it.

Wrapped in this shining cloak of adoration, she is swept ecstatically into marriage. But, unlike the male of the species, she is not content to drop that cloak and start scrubbing the kitchen as all-sufficient proof of her corresponding passion. Her home duties are proof of devotion, but they seldom assume for her the same role that her husband's work does for him—namely, a substitute for ardor. To her, love is a continuing emotional state. It does *not* become simply an established fact when two people join their lives.

The average woman is, I believe, love-conscious and love-anxious at least 60 percent of the time. Nature has designed her to be emotionally responsive, yielding, warm, sympathetic and sensitive. For these are the qualities and emotions that make for motherhood, that go with its very equipment—the womb that shelters, the breast that nourishes, the arms that comfort and carry. And they are also inevitably linked with a woman's major need and function, love.

I realize that there are plenty of stupid wives, nagging wives, wives who become dowdy and dull and break all the well-known rules for holding affection. On the other hand, more women would strive to be stimulating and beautiful if they tasted the sweet heady flavor of adulation more often. Love is a more potent beautifier than any cream, lotion or charm course on the market. Nearly everyone has observed some drab little creature who became downright stunning simply because some man thought her so. And nearly everyone has seen some truly gorgeous woman gradually fade because her man was so unobserving or chary of compliments that beauty itself became joyless and without meaning.

The husbands who really do care about their wives' appearance would find a little old-fashioned flattery doubly rewarding. They'd have partners to be prouder of on Ladies' Day at their luncheon clubs, and they'd actually save money. Lots of women buy clothes they don't need in the vague hope that if they change outfits often enough their husbands will eventually notice they exist. The man who's smart enough to convince his honey she's a knockout in anything she dons isn't likely to find her too bitter about wearing make-do's. No Schiaparelli original can make a female feel so robed in glory as the admiration of the man she loves.

Maybe this doesn't fall under the classification of romantic love. Maybe it's just old-fashioned bread-and-butter married love. But basically it's what every woman wants—to be cherished, to feel herself adored, to be drawn richly and consciously ever closer to her man.

Another thing the average American husband doesn't understand is the way women feel about sex. Women differ in their needs and responsiveness, just as men do. But more women are more passionate than a lot of men suspect, simply because the women are too modest to let on. I honestly think, however, that sexual satisfaction is not in itself nearly so important to a woman as the feeling of reassurance the relationship gives her—the reaffirmation of the fact that her husband has wanted to be close to her, to hold her in his arms, to be complete with her in a way that shuts the whole world out. Impotence would be a lot less common in men if they could understand that. Women don't so much seek physical thrills and bodily fulfillment as they seek a time and place of nearness, of going back spiritually—just two people alone together—to those far-lost moments of the past when each was supremely important to the other.

If I were a man, I would make it the first and last acts of my day to take my wife into my arms a few moments. I would make this drawing together so much a part of the fabric of our daily lives that either of us would feel lost without it. It would be the symbol of that blind hurtling together we first knew, a moment of closeness and strength exchanged with which to launch the day. And no matter how many other things had come thrusting between us, it would be a final seal of unity and communion at the day's end.

YOU'RE SMARTER

THAN YOU THINK

By John Kord Lagemann

W omen know everything," my grandfather once told me, "and Heaven help us if they ever find it out."

He was referring, of course, to feminine intuition—that mysterious faculty which enables women to answer questions before they're asked; predict the arrival of unexpected guests; identify social climbers, alcoholics and rivals as if they were plainly labeled; know without being told when their husbands have quarreled with the boss or daydreamed—just daydreamed, mind you—about another woman.

Ever since Eve took the first bite out of the apple, man has been asking woman how she knows all these things without any apparent reason for knowing. Nothing infuriates him more than to be told: "I just know, that's all."

Does intuition really exist? And if so, is it feminine? I decided to put the question to science.

Intuition, I learned, is a normal and highly useful function of human intelligence. This fact has been confirmed by each of the half dozen authorities I consulted. Though associated with high IQs in both sexes, it is more characteristic of women than of men.

Why? As Dr. Helene Deutsch, author of *The Psychology of Women,* points out, in adolescence a boy is interested primarily in asserting himself in action, while a girl's interests center around feelings, her own and others. Dr. Deutsch compares the adolescent girl to "someone listening in the dark and perceiving every noise with special acuteness." From the understanding she gains of her own emotions she is able by analogy to relive the emotions of others.

Women don't pay nearly as much attention as men to what people say, but they are apt to know a great deal more about the way people feel. One winter when I was living in New Hampshire my friend Mr. White coveted a corner pasture which his neighbor Mr. Perry stubbornly refused to sell. The men were no longer on speaking terms, but their wives went right on visiting over the phone. One night after a long and rambling party-line visit—in which the land issue was never mentioned—Mrs. White said to her husband, "I think Mr. Perry will sell that corner lot if you still want it." When I saw the Whites a few months later the deal had been completed.

Reduced to simplest terms intuition is a way of thinking without words—a short cut to the truth, and in matters of emotion the only way of getting there at all. Dr. Carl Jung defines it as "a basic psychological function which transmits perceptions in an unconscious way." This perception is based on the evidence of our physical senses. But because it taps knowledge and experience of which we aren't aware it is often confused with telepathy, clairvoyance or extrasensory perception. We all know the "psychic" card player who seems to read another's hand; actually he notes a telltale flutter of your eyelid or lip, a hesitation in speech, the tightening of a wrist muscle when your hand touches a card. He may not be aware himself of the clues he follows.

Civilization has substituted words and various other abstractions for the direct experience of seeing, hearing, smelling, tasting, touching and feeling. But our neglected senses still go right on operating, far better than we realize. Take the sense of smell, perhaps the least developed of the senses. We used to laugh at backwoods doctors who diagnosed certain diseases by sniffing the air near the patient. Then we discovered that these diseases really did produce chemical changes resulting in characteristic odors. Experiments have shown that the odor of a person's breath actually varies with changes in his emotional attitude. The distance over which we can unconsciously pick up the scent of another human being is unknown, but it is almost certainly greater than the length of a room. How can an odor of which you are not even aware mean anything to you? If you've ever been awakened slowly and deliciously by the aroma of coffee and bacon, you know the answer.

Last summer I saw an example of how the senses coöperate to produce intuition. On the boat from Woods Hole to Martha's Vineyard my wife nodded toward a young woman sitting nearby and remarked, "I'm sure I know her. Yet I can't remember having seen her before."

Impulsively we introduced ourselves and mentioned my wife's feeling. After the young woman had spoken, my wife said, "Now I know. You take phone calls for Dr. Miller."

"Why, yes, I do," the girl answered.

Why did my wife feel there was something familiar about the girl? "But don't you see?" she explained to me later. "She *looked* just the way she sounded over the phone." Simple as that. Come to think of it, though, can't almost any teen-ager spot a blind date from the way he or she sounded on the phone?

Most women are quite good at guessing age, particularly if the subject is another woman. If you don't believe it, try it sometime at a party. The difference between a girl of 23 and a girl of 25 is far too subtle to put into words. Men try to reason it out and usually their guesses are not better than chance or gallantry will allow. Yet with the aid of almost imperceptible clues women can often spot the difference.

One of the few attempts to observe intuition systematically was made by Dr. Eric Berne, a former staff psychiatrist with the Army Medical Corps, now a practicing psychoanalyst at Carmel, Calif. While interviewing men at an Army Separation Center, Dr. Berne and his colleagues tried to guess, before the patient had spoken, what his occupation had been in civilian life. All the patients were dressed in standard maroon bathrobes and cloth slippers. The doctors' guesses averaged well above chance. "On one occasion," Dr. Berne reports, "the occupations of 26 successive men were guessed correctly." Clues unconsciously detected in the men's eyes, gestures, facial expressions, speech, hands, and so on, probably explain this success.

As psychiatry and common sense have actually proved, you know a lot more than you are aware that you know. The mind tunes into consciousness only a few of the impressions which flow in from your sense organs. But your brain does not waste these impulses. It stores them up in your unconscious mind where they are ready to be used. Some physicians, for instance, have only to glance at a patient to diagnose correctly a disease which others cannot identify without painstaking examination. These intuitive doctors note many faint clues and match them with relevant information accumulated over a lifetime of experience.

Likewise, every intuitive person knows how to draw on his reserve of unconscious knowledge and experience in coping with the problems of everyday life. The American Chemical Society questioned 232 leading U. S. scientists, found that 83 percent of them depended on intuition in their research after intense conscious effort had failed to produce results. A similar study by Dr. Eliot Dole Hutchinson revealed that intuition played an important part in the creative work of 80 percent of a sample of 253 artists, musicians and writers.

The unconscious part of your brain never stops working. So when you're faced with a perplexing job, work on it as hard as you can. Then if you can't lick it, try sleeping on it or taking a walk or relaxing with friends. If you have primed yourself with all available facts, the answer is likely to "dawn" on you while your mind is seemingly at rest.

In the case of a purely personal decision, the important facts are your own deep feelings, and in this case you know intuitively what to do without the need for long preliminary deliberation. Dr. Sigmund Freud once told a friend, "When making a decision of minor importance I have always found it advantageous to consider all the pros and cons. In vital matters, however, such as the choice of a mate or a profession, the decision should come from the unconscious, from somewhere within ourselves. In the important decisions of our personal lives we should be governed by the deep inner needs of our nature."

Life is much more interesting for the intuitive person than for the nonintuitive. People mean more when you understand them from the inside out—and because of this, you mean more to them. That is what intuition is, really—finding new and deeper meanings in people and events, making more sense out of life. How can you develop your intuitive powers? Like any other form of thinking, intuition requires an alertness, sensitivity and discipline of mind which have to be cultivated.

Take off the blinders of habit and open your mind to what's going on around you. See people as they really are, not as you think they ought to be. Don't let prejudices distort your vision. Half the trick is to let people tell you about themselves unconsciously. The way a person stands, sits, shakes hands, smokes or sips a drink will be, to the intuitive man or woman, important clues in sizing up character.

Intuition isn't the enemy, but the ally of reason. Effective realistic thinking requires a combination of both.

Love Lines

» ONE GREAT THING about marriage is the fun of living two at a time. You get not only your own life's journey but an extra ticket through another life as well. Also, you get two points of view for your money. —Frances Lester Warner, *Inner Springs* (Houghton Mifflin)

» THE BEST CURE for a broken heart is to get it broken again.
—Sam Mentz, quoted by Frances Rodman in New York *Times Magazine*

» MARRIAGE is not a destination—it is a journey.
—Paul Popenoe in *Journal of Living*

» HE that marries for money earns it. —Proverb

» A MAN'S HEART may have a secret sanctuary where only one woman may enter, but it is full of little anterooms which are seldom vacant.
—Helen Rowland, *This Married Life* (Dodge)

» WHEN a woman told Somerset Maugham that she couldn't decide whether or not she was in love with a certain man, he said, "Madam, there is only one true test of love—could you use his toothbrush?" —Leslie F. Hannon in *New Liberty*

» A MAN and a woman should choose each other for life. A long life is barely enough for a man and woman to understand each other; and to understand is to love. The man who understands one woman is qualified to understand pretty well everything.
—J. B. Yeats, *Letters to His Son, W. B. Yeats, and Others,* ed. by Joseph Hone (Dutton)

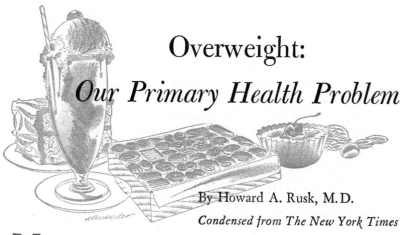

Overweight:
Our Primary Health Problem

By Howard A. Rusk, M.D.

Condensed from The New York Times

MANY PERSONS stepped on the scales this morning, noted they had gained a pound or two and silently resolved to lose weight. Some will follow through on their resolutions, but scientific studies have shown that most of the 25 million Americans who are overweight probably will forget it as soon as they sit down to their next meal.

The health of these overweight persons, five million of whom are seriously obese, is currently our nation's primary public-health problem. Although we rightfully pride ourselves on the advances we have made in reducing mortality in infancy, childhood and early adult life, relatively little progress has been made in reducing mortality in middle and later years. Our mortality rates for persons over 45 are 25 percent higher than for the same age groups in Norway, Denmark and the Netherlands. Overweight is a major underlying factor in many of the diseases that cause death after 45.

As *The American Journal of Public Health* editorialized recently, we hear a great deal about malnutrition in the underdeveloped areas of the world, but ours is a problem of an "overdeveloped" area. It is related as closely to our national future as malaria and malnutrition are to the poverty of some other lands.

Contrary to the general conception that overweight is a condition found primarily among those of high incomes, Dr. E. P. Luongo, medical director of the General Petroleum Corp., found in a series of 5000 physical examinations that the rate of overweight among executives and nonexecutives was about the same—one out of four. He noted that, because of improved living standards in recent years, the workman is just as likely to "dig his grave with his teeth" as the executive.

Dr. Louis I. Dublin and his associates at the Metropolitan Life Insurance Co. have shown that, of persons overweight up to 14 percent, the death rate from all causes is 22 percent higher than among persons of normal weight. Among persons who are overweight from 15 to 24 percent, the death rate is 44 percent higher than among those of normal weight, and among persons who are overweight 25 percent or more it is 75 percent higher.

A study of 50,000 overweight policyholders of the Metropolitan Life Insurance Co. showed they had a mortality rate 50 percent higher than among standard insurance risks. The death rates were particularly high for cardio-vascular-renal diseases, diabetes and diseases of the liver and gall bladder.

Another study, of Army officers, showed that sustained high blood pressure developed among overweights at an annual rate of 4.6 per thousand as compared with only 1.8 per thousand among those of normal weight. Heart disease, whatever its specific cause, is always aggravated by obesity.

It is true that some individuals are overweight because of physical, organic or functional deviations that need medical treatment. But for the great majority of overweight persons, the problem is simply one of eating more than the body needs. Studies have shown repeatedly that diet for such persons can be so adjusted to nutritional needs that weight can be brought to and maintained at normal.

Before embarking on a weight-reduction plan, however, the overweight person should consult a doctor without fail. Only a physician has the necessary knowledge and skill to consider and evaluate both the physical and emotional status of the individual, as well as his degree of overweight, to determine how much, how fast and with what program weight can be reduced.

The dieter should learn also something about food. The principle underlying a diet is to cut the daily intake of food to a point below the needs of the body without unbalancing the diet by omitting essential foodstuffs or so decreasing calories that the weight loss is too rapid and strength and well-being are impaired. The human body normally contains about 15 percent fat. This much is essential to good health and nutrition, but anything above is excessive. Dieters will benefit from reading popular pamphlets on weight control and nutrition available from the Metropolitan Life Insurance Co. and other organizations.

The person who is reducing need not have any special cooking nor need he waste his money on any of the so-called "health" foods. In fact, the unbalanced diets recommended by food faddists are lacking seriously in basic nutritional essentials and may seriously harm health.

Nor are drugs the answer. Any drug that can increase the body's rate of burning calories enough to effect weight reduction without dieting is potentially dangerous. One drug which was released during the early 1930's without medical approval caused weight loss, but it also caused deafness, blindness and paralysis.

No easy way to reduce is safe—no safe way to reduce is easy. The overweight person must learn that only a *permanent* change in his eating habits will bring lasting results.

MARTIN BUXBAUM, editor of *The Southern Dairy*, kissed his wife hello one evening and asked: "Well, how was everything today?"

"Pretty good. The latest issue of *Parents' Magazine* was a big help in straightening out a couple of young ladies who were acting up."

"What was the article?" asked Buxbaum.

"No article. I just rolled up the magazine and shellacked them good and proper."
                                                    —Bill Gold in Washington *Post*

As A YOUNG Frenchman pushed his son's carriage down the street, the youngster howled with rage. "Please, Bernard, control yourself," the father said quietly. "Easy there, Bernard, keep calm!"

"Congratulations, monsieur," said a woman who had been watching. "You know just how to speak to infants—calmly and gently." Then she said, "So the little fellow's named Bernard?"

"No, madame," corrected the father. "He's named André. *I'm* Bernard."
                                                    —Pierre-Jean Vaillard in *L'Anneau d'Or*

"A Man Don't Know
What He Can Do"

By Elise Miller Davis

JUST BEFORE midnight on February 18, 1952, Roy Gaby, driving for a Houston, Texas, trucking company, ran out of gasoline while returning from Waco in a heavy 14-wheel truck-trailer. From a house nearby he telephoned his wife, "SOS, honey, I'm out of gas."

Mrs. Gaby sighed, bundled up the baby and then set out to the rescue in the family car.

On the way home Mrs. Gaby drove ahead of Roy. About ten miles from Houston a speeding car, with an apparently drunken driver who never stopped, darted out of a side road, forcing Mrs. Gaby's car off the highway on the right. In the rear-view mirror she caught a glimpse of Roy's truck swerving to avoid a collision. Then she heard a crash.

The engine had smashed into a mammoth oak tree, the trailer had piled up on the cab and Roy was trapped in the twisted debris.

A passing motorist rushed into the village of Fairbanks and notified Deputy Sheriff Don Henry.

Henry decided to try "untelescoping" the wreck. "We attached a wrecker to the front of the mashed-in engine, hoping to pull it straight enough to get Gaby out. But the idea didn't work. We added the power of a truck at the front of the wrecker. Finally, two more trucks were attached to the rear, and they pulled in the opposite direction. But still, no soap."

Small flames appeared beneath the truck, and there was no extinguisher at hand. Halting passing drivers, Henry set helpers to working frantically at the crumpled doors with hammers and crowbars. The twisted doors refused to budge. Henry crawled onto the hood of the cab and turned his flashlight on the victim. The steering wheel was crushed against Gaby's waist and his feet were pinned between twisted brake and clutch pedals. Flames were licking his feet.

"I'm an accident investigator," Henry told me later, "and I've seen a lot of terrible sights. But I've never seen one more terrible and I've never felt more helpless. I looked at Mrs. Gaby and the baby, then back at the poor guy in the burning cab, and I felt like praying for a miracle."

At that moment, a husky Negro appeared out of the darkness.

"Can I help?" he asked quietly. Henry shook his head. Nobody could help if three trucks and a wrecker couldn't budge that cab, and by the time cutting torches and fire apparatus arrived it was going to be just too bad. The Negro calmly walked over to the cab, put his hands on the door and *wrenched it off!*

Speechless, the crowd watched the Negro reach in the cab and tear out the burning floor mat. Then he put out the flames around Gaby's legs—with his bare hands.

"It was just about then that I caught a glimpse of the big fellow's face," said one of the witnesses. "At first I thought he was in a trance. Then I saw that set expression for what it was—cold, calculated fury. I'd seen it before—at Pearl Harbor, on Okinawa. I remember thinking: *Why, that guy's not calm, he's enraged.* It was just as if he despised fire."

Swiftly, almost as if rehearsed, the Negro worked on, poking large arms into the truck cab. "He straightened that steering wheel like it was tin," the driver of the wrecker said. "With his left hand on the brake pedal and his right on the clutch, he all but uprooted the whole works to free Gaby's feet."

But the crucial job wasn't done. The victim still lay encased in what witnesses called "a squashed sardine can over a bonfire."

Patiently, then stubbornly, the big man struggled to squeeze in beside Gaby. The space was too tiny. Stepping back from the cab, he hesitated fleetingly. The flames were growing. He glared at them, slumped to a squatting position and began pushing into the cab, fighting crazily. At long last he was in far enough to rest his feet firmly on the floor-board. He started rising slowly. His muscles bulged in the half-light and the sleeves of his shirt tore.

"My God, he's trying to push up the top!" a woman's voice called.

Neck and shoulders against the caved-in cab roof, he pushed. Hard.

"We actually heard the metal give," reported a farmer who had come to the scene. Discussing the rescue afterward, Deputy Henry shook his head, still baffled. "And he held that top up until we could pull Gaby out."

In the excitement of attending Gaby, no one thought to thank the Negro or even ask his name. Later, at the hospital with Gaby, Deputy Henry told newsmen: "The mysterious Samson disappeared as quietly as he'd come. If I hadn't witnessed it I'd never believe a lone man could do a job we couldn't do with three trucks and a wrecker."

"I wish I knew his name," put in Mrs. Gaby. "He was a giant."

Actually 33-year-old Charles Dennis Jones is not a giant. He is six feet two inches tall and weighs 220 pounds. He'd been out to nearby Hempstead to change tires on a disabled truck when he came upon the accident. By morning the whole city of Houston was wondering about his identity. Newspapers throughout the country carried the story. But Jones didn't tell even his wife about his experience. His boss, C. C. Myers, became suspicious, however, when he noticed the big fellow walk away from a group of employes who were discussing the amazing rescue. Remembering the mission he'd sent Jones on the night before, Myers grabbed a photograph from company files and headed for the Sheriff's office. "Yes, that's him," agreed Deputy Henry.

And Myers knew immediately how Charlie Jones found the strength to lick that fire.

ONE December night 14 months before, Jones had come home to the three-room house where he lived with his wife, Mildred, and their five small children. Under one arm he carried a tiny pine tree and a single string of Christmas lights.

They'd had a lot of bad luck that year. Only two months before both his mother and Mildred's had died within a week, leaving grief, doctor bills, funeral expenses. But Evelyn Carol, his eight-year-old first-born, wanted some *real* Christmas-tree lights and he had them. He'd manage. He was healthy and husky and could stand a 16-hour day. Double work meant double pay. And they had a roof over their heads. Paid for.

Mildred left for church, where she was singing that evening. Jones tucked in the children. As he undressed, he wondered if he should risk leaving the tree lights on. He decided he would. Evelyn Carol wanted to surprise her mother and he'd promised. He fell asleep.

Mildred's pillow was still untouched when Jones awoke, sure he was having a nightmare. There was a burning in his nostrils, a crackling sound in his ears. He heard a child's cry: "Daddy!" Instantly he was on his feet, awake in a world on fire, pushing through choking waves of smoke, grabbing small bodies until he counted five, finding his way to the open window, pitching the children out.

People gathered. And Mildred came running through the darkness, crying his name. Then Jones heard a man's voice, maybe his own: "No, no—Evelyn Carol, come back, come back!" A child's answer: "But I must get my Christmas lights!" And like a fleeting spirit Evelyn Carol in a little white nightgown ran back toward the flames.

Later a neighbor told how the men couldn't hold Jones. How he'd raced after his child but hadn't reached her because just as he neared the dwelling its last remains exploded. How the blast had thrown Jones to the ground unconscious, and he'd been dragged out of danger.

The next morning, for the first time in ten years, Charles Dennis Jones failed to report to work at Robertson Transport. Everybody there had heard. When a man loses a child and his home, has four children to support and another one on the way, what can other men do?

Before nine o'clock a paper was circulating—from workshops to offices to yards. By noon it bore the names of 84 Robertson employes, and was sealed in an envelope and delivered to Charlie Jones. In the envelope Jones found $765.50.

The following day friends at Hughes Tool Co., where Mildred had formerly worked, sent in $80. By mail, from strangers, came $16. There were countless offers: Can you use an icebox? An army cot? A boy's coat, size 6? It seemed everyone had united to help the Jones family. Charlie began to work on a new home. He figured that before the new baby came he'd have his family back under their own roof.

You could understand why he always would hate fire.

Reading a newspaper account of Jones's heroic rescue, R. A. Childers, Houston businessman, wrote the papers, saying that he would give $400 to start a fund providing an annual college scholarship for a Negro high school graduate. The rescue had taken place during Brotherhood Week. "Could anything be more characteristic of brotherhood than the fact that Jones walked away without waiting for thanks?" Childers asked.

And so it came about in the new house Charlie and Mildred and their children had built with their own hands that they received a group of citizens who informed them of the proposed Charles D. Jones Endowment Fund. Jones heard the committee's proposal in his faded blue overalls, eyes glazed by unshed tears. His wife stood beside him, his children huddled near. He didn't say a word.

Finally, Mr. Childers broke the silence. Somehow Charlie must give a statement to the press. There was the mystery he might yet clear up. How in the name of heaven had he managed to wrench off a steel door, beat out flames with his hands, raise with his own back the crushed-in top of a driver's cab?

Charlie Jones looked at Childers and at the hushed group around him. He cleared his throat and said, simply:

"A man don't know what he can do until another man is hurting."

The Better Error

ELEANOR ROOSEVELT once brought a problem to Bernard Baruch. "My mind tells me to do it," she said, "but my heart tells me not to."

"When in doubt, follow your heart and not your mind," Baruch advised her. "When you make a mistake of the heart you don't feel so bad about it later."

—Leonard Lyons

A shoemaker who was far more than an expert workman

The Light in the Window

By Lois Mattox Miller

I MET HIM first on a summer day in 1936. I had rushed into his dingy little shop to have new lifts put on my slipper heels. He greeted me cheerily. "You're new in this neighborhood, aren't you?"

Yes, I admitted, I had moved into the apartment house at the end of the block only a week before.

"This is a fine neighborhood," he said. "You'll be happy here."

I sat there in my stocking feet, watching as he removed the old lifts and, with a sad tut-tut, examined the leather covering the heel—now worn through by a too long delay of this repair job. I was rushing to an appointment. "Please hurry," I begged.

He looked at me reproachfully over his spectacles. "Now, lady, we won't be long. I want to do a good job." He paused. "You see, I have a tradition to uphold."

A tradition? In this drab little shop without a thing to distinguish it from so many other cobbler shops on the side streets?

He must have sensed my surprise, for he smiled as he went on. "Yes, lady, I *inherited* a tradition. My father and my grandfather were shoemakers in Italy, and they were the best. My father always told me, 'Son, do the *best* job on every shoe that comes into the shop, and be proud of your fine work. Do that always, and you'll be doubly blessed —both happy and prosperous.'"

As he handed me the finished shoes, he said: "These will last a long time. These are good leather."

I left in a hurry, late for my appointment yet with a warm and grateful feeling. On my way home I passed the little shop again. There he was, bending over his last. To my surprise he waved cheerily. Thus began a rewarding friendship.

Those were disturbing years of depression and war. Daily as I passed his shop we exchanged a friendly handwave. At first I went in only when I had repair work to be done; then I found myself dropping in occasionally just for a chat.

He was surprisingly tall for an Italian, yet quite stooped from long years of toil. His hair was thin and gray, his face deeply lined. But I remember best his fine brown eyes, alive with kindness and humor. I remember how they flashed one day at the mention of Mussolini. "The dog!" he said. It was the strongest word I ever heard him use.

He was proud of his U. S. citizenship and everything American. Once, shortly after Pearl Harbor, when I complained of our slow-moving preparations for war, he looked at me in amazement. "But we're only getting started," he said. "We have the finest men, and we'll have the biggest machine. We'll do all right. We have great traditions to uphold."

He was the happiest man I've ever known. Often, as he stood in his shopwindow, hammering away at his last, he sang lustily. The Italians in our neighborhood called him *la luce alla finestra*—the light in the window.

Once, as we talked, he turned to wave cordially to a passer-by, then said to me: "There's a man I'd like to know. He's been passing here for years. I wish he'd stop in sometime, for he has a fine, honest face."

I did not tell him that I knew the man. But a week later he told me: "I was right about that man. He stopped in yesterday and we had a fine talk. There's a good man, if I ever saw one."

I knew then that the honesty and goodness of this gentle shoemaker had warmed another heart as it had mine.

Children—our sidewalks sprouted them—swarmed through his shop. They were always welcome. He would chuckle over their quarrels, and often stop his work to act as peacemaker.

One day I came away from my apartment angry and disgusted because of a sloppy job the painters had done. My friend waved to me as I went by, so I turned into his shop for solace. He let me rant about the incompetence and inefficiency of present-day workmen. They had no pride in their work, I argued; they didn't even want to work—just wished to collect their high wages and loaf.

He agreed. "There's a lot of that kind around, sure. But maybe they're not entirely to blame. Maybe their fathers had no pride in their work. That's tough on a kid. It deprives him of something important."

"What can be done about it?" I asked.

He waited a minute before answering, then looked at me squarely. "There is only one way. Every man or woman who hasn't inherited a prideful tradition must start building one. In this great country, where our wonderful freedom allows us to make an individual contribution, we must make it a good contribution. No matter what sort of work a man does, if he gives it his best each day, he's starting a tradition for his children to live up to—and making lots of happiness for himself."

I went abroad for a few months. Shortly after my return I walked down the street, looking forward to his surprise when he saw me.

There was no "light in the window." The door was closed. There was a little card: "Call for shoes at laundry next door."

I went into the laundry, full of apprehension. Yes, the old man had suffered a stroke two weeks ago, right there in his window. He had died a few days later.

"We sure miss him around here," the laundryman said. "He was so happy all the time."

I went away with a heavy heart. I would miss him, too. But he had left me something—a rare bit of wisdom I shall always remember: "If you have inherited a prideful tradition, you must carry it on; if you haven't, then start building one now."

TRY GIVING YOURSELF

By *Arline Boucher and John Tehan*

Condensed from Guideposts

RACIOUS GIVING requires no special talent, nor large amounts of money. It is compounded of the heart and the head acting together to achieve the perfect means of expressing our feelings. It is love sharpened with imagination. For, as Emerson explains, "The only gift is a portion of thyself."

A little girl gave her mother several small boxes tied with bright ribbons. Inside each were slips of paper on which the child had printed such messages as, "Good for two flower-bed weedings," "Good for two floor-scrubbings." She had never read Emerson, but unconsciously she put a large part of her small self into her gift.

When unexpected expenses wrecked a business girl's budget at Christmas, she hit upon a similar happy idea. Her presents that year were "time credit" slips which her friends could cash at their convenience. A young couple received slips entitling them to leave the baby with her for two week-ends. To a niece in college went an offer of her car for a Christmas vacation trip. An elderly shut-in could claim her time for five reading-aloud sessions. No costly presents gave so much satisfaction—both ways.

A young bride received a wedding present from an older woman. With it went a note, "Do not open until you and your husband have your first tiff." When there finally came a day of misunderstanding the bride remembered the package. In it she found a card box filled with her friend's favorite recipes—and a note, "You will catch more flies with honey than you will with vinegar." It was a wise woman indeed who gave of her experience with her gift.

Often the most successful gift is a spontaneous one. Act while the impulse is fresh—giving of yourself knows no special days.

Probably no gift ever thrilled a doctor more than a letter he received from a youngster on *her* birthday. "Dear Doctor, 14 years ago you brought me into this world. I want to thank you, for I have enjoyed every minute of it."

Family gifts should be the most satisfying because we know each member's wish and whim. Yet how often we make the stereotyped offerings—ties, candy or household utensils. One man I know is planning an unusual present for his wife. When I saw him coming out of a dancing studio, he explained: "I got tired of hearing my wife complain about my dancing. It's going to be a lasting birthday present for her—my dancing well."

An elderly lady on an Iowa farm wept with delight when her son in New York had a telephone installed in her house and followed it up with a weekly long-distance call.

Flowers are our first thought for a sick friend. But why not a more imaginative idea? A friend in a hospital received a flowerpot filled with dirt. On top was a packet of seeds with the note, "You'll have more fun growing your own!" A nurse told me about a woman patient whose recovery dated from the moment a neighbor brought her a pressure cooker, something she had always wanted.

In her autobiography, *His Eye Is on the Sparrow,* Ethel Waters tells about her gift to Rex Stout when he was convalescing. Though she was starring at the time in a Broadway play, she turned up early one morning at the hospital and, dressed as a nurse, carried in his breakfast tray. She spent the day with Stout, diverting him with chitchat, wheeling his chair, giving him all her attention. Friends of the author said that this was his most cherished gift.

In your own profession or business you have imaginative gift opportunities. One Christmas morning a Washington, D. C., woman was waiting for a trolley to go to the station when a taxi stopped beside her. The driver motioned her to get in. At the station when she fumbled in her purse for the fare, the driver said, "Nothing doing—I asked you. Merry Christmas." In memory of her sister who was killed in service during the war, a waitress often pays the checks of service-women who sit at her table.

All gifts that contain a portion of self signify that someone has been really thinking of us. One of the most useful and thoughtful travel presents a girl ever received was currency of the country to which she was going. A friend bought her some pesos from a bank so that she would have the correct money for tips and taxi fare when she first arrived in Mexico.

A GI stationed in Mississippi tells this story: "I made friends with a sharecropper who lived near camp. Though poor, he was the most contented man I had ever met. One day when I was grousing about not being able to borrow $20 that I needed, he handed me the money, saying it was a gift, not a loan. He explained it this way: 'If I lend you this money and for some reason you never return it, I must always think you have wronged me. If I give it to you as a gift, we're both happy. When you have the money and feel you want to make me a gift of $20, then we'll both be happy again.'"

A minister soliciting for a worthy cause was turned down by a curt letter which ended, "As far as I can see, this Christian business is one continuous give, give, give." The clergyman wrote back, "Thank you for the best definition of the Christian life I have ever heard."

Chances for heroic giving are rare, yet every day there are opportunities to give a part of yourself to someone who needs it. It may be no more than a kind word or a letter written at the right time. The important thing about any gift is the amount of yourself you put into it.

THE voluntary path to cheerfulness, if our spontaneous cheerfulness be lost, is to sit up cheerfully, and act and speak as if cheerfulness were already there. To feel brave, *act* as if we were brave, use all our will to that end, and courage will very likely replace fear. If we act as if from some better feeling, the bad feeling soon folds its tent like an Arab and silently steals away.   —William James

The Conscious Use of the Subconscious Mind

By Robert R. Updegraff

Condensed from Forbes

N EARLY ALL of us have had the experience of riding on a train with no one to talk to, or of sitting through a concert or lecture to which we were not really listening, and having ideas tumble over themselves in our minds. This is the subconscious mind at work, taking advantage of the relaxed state of the conscious mind. It is capable of doing much of our best thinking and of helping us solve our most perplexing problems. It can bring to bear on all our affairs far more wisdom and experience than our conscious minds command.

There is, of course, a time for concentrated application to our problems. But there is also a time to stop and smoke and whittle and let the subconscious mind do its part of the work. For, after all, it is accomplishment that we are all after, not activity.

Fehr, the French scientist, who made a study of the working habits of his contemporaries, says that 75 percent of the scientists stated that their important discoveries came to them when they were not actively engaged in research.

Most of us use our conscious minds entirely too hard, and as a result our thinking and our decisions are not as good as they should be. The trouble is, we are working with only half our minds, and with less than half of our accumulated experience and judgment. And as a consequence, we cheat ourselves of many hours of recreation which in themselves add to the effectiveness of our thinking. For relaxation is the key to the door of the subconscious mind. The subconscious mind works best when we are doing what we like best to do. A happy mind is a healthy mind and it puts drive back of a man's activities. As Henry David Thoreau put it, "A really efficient laborer will be found not to crowd his day with work."

How then may we *consciously* plan to use the subconscious mind, to take advantage of its power to improve our judgments and decisions, or to furnish us with bold new ideas or creative conceptions?

The process of thinking is strangely akin to the process of cooking. Although direct heat is ordinarily used, many dishes are better after long, slow cooking. To permit this, some ranges have fireless ovens in which the cooking is completed with retained heat.

The subconscious mind is a fireless cooker into which we can put our problems to finish the cooking on what might be called "retained thought." To do all of our mental cooking with our conscious minds is to burn mental energy wastefully, and at high cost to our nervous systems.

One rule always holds good: You must give your problems to your subconscious mind in the form of *definite assignments*, after assembling all the essential facts, figures and arguments. The cooking process must first be started by focusing our minds on this material long and intently enough to get it thoroughly heated with our best conscious thinking.

To start this focusing process, one method is to write on a sheet of paper the problem facing you, jotting down all important aspects. If there are pro and con sides, enumerate all the factors you can think of in two columns. *Then tear up the sheet and forget all about it.* Do something you want to do, something that will rest your mind.

Another way is to talk over the problem or situation with associates or members of your family, exploring every angle in detail. Get right down to cases—*but don't attempt to come to a decision.* End your discussion abruptly and set the whole matter aside to "cook."

Still a third method is to work consciously on the problem until you are just plumb fagged out mentally. At that point *put it entirely out of your mind.* Go fishing, golfing or motoring, or if it's night, go peacefully to bed.

One night in October 1920, Frederick Grant Banting, a young Canadian surgeon with so little practice that he had to teach to eke out a living, was working over his next day's lecture. His subject was diabetes. Hour after hour he pored over the literature of this dread disease, his head a whirling maze of conflicting theories, case histories, accounts of experiments with dogs. Finally he went wearily to bed.

At two in the morning he got up, turned on a light, and wrote three sentences in his notebook: "Tie off pancreatic duct of dogs. Wait 6 to 8 weeks for degeneration. Remove residue and extract." Then he went back to bed and slept.

It was those three magic sentences which led to the discovery of insulin. Banting's conscious mind had come to grips with one of the most baffling problems in medical science; his subconscious mind finished the job.

Sometimes the fireless-cooking process requires only a matter of hours, as in Banting's case. Again it may require days or weeks. And it may be necessary consciously to turn the heat on again once in a while to keep the cooking process going. But nearly always the subconscious mind can be depended upon to finish the cooking, and frequently with greater speed than if we rely on conscious thought alone.

Furthermore, it usually turns out a better product because it brings to bear all of one's accumulated life experience, including much that the conscious mind had long since forgotten. In an interview on his seventy-fifth birthday, Henry Ford referred to "instinct." "What is instinct?" asked his interviewer. "Probably the essence of past experience and knowledge stored up for later use," replied Mr. Ford.

A man of my acquaintance has acquired the habit of dropping into an easy chair in his office for 20 or 30 minutes each day, picking up a book and forgetting all his business concerns.

"I have never sat in that chair," he told me, "with any thought of developing an idea, but the minute my mind relaxes ideas begin to develop of themselves."

The renowned German physicist, Von Helmholtz, said that after thoroughly investigating a problem "in all directions," he found that "happy ideas come unexpectedly without effort like an inspiration. *But they have never come to me when my mind was fatigued or when I was at my working table.*"

Thornton Wilder, author of the Pulitzer prize novel, *The Bridge of San Luis Rey,* and the later Pulitzer prize play, *Our Town,* once confessed that his best story ideas came to him "on hikes and in the shower and places." Any place, it seems, other than at his desk!

Descartes, the famous French mathematician and philosopher, is said to have made his great discoveries while lying in bed in the mornings.

If you have not been consciously using your subconscious mind it may be a bit rusty, and you may have to make several tries before it will begin to function. Subconscious cerebration requires time, relaxation, a sense of leisure. Perhaps that is what the late Andrew Mellon had in mind when he said, "In leisure there is luck."

*Copyright 1938 by The Reader's Digest Association, Inc. (October 1938 issue)
Condensed from Forbes, September 15, 1938*

It's a Man's World

It's a man's world, all right. Just look at the difference in these descriptive words and phrases.

If a man doesn't marry, he's a "bachelor"—glamorous word. If a woman doesn't marry she's an "old maid."

When it's his night out he's "out with the boys." When it is her night out she's at a "hen party." What he hears at the office is "news." What she hears at a bridge party is "gossip."

If he runs the family he is "head of the house." If she runs it she "wears the pants in that family." If he is overly solicitous of her he is a "devoted husband." If she is overly solicitous of him he is "henpecked." If he keeps his eye on her at a party he is an "attentive husband." If she sticks close to him she is a "possessive wife."

In middle age he is "in the prime of life" or "at the peak of his career." At the same age she's "no spring chicken." If he is an easy spender he "does not deny his family anything." If she doesn't count the pennies she's "extravagant" or a "poor manager."

Gray hair gives him a distinguished look. If she has it, she's an old hag. If he hasn't any small talk he's "the quiet type." If she hasn't any she is "mousy."

It all depends on one thing—whether you're speaking of a man or a woman.　　　　　　　　　　　　　　　—Ruth Millett, NEA

I'd Want My Husband to Marry Again

By Eileen Morris   **Condensed from Chatelaine**

I F I SHOULD DIE, I'd want my husband to marry again—just as soon as he could win a woman willing to tolerate his driving and his jokes.

Many of my friends disagree with me. Snapped one, "The thought of some strange woman running my house, taking over my lovely things and lying in my bed makes me see red!" There is an unreasonable longing in most women's hearts that their love should be enough. But I contend it's time we turned the light of common sense on the prejudice against husbands' remarrying.

I'm not saying a man should rush to the altar with the first dreamboat who appears on the horizon. But I am asking for an end to the twisted thinking that says a man must not remarry "out of consideration" for his dead wife.

"Of course the question would not arise," one stiffish matron told me. "John is already 53. I should hope he would remember his age."

Let's face facts: Old age no longer means sitting safe in the chimney corner, rocking the years away. It is a happy, useful life into the 70's and 80's. At 53 John still has a lot of living ahead—why shouldn't he want the benefits of love and companionship in his later years?

The woman who wants them denied to him doesn't know what adult love is. She confuses love with absolute possession. Surely the real test of love is whether you put the other person's happiness first.

Let's be realistic: The normal, healthy life involves a partner. No matter how well liked, the widower is a fifth wheel, left out of social gatherings he would attend if married. Trivial as these things seem, they deepen his sense of isolation. And I want my husband to be happy.

The man who marries again pays his first wife a great compliment. If he wants to marry a second time, he must have liked marriage. Conversely, when a widower loudly declares he will never again become involved with Woman, I, for one, wonder what went on in that vine-covered cottage for 15 years!

I'd want my husband to marry again so he would have fresh purpose to his life. I'd want him to have someone to listen to his dreams and disappointments. An amiable woman who could fix his favorite dishes, plan a reading list and remember where he left the car keys.

If we have children I hope even more that my husband would re-marry. A child needs a family home with a father and mother who love him and each other. The absence of either parent is a handicap that can cripple a personality.

In the words of your marriage vows, you promised to love, honor and cherish *till death do us part*. The marriage covenant does not rob the surviving partner of the opportunity of building a new, enduring second marriage.

Courage begins when we can admit that there is no life without some pain, some frustration; that there is no tragic accident to which we are immune; and that beyond the normal exercise of prudence we can do nothing about it.

But courage goes on to see that the triumph of life is not in pains avoided, but in joys lived completely in the moment of their happening. Courage lies in never taking so much as a good meal or a day of health and fair weather for granted. It lies in learning to be aware of our moments of happiness as sharply as our moments of pain. We need not be afraid to weep when we have cause to weep, so long as we can really rejoice at every cause for rejoicing.

— Victoria Lincoln in *The Arts of Living* (Simon and Schuster)

The Best Advice I Ever Had

By
Konrad Adenauer
Chancellor, Federal Republic of Germany

THIS COUNSEL rang constantly in my ears when I was a boy: "Go the last mile—and enjoy it." It has stayed with me ever since, comforted me in difficult times and brought me moments of deep contentment.

It came from my father, who had gained it through experience. As a young soldier he did his duty so well that he was made an officer on the battlefield—in the Prussian Army an almost unheard-of achievement. Later, as a law-court clerk, he worked hard and well, earned a free conscience and so at home was a relaxed, contented man. Happiness to him was simply work's greatest by-product. "Only when you have done your *full* duty," he said, "are you completely happy." That is what he meant by "going the last mile."

Like most youngsters, I would have much preferred playing ball to conjugating Latin verbs, but Father insisted that mastering my studies was my chief duty. "Concentrate," he urged me, his pointed beard bristling with earnestness. "Do not let yourself be diverted until you are finished—not even if a cannon goes off at your elbow."

Thanks to his insistence I did well in school. Yet, despite Father's serious attitude toward work, our home was not a gray, joyless place. It rang with laughter and the sounds of good times well earned.

At the University of Munich my clear duty was to complete my studies as soon as possible in order to help support the family. Night after night I studied a lawbook by the light of a petroleum lamp. When I felt I had to go to sleep, I would remember my father's advice, and carry on. But how could I "go the last mile" every night?

Then it came to me. I filled my porcelain washbasin with water and put it on the floor beside me, took off my shoes and read on, barefoot. When my heavy head drooped with sleepiness, I plunged my feet into the cold water and shocked myself awake. Thanks to this stratagem, I finished the university in three years instead of four.

My father's counsel has helped me many other times since. I have never kept office hours. I have found that if you want to go the last mile you don't hear the clock strike six any more than you hear the cannon at your elbow.

I remember a meeting of the Cologne municipal council in 1918. As mayor, I wanted to see the old fortifications circling the city replaced not by factories or houses crowded together but by a refreshing green girdle of parks.

No one on the council agreed. I began to feel I would have to capitulate. Then Father's admonition popped into my head, and I went all the way in marshaling my data—contrasts between the health of people in large and small cities, charts on relative costs of government, the latest authentic information on every phase of the question. After I had presented the facts at several meetings, all the councilmen but one were convinced. Finally that one rose and said, "Let him have his way—he *will* have it anyhow!" I have sometimes thought that the people of Cologne have my father to thank for the beautiful greensward that now encircles the city.

When Nazism came to Germany I felt duty-bound to oppose it, for I clearly saw that it could only lead to slavery. Going all the way against it took me to an SS prison, where my wife and I spent a cheerless silver wedding anniversary. But I never regretted my stand. The sense of having done what seemed to me my complete duty gave me an inner serenity more precious than any physical comfort.

In fact, most of the happiness in what to me has been a very happy life has come, I believe, from the times I have "gone the last mile."

MARRIAGE
HAS IMPROVED

By Paul H. Landis

Professor of Rural Sociology, State College of Washington *Condensed from Redbook*

DESPITE all the head-shaking and talk about divorce rate, every sign points to the fact that marriage is better than it has ever been in our national history. It is high time that we look at what is right with marriage, rather than what is wrong with it. Our high divorce rate does not prove that marriage is heading for the institutional junk heap. It is, rather, a clear indication that modern couples demand more from marriage than their ancestors did.

When grandpa married 50 years ago, happiness was not the primary aim of his marriage. He was looking for a mate to help him make a living and rear a family. If happiness should come his way it would be welcomed. It would also quite probably be a surprise.

Today we have made happiness the first demand of marriage. It is doubtful that humanity has ever sought a goal in marriage so difficult —and yet so worthy of realization.

Three out of four couples live through their life span without shattering this dream. We cannot claim that all who remain loyal to the marriage pledge realize happiness fully; but many studies show that two thirds of all married couples are either "happy" or "very happy." The studies are not based solely on self-ratings; friends rate the marriage, too.

We have grown wiser, to be sure, and we no longer expect to find happiness ready-made, neatly boxed like the wedding gifts. Rather it must be achieved by a slow, sometimes painful struggle. But this wiser recognition does not lessen the concern with happiness; we have simply shifted from glib "happy" talk to the more realistic task of achieving happiness.

Marriage failure is often brought about by the fact that we demand the impossible. Somerset Maugham has suggested that American women seem to expect of their husbands "a perfection English women only hope to find in their butlers." And what a model of efficiency, romantic attraction and social competence the modern husband demands in his wife!

Consider what we require of a wife or husband emotionally. Because we Americans move frequently, we often become separated from relatives and lose track of old friends. Neighborhoods are large and impersonal, and even the people next door may be strangers. We cannot expect to find the neighborly companionship, loyalty and affection which our grandparents took for granted in the intimate community of yesterday. Yet we must have this warmth in our lives, or be miserably lonely. Today we demand of our husbands or wives all the affection and companionship formerly supplied by relatives and neighbors.

There are many respects in which yesterday's philosophy of marriage was inferior to that of today. A few generations ago most girls were taught that they must tolerate the intimate relation of marriage as a necessary yielding to male desire. Pleasure was incidental—and a little indecent. But today's young people are taught to expect emotional oneness in marriage through the fulfillment of mutual sex desire.

The wife of yesterday was supposed to bolster her husband's ego and to concentrate on helping him realize his wishes; hers were always secondary. The daily routine of housework and child care represented the limits of her world. Today's goal of equality embraces the hope that the wife will win a satisfying place for herself in the community through her own achievement.

On the strictly material side, we have gotten away from the long hours of work which so easily grind down the human spirit. Women's work in the old-fashioned family was literally never done. Today's woman, even in rural areas, has far more leisure, with freedom outside the home to enrich her life by work and diversions that make her a better wife, a more capable mother, a healthier individual. She enjoys marriage because she enjoys life in a way wives of previous generations could not possibly do.

Marriage has traditionally been for woman a necessity, if she were to find a secure and respected place in the community. Today custom permits her real independence in thought and behavior; not only is marriage optional, but the kind of marriage she will have is her choice as well. Because she is independent, she is a more lively, interesting and companionable wife.

The best test of success in marriage is the happiness of children in the home. A recent study at the State College of Washington asked college girls and their mothers whether or not they considered their childhood homes "happy." Compared with their mothers, more than twice as many of the present generation rated their childhood homes as "very happy."

It is natural that young people have absorbed much of our pessimism regarding marriage today. But in spite of the gloomy picture painted for them, they are marrying younger and a higher proportion are marrying than ever before. About 92 percent of all men and women in this country now marry, the highest record in our history. In fact, we are one of the most marrying people in the civilized world.

True, we do have too many divorces in certain circles. But if we make happiness the goal of marriage, as the tendency of our time has been, we must grant the right of divorce to those who fail after having exhausted every effort to find happiness with each other.

But this is not the end of our marriage system. In the "good old days" more marriages were broken than today, and far more children were orphaned than now. The difference is, of course, in the *way* families are broken. Then early deaths took a heavy toll. There is this to be said in favor of divorce: it leaves fewer orphans, for two divorces in three leave no offspring.

Most divorced persons today remarry—three fourths of them in less than five years. Actually, the divorced man or woman is more likely to marry than any person of similar age in the population. At 30, for example, 94 divorced women in 100 will remarry; but only 48 out of 100 spinsters of a comparable age will ever marry. Figures for divorced men are similar. Divorced persons have had the worst possible experience with marriage, and yet they are most willing of all to try again to find happiness through remarriage. This does not mean that we should encourage divorce. But we must acknowledge that in a second marriage many succeed in realizing the happiness which was absent in their first.

Too many young people still approach marriage in anxious ignorance. Even in college we teach more about raising crops and livestock than babies. The time has come when we should more seriously prepare the young for the all-important jobs of mate selection, marriage adjustment and parenthood.

It is time, too, to guide our youngsters in faith rather than despair. Marriage is not an outworn garment. The arrangement whereby a male provides for a mate and her young predates recorded history.

There is every reason to assume that marriage is here to stay. We have made marriage better, and we can keep on improving it.

++++++++++++

You Can't Trust Anybody?

"WHAT we call society," says S. I. Hayakawa, "is a vast network of mutual agreements." We cheerfully trust our lives to total strangers in the persons of locomotive engineers, subway motormen, airplane pilots, elevator boys, steamship captains, taxi drivers, traffic cops, and unhesitatingly consign all our worldly goods to bankers and insurance companies.

I asked a hotel manager, with experience in both Florida and New England, to estimate how many of his patrons turned out to be dead beats. "Oh, a quarter of one percent," he said. If this proportion were as much as ten percent, society would rock; charge accounts, installment buying, even ordinary banking would be impossible. If it were 25 percent, society would explode. Yet how many of us cherish the delusion that "you can't trust anybody these days"? If you couldn't, it is safe to say you wouldn't be here.

—Stuart Chase, *Roads to Agreement* (Harper)

FORGET IT!

By W. E. Sangster
Minister, The Central Hall, London

Condensed from Guideposts

I HAPPEN TO have a good memory. I can remember pretty well anything I want to. But more important, I have learned the truth that lies in the words of the French philosopher Henri Bergson: "It is the function of the brain to enable us not to remember but to forget."

Plenty of people are forgetful in an absent-minded way. Every article the great missionary Temple Gairdner possessed came back to his office through the post. Shoes, Bible, toothbrush, waistcoat followed one another in an unending stream. On one occasion, visiting in Birmingham, he met a friend on the street and put down his bag to make a note in his diary. Then he went blithely down the street minus the bag.

Perhaps this absent-mindedness isn't as funny as it sounds. Perhaps a wife whose birthday is forgotten by her husband doesn't think it hilarious. But if I were asked what causes more trouble in the world—the things forgotten which should have been remembered or the things remembered which should have been forgotten—I'm sure I should fix on the latter. What most of us need is not so much a good memory as a good forgettery.

Some forgetting is natural, a consequence of the passing of time and not the outcome of conscious effort. There is sense, as well as nonsense, in the old saying that time heals. For time brings new experiences—happy ones—and revives sweet memories to overlay the bitterness of loss.

The fact is that conscious memory has a preference for the pleasant. She is always trying to stuff painful experiences down the hole of oblivion and to preserve only the things we are glad to recall. Yet natural memory alone cannot deal with all unpleasant things. It starts us right but we must find ways of working with it.

One may not always be able to forget a tragic occurrence, but one can learn, in remembering it, not to be emotionally overwhelmed. The real danger in remembering the wrong things is that we remember them not as facts but as convulsive experiences, and we keep resentment, self-pity or embarrassment alive in our souls.

I meet people who seem to think that if someone has played them a dirty trick resentment is justified. Justified or not, resentment and the ache for revenge are poison. It is better to get rid of them, and the best way to get rid of them is to learn to forget.

If you say, "I *can't* forget," I will say, "You are wrong. You imply that the will has no power over the memory. But the will can be trained to do the work."

Immanuel Kant lived for years in entire and trustful dependence on his manservant, Lampe. Then, one sad day, he discovered that Lampe had systematically robbed him, and he felt compelled to sack his old servant. But how he missed him! In his journal this pathetic line appears: "Remember to forget Lampe."

Remember to forget! Here is one of the foremost philosophical figures of all time, and he studies to forget.

You forget by reversing the process of remembering. To remember, one must revive the image, hold it in the mind for so long, revive it again—and regularly; and then it's there for good.

Reverse that process. *Don't* revive the image. When it rises of itself, summoned by some association of ideas, turn your thoughts immediately from it. Have in the antechamber of your mind a few interesting themes always on call: things you find particularly absorbing and which have power to grip your thought and imagination. All of us have such themes—our work, our vacation plans, our sports or hobbies.

None of these substitute themes is of any use unless it has power to grip the mind, and what grips one mind may not grip another. A friend of mine, a shy soul, outwits the recollection of a public gaucherie by instantly remembering an occasion when he was a social success. I know another man who blots out unwanted memories by trying to write a poem, and another who daydreams about a fortune he plans to make. It does not matter what the substitue image is, if it can thrust the other thing from your attention. Prayer will not do if it is prayer *about the thing itself*. That keeps it in the memory. But prayer is excellent if it creates receptivity to love, forgiveness, peace and poise.

Dealt with in this way, the thing you want to forget loses mastery. Remember that the deeper laws of the mind are working with your will to help you forget. Most of the things you want to forget want to be forgotten; you are not working *against* but *with* nature if you learn to forget.

A recollection firmly rejected in a disciplined way recurs less and less frequently. Fewer and fewer will be its associations in your mind. When it does recur it will be as a cold fact only: the emotions will not be overheated by it. Thus you bring science to the aid of sense.

Restitution helps forgetfulness. No man should hope to forget the wrong things he's done till he has done also whatever he can to put them right. A false statement can be corrected, hurt feelings can be healed by honest apologies. To do everything you can to make amends helps your misdeeds into oblivion. A gnawing conscience keeps the memory terribly alert.

I saw the need and the possibility of forgetting years ago, and I've been at it long enough to know that my method works. Indeed, I proved it at Christmas. One of my guests had come a couple of days early and saw me sending off the last of my Christmas cards. He was startled to see a certain name and address on an envelope.

"Surely you are not sending a greeting to *him*," he said.

"Why not?" I asked.

"But you remember," he began, "18 months ago . . ."

I remembered then the thing the man had done to me. But I also remembered resolving at the time that I would remember to forget. And I had forgotten!

I posted the card.

Europe's outstanding oldsters belie the
concept of the "decline" of old age

A Second "Prime of Life"—After 70

By Martin Gumpert, M.D.
Author of "You Are Younger Than You Think," "The Anatomy of Happiness," etc.

Condensed from The New York Times Magazine

OLD AGE has long been misinterpreted, clouded by prejudices and conventional assumptions which are the harder to overcome because they have been accepted by the old people themselves throughout their lives. The aged have been considered the inescapable victims of human decline, nearer to death than to life, a sort of refuse which nature would take care of soon enough.

Once, on a trip to Europe I visited a number of persons of advanced age who have actively rejected this traditional concept. They are to me the pioneers of a future type of old person; they are participating creatively in life as long as life lasts.

We think of age 65 as the milestone where active life stops and old age and retirement begin. How arbitrary this artificial signpost is! The youngest person I interviewed in Europe was 77.*

In Italy I met 91-year-old Vittorio Emanuele Orlando, the only survivor of the prime ministers who concluded the Treaty of Versailles. He is a small man, but heavy set, with a full crop of white hair—a sort of friendly miniature lion, impulsive and agile. An active member of the Italian Senate, he is head of a successful law firm, president of the Rome lawyers' guild and professor at the University of Rome. In spite of violent political controversies—he is completely independent in his politics—he is treated with reverence as the "grand old man" of Italy. He sleeps well, has never been sick, takes long walks, drinks wine.

*Several of these men have died since this article was first published in 1951.

Another elderly Italian of incredible vitality is Dr. Raffaele Bastianelli, a surgeon of international reputation. At 87 he operates three times weekly, drives his own car, has daily office hours, does research, and even flew his own plane until five years ago. Bastianelli has had rheumatic arthritis and a bad stomach since he was 30, yet he is a tall, erect man who reads without glasses, whose hands do not show the slightest tremor.

Philosopher Benedetto Croce, 85, lives in the center of Naples, near the Italian Institute of Historical Studies which he founded and which houses his wonderful library and a lecture room where he teaches. He gets up at 8 a. m. and works for ten hours. He eats very little—no meat —but seems well nourished and looks like a kindly old walrus.

Croce suffered a stroke last year but has completely recovered—he speaks, hears and writes without difficulty. He, too, is active as a Senator and is of inexhaustible productivity. Two books by him were published in 1950; a new book of his philosophical essays is almost ready.

Bernhard Berenson, the art historian, 86, lives near Florence, surrounded by the most exquisite samples of Florentine painting, Asiatic and Egyptian sculpture, and a well-organized library of 50,000 books which someday will belong to Harvard. He has just published a book on the painter Caravaggio. Another book is ready for publication. If only, he says, he could stand at a corner with his hat and beg people to throw him their wasted hours.

George Santayana, the philosopher, 87, has lived for the past ten years in Rome. His eyesight is failing but his work goes on and he showed me the proofs of a voluminous new book. He reads Latin literature, is highly interested in modern poetry.

Edouard Herriot of France has just turned 79. He wakes at 7 a. m., has breakfast in bed and works until ten or 11. On three days he presides at the National Assembly; he is also president of his Radical Socialist Party. He sees countless official visitors. Every Saturday morning he drives to Lyons, of which he is the mayor. He spends Sunday with his wife in an old castle, Monday in his town house and with the city council. On Tuesday he goes back to Paris. He writes two articles every month, is preparing the second volume of his memoirs and in 1949 finished a book on Rodin.

He loves music and the theater, goes twice a month to the Comédie Française, and his greatest enjoyment is regular attendance at the circus, accompanied by small children. With all this goes a phlebitis of his left leg and chronic bronchitis.

In England there is Viscount Samuel, former British High Commissioner of Palestine, now 80, who has just published a work that deals with the interrelation of science, philosophy and religion. "This book wrote itself," he said. "It was a new subject to me. But the older I grow the easier I find the flow of ideas."

There is Bertrand Russell, preparing his autobiography at 79 and complaining that he is easily tired because he cannot walk more than five miles at a time. There is Lord Horder, a physician to the King, whom I visited in his Harley Street office the day after his 80th birthday. He puts in 12 hours of work daily, and writes poetry and takes care of his garden in his leisure time.

Among the notable women I talked with was Dr. A. Helen Boyle of Brighton, 81, the first woman president of the Royal Medico-Psychological Association. She practices psychiatry in London and Brighton and is now interested in founding a center to promote collaboration between clergy and physicians. Dr. Boyle eats what she likes, drinks enormous quantities of tea—and small ones of whisky—sleeps one hour in the afternoon and goes to bed at 2 a.m.

There is no fixed rule of physical behavior for a long and successful life; some of the persons I interviewed had never been seriously ill, some had been sick throughout their lives. Some are well-to-do, some are poor; but none of them seemed to be degraded by extreme poverty, none spoiled by extreme richness.

All of them seemed to enjoy their lives far beyond the average middle-aged individual, and none seemed afraid of death. They seemed to have a need for human warmth, human contact, for being talked to. Yet none showed the features of bitter despair and retardation which we so often encounter in older people; all of them were kind and thoughtful and emotionally sensitive. The most frequent complaint was a deficient memory for names.

All of these people have unceasingly used their intelligence, have continued to learn and to grow. They have never narrowed their interests; they are "modern" in the best sense of the word. The most constructive impression I had is that old age develops a creative urge and power of its own, of which we have hardly taken notice up to now.

Almost daily, among the old people I meet, I observe this need to create, this sudden wave of emotions, this craving for knowledge and human growth. Such enlargement of their existence has often developed, to their own surprise, for the first time in their lives. And I wonder whether life as a whole will not be richer and happier for all of us once we start discovering the unknown treasures of old age, now hidden under old age's miseries.

We sometimes call an old man's dotage "second childhood." I suggest that there is often, instead, a second prime of life which we should discover and explore and cherish.

Food to Grow On

No one seems to agree about what a well-balanced diet for children is, but here's what my two-year-old Johnnie eats:

Breakfast. Three bites of cereal, a sip of milk, a handful of rice (raw; he got it out of the box when the doorbell rang), a greenish ribbon, origin unknown (I saw it just before it disappeared), a dog biscuit (stolen from the dog) and a peach.

Lunch. A soft-cooked egg, half a glass of milk, two bites of soap (he wanted more, but I caught him), a rubber band (I got that just before it went down the hatch), and some toast (spread liberally with chlorophyll tooth paste when I was concentrating on the washing).

Dinner. A hamburger steak (complete with onions and ketchup because his daddy uses them and he won't eat it unless he gets the same), some peas, one bite of cottage cheese (deposited later on the rug), a glass of milk and a half bottle of hair oil (which he took on while his daddy and I were watching television).

My son is a healthy, red-cheeked boy, heavier and taller than other children of his age in the neighborhood, and the doctor says his diet is responsible.

—Letter from Mrs. D. W. McCarthy, in the Wichita, Kans., *Beacon*

There Is No Average Boy

By J. Roswell Gallagher, M.D.

School physician at Phillips Academy, Andover, Mass.

Condensed from The Atlantic Monthly

AM HAD just passed his 14th birthday; he weighed 150 pounds, was five feet ten inches tall, and might well have shaved every day. His ninth-grade teachers complained that he did not show the maturity which they felt a boy as big and as apparently grown-up should have. "He's always doing childish, silly things."

Sam's father was exasperated and his mother confused. "He's tired all the time, sleeps 14 hours at a stretch. He won't listen to us and he won't tell us anything. Do you think he's all right physically—is he normal?"

Billy lived down the street from Sam. Their parents had about the same interests, the boys had been fed about the same kind of food. But, at 16, Billy weighed only 115 pounds, was five feet four inches tall, and, although a little fuzz had recently begun to appear, had no real excuse for shaving. Until his third year in high school he had been a model boy. Then his marks fell off, he seemed inattentive, less willing to participate. At home he became uncommunicative, dodged family gatherings and parties. His mother anxiously took him to a doctor. The doctor sent mama out and discovered the real cause of the boy's unhappiness and anxiety—the fact that his growth and development had proceeded at a less rapid rate than usual.

Both Sam and Billy are normal boys. Adolescents vary tremendously in the rate and manner of their development. The *average* weight of one group of schoolboys was found to be 127 pounds, but the *range* in weight was 80 to 199! There is no correct average weight, or height, or grade level in school for any age; nor is there an average age at which boys should take responsibility, drive cars, stay out late or shave.

A boy can be well and happy and turn out to be a fine adult even though he weighs less than the average or has "grown six inches in the last year." Real abnormalities of growth are rare.

It is sensible to be interested in whether a boy is growing and maturing; but neither the rate of his growth nor whether he is "average" is of any significance; the most you can do about these matters is to give him food and affection. Don't worry or cause him to worry.

Boys want to feel security, affection, confidence in them. Their apparent indifference and their awkward steps toward independence are indicators of their inner needs and feelings. There is no quicker way to rob them of security than through oversolicitude, constant critical appraisal, and too frequent comparison with a chart or a neighbor's son.

Along with differences in physique go differences in intellectual interests, control of emotions, quality of judgment. It is easy to understand the teacher or parent who complains, "I wish he'd grow up," but it is unfortunate that the lad is so frequently criticized for being his real age. It is the rare boy who doesn't want to grow up—who doesn't want to behave in an adult fashion. And a rowdy this month may next month be viewing with disgust his classmates' uproarious behavior at the movies.

"When is Tom going to get interested in school? All he thinks about is jam sessions, girls and why we don't need the car as much as he does. When do boys usually get serious about school? Won't you please talk to him?"

I had no idea of the average age for a boy to get interested in school, but I found Tom a delightful conversationalist and he vastly improved my knowledge of swing. During the next two years Tom came in to see me frequently. School was rarely mentioned. The important thing is that *he* did the talking, that he had a listener who was slow to make suggestions or give advice. His parents had long since given up their exhortations and their half-serious threats—and then what some, who forget they are dealing with youth, call a miracle happened. Tom was in his senior year: he hadn't been near me for a month when one day he burst in, waved a list of school grades under my nose and let go comments about his ability as a scholar.

His elation was quickly spent but the academic zeal has persisted, and it is not that of a "grind"; it is that of a boy with real interest in studies, of a boy now attacking them with that great store of energy which he had been saving up all those years. It doesn't always happen, but I'm sure there is no "average" age at which it should appear.

Adolescents are not machines—new, shiny, repulsively similar, fresh off the assembly line. They are maddening as a lazy trout, unpredictable and surprising as a land breeze—and brimming with a capacity for change which we adults have lost. Standardization may be desirable for a chain-store product but, in people as in life, variety lends charm. The average is certainly no "better," no more desirable, than the unusual.

Courage

The courage that my mother had
    Went with her, and is with her still:
Rock from New England quarried;
    Now granite in a granite hill.

The golden brooch my mother wore
    She left behind for me to wear;
I have no thing I treasure more:
    Yet, it is something I could spare.

Oh, if instead she'd left to me
    The thing she took into the grave!—
That courage like a rock, which she
    Has no more need of, and I have.

—Edna St. Vincent Millay, *Mine the Harvest:*
A Collection of New Poems (Harper)

I Said I Would Fight— and I Did

By Albert Payson Terhune

THE CAR was making 50 miles an hour along the dark road. I was covering four miles an hour in the opposite direction, on the way back from my evening hike. The car went on under its own power. I didn't.

They got me home, somehow, and decanted me into a bed. The doctors, including a covey of specialists, inspected the remains. After I lay a few weeks in inert helplessness, they gave, in effect, this verdict:

I never could hope to do any more creative work. (Shell shock, presumably permanent, would see to that.) I never could hope to walk again. It would be wise to take off much of my right leg and at least three fingers of my right hand—perhaps the whole hand.

That was the prospect held out to a man who had always been a vigorous athlete and a busy writer.

I have seen a mighty swat and a pailful of ice water bring a maudlin drunk sharply back to his senses. In like manner that glum and multiple medical verdict yanked me out of doped drowsiness.

I told the gloomy prophets that they were wrong. There would be no amputation. Nor would there be a helpless and workless lifetime in bed. I said I was going to fight. I was going to win. And I did.

As a first step I refused to let them shoot any further morphia into me. True, morphia slowed down the eternal ghastly pain. But nobody can put up his best battle when he is doped.

Then I began to exercise. And never in my decades of athletics did I exercise so hard and so painfully. For many hours a day, at short intervals, I flexed and twisted the numbed leg and arm.

It was grueling work; the more so because for about three weeks it seemed hopeless. Then gloriously pringling pains began to blossom forth, and with them the ability to make some feeble rudimentary use of the crushed sinews. Day by day there was more and more life and more wholesome hurt in arm and leg.

Next I tried to hobble around my room on crutches. My first efforts resulted in eternal tumbles. It took two months to learn to keep some kind of balance. But at last I mastered the trick of crutch-walking.

From two crutches to a single crutch, a tiring but far shorter period of practice. Thence, in another two months, to a specially made cane. Keenly I missed the rocklike support of the crutch. I had to study the art of walking from an almost new angle.

At length came the day of days when I undertook to walk the whole 26-foot length of my room without the aid of even a stick. I fell three times. But I fell less and less often as the experiments went on.

I practiced walking, studying my gait in front of a big mirror. I was a sorry spectacle. I strove to correct each fault of foot and of body, as carefully as once I had tried to correct faults in my boxing, weight-throwing, running and fencing. You see, I had had long experience in such study. In less than ten months in all I could walk—if with a slight accent—nearly as well as the average man of my age.

As for the shell shock, my wife taught me how to quell that. She said: "If you have typhoid or a broken collar bone, there are a thousand doctors who can cure you. But nobody except yourself can cure your smashed nerves."

That was rare wisdom, though it cost me months of constant and effortful will power to profit by it. It was the toughest part of the whole fight. Yet the next year I, who "never could hope to do any more creative writing," had the second most lucrative season of my career.

The most valuable experience I have ever had was that unanimous Thumbs Down medical verdict. It made me fighting mad. And so it saved me from spending the rest of my long life idly in a wheel chair.

HOW TO HELP
SOMEONE IN SORROW

By Howard Whitman   Condensed from The Christian Advocate

OST OF US want to be helpful when grief strikes a friend, but often we don't know how. We may end up doing nothing because we don't know the right—and helpful—things to say and do. Because that was my own experience recently, I resolved to gather pointers which might be useful to others as well as to myself.

Ministers, priests and rabbis deal with such situations every day. I went to scores of them, of all faiths, in all parts of the country.

Here are some specific suggestions they made:

1. *Don't try to "buck them up."* This surprised me when the Rev. Arthur E. Wilson of Providence, R. I., mentioned it. But the others concurred. It only makes your friend feel worse when you say, "Come now, buck up. Don't take it so hard."

A man who has lost his wife must take it hard (if he loved her). "Bucking him up" sounds as though you are minimizing his loss. But the honest attitude, "Yes, it's tough, and I sure know it is," makes your friend feel free to express grief and recover from it. The "don't take it so hard" approach deprives him of the natural emotion of grief, stops up the safety valve God has given him.

2. *Don't try to divert them.* Rabbi Martin B. Ryback of Norwalk, Conn., pointed out that many people making condolence calls purposely veer away from the subject. They make small talk about football, fishing, the weather—anything but the reason for their visit.

The rabbi calls this "trying to camouflage death." The task of the mourner, difficult as it is, is to face the fact of death, and go on from there. "It would be far better," Rabbi Ryback suggested, "to sit silently and say nothing than to make obvious attempts to distract. The sorrowing friend sees through the effort to divert him. When the visitor leaves, reality hits him all the harder."

3. *Don't be afraid to talk about the person who has passed away.* Well-intentioned friends often shy away from mentioning the deceased. The implication is that the whole thing is too terrible to mention.

"The helpful thing," advised Rabbi Henry E. Kagan of Mount Vernon, N. Y., "is to talk about the person as you knew him in the fullness of his life, to re-create a living picture to replace the picture of death."

Once Rabbi Kagan called on a woman who had lost her brother. "I didn't know your brother too well," he said. "Tell me about him." The woman started talking and they discussed her brother for an hour. Afterward she said, "I feel relieved now for the first time since he died."

4. *Don't be afraid of causing tears.* When a good friend of mine lost a child I said something which made his eyes fill up. "I put my foot in it," I said, in relating the incident to the Rev. D. Russell Hetsler of Brazil, Ind. "No, you didn't," he replied. "You helped your friend to express grief in a normal, healthy way. That is far better than to stifle grief when friends are present, only to have it descend more crushingly when one is all alone."

Fear of causing tears, probably more than anything else, makes people stiff and ineffective. Visiting a friend who has lost his wife, they may be about to mention a ride in the country when they remember the man's wife used to love rides in the country. They don't dare speak of peonies because they were her favorite flower. So they freeze up.

"They really are depriving their friend of probably the greatest help they could give him," Pastor Hetsler commented. "That is, to help him experience grief in a normal way and get over it." Medical and psychological studies back up the pastor's contention that *expressing* grief is good and *repressing* it is bad. "If a comment of yours brings tears," he concluded, "remember—they are healthy tears."

5. *Let them talk.* "Sorrowing people need to talk," explained the Rev.

Vern Swartsfager of San Francisco. "Friends worry about their ability to *say* the right things. They ought to be worrying about their ability to *listen.*"

If the warmth of your presence can get your friend to start talking, keep quiet and listen—even though he repeats the same things a dozen times. He is not telling you news but expressing feelings that need repetition. Pastor Swartsfager suggested a measuring stick for the success of your visit: "If your friend has said a hundred words to your one, you've helped a lot."

6. *Reassure—don't argue.* "Everybody who loses a loved one has guilt feelings—they may not be justified but they're natural," Rabbi Joseph R. Narot of Miami pointed out. A husband feels he should have been more considerate of his wife; a parent feels he should have spent more time with his child; a wife feels she should have made fewer demands on her husband. The yearning, "If only I had not done this, or done that—if I only had a chance to do it now," is a hallmark of grieving.

These feelings must work their way out. You can give reassurance. Your friend must slowly come to the realization that he or she was, in all probability, a pretty good husband, wife or parent.

7. *Communicate—don't isolate.* Too often a person who has lost a loved one is overwhelmed with visitors for a week or so; then the house is empty. Even good friends sometimes stay away, believing that people in sorrow "like to be alone."

"That's the 'silent treatment,'" remarked Father Thomas Bresnaham of Detroit. "There's nothing worse." Our friend has not only lost his loved one—he has lost us too.

It is in that after-period, when all the letters of sympathy have been read and acknowledged and people have swung back into daily routine, that friends are needed most.

Keep in touch, Father Bresnaham urges. See your friend more often than you did before. See him for any purpose—for lunch, for a drive in the country, for shopping, for an evening visit. He has suffered a deep loss. Your job is to show him, by implication, how much he still has left. Your being with him is a proof to him that he still has resources.

8. *Perform some concrete act.* The Rev. William B. Ayers of Wollaston, Mass., told me of a sorrowing husband who lost all interest in

food until a friend brought over his favorite dish and simply left it there at suppertime. "That's a wonderful way to help, by a concrete deed which in itself may be small yet carries the immense implication that you care," Pastor Ayers declared.

We should make it our business, when a friend is in sorrow, to do at least one practical, tangible act of kindness. Here are some to choose from: run errands with your car, take the children to school, bring in a meal, do the dishes, make necessary phone calls, pick up mail at the office, help acknowledge condolence notes, shop for the groceries.

9. *Swing into action.* Action is the symbol of going on living.

By swinging into action with your friend, whether at his hobby or his work, you help build a bridge to the future. Perhaps it means painting the garage with him, or hoeing the garden. Or spending an afternoon with a woman friend mending the children's clothes, or browsing through antique shops.

In St. Paul, Minn., the Rev. J. T. Morrow told me of a man who had lost a son. The man's hobby had been refinishing furniture. When he called on him Pastor Morrow said, "Come on, let's go down to the basement." They sanded a table together. When Pastor Morrow left, the man said, "This is the first time I've felt I could go on living."

Sorrowing people, Pastor Morrow pointed out, tend to drop out of things. They're a little like the rider who has been thrown from a horse. If they are to ride again, better get them back on the horse quickly.

10. *"Get them out of themselves,"* advised Father James Keller, leader of the Christophers. Once you have your friend doing things for himself, his grief is nearly cured. Once you have him doing things for others, it *is* cured.

Grief runs a natural course. It will pass. But if there is only a vacuum behind it, self-pity will rush in to fill it. To help your friend along the normal course of recovery, guide him to a new interest.

Volunteer work for a charity, enrollment in a community group to help youngsters, committee work at church or temple are ways of getting people "out of themselves."

If you and I, when sorrow strikes our friends, follow even a few of these pointers, we will be helpful.

Ministers, priests and rabbis have a spiritual job to do; they can do that better than we can. But we have a practical job of helpfulness; we can do that better than they.

One of the clergymen I met on my rounds, the Rev. Loyal M. Thompson of Kewanee, Ill., carried with him for years—until it was worn to shreds—a bookmark which a woman had embroidered for him. On visits to people in sorrow he would show them the back of the embroidery, a senseless mass of threads going every which way. Then he would turn it over to the right side, and the threads spelled out "God Is Love."

We may not be able to explain what often seems senseless about death. But by our helpfulness we can give living proof of the right side of the embroidery.

Copyright 1953 by The Reader's Digest Association, Inc. (January 1954 issue)
Condensed from The Christian Advocate, December 3, 1953

When Mrs. Otis Skinner died, Alexander Woollcott sent a note of condolence which Mr. Skinner prized above all others. It read: "Dear Otis: You lucky bum! You had 40 blissful years together, you and that enchanting woman. How I envy you. A. Woollcott."

—John Mason Brown in *The Saturday Review*

SOME THINGS will never change. The voice of forest water in the night, a woman's laughter in the dark, the clean, hard rattle of raked gravel, the cricketing stitch of midday in hot meadows, the delicate web of children's voices in bright air—these things will never change.

The glitter of sunlight on roughened water, the glory of the stars, the innocence of morning, the smell of the sea in harbors, the feathery blur and smoky buddings of young boughs—these things will always be the same.

All things belonging to the earth will never change—the leaf, the blade, the flower, the wind that cries and sleeps and wakes again, the trees whose stiff arms clash and tremble in the dark—these things will always be the same, for they come up from the earth that never changes.   —Thomas Wolfe's *You Can't Go Home Again* (Harper)

Take God with You on Monday

Wallace C. Speers

Vice-President, James McCutcheon & Co.

As told to William Drake

Condensed from The American Magazine

I N THESE DAYS of fear and anxiety, when the very existence of the human race seems threatened, a solution for our difficulties lies at hand. It is the application of the great truths of religion to everyday life.

I am not a clergyman. I am a merchant engaged in buying and selling goods. I have never been a very pious person and believe I am practical and hardheaded. But during the past ten years, in coöperation with other laymen, I have been engaged in an experiment which clearly indicates that applied religion holds the answer to the problems which face us.

This experiment began one night in 1941 at my home in Montclair, N. J. Deeply disturbed about the state of the world, I had invited a dozen friends to my home, all successful businessmen whom I had known for years. "I've asked you here to see if we can figure out some way to make the world a better place for our children to grow up in," I told them.

That set off a talkfest which lasted until 2 a.m. Like me, most of these men practiced their religion on a one-day-a-week basis. Yet these businessmen were agreed that only through a wider acceptance of spiritual values could society be saved from eventual breakdown.

One man quoted G. K. Chesterton. "'Christianity has not failed,'" he said. "'It just never has been tried.'"

"We've left Christianity in the hands of the clergy for too long," another said. "The Twelve Apostles were laymen like us, yet they spread their faith to the ends of the earth. Maybe we can do something, too."

We resolved to try to find some workable pattern by which the laws of God for human conduct could be applied to industry, government and other human endeavors. Each man would do this in his own way, and we would get together occasionally and report our findings.

Out of that decision has grown the Laymen's Movement for a Christian World, of which I am chairman. We have never sought publicity or a large membership. Our organization, entirely nonsectarian and containing Catholics and Jews as well as Protestants, has only 1000 members scattered through 35 states and several nations in Europe. It was responsible for the inauguration of Laymen's Sunday, now observed annually by many churches throughout the nation. It also was largely responsible for the Prayer Room for people of all creeds in the United Nations headquarters in New York. We advocated the use of prayer in opening the U. N. General Assembly. And there have been many unpublicized results of our resolve to apply Christianity to everyday affairs.

Once a year we hold a national conference, and in some communities we meet briefly every week for prayer and consultation with one another. In New York some of our members go on occasion to a railway coach on Track 13, in Grand Central Terminal, where they are led in prayer by Ralston C. Young, a Negro redcap. Some of the members are national figures: Dwight D. Eisenhower, Francis B. Sayre, J. C. Penney, R. W. Woodruff, Thomas J. Watson, Conrad Hilton, John Q. Adams, Joseph F. Ford and John G. Ramsey. But the majority of us hold humbler positions in life. Among our members there are clerks, salesmen, garage mechanics, carpenters.

Working quietly as individuals and using religion, we have settled grave labor disputes; changed the working atmosphere in several large industries; injected spiritual values into some areas of education and community life; eradicated racial tensions in certain places. The results illustrate what can be done on a truly tremendous scale if more of us would apply the Lord's teachings to the world around us.

After that meeting in my home I began testing the efficacy of prayer.

I attended an important conference in a large New York club at which I became violently angry at a man who disagreed with me. I lost my head and gave him a fierce tongue-lashing. When I finished, an embarrassed silence fell over the conference table, followed by the expressed desire of several to abandon the project we were working on. In that moment, without anyone knowing what I was doing, I made one of my frequent "spot prayers."

"I've been stupid and lost my temper. God, please forgive me," I said. "Help me to see this other fellow's point of view, and help him to see mine."

When I looked up, the man whom I had just excoriated was actually grinning at me in a friendly way. In a few minutes we patched up our dispute and reached a sensible compromise. Had I not asked God's help, I'm sure that a useful enterprise would have been completely destroyed.

By talking with God frequently during the day I became a happier and more serene person, and created an atmosphere which made it easier for me to help others. I began applying religion directly to my business on a basis of live and *help* live instead of live and let live. In my home community I experimented with Christianity by serving on the school board, in an effort to bring a greater recognition of spiritual values to local education.

In many instances management-employe relations have been improved dramatically by simple Christian action on the part of an individual. One of our laymen, an industrial engineer in Chicago, prevailed upon a mine superintendent to try applying spiritual values to temporal situations. The superintendent did so. He singled out the most crotchety worker he could find and made a sincere effort to become friendly with him and help him solve his problems. After he had succeeded with that man, he repeated the process with all the men on his shift, one after the other.

The results were little short of miraculous. In less than a year's time the men on that crew were turning out so much more work than the other shifts in the mine that the company sent out a man from New York to investigate. It was thought they had discovered some new machine or technique which they were keeping secret.

It is impossible for us to separate spiritual values from any form of temporal activity if we wish for its successful long-term operation.

Another of our laymen, a famous brain surgeon, has put spiritual values to work in the operating room. Before every operation he lowers his head and prays. He does this for the same reason that he gathers around him the finest group of assistant surgeons available. He would be foolish, he says, if he did not avail himself of the help of the greatest physician of all—God.

A fire-insurance executive congratulated his adjusters in former years whenever they settled claims for less than the amount of damage actually sustained. Today he insists that they help clients not to underestimate their losses. The good will created has more than compensated for the extra money his company has paid out in settlements.

The ways in which laymen can put religious principles to work in everyday life are as limitless as the human imagination. The president of a large advertising agency is making his contribution to a better world by operating a unique job-finding forum in New York. Job-seekers are shown how to analyze their best employment qualifications, are advised how to apply for jobs, and guided toward jobs for which they are fitted. They are charged nothing for this service, but, in the altruistic spirit of the enterprise, are required to help others find positions as soon as they themselves obtain employment. Thousands of discouraged men and women have improved their status through the work of the forum. Some of them have stepped into jobs paying as much as $20,000 a year.

Another advertising executive, prominent in the Laymen's Movement, prays every morning that God grant him at least one opportunity during the day to be of service to other human beings. Not long ago he found one answer to his prayer in a magazine article describing deplorable conditions in certain women's prisons, where women became mentally ill because they were not provided with adequate clothing. The advertising man wrote to six large manufacturers of women's wear, suggesting that they donate some of their merchandise for the benefit of women prisoners.

The manufacturers shipped the ad man so many articles that they filled his office. Through prison-reform associations garments were sent to institutions where they were needed. Letters received from prison wardens and superintendents were almost tearfully grateful.

All around us, we have found, are opportunities for putting Christianity to work on a practical basis. The Laymen's Movement has not even scratched the surface of what needs to be done. Yet, as a small band of only 1000 men, we have proved that Christianity can be applied in a practical sense to temporal matters. What could not be accomplished by 100,000 laymen—or 100,000,000—who really worked with God to build a better world?

Feminine Figures

ONE MONTH not long ago my wife made a real effort to balance her checkbook. Instead of throwing away her canceled checks as she usually does, she matched them with her stubs. After one whole Sunday morning she handed me four sheets of typewritten figures with items and costs sitting neatly in their respective columns. I checked her total with the bank statement—and it balanced! Then, out of curiosity, I went over her list of items: Milkman—$11.25; Cleaner's—$4.60; and so forth. Everything was clear except for one item reading E.S.P.—$24.56.

"What does E.S.P. mean?" I asked warily.

"Error Some Place," she answered. —Robert S. Lee in *Ladies' Home Journal*

A WOMAN we know who could never keep her checkbook straight has solved her problem very neatly. It's an unorthodox method, but one that has enabled her to set up a Christmas-shopping fund as well. All she does is keep her checkbook without any cents. If a bill is for $7.20, she makes out a check for that amount, but in recording it and subtracting the amount from the balance, she calls it $8. If the amount is for $10.74, she enters $11. At the end of a month, after making out countless household and personal checks, she has a balance of about $20 that she thinks she spent but didn't. And at the end of the year, there it is—her Christmas fund. —"The Woman Who Sees" in New York *Sun*

Try to vary the habitual tempo of your work and play

Change Your PACE

By Hilton Gregory   *Condensed from The Rotarian*

ALL OF US have experienced at one time or another the feeling of renewal that comes from a change of pace. We may be walking or driving along slowly, and something happens that makes us speed up. New sensations occur; new thoughts cross the mind. We become more alert. Or if we have been walking breathlessly beyond our pace there is a feeling of relief, even repose, in slowing down.

The pace that kills is the pace that never changes; frequent change of pace will keep us from tedium on one hand or apoplexy on the other.

For most of us a change of pace means slowing down, but in many activities we should speed up. We may walk and talk too fast but think and work too slowly.

Everyone in journalism knows that as a deadline approaches the reporter, the make-up man, the people on the copy desk all turn out better work in half the time it takes when there is no pressure. The acceleration releases latent powers. I have seen men, when there is time, bone for an hour over a title or a heading—conjuring up, as the slow mind at work will, dozens that are no good. But as the last hour approaches, when there is no time to dally, their minds click and the captions come in a flash. It is not mere speed that does the trick, but speed that follows deliberation.

Experts in charge of reading clinics point out that the best way to get something out of the printed page is to read it fast, to set about to see how quickly it can be intelligently covered, because the mind may wander when reading is too slow. The chances are that you should change your reading pace from one of leisurely inspection to one of concentrated, swift consideration. On the other hand, if you have allowed yourself to become a hit-and-run reader, you may need to give more time. No one pace is adequate in reading. There are books to be read hastily and others to be read with loving delay.

I have a nephew whose slowness is the despair of his teachers, not to mention his kin. At the age of nine he gets his work done in his own good time. The other morning his mother suggested with wisdom that he write a letter before going to school. His other letters had taken as much as a day, off and on, to compose. In this case, his time was limited to 20 minutes in which to write his grandmother everything he could think of. The result was the best letter he had ever done. It was the change of pace that did it, by putting emphasis upon the preciousness of time and the importance of using it to maximum effect.

We've been kidding ourselves too long with the notion that we are rushed to death. We are rushed with the wrong things. In these we ought to slow down, but in others speed up. "Slow and easy" is no motto for an interesting life, as some contend. Indeed slowness may be a deterrent; often a man can get further with a difficult job by plunging into it full steam.

Not infrequently a change of pace is in itself a means of learning. Years of using the typewriter steadily—added to the fact that I never learned to write as a child—recently made it almost imperative that I improve my longhand. I discovered that I had been rushing pellmell through my words. I disciplined myself to write plainly, meticulously. Associates testify gratefully that the improvement is a long step toward legibility. And what was once a chore has become a pastime.

Thus a change in tempo may increase enjoyment whether or not it improves our work. If you are doing something tedious, it may become fun if done at a changed speed. Many tasks—to mention only cleaning house and writing letters—are oppressive in part at least because they are time-consuming. But if we make them an affair of dashing cavalry our attitude changes. The job becomes an adventure, or a contest at least. For, oddly enough, a job done at different speeds is not the same job at all. The motions and emotions connected with it are different. Many people who pine to change their jobs need only to change the pace with which they do their jobs—mix up their work and get variety into the tempo.

Change of pace is like what we call second wind; in moments of fatigue it sets up a fresh current of nervous energy. If you have been methodically moving around the house, making beds, dusting, sweeping, try shifting the flow of your energy into a different rhythm. Or in the office, vary rush typing with work at slower speed. As you work at any fatiguing task you'll find that change of tempo rewards you, like the second wind, with a glowing sense of power.

Nowhere in the simple acts of daily life does a change in pace make more difference than in eating. Most of us gulp our food, and we miss half the fun of eating. I was a fast eater, and so tried imagining that I was a slow-motion picture of myself. Then I really tasted for the first time foods I had been eating half-consciously all my life.

I live in one of the uncelebrated scenic spots of the United States. There are no travel folders to hymn its grandeur. Everyone rather accepts its charm as a matter of course, and one reason for this is that no one, save perhaps when mothering a new car, drives slowly enough to appreciate the region. Until I myself broke in a new car I never even saw an old tulip tree on the way to the station. Its top is broken by a generation of storms, some of its limbs are missing, yet it survives with a pride and strength that shame me in moments of trifling discouragement. It has been there for years but I never saw it while I was hellbent for nothing. And there is a cathedral of trees and rocks on the parkway not a mile from where I live—a place of quietness and strength. Even to glance at it thoughtfully in passing is to experience a moment of vespers. I had never been aware of this spot until I changed my pace.

Since in my work I have to talk a lot, I have fallen into the habit of talking rapidly. Lately I decided to alternate rapid speech with periods of slowing down, weighing each word, and letting its implications have full play. And this, I find, keeps the auditor's attention on edge, and makes me phrase more clearly the ideas I want to convey. But it does more—it affords me a new sense of confidence.

Haven't you, on the other hand, known dreary, hesitant people who ought to try talking fast for a change? While they fumble vaguely with facts, ideas and phrases, you'd like to jolt them into thinking a sentence swiftly through before they began it, so that words would follow one another with logical sequence and zip. Deliberate speeding up would not only add tremendously to their conversational effectiveness, but would also transform them by giving them a new and more sparkling personality.

In our method of thinking, above all, change of pace can be invaluable. The almost universal curse of worry is simply thought slowed down to a stumbling and circuitous walk. To think through and settle once for all a problem in the shortest possible time, and to act briskly and daringly on our decision, is to annihilate the problem of worry.

On the other hand, on busy days, try slowing down instead of speeding up. Linger over breakfast; pretend that you have a lifetime for the many things which must be crowded in before night. Live at slow motion. Instead of racing, make yourself stroll. And, paradoxically, when evening comes you will have actually done more work than if you had pushed yourself.

To live all one's life at *largo* would be deadly boring. The symphony you like or the musical composition that stirs you is neither fast nor slow throughout; it has as much variety in tempo as in mood. It is this in part that keeps your interest keyed to the theme.

If we are hectic and rushed it is not necessary to pull up stakes, move to the country and drive a horse to change the pace of living. It's not the city or business that wears us out; it's our response to it, our meeting life head-on without slowing down or speeding up. So if you are hitting a terrific pace, slow down. You don't have to slow down forever: it's the change you need. Or if you are going too slowly, if you are not alert but stodgy and graceless in your living, "step on it" a while. What's tedious in one speed may be delightful in another.

The Dangerous Years

STOPPING to chat with an old friend while shopping one day, I was astonished to note from the labels of the boxes he carried that he had bought flowers, perfume and lingerie. "Whatever are you buying such things for?" I asked impulsively. Then, horrified at myself, I started to babble apologies.

"It's all right," he said, smiling. "Some men, when they get to middle age, start looking for greener pastures but I . . . well, I thought I'd just fertilize the one I have." —Contributed by Mrs. M. E. Jensen

Do What You Want—
and Live Longer

By *Thurman B. Rice, M.D.*   Professor of public health, Indiana University

Condensed from The American Magazine

N O MATTER HOW I coax and threaten," a worried mother told me, "my Tommy simply will not eat his spinach. Whatever am I going to do?"

I suggested that she give him strawberries and cream instead. "You're not serious!" she gasped. I told her I never was more serious. Strawberries and cream happen to be packed with vitamins and minerals, and Tommy *liked* strawberries and cream while he detested spinach.

I am a strong believer in doing what you like. The very fact that you enjoy a thing is reason enough for doing it. This does not mean that I favor selfish indulgence or unbridled dissipation. It does mean that I'm in favor of getting more fun out of life.

Down through the centuries men have searched for some formula that would prolong the span of human existence—an elixir to endow men and women with eternal youth. The famous Pasteur Institute of Paris recently announced that it, too, is working on a "youth serum." The project is still in an experimental stage; but even if it were to succeed, how much better off would humanity be? What point is there in extending the span of one's existence if it simply means increasing the number of years in which to be old and futile?

Wouldn't it be more to the point to study ways and means of packing more living into the span of life already allotted to us?

A doctor friend has told me of a patient whom he inherited from his father. The patient is nearing 90 and apparently is in the best of health; yet my friend has never known him to draw an uncomplaining breath, or to be other than a burden to himself and a pain in the neck to those around him. For all his years, such a man can scarcely be said to have "lived" at all.

You're not truly living unless you get a kick out of life, you're simply existing. Yet I know plenty of people who actually go out of their way to deny themselves fun and enjoyment.

One man never does anything because it would be pleasant or enjoyable but always because it is his bounden obligation. He is one of those fellows of whom it is aptly said that they were "born old." His oppressive sense of duty makes him a bore to his acquaintances and a trial to his family. An overly conscientious woman considers it a sin to laugh since her husband died. Hugging her grief, she denies not only herself but her children the right to a happy, normal existence.

Many people make themselves miserable by adhering to a disagreeable "health" regimen under the mistaken notion that such practices are somehow good for them. They persist in sleeping beside open windows in cold weather though nose and throat specialists condemn the practice. Millions of American males start the day in fear and trembling with a cold shower that shocks the nervous system, leaves them chilled and under par and causes them to become drowsy by midmorning. They do it on the theory that it "hardens" them, whereas in a majority of cases it actually makes them more susceptible to colds.

One of my friends knocks himself out every morning doing setting-up exercises to keep himself fit. U. S. Army tests prove that recruits subjected to intensive calisthenics probably do not possess more physical endurance under combat conditions than soldiers who have had little or no "toughening."

I know a woman who feeds her family quantities of raw carrots, cracked wheat and brown sugar. Her meals are scientifically apportioned blends of proteins, carbohydrates, fats, minerals, vitamins and roughage; nevertheless, they are so unappetizing that her family fails to get much benefit.

Then there are people who ruin their lives by being overparticular about their physical surroundings. A woman in our town is a perfectionist and a fuss-budget. She makes both her family and visitors uncomfortable by her prissy insistence on having everything arranged just so—from chairs and ash trays in the living room to umbrellas and overshoes in the coat closet. Basically a well-intentioned wife and mother, this woman would be all right if only she could learn to relax and take things as they come.

And I know couples who are so determinedly conventional that they don't get fun even out of their amusements. They play bridge or golf not because they enjoy it but because it's "the thing to do."

Then there are those who have fallen into the habit of putting off the things that make for real living. One woman is forever buying a new suit or gown. But she rarely wears any of her smart clothes. She is saving them for some indefinite future occasion that never seems to arrive. Another young woman, a schoolteacher, went without her summer vacations for years in order to take more and more college courses. Last summer, having at last received her doctorate, she visited a summer resort for the first time. But she was so miserable there that she cut short her stay. It was too late—she had forgotten how to play. She isn't as good a teacher with a degree and a grouch as she was with no degree and a cheery outlook on life.

It's possible to wreck your life by trying to play things too safe. No man can be happy if he's excessively anxious about his home, his bank roll, his job or his health. When you get right down to it, *all* living involves risk. The people who try always to play it safe not infrequently find themselves more vulnerable to trouble than those who are willing to take some chances.

Many who entertain the notion that because a thing is unpleasant it must be good for them also believe that whatever is pleasant is bad. This is equally absurd. The world is full of good and pleasant things put there for our enjoyment: sun and rain and food and sleep and love and play and laughter. If we turn ʼur backs on them, are we not guilty of ingratitude to their Creator?

Living, as I see it, is an art, the most important art there is. Yet few people learn to practice it successfully. Mrs. Anne Mary ("Grandma") Moses probably offers the perfect example of the fun you can enjoy once you relax and start doing what you really want to do. Grandma Moses always wanted to paint, but she never got around to it till she was 78. Even in her 90's, unflustered by fame and wealth, she still painted for the sheer joy of it.

Nobody needs to go on living in the squirrel cage of a dull existence. Anybody who really wants to can emancipate himself and start enjoying life. The owner of a filling station far off the usual tourist routes in the Rocky Mountains was a man of obvious education and refinement. It eventually came out that he had been for a time a partner in a Manhattan law firm; but he hated the work and hated the life, in spite of all the money he was making. "So I quit and came out here," he says. "It may not be for everybody, but this part of the world suits me. My ulcers have disappeared; my nerves are steady again. I'm my own boss. Any time I feel like it I go fishing for a week. I don't make much money, but I'm having more fun than I ever had in my life."

The really successful man is the fellow who gets paid for doing the thing he likes to do. He'll not only be happier but the chances are he'll live longer, too. In the *Book of Proverbs* it is written: "A merry heart doeth good like a medicine." There's no other medicine to be compared with it.

The Heart of the Matter

WHEN Henry Norris Russell, the Princeton astronomer, concluded a lecture on the Milky Way, a woman asked him: "If our world is so little and the universe is so great, can we really believe that God pays any attention to us?"

"That, madam," replied Dr. Russell, "depends entirely on how big a God you believe in." —Quoted by Bill Gold in Washington *Post*

A MAN came to the Rev. B. J. Howard, of Orange County, North Carolina, and told him of all the troubles he had had during the past year. He wound up with: "I tell you right now, preacher, it's enough to make a man lose his religion."

"Seems to me, Jim," Mr. Howard told him quietly, "it's enough to make a man *use* his religion." —Carl Goerch in *The State*

WE DIDN'T GET A DIVORCE

Anonymous

O NE evening about three years ago my husband turned to me and said quietly, "Mary, I want a divorce."

We were sitting in front of the fire in our house in the country, so perfect a picture of connubial bliss that for a moment I couldn't believe he had spoken the words I heard. If we had just had an ugly quarrel I might have understood it, or if I had "let myself go" mentally and physically, as some women do after ten years of marriage.

True, we had not been madly in love with each other since the early years of our marriage. But we had sensibly substituted fondness for infatuation, and tolerance for passion. We had many interests in common and had learned to live and let-live together with mutual respect. Why, then, did John want a divorce?

Because, he said, he wanted to marry someone else.

Bewildered, I stared at the flames. A slow, stubborn anger filled me as I thought of our two young sons sleeping peacefully upstairs.

"Well, you can't have a divorce," I said. "The boys' happiness is more important than yours. You can't desert them now."

His answer was the irrefutable argument that by refusing him a divorce I should be maintaining merely the empty shell of a home. The psychological effect on the children would be even more disastrous than that of losing their father.

Hurt pride bubbled through my anger and I was sorely tempted to take the first train to Reno. Then I thought of the women I had known who had set their husbands free for the Other Woman. I remembered the confused misery in their eyes that lingered long after they had girded their hurt with hard-boiled armor. My imagination leaped ahead to the bickering over alimony and the custody of the children. Gradually I swallowed my pride.

I went to the city next morning and asked the advice of two men whose opinions I value highly. One is a doctor, the other a lawyer. They were of one accord:

"The Other Woman is never sufficient reason for breaking up a home in which there are children. John will get over it in time and it would be a tragedy for everyone concerned if he gets over it too late."

"But," I asked, "how can I be sure that he will get over it?"

"Nine times out of ten," they explained, " 'the Other Woman' is an empty phrase. She is merely a symptom that John has reached the stage when he is wondering whether he has eaten his cake or still has it. Because you are his wife you're probably not as glamorous to him as another woman. The routine of married life is at the root of this; not you or the Other Woman. If he divorces you and marries her, the chances are that the same thing will happen all over again."

"That sounds sensible," I agreed. "But how can I make him understand this?"

"By a trial separation. Give him a month or two living away from you and the children in order to think it over. He will have, in effect, a divorce, but no drastic steps will have been taken."

Both lawyer and doctor answered the question in my eyes. "Don't worry, Mary. He'll want to come back even before the time is up."

But we did not separate right away. My husband wasn't earning enough money to support two establishments. In order to remove that obstacle we moved back to town and I got a job. But soon we discovered that almost every cent I earned went right out to maids and sitters and nursery schools.

This put the divorce project back in my husband's lap. If he wanted to have his cake and eat it, too, he would have to earn more money. Right at the outset he would have to save up enough to cover my trip to Reno, the salary of the housekeeper while I was gone, and the lawyers' fees.

We settled down to wait. Although our relationship during that time was outwardly friendly, my position as wife in name only was difficult. The door was temptingly open for me to take the boys away from their father emotionally. Often it would have been comforting to cry on my elder son's shoulder and tell him his father was going to leave us. And it would have been easy to smother the baby with the fondness and affection I would normally have diverted to my husband. John was working nights and week-ends now and saw very little of the children. In spite of my efforts not to turn them against him they sensed a division in their parents and naturally sided with me.

So gradually John was forced to face the fact that part of the price he would have to pay for a divorce would be the loss of his sons. If it was difficult for me, it must have been far more difficult for him.

I know now that our thoughts were running in the same groove. I relived our courtship and wedding. I went back to those days of hardship and happiness when we were barely earning enough to live. And my husband has since told me that he kept remembering how hard we had both worked until we had enough money in the bank so I could quit my job and have a baby.

Neither of us could ever forget the night our first son was born, nor the arrival of our second. We recalled the thrill of at last finding just the country place we had dreamed of; the first exciting months when we had started the baby chicks and the garden. Indelible too was the memory of the dreadful illness that had almost taken both boys from us.

Waiting gave John plenty of time to feel the tug of the strong threads that had woven into the pattern of our past. We had got through the difficult adjustment years with flying color. Had it all been for nothing? How easy was it going to be to start all over again with someone else?

Thus while we waited we were actually making progress toward a better relationship.

Both partners in almost every marriage have at some time thought about divorce. Like many a wife, in moments of anger and disappointment I had wondered if my choice of a husband had been wise. For the sake of the children I had never allowed myself seriously to consider a break. Now I approached the subject from my own selfish point of view.

I did not want to face a future without a husband, and it would not be easy to get another one. I had thought of myself as an attractive, intelligent, independent woman. I promptly learned that I would not be independent until the boys were self-supporting, and the world, I found, was filled with attractive, intelligent, younger women without ties. In my business I met many attractive men and some who found me attractive, but those who had reached mental and emotional maturity were already married. I would not break up any other woman's home and the vision of the hide-and-seek existence of the gay divorcée of many affairs was distasteful.

I came to the conclusion that I had never before fully appreciated the value of a husband. For my own sake now I began to hope desperately that the divorce would never materialize.

When the time came to make the trial separation neither of us wanted to go through with it. But we did. And, as the lawyer and doctor had predicted, John wanted to come back after the first week.

Since his return he has been a better husband and a better father, and I have tried to be a better wife. He missed the boys intensely; consequently his patience with them has increased and he is more anxious to share in their guidance.

We are going back to the country next spring and I feel sure that we shall be there "for as long as we both shall live."

Just What They Needed

WHEN a girl applies for admission to Vassar, a questionnaire is sent to her parents. A father in a Boston suburb, filling out one of these blanks, came to the question, "Is she a leader?" He hesitated, then wrote, "I am not sure but I know she is an excellent follower."

A few days later he received this letter from the president of the college: "As our freshman group next Fall is to contain several hundred leaders, we congratulate ourselves that your daughter will also be a member of the class. We shall thus be assured of one good follower." — *The Journal of Education*

THE ART OF
STAYING AT HOME

By Charles W. Ferguson   *Condensed from Southwest Review*

STAY-AT-HOME" is a term commonly used for the person who *has* to stay at home. It conjures up untidy visions of the aged and infirm, the shut-ins, the unsociables. Yet there is an art to staying at home. And a good many of us, tired of aimless visiting, too much bridge and strenuous journeys to nowhere in particular, would like to practice it. We should like to stay at home with a greater sense of fitness and fun.

The kind of home you have, its size or its magnificence, is of slight importance. You don't need a vaulted temple for gracious living. Nor are there any hard-and-fast rules. Some find that ceremony helps— customs that lend dignity and importance to routine. I remember once running out of gas in the Connecticut hills and finding a retired broker all alone at table, wearing a dinner coat. It was a habit, and he said it seemed to make things more important. One young couple read aloud to each other. A family I often visit play fine phonograph records after dinner several evenings a week. Another couple find great amusement in reading the dictionary.

Practices of this sort, however, are auxiliaries at best. It is much more essential to understand, first of all, that a man's house is his castle, a refuge where he can do as he pleases. Obviously the first great step in mastering the art of staying home is to build up fortifications which make home a place of privacy and luxurious solitude.

The best thing is to have a schedule of privacy as rigid as your social calendar and stick with it at all costs. It is not stretching the truth too far, when someone calls up and asks if you are doing anything that evening, to say that you *are*—even if you intend only to read that book you've put off six months. And it can be gently suggested to friends that on certain nights you are simply not at home to anyone but yourself. Nights in are just as important as nights out: indeed, the former add endless zest to the latter.

Yet so few of us will pull up the drawbridge at sunset! We are like the woman Arnold Bennett speaks of—alive only in public. Our days and our nights are spent in being in public, or in preparing to be in public, or in recovering from the effects of being in public. Thoreau points out in one of his lightning flashes that "society is commonly too cheap. We meet at very short intervals, not having had time to acquire any new value for each other. We meet at meals three times a day and give each other a new taste of that old musty cheese that we are. We have had to agree on a certain set of rules, called etiquette and politeness, to make this frequent meeting tolerable. We live thick and stumble over one another."

Once you have the idea of the home as a refuge, the change wrought in your activities is automatic. Then comes quite naturally the will to be yourself. You begin to learn the pleasures of voluntary confinement, of taking the veil in the quietness of your own house. There is nothing anti-social about this attitude. "Our first duty to society," the Abbé Dimnet once said, "is to be somebody—that is to say, be ourselves; and we can only be ourselves if we are often enough by ourselves."

The first concrete thing likely to result from staying at home is the discovery that you are doing something you've always wanted to do. One couple have spent the past few months making a private guidebook for a trip they plan one day to take through Europe. Another couple have been spending their evenings classifying the negatives of hundreds of pictures taken in days when they roamed freely. There is something you want to do; but you'll never do it until you learn to stay at home. You've always wanted to learn French. Or you like geography. Or you think you can write or draw or do something with sculpture, or make furniture.

But to be constantly puttering about the house is still not the kind of solitude of which I am speaking. It would seem to most of us old-fashioned and queer if we set aside a definite period of the day in which to meditate. Yet, while "thinking can be dull, it also can be a glorious and exciting adventure," to quote Justice Holmes, who was a past master of the art of staying at home.

The first experiments in thinking creatively will probably result in disheartening failure. "That brain of yours will be hopping all over the place," Arnold Bennett wrote, "and every time it hops you must bring it back by force to its original position. The mind can be conquered only by never leaving it idle, undirected, masterless, to play at random like a child in the streets after dark."

It might help us to realize that thinking, after all, is only a process of talking to oneself—intelligently. When you learn to talk to yourself coherently, you will, if you persevere, discover a lively pastime. You will be forced to talk to yourself about something important. The reason conversation is at such a low ebb just now is that we do not know how to talk to ourselves.

Seated alone in your room, you begin to talk to yourself. You have innumerable vague notions about war, for instance, but you perhaps have never held a conversation with yourself about it. Try it. You must be exact—marshaling your notions, reconnoitering the subject, pitting contentions against each other. By the end of the evening you will be weary, but you will be better able to talk to others the next day.

Solitude is not always a matter of being grimly edifying. Much has been said in favor of purposive reading—reading with some lofty aim—but there is also reading for fun. It might be well if for a while we allayed our itch for culture and came to realize that there is real sport in the contacts of the mind with new ideas, in the repartee of great authors, in the free play of our minds with books and essays. Reading for fun by no means implies that the reading matter be frothy. I can imagine that some folks would enjoy reading philosophy for fun. Others could take history, others science, but in any case they would not read out of any compulsion of convention.

It is a struggle to learn any art, much more of a struggle to master it. It cannot be done in ten easy lessons. But you must admit this art of staying at home is important enough to be worth trying. Its cultivation would help solidify family life, stabilize our thinking, tone us up generally and develop self-sufficiency and serenity. What is required most of all is the realization that the gadabouts are missing something, that the satisfactions of a flea are greatly exaggerated. He is a happy man who has simplified his tastes to the point where a good book and a fire and a quiet evening are for him not a chore or a sign of increasing age, but a preference and a badge of wisdom and distinction.

Welcome Stranger

THE MORNING after we moved to a new residence in a town near New York, my doorbell rang. A woman was standing on the step, a friendly smile on her face, and in her hand was a tray with a pot of coffee, cups and some buns. She introduced herself as Mrs. Mills, my neighbor across the street. As we chatted over our coffee, she told me about the town, the names of the neighbors and some details about them—where the men worked, what they did. She invited the youngsters to her house to play with her children that afternoon. When she left, I felt nice and warm inside, and I thought of her visit all day long as I unpacked.

She'd just returned the children to me about five o'clock when the telephone rang. The voice turned out to be Mrs. Hart, who lived three doors away. "Mrs. Mills told me you'd just moved in, so I know you're busy and scarcely will have time to eat. But I've a stew ready. Bring your whole family over whenever you're hungry."

The next day another neighbor called to chat and acquaint me with more of the town. She mentioned good grocers, butchers, cleaners and laundries, and said the first time I went downtown she'd go along and introduce me to the merchants. She left me a neatly written list of stores and doctors, dentists and baby sitters.

Later we learned the friendly spirit those neighbors showed wasn't just casual. Feeling that old-fashioned neighborliness had slipped too far away, they'd got together and decided to get it back. They planned to take turns performing the various neighborly services. Now that we are neighbors ourselves, we'll have our own turn to make some other family's move such a pleasant surprise.

— Roberta Fleming Roesch in *Today's Woman*

Adventure At Dawn

By Lacy Bell Richter

Condensed from The Christian Science Monitor

HERE IS nothing more satisfying to me than the companionship of our George, just turned ten. Sometimes it is a quiet enjoyment on a Sunday evening with a new book; or a treasured moment during lunch hour when we tap our toes to a Gershwin melody. More often we sprawl Indian-fashion on the kitchen linoleum for a game of jacks while supper simmers.

If I whittle a tunnel for the electric train from an oatmeal box, I find George gazing at me in admiration. "You can run the train any time you want to, Mom! Just be sure to pull the switch afterward." There is no mistaking his sincerity. For a long moment I look into his upturned face. And there I see a child who is bewitchingly simple: a composite of thoughtfulness and elation, acrobatics and daydreaming, gripping every experience of his waking moments with the gusto of a frisky puppy.

One evening I was suddenly fired with the idea of going with George on his morning paper route. I wanted to see the doorways where he dropped the daily so regularly, regardless of the eccentricities of midwestern weather. I wanted to trek the cross-lot short cuts he had devised.

At 5:30 next morning the thermometer outside the kitchen window proclaimed a challenging five-below-zero. Clad in snowpants and an extra parka, I gripped the handle of the storm door and forced it open. Blasts of icy fury funneled the snow directly on our faces, leaving a razor-sharp sting. There were no steps, no outline of the driveway. "Let's follow the road—not so deep," shouted George. I saw him bend at an angle and plunge across the glistening whiteness. It was useless to talk—our words were whisked away with jet speed. We resorted to gestures until we reached the shelter of the store doorway where the paper bundles lay huddled in their heavy wrappings.

The first leg of the route lay along a narrow back street. Turning against the wind, George pointed out the best course between the apartment house and the tourist cabin, which lay just ahead. "Stay close to that line of trees, because there's a ditch you can't see," he advised. I could hear the rhythmic flop of his paper bag as he trudged along, glancing back over his shoulder from time to time to see if I was close on his heels. At the tourist cabin the door was hooked; so we anchored the paper under a snow shovel. I felt close to George at that moment. He, the guide, and I, the trainee—joining our forces against the elements for the righteous cause of enlightenment. "The paper must go through!"

Rounding the bank corner we saw Mr. Godfrey, the night watchman, approaching his patrol car. He gave us a hearty "Good morning."

"You're the first carrier I see, George. What's keeping the rest of 'em? Sa-ay! What brings your mother out in such a storm?" He swept the pillows of snow from the fenders. "Hop in! Take you to the top of Decker's Hill. Plow just went through."

The glint in George's eye matched the one I had seen the day he introduced us to his camp director, a sort of "we men" glint. He held the car door for me while Mr. Godfrey squeezed his sheepskinned bulk under the wheel. No one spoke as we jiggled along.

Watching the car go on its way, we took up the tortuous route, encouraged by the thought that the wind would be at our backs, sweeping us along with the last ten papers. The tin sign on the corner garage had set up an eerie tap-tapping. Shafts of light from kitchen windows cut into the billows of snow and occasionally a shirt-sleeved figure darted out to snatch the paper from its icy receptacle. The town was reluctantly shaking itself into the day's routine.

We divided the remaining papers between us, determined to maintain George's standing in the eyes of his customers. Bill Kaveny must have the sport page for breakfast reading and the trucker on the corner liked to take his paper with him to work.

Our paths converged under the street light, half a block from our back door. Conversation lagged. Like a pair of retrievers we were pointed homeward, to the warm kitchen, bowls of steaming oatmeal and release from our swaddling clothes. Neither of us proposed going around the block to avoid the hip-deep drifts in our back yard. We floundered through them with howls of laughter. In spite of our numb fingers and toes, the temptation to leave a snow-angel imprint beside the back porch was more than we could resist. Joining hands, we fell backward into the white expanse.

The dawn was bleak; but, as we lay side by side like two gingerbread men, a vibrant, glowing joy spearheaded from my fingertips to George's. The approaching day, frigid and sunless, had already laid at my feet a shining gift—an adventure with a little boy.

Man Trap

BRIDE: "Well, I finally landed a man, and what a chase! I made it my career, and prepared plans the way a general gets ready for his biggest battle. I joined a chess club, and took to hanging around airfields. I practiced skeet-shooting and made numerous calls for information about public questions at my favorite political headquarters. I played bit roles in an amateur theatrical group and joined a Sunday-morning party to read aloud to veterans in a hospital. I sold Red Cross memberships, concentrating on athletic clubs, university clubs and the Chamber of Commerce. I became secretary of the lecture forum of the church and saw to it that there was occasion for a brief announcement at each meeting. I took in as many formal weddings as my time permitted, for I figured I might pick up some constructive ideas in such an atmosphere of triumph. People thought I was public-spirited, patriotic, knowledge-hungry, self-sacrificing and progressive, when all along I had just one thing on my mind—how to cop a husband."

—American Freeman, quoted in The William Feather Magazine

> Most of us outgrow the shocks of
> childhood as we do our baby shoes

DON'T BLAME YOUR PARENTS

By Jacob H. Conn, M.D.
Assistant Professor of Psychiatry, Johns Hopkins University School of Medicine

As told to Edith M. Stern

THE UNSUCCESSFUL, the unhappy, at various periods in history, have blamed their plight on various things—fate, the gods, demons, innate cussedness or heredity. Today it is the fashion to hold one's parents accountable for every flaw, from plain laziness to mental illness: "I can't save money because my parents never taught me economy." "I'm a hypochondriac because my mother fussed so much about my health when I was little." "In childhood I wasn't permitted to think for myself."

A woman I know actually blamed her parents for her unattractive appearance. Asked why she didn't wave her hair, powder her nose or occasionally get a new hat, she answered plaintively, "When I was a child Mother always told me I wasn't good-looking." It did not occur to her that as an adult it was up to her, and nobody else, to make the most of her looks.

The current notion is that little children are emotionally fragile, that you can wreck a child's whole future by loving him too little or too much, by teaching him the facts of life too late or too soon, by being too strict or too indulgent. Such half-baked misinterpretations of the importance of the formative years ignore the fact that most human beings are blessed with an inner strength. Actually the average child is as tough psychologically as he is physically. Just as the body repels germs and viruses, so has the mind similar immunities and resistances to the unwise or unkind doings of parents.

History is full of examples of men and women who had unhappy childhoods and yet made a success of their lives. John Stuart Mill became a great philosopher and led a harmonious married life despite a father who never praised him, never allowed him to associate with other children, relentlessly forced him to study night after night. Beethoven's ne'er-do-well father drove and exploited him shamelessly. Florence Nightingale's parents hemmed her in by all the restrictions that went with Victorian gentility, and bitterly opposed her going into nursing.

Ordinary mortals likewise have the capacity to build worth-while lives despite a past full of psychological handicaps. I do not deny that "parental rejection" or "overdomination" may genuinely handicap some individuals. But a human being is not a machine that once set rolling in the wrong direction is unable to change its course. The essence of maturity or "adjustment" is to make the most of yourself with whatever you have, which includes your physique, your mental endowments, your social opportunities and your parents.

Almost daily in my practice I see patients who blame their failure to meet life on their parents instead of on themselves. A fearful, immature spinster wept that she "couldn't leave Mother." Yet her mother told me: "Doctor, I wish to goodness you'd help her, so that she'd go and get married." Nothing tied this woman to her mother's apron strings but knots of her own making.

"No wonder I'm the way I am," a seriously depressed man said to me. "Look!" He pulled from his pocket a yellowed newspaper clipping that told of his parents' double suicide 20 years before. He admitted that he had carried the clipping all those years. The heart of his problem was not the shocking memory but his compulsion to dwell on it.

Contrary to popular notion, mental illness or neuroticism is not caused by an event but by the way a person reacts to it. A disturbing incident is only the match which sets off the firecracker; it's the gunpowder within the cracker which actually causes the explosion. It is good old-fashioned character—a compound of inherited tendencies and our ability to tolerate disappointments—that determines whether we withstand childhood tragedies or whether they down us all our lives.

If it were true that what happens during childhood fixes us once and for all, everybody would be neurotic. Certain events in childhood are genuinely upsetting, among them weaning and a new baby in the family. But the normal individual outgrows the unhappy experiences of his childhood just as he outgrows his baby shoes.

The great majority of normal, healthy-minded youngsters manage, without special help, to cope matter-of-factly with their parents' antics. Just try to spoil a child who has such innate common sense that he doesn't need or want to be spoiled! Or try to dominate the average three-year-old. Children who do not have the neurotic need to be dependent will not be dominated. Maybe they react with tantrums. Maybe they argue. Maybe they are sullenly silent. But whatever their technique for maintaining their integrity, "Momism" won't and can't wreck them.

The psychiatrist's job does not consist, as many of my patients think, of breaking apart a person's past so that he can lay his failings, weaknesses and peculiarities right at his parents' door. All that a psychiatrist can do is to lead the patient to face the truth about his *own* wish to be dominated or sheltered or what not, and help him take a stand for himself. Once that point is reached, his past life matters very little. As Dr. Franz Alexander, distinguished Chicago psychoanalyst, put it: "The patient is suffering not so much from memories as from the incapacity to deal with the actual problems of the moment."

A single experience in adult life can so change human beings that it is sheer nonsense to maintain that their natures were immutably determined years before by what their parents said or did to them. A short illness turned St. Francis of Assisi from a frivolous, extravagant young man into a devout ascetic. Gay young blades marry and become serious and responsible husbands; gadabout young wives turn into settled stay-at-homes after the birth of a baby. The human organism is a going, changing concern, with the motives of the present its propelling force.

Too many of us with shortcomings are interested in asking, "How did it start?" Too few ask themselves, "Why do I keep it up?" Anyone who really wants to be grown-up emotionally must first make the frank self-admission, "I am worrisome—or thriftless, or hypochondriac, or irresponsible—because it suits some purpose of my own to be that way."

The cliché "There are no problem children, only problem parents" is as extreme and fallacious a swing of the pendulum as the Puritan idea that all children were imps of Satan. Even a little child can be responsible for his own bad upbringing, for it takes two to make an emotional bargain. When a father is too authoritarian it may well be that he is so because the child craves being bossed. When a mother prolongs treating Junior like a baby it may be because she responds to his own need for protection. Children are not mere lumps of clay which adults mold. In the parent-child relationship, as in marriage, one personality modifies and plays upon another.

Parents can set the stage for the drama of their children's lives. They can supply inspiring or uninspiring examples of conduct which will influence basic mental, physical and spiritual growth. But acceptance or rejection of the background they give is a matter of the child's individual character.

Marriage Brief

I KNOW a wise and witty woman who has been happily married for more than 40 years. Whenever one of her younger friends, who is about to be married, comes to her for advice, she replies: "Well, my dear, I most sincerely hope that you two will never have a difference of opinion. But if you *do* get into an argument, avoid the word 'always.'"

How simple, yet how sane! Think of the many, many occasions in a marriage when what might have been nothing worse than a trifling spark of disagreement has been fanned into a conflagration because one of the two parties had let drop this kind of remark:

"You *always* come tracking through the living room in your wet rubbers."

Or, "You *always* leave the cap off the tooth paste."

Or, "You *always* want to go home just when the party's being fun," or, "You *always* manage to get into long political discussions whenever Uncle George is around."

"Never say 'always' . . ." Of all the mottos for marriage I have heard, I think this one is the shortest and soundest. — Jan Struther in *This Week*

On Being

A REAL PERSON

By Harry Emerson Fosdick, D.D.   *Pastor of Riverside Church, New York City*

A condensation from the book

THE central business of every human being is to be a real person. We possess by nature the factors out of which personality can be made, and to organize them into effective personal life is every man's primary responsibility.

Without exaggeration it can be said that frustrated, unhappy people, who cannot match themselves with life, constitute the greatest single tragedy in the world. In mansion and hovel, among the uneducated and in university faculties, under every kind of circumstance people entrusted with building their own personalities are making a mess of it.

Three elements enter into the building of personality: heredity, environment and personal response. We are not responsible for our heredity; much of our environment we cannot control; but the power to face life with an individual rejoinder—*that* we are responsible for. When acceptance of this responsibility involves self-condemnation, however, an alibi almost invariably rushes to the rescue. All of us resemble the lawyer in the New Testament story, concerning whom we read: "But he, desiring to justify himself, said . . ." A college president says that after long dealing with students he is unsure whether B.A. stands for Bachelor of Arts or Builder of Alibis.

On the lowest level this desire to escape blame expresses itself in emphasis upon luck. Fortunate people "get the breaks," men say; personal failure is due not so much to mistake as to mischance. That luck represents a real factor in human experience is evident, and he who does not expect ill fortune as one of the ingredients of life is trying to live in fairyland. But nothing finer has appeared on earth than unlucky people who are real persons. The determining element in their experience is not so much what happens to them as the way they take it.

Glenn Cunningham, who ran fastest mile then on record, was crippled in boyhood in a schoolhouse fire. The doctors said that only a miracle could enable him to walk again—he was out of luck. He began walking by following a plow across the fields, leaning on it for support; and then went on to tireless experimentation to see what he could do with his legs, until he broke all records for the mile run.

Pilgrim's Progress came from a prison, as did *Don Quixote,* Sir Walter Raleigh's *History of the World* and some of the best of O. Henry's stories.

Bad luck is a poor alibi if only because good luck by itself never yet guaranteed real personality. Life is not so simple that good fortune suffices for it.

Many escape a sense of personal responsibility by lapsing into a mood of emotional fatalism. This is, curiously, one of the most comfortable moods in which a man can live. If he is an automaton, he is not responsible for anything.

On its highest level man's desire to escape responsibility expresses itself in ascribing all personal qualities to heredity and environment. This is a popular theory today. From intelligence quotients within to crippling environments without, it offers defenses for every kind of deficiency, so that no botched life need look far to find an excuse.

But consider the individual of superior inheritance and favorable circumstance. Must he necessarily be an admirable personality? Is *that* fate, willy-nilly, forced upon him? Certainly it does not seem so. The disastrous misuse of fine heredity and environment is too familiar a phenomenon to be doubted.

Handling difficulty, making the best of bad messes, is one of life's major businesses. Very often the reason victory is not won lies inside the individual. The recognition of this fact, however, by the individual concerned is difficult. At times we all resemble the Maine farmer laboriously driving his horses on a dusty road. "How much longer does this hill last?" he asked a man by the roadside. "Hill!" was the answer. "Hill nothing! Your hind wheels are off!"

The world is a coarse-grained place, and other people are often unfair, selfish, cruel. Yet, after all, we know the difference between a man who always has an alibi and the man who *in just as distressing a situation* habitually looks inward to his own attitudes and resources — no excuses, no passing of the buck. In any circumstance he regards himself as his major problem, certain that if he handles himself well that is bound to make some difference. Anyone can recognize the forthright healthy-mindedness of the youth who wrote home to his father after an unsuccessful football game, "Our opponents found a big hole in our line, and that hole was me."

When we succeed, when by dint of decision and effort we achieve a desired end, we are sure we had a share in *that*. We cannot slough off responsibility when we fail. We cannot eat our cake and have it too.

The beginning of worth-while living is thus to confront ourselves — unique beings, each of us entrusted with the makings of personality. Yet multitudes of people wrestle with every conceivable factor involved in the human situation before they face their primary problem — themselves. Our commonest human tragedy is correctly represented in a recent cartoon: A physician faces his patient with anxious solemnity, saying, "This is a very serious case; I'm afraid you're *allergic to yourself.*"

T HE common phrase "building a personality" is a misnomer. Personality is not so much like a structure as like a river — it continuously flows, and to be a person is to be engaged in a perpetual process of becoming.

The tests of successful personal living, therefore, are not neatly identical when applied to two persons in different situations or to the same person at different ages. Concerning one criterion, however, there is common agreement. A real person achieves a high degree of unity within himself. The often conflicting elements of personal experience, such as impulses, desires, emotions, must be coördinated.

Each of us deals continually with the underlying problem of a disorganized life. The ruffled man badly flurried because he has mislaid a pair of glasses, the hurried person trying to do something with too great haste and becoming flustered, the frightened person fallen into a panic, the choleric individual surprised by a burst of temper into loss of self-control—such examples from ordinary life remind us how insecure is our personal integration.

No virtue is more universally accepted as a test of good character than trustworthiness. Obviously, however, dependability is possible only in so far as the whole personality achieves a stanch unity that can be counted on.

Many of us frequently act "out of character." The general pattern of our lives may involve honesty, truthfulness and similar qualities— but not always. This is evident even with regard to a virtue like courtesy. How common is the person whose courtesy is unreliable! We all know him—polite today, morose and uncivil tomorrow; obliging and well bred in business, crabbed and sulky at home; affable with one's so-called "equals," gruff and snobbish with one's servants.

In a man with character, the responses to life are, in their quality, established and well organized; one can count on them. His various emotions, desires and ideas are no mere disparate will-o'-the-wisps. He has become a whole person, with a unifying pattern of thought and feeling that gives coherence to everything he does.

A "well-integrated" life does not mean a placid life, with all conflicts resolved. Many great souls have been inwardly tortured. Florence Nightingale had a desperate time finding herself, and wrote in her diary, "In my 31st year I see nothing desirable but death." Dwight L. Moody said, "I've had more trouble with D. L. Moody than with any other man I know."

In all strong characters, when one listens behind the scenes, one hears echoes of strife and contention. Nevertheless, far from being at loose ends within themselves, such persons have organized their lives around some supreme values and achieved a powerful concentration of purpose and drive.

The process by which real personality is thus attained is inward and spiritual. No environmental changes by themselves can so *push* a personality together as to bring this satisfying wholeness within. Even so fortunate an environment as a loyal and loving family cannot dispense a man from confronting himself. Thus Novalis said: "Only so far as a

man is happily married to himself, is he fit for married life." As for
material prosperity, that often disorganizes life rather than unifies it.
Indeed, nervous prostration is a specialty of the prosperous. Wealth, by
increasing the number of possible choices, is often far more disrupting
than satisfying.

A MODERN novelist describing one of his characters says, "He was
not so much a human being as a civil war." Every human being
sometime faces a situation where on the one side is his actual self, with
his abilities and circumstances, and on the other are ideal pictures of
himself and his achievements; and between the two is a gulf too wide
to be bridged. Here inward civil war begins.

To hold high ideals and ambitions is man's glory, and nowhere
more so than in the development of personality. This faculty, however, can function so abnormally that it tears life to pieces.

No well-integrated life is possible, therefore, without an initial act of
self-acceptance, as though to say: I, John Smith, hereby accept myself,
with my inherited endowments and handicaps and with the elements
in my environment that I cannot control, and, so accepting myself as
my stint, I will now see what I can do with *this* John Smith. So
Emerson put it: "There is a time in every man's education when he
arrives at the conviction that envy is ignorance; that imitation is suicide; that he must take himself for better, for worse, as his portion."

Alec Templeton entertains millions over the radio with his music
and amuses them with his whimsicalities. He is stone blind. The first
natural response to such crippling disadvantage is an imagination
thronged with pictures of the unattainable, and from the contrast between them and the actualities commonly spring resentment, self-pity,
inertia. The human story, however, has nothing nobler to present than
handicapped men and women who, accepting themselves, have illustrated what Dr. Alfred Adler called "the human being's power to turn
a minus into a plus."

Tension between our existent and our desired selves often arises
from high moral ideals, and nowhere is it more likely to be mis-
handled. Unselfishness and loyalty, for instance, are major virtues, but
a daughter under the thralldom of a possessive mother can so picture
herself as in duty bound to be unselfish and loyal that, without doing

her mother any real good, her life is blighted and her personality wrecked.

Ethical ideals in their application are relative to the individual. One man may have a calm, equable temperament that need never be ruffled; another may have to say, as Dr. Stephen Tyng did to one who rebuked him for asperity, "Young man, I control more temper every 15 minutes than you will in your whole lifetime."

WHEN self-acceptance is not achieved and the strain between the actual and the dreamed-of self becomes tense, the result is an unhappy and sometimes crushing sense of inferiority. One study of 275 college men and women revealed that over 90 percent suffered from gnawing, frustrated feelings of deficiency. They gave all sorts of reasons—physical incompetence, unpleasant appearance, lack of social charm, failure in love, low-grade intellectual ability, moral failure and guilt.

To be sure, the feeling of inferiority can never be taken at its face value as an indication of real lack. The runner-up in a championship tennis match may suffer wretchedly from a sense of inadequacy. However, the importance of the problem itself is made evident by the unhealthy ways in which it is commonly handled.

Some deal with it by the smoke-screen method. Feeling miserably inferior, and not wanting others to know it, the shy become aggressive, the embarrassed effusive, and the timid bluster and brag. One man, hitherto gentle and considerate in his family, suffered a humiliating failure. At once he began to grow harsh and domineering. Paradoxical though it is, when he felt superior he behaved humbly, as though he felt inferior; when he felt inferior he began to swagger as though he were superior.

Others, like the fox in Aesop's fable, call sour all grapes they cannot reach. The frail youth discounts athletics; the debauchee scoffs at the self-controlled as prudes; the failure at school scorns intellectuals as "highbrows." A major amount of cynicism springs from this source. Watch what people are cynical about, and one can often discover what they lack, and subconsciously deeply wish they had.

Still others find excuses based on an exaggerated acknowledgment of their inferiority. So one student who was struggling with failure said:

"I have thought it over carefully and I have come to the conclusion that I am feeble-minded!" Far from being said with despair, this was announced with relief; it was a perfect excuse; it let him out from all responsibility. Yet, factually it was absurd, and emotionally it was abnormal.

A MONG the constructive elements that make self-acceptance basic in becoming a real person is the principle of compensation. Deficiency can be a positive stimulus, as in the classic case of Demosthenes. Desiring to be an orator, he had to accept himself as a stammerer. He did not, however, conceal his humiliation with bluster and brag, nor decry eloquence as worthless trickery, nor resign himself to stammering as an excuse for doing nothing. He took a positive attitude toward his limitation, speaking against the noise of the waves with pebbles in his mouth until he could talk with confident clarity. To say that Demosthenes became a great orator *despite* his stammering is an understatement; the psychologist would add that he became a supremely effective orator *because* he stammered.

Some form of compensation is almost always possible. The homely girl may develop the more wit and charm because she is homely; the shy, embarrassed youth, with the temperament of a recluse, may be all the more useful in scientific research because of that.

Involved in such successful handling of recognized inferiority is the ability to pass from the defensive to the offensive attitude toward our limitations. John Smith accepts John Smith with his realistically seen limitations and difficulties, and positively starts out to discover what can be done with him.

Captain John Callender of the Massachusetts militia was guilty of cowardice at the Battle of Bunker Hill. George Washington had to order his court-martial. Callender re-enlisted in the army as a private, and at the Battle of Long Island exhibited such conspicuous courage that Washington publicly revoked the sentence and restored to him his captaincy.

Behind such an experience lies a basic act of self-acceptance—open-eyed, without equivocation or excuse—along with a shift from a defensive to an offensive attitude, that makes John Callender an inspiring person to remember.

I<small>N</small> <small>ACHIEVING</small> self-acceptance a man may well begin by reducing to a minimum the things that mortify him. Many people are humiliated by situations that need not be humiliations at all. To have what Ko-Ko called "a caricature of a face," to lack desired ability, to be economically restricted—such things are limitations, but if they become humiliations, it is because inwardly we make them so. One man developed an inferiority complex that haunted him all his life and ruined his career because he had curly hair of an unusual shade of red. Napoleon accepted himself—five feet two inches tall, and 43rd in his class at the *Ecole Militaire.* He never liked himself that way. Considering his imperial ambitions, his diminutive stature was a limitation, but had he made of it and of his scholastic mediocrity a humiliation, he probably never would have been Napoleon.

Life is a landscaping job. We are handed a site, ample or small, rugged or flat, whose general outlines and contours are largely determined for us. Both limitation and opportunity are involved in every site, and the most unforeseeable results ensue from the handling—some grand opportunities are muffed, and some utterly unpromising situations become notable. The basic elements in any personal site are bound to appear in the end no matter what is done with them, as a landscape still reveals its size and its major shapes and contours whatever the landscape architect may do. These basic elements, however, are to be accepted, never as humiliations, commonly as limitations, but most of all as opportunities and even as incentives.

One of the ablest women in this country, now the wife of a university president, was brought up in poverty. She recalls an occasion when, as a girl, she complained of her hardships. "See here," said her mother, "I have given you life; that is about all I will ever be able to give you. Now you stop complaining and do something with it."

Our most intimate and inescapable entrustment lies in our capacity to be real persons. To fail at that is to fail altogether; to succeed is to succeed supremely. Says Noah in the play *Green Pastures,* "I ain' very much, but I'se all I got." That is the place to start. Such self-acceptance is realistic, humble, self-respectful.

A <small>CERTAIN</small> "Charm School", promising to bestow "personality" on its clients, prescribes in the first lesson that one stand before a large mirror and repeat one's own name in a voice "soft, gentle and low" in order to impress oneself with oneself. But obsession with oneself can be one of life's most disruptive forces. An integrated personality is impossible save as the individual finds outside himself valuable interests, in devotion to which he forgets himself. To be whole persons we must get ourselves off our hands.

Self-centeredness is natural in early childhood. Many, however, never outgrow it. At 50 years of age they still are living on a childish pattern. Moralists censure them as selfish, but beneath the ethical is a psychological problem — they are specimens of arrested development. A novelist says of one of her characters: "Edith was a little country bounded on the north, south, east and west by Edith." Edith suffers from a serious psychological affliction. Egocentricity is ruinous to real personality. At the very best, a person completely wrapped up in himself makes a small package.

Being a real person is arrived at not so much by plunging after it as by indirection. A man escapes from himself into some greater interest to which he devotes himself, and so forgets himself into consecutive, unified, significant living.

Practical suggestions as to ways and means of getting out of ourselves must start close at home with the body. Many miserably self-centered folk need not so much a psychiatrist to analyze them or a minister to discuss morals with them as common sense in handling the physical basis of a healthy life.

The modern man needs constantly to be reminded that he cannot slough off his biological inheritance. Our bodies were made to use in hard physical labor. Any man who has found his appropriate recreation or exercise where he can let himself go in the lusty use of his major muscles knows what a transformation of emotional tone and mental outlook such bodily expenditure can bring.

One of the most durable satisfactions in life is to lose oneself in one's work. This is why more people become neurotic from aimless leisure than from overwork, and why unemployment is one of the worst of tragedies, its psychological results as lamentable as its economic ills.

THE PROBLEM of finding external interests weighs more heavily on some temperaments than on others. The "extrovert" readily takes part in objective practical affairs, is emotionally spontaneous and out-going, is relatively tough-minded when he is disapproved by others. The "introvert" is sensitive to disapproval, is given to introspection and self-criticism, and in general is more aware of the inner than of the outer world.

While everybody can recognize these two types, and each man can judge to which of them he himself is more closely akin, they do not constitute two mutually exclusive temperaments. Nor is the advantage altogether on either side. The balanced man is a synthesis of the two.

Abraham Lincoln had a tragic struggle with himself. In his early manhood he was not a unified and coherent person but a cave of Aeolus, full of storms, with the makings of neurotic ruin in him. In 1841 he said, "I am now the most miserable man living. If what I feel were equally distributed to the whole human family, there would not be one cheerful face on earth." He could easily have been an ex-treme example of the morbid "introvert," but he was not. He solved his obsessing inner problems by outflanking them. The amazing devel-opment of his latter years into great personality came not so much by centering attention on himself as by forgetting himself. His devotion to a cause greater than himself transformed what he had learned in his long struggle with himself into understanding, sympathy, humor, wis-dom. We cannot call him in the end either "introvert" or "extrovert." He combined them.

THE PERSONAL counselor constantly runs upon self-focused lives, miserably striving to find happiness through "self-expression." Pop-ularly, self-expression has meant: Let yourself go; knock the bungs from your emotional barrels and let them gurgle! As a protest against petty moralisms, this is easily explicable, and as a means of release to some individuals, tied hand and foot by senseless scrupulosities, it has had its value. The wise counselor wants self-expression too; but he wants it to be practiced in accord with the realistic psychological facts. Merely exploding emotions for the sake of the momentary self-centered thrill gets one nowhere, and in the end the constant repetition of such emotional self-relief disperses life and leaves it more aimless than it was before. Even in the sexual realm this is true. Says an eminent psy-chiatrist: "From the point of view of cure, the advice to go and 'express your instincts' is foolish. In actual experience I have never known a true neurosis cured by sexual libertinism."

Adequate self-expression is a much deeper matter than self-explosion. Its true exponent is not the libertine but the artist, the scientist, the fortunate mother absorbed in her family, the public-spirited businessman creatively doing something for his community, the teacher saying as Professor George H. Palmer did, "Harvard College pays me for doing what I would gladly pay it for allowing me to do." Such personalities, in eminent or humble places, really express themselves, and their common quality is not self-absorption but self-investment.

A⊤ LEAST two practical consequences follow from such successful expansion of the self.

For one thing, it gives a person a saving sense of humor. In anyone afflicted with abnormal self-concern, a deficient sense of humor is an inevitable penalty. Only people who live objectively in other persons and in wide-flung interests, and who therefore can see themselves impartially, can possibly have the prayer answered:

> O wad some Pow'r the giftie gie us
> To see oursels as ithers see us!

The egocentric's petition is habitually otherwise:

> O wad some Pow'r to others gie
> To see myself as I see me.

Nast, the cartoonist, one evening in a social group drew caricatures of each of the company. The result was revealing—each one easily recognized the caricatures of the others but some could not recognize their own. This inability to see ourselves as we look to others is one of the surest signs of egocentric immaturity.

Aristophanes, in his drama *The Clouds,* caricatured Socrates, and all Athens roared with laugher. Socrates, so runs the story, went to see the play, and when the caricature came on he stood up so that the audience might the better enjoy the comic mask that was intended to burlesque him. He was mature. He had got himself off his hands.

An extended self also results in power to bear trouble. In those who rise to the occasion and marshal their forces to deal with it, one factor commonly is present—*they are thinking about someone else besides themselves*. So one young American officer in the First World War wrote home: "You can truly think of me as being cheerful all the time. Why otherwise? I have 38 men with me. If I duck when a shell comes, all 38 duck, and if I smile, the smile goes down the line."

A person who has genuinely identified himself with other persons has done something of first-rate importance for himself without intending it. Hitherto he has lived, let us say, in a mind like a room surrounded by mirrors. Every way he turned he saw himself. Now, however, some of the mirrors change to windows. He can see through them to new interests.

ONE WAY or another we must do something with all the emotional drives native to our constitution. Such emotional urges as curiosity, pugnacity, fearfulness, self-regard, sexual desire are an essential part of us; we can either be ignobly enslaved by them or master them for the enrichment of our personality.

Curiosity is an emotional urge in all normal people, and its manifestations are protean. Peeping Toms, prying gossips, inquisitive bores, open-minded truth-seekers, daring explorers, research scientists are all illustrations of curiosity. Some uses of it produce the most despicable persons, while others produce the most admirable, but there is no escaping it. From this fact, which holds true of all our native drives, a double lesson comes: First, *no basic emotional factor in human nature is to be despised;* and second, *each of them can be ennobled by its use.*

Pugnacity is one of the most deeply rooted emotional drives in human nature, and combativeness is necessary to the continuance and advance of human life. The fighting spirit expresses itself in hard work, in bravely facing personal handicaps, in the whole range of attack on entrenched social evils.

If, however, we give this indispensable emotional drive gangway, the results are shattering. A chronic hatred or even a cherished grudge tears to pieces the one who harbors it. A strong feeling of resentment is just as likely to cause disease as is a germ. If one is so unfortunate as to have an enemy, the worst thing one can do, not to the enemy but to oneself, is to let resentment dig in and hatred become chronic.

When Edward Everett Hale in his later years said, "I once had an enemy, a determined enemy, and I have been trying all day to remember his name," he gave evidence not only of right-mindedness but of healthy-mindedness. So, too, Lincoln, rebuked for an expression of magnanimity toward the South during the Civil War, and told bitterly that he should desire rather to destroy his enemies, was not only morally but emotionally sound when he answered, "What, madam? Do I not destroy them when I make them my friends?"

F EAR is another indispensable element in the human make-up. Even in its simpler forms we cannot dispense with it; on the streets of a modern city a fearless man, if the phrase be taken literally, would probably be dead before nightfall. And fear can be a powerfully creative motive. In a profound sense schools spring from fear of ignorance, industry from fear of penury, medical science from fear of disease. But fear's abnormalities—hysteria, phobia, obsessive anxiety—tear personality to pieces.

Human life is full of secret fears, thrust into the attics and dark corners of personality. Fear of the dark, of cats, of closed places, of open places; fear of responsibility, of having children, of old age and death; guilty fears, often concerned with sins long passed; religious fears, associated with ideas of a spying and vindictive God and an eternal hell; and sometimes a vague fearfulness, filling life with anxious apprehension—such wretchedness curses innumerable lives.

The disruptive effect of such secret, chronic fearfulness is physically based. The adrenal glands furnish us in every frightening situation with "a swig of our own internal fight tonic." A little of it is stimulating; too much of it is poison. Habitual anxiety and dread constitute a continuous false alarm, turning the invaluable adrenal secretion from an emergency stimulant into a chronic poison.

To get our fear out into the open and frankly face it is of primary importance. As infants we started with fear of two things only—falling and a loud noise. All other fears have been accumulated since. To find out where and how we picked them up, to trace their development until we can objectively survey them as though they were another's and not our own, is half the battle. Often they can then be laughed off the scene.

Sometimes, however, the fear we find ourselves confronting is justified. In that case we are commonly defeated by the fallacy that dangerous situations are necessarily undesirable, whereas the fact is that there is *stimulus* in hazardous occasions.

Love of danger is one of the strongest motives in man. When life does not by itself present men with enough hazard, they go out looking for it. They seek it in their more active sports, in risky researches and explorations, in missionary adventures, in championing unpopular causes. To stand up to a hazardous situation, to let it call out in us not our fearfulness but our love of battle, is a healthy, inspiriting experience.

One of the sovereign cures for unhealthy fears is action. Dr. Henry C. Link gives this homely illustration from a mother: "As a young wife I was troubled with many fears, one of which was the fear of insanity. After the birth of our first child, these fears still persisted. However, we soon had another child and ended up by having six. We never had much money and I had to do all my own work. Whenever I started to worry about myself, the baby would cry and I would have to run and look after him. Or the children would quarrel and I would have to straighten them out. Or I would suddenly remember that it was time to start dinner, or that I must run out and take in the wash before it rained, or that the ironing had to be done. My fears were continually interrupted by tasks into which I had to put my back. Gradually my fears disappeared, and now I look back on them with amusement."

This story furnishes one explanation for the prevalence of emotional ills among prosperous and leisurely people. They have time to sit around, feeding their imaginations. In wartime they can listen over the radio to every news broadcast and commentator until, unlike a healthy soldier who has a job to do that he can put his back into, they become morbidly distraught over dangers concerning which they do nothing practical. In ordinary peacetime such people are the prey of endless imaginary woes, so that it is commonly true that those worry most who have least to worry about.

The dual nature of fear, as both good and evil, is nowhere better illustrated than in a man who dreads so much falling short of his duty that he dreads much less the cost of doing it. If one has anything positively to live for, from a child or a worthwhile day's work to a world delivered from the scourge of war, *that* is what matters.

Self-regard likewise is not to be despised or suppressed but educated and used.

When Charles Lamb said, "The greatest pleasure I know is to do a good action by stealth, and to have it found out by accident," he revealed how omnipresent is the wish for notice and attention that enhance self-esteem.

The cynic says that at the fountainhead of every so-called "unselfish" life are self-regarding motives. The cynic is right—but in his cynicism about it he is wrong. We all start as individual children, with self-regarding instincts. The test of us, however, lies in the objective aims and purposes which ultimately capture these forces in us and use them as driving power. A wise personal counselor, therefore, never tells anyone that he ought not to wish to feel important, but rather endeavors to direct that powerful wish into constructive channels.

From self-regard when it goes wrong spring vanity and avarice. Some people live habitually in the spirit with which Mascagni dedicated his opera *The Masks:* "To myself, with distinguished esteem and unalterable satisfaction." Yet we neither can nor should stop caring for ourselves. Our initial business in life is to care for ourselves so much that *I* tackles *Me,* determined to make out of him something worth while.

Probably it is in the realm of *sexual desire* that "sublimation"—redirection to a higher ethical level—is talked about most and understood least. Not all demands of the human organism can be sublimated. In satisfying physical hunger there is no substitute for food. When sex is thought of in its narrowest sense, it belongs in this class.

To the youth troubled by this elemental biological need, many sensible things can be said: that chastity is not debilitating and that sexual indulgence is not necessary to health; that interest in competing concerns is good therapy; that the general unrest accompanying unsatisfied sexual tension can often be relieved by vigorous action, fatiguing the whole body; that sexual desire is natural and right, to be accepted with gratitude and good humor as part of our constitutional equipment, and not sullied with morbid feelings of guilt at its presence; that nature, when left to itself, has its own ways of relieving the specific sex tension.

Sex, however, is far more deep-seated and pervasive in personality than at first appears. All the relationships of the family—maternal, paternal and filial—are grounded in this larger meaning of sex, all fine affection and friendship between brothers and sisters, and men and women, and all extensions of family attitudes to society at large, as in the love and care of children.

When one's life is thus thought of as a whole, sublimation of sex becomes meaningful. It is possible for one to choose a way of living that will channel one's devotions and creative energies into satisfying courses so that the personality *as a whole* finds contentment, even though specific sexual desires are left unfulfilled. So an unmarried woman, denied motherhood, can discover in nursing, teaching or social service an outlet for her maternal instincts that brings to her personality an integrating satisfaction.

That there must be some restraint on all our native drives is obvious. Picture a life in which all the native urges explode themselves together—self-regard, pugnacity, sexual desire, fear; obviously pandemonium would reign. The popular idea, therefore, that the restraint of basic emotional drives is in itself unhealthy is nonsense. The choice before us is not whether our native impulses shall be restrained and controlled but how that shall be done in the service of an integrated life.

THE MULTIPLE possibilities of use and misuse in handling our native drives root back in the essential quality of all emotional life, *sensitiveness*. One of the most important subjects of self-examination concerns the way we handle this primary quality. Let a man discover what he is characteristically touchy about and he will gain valuable insight into his personal problem.

Many people are extremely touchy to criticism. Their *amour-propre* squirms under adverse judgment. Sensitiveness to the opinion of others, without which social life could not go on at all, has in them been perverted into a disease.

Such abnormal persons take appreciation for granted and regard criticism as an impertinence. The normal person comes nearer taking criticism for granted and regarding appreciation as velvet. Emerson once made a speech that a minister sitting on the platform deeply disliked. The minister, in delivering the closing prayer, prayed, "We beseech Thee, O Lord, to deliver us from ever hearing any more such nonsense as we have just listened to." When Emerson was asked afterward what he thought about it, he remarked, "The minister seems a very conscientious, plain-spoken gentleman." Such healthy-mindedness is a necessary factor in a well-integrated personality.

O NE OF the commonest causes of personal disorganization is despondency. Some despondency is physically caused, but the moody dejections most people suffer are not altogether beyond their control.

A first suggestion for dealing with this problem is: *Take depression for granted*. One who expects completely to escape low moods is asking the impossible. To take low moods too seriously, instead of saying, This also will pass, is to confer on them an obsessive power they need not have.

A second suggestion is of daily importance: *We can identify ourselves not with our worse, but with our better, moods*. Deep within us all is that capacity. The ego, the central "I," can choose *this* and not *that* mood as representing the real self; it can identify itself with hopefulness rather than disheartenment, with good will rather than rancor.

All slaves of depression have this in common: They have acquired the habit of identifying their real selves with their low moods. Not only do they have cellars in their emotional houses, as everybody does, but they live there. While each of us has depressed hours, none of us needs to be a depressed person.

This leads to a third suggestion. *When depression comes, tackle yourself and do not merely blame circumstance*. Circumstances are often so tragic and crushing as to make dejection inevitable. Nevertheless, to deduce from the presence of misfortune the right to be a despondent person is a fatal error.

Life is an assimilative process in which we transmute into our own quality whatever comes into us. Walter de la Mare's lines have a wider application than at first appears:

It's a very odd thing—
As odd as can be,
That whatever Miss T. eats
Turns into Miss T.

Depressed persons can make depression out of any circumstances whatsoever. This truth is especially pertinent in a tragic era when the world is upset by catastrophic events. Not to be depressed by present calamities would reveal an insensitive spirit. Nevertheless, many today blame their emotional disorganization on the sad estate of the world, whereas their real problem is within themselves. As D. H. Lawrence wrote concerning one of his characters, "Poor Richard Lovatt wearied himself to death struggling with the problem of himself, and calling it Australia."

The fourth suggestion goes beyond self-tackling and says: *Remember others.* Emotions are contagious. One depressed person can infect a whole household and become a pest even to comparative strangers. If, therefore, Ian Maclaren's admonition is justified, "Let us be kind to one another for most of us are fighting a hard battle," good cheer and courage are among the most important kindnesses that we can show.

The fifth suggestion calls for deep resources of character: *Remember that some tasks are so important that they must be gone through with whether we are depressed or not.* Strong personalities commonly solve the problem of their despondency not by eliminating but by sidetracking it. They have work to do, a purpose to fulfill, and to *that,* whether or not they feel dejected, the main trunk line of their lives belongs.

To pull a personality together takes inner reserves of power—of power assimilated from beyond oneself.

As truly as a tree exists by means of chemical assimilation through roots and leaves, our own physical organisms sustain themselves by appropriated power. The entire cosmos furnishes the indispensable means by which we live at all. We are pensioners on universal energy, and our power is not fabricated in us but released through us.

This principle of released power does not stop at any supposed line separating man's physical from his spiritual experience. That our spirits are continuous with a larger spiritual life, and that in this realm also our power is not self-produced but assimilated, is the affirmation of all profound religious experience.

No more pathetic cases present themselves to the personal counselor than those whose only technique in handling their problems is to trust in the strength of their own volition. Soon or late they face problems to which such a technique is utterly inapplicable. When bereavement comes, for instance, bringing with it profound sorrow, to appeal to the will to arouse itself and solve the problem is an impertinence.

Such moments call for another technique altogether — the hospitable receptivity of faith.

Many people ask, "How does one get faith, if one does not have it? One cannot *will* to have faith." But faith is not something we *get;* it is something we *have*. Moreover, we have a surplus of it, associated with more curious objects than tongue can tell — faith in dictatorship or astrology or rabbits' feet, in one economic nostrum or another. That we have more faith than we know what to do with is shown by the way we give it to every odd and end that comes along.

Our trick of words — "belief" vs. "unbelief" — obscures this. No man can really become an unbeliever; he is psychologically shut up to the necessity of believing — in God, for example, or else in no God. When positive faiths die out, their place is always taken by negative faiths — in impossibilities rather than possibilities, in ideas that make us victims rather than masters of life; in philosophies that plunge us into Rabelais' dying mood: "Draw the curtain; the farce is played."

A friend once wrote to Turgenev: "It seems to me that to put oneself in the second place is the whole significance of life." Turgenev replied: "It seems to me that to discover what to put before oneself, in the first place, is the whole problem of life." Whatever one does put thus before oneself is always the object of one's faith; one believes in it and belongs to it; and whether it be Christ or Hitler, a chosen vocation or a personal friend, when such committal of faith is heartily made, it pulls the trigger of human energy.

Confidence that it is worth while constructively to tackle oneself, and the determination so to do, depends on faith of some sort. Distraught and dejected people almost inevitably ask: "Why should we bother to try to create an integrated and useful personality? Of what importance are we anyway?" These miserable folk perceive nothing worth living for, and the only cure for their futilitarian attitude is a positive faith.

Even though one goes no further than Robert Louis Stevenson in saying, "I believe in an ultimate decency of things," such faith has inestimable value. If one can go beyond Stevenson's affirmation, religion presents the most stimulating faith in human experience. It has said to every individual: Whatever you may fail at, you need not fail at being a real person; the makings of great personal life include handicaps, deficiencies, troubles and even moral failures; the universe is not a haphazard affair of aimless atoms but is organized around spiritual purposes; and personality, far from being a chance inadvertence, is the fullest and completest way of being alive and the most adequate symbol we have of the nature of God.

Thus religion is a basis for hopeful adventure and a source of available power in trying to make the most of our natural endowments and become what we ought to be. And he who undertakes that task is on the main highroad of creation's meaning and is accepting the central trust of life.